Albert Chaster

The powers, duties and liabilities of executive officers as between these officers and the public

Fourth Edition

Albert Chaster

The powers, duties and liabilities of executive officers as between these officers and the public
Fourth Edition

ISBN/EAN: 9783337280055

Printed in Europe, USA, Canada, Australia, Japan

Cover: Foto ©ninafisch / pixelio.de

More available books at **www.hansebooks.com**

THE POWERS, DUTIES, AND LIABILITIES

OF

EXECUTIVE OFFICERS

AS BETWEEN THESE OFFICERS AND THE PUBLIC.

A CONCISE ENQUIRY INTO THE LIMITS OF EXECUTIVE
AUTHORITY AND THE REMEDIES FOR BREACH
OR EXCESS THEREOF.

BY

A. W. CHASTER,

OF THE UNIVERSITY OF LONDON, LL.B.; AND OF THE MIDDLE TEMPLE AND WESTERN CIRCUIT,
BARRISTER-AT-LAW.

"Where freedom slowly broadens down
From precedent to precedent."
TENNYSON.

FOURTH EDITION.

LONDON:
WILLIAM CLOWES AND SONS, Limited,
27, FLEET STREET.
1891.

LONDON:
PRINTED BY WILLIAM CLOWES AND SONS, LIMITED,
STAMFORD STREET AND CHARING CROSS.

TO THE MEMORY OF
My Grandfather,
WALTER PRESTON CHASTER,
And my Father,
JOHN WEBBER CHASTER,
BOTH OF TOTNES,
WHO, WITHOUT THE ADVANTAGES OF WEALTH OR STATION,
DEVOTED MUCH OF THEIR LIVES TO THE CAUSE OF
GOVERNMENT
"OF THE PEOPLE, BY THE PEOPLE, FOR THE PEOPLE,"
THIS HUMBLE ENDEAVOUR
TO REDUCE TO A PRACTICAL FORM
THE TEACHINGS WHICH THEY INCULCATED,
IS AFFECTIONATELY INSCRIBED BY

THE AUTHOR.

PREFACE

TO THE

FOURTH EDITION.

THIS edition constitutes practically a new work. The matter which before was limited to a digest of the powers inherent in officers, has now been scientifically arranged and extended so as to include those exercised under warrants and orders whether of Superior Courts or of Courts or officers having lesser jurisdiction.

The aim has been to state every power and its qualification, if any, as concisely as possible consistent with accuracy and intelligibility, so that the work may still retain the limits of a handbook, instead of extending, as it otherwise would, to those of an encyclopædia. How nearly and with what degree of success that aim has been attained must be left to others more learned than the author to determine.

It should be mentioned that the powers are those only which are exercised under the ordinary law. Where the Habeas Corpus Act is suspended and Bills of Indemnity are subsequently passed, the condition is not easily distinguishable from that of civil war. *Inter arma leges silent.*

The collection of Forms in the Appendix is not intended to be complete. It is rather a selection of general Forms made for the better comprehension of the relative positions from a legal point of view, of those warrants and orders which are discussed in the first part of the work.

The author has to render his best acknowledgments to his brother Mr. J. N. Chaster, of the Middle Temple, for kindly preparing the lists of statutes and cases, the Appendix and Index with which the work, which now contains over 3000 references, is supplied.

8, NEW COURT,
   LINCOLN'S INN,
      October, 1891.

PREFACE

TO THE
FIRST EDITION.

THE accurate exercise and performance of their powers and duties, respectively, by executive officers, is of the essence of good government.

Partly on account of their system of payment (which is based in some cases at least on results), and of a desire to distinguish themselves and thus earn promotion, and partly on account of that imperfection which is inherent both in mankind and in all human institutions, there is, perhaps, at times a tendency among these officers, in their zeal for the service of the State, on the one hand, to exceed the authority with which the law has clothed them, and on the other to be forgetful of the obligations which are due from them to the public.

It is for those who may be in some measure, more or less, affected by such excess or breach of duty respectively, that the following pages have been collated.

5, NEW COURT,
    LINCOLN'S INN,
        October, 1886.

CONTENTS.

PART I.—WARRANTS AND ORDERS.

I.—WARRANTS AND ORDERS OF SUPERIOR COURTS AT COMMON LAW.

1.—THE KING A PARTY.

	PAGE		PAGE
Sergeant-at-Arms (Lords)	7	Tipstaff	12
Sergeant-at-Arms (Commons)	8	Gaoler	12
Sheriff	8		

2.—THE KING NOT A PARTY.

Sheriff	17	Admiralty Marshal	29

II.—WARRANTS AND ORDERS OF SUPERIOR COURTS NOT AT COMMON LAW, OF INFERIOR COURTS AND OFFICERS GENERALLY.

A.—AFTER ADJUDICATION.

1.—The King a Party.

Sheriff	35	Excise	38
Tipstaff	35	Taxes	39
High Bailiff	36	Gaolers	40
Constables	36		

2.—The King not a Party.

High Bailiff	40	Overseers	43
Constables	43	Highway Surveyors	45
Gaolers	43		

B.—WHERE NO ADJUDICATION.

1.—The King a Party.

Queen's Messengers	46	Customs	55
Post Officers	46	Excise	56
Minister, Churchwardens, and Overseers	46	Explosives Inspectors	57
		Wreck Receiver	58
Constables	47	Nuisance Inspector	58

2.—THE KING NOT A PARTY.

Constables 58	Overseers, Relieving and Asylum
Weights Inspectors . . . 60	Officers 61
Water Bailiffs 60	District Surveyors . . . 61
	Local Officers 61

C.—OTHER ORDERS.

Local Acts 62	Explosives 67
Bye-laws 62	Highways 67
Adulteration 65	Public Health 67
Canal Boats 66	Weights and Measures . . 74
Contagious Diseases . . 66	

PART II.—INHERENT POWERS.

Officers attending Courts . . 75	Factory Inspectors . . . 123
Sheriff 76	Mines Inspectors . . . 123
Constables 76	Merchant Shipping Inspectors . 124
Gaolers 111	Railway Inspectors . . . 127
Customs 113	Water Bailiffs 127
Excise 117	Alkali Works Inspectors . . 128
Taxes 120	Minister 130
Post 121	Churchwardens . . . 131
Contagious Diseases Inspectors . 122	Overseers, Relieving and Work-
Burial-Grounds Inspectors . 122	house Officers . . . 132
Inebriates Inspectors . . 122	Highway Surveyors . . 133
Cruelty to Animals Inspectors . 122	District Surveyors (Metrop.) . 135
Explosives Inspectors . . 122	Weights and Measures Inspectors 136

PART III.—LIABILITIES.

I.—UNDER WARRANTS AND ORDERS OF SUPERIOR COURTS AT COMMON LAW 137

II.—UNDER WARRANTS AND ORDERS OF SUPERIOR COURTS NOT AT COMMON LAW, OF INFERIOR COURTS AND OFFICERS GENERALLY . . . 144

    A.—AFTER ADJUDICATION . . . 144
    B.—WHERE NO ADJUDICATION . . 147
    C.—OTHER ORDERS 148

III.—UNDER INHERENT POWERS . . 150

    REMEDIES 153

    PROTECTION 153

1.—BREACH OF DUTY.

Civil Proceedings . . . 164	Criminal Proceedings . . 169
Action for Damages . . 164	Attachment 169
	Information 169
	Mandamus 170

2.—EXCESS OF POWER.

SELF DEFENCE 171

Fabrication of Evidence 171

Civil Proceedings . . . 172	Criminal Proceedings . . 201
Assault and Battery . . 172	Attachment 201
Extortion 175	Information 202
False Imprisonment . . . 181	Assault and Battery . . 203
Malicious Prosecution . . 185	Common Nuisance . . . 204
Public Nuisance . . . 188	Conspiracy 204
Slander 188	Extortion 206
Trespass to Personalty . . 192	False Imprisonment . . . 207
Trespass to Realty . . . 197	Inciting to commit Offence . 207
	Perjury 208
	Trespass to Realty . . . 209

APPENDIX.

I.—WARRANTS AND ORDERS OF SUPERIOR COURTS AT COMMON LAW 211

II.—WARRANTS AND ORDERS OF SUPERIOR COURTS NOT AT COMMON LAW, OF INFERIOR COURTS AND OFFICERS GENERALLY.

A.—AFTER ADJUDICATION 222
B.—WHERE NO ADJUDICATION . . . 239

INDEX 247

STATUTES.

	PAGE		PAGE
3 Edw. 1, c. 9	205	37 Geo. 3, c, 70, s. 1	50, 89
25 Edw. 3, st. 5, c. 2	51, 91	———, c. 123, s. 1	89
5 Ric. 2, c. 8	49	39 Geo. 3, c. 79, s. 3	49
15 Ric. 2, c. 2	49	39 & 40 Geo. 3, c. 94	47
8 Hen. 6, c. 9	49	41 Geo. 3, c. 23, s. 1	44
25 Hen. 8, c. 21, s. 20	46	———, s. 2	44
27 Hen. 8, c. 24, s. 8	143	42 Geo. 3, c. 119, s. 1	50
5 Ed. 6, c 16	50	———, s. 6	94
5 Eliz. c. 9, s. 3	50	———, s. 8	161, 162
———, c. 23, s. 2	10	43 Geo. 3, c. 61	97
18 Eliz. c. 5, s. 4	49	49 Geo. 3, c. 126, s. 3	51
29 Eliz. c. 4	19, 28, 175	51 Geo. 3, c. 155, s. 13	48
43 Eliz. c. 2	159	52 Geo. 3, c. 104, s. 1	89
7 Jac. 1, c. 5	159, 161, 162	53 Geo. 3, c. 127, s. 1	10
21 Jac. 1, c. 4, s. 4	161, 167	54 Geo. 3, c. 170, s. 12	44
———, c. 12, s. 3	160, 161, 162, 192, 197, 200	56 Geo. 3, c. 50, s. 1	11, 23
		———, s. 3	28
———, c. 15	49	———, s. 8	23
———, c. 16, s. 3	175, 185, 188	———, s. 9	167
13 Car. 2, c. 5	101	———, c. 138, s. 2	49
29 Car. 2, c. 3, s. 10	18	57 Geo. 3, c. 19, s. 23	101
———, c. 7, s. 6	16, 77	———, s. 25	49
31 Car. 2, c. 2, s. 5	14	———, s. 32	157, 159, 161, 162
1 W. & M. c. 18, s. 15	48		
———, s. 18	80	———, c. 93, s. 1	39, 44, 180
10 Will. 3, c, 23, s. 1	50	———, s. 6	203
7 Anne, c. 12, s. 4	7	58 Geo. 3, c. 70, s. 7	49
8 Anne, c. 14, s. 1	11, 25	59 Geo. 3, c. 12, s. 7	43
9 Anne, c. 10, s. 40	46, 202	60 Geo. 3, c. 1, s. 1	48
1 Geo. 1, st. 2, c. 5, s. 1	90	———, s. 2	79
2 Geo. 2, c. 25, s. 2	209	———, s. 5	157, 159, 161, 162
9 Geo. 2, c. 5, s. 4	51	1 & 2 Geo. 4, c. 88, s. 1	90
16 Geo. 2, c. 31	90	5 Geo. 4, c. 83, s. 3	96, 97
17 Geo. 2, c. 38, s. 7	44	———, s. 4	97, 98
———, s. 8	145, 161	———, s. 8	109
———, s. 10	159, 161	———, s. 13	52
19 Geo. 2, c. 21, s. 3	100	———, s. 19	157, 161
———, s. 11	161, 162	———, c. 84, s. 22	89
24 Geo. 2, c. 44, s. 6	146, 162	———, c. 113	90, 117
25 Geo. 2, c. 36, s. 1	50	6 Geo. 4, c. 78, s. 14	114
———, s. 5	49	———, s. 15	114
———, s. 6	49	———, s. 19	97
———, s. 7	49	———, s. 37	158, 161, 162
———, s. 8	49	7 & 8 Geo. 4, c. 17	39, 180
26 Geo. 3, c. 71, s. 7	71	———, c. 53, s. 22	51, 117, 118
33 Geo. 3, c. 55, s. 3	39	———, s. 28	11
———, c. 67, s. 1	51	———, s. 32	120
———, s. 3	51	———, s. 33	119
35 Geo. 3, c. 101	44	———, s. 34	56

STATUTES

Statute	PAGE
7 & 8 Geo. 4, c. 53, s. 38	116, 120
————, s. 40	120
————, s. 65	49
————, s. 86	38
————, s. 87	38
————, s. 88	38
————, s. 89	38
————, s. 90	38, 56
————, s. 91	38
————, s. 108	108
————, s. 118	161
————, c. 64, s. 12	52
————, s. 13	52
9 Geo. 4, c. 69, s. 1	50
————, s. 2	50
————, s. 9	50, 98
10 Geo. 4, c. 7, s. 28	50
————, c. 44, s. 1	54
————, s. 7	101
————, s. 9	110
————, s. 41	157, 158, 160, 161, 163
1 & 2 Will. 4, c. 22, s. 60	109
————, c. 41, s. 11	48
2 & 3 Will. 4, c. 53, s. 49	90
————, c. 75, s. 6	122
————, s. 17	122
3 & 4 Will. 4, c. 49	209
————, c. 82	209
————, c. 90, s. 41	43, 104
————, s. 55	99
4 & 5 Will. 4, c. 51, s. 25	120
5 & 6 Will. 4, c. 50, s. 14	133
————, s. 16	133
————, s. 22	133
————, s. 25	133
————, s. 26	133
————, s. 34	45
————, s. 35	133
————, s. 47	134
————, s. 51	45
————, s. 54	45
————, s. 55	134, 170, 202
————, s. 56	134, 170, 202
————, s. 57	134, 170, 203
————, s. 65	45
————, s. 67	134
————, s. 69	134
————, s. 72	134, 170
————, s. 73	133
————, s. 75	135
————, s. 78	135
————, s. 79	134
————, s. 85	45
————, s. 94	170
————, s. 109	157, 158, 159, 160, 161, 162, 163
————, c. 62, s. 13	50
————, s. 21	49
6 & 7 Will. 4, c. 11, s. 2	115
————, c. 37, s. 11	52

Statute	PAGE
1 Vict. c. 24	51
————, c. 36, s. 25	121, 202
————, s. 35	51
————, s. 36	51
————, s. 46	157, 158, 160, 163
————, c. 55, s. 3	173
————, c. 88	51, 90
1 & 2 Vict. c. 74, s. 1	43
————, s. 5	147
————, c. 110, s. 11	18
————, s. 12	21
2 & 3 Vict. c. 47, s. 26	103
————, s. 27	103
————, s. 28	103
————, s. 29	103
————, s. 30	103
————, s. 31	103
————, s. 32	103
————, s. 33	107
————, s. 34	102, 107, 109
————, s. 38	101
————, s. 39	110
————, s. 46	60
————, s. 47	54, 60
————, s. 48	54
————, s. 54	100, 101, 102, 208
————, s. 58	101, 103
————, s. 60	103
————, s. 61	110
————, s. 62	101
————, s. 63	103
————, s. 66	103, 109
————, s. 67	109
————, s. 68	109
————, s. 69	103
————, s. 70	110
————, s. 72	110
————, c. 71, s. 19	48
————, s. 20	48
————, s. 21	48
————, s. 22	48
————, s. 23	48
————, s. 24	48
————, s. 25	48
————, s. 51	145, 147
————, c. 93	48
————, s. 8	48
3 & 4 Vict. c. 18, s. 3	118
————, s. 5	120
————, c. 50, s. 6	100
————, s. 7	100
————, s. 8	100
————, s. 9	100, 109
————, s. 10	100
————, s. 11	100, 109
————, s. 12	100
————, s. 18	157, 158, 160, 161, 163
————, c. 72, s. 4	51
————, c. 96, s. 65	121

STATUTES.

XV

	PAGE		PAGE
3 & 4 Vict. c. 97, s. 13	51	10 & 11 Vict. c. 89, s. 15	105
5 & 6 Vict. c. 45, s. 12	49	———, s. 24	109
———, c. 51, s. 2	51	———, s. 26	106
———, c. 93, s. 13	120	———, s. 28	104, 105
———, c. 97, s. 2	163	———, s. 29	105
———, s. 3	161, 162	———, s. 30	105
———, s. 5	158	———, s. 31	105
6 & 7 Vict. c. 18, s. 81	49	———, s. 34	105
———, s. 86	59	———, s. 35	105
———, s. 89	49	———, c. 89, s. 36	60, 106
———, c. 73, s. 2	202	———, s. 61	105
———, c. 96, s. 1	191	———, s. 72	159
———, s. 3	50	———, c. 110, s. 10	132
———, s. 4	50	11 & 12 Vict. c. 12, s. 3	51, 91
———, s. 5	50	———, s. 4	51
7 & 8 Vict. c. 87, s. 4	106	———, s. 5	51
———, c. 96, s. 67	26	———, s. 6	51
———, c. 100, s. 6	97	———, s. 7	51
———, c. 101, s. 8	50	———, s. 8	51
———, s. 53	105	———, s. 9	51
———, s. 61	43	———, s. 10	51
8 & 9 Vict. c. 109, s. 2	55	———, c. 42, s. 1	37, 48
———, s. 5	55	———, s. 2	48
———, s. 6	54	———, s. 3	48
———, s. 7	54	———, s. 4	7, 48
———, s. 8	55	———, s. 5	48
———, s. 14	106	———, s. 9	48
———, s. 19	50	———, s. 10	48
———, s. 21	145	———, s. 11	48
———, s. 23	157, 158, 160	———, s. 12	48
———, c. 127, s. 8	23	———, s. 13	48
9 & 10 Vict. c. 74	71	———, s. 14	48
10 & 11 Vict. c. 14, s. 15	71	———, s. 15	48
———, s. 20	71	———, s. 16	48
———, s. 38	71	———, s. 17	202
———, s. 41	71	———, s. 19	59, 202
———, s. 154	71	———, s. 21	48
———, c. 27, s. 33	64	———, s. 24	48
———, s. 34	125	———, s. 25	48
———, s. 36	125	———, c. 43, s. 2	48, 58
———, s. 37	125	———, s. 3	48, 147
———, s. 39	126	———, s. 7	48
———, s. 40	126	———, s. 11	77
———, s. 41	126	———, s. 12	59
———, s. 44	126	———, s. 19	37, 48
———, s. 45	126	———, s. 20	54
———, s. 46	126	———, s. 36	39
———, s. 48	116	12 & 13 Vict. c. 92, s. 3	81
———, s. 52	126	———, s. 5	81
———, s. 53	126	———, s. 7	82
———, s. 58	126	———, s. 8	82
———, s. 65	126	———, s. 9	82
———, s. 72	127	———, s. 10	82
———, s. 79	127	———, s. 12	82
———, s. 91	159	———, s. 13	81
———, c. 34, s. 78	69	———, s. 19	108
———, s. 108	69	———, s. 27	157, 159, 160, 161, 162, 163
———, s. 131	71	———, s. 29	81
———, s. 219	159	———, c. 109, s. 26	10
———, c. 61	71	13 & 14 Vict. c. 101, s. 9	48
———, c. 85, s. 10	121		

STATUTES.

	PAGE
14 & 15 Vict. c. 19, s. 11	96
————, s. 12	48
————, c. 25, s. 2	26
————, c. 28, s. 12	74
————, c. 100, s. 29	51, 98
————, c. 102, s. 55	50
15 & 16 Vict. c. 56, s. 15	50
————, c. 76, s. 123	20
————, c. 81, s. 27	43
16 & 17 Vict. c. 30, s. 3	40
————, s. 9	14, 40
————, c. 96, s. 73	50
————, s. 74	50
————, s. 93	50
————, s. 122	50
————, s. 123	50
————, c. 119, s. 11	50
————, s. 12	54
————, s. 16	159
————, s. 17	157
17 & 18 Vict. c. 38, s. 13	159
————, c. 60, s. 3	81
————, c. 102, s. 2	40
————, s. 3	49
————, c. 104, s. 13	124, 125
————, s. 15	124
————, s. 102	116
————, s. 103	114, 116
————, s. 104	154, 162, 163
————, s. 105	113
————, s. 246	99
————, s. 300	114, 116
————, s. 306	124
————, s. 366	50
————, s. 441	124
————, s. 442	124
————, s. 444	125, 154
————, s. 445	125
————, s. 446	125
————, s. 451	58
————, s. 468	125
————, s. 469	41, 125
18 & 19 Vict. c. 15, s. 11	11, 18
————, c. 120, s. 82	74
————, s. 205	103
————, s. 206	101
————, s. 208	103
————, s. 224	159
————, s. 229	103
————, c. 122, s. 31	135
————, s. 42	135
————, s. 43	136
————, s. 50	136
————, s. 69	61
————, s. 80	60
————, s. 105	136, 157
————, s. 108	158, 160, 161, 162
————, c. 128, s. 8	122
19 & 20 Vict. c. 41, s. 6	50

	PAGE
19 & 20 Vict. c. 69, s. 6	104, 110
————, s. 31	104
————, c. 119, s. 12	51
————, s. 18	51
20 & 21 Vict. c. 81, s. 23	46
————, s. 25	47
————, c. 83, s. 1	52
————, c. 85, s. 50	50
21 & 22 Vict. c. 78, s. 31	50
————, c. 90, s. 38	50
————, c. 108, s. 23	50
22 Vict. c. 1, s. 1	47
22 & 23 Vict. c. 21, s. 36	35
————, c. 35, s. 24	51
23 & 24 Vict. c. 27, s. 24	118, 119
————, c. 32, s. 2	132
————, s. 3	80, 131
————, c. 75, s. 2	47
————, s. 12	50
————, s. 13	50
————, c. 114, s. 48	56
————, c. 135	106
————, c. 139	49
24 & 25 Vict. c. 53, s. 5	49
————, c. 94, s. 1	82
————, s. 3	82
————, s. 8	48
————, c. 96, s. 1	49, 50, 51, 94, 200
————, s. 4	95
————, s. 7	94
————, s. 8	94
————, s. 10	88
————, s. 11	88
————, s. 12	49, 86, 88
————, s. 13	49, 86, 88
————, s. 14	49, 95
————, s. 15	49, 95
————, s. 16	49
————, s. 17	96
————, s. 18	44
————, s. 19	95
————, s. 20	94
————, s. 21	95
————, s. 22	95
————, s. 24	95
————, s. 26	88, 95
————, s. 27	88
————, s. 28	88
————, s. 29	88
————, s. 30	88
————, s. 31	88
————, s. 32	88, 91
————, s. 33	91, 95
————, s. 34	95
————, s. 35	95
————, s. 36	95
————, s. 37	95
————, s. 38	88
————, s. 40	90
————, s. 41	90

STATUTES. xvii

Statute	Page
24 & 25 Vict c. 96, s. 42	84, 90
—, s. 43	90
—, s. 46	49
—, s. 47	49, 85, 91
—, s. 48	49, 91
—, s. 49	49, 91
—, s. 50	48, 90, 91
—, s. 51	48, 84, 85
—, s. 52	48
—, s. 56	87
—, s. 57	50, 87
—, s. 60	88
—, s. 61	88
—, s. 62	88
—, s. 63	88
—, s. 64	51, 88
—, s. 65	51, 95
—, s. 66	51, 95
—, s. 67	88
—, s. 68	49, 86
—, s. 69	49, 89
—, s. 70	49, 86, 89
—, s. 71	49, 89
—, s. 72	49, 89
—, s. 73	49, 89
—, s. 74	49, 89
—, s. 75	49, 94
—, s. 76	49, 94
—, s. 77	49
—, s. 78	49, 95
—, s. 79	49
—, s. 80	49, 95
—, s. 81	49, 95
—, s. 82	95
—, s. 83	95
—, s. 84	95
—, s. 88	95
—, s. 90	94
—, s. 91	90
—, s. 95	51, 95
—, s. 101	90
—, s. 103	52
—, s. 113	157, 158, 159, 160, 161, 163
— c. 97, s. 1	48, 51, 83
—, s. 2	48, 83
—, s. 3	48, 83
—, s. 4	48, 83
—, s. 5	48, 83
—, s. 6	48, 83
—, s. 7	48, 83
—, s. 8	48, 84
—, s. 9	84, 86
—, s. 10	86
—, s. 12	96
—, s. 13	96
—, s. 14	87
—, s. 15	89
—, s. 16	84
—, s. 17	84
—, s. 18	84
24 & 25 Vict. c. 97, s. 19	50, 87
—, s. 22	96
—, s. 23	96
—, s. 24	96
—, s. 25	50, 96
—, s. 26	84
—, s. 27	84
—, s. 28	89
—, s. 30	48, 90
—, s. 31	48, 83
—, s. 32	96
—, s. 33	48, 83
—, s. 35	90
—, s. 36	96
—, s. 37	96
—, s. 38	96
—, s. 39	96
—, s. 40	48, 85
—, s. 41	48, 96
—, s. 43	84
—, s. 44	84
—, s. 45	91
—, s. 46	91
—, s. 47	48, 90
—, s. 48	48, 84
—, s. 51	96
—, s. 54	96
—, s. 61	128
—, s. 63	96
—, s. 71	157-161, 163
— c. 98, s. 1	49, 86
—, s. 2	86
—, s. 3	86, 90
—, s. 4	86
—, s. 5	86
—, s. 6	86
—, s. 7	86
—, s. 8	84, 86
—, s. 9	48, 84
—, s. 10	48, 84
—, s. 11	48, 84
—, s. 12	86
—, s. 14	84
—, s. 20	86
—, s. 21	86
—, s. 22	86
—, s. 23	87
—, s. 34	87, 90
—, s. 36	87
—, s. 46	52
— c. 99, s. 2	49, 87, 90
—, s. 3	87, 90
—, s. 4	87, 90
—, s. 5	85
—, s. 8	91
—, s. 9	91
—, s. 10	92
—, s. 11	87, 91
—, s. 13	92
—, s. 14	85
—, s. 15	85, 92

b

STATUTES.

Statute	Page
24 & 25 Vict. c. 99, s. 16	92
————, s. 17	92
————, s. 18	86
————, s. 19	86
————, s. 20	92
————, s. 21	86
————, s. 22	91
————, s. 23	91
————, s. 24	85
————, s. 25	85
————, s. 27	107
————, s. 33	157–161, 163
———— c. 100, s. 1	50
————, s. 11	89, 90
————, s. 12	89
————, s. 13	89
————, s. 14	89
————, s. 15	48, 89
————, s. 16	91
————, s. 17	51, 91
————, s. 18	87
————, s. 21	85
————, s. 22	48, 85
————, s. 28	87
————, s. 29	87
————, s. 30	87
————, s. 36	7
————, s. 37	51
————, s. 44	173, 204
————, s. 45	173, 204
————, s. 48	90
————, s. 53	82
————, s. 54	48, 83
————, s. 55	48
————, s. 56	48, 83
————, s. 57	48, 84
————, s. 58	48, 83
————, s. 59	48
————, s. 61	51, 91
————, s. 66	82
————, s. 67	149
24 & 25 Vict. c. 109, s. 9	127
———— c. 10	127
————, s. 11	127, 128
————, s. 12	127
————, s. 14	127
————, s. 15	127
————, s. 16	127
————, s. 17	127
————, s. 18	127
————, s. 19	127
————, s. 20	127
————, s. 21	127
————, s. 34	60
———— c. 110, s. 7	59
25 & 26 Vict. c. 19, s. 21	127
———— c. 22, s. 31	91, 119
———— c. 53, s. 105	51
———— c. 63, s. 30	124
———— c. 67, s. 44	51
———— c. 89, s. 87	25
25 & 26 Vict. c. 89, s. 163	25
————, s. 166	51
———— c. 102, s. 75	73
———— c. 103, s. 40	50
———— c. 114, s. 2	107, 108
26 Vict. c. 13, s. 5	98
26 & 27 Vict. c. 10, s. 3	115
———— c. 29, s. 1	49
————, s. 2	49
————, s. 3	49
————, s. 4	49
———— c. 87, s. 5	51
27 & 28 Vict. c. 27, s. 12	48
———— c. 47, s. 6	81
———— c. 113, s. 66	128
————, s. 74	103
28 & 29 Vict. c. 34, s. 7	102
———— c. 36, s. 11	49
————, s. 16	59
———— c. 48, s. 18	101
———— c. 90, s. 12	74, 101, 110
————, s. 29	74
———— c. 104, s. 98	11
———— c. 121, s. 31	60
————, s. 37	128
————, s. 58	127
————, s. 64	127
————, s. 65	113, 115
———— c. 124, s. 6	48, 50
————, s. 8	48, 90
———— c. 126, s. 4	50
————, s. 17	111
————, s. 18	111
————, s. 37	49
————, s. 41	13
————, s. 43	111
————, s. 49	161–163
————, s. 50	158, 160
————, s. 63	111
————, s. 67	111
————, s. 82	13
————, sched. 1, r. 6	111, 170
————, r. 7	111
————, r. 8	111
————, r. 10	13, 111
————, r. 16	111
————, r. 19	111
————, r. 23	111
————, r. 24	14
————, r. 26	111
————, r. 28	111
————, r. 29	112
————, r. 32	112
————, r. 34	112
————, r. 38	112
————, r. 39	112
————, r. 41	112
————, r. 46	112
————, r. 47	112

STATUTES.

	PAGE
28 & 29 Vict. c. 126, sched. 1, r. 53	112
———————————————, r. 54	112
———————————————, r. 55	112
———————————————, r. 59	111
———————————————, r. 67	112
———————————————, r. 97	112
29 & 30 Vict. c. 37	50
——————, s. 10	52
—————— c. 39, s. 42	11
—————— c. 109, s. 9	49, 86
—————— c. 117, s. 15	40
——————, s. 21	100
——————, s. 31	50
—————— c. 118, s. 14	51, 94
——————, s. 19	59
——————, s. 33	94
——————, s. 42	40
——————, s. 43	40
30 & 31 Vict. c. 35, s. 10	40
—————— c. 84, s. 30	51
—————— c. 90, s. 10	118
—————— c. 105, s. 4	58
—————— c. 127, s. 4	25
—————— c. 128, s. 5	51
—————— c. 131, s. 19	51
——————, s. 35	90
—————— c. 134, s. 12	102
——————, s. 18	109, 110
——————, s. 23	101
——————, s. 25	105
31 & 32 Vict. c. 106, s. 2	110
—————— c. 110, s. 20	51
—————— c. 119, s. 5	51
32 & 33 Vict. c. 12, s. 10	94
—————— c. 52, s. 13	51
—————— c. 62, s. 4	48
——————, s. 5	9, 35, 36
——————, s. 6	12
——————, s. 7	48
——————, s. 8	48
——————, s. 9	48
——————, s. 10	48
——————, s. 11	48
——————, s. 12	48, 84
——————, s. 13	48
——————, s. 14	48
——————, s. 15	48
——————, s. 16	48
33 & 34 Vict. c. 23, s. 9	111
——————, s. 18	111
—————— c. 52, s. 8	49
—————— c. 57, s. 9	98, 110, 117, 119
——————, s. 10	106, 118
—————— c. 58, s. 4	90
—————— c. 61, s. 19	51
—————— c. 90, s. 4	49
——————, s. 5	49
——————, s. 6	49
——————, s. 7	49
——————, s. 8	49

	PAGE
33 & 34 Vict. c. 90, s. 10	49
——————, s. 12	49
——————, s. 21	115
——————, s. 23	56
——————, s. 25	56
——————, s. 28	154
——————, s. 29	154
—————— c. 102, s. 2	48
34 & 35 Vict. c. 31, s. 18	51
—————— c. 56, s. 1	108
——————, s. 2	43
—————— c. 78, s. 4	127
——————, s 10	51
—————— c. 79, s. 1	50
—————— c. 96, s. 18	99
—————— c. 105, s. 11	67
——————, s. 13	53
—————— c. 108, s. 7	132
——————, s. 8	132
—————— c. 112, s. 7	81
——————, s. 12	78
——————, s. 16	53
35 & 36 Vict. c. 15, s. 5	102
——————, s. 7	102
——————, s. 10	102
—————— c. 33, s. 9	59
—————— c. 60, s. 3	49
—————— c. 77, s. 17	124
—————— c. 94, s. 12	82
——————, s. 18	99
——————, s. 25	98
36 & 37 Vict. c. 38	36, 97, 105
—————— c. 60, s. 8	47
—————— c. 71, s. 17	127
——————, s. 19	127
——————, s. 20	127
——————, s. 36	127, 128
——————, s. 37	61
——————, s. 38	128
—————— c. 88	51, 90, 117
37 & 38 Vict. c. 36, s. 1	90
—————— c. 49, s. 3	99
——————, e. 10	99
——————, s. 16	106
——————, s. 17	52, 99
38 & 39 Vict. c. 17, s. 4	92
——————, s. 5	92
——————, s. 9	93
——————, s. 10	93
——————, s. 17	93
——————, s. 22	93
——————, s. 23	93
——————, s. 30	93
——————, s. 31	93
——————, s. 32	93
——————, s. 33	93
——————, s. 43	93
——————, s. 46	93
——————, s. 47	94
——————, s. 55	94, 123
——————, s. 56	94

STATUTES.

	PAGE		PAGE
38 & 39 Vict. c. 17, s. 58	58, 124	38 & 39 Vict. c. 55, s. 265	154
———, s. 63	94	———, s. 308	69
———, s. 64	94	——— c. 60, s. 16	49
———, s. 69	67, 94	——— c. 63, s. 6	65
———, s. 73	49, 52	———, s. 9	65
———, s. 74	53, 108, 154	———, s. 13	65
———, s. 75	53, 58	———, s. 14	65
———, s. 76	94, 123	———, s. 30	114
———, s. 77	82, 92	——— c. 70, s. 16	110
———, s. 78	92	———, s. 17	110
———, s. 80	94	——— c. 86, s. 5	49
———, s. 81	94	———, s. 7	205
———, s. 82	94	39 & 40 Vict. c. 36	49, 51, 113
——— c. 22, s. 1	121	———, s. 30	116
——— c. 24, s. 1	49	———, s. 47	113, 116
——— c. 25, s. 5	91	———, s. 51	116
———, s. 6	102	———, s. 52	113
———, s. 12	94	———, s. 54	113
——— c. 55	71	———, s. 61	116
———, s. 4	68	———, s. 73	116
———, s. 16	68	———, s. 74	116
———, s. 19	68	———, s. 75	115
———, s. 23	68	———, s. 93	116
———, s. 26	69	———, s. 94	116
———, s. 36	68	———, s. 95	115
———, s. 41	68	———, s. 102	113
———, s. 46	68	———, s. 134	113
———, s. 49	68, 69	———, s. 138	114
———, s. 54	68	———, s. 147	113
———, s. 62	68, 69	———, s. 179	116
———, s. 70	69	———, s. 181	116, 154
———, s. 75	69	———, s. 182	113
———, s. 85	69	———, s. 185	113
———, s. 91	70	———, s. 190	116
———, s. 94	68	———, s. 192	106
———, s. 97	69	———, s. 193	90
———, s. 102	69, 70	———, s. 194	113
———, s. 105	58	———, s. 196	113
———, s. 106	58	———, s. 199	116
———, s. 109	69	———, s. 202	114
———, s. 110	69	———, s. 203	114, 153
———, s. 116	70	———, s. 204	56
———, s. 117	69	———, s. 205	56
———, s. 119	52	———, s. 206	108
———, s. 120	68	———, s. 221	55
———, s. 121	68	———, s. 234	116
———, s. 124	58, 68	———, s. 236	40
———, s. 137	70	———, s. 257	115
———, s. 142	58	———, s. 268	157, 161
———, s. 144	67	———, s. 269	161
———, s. 150	68	———, s. 270	162, 163
———, s. 152	68	———, s. 271	159
———, s. 153	69	———, s. 272	158, 160, 161, 162, 163
———, s. 155	69	———, s. 273	202
———, s. 158	69	——— c. 61, s. 31	44
———, s. 171	104	——— c. 77, s. 4	122
———, s. 256	43	———, s. 10	122
———, s. 257	68	——— c. 80, s. 4	50
———, s. 258	68	———, s. 6	56
———, s. 264	157–160, 162, 163	———, s. 10	56

STATUTES.

	PAGE		PAGE
39 & 40 Vict. c. 80, s. 12	125	43 & 44 Vict c 24, s. 42	119
———, s. 13	125	———, s. 48	57
40 & 41 Vict. c. 13, s. 5	158	———, s. 127	118, 119
——— c. 21, s. 40	13, 170	———, s. 137	117–119
———, s. 41	13	———, s. 138	120
——— c. 60, s. 1	66	———, s. 139	118, 119
———, s. 5	66	———, s. 140	56, 119
———, s. 6	66	———, s. 141	118, 119
——— c. 68, s. 1	114	———, s. 143	120
41 & 42 Vict. c. 12, s. 4	106	———, s. 144	120
——— c. 14, s. 10	71	———, s. 145	118, 120
———, s. 11	71, 94	———, s. 146	120
——— c. 16, s. 68	51, 123	——— c. 41, s. 8	80
———, s. 70	123	44 & 45 Vict. c. 12, s. 5	114
———, s. 93	123	———, s. 11	113
———, s. 97	123	———, s. 12	113, 116
———, s. 98	123	——— c. 37, s. 11	129
——— c. 32, s. 21	136	———, s. 16	129
——— c. 39, s. 9	60	———, s. 17	129
——— c. 49, s. 48	60	——— c. 58, s. 7	86, 89
———, s. 86	71	———, s. 104	48
——— c. 73	30	——— c. 67, s. 2	54
——— c. 74, s. 15	69	———, s. 4	53
———, s. 21	69	——— c. 69, s. 4	49
———, s. 30	69	———, s. 6	47
———, s. 35	69	———, s. 16	49
———, s. 42	66	———, s. 28	47
———, s. 50	78, 92, 108	45 & 46 Vict. c. 36, s. 4	133
———, s. 51	67	——— c. 43, s. 8	23
———, s. 52	122	———, s. 14	39
———, s. 55	158, 159, 163	——— c. 50, s. 7	50
———, s. 61	92	———, s. 86	59
———, s. 62	92	———, s. 148	43
42 & 43 Vict. c. 19, s. 15	122	———, s. 193	104
———, s. 17	122	———, s. 226	158, 159, 163
———, s. 80	39	———, s. 227	110
———, s. 86	39	——— c. 74, s. 14	115
——— c. 21, s. 8	114	——— c. 75, s. 1	35
——— c. 30, s. 3	65, 66	———, s. 14	25, 66
——— c. 33, s. 12	49	46 & 47 Vict. c. 3, s. 2	86
——— c. 42, s. 9	110	———, s. 3	86
———, s. 38	110	———, s. 4	86
——— c. 49, s. 6	43	———, s. 5	86
———, s. 43	37	———, s. 8	123
43 & 44 Vict. c. 19, s. 9	40	——— c. 10, s. 3	115
———, s. 20	157–162	——— c. 22, s. 12	117
———, s. 22	40	——— c. 38	47
———, s. 86	120	——— c. 51, s. 6	90
———, s. 88	25, 121	——— c. 52, s. 24	35
———, s. 89	40	———, s. 25	35
———, s. 91	40	———, s. 40	44, 121
——— c. 20, s. 17	57	———, s. 46	178
———, s. 24	11	———, s. 51	35
———, s. 26	118	———, s. 100	36
———, s. 28	120	———, s. 119	35
———, s. 29	117–119	———, s. 145	28
———, s. 30	117, 119	———, s. 146	18
———, s. 35	117, 118	———, s. 163	48
——— c. 24, s. 20	49	——— c. 53, s. 17	71, 123
———, s. 40	118	——— c. 61, s. 34	23, 26

STATUTES.

	PAGE
47 & 48 Vict. c. 11, s. 3	61, 127, 128
———— c. 62, s. 3	113
———— c. 64, s. 2	40
————, s. 3	40
————, s. 4	40
————, s. 5	40
————, s. 15	47, 48
———— c. 76, s. 9	121
48 & 49 Vict. c. 18	101
———— c. 35, s. 2	69
———— c. 49, s. 6	158, 159
———— c. 52, s. 2	99, 132
———— c. 64, s. 4	85
———— c. 69, s. 4	48
———— c. 72, s. 9	72
———— c. 75, s. 2	78, 100
49 & 50 Vict. c. 32, s. 9	70
———— c. 41, s. 2	115
50 & 51 Vict. c. 28, s. 2	50
————, s. 3	50
————, s. 12	52
————, s. 13	50
————, s. 16	115
———— c. 29, s. 8	66, 114, 119
————, s. 10	66
———— c. 55, s. 8	6, 17, 98, 140
————, s. 10	17
————, s. 14	9
————, s. 15	182
————, s. 20	175
————, s. 25	142
————, s. 28	17
————, s. 29	143, 157, 167, 169, 181, 201
————, s. 34	143
————, s. 39	29, 175
———— c. 56, s. 5	37
———— c. 58, s. 39	124
————, s. 41	124
————, s. 71	124
51 Vict. c. 8, s. 6	119
51 & 52 Vict. c. 14, s. 6	115
———— c. 19	122
———— c. 24, s. 5	124
———— c. 33, s. 6	94, 120
———— c. 41, s. 85	135
———— c. 43, s. 35	145, 165
————, s. 37	36
————, s. 42	180
————, s. 43	180
————, s. 48	40
————, s. 49	168
————, s. 50	179
————, s. 52	147
————, s. 53	157–160
————, s. 54	146
————, s. 55	162
————, s. 56	188
————, s. 66	163
————, s. 112	40
————, s. 131	169

	PAGE
51 & 52 Vict. c. 43, s. 142	42
————, s. 143	42
————, s. 146	41
————, s. 147	41
————, s. 148	41
————, s. 152	42
————, s. 154	42, 179
————, s. 155	41
————, s. 156	41
————, s. 159	42
————, s. 160	42
————, s. 161	36
————, s. 162	36
———— c. 59, s. 6	116
————, s. 7	56
52 & 53 Vict. c. 11, s. 3	71
————, s. 4	52
———— c. 18, s. 3	94
————, s. 4	94
———— c. 21, s. 29	74, 136
———— c. 42, s. 2	115
———— c. 44, s. 1	49, 82
————, s. 3	82, 123
————, s. 4	59, 82, 110
———— c. 63, s. 31	33
————, s. 32	65
————, s. 36	33, 63
53 & 54 Vict. c. 5, s. 13	59, 61
————, s. 15	59, 61, 99, 132
————, s. 16	59
————, s. 19	59
————, s. 20	99, 132
————, s. 21	59, 61
————, s. 24	61, 132
————, s. 25	132
————, s. 26	132
————, s. 63	61
————, s. 64	61
————, s. 65	61
————, s. 66	61
————, s. 67	61
————, s. 68	61
————, s. 71	59
————, s. 79	61
————, s. 81	61
————, s. 85	59, 132
————, s. 86	59
————, s. 89	59
————, s. 315	203
————, s. 322	203
————, s. 324	203
————, s. 325	203
————, s. 331	160
———— c. 8, s. 31	118
———— c. 14, s. 4	122
———— c. 21, s. 27	202
————, s. 28	157–163
————, s. 29	153, 163
————, s. 30	119, 120
————, s. 31	119, 120

STATUTES.

	PAGE
53 & 54 Vict. c. 34, s. 3	69
————, s. 4	61
————, s. 5	68
————, s. 6	68, 69
————, s. 12	61
————, s. 21	69
———— c. 39, s. 23	20
———— c. 45, s. 25	78
———— c. 56, s. 1	114
————, s. 2	114, 153
————, s. 4	114
———— c. 59, s. 3	70
————, s. 17	70
————, s. 27	70
————, s. 28	70
————, s. 37	67
————, s. 44	71
———— c. 70, s. 31	70
————, s. 34	69
————, s. 77	67
———— c. 71, s. 7	35
————, s. 11	26
54 Vict. c. 8, s. 2	41
———— c. 15	115
———— c. 19	117
54 & 55 Vict. c. 22, s. 7	71
————, s. 8	71
———— c. 46, s. 10	202
———— c. 65, s. 2	59
————, s. 19	59
————, s. 25	61
———— c. 69, s. 2	81
————, s. 6	81
———— c. 75, s. 1	123
————, s. 2	123
————, s. 3	72
————, s. 4	68
————, s. 7	69
————, s. 25	123

	PAGE
54 & 55 Vict. c. 75, s. 37	123
———— c. 76, s. 2	72
————, s. 5	73
————, s. 6	73
————, s. 8	73
————, s. 9	72
————, s. 10	72
————, s. 12	43
————, s. 16	101
————, s. 17	109
————, s. 20	72
————, s. 23	72
————, s. 25	72
————, s. 26	72
————, s. 28	72
————, s. 29	72
————, s. 35	72
————, s. 37	72
————, s. 40	73
————, s. 41	73
————, s. 43	73
————, s. 47	74
————, s. 54	73
————, s. 55	73
————, s. 59	73
————, s. 60	73
————, s. 61	73
————, s. 66	73
————, s. 67	61, 73
————, s. 71	61
————, s. 82	73
————, s. 89	73
————, s. 95	72, 74
————, s. 96	73
————, s. 97	61, 74
————, s. 115	72
————, s. 124	154
————, s. 142	74, 106

CASES CITED.

A.

	PAGE
Aaron v. Alexander	183
Abley v. Dale	34
Abrahams v. Deakin	148
Abrath v. North Eastern Railway Co.	187
Ackland v. Paynter	165
Ackworth v. Kemp	192
Adair v. Shaw	167
Agnew v. Jobson	172, 203
Ainsley v. Kirkheaton	68
Aitkenhead v. Blades	16, 137
Alchin v. Wells	177
Aldred v. Constable	20, 27, 193
Alexander. The	29, 30
Allen v. Allen	24
—— v. Backhouse	181
—— v. Sharp	39
—— v. Wright	82
Alresford v. Scott	45
Alston v. Scales	198
Ames v. Waterlow	16
Anderson v. Hume	54
Andrews v. Cawthorne	130
—— v. Dixon	26
—— v. Marris	32, 34, 138, 144
Anon	59, 116
Appleby v. Franklin	172
Armory v. Delamirie	151
Arnitt v. Garnett	26
Ash v. Dawnay	16, 137
Ashcroft v. Bourne	34
Asher v. Calcraft	131, 132
Aspey v. Jones	146, 155
Astley v. Biddle	131
Atkins v. Kilby	146
Attorney-General v. Ansted	116
—— v. Briant	115
—— v. Delous	115
—— v. Forbes	199
—— v. Ford	12
—— v. Hurel	115
—— v. Leonard	11, 38
—— v. Lockwood	119
—— v. Metropolitan Board of Works	199
—— v. Pearson	132
—— v. Radloff	115
—— v. Richmond	199
—— v. Schiers	114
—— v. Trueman	11
—— v. Voudière	116
—— v. Warmsley	11
—— v. Weeks	116
Austin v. Dowling	182, 185
Avery v. Cheslin	23
Aylwin v. Evans	195

B.

	PAGE
Bach v. Holmes	94
Bagge v. Whitehead	167, 206
Bailey v. Windham	19
Baker v. Cave	33
—— v. Portsmouth	69
Ball v. Ward	104
Ballard v. Bond	132
Barber v. Lewis	187
Barker v. Braham	148
—— v. St. Quintin	192
Barlow v. Kensington	73
—— v. Terrett	74
Barnacott v. Passmore	127
Barnard v. Leigh	28
Barnes v. Chipp	65
—— v. Harding	18
—— v. Keane	33
Barrons v. Luscombe	146
Barry v. Arnaud	150, 168, 197
Barton v. Gill	166
Batchelor v. Vyse	193
Bateman v. Poplar	157, 199
Bates v. Wingfield	20, 27
Batten v. Gedge	198
Bax v. Jones	156
Bayley v. Manchester Ry. Co.	148
Beard v. Knight	42
Beatty v. Gillbanks	80, 171
—— v. Glenister	80
Beck v. Rebon	22
Beckwith v. Philby	82
Beddall v. Maitland	198
Beechey v. Sides	155
Beeston v. Marriott	25
Bell v. Crane	164
—— v. Hutchinson	24
—— v. Midland Ry. Co.	192

CASES CITED.

	PAGE
Bell v. Oakley	137, 146, 147, 194, 198
Bellencontre, In re	47
Bellyse v. M'Ginn	27
Bennett v. Bennett	189
Bennett	26
Berthier, Ex parte	28
Bessell v. Wilson	34
Besset, Ex parte	144
Bessey v. Windham	141
Bettesworth, In re	68
Birch v. Dawson	22
Bird v. Bass	196
—— v. Jones	182, 183, 207
Birley v. Chorlton	199
Bishop v. Hinxman	167
Bishop Auckland v. Iron Co.	70
Bissicks v. Bath Colliery Co.	177
Blades v. Armidale	20, 165
Blake v. Barnard	173
—— v. Beech	54
Bland v. Delano	178
Bloomer, The	30
Blunt v. Beaumont	174
Boden v. Smith	156, 161
Booth v. Cooper	185
Booth v. Clive	155
—— v. Ferrett	69, 74
—— v. Shadgett	60
—— v. Trail	152
Boothman v. Earl Surrey	143
Borjesson v. Carlberg	30
Bosley v. Davies	149
Bostock v. Saunders	56
Botten v. Tomlinson	201
Bowditch v. Balchin	76
—— v. Fosbury	183
—— v. Wakefield	68
—— v. Bowdler	13
Bows v. Fenwick	54
Box v. Allen	199
Boyfield v. Porter	158
Bracegirdle v. Oxford	199
Brackenbury v. Lawrie	167
—— v. Thorsby	135
Brackley v. Battersea	62
Bracy	32
Bradbury v. Cooper	191
Braddick v. Smith	166
Bradlaugh v. Erskine	138
—— v. Gossett	138
Brady v. Todd	148
Brainard v. Connecticut Ry. Co.	169, 170, 201
Braine v. Hunt	166
Braithwaite v. Skinner	164
Brand v. Hammersmith	140
Brasyer v. Maclean	167
Brecks v. Woltrey	131
Breese v. Jerdein	156
Brewis v. Hornsey	68
Brickill v. Hulse	196

	PAGE
Bridge v. Parsons	81
Brighton v. Strand	44
Brinsmead v. Harrison	17, 151
Brittain v. Kinnaird	34
Britton v. Cole	140
Broad v. Ham	186
Bromage v. Vaughan	19
Brooke v. Jenney	33, 45
Broughton v. Davis	10
—— v. Midland Great Western Ry. Co.	149
Brown v. Glenn	6, 7, 16
—— v. Holyhead	64
—— v. Jarvis	165
—— v. Parrott	24
—— v. Watson	138
Brownlow v. Tomlinson	133
Brunswick v. Sloman	151
Bryson v. Russell	155, 159
Buckland v. Butterfield	23
Buckle v. Bewes	178
Bullen v. Ansley	177
Bullock v. Dunlap	195
Burden v. Kennedy	21
Burder v. Selmes	131
Burdett v. Abbott	3, 5, 6
—— v. Coleman	5, 6
Burling v. Harley	155
Buron v. Denman	117, 153
Burridge v. Nicholetto	160
Burton v. Acton	63
—— v. Henson	131
—— v. Le Gros	145
Bush v. Barker	173
Busst v. Gibbons	186
Butterton v. Furber	163
Byne v. Moon	187

C.

	PAGE
Callous v. Tuffnel	22
Calvert v. Jolliffe	193
Cameron v. Reynolds	26, 142
Cann v. Clipperton	155, 156
Cant v. Parsons	184
Carlile v. Parkins	141, 165
Carman v. Truman	187
—— v. Stringer	60
Carr v. Royal Exchange Co.	161
Carratt v. Morley	32, 144
Carrett v. Smallpage	143
Carter v. Hughes	18
Casberd v. Attorney-General	10
Castioni, Ex parte	47
Castrique v. Behrens	187
Caswell v. Hundred House	106
Caudle v. Seymour	32
Cuzet v. De la Borde	8
Chamberlain v. Conway	64
—— v. King	155, 160

CASES CITED. xxvii

	PAGE
Chapman v. Auckland	157
—— v. Pickersgill	164
—— v. Robinson	134
Charinton v. Johnson	181
Charkich, The	30
Charleton v. Alway	121, 146, 194, 196
Chastenauf v. Capeyron	31
Chater v. Chigwell	194, 198
Chatfield v. Comerford	186
Cheasley v. Barnes	196
Chick v. Smith	20
Chinn v. Morris	184, 207
Chisholm v. Doulton	149
Christie v. Unwin	32, 33
Christopherson v. Barr	173
—— v. Burton	19
City Ry. Co. v. County Council	73
Clark v. Newsam	200
—— v. Postan	185
—— v. Woods	146, 147, 185
Clarke, In re	37
—— v. Bradlaugh	9, 19
—— v. Crowder	107
—— v. Hayne	54, 81
—— v. Higgins	105
—— v. Tucker	63
Clements v. Ohrly	186
Clerk v. Withers	28
Clew, In re	37
Clifton v. Hooper	165
Clutterbuck v. Jones	166
Cobbett, In re	13
—— v. Gray	64, 173
Cock v. Gent	161
Cocker v Musgrove	26, 193
Codd v. Cabe	52
Coffin v. Dyke	40
Cohen v. De las Rivas	176
—— v. Morgan	186
Colam v. Hall	82
—— v. Paget	81
Cole v. Coulton	108
Colegrave v. Dias Santos	22
Coleman v. Goldsmith	67
—— v. Goodwin	187
Collins v. Rose	147
Colls v. Coates	20, 177
Colman v. Goodwin	189
Colne Valley v. Trehane	69
Colyer v. Speer	26
Comus, The	30
Conder, Ex parte	178
Conybeare v. School Board of London	48
Cook v. Leonard	155
—— v. Nethercote	78
—— v. Palmer	27
Cooke v. Wildes	190
Cooper v. Asprez	4
—— v. Booth	56
—— v. Hill	175

	PAGE
Cooper v. Wandsworth	34, 134
Cope v. Barber	132
Copland v. Powell	155
Corbet v. Brown	142
Costar v. Hetherington	103, 173
Cotes v. Michill	32, 138, 139
Cottingham v. King	29
Cotton v. Brown	187
—— v. Radwell	146
Covell v. Laming	172
Coward v. Baddeley	78, 204
Cowler v. Jones	127
Cox v. Coleridge	59
—— v. Hakes	186
—— v. Leigh	26
Coyne v. Brady	54
Crane v. Lawrance	66
Crake v. Powell	164
Craycraft, In re	178
Creagh v. Gamble	99, 147, 182, 185
Crisp v. Anderson	151
Croasdill v. Radcliffe	135
Crockford v. Maidstone	135
Croft v. Allison	149
Cross, In re	98
Crowder v. Long	140
Crowther v. Ramsbottom	199
Crozier v. Cundy	52, 137, 147
Crumbie v. Wallsend	157
Crump v. Day	167
Cumming v. Green	191

D.

	PAGE
Dale	3, 10
Dalston v Coatsworth	151
Daly v. Webb	70
Danby v. Hunter	109, 135
Daniell v. James	96
—— v. Phillips	32
Danvers v. Morgan	156
Darby v. Ouseley	189
—— v. Waterlow	165
Dargan v. Davies	81
Davenport v. Rhodes	29
Davies v. Jenkins	183
Davis, Ex parte	98
—— v. Black	131
—— v. Curling	154
—— v. Marlborough	18
—— v. Jones	22
—— v. Stephenson	54
Dawson v. Clark	184
—— v. Vansandau	186
—— v. Wood	23
Danbury v. Cooper	59
Day v. King	33
De Gondouin v. Lewis	174, 195
De Medina v. Grove	187
De Moranda v. Dunkin	17

xxviii CASES CITED.

	PAGE
De Morgan v. Metropolitan Board of Works	79
D'Eyncourt v. Gregory	24
Dean v. Allarley	22
—— v. Taylor	174
—— v. Whitaker	24, 193
Delmar v Freemantle	166
Dempster v. Purnell	33
Dennis v. Whetham	166
Denny v. Thwaites	134
Dew v. Parsons	181
Dewdney v. Good	130
Dews v. Riley	34
Dick v. Badart	64
Dickinson, The	31
Dillon v. O'Brien	107
Ditcham v. Bond	199
Dixon	171
—— v. Board of Works	149
—— v. Ensell	167
—— v. Farrar	149, 153
Doe v. Filliter	191
—— v. Thorn	192
—— v. Young	151
Doggett v. Catterns	54
Doss v. Doss	197
Doswell v. Impey	145
Downing v. Butcher	184, 188
—— v. Capel	91
Drake, Ex parte	17
—— v. Sykes	141
Drewe v. Lainson	27
Dry Docks Co., In re	44
Dubois v. Keates	187
Dudley v. Warde	22
Duffie v. Spottiswoode	193
Dumerque v. Ramsey	24
Dundee, The	29, 30
Dunn v. Birmingham Canal Co.	149
Dunston v. Paterson	182
Durham, The Lady	30

E.

Eagleton v. Gutteridge	15, 199
East India Co. v. Skinner	44
Eastwood v. Miller	54
Ecklin v. Little	189
Edge v. Kavanagh	27
Edgell v. Francis	151, 185
Edmonds, Ex parte	35
Edwards, In re	13
—— v. Bridges	23
—— v. Farebrother	193
—— v. Hodges	160
—— v. Islington	155
—— v. Salmon	181, 207
Eggington	43
Eley v. Lytle	96
Elliott v. Osborne	81

	PAGE
Ellis v. Bridgworth	199
Elsie v. Smith	185
Elwes v. Mawe	22, 23, 24
Empson v. Soden	23
Entick v. Carrington	3, 146
Evans v. McCloughlan	119
—— v. Oakley	134
—— v. Wills	35
Everett v. Grapes	64
Everitt v. Davies	81
Eynde v. Gould	169, 201

F.

Farnley v. Ormsby	134, 168, 170
Farr v. Newman	25
Farrant v. Thompson	124
Fawcett v. York Ry.	133
Fecit v. Walsh	65
Feltham v. Terry	181
Fergusson v. Kinnoull	150, 164
Fermor v. Phillips	141
Fernandez, In re	3, 12, 139
Field v. Mitchell	196
Fielding v. Rhyl Commissioners	64
Fishermen of Faversham	64
Fitzjohn v. Mackinder	185
Flannagan v. Bishopwearmouth	97
Fletcher v. Bealey	199
Flewster v. Royle	76, 99
Flora, The	30
Flower v. Low Leyton	157
Floyd v. Bethel	29
Ford v. Leche	142
—— v. Wiley	81
Forde v. Skinner	203
Foster v. Dodd	34, 47, 147
—— v. Hilton	26
Foulger v. Newcomb	189
—— v. Taylor	42
Fowler v. Cookson	196
Foxall v. Barnett	185, 188
France v. Campbell	24
Francis v. Nash	21
Freegard v. Barnes	198
Freeman v. Arkell	187
—— v. Read	45, 194
Freston, In re	71
Frost v. Barclay	26
Fryer, Ex parte	35
Fuller v. Lane	131
Fulwood	83

G.

Galliard v. Laxton	43, 52, 58
Galloway v. Maries	54
Gardner v. Bygrave	79
Garnett v. Bradley	191

CASES CITED.

xxix

	PAGE
Garnett v. Ferrand	59
Garstin v. Asplin	195
Gartside v. Ratcliffe	157
Gawler v. Chaplin	21, 165, 193, 195
Gay v. Matthews	145
Gazard v. Cooke	128
Gent-Davis v. Harris	7
Geraldes v. Donison	181
Gerring v. Barfield	135
Gibbins v. Phillips	141
Gibbons v. Pepper	79, 204
Gibbs v. Stead	121
Gibson v. Preston	67
Gilbert v. Burtenshaw	191
Gimbert v. Coyney	194
Gladstone v. Padwick	20
Gladwell v. Blake	52, 77, 146
Glanibanta, The	31
Glasspoole v. Young	23, 193
Glynn v. Houston	76, 99, 148
Goff v. Great Northern Ry. Co.	149
Goode v. Langley	177
Goodwin v. Gibbons	144, 145
Gordon v. Harper	25
Gore v. Special Commissioners	128
Gosden v. Elphick	146
Gosset v. Howard	3, 138, 139
Grainger v. Hill	182, 196
Grand Junction v. Shugar	198
Grant v. Bagge	143
—— v. Moser	80
Great Western Ry. Co. v. Bailie	60
Greaves v. Keene	13, 183
Green v. Broad	156
—— v. Brown	166
—— v. Elgie	12, 139
—— v. Rowan	146
Greene v. Jones	140
Greenway v. Hurd	154, 156, 181
Gregg v. Smith	99
Gregory v. Brunswick	206
—— v. Cotterell	143
—— v. Derby	187
—— v. Hill	174
—— v. Sloman	28
Grey v. Smith	141
Griffin v. Coleman	78, 183
—— v. Deighton	130
Griffith v. Taylor	91, 155
Grindley v. Baker	75, 107, 114, 119
Grinham v. Willey	99
Groome v. Forester	32
Grymes v. Boweria	22
Guest v. Warren	151
Gully v. Smith	135

H.

Hadley v. Perks	103
Haigh v. Sheffield	54

	PAGE
Hale v. Cole	65
Haliday v. Phillips	131
Hall, Ex parte	166
—— v. Batley	148
—— v. Knox	108
—— v. Ley	17
—— v. Nixon	64
—— v. Richardson	95
—— v. Robinson	107
—— v. Roche	167
Hammersmith Rent-charge, In re	34
Hammond v. Bouyshe	34
Hancock v. Somes	103, 173
Handcock v. Baker	77, 210
Harbert	10
Hardwicke v. Moss	156
Hardy v. Murphy	80
Harley v. Harley	21
Harmonie, The	30
Harper v. Carr	146
Harris v. Mobbs	188
—— v. Slater	36
Harrison v. Barry	26
—— v. Bush	190
—— v. Hodgson	174
—— v. McL' Meel	106
—— v. Painter	17, 21
—— v. Wright	4, 32
Hart v. Basset	188, 204
Harvey v. Bridges	198
—— v. Harvey	9, 22
Hasker v. Wood	163
Hay v. Kitchen	174
Hayes v. Stevenson	97
Hayling Okey	199
Haythorn v. Bush	193
Heap v. Burnley Union	63
Hearson, In re	86
Hele v. Bexley	19
Helmore v. Smith	20
Hemming v. Hudson	174
Henderson v. Preston	13
Henley Co., In re	121
Hermitage v. Kilpin	35
Hescott	142, 206
Hewetson v. Sherwin	35
Howlett v. Crutchley	186
Hicks v. Faulkner	184, 186, 187
Hide v. Pettit	9
Hider v. Dorrell	156
Higginson v. Martin	145
Hill v. Barnes	117
—— v. Somerset	135
Hilliard v. Hanson	195
Hirst v. Molesbury	97
Hoare v. Silverlocke	189
Hobson, In re	19
—— v. Thellusson	167
Hodgson v. Gascoigne	21
—— v. Lynch	165
Hoe	19, 194

CASES CITED.

	PAGE
Hoey v. Felton	185
Hogg v. Ward	99, 183
Holden v. King	173
Holloway v. Turner	200
Holmes v. Sparkes	160, 164, 172
Holroyd v. Doncaster	183
Homer v. Cadman	79, 135
Hoop, The	30
Hooper v. Lane	6, 139, 140
Hope v. Evered	185
Hopkins v. Smithwick	68, 69
Hopton v. Thirlwall	128
Hordern v. Dalton	168
Horley v. Rogers	97
Horn v. Buller	22
Horsfall v. Holland	131
Howard v. Clarke	184, 187
——— v. Gosset	7, 138
Howell v. Jackson	99
Hoye v. Bush	144, 146, 184
Hoyle v. Hitchman	65
Huckle v. Money	151, 185
Hudson v. Shooter	94
Hughes v. Buckland	156
——— v. Lloyd	130
——— v. Smallwood	42
Hull v. Greenhill	18
Hume v. Druyff	12
——— v. Oldacre	150
Humphreys v. Stillwell	16, 190
Hunt v. Hooper	20
Hurrell v. Wink	44
Hutchings v. Morris	39
——— v. Reeves	3, 60
Hutchins v. Chambers	44
——— v. Denziloe	131
Hutchinson v. Johnson	19
Huth v. Clarke	64
Hyndman, Ex parte	37

I.

Imason v. Cope	173
Infant, In re	8
Ireland v. Bushell	166
Irving v. Wilson	155, 181, 195
Irwin v. Grey	150, 153
Iveson v. Moore	188

J.

Jackson, In re	14
——— v. Hill	143, 166
——— v. Stanhope	195
Jacobs v. Humphrey	27, 141, 165
——— v. Schmaltz	189
Jacobson v. Blake	195
Jagger v. Doncaster	69
James v. Brown	142

	PAGE
James v. Campbell	172
Jarmain v. Hooper	192
Jarratt v. Steele	130
Jason v. Dixon	121
Jenks v. Turpin	55
Jenkins v. Gettring	23
——— v. King	107
Jenoure v. Delmege	191
Jersey v. Uxbridge	18
Johnson	44
——— v. Croydon	63
——— v. Leigh	6, 15, 199
——— v. Northwood	174
——— v. Saunders	115
Jones v. Atherton	27
——— v. Chapman	197
——— v. Purcell	28
——— v. Perchard	143
——— v. Vaughan	162
——— v. Williams	167
——— v. Wood	141
——— v Wylie	173
Jordan v. Bincksc	21
Joule v. Taylor	154
Joyce v. Metropolitan Board of Works	74, 148
Julius v. Oxford (Bishop)	164, 165
Jupp v. Cooper	169, 201, 202
Justice v. Gosling	184

K.

Kavanagh v. Gudge	199
Keane v. Reynolds	145
Kearney v. Tottenham	174
Keene v. Dilke	196
Keet v. Smith	131
Keighly v. Bell	48, 59
Keightley v. Birch	26, 27
Kemplaud v. Macaulay	20
Kendal	32
——— v. Row	46
Kenyon v. Eastwood	36
Kerby v. Denbey	16, 137, 197, 200
Kershaw v. Johnson	60
Kinlyside v. Martin	24
Kinning v. Buchanan	34
Kirk v. Coates	65
Kyle v. Barber	202

L.

Labalmondiere v. Addison	77
Ladd v. Thomas	197
Lamacraft v. St. Thomas	68
Lamley v. E. Retford	156
Lamont v. Southall	194
Lancaster Co. v. Fitzhugh	194
Lane v. Cotton	150

CASES CITED.

	PAGE
Langdon v. Broadbent	69
Langrish v. Archer	97
Laugher v. Breffit	154, 162
—— v. Pointer	148
Law v. London Co.	21
Laws v. Eltringham	96
—— v. Telford	198
Lawton v. Lawton	22
—— v. Salmon	24
Lea v. Rossi	166
Leach v. Money	3
—— v. Thomas	22, 24
Leader v. Danvers	27
Leake, Ex parte	33
Leaper v. Smith	116
Lechmere v. Charlton	7
Lee v. Gansel	7, 15
—— v. Matthews	130, 168
—— v. Risdon	22, 24
—— v. Vesey	52
Leete v. Hart	82, 91
Lefanu v. Moregreen	192
Legg v. Evans	21, 24
Levy, In re	175
—— v. Edwards	80, 173, 203
Lewis, Ex parte	79
—— v. Fennor	81
—— v. Hammond	181
—— v. Vaughan	204, 205
—— v. Weston	68
Leyman v. Latimer	189
Linford v. Lake	174
Lithgow, Ex parte	178
Little v. Port Talbot Co.	125
Lloyd v. Davies	19, 137
—— v. Lloyd	107
Lockyer v. Offlen	114
London Co. v. Drake	24
—— and Devon Co., In re	25
—— and North Western Ry. Co. v. Richards	60
Long Wellesley	7
Long v. Bray	177
Longdill v. Jones	179
Loog v. Bean	190
Looker v. Halscomb	96
Lord Advocate v. Crookshanks	114
Love v. Attorney-General	116
Ludmore, In re	178
Lumley v. Gye	148, 149
—— v. Wagner	168
Lyne v. Leonard	128
Lyster v. Dolland	18

M.

	PAGE
M'Clenaghan v. Waters	171
M'Cloughlan v. Clayton	160, 184
M'Curday v. Driscoll	184
M'Kinnon v. Penson	133

	PAGE
M'Dougall v. Paterson	164
M'Gahey v. Alston	151
M'Pherson v. Daniell	189
Macartney v. Garbutt	7
Macdonald v. Lochrane	64
Macey v. Metropolitan Board of Works	199
Macgregor v. Galsworthy	156
Madrazo v. Willes	117
Magnay v. Burt	16
Mahon v. Miles	177
Maidman v. Malpas	130
Mallinson v. Carr	70
Marks v. Beyfus	170
Marshall v. Lamb	151
—— v. Smith	63
Marshalsea	33, 145
Martin, Ex parte	36
—— v. Bell	141
—— v. Shoppee	172
—— v. Upcher	156
Mason v. Birkenhead Commissioners	156
—— v. Paynter	165
Masper v. Brown	173
Masters v. Shawley	24
Mather v. Fraser	24
Matthews v. Biddulph	76
Mayhew v. Locke	37
—— v. Parker	33
Meirelles v. Banning	195
Mercer v. Woodgate	134
Merest v. Harvey	151, 200
Mesnil v. Dakyn	181
Metropolitan District v. Hill	149
Middlesex Sheriff	3
Midland Insurance v. Smith	172
Midland Ry. Co. v. Withington	154
Migotti v. Colvill	13
Miles v. Harris	177
Mill v. Hawker	133, 155, 198
Miller v. Searo	145
Milton v. Green	147
Milward v. Caffin	194
Minet v. Johnson	39
Minshall v. Lloyd	141
Mitchell v. Simpson	9, 17, 35
—— v. Tarbutt	150
—— v. Williams	186
Monck v. Hilton	97
Money v. Leach	137
Monk v. Cass	166
Moody v. Leach	70
Moon v. Raphael	141, 167
Moone v. Rose	183
Moore v. Adam	174
—— v. Shepherd	161
Morgan v. Leach	133, 168
Moriarty v. Brooks	173
Morley v. Greenhalgo	81
Morris v. Johnson	65

	PAGE
Morris v. Salberg	193
Morrish v. Murray	16, 199
Morse v. James	144
Mortimer v. Cradock	151
Mortimore v. Cragg	177
Morton v. Brammer	44
Mostyn v. Stock	28
Mullett v. Challis	165
Munro v. Watson	63
Mure v. Kaye	184
Murphy v. Manning	81
Musgrove v. Toy	115
Muskett v. Drummond	32

N.

Nalty v. Aylett	13
Nash v. Allen	19
—— v. Lucas	16
Naylor v. Collinge	22
Neate v. Hardinge	181
Newman v. Merriman	178
Newport Bridge, *In re*	164
Newsam v. Carr	188
Newton v. Harland	198
Nicholson v. Naylor	202
Nicol v. Beaumont	135
Nicols v. Hall	92
Norden	171
Nordstiernen, The	30
North v. Sheriff of Middlesex	167

O.

Oakes v. Wood	174
O'Brien v. Brabner	58, 185
—— v. Salisbury	192
Ogden v. Hesketh	141, 196
O'Kelly v. Harvey	174
Oldham v. Ramsden	54
Olding v. Wild	128
Olliet v. Bessey	144, 145
Opera Limited, *In re*	25, 178, 181
Original Co. v. Gibb	157
Osborne v. Millman	13
—— v. Veitch	173
Ostler v. Bower	166
Oughton v. Seppings	165

P.

Packington v. Culliford	167
Paddock v. Forester	153
Page, *Ex parte*	4
Pain v. Boughtwood	65
Pallister v. Pallister	142
Palmer v. Paul	199

	PAGE
Palomares, The	41
Panton v. Roberts	22
—— v. Williams	146
Pappin v. Maynard	135
Park, *In re*	35
Parkes v. Moore	16
Parkins v. Proctor	160
—— v. Scott	189
Parlement Belge, The	30
Parmiter v. Coupland	189
Parrott v. Mumford	140, 182
Parsons v. Bethnal Green	67
—— v. Lloyd	138, 139
Partridge v. Council of Medical Education	165
—— v. Elkington	180
Patchett v. Bancroft	39, 144
Payne v. Chapman	181
—— v. Revans	186
Peacock v. Bell	4
Pearce, *In re*	27
Pendlebury v. Greenhalgh	134
Penny v. Hanson	97
Penton v. Browne	15
Peppercorn v. Hoffman	52
Percival v. Stamp	16
Perkin v. Proctor	139, 145
Perkins Beach Lead Mine, *In re*	178
—— v. Vaughan	174, 184
Perkinson v. Gilford	166
Perrins v. Johnson	20
Peters v. Clarson	134, 155, 157
Phillips v. Canterbury	201
—— v. Gateshead JJ.	208
Pickard v. Paiton	19
Pidler v. Berry	64
Pilkington v. Cooke	177, 179
Piper v. Chappell	63
Pitcher v. King	165
Pitts v. Millar	81
Plater, *Ex parte*	36
Playfair v. Musgrove	16, 198, 199
Plumer v. Brisco	168
Plunkett v. Pearson	18
Pocock v. Moore	207
Pointon v. Hill	96
Poole	22, 23
Popham v. Pickburn	190
Porter v. Wotton	177
Poulton v. London and South Western Ry. Co.	149
Powell v. Hodgetts	184
—— v. Knights	81
Price v. Messenger	146
Prickett v. Gratrex	156
Primrose v. Laurence	190
Pugh v. Griffith	7, 16
Pullin v. Deffel	163, 194
Purcell v. Macnamara	187
—— v. Sowler	59, 61

CASES CITED. xxxiii

Q.

	PAGE
Queen v. London	186
Quick v. Staines	193
Quinby v. Liverpool	64
Quincey, *Ex parte*	22

R.

	PAGE
Ramsden v. Yeates	45
Ranken v. Harwood	20
Ratcliffe v. Burton	7, 15
Rawlings v. Till	79
Rawlins v. Ellis	48
Rawstone v. Backhouse	128
——— v. Wilkinson	177
Read v. Coker	146, 173
Reddell v. Stowey	193
Reece v. Taylor	174
Reed v. Nutt	173
Reeves v. Yeates	77
Regent Stores, The	121
R. v. Adams	88
— v. Adey	88
— v. Akers	115
— v. Allen	84
— v. All Saints	32, 33
— v. Ashton	103
— v. Asplin	87
— v. Atkinson	90
— v. Autey	87
— v. Avis	84
— v. Aylett	209
— v. Backhouse	16
— v. Bailey	7, 88, 89
— v. Bake	209
— v. Baker	203
— v. Bank of England	170
— v. Barfoot	114
— v. Barrett	151
— v. Barrow	90
— v. Bartlett	89
— v. Batstone	83
— v. Bawen	84
— v. Best	205
— v. Bethel	13
— v. Binney	145
— v. Bolland	86
— v. Bonkin	86
— v. Boulter	209
— v. Boulton	95
— v. Bowerman	94
— v. Bowers	89
— v. Brackenbridge	84
— v. Brice	85
— v. Brown	84, 91, 203
— v. Bullock	85
— v. Burgess	89
— v. Burns	80
— v. Burrell	83
— v. Burt	204

	PAGE
R. v. Bushell	202
— v. Cadman	83
— v. Cambridge	45
— v. Candy	115
— v. Carr	88
— v. Chapman	7, 52, 209
— v. Chester	170
— v. Child	83
— v. Christian	95
— v. Clarence	87
— v. Clarke	76, 98, 121
— v. Clinch	87
— v. Closs	86
— v. Coelho	86
— v. Coleridge	130
— v. Colvin	206
— v. Coney	79, 173
— v. Cook	54
— v. Cope	206
— v. Cosans	120
— v. Cotesworth	204
— v. Cox	106
— v. Cracknell	85
— v. Cross	204
— v. Crump	88
— v. Crunden	98
— v. Cruse	76
— v. Cubitt	116
— v. Cumming	86
— v. Cumpton	52
— v. Danser	139, 144
— v. Davis	85
— v. Davy	84
— v. Deane	21
— v. Devon, Sheriff of	9, 11
— v. D'Eyncourt	109
— v. Dixon	170
— v. Dobbins	106
— v. Downshire	45
— v. Druitt	205
— v. Eccles	205
— v. Edgall	83
— v. Elliott	98
— v. Ely, JJ.	145
— v. Evans	90
— v. Farrow	83
— v. Faulkner	84
— v. Fidler	89
— v. Fisher	89, 103
— v. Fitchie	87
— v. Flannagan	85
— v. Flitcher	120
— v. Flinton	97
— v. Ford	120, 121
— v. Foulkes	88
— v. Fox	170
— v. Fullagar	95
— v. Franks	92
— v. French	52
— v. Fretwell	87
— v. Fursey	80

c

CASES CITED.

	PAGE		PAGE
R. v. Ganz	47	R. v. Light	78, 80
— v. Gardner	206	— v. Lisle, Lord	11
— v. Gibbs	88	— v. Lockley	80
— v. Giles	86	— v. Loggan	207
— v. Gill	206	— v. London	43
— v. Gillham	207	— v. Londonthorpe	22
— v. Gloster, JJ.	44	— v. Long	104
— v. Goodhall	83	— v. Lovell	88
— v. Goole	68	— v. Mabel	203
— v. Gordon	151	— v. Macdaniel	205
— v. Gover	85	— v. Mackerel	89
— v. Graham	79, 80	— v. Magrath	84, 88
— v. Gray	89	— v. Manning	83
— v. Greenhalgh	95	— v. Marks	89
— v. Gregory	207	— v. Marsden	77, 78
— v. Griepe	209	— v. Marsh	11
— v. Hadfield	96	— v. Martin	85, 95
— v. Handsley	37	— v. Master	43
— v. Hardy	96	— v. Matthews	88, 89
— v. Harley	83	— v. Matthias	134
— v. Harris	98	— v. Mawbey	205
— v. Harvey	85	— v. McNaughten	79
— v. Haywood	85	— v. Mellish	88
— v. Hedges	22	— v. Menlis	142
— v. Herrmann	92	— v. Middlesex	37, 201
— v. Higgins	206, 208	— v. Middleton	88
— v. Hill	90	— v. Mitchell	87
— v. Hillard	85	— v. Mitton	7, 38
— v. Hodges	76	— v. Moorhouse, James	131
— v. Hodgkinson	99	— v. Mopsey	87
— v. Hollis	83, 88, 95	— v. Morton	86
— v. Holmes	98	— v. Moseley	199
— v. Honiton	44	— v. Myers	201
— v. Hood	33	— v. Neale	48, 59, 80
— v. Howarth	7, 77, 97	— v. Netherton	44
— v. Hughes	209	— v. Nettleton	89
— v. Hulcott	4, 33	— v. Newcastle	63
— v. Hulton	54	— v. Newman	95, 190
— v. Hunt	90	— v. Newmarket	45
— v. Isaac	83	— v. Nichol	209
— v. Isaacs	83	— v. Noakes	120
— v. James	13, 89, 121	— v. Noonan	143
— v. Jeans	85	— v. O'Donnel	109
— v. Jervis	91	— v. Orton	79
— v. John	92	— v. Otley	24
— v. Jolliffe	205	— v. Owen	91
— v. Jones	45	— v. Oxford, JJ.	45
— v. Jordan	36	— v. Page	92
— v. Joyce	87	— v. Paget	43
— v. Kay	87	— v. Palmer	9, 86
— v. Kent	45	— v. Parnell	205
— v. Kerrick	205	— v. Parsons	89, 206
— v. Kesteven	136	— v. Patience	52
— v. Kimmersley	205	— v. Pearson	88
— v. Kinnear	10	— v. Peddle	206
— v. Kirk	45	— v. Pedley	209
— v. Lambe	11	— v. Peel	52
— v. Lawrence	85	— v. Pembleton	96
— v. Lee	11	— v. Penson	84
— v. Lofroy	37	— v. Perring	201
— v. Lewis	86	— v. Phelps	82, 91

CASES CITED.

	PAGE
R. v. Phillips	209
— v. Pinney	48, 80, 169
— v. Plan	10
— v. Pollman	205
— v. Pratt	43
— v. Price	43
— v. Probert	83
— v. Pulham	91
— v. Quail	208
— v. Radford	92
— v. Ransford	208
— v. Reardon	91
— v. Reed	98
— v. Reynolds	90
— v. Richards	85, 206
— v. Richardson	170
— v. Ritson	86
— v. Robinson	95, 206
— v. Rose	120
— v. Rozier	54
— v. Russell	204
— v. St. Dunstan	22
— v. St. George	203
— v. St. Olave's	44
— v. Salmon	83
— v. Sanderson	11
— v. Sandoval	56
— v. Satchwell	84
— v. Saunders	37, 98
— v. Scofield	208
— v. Scott	170
— v. Sewers' Commissioners	63
— v. Shaw	209
— v. Shropshire County Court	168
— v. Simmonds	112
— v. Smith	85, 88, 89, 198
— v. Smyth	210
— v. Spanner	85
— v. Spencer	84, 89
— v. Spragg	206
— v. Spriggs	85
— v. Squire	88
— v. Stringer	84
— v. Surrey County Court	36
— v. Swallow	85
— v. Taylor	54, 84, 98, 130, 205
— v. Thallman	98
— v. Thompson	85, 115, 120, 205
— v. Thorn	87
— v. Thurborn	88
— v. Tithe Commissioners	165
— v. Tolson	84
— v. Topping	11
— v. Totnes	32
— v. —— Union	34
— v. Townsend	88
— v. Turner	205
— v. Vanderstein	86
— v. Vezzell	98
— v. Vreones	171, 206
— v. Wakefield	83

	PAGE
R. v. Watson	98
— v. Watts	56
— v. Webb	98, 104
— v. Weeks	85
— v. Weil	47, 86
— v. Wellard	98
— v. Wells	11
— v. Welsh	85, 92, 96
— v. West	89
— v. Wheeldon	85
— v. Wilkes	46
— v. Williams	104
— v. Wilson	47, 83, 84, 92, 209
— v. Wilts JJ.	152, 170
— v. Winton	169
— v. Wiseman	91
— v. Whitchurch	83
— v. Whittaker	98
— v. Wood	65, 98
— v. Woolf	11
— v. Young	79
— v. Zulueta	117
Reid v. Poyntz	141, 196
Rendsbury, The	30
Reynolds v. Barford	26
—— v. Monkton	132
Richards v. Cullerne	36
—— v. Easts	161
—— v. Johnston	23
—— v. Turner	184
Richardson v. Ardley	24
Ricket v. Metropolitan Ry. Co.	188
Rideal v. Fort	192
Riddell v. Pakeman	145
Rimmer v. Rimmer	174
Ritchings v. Cordingley	130
Riseley v. Ryle	195
Roberts v. Ball	9
—— v. Garrett	59
—— v. Hunt	133
—— v. Orchard	156
—— v. Woodward	136
Robins, Ex parte	170
Roccliffe, The	30
Roderick v. Aston	68
Rodriquez v. Tadmere	188
Rogers v. Kenny	24
Rollason v. Rollason	21
Rolles v. Newell	63
Roope v. D'Avigdor	172
Ross, Ex parte	27
Rothery v. Wood	26
Rouch v. Hall	66
Rowcliffe v. Edmonds	189
—— v. Murray	161
Rowe v. Brenton	153
—— v. Hawkins	173
Rowning v. Goodchild	150, 168
Royle v. Busby	178
Rudland v. Sunderland	63
Russell v. Horne	172

xxxvi   CASES CITED.

	PAGE
Russell v. Russell	34
Russen v. Lucas	207
Ruston v. Hatfield	165
Rutland (Countess)	138, 139
Ryan v. Shilcock	16

S.

Sairle v. Roberts	188
St. John (Rector) v. Parishioners	45
St. John v. Pigott	24
St. Luke v. Lewis	75
St. Pancras Vestry v. Batterbury	164
Salter v. Magapert	116
Sanderson v. Baker	140, 143, 192
Sandys v. Sindel	65
Sanson v. Rumsey	151
Saul v. Dawson	29
Saunders v. Warren	160
Sawle v. Paynter	20
Scarfe v. Hallifax	141
Scarlett v. Hanson	23, 166
Scott v. Lewis	166
—— v. Marshall	141
—— v. Morley	35
—— v. Sampson	191
—— v. Scholey	19
—— v. Shearman	168, 195
—— v. Waithman	168
Seaman v. Netherclift	190
Searle v. Blaise	178
Sedley v. Arbouin	14
Selmes v. Judge	156
Semayne	6, 15, 28
Seraglio, The	29
Sewell v. Taylor	98
Shaftesbury v. Russell	194
Sharp v. Key	19
Shattock v. Carden	166
Shaw v. Kirby	20
—— v. Morley	54
Sheers v. Brooks	16
Shepherd v. Hills	164
—— v. Wheble	141
Sherborn v. Bogle	73
—— v. Wells	100, 104
Shoreland v. Govett	199
Simmons v. Milligen	91, 184
—— v. Mitchell	189
Simpkins v. Robinson	39
Simpson v. Staff. Railway	200
—— v. Wells	134, 135
Sinclair v. Eldred	187
Six Carpenters	137, 152, 197
Slade	151
—— v. Hawley	166
Slattery v. Naylor	63
Slee v. Bradford	69
Sly v. Finch	27
—— v. Stevenson	146
Small v. Bickley	70

	PAGE
Smallcomb v. Buckingham	9, 19
Smart v. Hutton	140, 182
Smith, In re	10, 19
—— v. Bourchier	139, 145, 160
—— v. Critchfield	198
—— v. Hopper	155
—— v. Macdonald	187
—— v. Millar	192
—— v. Powditch	121
—— v. Pritchard	40, 140, 145
—— v. Reader	24
—— v. Reynolds	115
—— v. Shirley	77
—— v. Sydney	139
Sneary v. Abdy	178
Snow v. Hill	54
Snowball v. Goodricke	167
Snowden v. Davis	149, 178
Somerset v. Miller	65
Somerville v. Hawkins	190, 191
Sparrow v. Bristol	28
Speck v. Phillips	174
Speight v. Gosnay	189
Spencer	167
Squires v. Meyer	22
Stacey v. Chilworth	115
Stanley v. Powell	172
Stanton v. Styles	144
Stationers' Co. v. Salisbury	65
Stephens v. Meyers	172
—— v. Rothwell	177
Stevens v. Evans	44
—— v. Jeacocke	164
—— v. Midland Ry. Co.	185
Steward v. Lambe	24
Still v. Wells	59
Stimson v. Farnham	167
Stinson v. Browning	135
Stockdale v. Hansard	12, 138, 139
Stocken v. Carter	101
Stonehouse v. Elliott	82
Stonor v. Fowle	35
Stops v. Northampton, JJ.	152
Straight v. Gee	159
Stuart v. Bell	190
—— v. Whitaker	26
Summers v. Moseley	142
Surrey, Sheriff of, Re	177
Sutherland v. Murray	150
Sutton v. Johnstone	150, 164
—— v. Norwich	200
Swain v. Morland	166
Swan v. Sanders	81
Swenden	83
Syers v. Chapman	174
Symonds v. Kurtz	33

T.

Tancred v. Allgood	196
Taplin v. Atty	141

CASES CITED.   xxxvii

	PAGE
Tarleton v. McGawley	192
Tarlton v. Fisher	16, 138
Taylor v. Bekon	20
——— v. Clemson	4, 33
——— v. Cole	21, 199
——— v. Ford	187
——— v. Greenhalgh	134
——— v. Nisfield	156
——— v. Timson	131, 168
Terraz, Ex parte	47
Terry v. Huntington	150
Theobald v. Crichmore	154
Thomas v. Harris	175
——— v. Jones	128
——— v. Mirehouse	196, 197
——— v. Peck	179
——— v. The Queen	150
——— v. Russell	184
Thompson v. Clark	165
——— v. Failsworth	69
——— v. Farrar	56
Thoroughgood	20
Thorpe v. Stallwood	193, 197
Thresher v. East London Waterworks	24
Thurgood v. Richardson	26, 195
Thurston v. Mills	166
Thynne v. Sarl	29
Tinkler v. Wandsworth	69, 75, 199
Titley v. Foxall	174
Tobin v. The Queen	117, 150
Tollett v. Thomas	97
Tomkinson v. Russell	24
Tooley	171
Torquay v. Bridle	64
Tottenham v. Rowell	68
Townend v. Yorks. Sheriff	177
Triggs v. Lester	62
Triminger v. Keene	142
Tulk v. Metropolitan Board of Works	98
Tullidge v. Wade	151, 174
Turnbull v. Appleton	97
Turner v. Bridget	28
——— v. Fellgate	32, 138, 139
——— v. Ford	106
——— v. Morgan	107
Twyman v. Knowles	168
Tyler v. Leeds	167
Tyson v. Parke	19

U.

Umphelby v. McLean	155
Underden v. Burgess	178
Unwin v. Hanson	45, 198
Upton v. Wils	29
Usher v. Luxmoore	96
Utting v. Berney	185

V.

	PAGE
Valpy v. Manley	181
Van Boven	115
Van Sandau, Ex parte	59
——— v. Turner	12
Vaughan v. Taff Vale	149
Victor, The	30
Villars, Ex parte	28, 166
Vinter v. Hind	70
Vulture, The	30

W.

Walker v. Horner	135
——— v. Sharman	192
Waller v. Weedale	166
Walter, In re	35
Walthamstow v. Staines	68
Walwyn v. Awberry	19
Ward	22
——— v. Macaulay	25
Wardour v. Beresford	151
Warne v. Varley	75, 107, 114, 119
Warner v. Riddiford	182
Warren, Ex parte	26
Warwick v. Foulkes	183
Waterhouse v. Keen	155
Watkin v. Hall	189
Watson v. Bodell	4, 37
Watts v. Lucas	128
Weaver v. Lloyd	191
Webb v. Beaven	189
——— v. Catchlove	170
Webber v. Hutchins	20
Weiss v. Smith	139
Wells v. Gibbs	9
Westmoreland v. Smith	27
Weston v. Woodcock	24
Wetherell v. Howell	24
Whale v. Booth	25
Whalley v. Williamson	16
Wheeker v. Webb	65
Wheeler v. Whiting	80
Whitbread v. Brooksbank	181
Whitchurch, Ex parte	7
White v. Binstead	26
——— v. Morris	141, 155
——— v. Redfern	70
Whitehead v. Bennett	22
Whitehouse v. Atkinson	141, 197
Whitehurst v. Fincher	54
Whitfield v. Despencer	150
Wicks v. Fentham	186, 187
Wilcoxon v. Searby	42
Wilde v. Waters	24
Wilkes v. Hungerford Market Co.	188
——— v. Wood	3
Wilkins v. Day	135, 188
——— v. Hemsworth	34, 147
Willans v. Taylor	187

d

CASES CITED.

	PAGE
Willem III., The	30
Williams v. Blackwall	128, 194
—— v. Evans	135
—— v. Glenister	80, 132, 184
—— v. Jones	204, 207
—— v. Lyons	206
Willis v. McLachlan	59
Wilson v. Barker	148
—— v. Stewart	149
—— v. Tunman	148
Windham v. May	24
Winterbourne v. Morgan	197
Wintle v. Freeman	166, 167
Withall v. Francis	60
Withers v. Henley	183
Wolf, Ex parte	205
Wood v. Burgess	115
—— v. Chessal	161
—— v. Durham	191
—— v. Lane	182
—— v. Venton	64
—— v. Wood	21, 24, 34
Woodgate v. Knatchbull	143, 206
Wooding v. Oxley	80
Woodland v. Fuller	201
Woodman v. Gist	143
Woods v. Finnis	28, 140
Woodward v. Billericay	45, 157
Woolford's Trustee v. Levy	181

	PAGE
Woolley v. Corbishley	134
Wordsworth v. Harley	157
Worral Co. v. Lloyd	18
Worth v. Torrington	131
Wortley v. Notts	65
Wray v. Reynolds	60
Wren v. Pocock	109
Wright, Ex parte	59
—— v. Child	142
—— v. Court	77
—— v. Mills	20
Wyatt v. White	52
Wylie v. Birch	166
Wyllie v. Mott	131
Wyman v. Knight	8
Wyndham v. Cole	130
Wynne v. Ingleby	24

Y.

	PAGE
Yates v. Rutledge	26
Yewdall v. Craven	44
Young v. Davis	133, 168
—— v. Edwards	64
—— v. Gattridge	70
—— v. Higgon	156
Yourrell v. Proby	165

THE POWERS,
DUTIES, AND LIABILITIES
OF
EXECUTIVE OFFICERS

AS BETWEEN THESE OFFICERS AND THE PUBLIC.

INTRODUCTION.

An executive officer, properly so called, is, I assume, an officer employed by the State to put into actual execution the laws, or some portion of the laws, of his country. Taking this as the definition upon which this work is based, it is a natural consequence that the following officers, all of whom come within the term "executive" in its wide signification, are not included within it. First, military and naval officers, who act under the orders of their commander, and who in ninety-nine cases out of a hundred are employed actively, outside the country, to deal with those foes whom it is to our interest politically to force into submission. Secondly, judicial officers, whose duty it is to interpret the laws, statutory or otherwise, but who are not themselves personally engaged in putting the laws into active operation. Thirdly, those officers whose business it is to perform purely ministerial functions and none other, such as those in the ordinary clerical establishments of our great public departments and the like, and who never, under any circumstances, come into collision, in their official capacities, with any member of the public.

Having thus positively and negatively determined shortly, what I mean in this work by the term "executive officer," I would observe that the powers which are exercised by these men, when considered in the aggregate, are enormous. They, in fact, carry on between them the whole business of active government in this country; and when we remember that every single case, either of excess of power or breach of duty towards any member of the public, contains within it as its kernel the all-important questions of the rights and liberties of the people, it will be seen that it is impossible to over-rate the necessity of closely scrutinizing their labours. Professor Dicey, in his able work on the Constitution, in this connection, says as follows:— "Unintelligent students may infer that the law of the constitution is to be gathered only from notorious judgments which embalm the results of grand constitutional or political conflicts. This is not so. Scores of unnoticed cases .... touch upon or decide principles of constitutional law. Indeed every action against a constable or collector of revenue enforces the greatest of all such principles, namely that obedience to administrative orders is no defence to an action or prosecution for acts done in excess of legal authority."

It is impossible, having regard to the fallibility of human nature and the system of administration, to suppose that these officers are invariably in the right, or even to credit them on all possible occasions with purity of motive. Over-zeal for the public service and individual interest will, in spite of all precautions, from time to time exhibit themselves. It is against such exhibitions that this work is mainly directed. Hitherto there would appear to have been nothing like a direct exterior check upon the powers of these officers, and the natural tendency therefore is—no matter how carefully any system may be administered—not only for these men to exalt their functions as between themselves and the public, but possibly also for them to become a danger of no petty magnitude to the community.

It is for these reasons that this work has been prepared. Its object is to furnish the profession and the public with a treatise from which may be ascertained what these officers have the power to do, and what not to do, as against any member of the public, and what remedies are pursuable in case the officer has either exceeded his power or fallen short of his duty to the individual. It is conceived, therefore, that it cannot fail to be of interest and value.

The liberties of the people of this country have, it must not be forgotten, been purchased with the blood and treasure of our ancestors, and have been maintained by the mental and physical labours of thousands of earnest and good men who have preceded us. To preserve those liberties intact is both the right and duty of us all.

That this work may, in some humble degree, minister to that end, is the prayer of the author.

PART I.

WARRANTS AND ORDERS.

A WARRANT may be defined as a written authority under the hand and seal (*a*) of some Court, or judicial or other officer authorized by law to issue the same, commanding the person or persons to whom it is addressed to arrest or detain, or produce or release, the body, or to search the premises, or seize or levy, or suspend execution on the goods or lands of some person named therein (*b*). *Warrant, definition.*

In every instance save those of warrants of superior Courts at common law (*c*), viz. the Parliament, the High Court, and those of Assize and Arches (*d*), the cause of issue must appear on the face thereof; and where the process is in contempt, the period of detention be specified (*e*). *Cause of issue and period of detention to appear when.*

Warrants are therefore, when regarded as to their legal effect, of two kinds, namely (1) those issued by superior Courts according to the course of the common law, and (2) those of inferior Courts at common law and of any Court or officer under statutory jurisdiction (*f*). *Two kinds.*

The distinction between these two kinds, although rather a nice one, is important from the point of view of the liability of the officer entrusted with the execution. The principle may be thus expressed:— *Distinction between them.*

Whereas, under a warrant of the first kind, the presumption is that the Court from which it issues had jurisdiction to order the particular thing or things to be done, no matter what the order may be, so as to throw the *onus* of proving no jurisdiction generally on the party attacking it; in the case of a warrant of the second kind, the presumption only extends to the matter actually appearing on its face. But, in either case, if on investigation it be found that there was no jurisdiction, being beyond the scope of the powers delegated to the Court or officer *Goes to the jurisdiction.*

(*a*) Those of superior Courts are sometimes not sealed.

(*b*) Any warrant which purports to relate to an unknown person or where alleged offence is the cause of issue, to an offence not yet committed, is void: *Leach* v. *Money*, 19 St. Tr. 1001; *Entick* v. *Carrington*, *ib*. 1030; *Wilkes* v. *Wood*, *ib*. 1153. The only exceptions are search warrants which are generally directed against premises and not against persons; and see *Hutchings* v. *Reeves*, *post*, p. 60.

(*c*) *Burdett* v. *Abbott*, 14 East, 1; *In re Fernandez*, 10 C. B. 1; *The Sheriff of Middlesex*, 11 Ad. & E. 273.

(*d*) See the judgment of Brett, L.J., *Dale's Case*, 6 Q. B. D. 455.

(*e*) 2 Inst. 52.

(*f*) See the judgment of Parke, B., *Gossett* v. *Howard*, 10 Q. B. 452, *et seq.*

issuing it, the warrant is bad, and no justification to the officer who executes it.

"The rule for jurisdiction is that nothing shall be intended to be out of the jurisdiction of a superior Court but that which specially appears to be so, ... nothing shall be intended to be within the jurisdiction of an inferior Court but that which is expressly alleged" (*g*).

Orders of two kinds. With regard to orders, they are to be divided into two main classes, namely (1) those which are similar in form and in regard *Like warrants.* to the principles of law applicable thereto to warrants, and may therefore not improperly be classed with warrants, and (2) those *Unlike warrants.* which have no similarity to warrants, but constitute merely the relationship of principal and agent between the person or body issuing and the person executing them.

Jurisdiction to make. In regard to orders of the first kind, it has been laid down that in so far as the jurisdiction to make them, must appear on the face thereof, the rule is equally applicable to them as it is *Verbal of Courts of record.* to warrants (*h*), and here it is to be observed that where orders are made verbally by Courts of record (*i*), they are presumed to be in writing, "for there is or ought to be a record of such order" (*j*).

As to orders of the second kind—those which constitute merely the relationship of principal and agent, they fall into a different category. They will be found discussed in a separate chapter.

Authority co-extensive with validity. The authority of every officer is dependent on the validity of the proceedings (*k*).

(*g*) *Peacock v. Bell*, 1 Saund. 74; *Taylor* v. *Clemson*, 2 Q. B. 1031; *Harrison* v. *Wright*, 13 M. & W. 816; Com. Dig. Pl. 3 M. 24, and see Part III., *post*.
(*h*) *R.* v. *Hulcott*, 6 T. R. 583.

(*i*) This includes Quarter Sessions.
(*j*) Per Parke, B., *Watson* v. *Bodell*, 14 M. & W. 70.
(*k*) *Ex parte Page*, 17 Ves. 59; *Cooper* v. *Asprey*, 3 B. & S. 932; 36 L. J. Q. B. 209.

I.—WARRANTS AND ORDERS OF SUPERIOR COURTS AT COMMON LAW.

Warrants and orders of superior Courts at common law range themselves into two categories, which may sufficiently accurately be described as (1) those to which the king is a party, and (2) those to which the king is not a party. "The phrase 'where the king is a party' is not a correct statement of the law. The question is whether the process be issued at the instance of a private person in the assertion of a private right, or at the instance of a public authority in the assertion of a public right, where the public weal is interested in the execution of it" (*a*). *Warrants and Orders of Superior Courts at common law. Of two kinds, which correspond with (1) absolute and (2) relative duties.*

This description appears to tally (so far as concrete can with abstract law) with that given by modern writers in jurisprudence of those absolute duties which the individual owes to the State, those which are correlative with *natural* rights, *i.e.* those rights which are essential to man's existence in society; as distinguished from those relative duties which correspond with those rights which are the creatures merely of positive law, and of which it has been said that "when they have not the ethical sanction which is derivable from the laws of human life, as carried out under social conditions, they have no sacredness and may rightly be challenged."

The distinction which exists in our law between *mala in se* and *mala quia prohibita* is practically identical (*b*).

I.—THE KING A PARTY.

The first point which arises for consideration in regard to the execution of warrants and orders to which the king is a party, is as to the amount of force which may be employed for that purpose. And it seems quite clear that *any* degree of force may be resorted to which is *necessary* to carry the execution into effect, the *onus* of proving such necessity resting on the officer who resorts to it (*c*). Lord Ellenborough, C.J., in the case last cited, adverting to the allegation in the defence that the employment of the military was necessary to assist at the execution of a warrant of the Speaker, says: "Now what application has the military force to the entry? None at all. Not that it is not competent to use military force, or any force which may be necessary for the execution of a warrant of this kind; the *1. King a Party. What force may be employed. Onus of proving necessity of resorting to, on whom. Lord Ellenborough on use of.*

(*a*) Per Att.-Gen., *arg. Burdett* v. *Abbott*, 14 East, 116.
(*b*) See Steph. Comm. 8th ed.
(*c*) *Burdett* v. *Coleman*, 14 East, 190.

degree and quality of the force must vary according to the exigency of the case. The first duty of the officer who is entrusted with the execution of process is to take care that it is executed effectually and with as little injury to the individual or to the public as may be." And in that case evidence was tendered and admitted to shew the danger and difficulty of executing the warrant by force against the plaintiff in his own house without the aid and protection of the military (d).

Military when employed, to be under magistrate.
When it is necessary to resort to the expedient of employing the military, that force must act under the direction of the civil magistrate (e).

Sheriff may raise posse comitatus.
In regard to warrants of the High Court, the duty of executing which is imposed on the sheriff, it is laid down by statute that if he finds any resistance in such execution he shall take with him the power of the county and shall go in proper person to do execution, and may arrest the resisters and commit them to prison (f).

Power to break doors.
The next point is as to breaking doors. In *Semayne's Case* (g), it was laid down that: (1) In all cases where the king is a party the [officer] (if the doors be not open) may break the party's house either to arrest him or to do other execution of the king's process if otherwise he cannot enter. But before he breaks it he ought to signify the cause of his coming, and to make request to open the doors.

Of third person.
(2) The house of any one is not a castle or privilege but for himself, and shall not extend to protect any person who flies to his house or the goods of any other which are brought or conveyed into his house, to prevent a lawful execution, and to escape the ordinary process of law; and therefore in such cases after denial on request made the [officer]

Officer acts here at his peril.
may break the house. But he does this at his peril, for if it turn out that the defendant was not in the house, or had no property there he is a trespasser (h).

This protection which the law casts around dwellings is confined to dwellings only and does not extend to outhouses (i).

On escape.
After an escape a man's own house or that of a stranger is no sanctuary, and may be broken after notice of the purpose and demand of admission and refusal (j).

Breaking at what time.
According to the opinion of the Attorney-General above cited, this breaking is limited to the daytime (k), which means presumably exclusive of night and twilight (l); but in treason or felony it seems it may take place at any time (m).

Inner doors.
Having obtained admission the officer may break inner

(d) *Burdett* v. *Coleman*, 14 East, 183.
(e) Opinion of Att.-Gen., 65 Com. Jour. 264; Hans. Deb. xvi., 257, 454 h.
(f) 50 & 51 Vict. c. 55, s. 8 (2). This power extends to the Under-Sheriff: Dalt. 104.
(g) 5 Coke, 91. See *Burdett* v. *Abbott*, 14 East, 157; 5 Dow. 165.
(h) *Johnson* v. *Leigh*, 1 Marsh, 565; 6 Taunt. 246.
(i) *Brown* v. *Glenn*, 16 Q. B. 257.
(j) 1 East, P. C. 324.
(k) *Supra*.
(l) 3 Inst. 63; 4 Black. 224.
(m) 1 East, P. C. 324.

doors (*n*), whether the defendant be therein at the time or not (*o*). He may also break out in order to complete the execution (*p*). {Breaking out.}

Although the officer may force an entrance, he is not authorized in remaining in the house more than a sufficient time to execute the warrant, and in case of an arrest, if the party be from home he is not justified in there awaiting his return (*q*). {Remaining on premises.}

Under such a warrant execution on a Sunday is valid (*r*), and it seems that an officer of the law in executing process is not limited to any time of the day or night (*s*). {Time of execution.}

There is no privilege from arrest in these cases (*t*). Ambassadors however, and their servants, if the servant be not carrying on business, although a British subject (*u*), are protected by 7 Anne, c. 12, s. 4, and clergymen attending service *eundo morando et redeundo* by 24 & 25 Vict. c. 100, s. 36. Arrest in such cases is a misdemeanour (*v*). {Privilege.}

When a warrant is given to a defendant for his perusal and he refuses to return it, it appears that the officer has a right to take it from him, and even to coerce his person to obtain the possession of it, provided he use no more violence than is necessary to effect that purpose (*w*). And the taking away of such a warrant even if not recovered does not affect the validity of the execution (*x*). {Officer may recover possession of warrant.}

The production of a warrant is not apparently unless demanded a condition precedent to its execution (*y*).

Warrants of superior Courts, unless restricted by what appears upon their face, extend all over the kingdom (*z*). {Jurisdiction.}

THE SERGEANT AT ARMS (LORDS).

This officer is employed by the House of Lords to execute its orders against persons committed for contempt (*a*). The order of the House is signed by the Clerk of the Parliaments, and is the authority under which the officer acts (*b*). {Sergeant at Arms (Lords). Order to.}

(*n*) *Lee* v. *Gansel*, Cowp. 1; Lofft. 374.
(*o*) *Ratcliffe* v. *Burton*, 3 B. & P. 223.
(*p*) *Pugh* v. *Griffith*, 3 N. & P. 187; 7 A. & E. 827.
(*q*) *Howard* v. *Gossett*, C. & M. 382.
(*r*) *Ex parte Whitchurch*, 1 Atk. 55, and as to warrants of justices in indictable offences, see 11 & 12 Vict. c. 42, s. 4.
(*s*) *Per* Campbell, C.J.: *Brown* v. *Glenn*, 16 Q. B. 257.
(*t*) *In re Freston*, 11 Q. B. D. 545; *Long Wellesley*, 2 R. & M. 639; *Lechmere Charlton*, 3 My. & C. 354; *Gent-Davis* v. *Harris*, 40 Ch. D. 190; 58 L. J. Ch. 162; 60 L. T. 355; 37 W. R. 151; 5 Ti. Rep. 89.
(*u*) *Macartney* v. *Garbutt*, 24 Q. B. D. 368.
(*v*) See *post*, p. 202.
(*w*) *R.* v. *Milton*, 3 C. & P. 31.
(*x*) *R.* v. *Bailey*, L. R. 1 C. C. 347; 41 L. J. M. C. 61; 12 Cox, C. C. 129.
(*y*) *R.* v. *Howarth*, 1 Moo. C. C. 207; *R.* v. *Chapman*, 12 Cox, C. C. 4.
(*z*) 4 Bl. Comm. 291.
(*a*) In case of committal of a member the order goes to Black Rod. Macqueen H. L. 68.
(*b*) May's Parl. Prac., 9th ed., pp. 77 and 89. For the form, see App. I., 1.

Duty under.	The order usually requires the sergeant to take into custody the person named therein, and to bring him to the bar of the House.
Warrant of Lord Chancellor.	The order of the High Court to arrest a person under attachment on a return of *non est inventus* by the sheriff, or to obtain the custody of a ward of Court is directed to this officer, but is seldom now issued (*c*). In the first case it appears that the defendant is not entitled to release without a certificate from the sergeant that his fees have been paid (*d*), but it is believed that all the sergeant's fees have beeen abolished.
Verbal order.	As has been above stated, a verbal order of the Lords to this officer is tantamount to a warrant (*e*).

The Sergeant at Arms (Commons).

Sergeant at Arms (Commons). Speaker's warrant; duty under.	The warrant of the Speaker of the House of Commons is addressed to this officer (*f*). The duty of the sergeant is to take into custody the person named therein and to detain him during the pleasure of the House. The practice is to require the offender to attend at the bar to be discharged on payment of the fees, which are in the nature of a fine (*g*). He cannot, however, be detained in any case after the prorogation (*h*).
Verbal order.	As has been above pointed out, a verbal order of the Speaker amounts to a warrant (*i*). When the Speaker is accompanied by the mace he has power to order persons into custody for disrespect or breach of privilege committed in his presence (*j*).

The Sheriff.

The Sheriff.	The warrants (or, as they are usually called in this case, writs) of the High Court, save that issued on a committal for contempt, are directed to this officer. They are as follow:—

Assistance.

Assistance. When issued. Duty.	This writ issues where there has been a decree or order directing the possession of chattel property to be given up (*k*). The duty of the sheriff is to put the plaintiff in possession of

(*c*) Braithwaite's Pr. 286, 288. See *In re an Infant*, 7 T. L. R. 580; 64 L. T. 732. For the Form, see App. I., 1a.
(*d*) Cons. Ord. xxx., r. 9.
(*e*) *Ante*, p. 4.
(*f*) For the form, see App. I., 2.
(*g*) 82 Com. Jour. 397; 87 *ib.* 365; 97 *ib.* 240; 106 *ib.* 289. The fines are now paid into the Fee Fund, and are not received by the sergeant.
(*h*) May, p. 109.

(*i*) *Ante*, p. 4.
(*j*) May, pp. 89 and 100. The House of Commons is not strictly a superior Court, although its warrants are construed in like manner. This will appear *infra*, p. 138.
(*k*) *Wyman* v. *Knight*, 39 Ch. D. 165; 57 L. J. Ch. 886; 59 L. T. 164; 37 W. R. 76. *Cazet* v. *de la Borde*, 23 W. R. 110. For the Form, see App. I. 3.

the property in question. A previous demand of possession is not necessary (*l*).

For the fee payable, see *post* (*m*). There is no poundage (*n*.) Fee.

Attachment.

This writ issues to arrest for a contempt of Court (*o*). It is considered as issued on the first moment of the day of issue (*p*), and must be indorsed with a recital of the particular contempt. *Attachment for contempt, indorsement,*

The duty of the sheriff is to take the defendant and keep him in custody, so that he may have him in court at the return of the writ. *duty.*

The property of a defendant may be taken in execution notwithstanding an attachment (*q*).

Where this writ had issued against a party to an action for non-compliance with an order for the delivery over of deeds and documents, the officer charged with the execution might, it was held, break the outer door of the party's house in order to execute it (*r*); and where a defendant was committed under sec. 5 of the Debtors Act, 1869, for non-payment of a debt, it was decided that sec. 14 of the Sheriffs Act, 1887 (*s*), did not apply, the attachment being not for debt, but for contempt (*t*). *Breaking doors.*

For the fee payable, see *post* (*u*). There is no poundage (*v*.) Fee.

Bench Warrant.

This warrant is issued by a judge of the High Court to bring before him any person charged with felony (*w*), or by a judge of assize in case of felony or misdemeanour (*x*). *Bench warrant. When issued.*

Capias ad Respondendum.

This writ is employed only in outlawry. The sheriff's duty is to take the defendant and produce him in Court (*y*). *Capias ad Respondendum. When issued.*

Capias Utlagatum.

This writ, which is practically obsolete, issues in cases of outlawry, and requires the sheriff to take the defendant and have him in Court on a certain day (*z*). *Capias utlagatum. When issued.*

(*l*) Cons. Ord. xxix., 1.
(*m*) Page 175.
(*n*) *R.* v. *Sheriff of Devon,* 3 Dowl. 10.
(*o*) For form, see App. I. 4.
(*p*) *Smallcombe* v. *Buckingham,* Carth. 419. See *Clarke* v. *Bradlaugh,* 8 Q. B. D. 63.
(*q*) *Roberts* v. *Ball,* 1 Jur. N. S. 585; *Hide* v. *Pettit,* 1 Ch. Ca. 91; *Wells* v. *Gibbs,* 3 Beav. 399.
(*r*) *Harvey* v. *Harvey,* 26 Ch. D. 644; 51 L. T. 508; 33 W. R. 76; 48 J. P. 468.
(*s*) This section is apparently obsolete.
(*t*) *Mitchell* v. *Simpson,* 23 Q. B. D. 373; 25 *ib.* 183; 58 L. J. Q. B. 425.
(*u*) Page 175.
(*v*) *R.* v. *Palmer,* 2 East, 411; *R.* v. *Sheriff of Devon,* 3 Dowl. 10.
(*w*) 1 Ch. Cr. Law, 36.
(*x*) *Ib.* 339. For Form, see App. I. 5.
(*y*) See Crown Office Forms.
(*z*) *Ibid.*

Contumace Capiendo.

Contumace capiendo.
When issued.
To be produced in Court and delivered to the sheriff.

This is employed for the attachment of a contumacious clergyman, and is issued either with or without proclamations (*a*).
The duty of the sheriff is to take the defendant and keep him in custody pending the order of the Court.
The provisions of 5 Eliz. c. 23, s. 2, incorporated by 53 Geo. 3, c. 127, s. 1, that this writ should be brought into the Court of Queen's Bench, and there, in the presence of the justices, be opened and delivered of record to the sheriff, are not impliedly repealed by 12 & 13 Vict. c. 109, s. 26. Where, therefore, a clergyman was arrested on this writ without this formality being complied with, he was ordered to be discharged from custody (*b*).

Exigent.

Exigent.

By this writ, which is practically obsolete, the sheriff is required to take the person named therein and render him in Court on a certain day (*c*).

Extent.

Extent.
When issued.

This writ is the one employed by the Crown to recover a debt due to itself (*d*).
Under it the debtor may be taken and imprisoned, the Debtors' Act, 1869, which abolished imprisonment for debt not extending to those at the suit of the Crown (*e*). Arrest is not now, however, usually resorted to (*f*).

What may be taken.
Goods.

"The sheriff is authorised to take on one writ the person, goods, lands, and debts" of the debtor (*g*). All goods and chattels except necessary victuals of himself and family, and oxen and beasts of the plough (*h*), including those conveyed away fraudulently to defeat the execution (*i*) and specialties (*k*).

Lands.

The sheriff may concurrently seize the lands of the debtor. A freehold estate (*l*) and that vested in trustees (*m*), an equity of redemption (*n*), and an equitable mortgage by deposit, if there is reason to believe that the mortgagee knew of the claim of the Crown (*o*), may be seized, and so may leaseholds either as goods or lands (*p*).

What may not be taken.
Goods.

As to what cannot be taken, this includes goods pawned or pledged or demised or lent prior to the *teste* of the writ for a

(*a*) For Form, see App. I. 6.
(*b*) *Dale's Case*, 6 Q. B. D. 376.
(*c*) For the Form, see Crown Office Rules.
(*d*) For Form, see App. I. 7.
(*e*) *In re Smith*, 2 Ex. D. 47.
(*f*) *R.* v. *Kinnear*, 3 Price, 566; *R.* v. *Plan*, ib. 94.
(*g*) Chit. Prerog. 262, 264.
(*h*) West, Extents, p. 172.
(*i*) West, Extents, p. 115.
(*k*) Ibid. p. 171.
(*l*) Harbert, 3 Rep. 12.
(*m*) Ibid.
(*n*) Wat. 2nd ed. 367.
(*o*) *Broughton* v. *Davis*, 1 Price, 216; *Casberd* v. *Att.-Gen.*, 1 Dan. 238.
(*p*) Wat. p. 361.

term certain, during the term or wherever a third person has a lien as an agent or factor or otherwise (*q*) until such lien is satisfied (*r*). And it is the same with a sum of money payable on a negotiable instrument not arrived at maturity (*s*), and with property vested in trustees for a bankrupt (*t*), or assigned to creditors without fraud (*u*).

As to lands, where a judgment has been obtained against them before the commencement of the Crown suit, whether an *elegit* thereunder has been sued out or not, they are not seizeable (*v*), nor are copyholds (*w*), nor those vested in a purchaser or mortgagee (*x*). Lands.

Under an *extent* against partners the rule is the same as that under a *fi. fa.* (*y*). Partners.

An appraisement must be made by a jury summoned for the purpose (*z*). Appraisement.

Where writs of the subject and of the Crown concur, that of the Crown takes priority so long as that at the suit of the subject remains unexecuted (*a*), "in other words, until the property in the goods is changed" (*b*). And this priority extends as against the landlord for rent due (*c*), and also to growing crops (*d*). Priority.

And where the Crown has a *lien*, as under the excise laws (*e*), it will override that of the subject (*f*). It is, however, only commensurate with the interest of the debtor (*g*), but can only be discharged by an actual *bonâ fide* sale (*h*). The fees payable are stated *post* (*i*). There is no poundage (*k*). Fees.

Levari Facias.

This writ issues against the inhabitants of a township or a Crown debtor, on conviction and fine (*l*). Levari facias.

In the latter case, where there is imprisonment, the writ may issue before the expiration of the term of imprisonment (*m*). When issued.

If the debtor's goods be *bonâ fide* sold, the claim of the Crown

---

(*q*) *R.* v. *Lee*, 6 Price, 369.
(*r*) West, p. 116.
(*s*) Wat. p. 369.
(*t*) *R.* v. *Marsh*, McLel. & Y. 259.
(*u*) West, p. 115.
(*v*) West, p. 160.
(*w*) *R.* v. *Ld. Lisle*, Parker, 195.
(*x*) 18 & 19 Vict. c. 15, s. 11; and see *R.* v. *Lambe*, McLel. 402; 13 Price, 649; and 28 & 29 Vict. c. 104, s. 48; and 29 & 30 Vict. c. 39, s. 42.
(*y*) *R.* v. *Sanderson*, Wight, 50; and see *post*, p. 20.
(*z*) West, p. 115.
(*a*) *Per* Macdonald, C.B.: *R.* v. *Wells*, 16 East, 278, n.
(*b*) *Per* Chitty, J.: *Att.-Gen.* v. *Leonard*, 38 Ch. D. 626; 23 L. T.
71; 4 Ti. Rep. 479.
(*c*) 8 Anne, c. 14, s. 1.
(*d*) 56 Geo. 3, c. 50.
(*e*) *Att.-Gen.* v. *Warmesley*, 12 M. & W. 179; 13 L. J. Ex. 66.
(*f*) 7 & 8 Geo. 4, c. 53, s. 28; 44 Vict. c. 20, s. 24.
(*g*) *R.* v. *Topping*, McLel. & Y. 544.
(*h*) *Att.-Gen.* v. *Trueman*, 11 M. & W. 694; 13 L. J. Ex. 70.
(*i*) Page 175.
(*k*) *R.* v. *Sheriff of Devon*, 3 Dowl. 10.
(*l*) For Form, see Crown Office Rules.
(*m*) *R.* v. *Woolf*, 2 B. & Ad. 609; 1 Chit. 428.

will be defeated unless there be a *lien*, as in the case of duties of excise (*n*).

Ne Exeat Regno.

Ne creat regno.
When issued.

This writ issues when there is reason to believe that a person is about to quit the country whose presence is required in the course of proceedings then pending, and the Court is satisfied that his absence will embarrass the plaintiff in such proceedings (*o*).

Duty.

The duty of the sheriff is to take the defendant, and keep him until he give the required security; but, after final judgment in the action, he must be discharged (*p*).

Fee.

For the sheriff's fee, see *post* (*q*).

Nocumento amovendo.

Nocumento amovendo.
When issued.
Duty.

This writ issues to remove a wall or other thing which has been adjudged a nuisance (*r*).

The sheriff's duty is to remove the nuisance according to the terms of the writ.

THE TIPSTAFF.

Tipstaff.
Warrants and orders of committal.

Warrants and orders of committal of the High Court are delivered to this officer for execution (*s*), and, as has been already seen, where the order is verbal, it is of equal force with a warrant (*t*).

Jurisdiction to issue.

Superior Courts have power to punish by fine and imprisonment for contempt, whether committed in the face of the Court or not (*u*). But where the warrant recites an order which is clearly informal and bad, it will afford no justification (*v*).

Duty.

The duty of the tipstaff is to arrest the defendant, and deliver him over for detention to the gaoler.

Fee.

The fee payable on an arrest is £1 1*s.*, together with reasonable charges for travelling, &c.

THE GAOLER.

Gaoler.
Lords' order.

The order of the Lords to this officer requires him to detain the prisoner "during the pleasure of the House" (*w*). The duration of the session is immaterial in this case (*x*).

(*n*) *Att.-Gen.* v. *Ford*, 8 Price, 364, and see *supra*.
(*o*) For the Form, see App. I. 8. The writ is ordinarily now issued in connection with applications under sec. 6 of the Debtors Act, 1869.
(*p*) *Hume* v. *Druyff*, 8 Ex. 214.
(*q*) Page 175.
(*r*) For Form, see App. I. 9.
(*s*) For the Form, see App. I. 10.
(*t*) Page 4.
(*u*) 4 Black. 285, and see *Van Sandau* v. *Turner*, 6 Q. B. 773.
(*v*) *Green* v. *Elgie*, 5 *ib.* 99; *Ex parte Fernandez*, 10 C. B. N. S. 3.
(*w*) For Form, see App. I. 11.
(*x*) *Per* Denman, C.J.: *Stockdale* v. *Hansard*, 9 A. & E. 1; 43 Lords Journ. 105.

WARRANTS AND ORDERS. 13

The warrant of the Speaker is to the same effect (*y*); but, on the prorogation of Parliament, the prisoner is entitled to immediate discharge (*z*). *Speaker's warrant.*

In the case of the writs of the High Court, a statutory duty is imposed on the gaoler to detain the prisoner (*a*); and where a prisoner is brought up by the serjeant-at-arms, an order is (if necessary) made to turn him over to the gaoler (*b*). *High Court.*

As to the warrant of committal which is executed by the tipstaff, where the committal is by way of punishment and not by way of process, it ought to be certain as a sentence, and the term of imprisonment should be specified (*c*).

In the case of prisoners sentenced at the assizes, there is no warrant, but a copy of the calendar is delivered to the gaoler, and is the authority under which he detains the prisoners. This is signed by the judge (*d*). *Assizes.*

Where persons are committed for seditious libel or contempt, they are to be treated as first-class misdemeanants (*e*). *First class misdemeanants.*

But this does not apply to a prisoner committed for acting as a solicitor when not duly qualified (*f*).

On the receipt of a pardon or remission, or order of release, or to admit to bail, the gaoler must release according to the terms thereof (*g*). *Pardon, release, bail.*

In attachment and committal, if the term of imprisonment does not appear on the writ or order, application to the Court must be made for discharge (*h*); but no such application is necessary where the term does so appear (*i*). *Discharge.*

A person sentenced to imprisonment for one calendar month is entitled to be discharged on the day of the succeeding month immediately preceding the day corresponding to that from which his sentence takes effect (*j*). And the time runs from the date of the warrant of commitment, and not from that of the original arrest (*k*); and when the term expires on a Sunday, the prisoner is entitled to discharge on the preceding day (*l*).

A prisoner is not to be discharged if the surgeon certify unfitness, unless he requires to be so (*m*). On discharge, he

(*y*) For Form, see App. I. 12.
(*z*) May, p. 109.
(*a*) 28 & 29 Vict. c. 126, s. 82.
(*b*) For Form of Order, see App. I., No. 12a.
(*c*) Crawford, 13 Q. B. 629; *R.* v. *James*, 5 B. & Ald. 894, and see *In re Cobbett*, 7 Q. B. 187.
(*d*) *R.* v. *Bethel*, 5 Mod. 22; Christ. Black. iv., 4044.
(*e*) 40 & 41 Vict. c. 21, ss. 40, 41.
(*f*) *Osborne* v *Millman*, 18 Q. B. D. 471; 56 L. J. Q. B. 263; 56 L. T. 808; 35 W. R. 397; 51 J. P. 437.
(*g*) For the Forms, see App. 1., 13, 14, and *cf.* 22 and App. II., No. 9a. As to licenses, see 27 & 28 Vict. c. 112, Sched. Pardons and remissions are a branch of the Royal Prerogative. They do not, therefore, fall in this category, but, of course, must receive the like attention.
(*h*) *Nalty* v. *Aylett*, 30 L. T. 783; *Greares* v. *Keane*, 4 Ex. D. 73.
(*i*) *Re Edwards*, 21 Ch. D. 230.
(*j*) *Migotti* v. *Colvill*, L. R. 4 C. P. D. 233.
(*k*) *Henderson* v. *Preston*, 21 Q. B. D. 362; 4 Ti. Rep. 632, 696; 36 W. R. 83; 57 L. J. Q. B. 607; 52 J. P. 820, and see *Bowdler's Case*, 17 L. J. Q. B. 243; 12 Q. B. 612; 12 J. P. 708.
(*l*) 28 & 29 Vict. c. 126, s. 41.
(*m*) *Ibid.*, Sched. I., r. 10.

is entitled to his clothes, unless destroyed, in which case proper clothing is to be provided (*n*).

Habeas corpus.
On receipt of a *habeas corpus* or of an order to produce in Court, which is to the same effect (*o*), the gaoler must produce the body of the prisoner in the Court as required.

In the case of a *habeas corpus*, the Lord Chancellor would appear to have *ex officio* the right to issue this writ in any case of a person under disability which appears to him to be a proper one for such issue (*p*).

Commitment, copy of.
This officer is also required, within six hours after demand, to deliver a true copy of the commitment of any prisoner in his custody (*q*), and this has been held to apply to the case of a person detained under warrant of the Chief Secretary for Ireland (*r*).

(*n*) Sched. I., r. 24.
(*o*) 16 & 17 Vict. c. 30, s. 9. For the Forms, see App. I., 15, and App. II., 19.
(*p*) See the remarks of the L. C. in *Re Jackson*, 55 J. P. 246; 39 W. R. 407; 64 L. T. 679.
(*q*) 31 Car. II. c. 2, s. 5, penalty for neglect or refusal £100 for first offence, and £200 and discharge from office for second offence.
(*r*) *Sedley* v. *Arbouin*, 3 Esp. 173.

2.—THE KING NOT A PARTY.

The principal point for consideration in regard to the execution of warrants and orders to which the king is not a party is as to the breaking of doors; and the general rule is, that in such cases outer doors cannot be broken.

2. *King not a party.* Breaking doors.

In *Semayne's* case it was resolved that, (4.) " In all cases where the door is open the [officer] may enter the house, and do execution about suit of any subject either on building or on goods. But it is not lawful on request made and denial, at the suit of a common person, to break the defendant's house so as to execute any process at the suit of any subject" (*a*).

If an officer attempt to force his way into a house in execution of civil process, and be resisted and killed, it is manslaughter only (*b*).

On the other hand, where a person conceals himself or deposits his goods in the house of a third party, in order to defeat the execution, the doors of such house may be broken.

Third person's house.

In the same principal case it is laid down that, (5.) The house of any one is not a castle or privilege, but for himself, and shall not extend to protect any person who flies to his house, or the goods of any other person which are brought or conveyed into his house, to prevent a lawful execution and to escape the ordinary process of law; and therefore in such case, after denial on request made, the [officer] may break the house. But he does this at his peril; for, if it turn out that the defendant was not in the house, or had no property there, he is a trespasser (*c*).

Officer breaks at his peril.

These rules extend to dwellings only, and not to outhouses (*d*).

If he be forcibly ejected after lawful entry, he may break open to re-enter (*e*).

Having obtained admission, he may break inner doors, although defendant be not therein at the time (*f*); but he must first demand admittance (*g*), and cupboards, trunks, &c., may be broken (*h*).

Inner doors.

If by lifting the latch of the outer door or opening in the ordinary way, he enters, he is justified if he had reasonable ground (*i*) to believe that the execution-debtor or his goods were

What a breaking.

(*a*) 5 Coke, 91.
(*b*) 1 East, P. C. 321.
(*c*) *Johnson* v. *Leigh*, 1 Marsh. 565; 6 Taunt. 246.
(*d*) *Penton* v. *Browne*, 1 Sid. 141.
(*e*) *Eagleton* v. *Guttridge*, 11 M. & W. 465.

(*f*) *Lee* v. *Gansel*, Cowl; Lofft. p. 374.
(*g*) *Ratcliffe* v. *Burton*, 3 B. & P. 223.
(*h*) *Lee* v. *Gansel*, ubi supra.
(*i*) See the cases, *post*, p. 82.

there (*j*). The lifting of such a latch, or drawing back a sliding bar in the ordinary way, is not a breaking (*k*).

The house where the execution-debtor resides—that is, where he sleeps—may be considered to be his own house, although he is not the proprietor thereof (*l*).

Entry obtained by fraud.
The entry is not illegal by reason only of being obtained by fraud or deceit (*m*).

Window.
If a hole in the outer wall be intended for a window or door, the officer is justified in entering, otherwise not (*n*). If a window be shut, but not fastened, it may not be opened (*o*).

Breaking out.
The officer being lawfully inside, may break the outer door in order to carry away the goods seized (*p*); and it has been held that, where a sheriff breaks a house to seize goods, the execution is valid, although he is a trespasser (*q*).

Breaking does not affect execution on goods.

Arrest on unlawful entry.
If the original entry is unlawful, so is the continuance there, and the officer cannot avail himself of such entry to execute a warrant of arrest (*r*). An arrest effected by the illegal breaking of a door is altogether void, and renders the officer liable to action not only for the breaking, but also for the assault and false imprisonment (*s*).

Continuing in possession.
Continuing on premises more than a reasonable time, or beyond that allowed by law, is good ground for an action of trespass (*t*), and the officer cannot plead justification in such case (*u*).

As to the sheriff, if he continue in possession after the return day of the writ he becomes a trespasser *ab initio* (*v*), but this will not subject him to the allegation of a new trespass after the acts which he justifies under the execution (*w*).

Time.
It appears that execution may take place at any time (*x*), but that on a Sunday is not permissible (*y*), except in the case of a subsequent arrest after an escape (*z*).

Privilege.
Where privilege exists it may be claimed. But this does not concern the officer (*a*), except in the case of ambassadors and their servants, and clergymen, the arrest of whom as has been seen is a misdemeanour (*b*).

(*j*) *Morrish* v. *Murray*, 13 M. & W. 57.
(*k*) *Ryan* v. *Shilcock*, 7 Ex. 77; 21 L. J. Ex. 58.
(*l*) *Sheers* v. *Brooks*, 2 H. Bl. 122.
(*m*) *R.* v. *Backhouse*, Lofft. 61.
(*n*) *Whaley* v. *Williamson*, 7 C. & P. 294.
(*o*) *Nash* v. *Lucas*, L. R. 2 Q. B. 590.
(*p*) *Pugh* v. *Griffith*, 3 N. & P. 187.
(*q*) *Percival* v. *Stamp*, 9 Ex. 167.
(*r*) *Hooper* v. *Lane*, 6 H. L. C. 535; 3 Jur. N. S. 1026; 27 L. J. Q. B. 75; *Humphreys* v. *Stillwell*, 2 Bing. N. C. 619; 5 Sc. 51.
(*s*) *Kerby* v. *Denby*, 1 M. & W. 336; 2 Gale, 31.
(*t*) *Ash* v. *Dawnay*, 8 Ex. 237; 22 L. J. Ex. 59.
(*u*) *Playfair* v. *Musgrove*, 14 M. & W. 239; 3 D. & L. 72; 9 Jur. 783; 15 L. J. Ex. 26.
(*v*) See *post*, p. 152.
(*w*) *Aitkenhead* v. *Blades*, 5 Taunt. 198; 1 Marsh. 17.
(*x*) Per Campbell, C.J.: *Brown* v. *Glenn*, 16 Q. B. 257.
(*y*) 29 Car. II. c. 7, s. 6.
(*z*) *Parkes* v. *Moore*, 2 Salk. 226.
(*a*) *Tarlton* v. *Fisher*, 2 Doug. 671; *Maquay* v. *Burt*, 5 Q. B. 381; *Ames* v. *Waterlow*, L. R. 5 C. P. 53.
(*b*) *Ante*, p. 7.

Arrest for debt is apparently obsolete (*c*), except in the case of commitments in civil matters by justices (*d*).

Arrest for debt.

THE SHERIFF.

By 50 & 51 Vict. c. 55, s. 8 (2), the sheriff is required to execute the king's writs, and "if he shall find any resistance in such execution he shall take with him the power of the county, and shall go in proper person (*e*) to do execution, and may arrest the resisters and commit them to prison."

Sheriff. Posse com.

He is bound to enter a liberty or franchise whenever the writ contains the *non-omittas* clause.

Entering liberty.

Every sheriff shall at the expiration of his term of office make out and deliver to the incoming sheriff a correct list and account under his hand . . . of all rolls and writs in his hand not wholly executed by him (*f*).

Outgoing, duty of.

The incoming sheriff shall thereupon sign and give to the outgoing sheriff a duplicate of such account which shall be a good and sufficient discharge to him (*g*).

Incoming, duty of.

A sheriff shall not be called upon to return to any writ after the expiration of six months from the time he held office (*h*). No return is now to issue, but a notice to him shall have the same effect (*i*). He must if required give a receipt for the writ (*j*).

Return to writ.

Receipt.

Delivery.

This writ issues for the recovery of specific chattel property (*k*). If the same cannot be found the sheriff is to distrain the defendant by all his lands and chattels, and the writ is then executed in the same manner as that of *distringas* (*l*).

Delivery. When issued.

Duty of sheriff.

A judgment does not change the property in the detained chattel until satisfaction of the value found by the judgment even though the satisfaction has been prevented by the bankruptcy of the defendant, and accordingly the plaintiff in an action of detinue was held entitled, although the defendant had become bankrupt, to have the chattel delivered to him (*m*).

For the sheriff's fee see *post* (*n*).

Fee.

(*c*) *Mitchell* v. *Simpson*, 23 Q. B. D. 373; 25 *ib.* 183; 6 Ti. Rep. 391; 58 L. J. Q. B. 425; 61 L. T. 248; 37 W. R. 798; 53 J. P. 328, 694.

(*d*) See *post*, p. 43.

(*e*) This includes the under-sheriff, Dalt. 104.

(*f*) Sect. 28 (1). This does not apply after seizure and sale: *Harrison* v. *Paynter*, 6 M. & W. 387.

(*g*) Sect. 28 (2).

(*h*) Sect. 28 (3).

(*i*) Order 52, r. 11; and see *Hall* v. *Ley*, 12 C. D. 795. In the case of a special bailiff, as to which see *post*, p. 142, he cannot be ordered to return: *De Moranda* v. *Dunkin*, 4 T. R. 119.

(*j*) Sect. 10 (1).

(*k*) For the Form, see App. I. 16.

(*l*) See *post*, p. 28.

(*m*) *Ex parte Drake*, 5 C. D. 866; *Brinsmead* v. *Harrison*, L. R. 7 C. P. 547.

(*n*) Page 175.

Elegit.

Elegit. When issued.
This writ is employed in the execution of process against the lands of the judgment debtor (*o*).

Inquisition to be held.
In order to ascertain the lands, the sheriff must hold an inquisition (*p*). There is no actual delivery in execution, but on the finding of the inquisition the sheriff returns to the writ (*q*).

What may be taken. Lands generally, in trust.
The sheriff is to " make and deliver execution unto the party in that behalf suing of all such lands tenements, rectories, tithes (*r*), rents and hereditaments including lands and hereditaments of copyhold or customary tenure as the person against whom execution is so sued, or any person in trust for him, shall have been seized or possessed of at the time of entering up the said judgment or at any time afterwards or over which

Subject to appointment.
such person shall at the time of entering up such judgment, or at any time afterwards have any disposing power which he might without the assent of any other person exercise for his own benefit (*s*)."

Mansion. Estates held from Crown. Public land. Wife's land.
This includes a mansion-house excepted from the leasing power of a tenant for life. Estates granted by the Crown for the maintenance of dignities with reversion to the Crown (*t*), land held by a public body for a public purpose (*u*), other than that held not for the district generally, but for a contributory place in which case it can only be taken in execution for judgment debts of such place (*v*), and a wife's land vested in the husband during the coverture (*x*).

No interest for subsequent writ.
Where lands are taken under this writ there is no interest in them seizable under a subsequent writ (*y*).

What may not be taken. Land sold or mortgaged. Equity of redemption.
As to what may not be taken this includes estates vested in purchasers or mortgagees (*z*), an equity of redemption (*a*), and as to trust estates it has been held that where land is vested in a long term of years in a trustee in trust to permit a person to receive the rents and profits until default in payment of a rent-charge, or until the person should insure the premises, and in case of such default to pay to a third person out of the rents and profits a certain rent-charge, this was not seizable under an *elegit* against the first *cestui que trust* (*b*). But a simple trust

(*o*) 46 & 47 Vict. c. 52, s. 146. For Form, see App. I. 17.
(*p*) Co. Litt. 289 b.
(*q*) *Barnes* v. *Harding*, 1 C. B. N. S. 568.
(*r*) As to ecclesiastical execution, see *post* p. 19.
(*s*) 1 & 2 Vict. c. 110, s. 11; and see 29 Car. 2, c. 3, s. 10.
(*t*) *Davis* v. *Marlborough*, 2 Swan. 122.
(*u*) *Worral Co.* v. *Lloyd*, L. R. 1 C. P. 719.
(*v*) *Jersey* v. *Uxbridge*, 55 J. P. 165; 7 T. L. R. 568.
(*x*) Dalt. 136; and see *post*, p. 25.
(*y*) *Carter* v. *Hughes*, 2 H. & N. 714.
(*z*) 18 & 19 Vict. c. 15, s. 11.
(*a*) *Lyster* v. *Dolland*, 3 Br. C. C. 478; 1 Ves. 431; *Plunkett* v. *Pearson*, 2 Atk. 292.
(*b*) *Hull* v. *Greenhill*, 4 B. & Ald. 684.

estate even for the life of the party is seizable (c). A benefice including the glebe of a parsonage, a vicarage, or an advowson in gross, or a churchyard cannot be taken (d), but a bishop's lands probably may be (e). Trust.
Ecclesiasti-
cal land.

Rent-arrears, a rent-seck or an office is exempt. For the execution creditor to be entitled to rent it must be due before the delivery of the writ to the sheriff (f). But a tenant need not attorn in order for the plaintiff to sue for rent subsequently accruing (g). Rent.

A remainder or reversion is not seizable (h).

The sheriff must make a return (i), where anything has been done under the writ (j). But such return is not necessary to complete seizure under sect. 45 of the Bankruptcy Act, 1883 (k). Remainder or rever-sion.
Return.

There is no sale under this writ (l). No sale.

For the fees payable, see *post* (m). The poundage is £5 per cent. on the first £100, and £2½ per cent. afterwards (n), and this is confined to the yearly value (o). Fees.
Poundage.

Fieri Facias.

This writ is employed in execution on the goods of the judgment debtor (p). *Fieri facias.*

Where the sheriff returns that the defendant is a beneficed clerk and has no goods or chattels or any lay fee in his baili-wick, a like writ is directed to the bishop for execution (q). When issued.
Ecclesias-tical.

The creditor in this case must exhaust the temporal before recourse to the spiritual goods (r). The liability of the bishop is the same as that of the sheriff (s).

Where more than one writ is in the sheriff's hands he must execute that which was first delivered to him (t), unless fraudulent, and in that case execute the other or others (u). The fraction of a day is sufficient to give priority (v). An execution levied by a special bailiff on a subsequent writ may be recovered Priority.

(c) *Scott* v. *Scholey*, 8 East, 485; *Hele* v. *Bexley*, 17 Beav. 14.
(d) Wat. p. 309.
(e) Dalt. p. 136.
(f) *Sharpe* v. *Key*, 8 M. & W. 379.
(g) *Lloyd* v. *Davies*, 2 Ex. 103; 18 L. J. Ex. 80.
(h) *In re Smith*, L. R. 9 Ch. 373.
(i) See ante. p. 17.
(j) *Hoe*, 5 Rep. 90 a.
(k) *Re Hobson*, 2 Ti. Rep. 884. This section denies to creditors the benefit of an execution unless it is completed before bankruptcy.
(l) Co. Litt. 289 b.
(m) Page 175.
(n) 29 Eliz. c. 4.
(o) *Nash* v. *Allen*, 1 Dav. & M. 16;

Tyson v. *Parke*, 2 Ld. Ray. 1212; Salk. 333.
(p) For the Form, see App. I. 18.
(q) Order 43, r. 3.
(r) *Bromage* v. *Vaughan*, 7 Ex. 223.
(s) *Walwyn* v. *Auberry*, 2 Mod. 257; *Pickard* v. *Paiton*, 1 Sid. 276. In the event of a vacancy in the see, the writ goes to the archbishop.
(t) *Hutchinson* v. *Johnson*, 1 T. R. 729.
(u) *Bailey* v. *Windham*, 1 Wils. 44; *Christopherson* v. *Burton*, 3 Ex. 160; 18 L. J. Ex. 60.
(v) *Smallcomb* v. *Buckingham*, Canth. 419. See *Clarke* v. *Bradlaugh*, 8 Q. B. D. 63.

by the sheriff as received to his use (*w*). But if he is directed not to execute the first writ until a future day, he may execute another delivered before that day (*x*). If after execution of the first there is a surplus, this must be applied to the second and so on (*y*). Where a writ is renewed it is entitled to priority from the time of the original delivery (*z*); but while it is withdrawn he cannot enter without further instructions from the execution creditor, and may execute a subsequent writ without notice to such creditor (*a*).

<small>Writ to agree with judgment.</small>
The writ must agree with the judgment in the mandatory part (*b*).

<small>Death of debtor.</small>
If the debtor die after the writ has issued, execution may be levied on goods in the hands of the executor (*c*). The death of the execution creditor after the issue of the writ will not affect the execution (*d*).

<small>Death of creditor.</small>

<small>Duty of sheriff.</small>
The duty of the sheriff is to seize only so much as will satisfy the writ together with poundage fees and expenses (*e*), and interest where it is for the recovery of money at the rate of £4 per cent. from the judgment or more where agreed on (*f*). The sheriff must on seizure leave a man in possession until the sale takes place (*g*), which must be within a reasonable time (*h*). A seizure of part in the name of the whole is good (*i*).

<small>Payment of debt.</small>
The defendant instead of allowing the writ to be executed may pay the debt and costs (*j*); a tender before seizure is equivalent to payment (*k*).

<small>Partners.</small>
Where a judgment is against partners in the name of the firm, execution may issue (1) against any person who has admitted on the pleadings that he is or has been adjudged a partner; (2) against any property of the partners as such; (3) against any person who has been served as a partner with a writ of summons, and has failed to appear (*l*). The sheriff can only sell such assets as are seizable, not book-debts or goodwill (*m*).

No writ of execution against partnership property can now issue for a partner's separate debt (*n*).

(*w*) Sawle v. *Paynter*, 1 D. & Ry. 307.
(*x*) *Kempland* v. *Macaulay*, Peake N. P. C. 66; *Hunt* v. *Hooper*, 1 D. & L. 628.
(*y*) *Aldred* v. *Constable*, 6 Q. B. 370.
(*z*) Order 42, r. 20.
(*a*) *Shaw* v. *Kirby*, 52 J. P. 182.
(*b*) *Webber* v. *Hutchins*, 8 M. & W. 319.
(*c*) *Ranken* v. *Harwood*, 10 Jur. 794; *Chick* v. *Smith*, 8 Dowl. 337; *Wright* v. *Mills*, 28 L. J. Ex. 223.
(*d*) *Thoroughgood*, Noy. 73.
(*e*) 15 & 16 Vict. c. 76, s. 123.

(*f*) Order 42, r. 16.
(*g*) *Blades* v. *Arnidale*, 1 M. & S. 711.
(*h*) *Bates* v. *Wingfield* 2 N. & M. 83.
(*i*) *Gladstone* v. *Padwick*, L. R. 6 Ex. 203.
(*j*) *Taylor* v. *Bekon*, 2 Lev. 203.
(*k*) *Colls* v. *Coates*, 11 A. & E. 826; 3 P. & D. 511.
(*l*) Order 42, r. 8.
(*m*) *Helmore* v. *Smith*, 36 W. R. 3; cf. *Perrens* v. *Johnson*, 3 Sm. & G. 419; 3 Jur. N. S. 975.
(*n*) 53 & 54 Vict. c. 39, s. 23.

Where an insufficient levy is made, there may be a further levy under the same writ, or a second writ may issue (*o*). *Further levy.*

All goods and chattels, with certain exceptions, may be seized, provided they can be sold (*p*), including corn, potatoes, and other crops which yield an annual profit (*q*). But where growing crops had been seized and a writ of possession was subsequently delivered to the sheriff in ejectment at the suit of the landlord founded on a demise made long before the issue of the *fi. fa.* the sheriff was not bound to sell them as they could not be considered as belonging to the tenant (*r*). As to money it is laid down by 1 & 2 Vict. c. 110, s. 12, that the sheriff or his officer "may and shall seize and take any money (*s*), or bank notes (whether of the Bank of England or otherwise), and any cheques, bills of exchange, promissory notes, bonds, specialties, or other securities for money (*t*), belonging to the person against whose effects such writ of *fi. fa.* shall be sued out, and may and shall pay or deliver to the party suing out such execution any money or bank notes which shall be so seized or a sufficient part thereof, and may and shall hold any such cheques, bills of exchange, promissory notes, bonds, specialties, or other securities for money as a security or securities for the amount by such writ of *fi. fa.*, directed to be levied and raised," and after providing for the manner of recovery, continues, "and may and shall pay over to the party suing out such writ the money so to be recovered, or such part thereof as shall be sufficient to discharge the amount by such writ directed to be levied, and if after satisfaction of the amount so to be levied together with sheriff's poundage and expenses any surplus shall remain in the hands of such sheriff or other officer, the same shall be paid to the party against whom such writ shall be so issued." *What may be taken. Corn, &c. Money.*

In the case of a ship, seizure before sale is apparently not necessary (*u*). *Ship.*

Chattel interests such as leases for years are seizable (*v*); but a tenant cannot be turned out of possession when he has taken a term, under an execution against the landlord (*w*), nor to give place to a purchaser (*x*). As to fixtures, those which may be removed by the tenant during his term may be seized and sold in execution against him, and these include arras hangings (*y*), *Lease. Fixtures.*

(*o*) *Jordan* v. *Binckse*, 18 L. J. Q. B. 277; *Gawler* v. *Chaplin*, 18 L. J. Ex. 42.

(*p*) *Francis* v. *Nash*, Ca. t. Hard. 53; *Legg* v. *Evans*, 6 M. & W. 41.

(*q*) 2 Gilb. Ex. 19; Wat. p. 253.

(*r*) *Hodgson* v. *Gascoigne*, 5 B. & Ad. 58.

(*s*) This does not extend to a mere debt: *Wood* v. *Wood*, 4 Q. B. 397; *Harrison* v. *Paynter*, 6 Q. B. 387.

(*t*) This does not include title-deeds. But a policy of insurance may be taken: *Law* v. *London Co.*, 1 K. & J. 223—and pawnbroker's pledges: *Rollason* v. *Rollason*, 34 Ch. D. 495.

(*u*) *Harley* v. *Harley*, 11 Ir. Ch. R. 451.

(*v*) Com. Dig. Execution.

(*w*) *Taylor* v. *Cole*, 3 D. & E. 292.

(*x*) *R.* v. *Deane*, 2 Show. 85; see *Burden* v. *Kennedy*, 3 Atk. 739.

(*y*) Sewell, p. 231.

barn on blocks (*z*), beds fastened to ceiling (*a*), bins (*b*), blinds (*c*), book cases (*d*), buildings on blocks, rollers, pillars, &c. (*e*), cabinets (*f*), chimney backs (*g*), glasses (*h*), and pieces (*i*), cider mills (*j*), cisterns (*k*), clock cases (*l*), coffee mills (*m*), colliery machines (*n*), cooling coppers (*o*), counters (*p*), coppers (*q*), cranes (*r*), cupboards (*s*), desks and drawers (*t*), dutch barns (*u*), engines (*v*), fire engines (*w*), furnaces (*x*), furniture, fixtures put up as (*y*), gas-pipes (*z*), glass fronts (*a*), grates (*b*), hangings (*c*), iron chests (*d*), and malt mills (*e*), ovens (*f*), safes (*g*), jacks (*h*), lamps (*i*), looking-glasses (*j*), machinery let into cups or sets of timber (*k*), or capable of removal without damage to building (*l*), mash-tubs (*m*), mills and posts or erections on brick foundations (*n*), partitions (*o*), pattens, erections on (*p*), pier-glasses (*q*), pictures (*r*), plant and pipes of brewers, distillers, &c. (*s*), presses (*t*), pumps slightly attached (*u*), ranges (*v*), reservoirs (*w*), shelves (*x*), sinks (*y*), shrubs planted for sale (*z*), stoves (*a*), tapestry (*b*), tubs (*c*), turret clocks (*d*), vessels on brickwork (*e*), varnish houses (*f*), vats and utensils used for trade (*g*), wainscot fixed by screws (*h*), and window-sashes not beaded into frames (*i*).

(*z*) *Callous* v. *Tuffnell*, Bull N. P. 3.
(*a*) *Ex parte Quincey*, 1 Atk. 477.
(*b*) Am. & Fer. 278 n.
(*c*) *Colegrave* v. *Dias Santos*, 1 B. & C. 77.
(*d*) See note (*b*).
(*e*) *Elwes* v. *Mawe*, 3 East, 38; 2 S. L. C. 182.
(*f*) See note (*b*).
(*g*) *Harvey* v. *Harvey*, 2 Str. 117.
(*h*) *Beak* v. *Rebors*, 1 P. Wms. 94.
(*i*) *Leach* v. *Thomas*, 7. C. & P. 328.
(*j*) *Lawton* v. *Lawton*, 3 Atk. 12.
(*k*) See note (*b*).
(*l*) 4 Burn. Ecc. Law, 7th ed. 301.
(*m*) *R.* v. *Londonthorpe*, 6 T. R. 379.
(*n*) See note (*j*).
(*o*) See note (*c*).
(*p*) See note (*b*).
(*q*) *Poole*, 1 Salk. 368.
(*r*) See note (*b*).
(*s*) *R.* v. *St. Dunstan*, 4 B. & C. 686.
(*t*) See note (*b*).
(*u*) *Dian* v. *Allarley*, 3 Esp. 11.
(*v*) *Dudley* v. *Ward*, Amb. 113;
Whitehead v. *Bennett*, 27 L. J. Ch. 474.
(*w*) *Ibid*.
(*x*) *Squier* v. *Meyer*, 2 Free. 249.
(*y*) *Birch* v. *Dawson*, 4 N. & M. 22; 2 Ad. & E. 37.
(*z*) Am. & Fer. 278 n.
(*a*) *Ibid*.
(*b*) *Lee* v. *Risdon*, 7 Taunt. 191.
(*c*) See note (*g*), *sup*.

(*d*) See note (*m*), *sup*.
(*e*) See note (*l*), *sup*.
(*f*) Am. & Fer. 278.
(*g*) See note (*l*), *sup*.
(*h*) See note (*f*).
(*i*) *Davis* v. *Jones*, 2 B. & Ald. 165.
(*j*) See note (*v*), *sup*.
(*k*) *Colegrave* v. *Dias Santos*, 1 B. & C. 77.
(*l*) *Ward*, 4 Leon. 241.
(*m*) See note (*f*).
(*n*) *Ward*, 4 Leon. 241.
(*o*) Am. & Fer., *ubi sup*.
(*p*) *Naylor* v. *Collinge*, 1 Taunt. 19.
(*q*) *Beak* v. *Rebors*, *ubi sup*.
(*r*) *Ibid*.
(*s*) *Lawton* v. *Lawton*, *ubi supra*.
(*t*) See note (*f*).
(*u*) *Grymes* v. *Bowerin*, 6 Bing. 437; 3 T. & I. 333.
(*v*) See note (*f*).
(*w*) See note (*u*).
(*x*) See note (*f*).
(*y*) *Ibid*.
(*z*) *Ibid*.
(*a*) *R.* v. *St. Dunstan*, *ubi sup*.
(*b*) *Harvey* v. *Harvey*, *ubi sup*.
(*c*) *Colegrave* v. *Dias Santos*, *ubi sup*.
(*d*) See note (*f*), *sup*.
(*e*) *Horn* v. *Baker*, 9 East, 215.
(*f*) *Penton* v. *Roberts*, 2 East, 88.
(*g*) *Whitehead* v. *Bennett*, *ubi sup*.
(*h*) See note (*s*), *sup*.
(*i*) *R.* v. *Hedges*, 1 Leach, C. C. 201; 2 East, P. C. 590.

. Under the Agricultural Holdings Act, engines, machinery, fencing, &c., erected by the tenant on such a holding are *primâ facie* his property, and therefore liable to be taken in execution against him (*k*), provided that all rent is paid, the removal does not cause damage, and such damage is made good, and the landlord on a month's notice, elects not to purchase the same.

As to what may not be taken, it appears that actual necessaries such as tools, bedding, &c., to the value of £5 are exempt (*l*), as also is straw threshed or unthreshed, or any straw of crops growing, or any chaff colder, or turnips, or manure, compost ashes or seaweed in any case whatever, or hay, grass or grasses, whether natural or artificial, nor any tares, or vetches, nor any roots or vegetables being produce of such lands in any case where according to any covenant or written agreement entered into and made for the benefit of the owner or landlord of any farm, such hay, &c., ought not to be taken off or withholden from such lands, or which by the tenor or effect of such covenants or agreements ought to be used or expended thereon, and of which covenants or agreements such sheriff or other officer shall have received a written notice before he shall have proceeded to sale (*m*). {What may not be taken. Necessaries. Farm stuffs.}

Things which yield no annual profit, or which are produced without man's labour (*n*)—clover, rye, or artificial grass growing under corn, and meadow grass or fruit growing—are exempt (*o*). So also are goods which do not actually belong to the defendant (*p*), or which have passed without fraud under a bill of sale (*q*). These must be registered to be valid within seven days of execution (*r*). And in these cases the sheriff is not bound to interplead, but is at liberty to withdraw, though the value of the goods seized exceed the sum secured by the bill of sale (*s*). {Crops produced without labour. Goods not defendant's.}

Landlords' fixtures are also exempt. These are agricultural erections (*t*), alehouse bar (*u*), barns fixed (*v*), beast-house (*w*), bench (*x*), boilers built in (*y*), box border (*z*), carpenter's shop (*a*), cart-house (*b*), chimney-pieces (*c*), cornices affixed (*d*), conservatories (*e*), doors (*f*), dressers (*g*), fold-yard walls (*h*), fruit {Fixtures.}

(*k*) 46 & 47 Vict. c. 61, s. 34.
(*l*) 8 & 9 Vict. c. 127, s. 8.
(*m*) 56 Geo. 3, c. 50, ss. 1, 8.
(*n*) 2 Gilb. Ex. 19.
(*o*) Wat. 253.
(*p*) *Glasspoole* v. *Young*, 9 B. & C. 696; *Dawson* v. *Wood*, 3 Taunt. 256; *Edwards* v. *Bridges*, 2 Stark, 396.
(*q*) *Glasspoole* v. *Young*, ubi supra, and see *Richards* v. *Johnston*, 4 H. & N. 660; 1 F. & F. 447.
(*r*) 45 & 46 Vict. c. 43, s. 8.
(*s*) *Scarlett* v. *Hanson*, 12 Q. B. D. 213.
(*t*) *Elwes* v *Mawe*, ubi sup.
(*u*) 2 Bl. 111.

(*v*) See note (*t*).
(*w*) Ibid.
(*x*) Am. & Fer. 68, 155.
(*y*) *Jenkins* v. *Guttring*, 2 J. & H. 520.
(*z*) *Empson* v. *Soden*, 1 N. & M. 720.
(*a*) See note (*t*), sup.
(*b*) Ibid.
(*c*) *Poole*, 1 Salk. 368.
(*d*) *Avery* v. *Cheslyn*, 5 N. & M. 372; 3 Ad. & E. 75.
(*e*) *Buckland* v. *Butterfield*, 4 Moo. 440; 3 B. & B. 54.
(*f*) 2 Bl. 111.
(*g*) Ibid.
(*h*) See note (*t*), sup.

trees and shrubs (*i*), fruit-house (*j*), glasses in panels fixed (*k*), windows (*l*), grates (*m*), hearth (*n*), keys and locks (*o*), ladders fixed (*p*), lime-kilns (*q*), machinery, moveable part essential to fixture (*r*), mill machinery (*s*) or stones (*t*), ovens (*u*), partitions (*v*), pillars on a dairy floor (*w*), pineries fixed (*x*), pumphouse (*y*), ranges and set-pots (*z*), racks in stables (*a*), saltpans (*b*), slabs of marble (*c*), statues, vases, part of design, fixed (*d*), strawberry beds (*e*), tapestry fixed (*f*), wagonhouse (*g*), windmills (*h*).

The tenant may renounce his right to remove his fixtures, and, in that case, they could not be taken (*i*). If he mortgage them, the mortgagee may enter and seize them (*j*) during the tenancy (*k*).

Goods deposited as security, held by lien.
Held by trustee or agent.

Goods deposited as a security for a debt are not seizable (*l*), nor those which are held by way of lien (*m*). Nor money in the hands of a trustee for the debtor (*n*), or of an auctioneer properly employed by him (*o*); nor that left with the sheriff in part payment of the debt (*p*), or by a subsequent sheriff (*q*). Money levied by the sheriff is not seizable under a writ against the creditor (*r*).

In hands of sheriff.
Goods sold.
Goods lent.

Cut grass in the possession of a debtor, but sold by him before execution, is not seizable (*s*), nor goods lent on hire; but the owner of such goods must, in this instance, inform the sheriff on seizure that they are lent for a term only (*t*); and in that

(*i*) *Windham* v. *May*, 4 Taunt. 316.
(*j*) See note (*t*), *sup.*
(*k*) *Allen* v. *Allen*, More, 112.
(*l*) 11 Co. Rep. 64.
(*m*) *Lee* v. *Risdon*, 7 Taunt. 191; *Richardson* v. *Ardley*, 38 L. J. Ch. 308.
(*n*) See note (*t*), *sup.*
(*o*) *St. John* v. *Pigott*, 2 Bul. 103.
(*p*) *Wilde* v. *Waters*, 16 C. B. 637.
(*q*) *Thrasher* v. *E. London Waterworks*, 2 B. & C. 608.
(*r*) *Mather* v. *Frazer*, 25 L. J. Ch. 361.
(*s*) *Farrant* v. *Thompson*, 5 B. & Ad. 826.
(*t*) Am. & Fer. 64.
(*u*) *Wynne* v. *Ingleby*, 5 B. & Ald. 625.
(*v*) *Kinlyside* v. *Martin*, 2 Bl. 111.
(*w*) *Leach* v. *Thomas*, 7 C. & P. 328.
(*x*) See note (*e*), *sup.*
(*y*) *Elwes* v. *Mawe*, *ubi sup.*
(*z*) See note (*u*).
(*a*) 2 Vent. 114.
(*b*) *Lawton* v. *Salmon*, 1 H. Bl. 260.
(*c*) See note (*k*), *sup.*

(*d*) See note (*k*), *sup.*
(*e*) *Wetherell* v. *Howell*, 1 Camp. 227.
(*f*) *D'Eyncourt* v. *Gregory*, L. R. 3 Eq. 382.
(*g*) See note (*y*). *sup.*
(*h*) *Steward* v. *Lambe*, 4 Moo. 25; 1 B. & B. 506; *R.* v. *Otley*, 1 B. & Ad. 161.
(*i*) *Dumerque* v. *Ramsey*, 2 H. & C. 777.
(*j*) *London Co.* v. *Drake*, 6 C. B. N. S. 798.
(*k*) *Weston* v. *Woodcock*, 7 M. & W. 14; *Smith* v. *Reader*, 27 L. J. Ex. 85.
(*l*) *Rogers* v. *Kenny*, 9 Q. B. 592.
(*m*) *Legg* v. *Evans*, 6 M. & W. 36.
(*n*) *France* v. *Campbell*, 6 Jur. 105.
(*o*) *Brown* v. *Parrott*, 4 Beav. 585.
(*p*) *Bell* v. *Hutchinson*, 2 D. & L. 43; 13 L. J. Q. B. 244.
(*q*) *Masters* v. *Stanley*, 8 Dow. 169.
(*r*) *Wood* v. *Wood*, 12 L. J. Q. B. 141.
(*s*) *Tomkinson* v. *Russell*, 6 East, 602.
(*t*) *Dean* v. *Whitaker*, 1 C. & P. 347.

case the sheriff can only seize the interest of the debtor (*u*). *In hands of executor.* Goods of a testator in the hands of an executor are exempt under a writ against such executor (*v*).

As to husband and wife, since the Married Women's Property *Of wife.* Act, 1882, their property respectively continues separate in the absence of settlement. By sect. 14 a husband is liable for the debts of his wife, and for all contracts entered into, and for all wrongs committed by her before marriage, including any liabilities to which she may be subject under the Companies Acts to the extent of all property whatsoever belonging to her which he shall have acquired or become entitled to from or through her, after deducting therefrom any payments made by him and any sums for which judgment may have been *bonâ fide* recovered against him in any proceeding at law in respect of any such debts, contracts, or wrong, for or in respect of which his wife was liable before her marriage (*w*).

By 25 & 26 Vict. c. 89, s. 163, where any company is being *Company's effects.* wound up by or subject to the supervision of the Court, any execution put in force (*x*) against the estate or effects of the said company after the commencement of the said winding-up shall be void. Except by leave of the Court (*y*). Where the sheriff was in possession before, but received moneys after the commencement of the winding-up, he was ordered to account to the liquidator for all moneys so received (*z*).

By 30 & 31 Vict. c. 127, s. 4, the engines, tenders, carriages, trucks, machinery, tools, fittings, materials, and effects, constituting the rolling-stock and plant used or provided by a company for the purposes of the traffic on their railway, or of their stations or workshops shall not, after their railway, or any part thereof, is open for public traffic, be liable to be taken in execution. And this includes the case of plant going over to the contractor on completion of the line (*a*).

A cost-book mining company is a partnership only (*b*).

Where taxes are in arrear the goods are not seizable unless *Taxes in arrear.* the execution creditor before sale or removal pay the collector such arrears, provided they be not claimed for more than one year (*c*).

Where rent is in arrear the goods cannot be taken unless *Rent in arrear.* before removal such arrear be paid to the landlord, provided the claim be not for more than one year (*d*). And this is extended in the case of weekly tenements, or in that of any term less than

---

(*u*) *Gordon* v. *Harper*, 7 T. R. 9, see *Ward* v. *Macaulay*, 4 D. & E. 489.
(*v*) *Farr* v. *Newman*, *ib.* 621, see *Whale* v. *Booth*, *ib.* 642.
(*w*) 45 & 46 Vict. c. 75.
(*x*) See *In re Lond.* v. *Devon Co.*, L. R. 12 Eq. 190.
(*y*) Sect. 87.

(*z*) *In re The Opera, Limited*, 62 L. T. 859; 64 *ib.* 313; 38 W. R. 637; 39 *ib.* 398; W. N. (90) 104.
(*a*) *Beeston* v. *Marriott*, 4 Giff. 436; 11 W. R. 896.
(*b*) 1 Lind. 4th ed. p. 694; see *ante*, p. 20.
(*c*) 43 & 44 Vict. c. 19, s. 88 (1).
(*d*) 8 Anne, c. 14, s. 1.

26 EXECUTIVE OFFICERS.

Tenant's fixtures.
a year to four such terms (*e*); and applies also to the case of growing crops (*f*).
Where a tenant's fixtures become the property of the landlord by the terms of the Agricultural Holdings Act not having been complied with (*g*), they cannot be seized in execution against the tenant.

Landlord, whom under Act of Anne.
As to the above-cited statute of Anne, it has been held not to apply to a ground landlord (*h*), but it does to a lessee and under-tenant (*i*). It also applies to forehand rents (*j*).

Tenancy to be in existence. Notice. Removal of goods. Sheriff to withdraw unless landlord take undertaking. Bona fides of claim.
The tenancy must be actually in existence at the time of seizure (*k*), but the claim of the landlord is confined to rent due at that time (*l*). The sheriff must have notice of such claim while the goods are in his hands (*m*), or knowledge thereof, which is equivalent thereto (*n*). The goods must be actually removed for the Act to apply (*o*), and the fact that a sufficient distress remained is no defence (*p*). In such case the sheriff's duty is to withdraw (*q*), unless the landlord's agent takes from the officer an undertaking and consents to the sale (*r*).
The sheriff must inquire into the *bona fides* of the claim (*s*); but the execution-creditor, if he assents to the proceedings, cannot afterwards turn round if a mistake has been made (*t*).

Venditioni Exponas.

Venditioni exponas. What.
This writ is in aid of that of *fi. fa*, and is a command to the sheriff to sell the goods (*u*). On receipt thereof it is his duty to sell for as much as he is able (*v*). He need not, of course, delay sale until the issue of this writ.

Bankruptcy supervening.
By 53 & 54 Vict. c. 71, s. 11: (1.) Where the goods of a debtor are taken in execution, and before the sale thereof, or the completion of the execution by the receipt or recovery of the full amount of the levy, notice is served on the sheriff (*w*) that a receiving order has been made against the debtor, the sheriff

---

(*e*) 7 & 8 Vict. c. 96, s. 67.
(*f*) 14 & 15 Vict. c. 25, s. 2.
(*g*) 46 & 47 Vict. c. 61, s. 34, see *ante*, p. .
(*h*) *Bennett*, Stra. 787.
(*i*) *Thurgood* v. *Richardson*, 7 Bing. 428.
(*j*) *Harrison* v. *Barry*, 7 Price, 690; *Yates* v. *Rutledge*, 5 H. & N. 249; 29 L. J. Ex. 117.
(*k*) *Cox* v. *Leigh*, L. R. 9 Q. B. 333; 22 W. R. 730; 30 L. T. N. S. 444.
(*l*) *Reynolds* v. *Barford*, 7 M. & G. 449; 8 Sc. N. R. 233; 2 D. & L. 327; 8 Jur. 961; 13 L. J. C. P. 177.
(*m*) *Armitt* v. *Garnett*, 3 B. & Ald. 440.
(*n*) *Andrews* v. *Dixon*, *ib.* 645.

(*o*) *White* v. *Binstead*, 13 C. B. 304; 22 L. J. C. P. 115.
(*p*) *Colyer* v. *Speer*, 2 B. & B. 67.
(*q*) *Foster* v. *Hilton*, 1 Dow. 35; *Cocker* v. *Musgrove*, 15 L. J. Q. B. 365; 9 Q. B. 223; 10 Jur. 922.
(*r*) *Rothery* v. *Wood*, 3 Camp. 24.
(*s*) *Frost* v. *Barclay*, 3 Ti. Rep. 617.
(*t*) *Stuart* v. *Whitaker*, Ry. & M. 310.
(*u*) *Cameron* v. *Reynolds*, Cowp. 406. For the form, see App. 1. 19.
(*v*) *Keightley* v. *Birch*, 3 Camp. 524.
(*w*) That on the bailiff is not sufficient: *Ex parte Warren*, 15 Q. B. D. 48.

shall on request deliver the goods, and any money seized or received in part satisfaction of the execution, to the official receiver or trustee under the order, but the costs of the execution (*x*) shall be a first charge on the goods or money so delivered, and the official receiver or trustee may sell the goods, or an adequate part thereof, for the purpose for satisfying the charge. (2.) Where under an execution in respect of a judgment for a sum exceeding £20, the goods of a debtor are sold, or money is paid in order to avoid sale, the sheriff shall deduct the costs of the execution (*x*) from the proceeds of the sale or the money paid, and retain the balance for fourteen days (*y*); and if within that time notice is served on him (*z*) of a bankruptcy petition having been presented against or by the debtor, and a receiving order is made against the debtor thereon, or on any other petition of which the sheriff has notice, the sheriff shall pay the balance to the official receiver, or, as the case may be, to the trustee, who shall be entitled to retain the same as against the execution creditor.

Where the sheriff is in possession under several writs, and receives notice as above, only those writs are entitled to be paid which are for less than £20, and which would have been paid had not bankruptcy supervened (*a*). And where he has several writs it is immaterial under which he sells (*b*).

The goods must be sold within a reasonable time after seizure (*c*) and before the return of the *vend. exp.* (*d*). He is responsible for their safe custody until sale (*e*). The sale must be for not much below the real value (*f*), and is for ready money and immediate delivery. He is not therefore justified in selling more than necessary to satisfy the writ on the speculation that the actual delivery may be prevented by loss or accident (*g*). If an adequate price be obtained they must be sold, and the plaintiff may be the purchaser (*h*). If not sold he must return that they remain in his hands for want of buyers (*i*).

Within reasonable time. Safe custody. Real value Ready money. Immediate delivery. Must be sold, when. Return otherwise.

Where a tenant entered under an agreement for a lease and paid the stipulated rent, it was held that a tenancy from year to year was created, which the sheriff might sell under this writ (*j*). Where a lease and fixtures are taken they may be

Annual tenancy. Lease and fixtures.

(*x*) See the cases, *post*, p. 178.
(*y*) These run from time of sale, and not from that of receipt of proceeds by sheriff: *Ex parte Ross*, 21 Q. B. D. 472; 36 W. R. 845; 88 L. J. Q. B. 19; 59 L. T. 341.
(*z*) That on the bailiff is not sufficient: *Bellyse* v. *M'Ginn*, [1891] 2 Q. B. 227.
(*a*) *In re Pearce*, 14 Q. B. D. 966.
(*b*) *Jones* v. *Atherton*, 7 Taunt. 56; 2 Marsh. 375; *Drewe* v. *Lawson*, 11 Ad. & E. 529; 3 P. & D. 245.
(*c*) *Bates* v. *Wingfield*, 2 N. & M. 831.
(*d*) *Jacobs* v. *Humphrey*, 2 C. & M. 413.
(*e*) *Sly* v. *Finch*, Cro. Jac. 518.
(*f*) *Keightley* v. *Birch*, *ubi supra*; and see *Edge* v. *Kavanagh*, 24 L. R. Ir. 1.
(*g*) *Aldred* v. *Constable*, 6 Q. B. 370; *Cook* v. *Palmer*, 6 B. & C. 739.
(*h*) *Leader* v. *Danvers*, 1 B. & P. 360.
(*i*) *Keightley* v. *Birch*, *ubi supra*.
(*j*) *Westmoreland* v. *Smith*, 1 M. & R. 137.

28 EXECUTIVE OFFICERS.

Assignment of term. — sold separately if there is difficulty in finding a purchaser for the whole (*k*); and where an outgoing tenant has agreed to assign the remainder of his term, it may be sold before an actual assignment, and have set on it the value agreed to be given (*l*).

Payment. — If payment is made to the sheriff before sale, that is a bar to further execution (*m*).

Farm produce. — By 56 Geo. 3, c. 50, s. 3, the sheriff may sell the crops or produce mentioned in sec. 1 (*n*) subject to an agreement to expend it on the land.

Auction when advertised. — By 46 & 47 Vict. c. 52, s. 145, where the sheriff sells goods of a debtor under an execution for a sum exceeding £20 (including legal incidental expenses) the sale shall, unless the Court from which the process issued otherwise orders, be made by public auction and not by bill of sale or private contract, and shall be publicly advertised on and during three days next preceding the day of sale.

This section does not seem to apply where the goods are sold to levy a sum not exceeding £20, including legal incidental expenses, although judgment has been entered for a greater sum (*na*), but it could probably not be evaded by selling portions at different times of less than £20 if the total to be levied exceeded that amount (*nb*).

Fees. — For the fees, see *post* (*o*). The poundage is £5 per week on the first £100 and 2½ per cent. after (*p*).

Distringas.

Distringas. When issued. — This writ, which issues against a sheriff who has gone out of office and returns that he has seized the goods, but that they remain in his hands for want of buyers, is also in aid of that of *fi. fa.*

Duty. — The duty of the sheriff is expressed on the face thereof (*q*).

Possession.

Possession. When issued. — This writ is employed in actions for the recovery of land to put a successful plaintiff into possession of the premises (*r*).

Breaking doors. — The rule as to breaking doors under this writ is contained in *Semayne's Case* (*s*), the second resolution in which is that where any house is recovered by any real action the sheriff may break the house and deliver the seisin or possession to the plaintiff.

(*k*) *Barnard* v. *Leigh*, 1 Stark. 43.
(*l*) *Sparrow* v. *Earl of Bristol*, 1 Marsh. 10.
(*m*) *Woods* v. *Finnis*, 7 Ex. 570; *Gregory* v. *Sloman*, 1 E. & B. 368.
(*n*) See *ante*, p. 23.
(*na*) *Ex parte Berthier*, 7 Ch. D. 882; *Turner* v. *Bridget*, 8 Q. B. D. 392; *Mostyn* v. *Stock*, 9 ib. 432.

(*nb*) *Ex parte Villars*, 9 Ch. 732; *Jones* v. *Purcell*, 11 Q. B. D. 430.
(*o*) Page 176.
(*p*) 29 Eliz. c. 4.
(*q*) 1 Chit. Arch. 575; *Clerk* v. *Withers*, 6 Mod. 300. For Form, see App. I. 20.
(*r*) Ibid. 21.
(*s*) 5 Coke, 91.

The sheriff's duty is to deliver the property to the plaintiff, **Duty.** and for this purpose he must remove all persons off the premises **Persons to** unless the plaintiff recovers only an undivided portion, in which **be re-** case he cannot turn persons out of possession, but can only put **moved** the plaintiff in possession of the portion to which he is entitled (*t*). If persons be left on the premises it is not a complete **unless they** execution, unless they attorn to the plaintiff (*u*). **attorn.**

No notice is necessary to the persons actually in possession (*v*).

It is necessary that the plaintiff point out to the sheriff the **Plaintiff to** precise lands to which he is entitled (*w*); if more be taken the **point out** Court will order restitution (*x*), and if no person attend the **lands.** sheriff on behalf of the plaintiff to be put in possession, this is a good return (*y*).

It is usual for the lessor of the plaintiff to give the sheriff an **Indemnity.** indemnity for executing the writ (*z*).

The delivery of part is sufficient (*a*), unless it be in the **Delivery of** possession of several persons, or an undivided share (*b*). **part.**

For the fees, see *post* (*c*). The poundage is 1s. in the pound **Fees.** on the yearly value of the lands up to £100, and 6d. in the **Poundage.** pound for every £ above that sum (*d*).

Supersedeas.

This is a general writ, varying in form with the previous writ **Super-** issued, and requires the sheriff to supersede the execution under **sedeas.** such previous writ (*e*). **What.**

THE ADMIRALTY MARSHAL.

The warrant of the Admiralty Division for the arrest of a **Admiralty** ship, cargo, or freight, is addressed to this officer (*f*), and his **Marshal,** substitutes, and commands them to detain the property mentioned **warrant of** therein in safe custody until the further order of the Court (*g*).

When this officer sends by telegram to his substitute at an **Notice of** outport notice of the issue of the warrant, and the substitute **issue.** communicates it to the master of the vessel, it is a contempt of Court to move the vessel from the place where she is lying (*h*).

(*t*) 1 Chit. Arch. 851.
(*u*) *Upton* v. *Wills*, 1 Leon. 145.
(*v*) *Minet* v. *Johnson*, 6 Ti. Rep. 417.
(*w*) *Davenport* v. *Rhodes*, 11 M. & W. 608; *Thynne* v. *Sarl* [1891] 2 Ch. 79; 64 L. T. 781.
(*x*) *Cottingham* v. *King*, 1 Burr. 627.
(*y*) Wat. p. 322.
(*z*) Com. Dig. Ex. A. 3.
(*a*) *Cottingham* v. *King*, *ubi supra*;
Floyd v. *Bethel*, 1 Rol. 420.
(*b*) *Saul* v. *Dawson*, 3 Wils. 47.
(*c*) Page 175.
(*d*) 50 & 51 Vict. c. 55, s. 39 (5).
(*e*) For general Form, see App. I. 22.
(*f*) Or the officer of Customs. *The Alexander*, 1 Dods. 282; *The Dundee*, 1 Hagg. 124.
(*g*) Order v. r. 16 (38). For the Form, see App. I. 23.
(*h*) *The Seraglio*, 10 P. D. 120.

30   EXECUTIVE OFFICERS.

Jurisdiction. The jurisdiction extends to England and Wales and three miles from the coast (*i*). Where the officer, on finding that the vessel had sailed, pursued her, and overtaking her within the jurisdiction, seized her, brought her back into port and dismantled her, the arrest was held illegal (*j*), and so also was a subsequent detention effected by parties acting in concert with the original arresters, after she had been so brought back into port (*k*).

Arrest after departure.

Service of warrant. Service of the warrant must be made, and this is done by affixing it to the mast or hull (*l*). An arrest so effected extends not only to the vessel (*m*), but to sails and rigging taken on shore for the purpose of safe custody (*o*), and all other things of a like kind appurtenant to the ship, but in salvage cases the personal luggage of passengers is exempt (*p*), and so are seamen's clothes (*q*).

Arrest of cargo The cargo may be proceeded against in respect of liability attaching to it, or simply as security for freight which is due (*r*), and part may be seized for that due on the whole (*s*). If the cargo be on board and proceeded against specifically and named in the warrant, or if not so named, is proceeded against for freight, the arrest of the ship arrests the cargo (*t*). But if landed and warehoused or transshipped it is otherwise, and here service must be effected by placing the warrant on the cargo, or if access to it be refused, by leaving a copy with the custodian thereof (*u*).

when included in that of ship.

When not.

Service here.

Effect of arrest. The arrest binds the whole property, however great its value, and whether there be a possessory lien on it or not (*v*). If the property be already in the hands of the sheriff the warrants take priority in order of time (*w*).

Priority.

Safe custody. The marshal is responsible for the safe custody of property while under arrest (*x*).

Caveat.

Effect on release. Where a *caveat* has been entered against the release of the property, he is bound to give notice to the party entering the same before he releases (*y*). Otherwise he must, on receipt of a release, release the property, and this extends to all property mentioned therein, whether it be in the same or different

(*i*) 41 & 42 Vict. c. 73.
(*j*) *Borjesson* v. *Carlberg*, 3 App. Cas. 1316.
(*k*) *Ibid*. 1322.
(*l*) Order ix. r. 12 (59).
(*m*) Public ships are exempt. *The Comus*, 2 Dod. 464; *The Charkieh*, L. R. 4 A. & E. 59; *The Parlement Belge*, 4 P. D. 129; 5 *ib*. 197.
(*o*) *The Alexander*. *The Dundee*, *ubi supra*.
(*p*) *The Willem III*. L. R. 3 A. & E. 487.
(*q*) *The Vulture*, Prit. Ad. Dig. II. 514.
(*r*) *The Lady Durham*, 3 Hagg.

200; *The Victor*, Lush. 72.
(*s*) *The Roecliffe*, 2 A. & E. 363.
(*t*) Where freight is not to be arrested a note is appended to the *præcipe*.
(*u*) Order x. r. 13 (60); ix. r. 14 (61).
(*v*) *The Harmonie*, 1 W. Rob. 178; *The Nordstiernen*, Swa. 260.
(*w*) Order xlii. r. 29; *The Flora* 1 Hagg. 298; *The Bloomer*, 11 L. T., N. S. 46.
(*x*) *The Hoop*, 4 Rob. 145; *The Rendsbury*, 6 *ib*. 157.
(*y*) Order xxix. r. 6 (327).

places (z). In a suit of restraint the required security must first be given (a).

In a suit of possession the marshal must deliver the ship to the plaintiff (b). *Delivery.*

Commissions of appraisement (c), delivery, and removal (d) are addressed to this officer, and require him to appraise and certify the value or unload or remove the goods, as the case may be. *Commissions of appraisement, &c.*

Where there is an order for sale the marshal or his substitutes must sell and pay the proceeds into Court (e). The sale, in the absence of other order must be by public auction (f). If it has been already appraised it cannot be sold for less than the appraisement (g). *Sale by auction. Appraisement, effect of.*

The sale being effected the marshal must deliver the property to the purchaser, and if required execute a bill of sale to him (h).

For the fees payable, see *post* (i). *Fees.*

(z) Order xxix. r. 4 (322). For Form, see App. I. 24.
(a) *The Dickenson. The Giannibanta*, 10 P. D. 15; 33 W. R. 400.
(b) Ibid.
(c) For the Form, see App. I. 25.
(d) These Forms are adapted from the last-named.
(e) Order li. r. 14 (693).
(f) Coote, 108.
(g) Ibid.
(h) *Chastenauf* v. *Capeyron*, 7 App. Cas. 127.
(i) Page 179.

II. WARRANTS AND ORDERS OF SUPERIOR COURTS, NOT AT COMMON LAW: OF INFERIOR COURTS AND OFFICERS GENERALLY.

Warrants and orders of superior Courts, not at common law: of inferior Courts and officers generally.

As was stated at the outset of the last chapter warrants and orders of superior Courts, not at common law, of inferior Courts and officers generally, occupy in law a position different from those of superior Courts which issue according to the course of the common law. In regard to these last, all that the officer has to do is to satisfy himself that the warrant or order issues in a due and regular manner, and he will then be justified in executing it, for " he ought not to examine the judicial act of the Court, whose servant he is, nor exercise his judgment touching the validity of the process in point of law, but is bound to execute it, and is therefore protected by it (a).

Omnia præsumuntur ritè esse acta not applicable here.

Necessary ingredients therefore.

Cause of issue, period of detention, facts giving jurisdiction.

But when we come to consider warrants and orders which issue under statutory authority, or of inferior Courts at common law, the case is different, and the reason for this distinction is that in the case of Courts and officers other than the superior Courts acting according to the course of the common law, the maxim *Omnia præsumuntur ritè esse acta* does not apply to give jurisdiction (b). Such a warrant or order therefore must contain not only the cause of issue and the period of detention (if any) (c), but facts sufficient to shew jurisdiction to make the particular order must also appear on the face of the instrument (d), otherwise it is no justification to the officer who executes it (e).

Certain date, apt conclusion.

The *mittimus* ought to have these circumstances. It must contain a certain cause, and therefore, if it be for felony, it ought not to be generally *pro felonia*, but it must contain the special nature of the felony, so that it may appear to the judges upon a *habeas corpus* whether it be felony or not. It must have a certain date, and an apt conclusion (f), such as "him safely to keep until he may be dealt with by law " (g).

Where commissioners committed a bankrupt for not answering questions, the Court ordered his discharge, as the questions were

---

(a) Turner v. Felgate, 1 Lev. 95; Cotes v. Michill, 3 ib. 20.
(b) Per Holroyd, J.: R. v. All Saints, 7 B. & C. 790. See R. v. Totnes, 11 Q. B. 80.
(c) 2 Inst. 52.
(d) Harrison v. Wright, 13 M. & W. 816; Christie v. Unwin, 11 A.& E. 373; Muskett v. Drummond, 10 B. & C. 153.

(e) Andrews v. Morris, 1 Q. B. 17; Carratt v. Morley, ib. 28.
(f) 2 Hale P. C. 122; Kendal, 5 Mod. 78; Caudle v. Seymour, 1 G. & D. 434; 1 Q. B. 889; 5 Jur. 1196.
(g) 2 Inst. 52; Bracy, 1 Ray. 99; Groome v. Forrester, 5 M. & S. 314; Daniell v. Phillips, 1 Cro. M. & R. 662.

not specified so that the Court might judge of their legality (*h*). And where a warrant left a blank for the Christian name of the person to be apprehended, giving no reason for the omission, it was held too general, and a resistance to such an arrest lawful, and the killing of the person attempting to execute it not murder (*i*). But a warrant to arrest a party to the end that he may become bound at the next sessions has been held to mean those next after the arrest, and therefore the officer may in such case justify an arrest after the sessions next ensuing the date of the warrant (*j*). It can, however, only be executed by the person to whom it is addressed (*k*). To be executed by addressee.

Where it appears on the face of the proceedings that there is jurisdiction, it will be intended that the proceedings are regular (*l*), otherwise no such intendment will be made (*m*). And where the Court or officer has merely proceeded erroneously in the issue of process, but not without jurisdiction, the executing officer will be justified (*n*). Where proceeding deemed regular. Erroneous process.

There appears to be no distinction between warrants and orders so far as regards the question of jurisdiction (*o*). In orders as well as in warrants the facts conferring jurisdiction must appear thereon. "We cannot intend for or against the order, but must decide according to the words. However high the authority may be where a special statutory power is exercised the person who acts must take care to bring himself within the terms of the statute. Whether the order be made by the Lord Chancellor or by a justice of the peace, the facts which gave the authority must be stated " (*p*). No distinction between warrants and orders as to jurisdiction.

And where any Act confers a power to make, grant, or issue any instrument, expressions used in the instrument are, unless the contrary intention appears, to have the same respective meanings as in the Act conferring the power (*q*).

There is, however, an important distinction which must be here pointed out between the cases where warrants and orders of the class we are now considering, issue (1) after adjudication, and (2) where there has been no adjudication. And this distinction is mainly important in regard to the liability of the officer who executes the process. It may be thus stated :— True distinction is between warrants and orders, where issue (*a*) after adjudication, (*b*) where no adjudication.

Where an officer executes a warrant or order made under statutory jurisdiction, or of an inferior Court at common law, after an adjudication, he is protected where it appears on the

(*h*) *Ex parte Leake,* 9 B. & C. 240.
(*i*) *R.* v. *Hood,* 1 Moo. C. C. 281.
(*j*) *Mayhew* v. *Parker,* 8 T. R. 110; 2 Esp. 683.
(*k*) *Symonds* v. *Kurtz,* 61 L. T. 559; 53 J. P. 727; 5 Ti. Rep. 511.
(*l*) *Barnes* v. *Keane,* 15 Q. B. 75; *Baker* v. *Care,* 1 H. & N. 674.
(*m*) *Dempster* v. *Purnell,* 4 Sc. N. R. 39.
(*n*) *The Marshalsea,* 10 Rep. 68 b,

76 a.
(*o*) *R.* v. *Hulcott,* 6 T. R. 583; *R.* v. *All Saints,* 7 B. & C. 785; *Day* v. *King,* 5 A. & E. 367.
(*p*) Per Coleridge, J.: *Christie* v. *Unwin,* 11 A. & E. 373; and see *Brook* v. *Jenney,* 2 Q. B. 275: and *Taylor* v. *Clemson, ib.* 978.
(*q*) 52 & 53 Vict. c. 63, s. 31; and as to the time of coming into operation, see s. 36.

D

34   EXECUTIVE OFFICERS.

Distinction stated after adjudication.
No adjudication.

face of the instrument that (1) the Court or person from which it issues had jurisdiction, or (2) apparently had jurisdiction to issue such warrant or order (*r*).

Where, however, he executes such a warrant or order where there has been no previous adjudication, the protection is confined to the case only where the jurisdiction to make it appears on the face of the instrument, and in the event such jurisdiction has been properly exercised, and does not extend to the second case above-mentioned, namely, where it reasonably appears to have been within the jurisdiction, although it subsequently turn out to be in excess of it (*s*).

This, therefore, constitutes the main dividing line between the classes of warrants and orders we are now considering, and we shall therefore proceed to discuss them under those heads respectively.

A.—AFTER ADJUDICATION.

A. After adjudication.
Two kinds.

These warrants and orders range themselves into the same two categories as do those of superior Courts at common law, namely, (1) those to which the king is and (2) is not a party. It will not be necessary here to re-enumerate the incidents which specially appertain to those two classes, as that has been already done in the last chapter (*t*). Where the king is a party it matters not of course whether the particular warrant or order issues at common law or under statutory authority, or from a superior or an inferior Court. In either case the incidents and powers attendant on its execution are identical. And it is the same with those to which the king is not a party.

Adjudication, what is.

As to what is an adjudication, the principle contained in the maxim *audi alteram partem* is here applicable (*u*). It has been laid down that no man is to be condemned, punished, or deprived of his property in any judicial (*v*) or other similar proceeding (*w*) unless he has had opportunity of being heard (*x*). And this rule has been held to apply to judges of inferior Courts (*y*), to justices (*z*), and to cases arising under the Metropolis Management Act (*a*). It prevails universally unless excepted by the express wording of the Act conferring the power (*b*).

(*r*) *Andrews* v. *Marris*, 1 Q. B. 17; *Ashcroft* v. *Bourne*, 3 B. & Ad. 684; *Brittain* v. *Kinnaird*, 1 B & P 432.
(*s*) *Foster* v. *Dodd*, L. R. 3 Q. B. 67; *Wilkins* v. *Hemsworth*, 7 A. & E. 807.
(*t*) *Ante*, p. 5,¶15.
(*u*) *Wood* v. *Wood*, L. R. 9 Ex. 190; 43 L. J. Ex. 190; 30 L. T. 815; 22 W. R. 709.
(*v*) *Re Hammersmith Rent-charge*, 4 Ex. 96.
(*w*) See *Russell* v. *Russell*, 14 Ch. D.

471; 49 L. J. Ch. 268; 42 L. T. 112.
(*x*) *Wood* v. *Wood*, *ubi sup.*
(*y*) *Kinning* v. *Buchanan*, 8 C. B. 271; *Abley* v. *Dale*, 10 C. B. 62; *Dews* v. *Riley*, 11 C. B. 734.
(*z*) *Bessell* v. *Wilson*, 1 E. & B. 489; *Hammond* v. *Beuyshe*, 13 Q. B. 869; *R.* v. *Totnes Union*, 7 Q. B. 690.
(*a*) *Cooper* v. *Wandsworth*, 14 C. B. N. S. 180.
(*b*) *Re Hammersmith Rent-charge*, *ubi sup.*

1.—THE KING A PARTY.

The Sheriff.

Courts of assize and quarter sessions are authorized to issue to this officer a writ (or warrant) for the recovery of fines, estreats, recognizances, and the like (c).

This writ, the form of which is settled by the schedule to the Act 22 & 23 Vict. c. 21 (d), empowers the sheriff to levy the amount of the fine, &c., and, in the event of such amount not forthcoming, to take the defendant and lodge him in gaol until payment or until discharged by due course of law.

If the defendant be not in his county he may issue his warrant to the sheriff of the county where the offender is found, who is required to execute it (e).

[margin: 1. King a Party. Sheriff. Warrant, &c., for fines. Duty. Offender out of jurisdiction.]

The Tipstaff.

The warrants of the Bankruptcy Division of the High Court are addressed to this officer.

By the Bankruptcy Act, 1883, sects. 24 & 25, the judge of that division has power to commit a debtor for offences against those sections, and the powers under such warrants are expressly made equivalent to the class now under consideration (f).

And orders made under sect. 5 of the Debtors Act, 1869, for the committal of a defendant also fall within this class (g).

This order does not apply in case of non-payment by a married woman of a judgment-debt payable out of her separate estate under 45 & 46 Vict. c. 75, s. 1 (2) (h).

There must be evidence of means to pay, but it is not necessary that those means should have been derived from the debtor's earnings or a fixed income (i), and it is sufficient if there has been the means to pay any part of it (j).

It includes costs (k), and may be exercised if payment is to be by instalments (l). It need not be executed within a year, but remains in force as long as the judgment (m).

[margin: Tipstaff. Warrants in bankruptcy. Orders under Debtors Act, s. 5. On married woman. Evidence of means to pay. Costs. Instalments. Limitation.]

(c) See *Ex parte Edmonds*, 23 J. P. Rep. 56; 52 J. P. 230; and see *Re Walter*, 55 J. P. 276.
(d) For the Form, see App. II. 1.
(e) 22 & 23 Vict. c. 21, s. 36.
(f) See ss. 51 and 119, and 53 & 54 Vict. c. 71, s. 7, and for the Forms, App. II. 2–5.
(g) *Mitchell* v. *Simpson*, 23 Q. B. D. 373; 25 *ib.* 183. For Form, see App. II. 6.
(h) *Scott* v. *Morley*, 20 *ib.* 120; 36 W. R. 67; 57 L. J. Q. B. 43; 4 Ti.
(i) *In re Park*, 14 Q. B. D. 597.
(j) *Ex parte Fryer*, 17 *ib.* 718.
(k) *Hewitson* v. *Sherwin*, L. R. 10 Eq. 53.
(l) *Evans* v. *Wills*, 1 C. P. D. 229; *Stonor* v. *Fowle*, 13 App. Cas. 20; 36 W. R. 742.
(m) *Hermitage* v. *Kilpin*, L. R. 9 Ex. 205.

THE HIGH BAILIFF.

High Bailiff (n). The warrants and orders of the County Court in this category are the following:—

Committal in Equity and Admiralty. Warrants of committal under the Equity or Admiralty jurisdiction (o), the jurisdiction here being as great as that of the High Court (p), whether the order be final or interlocutory (q).

Bankruptcy. Under the Bankruptcy Act, 1883, s. 100, this Court has all the powers of the Bankruptcy Division, and its orders may be enforced in like manner (r).

Contempt. Warrants of committal for wilful insult to the judge or any juror, or witness, or any registrar, bailiff, or officer of the Court, or in going to or returning from the Court, or wilful interruption of the proceedings of the Court, or other misbehaviour in Court (s).

To observe to a judge in the course of, and in reference to his judgment, that "that is a most unjust remark," is an insult, and if not withdrawn amounts to such a wilful insult as is contemplated by these sections (t).

Verbal order. The judge may under these sections verbally order this officer to take into custody the offender and detain him until the rising of the Court. And such order amounts to an adjudication as to the fact of wilful insult (u).

Orders under Debtors Act, s. 5. Orders of committal made under sect. 5 of the Debtors Act, 1869. These must be exercised only by a judge or his deputy, and by an order made in open Court shewing on its face the ground on which it is issued (v). The order need not be then and there drawn up (w).

CONSTABLES.

Constables. The warrants and orders of this class which are executed by these officers are:—

Committal by quarter sessions. Those of quarter sessions who may commit by order to the custody of its officers without warrant "for there is or ought to be a record of such commitment, and the order given *sedente*

(n) The duties of this officer are in some cases performed by the registrar, but the liability in such cases is the same as that of the high bailiff: 51 & 52 Vict. c. 43, s. 37.

(o) Jud. Act, 1873, s. 89; Order xlii. r. 5. For general Forms of committal for neglect to obey order, see App. II. 7, 8.

(p) *Ex parte Martin*, 4 Q. B. D. 212.

(q) *Richards* v. *Cullerne*, 7 *ib.* 623, and see *R.* v. *Surrey County Court*, 13 *ib.* 966.

(r) See *supra*, and the Forms there referred to.

(s) 51 & 52 Vict. c. 43, ss. 161, 162.

(t) *R.* v. *Jordan*, 36 W. R. 589. For Form, see App. II. 9.

(u) See *R.* v. *Jordan, ubi sup.; Ex parte Plater*, 12 W. R. 823; 33 L. J. M. C. 142.

(v) See *Kenyon* v. *Eastwood*, 4 Ti. Rep. 451; 23 L. J. N. 71.

(w) *Harris* v. *Slater*, *ib.* 120; W. N. (1888) 186. For the Form, see App. II. 6, and see *ante*, p. 35.

curiâ would probably be a protection to the officer" (*x*). In the case of prisoners sentenced at the sessions there is a calendar as at the assizes (*y*). Calendar.

The coroner has power to order the arrest by warrant of a person found by the verdict of the jury guilty of murder or manslaughter (*z*), also of a witness for contempt of a summons (*a*), or for refusing to (1) give evidence, (2) sign his information, or (3) enter into recognizances (*b*). Warrant of coroner.

Inferior Courts of Record have power to commit for contempt only when committed in the face of the Court (*c*). Inferior Courts, power in contempt.

Justices may order arrest by warrant for not appearing to a summons or to answer a charge (*d*). And warrants of commitment either for punishment or for trial other than in civil matters (*e*) fall in this category (*f*). They must be executed by the constable to whom addressed (*ff*), and no conditions can be annexed by the justices to the performance of the duty imposed, which the law does not warrant (*g*). Committal by justices.

The warrants of distress which issue on a conviction or order by justices, other than those issued in civil matters, are to be here included (*h*). Distress warrants.

The conviction or order is enforced by this means in all cases save those under the Game, the Malicious Injury to Property and Person and a few other Acts, where the statute neither directs the same to be so levied or no mode of levying the penalty is provided (*i*).

By 42 & 43 Vict. c. 49, s. 43 (1), these warrants are to be executed by or under the direction of a constable, (2) save so far as the person against whom the distress is levied otherwise consents in writing, the distress shall be sold by public auction, and five clear days at least shall intervene between the making of the distress and the sale, and where written consent is so given as aforesaid, the sale may be made in accordance with such consent. How executed. Sale by auction.

(3.) Subject as aforesaid the distress shall be sold within the period fixed by the warrant, and, if not so fixed, then within the period of fourteen days from the date of the making of the distress unless the sum for which the warrant was issued and Within what time. Extent of sale.

(*x*) Per Parke, B., *Watson* v. *Bodell*, 14 M. & W. 70; 2 Hale P. C. 122, and see *In re Clarke*, 2 Q. B. 619.
(*y*) See *ante*, p. 13.
(*z*) 50 & 51 Vict. c. 56, s. 5. For the Form, see App. II. 10, 11.
(*a*) Jervis, 5th ed. p. 47. This warrant is also addressed to the coroner's officer. For the Form, see App. II. 12.
(*b*) App. II. 13.
(*c*) *R.* v. *Lefroy*, L. R. 8 Q. B. 134; 42 L. J. Q. B. 121.
(*d*) 11 & 12 Vict. c. 42, s. 1.
(*e*) See *post*, p. 43.

(*f*) For Forms, see App. II. 14, 15. Justices cannot apparently commit for contempt merely: *Mayhew* v. *Locke*, 7 Taunt. 63; *Ex parte Hyndman*, 50 J. P. 151.
(*ff*) *R.* v. *Saunders*, L. R. 1 C. C. 75; 36 L. J. M. C. 87; 10 Cox C. C. 445; 16 L. T. 331; 15 W. R. 752.
(*g*) *R.* v. *Middlesex*, 12 L. J. M. C. 36; *R.* v. *Handsley*, 7 Q. B. D. 398.
(*h*) For Form, see App. II. 16.
(*i*) 11 & 12 Vict. c. 43, s. 19, and see s. 17; and *Re Clew*, 8 Q. B. D. 511; 51 L. J. M. C. 140; 46 L. T. 482; 30 W. R. 704; 46 J. P. 534.

38 EXECUTIVE OFFICERS.

also the charges for taking and keeping the said distress are sooner paid.

Goods not to be removed,
(4.) Subject to any directions to the contrary given by the warrant of distress, where the distress is levied on household goods, the goods shall not, except with the consent in writing of the person against whom the distress is levied, be removed from the house until the day of sale, but so much of the goods *but to be impounded.* shall be impounded as are in the opinion of the person executing the warrant sufficient to satisfy the distress, by affixing to the articles a conspicuous mark. . . .

Costs.
Overplus.
(7.) A constable charged with the execution of a warrant of distress shall cause the distress to be sold, and may deduct out of the amount realised by such sale all costs and charges actually incurred in effecting such sale (*j*), and shall render to the owner the overplus, if any, after retaining the amount of the sum for which the warrant was issued, and the proper costs and charges of the execution of the warrant.

Superseded on payment of debt and costs.
(8.) Where a person pays or tenders to the constable charged with the execution of a warrant of distress, the sum mentioned in such warrant, or produces the receipt for the same of the clerk of the Court of summary jurisdiction issuing the warrant, and also pays the amount of the costs and charges of such distress up to the time of such payment or tender, the constable shall not execute the warrant.

What may not be taken.
By sect. 21 (2) wearing apparel and bedding of a person and his family, and, to the value of £5, the tools and implements of his trade, shall not be taken.

Priority of warrant.
In the event of another and civil execution being in at the same time, these warrants being ones in which the king is interested have priority (*k*).

EXCISE.

Excise.
The only warrants which fall within this class and are directed to these officers are levy and commitment warrants, which are regulated by 7 & 8 Geo. 4, c. 53, ss. 86-91.

Levy warrant. Sale. For penalty and costs. Overplus to owner. Warrant to be shewn and copy permitted to be taken.
The sale under a levy warrant must take place between four and eight days after issue, unless the penalties or sums are sooner paid or satisfied (*l*).

The officer making such levy is to deduct the penalty or sum for which such levy shall be made, and all reasonable charges and expenses attending such levy, and return the overplus to the proprietor of the goods, and such officer shall if required shew the warrant to the person upon whose goods the levy shall be made, and suffer such person to take a copy thereof (*m*).

(*j*) Sub-s. (5) imposes a summary penalty of £5 for excessive charges or other exaction.
(*k*) See *Att.-Gen.* v. *Leonard, ante,* p. 11.

(*l*) Sect. 88. The warrant is of the same kind as that of distress. See *ante,* p. 37.
(*m*) Sect. 89, and see *R.* v. *Mitton, ante,* p. 7.

Where an action was brought against these officers for detention of goods after the penalty had been paid it was held that the action would not lie as there had been no demand for their return (*n*). Demand condition precedent to action for illegal detention.

The warrant of commitment is of the same kind as that ordinarily issued by justices (*o*). Commitment.

Taxes.

Warrants of the commissioners for levying distresses on non-payment of taxes and of commitment of defaulters are executed by the collectors (*p*). Taxes.

By 42 & 43 Vict. c. 19, s. 86 (3), a levy or warrant to break open shall be executed by or under the direction and in the presence of the collector. Distress warrant.

By sub-sect. (2), the breaking must take place in the daytime. Breaking in daytime.

(4.) Every distress shall be kept for the space of five days at the costs and charges of the person so refusing to pay. Distress to be kept five days.

(5.) If the sum due not then paid, the said distress shall be appraised by two or more of the inhabitants, or other sufficient persons, and there be sold by public auction by the said collector or his deputy for the payment of the said money, the overplus, if any, after deducting the said money, and also the costs and charges of taking, keeping, and selling the said distress, to be restored to the owner. Appraised. Sale by auction. Overplus to owner.

(6.) The powers conferred by 33 Geo. 3, c. 55, may be employed under this Act. These powers are contained in sect. 3, which was repealed by 11 & 12 Vict. c. 43, s. 36, but which it is presumed is revived by this sub-section. In the event of no sufficient distress being found in the district, it authorizes a justice of a foreign jurisdiction to back the warrant in order that distress may be levied there. Execution in foreign jurisdiction.

The amount assessed must be paid unless the plaintiff appeal (*q*). Appeal.

By sect. 80 (1) of the same Act no goods are to be taken in execution except at the suit of the landlord for rent. Landlord's claim.

A bill of sale is no protection in respect of chattels which but for such bill of sale would have been liable to distress under a warrant for the recovery of taxes, and poor and other parochial rates (*r*). Bill of sale, effect of.

By 57 Geo. 3, c. 93, s. 1, and 7 & 8 Geo. 4, c. 17, distresses for taxes under £20 are not to be charged for otherwise than as in the schedule to the first Act (*s*). Charges.

One warrant for several duties is sufficient (*t*). One warrant for several duties.

(*n*) *Hutchings* v. *Morris*, 6 B. & C. 464.
(*o*) See *ante*, p. 37.
(*p*) For the Forms, see App. II. 17, 18.
(*q*) *Simpkins* v. *Robinson*, 45 L. T. 221, and see *Allen* v. *Sharp*, 2 Ex. 352; 17 L. J. Ex. 209.
(*r*) 45 & 46 Vict. c. 43, s. 14.
(*s*) See *post*, p. 180.
(*t*) *Patchett* v. *Bancroft*, 7 T. R. 367.

EXECUTIVE OFFICERS.

Commitment warrant.

As to the warrant of commitment the power of the commissioners is to commit a defaulter until payment of the sum due together with the costs and expenses of apprehension and conveyance to gaol (*u*).

THE GAOLER.

Gaoler.

The warrants above-mentioned which are executed by the tipstaff, the high bailiff and constables, excise and taxes officers, respectively, are also addressed to this officer.

In default of sureties for the peace. Customs. First class misdemeanants. Warrants of Secretary of State and County Court and order of High Court to bring up prisoner. Removal to asylum. To reformatory school. Discharge.

For not entering into recognizances or finding sureties to keep the peace, the imprisonment is not to exceed 12 months (*v*), and for non-payment of a penalty under the Customs Act 6 months (*w*).

Prisoners committed for contempt of Court are to be treated as first-class misdemeanants (*x*).

The warrant of the Secretary of State and of the County Court (*y*), and the order of the Court to bring up a prisoner for trial (*z*) go to this officer. The two first-mentioned are made of equal force with a *habeas corpus* (*a*).

The Secretary of State may issue a warrant to remove an insane prisoner to an asylum (*b*), and a justice to remove a prisoner to a reformatory school (*c*).

As to the discharge of prisoners, see *ante* (*d*).

2.—THE KING NOT A PARTY.

THE HIGH BAILIFF.

2. King not a Party. High Bailiff. Arrest for assault or rescue. Liability of high bailiff.

With reference to the powers of this officer in execution, it is enacted that if any officer or bailiff shall be assaulted while in the execution of his duty (*e*), or if any rescue shall be made or attempted of any goods levied under process of the Court, the officer may apprehend the offender and bring him before the judge (*f*).

In such case it has been held that the high bailiff is not liable for the act of his officer (*g*).

(*u*) 43 & 44 Vict. c. 19, ss. 22 and 89.
(*v*) 16 & 17 Vict. c. 30, s. 3.
(*w*) 39 & 40 Vict. c. 36, s. 236.
(*x*) *Ante*, p. 13.
(*y*) 16 & 17 Vict. c. 30, s. 9, and 51 & 52 Vict. c. 43, s. 112. For the Form, see App. II. 19.
(*z*) 30 & 31 Vict. c. 35, s. 10.
(*a*) See *ante*, p. 14.
(*b*) 47 & 48 Vict. c. 64, ss. 2–5. For Form, see App. II. 20.
(*c*) 29 & 30 Vict. c. 117, s. 15. For Form, see App. II. 21. As to industrial schools, see cap. 118, ss. 42, 43.
(*d*) See *ante*, p. 13; and as to discharge under the Taxes Acts, 43 & 44 Vict. c. 19, s. 9.
(*e*) Where the officer had left for refreshment and was assaulted on his return, it was held within the section: *Coffin* v. *Dyke*, 48 J. P. 757.
(*f*) 51 & 52 Vict. c. 43. s. 48.
(*g*) *Smith* v. *Pritchard*, 8 C. B. 565.

Admiralty.

The warrant in Admiralty matters is to arrest and detain a ship or cargo pending the further order of the Court (*h*). *Admiralty. Warrant of arrest.*
Service of the warrant is to be effected in the same manner as that in the High Court (*i*), and the warrant may be executed on Sunday, Good Friday, or Christmas Day (*j*). Service by a clerk in the high bailiff's office is irregular (*k*). *Service thereof. Time.*
The property must be released on receipt of an order to that effect (*l*); but in a salvage action the property must be first appraised unless the plaintiff otherwise consents (*ll*). *Release. In action for salvage.*

Delivery.

This warrant issues for the delivery of specific property, and if the property cannot be found the lands and chattels of the defendant may be distrained (*m*). *Delivery.*

Execution on Goods.

This warrant authorizes the officer to levy or cause to be levied by distress and sale of the goods and chattels of the defendant, the sum recovered by the judgment and the costs of the execution (*n*). *Execution on goods.*
Under it, the officer may seize and take any of the goods and chattels of such person (excepting the wearing apparel and bedding of such person or his family, or the tools and implements of his trade to the value of £5), and any money or bank notes, cheques, bills of exchange, promissory notes, bonds, specialties, or securities for money (*o*). *What may be taken.*
Such securities are to be held by the high bailiff as security for the amount directed to be levied (*p*).
The execution is to be superseded on the payment of the debt and costs (*q*). *Execution superseded.*
A claimant of goods taken in execution must deposit their values or pay the costs of keeping possession in order to prevent their being sold (*r*). *Claimant of goods taken.*

(*h*) For the Form, see App. II. 22. This warrant does not issue strictly always after adjudication, but in Admiralty matters the power of this Court are as great as those of the High Court, see *ante*, p. 29.
(*i*) County Court Rules, 1889, Order xxxix., rr. 12, 13, and see *ante*, p. 29.
(*j*) *Ibid.* r. 11.
(*k*) *The Palomares*, 10 P. D. 36.
(*l*) County Court Rules, 1889, Order xxxix., r. 20.
(*ll*) *Ibid.* r. 21. As to the receiver selling under an order, see 17 & 18 Vict. c. 104, s. 469.
(*m*) Order xxv., r. 50. For the Form, see App. II. 23, and see also *ante*, p. 17.
(*n*) 51 & 52 Vict. c. 43, s. 146. For Form, see App. II. 24. As to the duties of the officer of the Court in distraint for the recovery of tithe rent charge leviable on lands occupied by an owner, see 54 Vict. c. 8, s. 2.
(*o*) Sect. 147.
(*p*) Sect. 148.
(*q*) Sect. 155.
(*r*) Sect. 156.

Landlord. If within five clear days from the taking in execution or before removal, the landlord claim in writing for rent in arrear, the bailiff shall in addition distrain for the rent so claimed and the costs thereof, and shall not within five days sell unless the goods be perishable or on request in writing of the defendant. On sale, he shall pay first the costs, then the landlord four weeks where weekly rental, two terms where less than a year, or one year in any other case, and then the amount for which the warrant issued (*s*).

This section does not authorize the distraint and sale of goods of a stranger (*t*), where the bailiff is wrongfully in possession, but where he is rightfully in possession it is otherwise (*u*).

Bailiffs as brokers. The bailiffs may act as brokers and take the poundage allowed by the Act (*v*).

Sale. As above stated the sale is not to take place until the end of five days, and in the meantime the goods are to be deposited by the bailiff in some fit place, or remain in the custody of a fit person approved by the high bailiff. The sale must be made by one of the brokers or appraisers appointed under the Act (*w*).

In the case of a ship, an inventory and valuation must be first made and on completion of the purchase the high bailiff must if required execute a bill of sale to the purchaser at his expense (*x*).

Priority. Where execution issues from the High Court and County Court the writs take priority in order of time (*y*).

Bankruptcy. Where bankruptcy supervenes, the execution is superseded in the same manner as in the High Court (*z*).

Fees, &c. For the fees and poundage payable to this officer, see *post* (*a*).

Possession.

Possession. This warrant is employed in actions for the recovery of land (*b*).

Entry under. It authorizes the high bailiff to give possession, and for this purpose he may enter on the premises with such assistants as he shall deem necessary between 9 A.M. and 4 P.M. (*c*).

Continuance of warrant. The warrant is to bear date next after the day named by the judge for delivery of possession, and is to continue in force for three months (*d*).

Fees, &c. For the fees &c., see *post* (*e*).

(*s*) Sect. 160.
(*t*) *Beard* v. *Knight*, 27 L. J. Q. B. 359; 8 El. & Bl. 865, and see *Wilcoxson* v. *Searby*, 29 L. J. Ex. 154; *Foulger* v. *Taylor*, 5 H. & N. 202; 29 L. J. Ex. 154.
(*u*) *Hughes* v. *Smallwood*, 25 Q. B. D. 306; 59 L. J. Q. B. 503; 63 L. T. 198; 55 J. P. 182.
(*v*) Sect. 159.
(*w*) Sect. 154.
(*x*) Order xxxix., rr. 29, 31.
(*y*) 51 & 52 Vict. c. 43, s. 152.
(*z*) See *ante*, p. 26.
(*a*) Page 179.
(*b*) For Form, see App. II., 25.
(*c*) Sect. 142.
(*d*) Sect. 143.
(*e*) Page 179.

CONSTABLES.

The warrants and orders of justices in civil matters fall within this category (*f*). *Constables.*

Commitments for non-payment of rates are in the nature of civil process (*g*), and so also it has been held is a conviction on an information for not delivering up books to a town-council (*h*). And it is the same with all cases of civil debts (*i*). *Commitment in civil matters.*

The constable must have the warrant in his possession at the time of executing it (*j*).

The powers under warrants of distress have been already enumerated (*k*). *Distress.*

In the case of recovery of tenements the warrant commands them within not less than twenty-one or more than thirty days of its date to enter the premises (by force if needful), and give possession to the landlord or agent. Such entry is not to be made on Sunday, Good Friday, or Christmas Day, nor except between 9 A.M. and 4 P.M. (*l*). *Recovery of tenements. Entry by force. Time.*

In the Metropolis a justice may order a constable to execute an order with reference to nuisances in which cases the officer is to be in the same position as an officer of the local authority (*m*). *Nuisance.*

GAOLERS.

The only warrants of this class addressed to these officers are commitments in civil matters. The persons so detained are in the class of debtors. The duty of the gaoler in such case is pointed out *infra* (*n*). *Gaolers. Civil commitments. Debtors.*

OVERSEERS.

Warrants of distress for poor-rates are executed by these officers (*o*). Paid assistant overseers have the same powers as overseers (*p*); but local collectors of rates have not. In this case the Summary Jurisdiction Act applies and the warrant must be executed by a constable (*q*). *Overseers. Paid assistants. Local collector.*

(*f*) See *R.* v. *Paget*, 51 L. J. M. C. 9; 8 Q. B. D. 151; 45 L. T. 794; 46 J. P. 151; 30 W. R. 336, and *R.* v. *Pratt*, L. R. 5 Q. B. 176; 39 L. J. M. C. 73; 18 W. R. 626.
(*g*) *R.* v. *London*, 34 L. J. M. C. 193; *R.* v. *Master*, 38 *ib.* 73. For the Form, see App. II. 26.
(*h*) *Eggington*, 2 El. & Bl. 717.
(*i*) 42 & 43 Vict. c. 49, s. 6.
(*j*) *Galliard* v. *Laxton*, 2 B. & S. 363; 9 C. C. 127; 8 Jur. 692; 31 L. J. M. C. 123; 10 W. R. 353; 5 L. T. 835.
(*k*) *Ante*, p. 37.
(*l*) 1 & 2 Vict. c. 74, s. 1. For Form, see App. II. 27. An order to destroy dogs is made under 34 & 35 Vict. c. 56, s. 2.
(*m*) 54 & 55 Vict. c. 76, s. 12. For general Form of warrant, see App. II. No. 53.
(*n*) Page 111.
(*o*) *R.* v. *Price*, 5 Q. B. D. 300; 49 L. J. M. C. 49. For Form, see App. II. 16. As to county rates, see 15 & 16 Vict. c. 81, s. 27, and as to borough, see 45 & 46 Vict. c. 50, s. 148.
(*p*) 59 Geo. 3, c. 12, s. 7; 7 & 8 Vict. c. 101, s. 61.
(*q*) 38 & 39 Vict. c. 55, s. 256; 3 & 4 Will. 4, c. 90.

44 EXECUTIVE OFFICERS.

Levy.
In the county.
In another county.
The goods of any person assessed and refusing to pay poor-rates may be levied not only in the place for which such assessment was made; but in any other place within the same county or precinct, and if sufficient distress cannot be found within the said county or precinct on oath made before some justice of any other county or precinct (which oath shall be certified under the hand of such justice on the said warrant), such goods may be levied in such other county or precinct by virtue of such warrant or certificate (*r*).

Demand.
There must be a demand before levy (*s*), and that of the exact sum demanded (*t*), but it need not be personal (*u*). There can, however, apparently be no levy upon the representative of a person who dies before it is paid (*v*). Money may be distrained as well as goods (*vv*).

Costs.
The cost of the levy and of the broker or other officer for his attendance may also be levied (*w*).

Appeal.
On appeal from any poor-rate which is either amended or quashed, the sum assessed may notwithstanding be levied and applied in satisfaction of the next effective rate (*x*). Notice of appeal does not prevent distress; but no greater sum shall be proceeded for than that assessed in the last effective rate (*y*).

Bill of sale, effect of.
As to the effect of a bill of sale, see *ante* (*z*).

Bankruptcy.
Where bankruptcy supervenes there is no power to distrain; but the claim must be proved as a debt which is entitled to preferential payment (*a*).

Company
Distress levied against the estate or effects of a company in liquidation is void (*b*). But where they had levied an injunction was refused unless the liquidator paid the amount due (*c*).

Excessive charges.
By 57 Geo. 3, c. 93, s. 1, distresses for rates under £20 are not to be charged for otherwise than as in the schedule thereto (*d*).

Removal of paupers.
Orders for the removal of paupers are addressed to these officers or the guardians (*e*).

Such orders must contain description of the pauper (*f*), and actual chargeability (*g*); but not the grounds on which the justices arrive at their conclusion (*h*).

(*r*) 17 Geo. 2, c. 38, s. 7; 54 Geo. 3, c. 170, s. 12.
(*s*) *East India Company* v. *Skinner*, 1 Bott. 249.
(*t*) *Hurrell* v. *Wink*, 8 Taunt. 369; *Morton* v. *Brammer*, 29 L. J. M. C. 218; 2 L. T. 600.
(*u*) *R.* v. *JJ. Gloucester*, 24 J. P. 39; *Yewdall* v. *Craven*, 29 *ib.* 197; 11 L. T. 368.
(*v*) *Stevens* v. *Evans*, 2 Burr. 1152.
(*vv*) *Hutchins* v. *Chambers*, 1 *ib.* 579.
(*w*) 39 & 40 Vict. c. 61, s. 31.
(*x*) 41 Geo. 3, c. 23, s. 1.
(*y*) Sect. 2.
(*z*) Page 39.
(*a*) 46 & 47 Vict. c. 52, s. 40.
(*b*) *Ante*, p. 25.
(*c*) *Re Dry Docks Co.*, 4 Ti. Rep. 737; W. N. 1888, 188.
(*d*) *Post*, p 180.
(*e*) 35 Geo. 3, c. 101; *R.* v. *St. Olave's*, 3 Salk. 256.
(*f*) *Johnson*, 2 *ib.* 485. For Form, see App. II. 28.
(*g*) *R.* v. *Netherton*, Burr. 139.
(*h*) *R.* v. *Honiton*, *ib.* 680. See *Brighton* v. *Strand*, [1891] 2 Q. B. 156; 64 L. T. 722.

HIGHWAY SURVEYORS.

The power of highway surveyors for the recovery of rates for the highway is the same as that of overseers (*i*). *Highway surveyors.*

Where the surveyor distrained for this rate under the warrant of a justice against a person not liable to pay he was held liable for executing the warrant (*j*). But a rate not appealed from may be enforced (*k*). *Highway rate.*

The certificate of justices for diverting or stopping up a highway also falls in this category (*l*). This must be confirmed by Quarter Sessions. The certificate must state actual inspection by the justices (*m*), together (*n*), and consent of the owner (*o*). It must not delegate to the surveyor a discretion (*p*), and no part of any consecrated ground may be taken (*q*). *Diverting highways.*

And a licence from justices for gathering stones (*r*), and materials (*s*), belongs to this class. And so also does an order to lop trees (*t*). Such an order does not confer a power to top (*u*). *Materials. Trees.*

The order must specify the extent to which the owner is required to cut the hedges (*v*); but service on the occupier is sufficient (*w*).

(*i*) 5 & 6 Will. 4, c. 50, s. 34.
(*j*) *Freeman* v. *Read*, 32 L. J. M. C. 226; 10 Jur. 149.
(*k*) *R.* v. *Oxfordshire, JJ.*, 18 L. J. M. C. 222; 14 Jur. 575.
(*l*) Sect. 85. For Form, see App. II. 29.
(*m*) *R.* v. *Downshire*, 4 A. & E. 721; *R.* v. *Jones*, 12 *ib.* 684.
(*n*) *R.* v. *Cambridge. JJ.*, 4 *ib.* 111; *R.* v. *Kent, JJ.*, 10 B. & C. 477.
(*o*) *R.* v. *Kirk*, 1 B. & C. 21, and see *R.* v. *Kent, JJ.*, 1 B. & C. 622.
(*p*) *R.* v. *Newmarket Co.*, 19 L. J. M. C. 241.
(*q*) *Rector of St. John's* v. *Parishioners*, 2 Rob. 515.

(*r*) Sect. 51, and see *Alresford* v. *Scott*, 7 Q. B. D. 210; 50 L. J. M. C. 103. For Form, see App. II. 30.
(*s*) Sect. 54. Certain places are excepted from this section, but the materials may be carried over or through them: *Ramsden* v. *Yeates*, 6 Q. B. D. 583; 50 L. J. M. C. 135.
(*t*) 5 & 6 Will. 4, c. 50, s. 65. For Form, see App. II. No. 30a.
(*u*) *Unwin* v. *Hanson*, 1891, 2 Q. B. 115; 7 T. L. R. 488.
(*v*) *Brook* v. *Jenny*, 2 Q. B. 265; 6 *ib.* 223; 1 G. & D. 567; 11 L. J. M. C. 10; 5 J. P. 734.
(*w*) *Woodard* v. *Billericay*, 11 Ch. D. 214.

B.—WHERE NO ADJUDICATION.

B. Where no adjudication.

The warrants and orders under this head also range themselves under those to which the king is or is not a party.

1.—THE KING A PARTY.

QUEEN'S MESSENGERS.

1. King a Party. Queen's messengers. Warrant for treason.

The Secretary of State (*a*) has power at common law to issue to these officers a warrant for the arrest of a person charged with treason or other offences affecting the Government (*b*).

POST OFFICERS.

Post officers. Warrant to open, &c., letters.

The Secretary of State has power also to issue to these officers warrants for the opening, detaining, and delaying of post letters. There must be an express warrant for every such opening, detaining, or delaying (*c*). This is a prerogative warrant (*d*).

MINISTER, CHURCHWARDENS, AND OVERSEERS.

Minister, churchwardens and overseers. Warrant of coroner to exhume. Orders of Privy Council as to burial-grounds.

The coroner has power at common law to issue a warrant requiring these officers to exhume the body of a person within a reasonable time after burial upon which it is his intention to hold an inquest (*e*).

Orders of the Privy Council issue directing such acts to be done by and under the direction of the churchwardens or such other person as may have the care of any vaults or places of burial, as shall prevent them from becoming or continuing dangerous or injurious to the public health (*f*). If not done

---

(*a*) As to the visitation of religious houses, see 25 Hen. 8, c. 21, s. 20.

(*b*) 1 Ch. Cr. Law, 34, 107; Hawk. P. C. b. 2, c. 16; *Kendal* v. *Row*, 1 Ld. Ray. 65; *R.* v. *Wilkes*, 2 Wils. 151. A like power is conferred on the Privy Council, but this is obsolete. For the Form, see App. II. 31.

(*c*) 9 Anne, c. 10, s. 40. There is no special Form in this case. As a matter of practice it is seldom employed. Cases have occurred in recent years in which letters have been tampered with, and the Home Secretary has publicly disclaimed any knowledge of the matter. Such tampering is a misdemeanour, see *post*, p. 202.

(*d*) Ordinances of 1656, 25, 5, 1663 and 25, 8, 1683, by which the Post Office was established.

(*e*) Jervis, 5th ed., p. 47. For Form, see App. II. 32.

(*f*) 20 & 21 Vict. c. 81, s. 23. These appear in the *London Gazette*.

within a reasonable time, the Secretary of State may by writing under his hand authorize and direct the churchwardens to do and complete the same (*g*). *Of Secretary of State for same purpose.*

These orders apply only to existing burial-grounds. Where, therefore, they were issued in regard to a disused ground, they were held no defence in an action against the churchwardens for trespass (*h*).

Orders of the Secretary of State to remove any body which may have been interred (*i*). *For removal of dead body.*

This section seems to be relied on by the Secretary of State as a sufficient authority to him to order exhumation in any case where that course appears desirable or necessary. This is, perhaps, doubtful.

CONSTABLES.

The following warrants and orders of this class are executed by constables. *Constables.*

The Secretary of State issues his warrant under the Extradition Act (*j*), and any person to whom such warrant is directed may receive, hold in custody, and convey within the jurisdiction of the foreign State the criminal mentioned therein; and if the criminal escapes out of any custody to which he may be delivered on or in pursuance of such warrant, he may be retaken in the same manner as any person accused of any crime (*k*). *Warrants of Secretary of State. Extradition.*

This Act applies only subject to treaty (*l*), and generally not to offences of a political character (*m*). If the description of the offence is sufficient, the warrant will be good (*n*). A person already in custody may be detained (*o*).

The Act applies to all persons of whatever nationality committing the specified crimes in the treaty countries, unless by treaty specially exempted (*p*).

The offences in the schedule to the Act (*q*) are all indictable by our law.

Also under the Fugitive Offenders Act (*r*), and in this case there is the same proviso as to retaking on an escape (*s*). *Fugitive offenders.*

And under the Criminal Lunatics Acts (*t*) such warrant may *Criminal lunatics.*

(*g*) 22 Vict. c. 1, s. 1. No Form for general use under this Act has yet been settled.

(*h*) *Foster* v. *Dodd*, L. R. 3 Q. B. 67.

(*i*) 20 & 21 Vict. c. 81, s. 25. For Form, see App. II. 33.

(*j*) 33 & 34 Vict. c. 52, s. 11. For the Form, see App. II. 34.

(*k*) Ibid. See *post*, p. 82.

(*l*) See *R.* v. *Wilson*, 3 Q. B. D. 42.

(*m*) *Ex parte Castioni*, 1891, 1 Q. B. 149; 39 W. R. 202.

(*n*) *Ex parte Terraz*, 4 Ex. D. 63;

In re Bellencontre, 7 T. L. R. 315; 39 W. R. 381; 1891, 2 Q. B. 122; 64 L. T. 461.

(*o*) *R.* v. *Weil*, 9 Q. B. D. 701.

(*p*) *R.* v. *Ganz*, ib. 93.

(*q*) And see 36 & 37 Vict. c. 60, s. 8.

(*r*) 44 & 45 Vict. c. 69, s. 6. For Form, see App. II. 35. This is addressed to the keeper of the prison.

(*s*) Ibid. s. 28.

(*t*) 47 & 48 Vict. c. 64, s. 15, and see 23 & 24 Vict. c. 75, s. 2; 39 & 40 Geo. 3, c. 94, and 46 & 47 Vict. c. 38.

be executed by any constable, as if it were for the arrest of a person charged with an offence (*u*).

Quarter sessions bench warrant.
Quarter sessions have power to issue a bench warrant for the arrest of a person charged with felony or misdemeanour (*v*).

Riot.
Where a riot exists, a justice present may verbally order its dispersal. One hour after the reading of the proclamation the justice may order the mob to be fired into or charged sword in hand (*w*).

Warrants of justices.
But the warrants which are addressed to constables for execution are principally those of justices of the peace out of sessions.

Treason, felony, or other indictable offence.
In all cases of treason felony or other indictable offence (*x*), the warrants issued fall within this category (*y*).

(*u*) 47 & 48 Vict. c. 64. See App. II., 18, for the Forms. As to the warrants of the Secretary of State for War for billeting soldiers, see 44 & 45 Vict. c. 58, s. 104.
(*v*) 1 Ch. Cr. Law, 339. For the Form, see App. I., 5.
(*w*) *R.* v. *Neale*, 9 C. & P. 431; *R.* v. *Pinney*, 5 *ib.* 254; *Keighley* v. *Bell*, 4 F. & F. 790.
(*x*) *Rawlins* v. *Ellis*, 16 M. & W. 172; and see *Conybeare* v. *The School Board for London*, 63 L. T. 635; 39 W. R. 288; 55 J. P. 151.
(*y*) Warrants generally are granted under 11 & 12 Vict. c. 42, ss. 1–5, 9–16, 21, 24, and 25; 11 & 12 Vict. c. 43, ss. 2, 3, 7, and 19; and as regards the Metropolis, under 2 & 3 Vict. c. 71, ss. 19–25. Indictable offences are :—

Abduction	24 & 25 Vict. c. 100, ss. 54–56.
Abettors in misdemeanour . .	24 & 25 Vict. c. 94, s. 8.
Abortion	24 & 25 Vict. c. 100, ss. 58, 59.
Animals, killing or maiming .	24 & 25 Vict. c. 97, ss. 40, 41.
Aqueducts, &c., injuring . .	——————, s. 33.
Admiralty, uttering false certificates	28 & 29 Vict. c. 124, s. 6.
personating person entitled .	—————— s. 8.
Aliens, false declaration . .	33 & 34 Vict. c. 102, s. 2.
Arms, training to use . . .	60 Geo. 3, c. 1, s. 1.
Arson	24 & 25 Vict. c. 97, ss. 1–8.
Assault committed, &c., on female	Common law.
on parish officer . . .	13 & 14 Vict. c. 100, s. 9.
on county constable . .	1 & 2 Wm. 4, c. 41, s. 11.
promoting another to do so .	2 & 3 Vict. c. 93, s. 8.
on person arresting . .	14 & 15 Vict. c. 19, s. 12.
Attempt to commit felony . .	Common law.
Bank notes, making . . .	24 & 25 Vict. c. 98, ss. 9–11.
Bankrupt—frauds . . .	32 & 33 Vict. c. 62, ss. 4–16. 46 & 47 Vict. c. 52, s. 163.
Bigamy	24 & 25 Vict. c. 100, s. 57.
Blasphemous libel . . .	Common law.
Bribery at elections . . .	" "
Bridges, malicious injury . .	24 & 25 Vict. c. 97, ss. 30, 31.
Buoys, interfering with . .	——————, ss. 47, 48.
Burglary	24 & 25 Vict. c. 96, ss. 50–52.
Carnal knowledge, attempt . .	Common law.
Chain, cables, &c., malicious injury	27 & 28 Vict. c. 27, s. 12.
Challenge to fight . . .	Common law.
Cheating by false weight . .	
Child, stealing	24 & 25 Vict. c. 100, s. 59.
Children under 13, carnal abuse .	48 & 49 Vict. c. 69, s. 4.
Chloroform, administering with intent	24 & 25 Vict. c. 100, s. 22.
Choke, attempt to . . .	——————, s. 15.
Church or meeting-house . .	1 Wm. & M. c. 18, s. 15.
disturbing . . .	51 Geo. 3, c. 155, s. 13.

WARRANTS AND ORDERS. 49

These warrants are of three kinds, namely arrest, search, and remand.

Coin offences	24 & 25 Vict. c. 99.
Combinations, unlawful	39 Geo. 3, c. 79, s. 3.
	57 Geo. 3, c. 19, s. 25.
Compounding felony	Common law.
misdemeanour	"
informations	18 Eliz. c. 5, s. 4.
	56 Geo. 3, c. 138, s. 2.
Conspiracies	Common law.
Contract of service, breaking	38 & 39 Vict. c. 86, s. 5.
Constable, refusing to assist, when required	Common law.
Copyright, false registration	5 & 6 Vict. c. 45, s. 12.
Crime, extortion by accusing of	24 & 25 Vict. c. 96, ss. 46–49.
Cruelty to those under one's control	Common law.
to children	52 & 53 Vict. c. 44, s. 1.
Customs offences	39 & 40 Vict. c. 36.
Dead body, disinterring	Common law.
Declaration, making false	5 & 6 Will. 4, c. 62, s. 21.
Deer taking	24 & 25 Vict. c. 96, ss. 12–16.
Desertion, army	42 & 43 Vict. c. 33, s. 12.
navy	29 & 30 Vict. c. 109, s. 9.
Disobedience of order of justices, or direction under statute with no penalty	Common law.
Disorderly house, keeping	25 Geo. 2, c. 36, ss. 5–8.
	58 Geo. 3, c. 70, s. 7.
Election offences	6 & 7 Vict. c. 18, ss. 81, 89.
	28 & 29 Vict. c. 36, s. 11.
	17 & 18 Vict. c. 102, ss. 2, 3.
	26 & 27 Vict. c. 29, s. 1–4.
	24 & 25 Vict. c. 53, s. 5.
municipal	35 & 36 Vict. c. 60, s. 3.
Embezzlement	24 & 25 Vict. c. 96, ss. 68–81.
Entry, forcible	5 Ric. 2, c. 8.
	15 Ric. 2, c. 2.
	8 Hen. 6, c. 9.
	21 Jac. 1, c. 15.
Escape of felon, aiding	28 & 29 Vict. c. 126, s. 37.
rescue in felony or misdemeanour	Common law.
Excise offences	7 & 8 Geo. 4, c. 53, s. 65.
	43 & 44 Vict. c. 24, s. 20.
Explosives	38 & 39 Vict. c. 17, s. 73.
Extradition	33 & 34 Vict. c. 52, s. 8.
Extortion by colour of office	Common law.
False imprisonment	" "
False pretences	" "
Falsification of accounts	38 & 39 Vict. c. 24, s. 1.
Felony, misprision of	Common law.
Fireworks, nuisance by	23 & 24 Vict. c. 139.
Fish stealing	24 & 25 Vict. c. 96.
Foreign enlistment	33 & 34 Vict. c. 90, ss. 4–7.
shipbuilding	——————, s. 8.
aiding equipment	——————, ss. 10, 12.
Forgery	24 & 25 Vict. c. 98.
Friendly societies circulating false copies of rules	38 & 39 Vict. c. 60, s. 16.
Fugitive offenders	44 & 45 Vict. c. 69, ss. 4, 16.

E

50 EXECUTIVE OFFICERS.

Arrest.

**Arrest.
Jurisdiction backing.**

The warrant of arrest can be executed only within the jurisdiction of the magistrate who issues it (z), otherwise it must be

Game offences	9 Geo. 4, c. 69, ss. 1, 2, 9.
Gaming, cheating at play	8 & 9 Vict. c. 109, s. 19.
Gaming-house, keeping	Common law.
	16 & 17 Vict. c. 119, s. 11.
Hopbinds, destroying	24 & 25 Vict. c. 97, s. 19.
false marking bags	29 & 30 Vict. c. 37.
Housebreaking	24 & 25 Vict. c. 96, s. 57.
Indecent exposure	Common law.
prints	" "
Industrial schools	29 & 30 Vict. c. 117, s. 31.
Jesuits	10 Geo. 4, c. 7, s. 28.
Kidnapping	Common law.
Larceny	24 & 25 Vict. c. 96.
Libel against Queen	Common law.
administration of justice	
publishing against person	6 & 7 Vict. c. 96, ss. 3–5.
Lodger, false declaration	34 & 35 Vict. c. 79, s. 1.
Lotteries	10 Will. 3, c. 23, s. 1.
	42 Geo. 3, c. 119, s. 1.
Lunatics, offences against	16 & 17 Vict. c. 96, ss. 73, 74, 93, 122, 123.
criminal	23 & 24 Vict. c. 75, ss. 12, 13.
Maintenance	Common law.
Manslaughter	24 & 25 Vict. c. 100.
Medical practitioner, false registration	21 & 22 Vict. c. 90, s. 38.
Merchandise marks	50 & 51 Vict. c. 28, ss. 2, 3, 13.
Merchant shipping	17 & 18 Vict. c. 104, s. 366.
	19 & 20 Vict. c. 41, s. 6.
	14 & 15 Vict. c. 102, s. 55.
	39 & 40 Vict. c. 80, s. 4.
Municipal corporations, appropriating money of	45 & 46 Vict. c. 50.
Mint, conveying tools, &c., out of	24 & 25 Vict. c. 97, s. 25.
Murder	24 & 25 Vict. c. 100.
Music and dancing unlicensed	25 Geo. 2, c. 36.
Mutiny	37 Geo. 3, c. 70.
Nuisance on highway	Common Law.
Oaths, taking unlawful	5 & 6 Will. 4, c. 62, s. 13.
Office, buying or selling	5 Ed. 6, c. 16.
	49 Geo. 3, c. 126, s. 3.
Penal servitude, at large during	28 & 29 Vict. c. 126.
Personation	28 & 29 Vict. c. 124.
Perjury	5 Eliz. c. 9, s. 3.
	21 & 22 Vict. c. 78, s. 31.
	20 & 21 Vict. c. 85, s. 50.
	21 & 22 Vict. c. 108, s. 23.
Pharmacy, false registration	15 & 16 Vict. c. 56, s. 15.
Poor-officer promoting marriage of mother of bastard	7 & 8 Vict. c. 101, s. 8.
injuring rate-book, or false evidence to assessment committee	25 & 26 Vict. c. 103, s. 40.

(z) For Form, see App. II. 36.

backed before execution by a magistrate in whose jurisdiction the execution is required to be made (*a*), except that of a police magistrate issued under the Extradition Act (*b*). Offences against

Piles, cutting	24 & 25 Vict. c. 97.
Piracy	7 Will. 4, & 1 Vict. c. 88.
Post office	7 Will. 4, & 1 Vict. c. 36, ss. 35, 36.
Pound, breach	Common law.
Prize-fights	" "
Queen, firing at	5 & 6 Vict. c. 51, s. 2.
Railway offences	3 & 4 Vict. c. 97, s. 13.
	24 & 25 Vict. c. 97.
	31 & 32 Vict. c. 119, s. 5.
	34 & 35 Vict. c. 78, s. 10.
Rape	Common law.
Real estate, false statement as to title	25 & 26 Vict. c. 53, s. 105.
	25 & 26 Vict. c. 67, s. 44.
Receiving stolen goods	24 & 25 Vict. c. 96, s. 95.
Reformatory schools	29 & 30 Vict. c. 118.
Registration of marriage, false declaration	7 Will. 4, c. 24.
	3 & 4 Vict. c. 72, s. 7.
	19 & 20 Vict. c. 119, ss. 12, 18.
Rescue	14 & 15 Vict. c. 100, s. 20.
Riot	Common law.
Robbery	24 & 25 Vict. c. 96.
Sacrilege	
Sea-banks, interfering with	24 & 25 Vict. c. 97.
Savings banks	26 & 27 Vict. c. 87, s. 5.
Seamen, preventing ship loading	33 Geo. 3, c. 67, ss. 1, 3.
Signals, altering	24 & 25 Vict. c. 97.
Slave trade	36 & 37 Vict. c. 88.
Sluices, opening	24 & 25 Vict. c. 97.
Smuggling	7 & 8 Geo. 4, c. 53.
	39 & 40 Vict. c. 36.
Soliciting commission of offence	Common law.
Suicide, attempt	"
Tampering with witness	31 & 32 Vict. c. 110, s. 20.
Trades unions	34 & 35 Vict. c. 31, s. 18.
Trade-offences	25 & 26 Vict. c. 89, s. 168.
	30 & 31 Vict. c. 131, s. 19.
	33 & 34 Vict. c. 61, s. 19.
Treason	25 Ed. 3, s. 5.
Treason-felony	11 & 12 Vict. c. 12, ss. 3–10.
Treasure-trove, selling	Common law.
Unnatural crime	24 & 25 Vict. c. 100, s. 61.
Unwholesome meat, offering for sale	Common law.
Vaccination, false certificate	30 & 31 Vict. c. 84, s. 30.
Vendors selling deeds	22 & 23 Vict. c. 35, s. 24.
Vessels, malicious injury	24 & 25 Vict. c. 97.
Viaducts, malicious injury	
War stores offences	30 & 31 Vict. c. 128, s. 5.
Wife, exposing for sale	Common law.
Witchcraft, pretending	9 Geo. 2, c. 5, s. 4.
Workshop regulation, offences against	41 & 42 Vict. c. 16.
Wreck, impeding escape	24 & 25 Vict. c. 96, ss. 64–66.
interfering with	24 & 25 Vict. c. 100, ss. 17, 37.

(*a*) 4 Black. 20.   (*b*) 33 & 34 Vict. c. 52, s. 13.

the Coin, Explosives, Forgery, Larceny, Malicious Injury, Merchant Shipping, and Post Office Acts, are triable where the offender is found (*c*). It may be executed without being backed, not only by apprehending the offender at any place in the district of the justice's jurisdiction, but also where there is fresh pursuit at any place in the next adjoining county or place, and within seven miles of the border of such district. And offences committed on a vehicle are triable in any place through which such vehicle passed (*d*). If it be directed to all constables in the jurisdiction of the justice, it may be executed by any peace-officer for any parish, township, hamlet, or place within such jurisdiction (*e*). If it be directed to a particular officer, it must be executed by him (*f*).

By whom executed.

In all cases other than treason and felony (*g*) the officer is bound to have the warrant on him at the time of the arrest, otherwise the arrest will be illegal, resistance thereto will be lawful (*h*), and the killing of the officer in order to prevent the arrest will be manslaughter only (*i*).

When warrant must be in possession of officer.

Search.

A search warrant is confined to comparatively few cases, such as stolen property (*j*), obscene books (*k*), explosives (*l*), unwholesome food (*m*), hops improperly marked (*n*), merchandize marks (*o*), licensing (*p*), vagrants (*q*), and forged instruments (*r*).

Search.

Where the property sought for is found on the premises searched, a warrant of apprehension seems to be involved in this warrant, so that the arrest (if any) would take place under the warrant, and not of the constable's own motion (*s*). But if he seizes other property than that named, he will be liable to an action of trespass (*t*); and so also will he be if he stay an unreasonable time on the premises (*tt*).

When warrant of arrest implied.

Seizure to be limited to property named.

(*c*) See *R.* v. *Peel*, 32 L. J. M. C. 65; 9 Cox, C. C. 220; 8 Jur. 1185; 7 L. T. 336; 11 W. R. 40; 26 J. P. 757.
(*d*) 7 Geo. 4, c. 64, ss. 12 and 13; *R.* v. *French*, 8 Cox C. C. 252.
(*e*) *R.* v. *Cumpton*, 5 Q. B. D. 341; 49 L. J. M. C. 41; 42 L. T. 543; 28 W. R. 539; 40 J. P. 489.
(*f*) Steph. Crim. Proc. Art. 104, and see *Gladwell* v. *Blake*, 1 C. M. & R. 636; 5 Tyr. 186; *Lee* v. *Tesey*, 1 H. & N. 30; 25 L. J. Ex. 271; and *R.* v. *Patience*, 7 C. & P. 775.
(*g*) For a list of these offences, see *post*, p. 82.
(*h*) *Codd* v. *Cabe*, 1 Ex. D. 352; 45 L. J. M. C. 101; 34 L. T. 453; 12 Cox C. C. 202; *Galliard* v. *Laxton*, 2 B. & S. 363; 9 C. C. C. 127; 8 Jur. N. S. 642; 31 L. J. M. C. 123; 10 W. R. 353; 5 L. T. N. S. 835.
(*i*) *R.* v. *Chapman*, 12 Cox, C. C. 4.
(*j*) 24 & 25 Vict. c. 96, s. 103. For Form, see App. II. 37.
(*k*) 20 & 21 Vict. c. 83, s. 1.
(*l*) 38 & 39 Vict. c. 17, s. 78.
(*m*) 38 & 39 Vict. c. 55, s. 119; 52 & 53 Vict. c. 11, s. 4; and see 6 & 7 Will. 4, c. 37, s. 11.
(*n*) 29 & 30 Vict. c. 37, s. 10.
(*o*) 50 & 51 Vict. c. 28, s. 12.
(*p*) 37 & 38 Vict. c. 49, s. 17.
(*q*) 5 Geo. 4, c. 83, s. 13.
(*r*) 24 & 25 Vict. c. 98, s. 46.
(*s*) *Wyatt* v. *White*, 29 L. J. Ex. 193.
(*t*) *Crozier* v. *Cundy*, 6 B. & C. 232; 9 D. & R. 224.
(*tt*) *Peppercorn* v. *Hoffman*, 9 M. & W. 628.

In connection with this branch there are two cases which require special mention, the first being that of stolen property, and the second that of explosives.

As to stolen property, it is laid down that a constable may, when duly authorized by any chief officer of police, search and seize and secure any property he may believe to have been stolen, in the same manner as he would be authorized to do if he had a search warrant, and the property seized (if any) corresponded to the property described in such search warrant. Stolen property, order of chief officer of police.

It shall be lawful for any chief officer of police to give such authority as aforesaid in the following cases or either of them:—

(1.) When the premises to be searched are, or within the preceding twelve months have been, in the occupation of any person who has been convicted of receiving stolen property or of harbouring thieves; or, Premises occupied by convicted persons.

(2.) When the premises to be searched are in the occupation of any person who has been convicted of any offence involving fraud or dishonesty, and punishable by penal servitude or imprisonment.

And it shall not be necessary for such chief officer of police, on giving such authority to specify any particular property, but he may give such authority if he has reason to believe generally that such premises are being made a receptacle for stolen goods (*u*).

As to explosives, any officer of police who has reasonable cause to suppose that any offence against the Explosives Act is being committed in respect of any carriage (not being on a railway), or any boat conveying, loading, or unloading any explosive, and that the case is one of emergency, may stop, enter, inspect, and examine such carriage or boat, and generally take such precautions as may be necessary to remove any danger, as if the explosives were liable to forfeiture. Explosives.

In such case he is to be in the same position *as if* armed with a search warrant granted under this Act (*v*).

Similar power is conferred on constables or any officer authorized by the local authority in the case of the hawking of petroleum (*w*). Here the amount conveyed is not to exceed twenty gallons, to be in closed vessel, which must be properly ventilated; lights not to be brought near; carriage not to permit of escape; escape into part of house or drain to be pre- Petroleum.

(*u*) Chief officer means in London the commissioners; elsewhere the chief constable, or other officer in command or any person authorized by him; 34 & 35 Vict. c. 112, ss. 16, 20.

(*v*) 38 & 39 Vict. c. 17, s. 75. By s. 73, a superintendent or a government inspector may, in case of emergency, issue an order to enter premises, &c., to a constable or officer of the local authority. Such an order would amount to a warrant. And by s. 74 those officers or a justice may order the substance seized to be destroyed or rendered harmless. But a sample must first be taken and a portion thereof given to the owner or person having control of the explosive at the time of seizure.

(*w*) 44 & 45 Vict. c. 67, s. 4; 34 & 35 Vict. c. 105, s. 13.

vented; to be properly stored when not being hawked; all precautions to be taken to prevent accident; no other explosive to be in same carriage while being used (*x*).

Remand.

Remand. A warrant of remand is granted to detain a person charged in custody pending the further hearing of the case (*y*); and, in certain cases, the order may be verbal (*z*).

Metropolitan. Betting. As regards the Metropolis, it is laid down that the Commissioner (*a*) may issue an order in writing authorizing a superintendent to enter any house, office, room, or place within the metropolitan police district kept or used as a betting-house or office contrary to the Act, with such constables as shall be directed by the Commissioner to accompany him, and, if necessary, to use force for the purpose of effecting such entry either by breaking open doors or otherwise. Having entered he may arrest all persons found therein, and seize all lists, cards, or other documents relating to racing or betting there found (*b*).

What is house, room, office, or place. With regard to what is such a house, office, room, or place, it has been held, and may now be taken as settled, that any kind of inclosure, whether covered or not, with or without an erection, may come within the Act (*c*). But a table in Hyde Park (*d*), or a club where members bet with one another is not (*e*). The owner is not liable if he take no part (*f*), nor is a person betting in an inclosure if he do not remain in a fixed place (*g*).

Common gaming-house. A similar power is conferred on the Commissioner in the case of a common gaming-house, and inasmuch as a betting-house is within the Gaming House Act, the entry into a betting-house is usually effected by an order under this Act (*h*).

(*x*) 44 & 45 Vict. c. 67, s. 2.
(*y*) For the Form, see App. II. 38.
(*z*) 11 & 12 Vict. c. 43, s. 20.
(*a*) This officer is a justice: 10 Geo. 4, c. 44, s. 1.
(*b*) 16 & 17 Vict. c. 119, s. 12. For Form, see App. II. 39. The persons arrested need not be actually engaged in contravention of the Act: *Anderson* v. *Hume*, 46 J. P. 825; *Blake* v. *Beech*, 1 Ex. D. 320; 45 L. J. M. C. 111; 40 J. P. 678; 34 L. T. 674. But the betting must be on the premises: *Davis* v. *Stephenson*, 24 Q. B. D. 529; 59 L. J. M. C. 73; 62 L. T. 436; 38 W. R. 492; 54 J. P. 565; 6 T. L. R. 242.
(*c*) *Eastwood* v. *Miller*, L. R. 9 Q. B. 443; *Shaw* v. *Morley*, L. R. 3 Ex. 137; *Haigh* v. *Sheffield*, L. R. 10 Q. B. 102; *Galloway* v. *Maries*, 8 Q. B. D. 275; 50 W. R. 151; 51 L. J. M. C. 53; 45 L. T. N. S. 763; 46 J. P. 326. See *Bows* v. *Fenwick*, L. R. 9 C. P. 339; *Clarke* v. *Hayne*, 2 E. & E. 281; *Coyne* v. *Brady*, 12 Ir. C. L. 577.
(*d*) *Doggett* v. *Catterns*, 19 C. B. N. S. 765; 34 L. J. C. P. 159.
(*e*) *Oldham* v. *Ramsden*, 44 L. J. C. P. 309; 32 L. T. 825; 39 J. P. 583; *R.* v. *Rozier*, 1 B. & C. 272; *R.* v. *Taylor*, 3 B. & C. 502.
(*f*) *R.* v. *Cook*, 48 J. P. 351; 32 W. R. 795.
(*g*) *Snow* v. *Hill*, 14 Q. B. D. 588, followed in *Whitehurst* v. *Fincher*, 17 Cox, 70; and see *R.* v. *Hulton*, 7 Ti. Rep. 491.
(*h*) 8 & 9 Vict. c. 109, ss. 6 and 7; and see 2 & 3 Vict. c. 47, s. 48.

The case of *Jenks* v. *Turpin* (*i*) contains a *résumé* of the statute and common law relating to gaming; and from the judgments of Hawkins and Smith, JJ., there can be little doubt as to what is a common gaming-house. *Jenks* v. *Turpin*.

A common gaming-house is "a house in which a large number of persons are invited habitually to congregate for the purpose of gaming (*j*). Definition.

"In default of other evidence, it shall be sufficient to prove: (1) that such house or place is kept or used for playing therein at any unlawful game, and that a bank is kept there by one or more of the players exclusively of the others; or (2), that the chances of any game played therein are not alike favourable to all the players, including among the players the banker or other person by whom the game is managed, or against whom the other players stake, play, or bet" (*k*). Evidence in support.

It is immaterial whether the bank is kept by the owner, occupier, or keeper of the house, or by one of the players.

A house is not less a common gaming-house because gaming therein is restricted to the members of a club who resort thereto. Club.

"To no gaming-house is the public at large invited to go without restriction of some sort or other . . . If the admission of 500 persons does not make it a common gaming-house, it might equally be said that the admission of 5000 would not. The law does not require that it shall be a public gaming-house: a common gaming-house is that which is forbidden" (*l*).

If the house be not exclusively devoted to gaming, that will not prevent it from coming under the description if such be the fact. House not entirely devoted to gaming.

The following games are unlawful at the present day: Ace of hearts, pharaoh (or faro), baccarat, basset, hazard, passage, roulet, every game of dice except backgammon, and every game of cards which is not a game of mere skill, and any other game of mere chance. Unlawful games.

Customs.

The warrants which are addressed to Customs officers, and which fall in this category, are— *Customs.*

Arrest,

which is granted by justices under 39 & 40 Vict. c. 36, s. 221 (*m*), and may be executed without backing anywhere in the United Kingdom. Arrest.

Search,

which is either under a writ of assistance issuing from the High Search.

(*i*) 13 Q. B. D. 505; 52 L. J. M. C. 161; 50 L. T. 808; 49 J. P. 20.
(*j*) 13 Q. B. D. 516.
(*k*) 8 & 9 Vict. c. 109, ss. 2, 5, 8.
(*l*) 13 Q. B. D. 515.
(*m*) For Form, see App. II. 36.

56   EXECUTIVE OFFICERS.

Court, or justice's warrant under sects. 204 and 205 of the same Act (*n*).

The writ of assistance apparently confers no further power than the justice's warrant (*o*); and in an action of trespass thereunder, entry can only be justified by the event (*p*).

Sea fisheries. The warrant of justices under the Sea Fisheries Act, 1888, to enter suspected places is executed by these officers (*q*).

Secretary of State. Foreign enlistment. And so also is the warrant of the Secretary of State to search a ship believed to be fitted out contrary to the provisions of the Foreign Enlistment Act (*r*), and, if necessary, to detain her (*s*).

Detention.

Merchant shipping. Those officers (or those of the Board of Trade) may by order of the detaining officer provisionally or finally detain a ship as unsafe (*t*).

The question in these cases is whether the facts with regard to the ship as she lays in port which would have been apparent to a person of ordinary skill on examining her and inquiring about her would have given him reasonable and probable cause to suspect her safety (*u*).

Excise.

Excise. The warrants in this class to these officers are—

Arrest,

Arrest. which is issued under 7 & 8 Geo. 4, c. 53, s. 90 (*uu*).

Search,

Search. which issues under sect. 34 of the same Act, sect. 48 of 23 & 24 Vict. c. 114, and sect. 140 of 43 & 44 Vict. c. 24. This last may be executed in the night, provided it be in the presence of a constable (*v*).

Distress.

Distress. Brewer. If any duty payable by a brewer remain unpaid, the collector may by warrant empower any person to distrain all beer, malt,

(*n*) App. II. 37 and 40.
(*o*) Per Kelly, *arg.* in *R.* v. *Watts*, 2 B. & Ad. 172.
(*p*) Per De Grey, C.J., in *Bostock* v. *Saunders*, 2 W. Bla. 912, upheld by Lord Mansfield in *Cooper* v. *Booth*, 3 Esp. 135, though the principal decision was overruled.
(*q*) 51 & 52 Vict. c. 59, s. 7. No Form is yet settled.
(*r*) 33 & 34 Vict. c. 90, s. 25. No form for general use under this Act has yet been settled.

(*s*) 33 & 34 Vict. c. 90, s. 23, and see *R.* v. *Sandoval*, 56 L. T. 526; 35 W. R. 500; 51 J. P. 709; 16 Cox, C. C. 206.
(*t*) 39 & 40 Vict. c. 80, s. 6. For the Form, see App. II. 41.
(*u*) *Thompson* v. *Farrer*, 9 Q. B. D. 372. As to compensation where no reasonable cause for detention, see s. 10.
(*uu*) For the Form, see App. II. 36.
(*v*) *Ibid.* 37.

or other materials for brewing, vessels and utensils belonging to the brewer, or in any premises in the use or possession of the brewer, or of any person on his behalf or in trust for him, and to sell the same by public auction, giving six days' previous notice of the sale.

The proceeds to be applied toward payment of the costs and expenses of the distress and sale, and of the payment of the duties due; and the surplus, if any, to be paid to the brewer.

Before the day of sale, the brewer may remove the whole or any part of the beer, malt, or other materials distrained on paying to the collector towards payment of the duty the true value of such beer, malt, or other materials (*w*).

The procedure as to distillers is the same, except that permits for removal are, on application, to be granted as if the distress had not been made (*x*). *Distiller.*

Explosives Inspectors.

Any of the following officers—namely, any Government inspector under this Act, any chief officer of police, and any superior officer appointed for the purposes of this Act . . . may for the purpose of ascertaining whether the provisions of this Act with respect to the conveyance, loading, unloading, and importation of an explosive are complied with (*y*), enter, inspect and examine at any time, and as well on Sundays as on other days, the wharf, carriage, ship, or boat of any carrier or other person who conveys goods for hire, or of the occupier of any factory magazine on shore, or of the importer of any explosive on or in which wharf, carriage, ship, or boat he has reasonable cause to suppose an explosive to be for the purpose of or in course of conveyance, but so as not to unnecessarily obstruct the work or business of any such carrier, person, occupier, or importer. *Explosives inspectors. Entry on wharfs, &c.*

Any such officer if he find any offence being committed under this Act in any such wharf, carriage, ship, or boat, or on any public wharf, may seize and detain or remove the said carriage, ship, or boat, or the explosive, in such manner and with such precautions as appear to him to be necessary to remove any danger to the public, and may seize and detain the said explosive as if it were liable to forfeiture. *Seizure and detention.*

Any officer above-mentioned in this section, and any officer of police, or officer of the local authority who has reasonable cause to suppose that any offence against this Act is being committed in respect of any carriage (not being on a railway), or any boat conveying, loading, or unloading any explosives, and that the case is one of emergency, and that the delay in obtaining a warrant will be likely to endanger life, may stop and enter, inspect

---

(*w*) 43 & 44 Vict. c. 20, s. 17.
(*x*) 43 & 44 Vict. c. 24, s. 48. For

Form of warrant, see App. II. 42.
(*y*) See *post*, p. 92.

and examine such carriage or boat, and by detention or removal thereof or otherwise take such precautions as may be reasonably necessary for removing such danger in like manner as if such explosive were liable to forfeiture.

Officer deemed in possession of warrant.

Every officer shall for the purpose of this section have the same powers and be in the same position as if he were authorized by a search warrant granted under this Act (z).

WRECK RECEIVER.

Wreck receiver. Search.

The justices have power under 17 & 18 Vict. c. 104, s. 451, to issue a warrant to this officer to search for and seize concealed wreck (a). Under such a warrant he may enter any house or other place and any ship or boat.

NUISANCE INSPECTOR.

Nuisance inspector.

The justices may by order authorize these officers to remove infected persons (b) or bodies (c) from premises.

2.—THE KING NOT A PARTY.

CONSTABLES.

2. King not a Party. Constables.

The warrants and orders of justices issued and made in all cases other than treason felony and other indictable offence (d) fall within this category (e).

Such are warrants of arrest where there has been no adjudication in cases of mere misdemeanour (f).

The constable must have the warrant in his possession at the time of executing it (g).

A warrant in such a case "forthwith to arrest and take before a magistrate," does not mean to take forthwith before a magistrate (h).

Examine premises, alleged nuisance.

Orders to examine premises in cases of alleged nuisance, in which case the officer is clothed with the like powers as an officer of the local authority (i). And where the local authority is in default, this power may be conferred by the Local Government Board (j).

(z) 38 & 39 Vict. c. 17, s. 75.
(a) For the Form, see App. II. 37.
(b) 38 & 39 Vict. c. 55, s. 124.
(c) Ibid. s. 142. For Forms, see App. II. 43, 44.
(d) For these offences, see *ante*, p. 48.
(e) As to the powers of councils of conciliation, see 30 & 31 Vict. c. 105, s. 4.
(f) 11 & 12 Vict. c. 43, s. 2.

(g) *Galliard* v. *Laxton*, 2 B. & S. 363; 9 C. C. C. 127; 8 Jur. 642; 31 L. J. M. C. 123; 10 W. R. 353; 5 L. T. 835.
(h) *O'Brien* v. *Brabner*, 49 J. P. 227; 78 L. T. N. 409.
(i) 38 & 39 Vict. c. 55, s. 105. For the Form, see App. II. 45. It may be directed to the officer of the local authority in the first instance.
(j) Ibid. s. 106.

Orders to inspectors and sergeants of police to visit the places of business of registered dealers in old metals (*k*). Dealers in old metals.

Orders as to the apprehension or detention of an alleged lunatic (*l*). They may by order of a justice convey a lunatic to an institution for lunatics (*m*) which may be suspended, provision being made for temporary detention (*n*). They may by warrant of a justice duly backed arrest a lunatic escaped from Scotland or Ireland (*o*), and under that of the Secretary of State remove a lunatic to a vessel to be conveyed to his own country (*p*). They may also by order in writing of the master of an institution retake an escaped lunatic (*q*). Lunatics.

And orders that children to whom the Industrial Schools Act applies may be taken to the workhouse (*r*). Remove children to workhouse.

The following are verbal orders:— Verbal orders.

In the case of persons disturbing a petty sessional Court, the justices have power at common law to order their removal (*s*). A like power is conferred on revising barristers when sitting (*t*). Disturbing sessions, or revising barristers Court.

A coroner may order the forcible exclusion of a party from the Court (*u*), and so may a justice on a preliminary inquiry, even though he be the attorney of the party accused (*v*); but if the inquiry be final and of a judicial nature all persons have a right to be present (*w*). Removal from coroners and justices Courts.

As to witnesses it seems that they may be requested to leave the Court during the hearing; but that if they do not choose to obey, their evidence cannot be rejected on that account (*x*). Witnesses.

Out of sessions justices may verbally commit offenders in cases of breach or apprehended breach of the peace (*y*). Justices not sitting breach of peace.

And where an unlawful assembly or rout exists, order its dispersal (*z*). Unlawful assembly.

A returning officer at an election may order a person who misconducts himself at a polling station to be removed by a constable (*a*); or, if such person commit any offence there, to be arrested (*b*). Returning officer.

With regard to local authorities generally, there would appear to be no power at common law to sit with closed doors (*c*). But this would apparently not apply to meetings of committees. Local authorities.

(*k*) 24 & 25 Vict. c. 110, s. 7. For Form, see App. II., 46.
(*l*) 53 & 54 Vict. c. 5, ss. 13, 15, 21, and see 54 & 55 Vict. c. 65, ss. 2, 19.
(*m*) 53 & 54 Vict. c. 5, s. 16.
(*n*) Sect. 19.
(*o*) Sects. 86, 89.
(*p*) Sect. 71.
(*q*) Sect. 85. For Forms, see App. II. 47, 48, 49.
(*r*) 29 & 30 Vict. c. 118, s. 19, and see 52 & 53 Vict. c. 44, s. 4.
(*s*) See *Ex parte Van Sandau*, 1 Phil. 445.
(*t*) 28 & 29 Vict. c. 36, s. 16.
(*u*) *Garnett* v. *Ferrand*, 6 B. & C. 618.
(*v*) 11 & 12 Vict. c. 42, s. 19. *Cox* v. *Coleridge*, 1 B. & C. 37.
(*w*) 11 & 12 Vict. c. 43, s. 12. *Daubeny* v. *Cooper*, 10 B. & C. 237, and see *Willis* v. *Maclachlan*, 1 Ex. D. 376.
(*x*) *Roberts* v. *Garrett*, 6 J. P. 154; *Ex parte Wright*, 39 ib. 85.
(*y*) *Still* v. *Wells*, 7 East, 533; *Anon.*, Lofft. 243.
(*z*) *R.* v. *Neale*, 9 C. & P. 431; *Keighley* v. *Bell*, 4 F. & F. 790.
(*a*) 35 & 36 Vict. c. 33, s. 9.
(*b*) 6 & 7 Vict. c. 18, s. 86; 45 & 46 Vict. c. 50, s. 86.
(*c*) *Purcell* v. *Sowler*, 2 C. P. D. 219.

EXECUTIVE OFFICERS.

Order in writing of commissioner in Metropolis as to cock-fighting, &c.
Dramatic entertainments.
Dangerous structures.

As regards the Metropolis, the Commissioner may by order in writing authorize a superintendent constable, with such constables as he thinks necessary, to enter any premises kept or used for the purpose of cock-fighting, &c., and to take into custody all persons found therein without lawful excuse (*d*).

A similar power is conferred in the case of an unlicensed theatre at any time when the same shall be open for the reception of persons resorting thereto (*e*).

And a magistrate may authorize one of these officers to remove persons from dangerous structures (*f*).

WEIGHTS INSPECTORS.

Weights inspectors.
Warrant to enter.
Seizure.

The warrant of a justice to inspect measures, weights, and scales is executed by these officers (*g*). Acting thereunder he may seize and detain any weight, measure, scale, balance, or steelyard which is liable to forfeiture, and may, for the purpose of such inspection, enter any place, whether a building or in the open air, whether open or inclosed, where he has reasonable cause to believe that there is any weight, &c., which he is authorized by the Act to inspect (*h*).

Where there is no fraud there is no offence (*i*), nor where the weights are against the seller himself (*j*).

WATER BAILIFFS.

Water bailiffs.
Warrant of justice to enter.
Order of justice as to land.

The warrant of a justice to enter suspected places, either by day or night, and there seize all illegal engines, or any salmon illegally taken, is addressed to these officers, and continues in force for one week (*k*).

Justices may by order authorize these officers during twenty-four hours from the time of issue to enter and remain on land near a salmon river for the purpose of detecting offences (*l*).

(*d*) 2 & 3 Vict. c. 47, s. 47. The same power is conferred on local authorities by 10 & 11 Vict. c. 89, s. 36. There are no Forms under these enactments.

(*e*) 2 & 3 Vict. c. 47, s. 46. No Form is settled under this enactment.

(*f*) 18 & 19 Vict. c. 122, s. 80. For Form, see App. II. 50.

(*g*) A general warrant is sufficient. *Hutchings* v. *Reeves*, 9 M. & W. 747; 11 L. J. M. C. 109; 6 Jur. 439; 6 J. P. 313.

(*h*) 41 & 42 Vict. c. 49, s. 48. There need be no weight there: *Kershaw* v. *Johnson*, 1 C. & K. 329, and see *Wray* v. *Reynolds*, 1 E. & E. 165. For the Form, see App. II. 51.

(*i*) *Withall* v. *Francis*, 42 J. P. 612.

(*j*) *Booth* v. *Shadgett*, L. R. 8 Q. B. 352; 42 L. J. M. C. 98; 21 W. R. 845; 29 L. T. 30; 37 J. P. 743. See *L. & N. W. Ry.* v. *Richards*, 2 B. & S. 326; 8 Jur. 539; 26 J. P. 181; 5 L. T. 792; *Gt. W. Ry.* v. *Bailie*, 34 L. J. M. C. 31; 5 B. & S. 928; 11 Jur. 264; 13 W. R. 203; 29 J. P. 229; 11 L. T. 418, and *Carr* v. *Stringer*, 9 B. & S. 233; L. R. 3 Q. B. 433; 37 L. J. M. C. 120; 16 W. R. 859; 18 L. T. 399; 32 J. P. 517.

(*k*) 24 & 25 Vict. c. 109, s. 34, and see *post*, p. 127. For the Form, see App. II. 37. Extended to all fresh-water fish by 41 & 42 Vict. c. 39, s. 9.

(*l*) 28 & 29 Vict. c. 121, s. 31. For the Form, see App. II. 52. This warrant and order may be addressed to conservators.

Conservators may by order authorize these officers at all reasonable times to enter, remain upon, and traverse any lands not being a dwelling-house or the curtilage thereof, adjoining or near a salmon river, for the purpose of preventing any breach of the Salmon Fishery Acts. Such order continues in force for two months (*m*). *Of conservators.*

OVERSEERS.

Justices may, by order addressed to these officers, cause a lunatic to be apprehended (*n*), and they may by order to workhouse officers, require his release (*o*). The guardians have the same power (*p*). *Overseers. Arrest of lunatic.*

Guardians, it appears, have a right to sit with closed doors (*q*). *Workhouse officers.*

The visitors of an asylum may by order require the removal of a lunatic, and may address the same to a relieving officer or any of these officers (*r*). They may also order a discharge (*s*). *Asylum officers.*

DISTRICT SURVEYORS.

The County Council may by order require a survey to be made of dangerous structures (*t*). *District surveyors. Survey of dangerous structures.*

LOCAL OFFICERS.

Justices may by order addressed to these officers, where infectious disease attributable to milk exists, empower them to inspect dairies, *i.e.* places from which milk is supplied or in which it is kept for sale (*u*), or, upon proper cause shewn, order the detention of a person in hospital (*v*), and in this case hospital officers or inspectors of police are to do necessary acts for enforcing the execution thereof. *Local officers. Inspection. Detention.*

The like powers are conferred on justices in the Metropolis, together with that of authorizing an officer to enter underground dwellings for inspection (*w*).

(*m*) 36 & 37 Vict. c. 71, s. 37. Extended to any freshwater fish by 47 & 48 Vict. c. 11, s. 3. No Form has yet been settled under this enactment.

(*n*) 53 & 54 Vict. c. 5, ss. 13, 15, 21, and see 54 & 55 Vict. c. 65, s. 25. For the Forms, see App. II. 47, 48, 49. As to temporary detention in a workhouse, see 53 & 54 Vict. c. 5, ss. 21, 24.

(*o*) Sect. 68.
(*p*) Sect. 81.

(*q*) *Purcell* v. *Sowler*, 2 C. P. D. 219.
(*r*) Sects. 63–67.
(*s*) Sect. 79. For the Forms, see App. II. 47–49.
(*t*) 18 & 19 Vict. c. 122, s. 69.
(*u*) 53 & 54 Vict. c. 34, s. 4.
(*v*) Sect. 12. There are no special Forms under this Act.
(*w*) 54 & 55 Vict. c. 76, ss. 67, 71, 97. For general Form of warrant, see App. II. No. 53.

C.—OTHER ORDERS.

C. Other orders.
Principal and agent.

The orders which remain to be considered are (*a*) those which constitute the officer executing them the agent simply of the person or authority making them. In some cases this agency is express, in others it is to be implied from the circumstances, but the principle applicable to both is the same.

No question arises here as to whether the king is, or is not, a party. The powers conferred are of a lower order than those of warrants and orders which have been above discussed, and are, generally speaking, those of local and departmental authorities, made for local purposes and applied locally.

LOCAL ACTS.

Local Acts.

Local Acts confer upon local authorities, sometimes called commissioners, powers to do certain things, and officers are directed to be appointed in pursuance of the Acts for the purpose of carrying the provisions of the statutes into execution.

Such officers are, while acting within the scope of the powers delegated to them, the agents of the body entrusted with the execution of the Act (*b*).

A power, in such an Act to seize wares, merchandize, &c., placed on footways or carriageways, and not removed when required by the authority, may be exercised without any previous proceedings before justices (*c*).

BYE-LAWS.

Bye-laws.
What.
Revenue.
Post.
Traffic (metropolis) and (towns).
Gaols.
Burial grounds.
Local.
Power to make.

Under the denomination of bye-laws are to be included the regulations which are made for the management of the revenue, or of the Post Office, to regulate traffic in the Metropolis, and in towns, by the Home Secretary in regard to the management of goals, and the execution of the Acts relating to burial-grounds, and those of local authorities, made either for general purposes or under the Acts for the regulation of piers, harbours, and docks.

The power to make such regulations is to be found in the

(*a*) Summonses issued by Courts or justices are not within the purview of the work. They are purely "administrative," as distinguished from "executive."

(*b*) See *post*, p. 148. As to the imposition of a penalty under such an Act, see *Triggs* v. *Lester*, 30 J. P. 228.

(*c*) *Brackley* v. *Battersea*, 23 Q. B. D. 486; 58 L. J. Q. B. 589.

statutes which confer the general powers on the different authorities, and if in making the bye-law, the power conferred, or the general law of the land is exceeded, it is void (*d*).

A bye-law is a law made by some authority less than the sovereign or Parliament, in respect of a matter specially or impliedly referred to that authority, and not provided for by the general law of the land (*e*). {Definition.}

The necessary ingredients of its validity are:—
1. Consistent with and not repugnant to the general law
2. Certain, *i.e.* not ambiguous, and affording complete direction to those who are to obey it, and have definite penalties for its breach, which must not be excessive (*f*). There may be power to mitigate the penalty (*g*).
3. General in its application, *i.e.* obligatory on all persons equally.
4. Reasonable (*h*). In determining whether or no a bye-law is reasonable, it is material to consider the relation of its framers to the locality affected by it and the authority by whom it is sanctioned (*i*).

{Necessary ingredients.
1. Consistent with law.
2. Certain.
3. General
4. Reasonable.}

Where a council made a bye-law under the Municipal Corporations Act, 1882, s. 23, that no person not being a member of Her Majesty's army or auxiliary forces, acting under the orders of his commanding officer, should sound or play upon any musical instrument in any of the streets of the borough on Sunday, it was held unreasonable (*j*). And so also, was one where a penalty was imposed on every person who in any street shall sound or play upon any musical or noisy instrument, or shall sing, recite, or preach in any street without having previously obtained a licence in writing from the mayor (*k*). And so was one made under the Public Health Act, that "no person shall commence the erection of a building in a new street unless and until the kerb of each footpath therein shall have been put on such a level as may be fixed and approved by the urban sanitary authority" (*l*). And one prohibiting the keeping of swine within fifty feet of a dwelling-house (*m*), or requiring a new fee for the commencement of each new period of granting licences (*n*), or notice as to the erection of temporary

---

(*d*) As to time of coming into operation, see 52 & 53 Vict. c. 63, s. 36. Bye-laws must be construed strictly. See *Rolles* v. *Newell*, 25 Q. B. D. 335; 59 L. J. Q. B. 423; 63 L. T. 384; 39 W. R. 96.
(*e*) See Lumley, p. 2.
(*f*) *Clarke* v. *Tucker*, 2 Ventr. 183.
(*g*) *Piper* v. *Chappell*, 14 M. & W. 624.
(*h*) See *Marshall* v. *Smith*, L. R. 8 C. P. 416.
(*i*) Per Lord Hobhouse, *Slattery* v. *Naylor*, 13 App. Cas. 452.

(*j*) *Johnson* v. *Croydon*, 16 Q. B. D. 708.
(*k*) *Munro* v. *Watson*, 57 L. T. 366; 51 J. P. 660.
(*l*) *Rudland* v. *Sunderland*, 33 W. R. 164. See *R.* v. *Newcastle-on-Tyne*, 60 L. T. 963; 53 J. P. 788; and *Burton* v. *Acton*, 51 J. P. 566.
(*m*) *Heap* v. *Burnley Union*, 12 Q. B. D. 617; 53 L. J. M. C. 76; 32 W. R. 661; 48 J. P. 359.
(*n*) *R.* v. *Commissioners of Sewers*, 22 L. T. 552.

structures (*o*), or prohibiting building on an open space in the rear of new buildings (*p*).

5. Not ultrâ vires.

5. Not *ultrâ vires*, *i e*. within the scope of the authority delegated in the particular case (*q*).

The Secretary of State is liable in trespass if a person be removed from one part of a prison to another in which he is not legally confined, under a general order made by him for the classification of prisoners which he had no legal authority to make (*r*).

A bye-law respecting non-compliance with the requirements of a board is probably *ultrâ vires* (*s*). And so also is one giving power to such board to pull down buildings erected contrary to the bye-laws (*t*).

Where undertakers, under 10 & 11 Vict. c. 27, s. 33, provided that no lumpers should be allowed to work on board any vessel in the dock but such as were authorized by the company, unless permission in writing had been previously obtained from the superintendent of the dock, and that servants of the company only should be allowed to work within the dock premises, whether on ship, lighter, or shore, they were held *ultrâ vires* (*u*). And the same was held where it was laid down that no person should purchase, barter for, or deal in marine stores or other second-hand goods in or about the dock or premises without first obtaining permission in writing from the company (*v*). And also as to one made by a municipal corporation that parents should be liable to a penalty if they suffered a child to be selling articles in the street after a certain hour (*w*). And one made by a local board that a person should not cause or suffer any fowl to enter and remain in pleasure-grounds (*x*).

Where power was conferred on conservators to make bye-laws to regulate the use of nets, and a bye-law was made thereunder prohibiting during a certain season the use of any net except a trawl, it was held *ultrâ vires* (*y*).

Good or bad in part.

A bye-law may be good in part and bad in part, if the two parts be distinct (*z*). There is no dispensing power in the

Dispensing power.

(*o*) *Fielding* v. *Rhyl Commissioners*, 3 C. P. D. 272.
(*p*) *Quimby* v. *Liverpool*, 53 J. P. 213.
(*q*) As to a rule made by a delegated authority of the local authority, see *Huth* v. *Clarke*, 25 Q. B. D. 391; 59 L. J. M. C. 120; 63 L. T. 348; 38 W. R. 655; 6 T. L. R. 373.
(*r*) *Cobbett* v. *Grey*, 4 Ex. 729; 19 L. J. Ex. 137.
(*s*) *Young* v. *Edwards*, 33 L. J. M. C. 227. But see *Hall* v. *Nixon*, L. R. 10 Q. B. 152.
(*t*) *Brown* v. *Holyhead*, 32 L. J. Ex. 25.

(*u*) *Dick* v. *Badart*, 10 Q. B. D. 387; 48 L. T. 391; 47 J. P. 422; 5 Asp. M. C. 49.
(*v*) *Chamberlain* v. *Conway*, 5 Ti. Rep. 44.
(*w*) *Macdonald* v. *Lochrane*, 51 J. P. 629.
(*x*) *Torquay* v. *Bridle*, 47 J. P. 183; and see *Everett* v. *Grapes*, 3 L. T. N. S. 669.
(*y*) *Pidler* v. *Berry*, 59 L. T. 230; 53 J. P. 6; 4 Ti. Rep. 627; and see *Wood* v. *Venton*, 54 J. P. 662.
(*z*) *The Fishermen of Faversham*, 8 T. R. 357.

makers thereof (a). But now, where an Act confers a power to make any rules, regulations, or bye-laws, the power shall, unless the contrary intention appears, be construed as including a power exercisable in a like manner, and subject to like consent and conditions, if any, to rescind, revoke, amend or vary such rules, regulations and bye-laws (b).

Confirmation by a superior authority does not render a bad bye-law valid. Where the Lord Chancellor was reported to have confirmed a bye-law it was said, "it is never the better for that, for that is done of course. If the orders be not good, let the parties look to that at their peril" (c).

Confirmation.

ADULTERATION.

Any medical officer of health, inspector of nuisances or inspector of weights and measures, or any inspector of a market, or any police constable . . . may procure any sample of food or drugs (d).

The officer purchasing shall, after the purchase, forthwith (e) notify to the seller or his agent his intention to have the same analysed by the public analyst (f), and shall offer to divide the article into three parts to be then and there separated, and each part to be marked and sealed or fastened up in such manner as its nature will permit, and shall, if required to do so, proceed accordingly, and shall deliver one of the parts to the seller or his agent (g).

To constitute an offence against sect. 6 of the Act, which prohibits the sale not of the nature, substance, and quality demanded, a false representation of the "nature, substance, and quality" must be made at the time of the sale (h).

But under sect. 9, which prevents the sale of a deteriorated article without notice, knowledge that it is deteriorated is immaterial (i). Under this section there may be, in the case of milk delivery in cans, an offence as to each can (j).

These officers may, without going through the form of purchase provided by the principal Act, but otherwise acting in all respects in accordance with the provisions of the said Act as to

Adulteration. Samples. Notification of analysis. Division of samples. Offence, what. Margarine.

(a) *Wortley* v. *Notts,* 21 L. T. N. S. 582.
(b) 52 & 53 Vict. c. 63, s. 32.
(c) *Stationers' Co.* v. *Salisbury,* Comb. 222; *R.* v. *Wood,* 5 E. & B. 49.
(d) 38 & 39 Vict. c. 63, s. 13. See *Hale* v. *Cole,* 55 J. P. 376. The purchase may take place in a shop or in streets, and public places of resort: 42 & 43 Vict. c. 30, s. 3.
(e) Two minutes later is forthwith: *Somerset* v. *Miller,* 54 J. P. 614.
(f) See *Wheeler* v. *Webb,* 51 J. P. 661; *Barnes* v. *Chipp,* 47 L. J. M. C. 85; 3 Ex. D. 176; 38 L. T. 570; 26 W. R. 635.
(g) 38 & 39 Vict. c. 63, s. 14.
(h) *Kirk* v. *Coates,* 16 Q. B. D. 49; 55 L. J. M. C. 182; 54 L. T. 178; 50 J. P. 148; 34 W. R. 295; *Sandys* v. *Sindell,* 3 Q. B. D. 449; 47 L. J. M. C. 115; 39 L. T. 118; 26 W. R. 814; 42 J. P. 550; *Hoyle* v. *Hitchman,* 4 Q. B. D. 233; and see *Morris* v. *Johnson,* 54 J. P. 612.
(i) *Pain* v. *Boughtwood,* 24 Q. B. D. 353; 59 L. J. M. C. 45; 62 L. T. 284; 38 W. R. 428; 54 J. P. 469; 16 Cox C. C. 747; 6 Ti. Rep. 167.
(j) *Fecit* v. *Walsh,* 55 J. P. 277; 39 W. R. 525; [1891] 2 Q. B. 304.

dealing with samples, take for the purpose of analysis samples of any butter or substances purporting to be butter which are exposed for sale (*k*), and not marked "margarine" (*l*).

In the case of importation or manufacture in the United Kingdom they may procure samples for analysis if they shall have reason to believe that the provisions of the Act are infringed by its conveyance not consigned as margarine, and examine and take samples from any package (*m*).

Milk.

They may also procure at the place of delivery any sample of any milk in the course of delivery to the purchaser or consignee in pursuance of any contract (*n*).

No notification.

No notification to the seller as above-mentioned is necessary in the case of milk samples (*o*).

Canal-Boats.

Canal boats. Inspection.

Where any person duly authorized by a registration or sanitary authority (or by a justice of the peace) has reasonable cause to suppose either that there is any contravention of this Act (*p*) on board a canal-boat or any person suffering from an infectious disorder, he may, on producing (if demanded) either a copy of his authorization or some other sufficient evidence, enter by day such canal-boat and examine the same and every part thereof . . . and may if need be detain the boat for the purpose, but for no longer time than is necessary.

Master to render assistance.

The master shall, if required by such person, produce to him the certificate of registry (if any) of the boat, and permit him to examine and copy the same, and shall furnish him with such assistance and means as such person may require for the purpose of his entry and examination of and departure from the boat in pursuance of this section (*q*).

Contagious Diseases.

Contagious diseases. Entry.

Contagious diseases inspectors employed by the local authority have the same powers as constables have under the Act (*r*).

They may at any time on giving reasons in writing, if required, enter any land, dairy or cowshed to which the Act applies, or milk-shop, or stores, or other building or place where they have reasonable grounds to suppose : (a.) disease exists or has within fifty-six days existed ; (b.) the carcase of a diseased or suspected animal is or has been kept, buried, destroyed, or

(*k*) These words must be construed strictly: *Crane* v. *Lawrence*, 25 Q. B. D. 152; 59 L. J. M. C. 110; 63 L. T. 197; 38 W. R. 620; 54 J. P. 471; 6 Ti. L. R. 370.
(*l*) 50 & 51 Vict. c. 29, s. 10.
(*m*) Sect. 8.
(*n*) 42 & 43 Vict. c. 30, s. 3.
(*o*) *Rouch* v. *Hall*, 6 Q. B. D. 17;
50 L. J. M. C. 6; 44 L. T. 183; 29 W. R. 304; 45 J. P. 220.
(*p*) Registration required by s. 1; education of children by s. 6.
(*q*) 40 & 41 Vict. c. 60, s. 5; and see 47 & 48 Vict. c. 75, s. 4.
(*r*) 41 & 42 Vict. c. 74, s. 42; and see *post*, p. 92.

otherwise disposed of; or (c.) there is anything in respect whereof there has been a failure to comply with the provisions of the Act, an order, or a regulation of the local authority (*s*).

As to slaughter-houses, see 7 & 8 Vict. c. 87, s. 4, cited, *post* (*t*).

EXPLOSIVES.

Any officer authorized by the local authority may, on producing, if demanded, either a copy of his authority ... or some other sufficient evidence, require the occupier of any store (not subject to the inspector of mines), or any registered premises, or any small firework factory, to shew him every or any place and all or any of the receptacles in which any explosive or ingredient of an explosive or regulated by this Act (*u*), that is in his possession is kept, and to give him samples of such explosive ingredient or substance, or of any substance which the officer believes to be an explosive, or such ingredient or substance (*v*). *Explosives. Inspection of stores.*

Samples.

He may also purchase any petroleum from any dealer in it, and on producing a copy of his appointment, or other sufficient authority, require such dealer to shew him every or any place, and all or any of the vessels in which any petroleum in his possession is kept, and give him samples of such petroleum on payment of the value thereof (*w*). *Petroleum.*

As to the power of officers of the local authority to arrest for offences, see *post* (*x*). *Arrest.*

HIGHWAYS.

The surveyors in urban districts are the officers of the local authority (*y*). The powers generally will be found stated, *post* (*z*). *Highways.*

These officers may inspect platforms erected on public occasions under the Public Health Amendment Act, where that Act is adopted (*a*), and may enter premises for the purpose of surveying and valuing which the local authority are entitled to take under the Housing of the Working Classes Act, at all reasonable times by day on giving twenty-four hours notice (*b*). *Entry. Inspection.*

PUBLIC HEALTH.

The powers conferred by this Act, and those incorporated therewith, upon local authorities, which are here enumerated, *Public health.*

(*s*) Sect. 51.
(*t*) Page 106.
(*u*) See *post*, p. 92.
(*v*) 38 & 39 Vict. c. 17, s. 69.
(*w*) 34 & 35 Vict. c. 105, s. 11; and see *Coleman* v. *Goldsmith*, 43 J. P. 718.
(*x*) Page 92.
(*y*) 38 & 39 Vict. c. 55, s. 144.
(*z*) Page 133.

(*a*) 53 & 54 Vict. c. 59, s. 37.
(*b*) 53 & 54 Vict. c. 70, s. 77. The liability of the local authority is no greater than that of the surveyor in rural districts: *Gibson* v. *Preston*, L. R. 5 Q. B. 218; 39 L. J. Q. B. 131; 22 L. T. 293; 34 J. P. 342; *Parsons* v. *Bethnal Green*, L. R. 3 C. P. 56; 37 L. J. C. P. 62; 17 L. T. 211.

are those where they are authorized to interfere to some extent with the property of an individual. As to the general principle of law applicable in such cases, see *ante* (*c*).

The local authority may order the following things to be done, namely :—

Drains, &c.   The carrying of sewers and water-mains through private lands, if, on the report of the surveyor, it is by him deemed necessary (*d*). "Necessary" means for the efficient discharge of the duty in the way most for the public benefit. The Court will not interfere with the *bonâ fide* determination of the surveyor (*e*).

They need not purchase the lands (*f*), but in case of a sewer it must not amount to a nuisance (*g*).

They may perhaps place ventilating shafts to drains against private buildings (*h*), enforce the drainage of undrained houses (*i*). enforce privy accommodation (*j*), and examine the same on complaint (*k*).

Drains cannot be disconnected by the local authority unless the connection has been made contrary to the Act (*l*).

Streets.   They may sewer, level, pave, metal, flag, channel, make good, and light, after notice not attended to, and charge expense on the owner or occupier, fronting, adjoining or abutting streets, not being highways, repairable by the inhabitants (*m*). But an incumbent or minister of a church, &c., exempt from poor-rates is not so liable (*n*).

This exemption does not apply to trustees of a chapel and buildings not wholly devoted to religious purposes (*o*).

Houses and workshops.   They may purify houses after certificate of the medical officer that they are unwholesome and refusal to purify on the part of the occupier (*p*).

Filth.   And remove filth on the certificate of the inspector (*q*).

Infected persons.   And remove infected persons (*r*) and destroy the bedding (*s*).

Gas and water.   And remove gas and water-pipes where the owner refuses to

(*c*) Page 62.
(*d*) 38 & 39 Vict. c. 55, ss. 16, 54.
(*e*) *Lewis* v. *Weston*, 40 Ch. D. 55.
(*f*) *Roderick* v. *Aston*, 5 Ch. D. 328; 46 L. J. Ch. 804; 36 L. T. 328; 41 J. P. 516.
(*g*) *Lamacraft* v. *St. Thomas*, 42 L. T. 365; 44 J. P. 441.
(*h*) See *Hopkins* v. *Smethwick Local Board*, 24 Q. B. D. 712; 6 T. Rep. 174; and 38 & 39 Vict. c. 55, s. 19.
(*i*) Sect. 23.
(*j*) Sect. 36.
(*k*) Sect. 41.
(*l*) *Ainsley* v. *Kirkheaton*, 7 T. L. R. 323; 55 J. P. 230.
(*m*) 38 & 39 Vict. c. 55. ss. 4, 150, 257, 258: *Walthamstow* v. *Staines*,

W. N. 1891, 82. See *R.* v. *Goole*, 39 W. R. 608.
(*n*) Sect. 151.
(*o*) *Brewis* v. *Hornsey*, 64 L. T. 288; 55 J. P. 389. See *Re Bettesworth*, 37 Ch. D. 535; 58 L. T. 796; *Bowditch* v. *Wakefield*, L. R. 6 Q. B. 567; 25 L. T. 88; *Tottenham* v. *Rowell*, 15 Ch. D. 378; 43 L. T. 616.
(*p*) 38 & 39 Vict. c. 55, ss. 46, 94, 120; and 53 & 54 Vict. c. 34, ss. 5 and 6. Entry under the latter Act must be between 10 A.M. and 6 P.M., see s. 17; as to workshops, see 54 & 55 Vict. c. 75, s. 4.
(*q*) 38 & 39 Vict. c. 55, ss. 49, 62.
(*r*) Sect. 124.
(*s*) Sect. 121.

WARRANTS AND ORDERS. 69

comply with notice (*t*), and compel persons to have a proper water supply (*u*).

This latter power is not repealed by the Public Health Water Act (*v*).

They may slaughter diseased cattle (*w*), and prohibit their landing (*x*). Cattle.

Under the order of justices—

They may remove dangerous buildings (*y*) or those erected contrary to bye-laws (*z*). The last-mentioned power cannot be exercised without giving the owner an opportunity of shewing cause against it (*a*). Buildings.

And enter to abate nuisances (*b*) after disobedience of order of abatement (*c*). Nuisances.

They may also close wells (*d*), cellars (*e*), and close or demolish houses unfit for habitation (*f*), and destroy unsound meat (*g*). Wells. Houses. Meat.

Where a person is not in default and his property is damaged or destroyed he may obtain compensation (*h*). Compensation.

Factories may be examined in order to ascertain whether there is proper precaution against fire (*i*). Factories.

The officers of the board are to be allowed to inspect premises where infectious disease has occurred, between 10 A.M. and 6 P.M., on producing their authority (*j*), if the authority has adopted the amending Act (*k*), and common lodging-houses at all times (*l*). Inspection.

As to nuisances they must be admitted into any premises for the purpose of examining as to any nuisance thereon or of enforcing the provisions of any Act (*m*), requiring fireplaces and furnaces to consume their own smoke, at any time between 9 A.M. and 6 P.M., or in case of nuisance arising from business, at Nuisances.

(*t*) Sect. 153.
(*u*) Sect. 62.
(*v*) *Colne Valley* v. *Treharne*, 50 L. T. 617; 48 J. P. 279.
(*w*) 41 & 42 Vict. c. 74, s. 21.
(*x*) Sects. 15, 30, and 35.
(*y*) 38 & 39 Vict. c. 55, s. 26.
(*z*) Sects. 155 and 158, and 10 & 11 Vict. c. 34, s. 78.
(*a*) *Hopkins* v. *Smethwick, ubi sup.* See *Baker* v. *Portsmouth*, 47 L. J. Ex. 223; 3 Ex. D. 10; 37 L. T. 822; 42 J. P. 278; 26 W. R. 303; *Thompson* v. *Failsworth*, 46 J. P. 21; *Slee* v. *Bradford*, 9 Jur. 815; 8 L. T. 491; *Jagger* v. *Doncaster*, 54 J. P. 438
(*b*) 38 & 39 Vict. c. 55, ss. 49, 102.
(*c*) *Tinkler* v. *Wandsworth*, 27 L. J. Ch. 342; 4 Jur. 293; 2 De G.

& J. 261; 22 J. P. 224. The definition of nuisance is practically identical with that in the Metropolis Act. See *post*, pp. 70, 72.
(*d*) 38 & 39 Vict. c. 55, s. 70.
(*e*) Sect. 75.
(*f*) Sects. 97, 109, 110; 48 & 49 Vict. c. 35, s. 2; 53 & 54 Vict. c. 70, s. 34.
(*g*) 38 & 39 Vict. c. 55, s. 117.
(*h*) Sects. 155, 308.
(*i*) 54 & 55 Vict. c. 75, s. 7.
(*j*) 53 & 54 Vict. c. 34, s. 6.
(*k*) Sects. 3 and 21.
(*l*) 38 & 39 Vict. c. 55, s. 85. See *Langdon* v. *Broadbent*, 37 L. T. 434; 42 J. P. 56; and *Booth* v. *Ferrett*, *post*, p. 74.
(*m*) 10 & 11 Vict. c. 34, s. 108.

any time when business carried on (*n*). Also where a nuisance exists or an order of abatement or prohibition has been made, between the hours aforesaid until the nuisance is abated or the works completed, and such order of abatement or prohibition not having been complied with, they must be admitted in order to abate the same (*o*).

A nuisance is any premises in such a state as to be a nuisance, pools, ditches, &c., so kept, or animals, or accumulations or deposits, or houses overcrowded, factories, workshops, &c., not cleanly kept, or ventilated or overcrowded, or fireplaces and furnaces not consuming their own smoke, or chimneys sending forth quantities of black smoke (*p*).

Dairies. Epidemics. These powers are extended to dairies, cow-sheds and milk-shops (*q*), and apply also to the execution of regulations issued by the Local Government Board on the breaking out of epidemic diseases (*r*).

Public health amendment. Working classes, housing. Food. Under the Public Health Amendment Act, if adopted (*s*), they may enter premises to see whether chemical refuse or steam be turned into sewers (*t*), or to sweep courts and passages, in which case the expense may be charged on the occupier (*u*). They may also, on the representation of four householders, inspect buildings unfit for habitation (*v*).

Any medical officer of health or inspector of nuisances may at all reasonable times (*w*) inspect and examine any animal (*x*), carcase, meat, poultry, game, flesh, fruit, fish, vegetables, corn, bread, flour, or milk exposed for sale or deposited in any place (*y*) for the purpose of sale or of preparation for sale (*z*), and intended for the food of man; . . . and if any such animal, &c., appears to be diseased, unsound, unwholesome, or unfit for food, he may seize (*a*) and carry away the same in order to have the same dealt with by a justice (*b*).

(*n*) 38 & 39 Vict. c. 55, s. 102. Under s. 91 it was held an accumulation may be a nuisance though not injurious to health: *Bishop Auckland v. Iron Co.*, 10 Q. B. D. 138; 54 L. J. M. C. 38; 48 L. T. 223; 31 W. R. 288; 47 J. P. 389.
(*o*) *Ibid.* s. 102.
(*p*) 38 & 39 Vict. c. 55, s. 91.
(*q*) 49 & 50 Vict. c. 32, s. 9.
(*r*) 38 & 39 Vict. c. 55, s. 137.
(*s*) 53 & 54 Vict. c. 59, s. 3.
(*t*) Sect. 17.
(*u*) Sect. 27.
(*v*) 53 & 54 Vict. c. 70, s. 31.
(*w*) This was held not to extend to Sunday afternoon, where a man lived half a mile from his shop: *Small v. Bickley*, 32 L. T. 726.
(*x*) Includes live animals: *Moody v. Leach*, 44 J. P. 459.
(*y*) This applies to a yard belonging to a shop: *Young v. Gutteridge*, L. R. 4 Q. B. 166; and to meat passing from a slaughter-house to a factory of preserved meats: *Daly v. Webb*, 4 C. L. Ir. 309; 18 W. R. 631; and see *Mallinson v. Carr*, [1891] 1 Q. B. 48; 39 W. R. 270; 55 J. P. 102.
(*z*) But not after sale: *Vinter v. Hind*, 10 Q. B. D. 63; 52 L. J. M. C. 93; 48 L. T. 359; 31 W. R. 198; 47 J. P. 373.
(*a*) No notice is necessary: *White v. Redfern*, 5 Q. B. D. 15; 49 L. J. M. C. 19; 41 L. T. 524; 28 W. R. 168; 44 J. P. 87.
(*b*) 38 & 39 Vict. c. 55, s. 116. This section is by the Public Health Amendment Act, where adopted, extended to all articles of food: 53 & 54 Vict. c. 59, s. 28.

This power is extended to horse-flesh intended for sale for Horseflesh.
food, and exposed for sale in any place not advertised for the
sale thereof (c).

The medical officer has all the powers of entry and inspection Bake-
of bakehouses as an inspector under the Factory Act (d). houses.

The local officer may remove persons offending against any Baths and
bye-laws made under the Baths and Wash-houses Acts (e), and wash-
refuse admittance to any person who may have been convicted houses.
of an offence against the bye-laws or public decency (f).

The inspector of provisions may seize unwholesome meat or Markets
provisions in the market or fair, and carry the same before a and fairs.
justice (g), and may arrest an unknown offender (h). He may
enter any building erected for slaughtering cattle, and seize and
carry away such as appears unfit for food (i).

On refusal to pay toll (j) he may distrain all or any of the
cattle or other articles in respect of which it is payable belonging to the person liable to pay (k).

He may also at all reasonable times weigh or measure all
goods sold, offered, or exposed for sale (l).

Under the Public Health Amendment Act, when adopted, Parks.
the local authority may close parks and pleasure-grounds for
twelve days in the year, not more than four being consecu-
tive (m).

The inspector of nuisances, officer of health, or any other Slaughter-
officer appointed for that purpose, may at all reasonable times, houses.
with or without assistants, enter into and inspect buildings or
places kept or used for the sale of butcher's meat or for slaughtering cattle, and examine whether any cattle, or the carcase of any
such cattle, is deposited there, and, if it appear unfit for food,
seize and carry the same before a justice (n).

If a person offer for sale any cattle, &c., at such slaughter-
house, and be unable or refuse to give an account of how he
came by it, the officer may seize the cattle and give the person
into custody (o).

Where any person duly authorized by a sanitary authority Tents and
(or by a justice) has reasonable cause to suppose either that vans.
there is any contravention of this Act, or of any bye-law made
thereunder, in any tent, van, shed, or similar structure, or
any person suffering therein from a dangerous infectious disorder, he may, on producing (if demanded) his authority or

(c) 52 & 53 Vict. c. 11, s. 3.
(d) 46 & 47 Vict. c. 53, s. 17, and see *post*, p. 123.
(e) 9 & 10 Vict. c. 74; 10 & 11 Vict. c. 61; 41 & 42 Vict. c. 14, s. 10; 38 & 39 Vict. c. 55.
(f) 41 & 42 Vict. c. 14, s. 11. As to museums and gymnasiums, see 54 & 55 Vict. c. 22, ss. 7 and 8.
(g) 10 & 11 Vict. c. 14, s. 15.

(h) Sect. 154.
(i) Sect. 20.
(j) These must be set up conspicu-ously: s. 41.
(k) Sect. 38.
(l) 41 & 42 Vict. c. 49, s. 86.
(m) 53 & 54 Vict. c. 59, s. 44.
(n) 10 & 11 Vict. c. 34, s. 131.
(o) 26 Geo. 3, c. 71, s. 7.

72   EXECUTIVE OFFICERS.

other sufficient evidence, enter by day (*p*) such tent, &c., and examine the same and every part thereof (*q*).

Workshops. The sanitary authority and their officers shall have all such powers, as to entry and inspection for the purposes of purification of workshops, as an inspector of factories has generally as regards factories (*r*).

Metropolis.

Nuisances. The definition of nuisance in the Metropolitan Act is practically identical with that in the Public Health Act, with the additions of (1) absence from premises of water fittings, and (2) tents and vans kept so as to be a nuisance (*s*).

Manure, &c. The sanitary authority may sell manure, &c., collected by them either by public auction or otherwise (*t*).

Their right of entry is to be subject in all cases to the production of a written document shewing such right (*u*).

Entry. They may enter from time to time any premises (a.) to examine any nuisance liable to be dealt with under the Act at any hour by day; or where nuisance arises from a business, when the business is carried on (b.) where a nuisance is ascertained to exist, or order made, then at any such hour as aforesaid until abated or the works completed; (c.) where order not complied with or infringed, then at all reasonable hours, including all hours in which business is in progress or usually carried on (*v*).

They may enter slaughter-houses or knackers' yards at any hour by day, or when business is in progress, to examine whether there is any contravention of the Act or bye-laws made thereunder (*w*); and trade-works or steam-vessels, to enforce the Act as to smoke consumption (*x*); and after notice not complied with, they may lime-wash, cleanse, or purify workshops and bakehouses (*y*).

The County Council have the like power of entry for the execution of orders and regulations as to dairies (*z*).

The sanitary authority must remove refuse free, and trade refuse on reasonable remuneration (*a*); and obnoxious matter may be removed by them on the requisition of the inspector, and taken possession of after notice not complied with (*b*).

They may also enter and execute works as to water-closets (*c*)

(*p*) Between 6 a.m., and 9 p.m.
(*q*) 48 & 49 Vict. c. 72, s. 9. This does not apply to tents of Her Majesty.
(*r*) 54 & 55 Vict. c. 75, s. 3, and see *post*, p. 123.
(*s*) 54 & 55 Vict. c. 76, ss. 2, 23 and 95.
(*t*) Sect. 9.

(*u*) Sect. 115.
(*v*) Sect. 10.
(*w*) Sect. 20.
(*x*) Sect. 23.
(*y*) Sects. 25, 26.
(*z*) Sect. 28.
(*a*) Sect. 29.
(*b*) Sect. 35.
(*c*) Sect. 37.

after such notice. But this power must only be exercised with reference to each particular case (*d*).

And examine water-closets; and for that purpose, or to ascertain the course of a drain, they may at all reasonable times by day, after twenty-four hours' notice on the occupier or owner, or in emergency without notice, enter and cause the ground to be opened, doing as little damage as possible. If in good order, the authority to pay the expenses, otherwise not (*e*). And where water-closets are improperly made or altered, after notice not complied with, enter and make necessary alterations (*f*).

They may cleanse and cover offensive ditches, damage to mills, &c., being made good (*g*). *Ditches.*

In case of certain infectious diseases, viz. small-pox, cholera, diphtheria, membranous croup, erysipelas, scarlatina, scarlet fever, typhus, typhoid, enteric, relapsing, continual or puerperal fever (*h*), they may order the destruction of unfit bedding or disinfect bedding, paying compensation for damage; and after notice not complied with, cleanse and disinfect infected premises, entering by day, temporary shelter to be provided for families (*i*). *Infectious disease.*

And in case of epidemics, they may enter any premises or vessel for the purpose of executing or superintending the execution of regulations (*j*).

Under order of a justice—

Of abatement, prohibition or closing not complied with, they may enter the premises and do what is necessary in execution thereof (*k*). In case of appeal, if immediate abatement required, if appeal be successful, the damage is to be made good (*l*). *Justice's order.*

They may close wells (*m*), and remove persons suffering from any dangerous infectious disorder to a hospital, where they are without proper lodging or accommodation, or lodged in a tent or van, or on board a vessel (*n*).

And cleanse underground dwellings (*o*).

And remove dead bodies to mortuaries (*p*).

The local authority may take down buildings beyond the general line (*q*).

Where this section was found inconsistent with a special Act, it was held the justice had no jurisdiction to make the order (*r*). And in any case a verbal order is insufficient (*s*).

(*d*) *Tinkler* v. *Wandsworth*, 27 L. J. Ch. 342; 30 L. T. 146; 22 J. P. 223. See *St. Luke* v. *Lewis*, 31 L. J. M. C. 73; 1 B. & S. 865; 5 L. T. 608, and *Sherborne* v. *Boyle*, 46 J. P. 675.
(*e*) Sect. 40.
(*f*) Sect. 41.
(*g*) Sect. 43.
(*h*) This list may be extended by order of the sanitary authority: Sect. 55.
(*i*) Sects. 59, 60, 61.
(*j*) Sect. 82.
(*k*) Sects. 5, 8.
(*l*) Sect. 6.
(*m*) Sect. 54.
(*n*) Sects. 66, 67.
(*o*) Sect. 96.
(*p*) Sect. 89.
(*q*) 25 & 26 Vict. c. 102, s. 75.
(*r*) *City Ry.* v. *County Council*, W. N. 1891, 94.
(*s*) *Barlow* v. *Kensington*, 11 App. Cas. 257; 55 L. J. Ch. 680; 55 L. T. 221; 34 W. R. 521; 50 J. P. 691.

EXECUTIVE OFFICERS.

Officers, food. As to officers of the authority, the power to inspect food is practically identical with that under the Public Health Act (*t*).

Tents and vans. And the power as to tents and vans is the same as in the previous Act (*u*).

Underground rooms. They may enter underground rooms for inspection at any hour by day (*v*).

Drains. Any surveyor or inspector, or such other person as the vestry may appoint, may inspect any drain or other works within the parish or district of such vestry, and for that purpose at all reasonable times in the day time after twenty-four hours' notice to the occupier; or in case of emergency, without such notice, may enter upon any premises, and cause the ground to be opened in any place they think fit, doing as little damage as possible (*w*).

Common lodging-houses. Common lodging-houses are open to inspection at all times (*x*). But such a house, maintained as a charitable institution, is not within the Act (*y*).

Fires. In case of fire, the officer in charge of the fire brigade may remove persons who interfere with the operations, and take all measures expedient for the protection of life and property, with power to break into or through, or take possession of, or pull down, any premises to put an end to the fire, doing as little damage as possible, and to shut off mains in any district for a greater supply of water (*z*).

He need not take possession of premises (*a*).

The brigade must render assistance to the salvage corps, and hand over property saved to them (*b*).

WEIGHTS AND MEASURES.

Weights and measures. As to the power of the local authority to weigh coal, see 52 & 53 Vict. c. 21, s. 29 (*c*).

Coal.

(*t*) 54 & 55 Vict. c. 76, s. 47, see *ante*, p. 70, and *Barlow* v. *Terrett*, 1891, 2 Q. B. 107; 39 W. R. 640.
(*u*) Sect. 95, see *ante*, p. 71.
(*v*) Sect. 97.
(*w*) 18 & 19 Vict. c. 120, s. 82; 54 & 55 Vict. c. 76, s. 142.
(*x*) 14 & 15 Vict. c. 28, s. 12.
(*y*) *Booth* v. *Ferrett*, 25 Q. B. D. 87; 59 L. J. M. C. 136; 63 L. T.

346; 38 W. R. 718; 55 J. P. 7; 6 T. L. R. 337.
(*z*) 28 & 29 Vict. c. 90, s. 12. Damage done is deemed damage by fire within the meaning of any policy.
(*a*) *Joyce* v. *Metropolitan Board of Works*, 44 L. T. 811.
(*b*) Sect. 29.
(*c*) *Post*, p. 136.

PART II.
INHERENT POWERS.

As nearly all the inherent powers of officers are conferred by statute, it should be premised here that, where a power is conferred by statute, it must be pursued strictly, or it will afford no justification in the event of action arising on account of its exercise. This principle will be found laid down in the case of *Warne* v. *Varley* (a). There searchers of leather had been appointed under statute, who were authorized to seize leather insufficiently dried, in order to carry it before officers called triers. It was held that this authority did not extend to the seizure of any leather which was sufficiently dried, though *in their judgment* it was not so, and that such a seizure having taken place, they were liable to an action of trespass. *Inherent powers. To be pursued strictly.*

But, although this is the general principle, it must be read in conjunction with those protective clauses of statutes which have been passed for the relief of officers when acting or neglecting to act *bonâ fide*, in the belief that they were discharging their duty, and which will be found discussed *infra* (b). *Qualification.*

OFFICERS ATTENDING COURTS.

In the case of all officers attending Courts, it is obvious that, whether the Court be the High Court of Parliament or a petty sessions, the object of their attendance is to secure order and decorum during the sittings thereof. It is presumed, therefore, that it follows that they have in their own persons power to take such steps as may be reasonably necessary to secure the maintenance of such order and decorum without any specific instructions for that purpose; and that to this end they may remove any persons who make a disturbance, or prevent from entering those who are in an improper state (c). *Officers attending Courts. To preserve decorum.*

In cases involving charges of indecency, women have usually been denied admittance; but it seems they are entitled to be present if they think fit (d). *Cases of indecency.*

The disturbing of a meeting of justices would appear to constitute a breach of the peace (e).

(a) 6 T. R. 443, and see *Grindley* v. *Baker*, 1 B. & P. 229.
(b) Page 154.
(c) May, Parl. Prac. 9th ed. p. 89.

(d) Liverpool Assizes, May, 1891.
(e) See the opinion of the Attorney-General, Stone, 23rd ed. p. 645.

Sheriff.

Sheriff.
Jury.

When a jury has been empanelled, they are strictly in the custody of the sheriff until their verdict be given (*f*). In practice, however, this rule is relaxed, except on the trial of persons for serious crimes.

Where they are detained, a bailiff is sworn to keep them together, and not to suffer any to speak to them (*g*).

Constables.

Constables.
Duty.

The duty of constables is to preserve the peace, and where any serious offence against the law is committed, to seize and detain the offender.

Force, use of.

If resisted in the execution of duty, they may repel force by force, provided it is proportioned to the injury it is intended to prevent (*h*).

Aiding other officers.

Under a number of statutes these officers are required to lend their assistance to other officers, either to effectuate the execution of some warrant or some power which such other officer has in his own person. In such cases, it has been held, the constable is in the execution of his duty (*i*); but if he act purely ministerially, and is not guilty of any excess, he is not liable while so acting (*j*); and if protection be afforded to these other officers, he is usually entitled to share it (*k*).

Infants.
Lunatics.
Married women.

Three classes of persons, viz. infants, lunatics, and married women, are under certain circumstances excused from the consequences of criminal acts; but this is a matter for the judge or magistrate, and would not generally affect the duty of a constable to act in such cases (*l*).

Arrest.

Arrest.

The inherent power of a constable to arrest is confined to cases of treason, felony, or reasonable suspicion thereof, breach of the peace committed in his view, and those misdemeanours which are specially provided for by statute, and detailed below (*m*).

Time.

With regard to the time of arrest, it appears that on a criminal charge it may take place at any time of the day or night (*n*);

(*f*) Hale, P. C. II., p. 296.
(*g*) Ibid.
(*h*) 1 East, P. C. 297.
(*i*) *R.* v. *Clarke*, 4 N. & M. 671; 3 A. & E. 287; 1 H. & W. 252.
(*j*) Cf., *Flewster* v. *Royle*, and *Glynn* v. *Houston*, &c., *post*, p. 99.
(*k*) See *post*, p. 153.
(*l*) See on this, 1 Hale, 25-28, 44, 434, 516; *R.* v. *Hodges*, 8 C. & P. 195; *R.* v. *Cruse*, ib. 541.

(*m*) A person cannot be arrested on suspicion of having committed a misdemeanour: *Matthews* v.*Biddulph*, 4 Sc. N. R. 54; 11 L. J. M. C. 13; 1 D. P. C. 216; *Bowditch* v. *Balchin*, 19 L. J. Ex. 337; 5 Ex. 378; 15 L. T. 232; 14 J. P. 449.

(*n*) Greenwood, Magist. Guide, 3rd. ed., p. 129.

and in cases of treason, felony, and breach of the peace, on Sunday also (*o*).

As to breaking doors, it seems that that can take place only in two cases:— {Breaking doors.}

1. In an affray which occurs in his view, he may pursue the affrayers, and if they fly to a house into which he is not permitted to enter, he may in the immediate pursuit break the doors to apprehend them (*p*). Or if there be an affray in a house, and the doors be shut, whereby there is likely to be manslaughter or bloodshed committed (*q*), provided the life of some person in the house is really in danger, and there be calls for assistance (*r*). Or if there be any disorderly drinking or noise at an unseasonable time of the night, especially in inns, a constable demanding entrance and being refused, may break open the doors to see and suppress the disorder (*s*). {In (1.) affray.}

2. If a felony be committed, and there be reasonable ground of suspicion (*t*) that the felon was in the house (*u*), or if a felony will probably be committed unless he interfere, and there are no other means of entering (*v*), he may in immediate pursuit (*w*) break the door. {In (2.) felony.}

In all other cases a warrant is apparently necessary (*x*).

A constable cannot justify handcuffing a prisoner unless he has attempted to escape, or it be necessary in order to prevent his doing so (*y*). {Handcuffs.}

Where the circumstances are such that a man must know why a person is about to apprehend him, he need not be told, and the arrest will be legal, and resistance illegal, as if he had been told (*z*). {Stating cause of arrest.}

The jurisdiction of justices to hear and determine is limited to six months from the commission of the offence (*a*); and time runs as soon as the defendant's default or liability is complete (*b*). In indictable offences there is no such limitation. {Jurisdiction.}

A constable has no authority at common law to act out of his vill (*c*). But a police authority may now enter into an agreement with another authority to aid such other authority either generally or for any particular time. And under such an agree-

---

(*o*) 29 Car. 2, c. 7, s. 6.
(*p*) 2 Hawk. P. C. c. 14, s. 8.
(*q*) 2 Hale, P. C. 95; *Smith* v. *Shirley*, 3 C. B. 142.
(*r*) *Handcock* v. *Baker*, 2 B. & P. 260.
(*s*) 2 Hale, P. C. 95.
(*t*) See *post*, p. 82.
(*u*) 2 Hale, P. C. 95.
(*v*) Greenwood, p. 209.
(*w*) See *post*, p. 78, and *R.* v. *Marsden*, *post*, p. 78.
(*x*) 2 Hale, P. C. 95.
(*y*) *Wright* v. *Court*, 4 B. & C. 596; 6 D. & R. 625.
(*z*) *R.* v. *Howarth*, 1 Moo. C. C. 207.
(*a*) 11 & 12 Vict. c. 43, s. 11.
(*b*) *Labalmondiere* v. *Addison*, 1 El. & El. 41; 28 L. J. M. C. 25; 5 Jur. 431; 23 J. P. 261; *Reeves* v. *Yeates*, 1 H. & C. 435; 31 L. J. M. C. 241; 8 Jur. 751; 10 W. R. 779; 26 J. P. 808.
(*c*) 1 Hale, P. C. 459, and see *Gladwell* v. *Blake*, 1 C. M. & R. 636; 5 Tyr. 186.

ment the constables of the aiding force are deemed to have all powers and privileges of the aided force (*d*).

In felonies, and under the Coin, Gaming, Highway, Industrial Schools, Larceny, Night Offenders, and Vagrant Acts (*e*), any person may arrest, which words include, of course, a constable out of his jurisdiction. In such case he would not be acting in execution of his duty, and could not therefore claim the privileges accorded to a constable when so acting.

Authority to arrest is confined to the following cases:—

Affray.

Where there is an affray, *i.e.* the fighting of two or more persons in some public place to the terror of Her Majesty's subjects (*f*). No quarrelsome or threatening words, are sufficient (*g*); but there need be no actual violence; as where persons arm themselves with dangerous and unusual weapons (*h*). Here the constable may arrest and carry the affrayers before a justice, or detain them till their heat be over. But it is essential that the party should have been engaged in the affray, and that the constable should have had view of the affray while the party was so engaged in it, and that the affray was still continuing at the time of apprehension (*i*). If they fly into a house he may in the immediate pursuit break in to apprehend them (*j*).

Assault and battery.

To justify an arrest for an assault and battery in a constable's view, it must be such as would justify a criminal charge (*k*).

Where a man in the presence of a constable raised a shovel as if to strike his wife, swearing that he would have murdered her were it not for the presence of the constable, and afterwards for about twenty minutes continued to use violent language towards his wife, and then left his house professing an intention of going to his father's to sleep; and after he had gone a few yards the constable arrested him, he was held justified in doing so (*l*). But where upon an assault on a constable in the execution of his duty, a delay of over an hour occurred, when the house of the prisoner was forced and he was arrested therein, the arrest was held illegal (*m*). And so also is one on the charge of another constable which is not well founded (*n*).

A prize-fight is an assault, and this has been held to be such a fighting, whether with gloves or not, that injury to one of the

(*d*) 53 & 54 Vict. c. 45, s. 25. The Secretary of State may in case of emergency authorise a contingent of metropolitan constables to assist the local force.
(*e*) See these statutes cited, *infra*.
(*f*) 1 Hawk. P. C. c. 63, s. 13.
(*g*) Ibid., s. 3.
(*h*) Sects. 2, 4.
(*i*) *Cook* v. *Nethercote*, 6 C. & P. 741.
(*j*) 2 Hawk. P. C. c. 14, s. 8.
(*k*) *Coward* v. *Baddeley*, 4 H. & N. 481; 5 Jur. N. S. 414. As to assault on officers, see 34 & 35 Vict. c. 112, s. 12; 41 & 42 Vict. c. 74, s. 50; and 48 & 49 Vict. c. 75, s. 2.
(*l*) *R.* v. *Light*, 27 L. J. M. C. 1; D. & B. C. C. 232.
(*m*) *R.* v. *Marsden*, L. R. 1 C. C. 131; 37 L. J. M. C. 80; 11 Cox, C. C. 90; 18 L. T. 298; 32 J. P. 436.
(*n*) *Griffin* v. *Coleman*, 4 H. & N. 265; 28 L. J. Ex. 134.

combatants is likely to ensue (*o*); all persons aiding and abetting therein are guilty of assault, but the mere presence of a person is not conclusive of aiding or abetting (*p*).

A battery includes beating and wounding. To beat means not merely to strike forcibly with the hand, or a stick, or the like, but includes every touching or laying hold (however trifling) of another's person or clothes in an angry, revengeful, rude, insolent, or hostile manner (*q*)., as *e.g.* thrusting or pushing him in anger (*r*), holding him by the arm (*s*), spitting in his face, jostling him out of the way (*t*), pushing another against him (*u*), throwing a squib at him (*v*), striking a horse on which he is riding by which he is thrown (*w*). If one strike at another and miss him it is an assault only. A wounding is where the violence is so great as to draw blood (*x*).

No battery can occur by mere misadventure (*y*), nor where a parent moderately corrects his child (*z*), or a master his servant or scholar (*a*), or if the defendant committed it merely in his own defence (*b*), or in defence of a husband, wife, child, parent, master, or servant (*c*).

Any meeting whatever of great numbers of people with such circumstances of terror as cannot but endanger the public peace and raise fears and jealousies among the King's subjects, seems properly to be called an unlawful assembly, as where great numbers, complaining of a common grievance, meet together armed in a warlike manner, in order to consult together concerning the most proper means for the recovery of their interests, for no man can foresee what may be the event of such an assembly (*d*). Assembly unlawful.

Illegal drilling constitutes an unlawful assembly (*e*), and so also would it appear to be where parties assemble together to obstruct the officers of the law (*f*). Any assembling together in thoroughfares for the purpose of peaceably passing along is lawful. But there is apparently no common law right of stationary meeting in any thoroughfare or public place (*g*).

(*o*) *R.* v. *Orton*, 39 L. T. 293; 14 Cox, C. C. 266; *R.* v. *Young*, 10 *ib.* 371.
(*p*) *R.* v. *Coney*, 8 Q. B. D. 534; 37 L. J. M. C. 66; 15 Cox, C. C. 46; 46 L. T. 307; 30 W. R. 678; 46 J. P. 404.
(*q*) 1 Hawk. c. 62, s. 2; *Rawlings* v. *Till*, 3 M. & W. 28.
(*r*) *Per* Holt. C.J., 6 Mod. 142.
(*s*) *Ibid.* 172.
(*t*) *Ibid.* 149.
(*u*) Bull, N. P. 16.
(*v*) 2 W. Bl. 892.
(*w*) 1 Mod. 24.
(*x*) *Post*, p. 87.
(*y*) *Gibbon* v. *Pepper*, 2 Salk. 637; *R.* v. *Gill*, 1 Str. 490.
(*z*) Com. Dig. Pl. 3 M. 19; 1 Hawk. c. 60, s. 23.
(*a*) See *Gardner* v. *Bygrave*, 6 T. L. R. 23.
(*b*) 1 Sid. 246; 1 Rol. Rep. 19.
(*c*) 2 Rol. Abr. 546 d.; 1 Hawk. c. 60, ss. 23, 24.
(*d*) 1 Hawk. P. C. c. 65, s. 9.
(*e*) 60 Geo. 3, c. 1, s. 2.
(*f*) *Per* Fitzgerald, J., *R.* v. *McNaughten*, 14 Cox, C. C. 576.
(*g*) *R.* v. *Graham*, 32 Sol. J. 179; 16 Cox, 420. *Cf. De Morgan* v. *Metropolitan Board of Works*, 49 L. J. M. C. 58; 28 W. R. 489, and *Homer* v. *Cadman*, 34 *ib.* 413. As to Trafalgar Square, see *Ex parte Lewis*, 21 Q. B. D. 191; 57 L. J. M. C. 108; 59 L. T. 338; 37 W. R. 13; 52 J. P. 773.

A lawful assembly may become unlawful if during its course seditious words are spoken of such a nature as to produce a breach of the peace (*h*).

Where persons assembled with others for a lawful purpose, and with no intention of carrying it out unlawfully, but with the knowledge that their assembly would be opposed, and with good reason to suppose that a breach of the peace would be committed by those who opposed it, they could not be convicted of an unlawful assembly (*i*).

The local authority responsible for the maintenance of order may, in their discretion, issue notices warning persons not to attend a meeting, but a meeting held there subsequently is not an unlawful assembly by reason only of the existence of such a notice (*j*). Any one who reads it however is aware of the character of the meeting and thus affected with responsibility for attending it (*k*).

An assembly being unlawful may be dispersed (*l*).

Brawling. Any person making any disturbance in any church, chapel, or churchyard may be immediately apprehended by any constable and taken before a justice (*m*). The disturbance must be wilful and intentional (*n*).

Breach of the peace. As was above stated, the constable may arrest for a breach of the peace committed in his view. But it must be actual (*o*), and he may arrest as soon after as he conveniently can, so as it come within the expression "recently" (*p*). The continued ringing at a door-bell without cause or excuse is not itself such a breach, but it is eminently calculated to lead to it, and if it is done and persisted in, in view of the constable, he may arrest (*q*).

The disturbance and annoyance of a public meeting by putting questions to the speakers, making observations on their statements, and saying "that is a lie," is not a breach of the peace (*r*). Nor is using loud words in the street (*s*), and arrest in such case is unjustifiable (*t*). But if a constable be engaged in preventing a breach of the peace, and a person stands in his way to hinder his doing so, he may arrest such person (*u*).

Child exposure. A person about to expose an infant whereby its life may be endangered may be arrested (*v*).

(*h*) *R.* v. *Burns*, 16 C. C. C. 355.
(*i*) *Beatty* v. *Gillbanks*, 9 Q. B. D. 308; 51 L. J. M. C. 117; 47 L. T. 194; 31 W. R. 275; 46 J. P. 789, and see *Beatty* v. *Glenister*, W. N. 1884, 93; 51 L. T. 304.
(*j*) *R.* v. *Graham, ubi sup.*
(*k*) *R.* v. *Fursey*, 6 C. & P. 81.
(*l*) *R.* v. *Neale*, 9 *ib.*, 431. Soldiers employed in suppressing such an assembly have the same powers, and are under the same liabilities as constables: *R.* v. *Pinney*, 5 *ib.*, 254.
(*m*) 1 Will. & M. c. 18, s. 18; 23 & 24 Vict. c. 32, s. 3; 43 & 44 Vict. c. 41, s. 8.
(*n*) *Williams* v. *Glenister*, 2 B. & C. 699, and see *post*, p. 132.
(*o*) *Wheeler* v. *Whiting*, 9 C. & P. 262.
(*p*) *R.* v. *Light*, D. & B. C. C. 232; 27 L. J. M. C. 1.
(*q*) *Grant* v. *Moser*, 5 M. & G. 123; 6 Sc. N. R. 466.
(*r*) *Wooding* v. *Oxley*, 9 C. & P. 1.
(*s*) *Hardy* v. *Murphy*, 1 Esp. 294.
(*t*) *R.* v. *Loekley*, 4 F. & F. 155.
(*u*) *Levy* v. *Edwards*, 1 C. & P. 40.
(*v*) Arch. J. P. 122.

A convicted person, at large on licence, who a constable may **Convicted**
reasonably suspect (*w*) of having committed any offence or **persons.**
broken any of the conditions of such licence (*x*) may be apprehended. And so also may persons twice convicted if they are
found getting their living by dishonest means, or found under
suspicious circumstances, or found on premises without being
able to give a satisfactory account of themselves (*y*).

A constable may on his own view arrest offenders against the **Cruelty to**
Cruelty to Animals Act. The offences are—cruelly beat, ill- **animals.**
treat, over-drive, abuse, or torture, or cause this to be done, to
any animal (*z*). Animal means horse, mare, gelding, bull, ox,
cow, heifer, steer, calf, mule, ass, sheep, lamb, hog, pig, sow,
goat, dog, cat, or any other domestic animal (*a*), whether a
quadruped or not (*b*).

Cutting cocks' combs for fighting or winning prizes is within
the section (*c*), and so is dishorning (*d*). But operating for the
purpose of improving an animal is not (*e*). Nor is mere passive
cruelty by not killing a wounded animal (*f*), unless there be
evidence of its being kept in such a manner as to amount to
torturing (*g*).

Keeping, or using, or acting in the management of any place
for the purpose of fighting or baiting any animal (*h*), or aiding
thereat.

This offence must be committed in a place usually kept for
the purpose (*i*). Hunting rabbits in an inclosed area of four
acres is not within the section (*j*).

Persons impounding animals not providing food and water (*k*).
This does not apply to the pound-keeper (*l*).

(*w*) See *post*, p. 82.
(*x*) *I.e.*, by conviction or failure to report to police: s. 4; 27 & 28 Vict. c. 47, s. 6.
(*y*) 34 & 35 Vict. c. 112, s. 7; and see 54 & 55 Vict. c. 69, ss. 2 and 6.
(*z*) 12 & 13 Vict. c. 92, s. 13 (2). There is no offence if defendant did not know of the pain caused: *Elliott* v. *Osborne*, 55 J. P. 277.
(*a*) Sect. 29.
(*b*) 17 & 18 Vict. c. 60, s. 3. It includes cocks: *Bridge* v. *Parsons*, 3 B. & S. 302; 32 L. J. M. C. 95; 9 Jur. N. S. 796; 7 L. T. 784; 11 W. R. 424, and linnets: *Colam* v. *Paget*, 53 L. J. M. C. 64; 12 Q. B. D. 66; 32 W. R. 289; 44 J. P. 263, but not young unacclimatised parrots: *Swan* v. *Sanders*, 50 L. J. M. C. 67; 44 L. T. 424; 45 J. P. 522; 29 W. R. 538; 14 Cox, C. C. 566.
(*c*) *Murphy* v. *Manning*, 2 Ex. D. 307; 46 L. J. M. C. 211; 36 L. T. 592; 41 J. P. 104; 25 W. R. 540.

(*d*) *Ford* v. *Wiley*, 5 Ti. Rep. 453; 53 J. P. 324; 37 W. R. 709; 58 L. J. M. C. 145.
(*e*) *Lewis* v. *Fermor*, 18 Q. B. D. 532; 56 L. J. M. C. 45; 56 L. T. 236; 35 W. R. 378; 51 J. P. 371; 16 Cox, C. C. 176.
(*f*) *Powell* v. *Knights*, 38 L. T. 607; 42 J. P. 597; 26 W. R. 721.
(*g*) *Everitt* v. *Davies*, 38 L. T. 360; 42 J. P. 248; 26 W. R. 332.
(*h*) 12 & 13 Vict. c. 92, s. 3.
(*i*) *Clarke* v. *Hague*, 29 L. J. M. C. 105; 6 Jur. N. S. 273; 8 W. R. 363; 2 L. T. 85; 24 J. P. 517; *Morley* v. *Greenhalgh*, 32 L. J. M. C. 93; 3 B. & S. 374; 9 Jur. N. S. 745; 7 L. T. 624; 27 J. P. 197.
(*j*) *Pitts* v. *Millar*, L. R. 9 Q. B. 380; 43 L. J. M. C. 102; 30 L. T. 328; 38 J. P. 615.
(*k*) 12 & 13 Vict. c. 92, s. 5.
(*l*) *Dargan* v. *Davies*, 2 Q. B. D. 118; 46 L. J. M. C. 122; 35 L. T. 810; 41 J. P. 468.

Persons keeping slaughter places to affix names (*m*).

Neck hair to be cut before slaughter, to be killed within three days, and food and water meanwhile provided (*n*).

Cattle for slaughter not to be employed (*o*).

Description of cattle slaughtered to be entered in book (*p*).

Conveying so as to cause unnecessary suffering (*q*).

Cruelty to children. — Persons committing offences against the Cruelty to Children Act may be arrested if the offence be committed in the constable's view, and the person's name and address cannot be astertained, and the child may be taken to a place of safety (*r*).

The offences are—ill-treatment and neglect (*s*); causing child to beg (*t*).

Dice. — Persons playing with false dice may be arrested (*u*).

Drunkenness. — So also may every person who in any highway or other public place, whether a building or not, is guilty while drunk of riotous or disorderly behaviour, or who is drunk while in charge on any highway or other public place of any carriage, horse, cattle, or steam-engine, or who is drunk while in possession of any loaded fire-arms (*v*).

Escape. — Offenders who have escaped cannot be retaken without warrant, unless the original offence was one for which no warrant was required (*w*).

Explosives. — Constables may remove persons who enter factories, magazines, or stores of explosives without permission (*x*).

Felony. — With respect to felonies, inasmuch as they form a class to themselves, it is as well that they should be arranged alphabetically under this head.

A constable has power to arrest in case of felony committed, or reasonable suspicion that it has been committed (*y*); or, as regards offences against the person, that it is about to be committed in the night-time (*z*). Similar provisions are contained in the Larceny and Malicious Injury to Property Acts.

Accessories before and after the fact are now liable in all respects as principals (*a*).

With regard to what is reasonable suspicion, the grounds must be such as would lead a reasonable person acting without passion or prejudice to come to that conclusion (*b*).

Abduction. — Abduction of a woman for lucre or under twenty-one (*c*).

If the woman be taken away at first by consent, and after-

(*m*) 12 & 13 Vict. c. 92, s. 7.
(*n*) Sect. 8.
(*o*) Sect. 9. This is not confined to licensed slaughter-houses: *Colam* v. *Hall*, L. R. 6 Q. B. 206.
(*p*) Sect. 10.
(*q*) Sect. 12.
(*r*) 52 & 53 Vict. c. 44, s. 4.
(*s*) Sect. 1.
(*t*) Sect. 3.
(*u*) Arch. J. P. 123.
(*v*) 35 & 36 Vict. c. 94, s. 12.

(*w*) 2 Hawk. c. 14, s. 9.
(*x*) 38 & 39 Vict. c. 17, s. 77.
(*y*) *Beckwith* v. *Philby*, 6 B. & C. 635; 9 D. & R. 487; *Stonehouse* v. *Elliott*, 6 T. R. 315; *R.* v. *Phelps*, Car. & M. 180.
(*z*) 24 & 25 Vict. c. 100, s. 66.
(*a*) 24 & 25 Vict. c. 94, ss. 1 and 3.
(*b*) *Allen* v. *Wright*, 8 C. & P. 522; *Leete* v. *Hart*, 37 L. J. C. P. 157; L. R. 3 C. P. 322; 32 J. P. 407.
(*c*) 24 & 25 Vict. c. 100, s. 53.

wards refuse to continue with the offender, and be forcibly detained by him, it is sufficient (*d*). And so if she be forcibly taken away, and afterwards married or defiled by her consent (*e*), or if it be effected by fraud (*ee*).

Of any woman by force (*f*).
Of a girl under fourteen (*g*)
Abortion, attempt to procure (*h*).   Abortion.

The administration of a drug must be by the defendant (*i*), but mere delivery is not sufficient (*j*), although the defendant need not be present at the time of taking the drug (*k*). The drug must be a poison or noxious thing (*l*), and the offence is complete whether the woman be or be not with child, and may be committed by the woman herself (*m*).

Aqueducts, bridges or piles, malicious injury to (*n*).   Aqueducts, &c.
Arson of a church or chapel (*o*).   Arson.
Of a dwelling-house (*p*).
Of an out-house, factory &c. (*q*).
An unfinished structure is not within this section (*r*).
Of buildings belonging to railways and canals (*s*).
Of public buildings (*t*).
Of other buildings (*u*).
An unfinished dwelling-house is within this section (*v*).

If a man by wilfully setting fire to his own house burn that of a neighbour it is sufficient (*w*). The absence of malice or spite to the owner is no answer (*x*), nor that the burning is trifling (*y*).

Of goods in buildings (*z*).

This does not extend to throwing a light into a letter box (*a*), nor to setting fire to goods to injure the owner of the goods, but not of the house (*b*).

(*d*) 1 Hawk. c. 41, s. 7.
(*e*) *Fulwood*, Cro. Car. 488; *Swenden*, 5 St. Tr. 450.
(*ee*) *R.* v. *Wakefield*, 1 Lew. Cr. C. 1; *R.* v. *Burrell*, 33 L. J. M. C. 54; 1 L. & C. 354; 12 W. R. 149; 9 L. T. 426.
(*f*) 24 & 25 Vict. c. 100, s. 54.
(*g*) Sect. 56.
(*h*) Sect. 58.
(*i*) *R.* v. *Harley*, 4 C. & P. 369.
(*j*) *R.* v. *Cadman*, 1 Moo. C. C. 114.
(*k*) *R.* v. *Wilson*, 26 L. J. M. C. 18; 1 D. & B. C. C. 126; 7 Cox, C. C. 190; 2 Jur. N. S. 1146; 5 W. R. 70; 20 J. P. 774; *R.* v. *Farrow*, 1 D. & B. C. C. 164; 3 Jur. N. S. 167; 5 W. R. 269; 21 J. P. 118.
(*l*) *R.* v. *Isaacs*, 1 L. & C. C. C. 220; 32 L. J. M. C. 52; 9 Cox, C. C. 228; 11 W. R. 95; 7 L. T. 477; *R.* v. *Hollis*, 12 Cox, 463; 28 L. T. 455.
(*m*) *R.* v. *Goodhall*, 1 Den. 187; 2 C. & K. 293; *R.* v. *Whitchurch*, 24 Q. B. D. 420.
(*n*) 24 & 25 Vict. c. 97, ss. 31, 33.
(*o*) Sect. 1.
(*p*) Sect. 2.
(*q*) Sect. 3.
(*r*) *R.* v. *Edgell*, 11 Cox, C. C. 132; 32 J. P. 168.
(*s*) Sect. 4.
(*t*) Sect. 5.
(*u*) Sect. 6.
(*v*) *R.* v. *Manning*, 1 C. C. R. 338; 41 L. J. M. C. 11; 36 J. P. 228; 12 Cox, C. C. 106; 25 L. T. 573.
(*w*) *R.* v. *Probert*, 2 East, P. C. 1030; *R.* v. *Isaac, ib.* 1031.
(*x*) *R.* v. *Salmon*, R. & R. 26.
(*y*) 1 Hawk. c. 39, s. 17; 3 Inst. 66.
(*z*) 24 & 25 Vict. c. 97, s. 7.
(*a*) *R.* v. *Batstone*, 10 Cox, C. C. 20.
(*b*) *R.* v. *Child*, 1 C. C. R. 307; 40 L. J. M. C. 127; 12 Cox, C. C. 64; 35 J. P. 805; 24 L. T. 556.

84 EXECUTIVE OFFICERS.

Attempts to fire buildings (*c*).
Damaging house with gunpowder, &c., whereby the life of anyone is endangered (*d*).
This does not extend to mere wanton mischief (*e*); but includes persons imperilled outside the building (*f*).
Setting fire to crops, &c. (*g*).
This does not apply to a single tree (*h*).
Firing stacks of corn, &c. (*i*).
Flax in seed is included (*j*); but straw in a lorry *in transitû* (*k*), or wood in a temporary loft is not (*l*).
Attempts to fire stacks, &c. (*m*).
It is sufficient if the attempt be abandoned before being actually made (*n*).
Firing mines or attempts (*o*).
Firing ships or attempts (*p*).
The firing must not be the result of accident (*q*).

Assault. Assault with intent to rob (*r*).
Actual violence is not necessary. Assaulting and threatening to charge with an infamous crime is within the section (*s*).

Bank notes, making. Bank-notes, exchequer bills, &c., or paper making (*t*). This applies to notes of a Scotch bank (*u*).

Bankrupt. Bankrupt absconding with £20 and upwards (*v*). This does not extend to a minor (*w*).

Bigamy. Bigamy (*x*).
It is sufficient if a person goes through the form and ceremony of a second marriage, though it be unlawful and void (*y*). But a belief in good faith and on reasonable grounds that the husband or wife is dead is a good defence (*z*).

Buoys. Buoys, boats, &c., interfering with (*a*).
Burglary. Burglary (*b*).
This must take place between 9 P.M. and 6 A.M. There must

(*c*) 24 & 25 Vict. c. 97, s. 8.
(*d*) Sect. 9.
(*e*) R. v. *Brown*, 3 F. & F. 821.
(*f*) R. v. *M'Grath*, 14 Cox, C. C. 598.
(*g*) 24 & 25 Vict. c. 97, s. 16.
(*h*) R. v. *Davy*, 1 Cox, C. C. 60.
(*i*) Sect. 17.
(*j*) R. v. *Spencer*, 26 M. C. L. J. 16; 1 D. & B. 131; 7 Cox, C. C. 189; 2 Jur. N. S. 1212; 5 W. R. 70; 20 J. P. 775.
(*k*) R. v. *Satchwell*, L. R. 2 C. C. 21; 42 L. J. M. C. 63; 21 W. R. 612; 37 J. P. 421; 28 L. T. 569.
(*l*) R. v. *Aris*, 6 C. & P. 348.
(*m*) 24 & 25 Vict. c. 97, s. 18.
(*n*) R. v. *Taylor*, 1 F. & F. 571.
(*o*) 24 & 25 Vict. c. 97, ss. 26, 27.
(*p*) Sects. 43, 44.
(*q*) R. v. *Faulkner*, 13 Cox, 550.
(*r*) 24 & 25 Vict. c. 96, s. 42.
(*s*) R. v. *Stringer*, 2 Moo. C. C.

261; 1 C. & K. 188.
(*t*) 24 & 25 Vict. c. 98, ss. 8-11, 14.
(*u*) R. v. *Brackenbridge*, 1 C. C. R. 133; 37 L. J. M. C. 86; 11 Cox, C. C. 96; 18 L. T. 369; 16 W. R. 816.
(*v*) 32 & 33 Vict. c. 62, s. 12.
(*w*) R. v. *Wilson*, 5 Q. B. D. 28; 49 L. J. M. C. 13; 41 L. T. 480; 44 J. P. 105.
(*x*) 24 & 25 Vict. c. 100, s. 57.
(*y*) R. v. *Allen*, 1 C. C. R. 397; 41 L. J. M. C. 97; 12 Cox, C. C. 193; 20 W. R. 756; 36 J. P. 820; 26 L. T. 664; R. v. *Bawen*, 1 Cox, C. C. 33; 7 J. P. 530; R. v. *Penson*, 5 C. & P. 412.
(*z*) R. v. *Tolson*, 23 Q. B. D. 168; 58 L. J. M. C. 97; 16 Cox, C. C. 629; 60 L. T. 899; 37 W. R. 716; 54 J. P. 4.
(*a*) 24 & 25 Vict. c. 97, s. 48.
(*b*) 24 & 25 Vict. c. 96, s. 51.

be a breaking, but it is not a breaking to open a window or aperture which is already open and should be fastened (c); but an entry by a chimney is a breaking (d). It may be on one night and the entry on another (e). It must take place in a dwelling-house, which includes every permanent building. The residence of care-takers is not sufficient (f), nor where the owner or occupier is not yet in actual occupation (g); outhouses must be connected with a covered way. There must be an entry (h) though with any part of the body or an instrument is sufficient (i).

Burglary by breaking out (j).

This extends to the case of larceny by lodgers (k). On an attempt it is unnecessary to establish entry (l).

Cattle, killing or maiming (m), &c.   Cattle.

Maiming without wounding must entail permanent injury (n). The wounding need not be done with an instrument (o), and it is sufficient if it be done recklessly (p).

Children under thirteen, carnally abusing (q).   Children, abuse of.

Where the girl assented the conviction was quashed (r).

Chloroform, administering with intent (s).   Chloroform, administering, &c.

Choking, attempt to, with intent (t).

Coin clippings, possessing (u).

Coin tools, &c., making (v).   Choking.

This extends to a mould (w), and to a galvanic battery (x).

Conveying tools or coins, &c., out of the mint (y).   Coins, clippings, possessing tools, &c.

Copper, counterfeiting or dealing in, having three or more pieces after previous conviction (z).

Crime, accusing of, extorting by (a).   Copper.

The guilt or innocence of the party threatened is immaterial (b).   Crime.

(c) 1 Hale, 551; 3 Inst. 64; R. v. Lewis, 2 C. & P. 628; R. v. Spriggs, 1 M. & R. 357; R. v. Swallow, 2 Russ. C. & M. 9.
(d) R. v. Brice, R. & R. 341.
(e) 1 Hale, 551.
(f) R. v. Smith, 2 E. P. C. 497; R. v. Flannagan, R. & R. 187.
(g) R. v. Hillard, 2 E. P. C. 498; R. v. Thompson, ib.; 2 Leach, 771.
(h) 1 Hale, 551.
(i) R. v. Davis, R. & R. 499.
(j) 24 & 25 Vict. c. 96, s. 51.
(k) R. v. Wheeldon, 8 C. & P. 747; R. v. Lawrence, 4 ib. 231.
(l) R. v. Spanner, 12 Cox, C. C. 155.
(m) 24 & 25 Vict. c. 97, s. 40.
(n) R. v. Jeans, 1 C. & K. 539; R. v. Haywood, 2 E. P. C. 1076; R. & R. 16.
(o) R. v. Bullock, L. R. 1 C. C. 115; 37 L. J. M. C. 47; 11 Cox, C. C. 125;
16 W. R. 405; 32 J. P. 102; 17 L. T. 516.
(p) R. v. Welch, 1 Q. B. D. 23; 45 L. J. M. C. 17; 13 Cox, C. C. 121; 33 L. T. 753; 24 W. R. 280.
(q) 48 & 49 Vict. c. 64, s. 4.
(r) R. v. Martin, 2 Moo. C. C. 123.
(s) 24 & 25 Vict. c. 100, s. 22.
(t) Sect. 21.
(u) 24 & 25 Vict. c. 99, s. 5.
(v) Sect. 24.
(w) R. v. Weeks, 8 Cox, C. C. 455; 7 Jur. N. S. 472; 30 L. J. M. C. 141; L. & C. 18; 25 J. P. 357; 4 L. T. 373.
(x) R. v. Gover, 9 Cox, 282.
(y) 24 & 25 Vict. c. 99, s. 25. See R. v. Harvey, L. R. 1 C. C. 284; 40 L. J. M. C. 63.
(z) 24 & 25 Vict. c. 99, ss. 14, 15.
(a) 24 & 25 Vict. c. 96, s. 47.
(b) R. v. Cracknell, 10 Cox, C. C. 408; R. v. Richards, 11 ib. 43.

86 EXECUTIVE OFFICERS.

Deer. Deer stealing (*c*).
Desertion. Desertion army (*d*), or navy (*e*).
As to naval officers, it has been laid down that to be deserters they must be borne on the books of a ship in commission (*f*).
Embezzlement. Embezzlement (*g*).
This offence is similar to larceny (*h*).
Escape. Escape or aiding, in case of felony (*i*).
Explosion. Explosion with intent, or attempts (*j*), or making, or having possession of explosive substances under suspicious circumstances (*k*).
Extradition. As to extradition cases, it seems an open question whether a constable would be justified in arresting a fugitive on reasonable suspicion that he had committed a crime which would be felony if committed here (*l*).
Foreign gold. Foreign gold or silver, counterfeiting or dealing in (*m*).
Forgery. Forgery (*n*).
At common law this is the fraudulent making or alteration of a writing to the prejudice of another man's right (*o*). The slightest alteration of a genuine instrument in a material part whereby a new operation is given to it is sufficient (*p*). The name forged may be that of a fictitious person (*q*), provided the name be assumed for the purposes of fraud (*r*). It must be of some document or writing, and does not include painting an artist's name on a picture (*s*). It must be uttered, offered or disposed of, although that to an innocent agent or accomplice is sufficient (*t*).
Of Great Seal, powers of attorney, dividend warrants, &c. (*u*).
Of bank-notes (*v*).
Of deeds, bonds, &c. (*w*).
This includes a fraudulent demise (*x*), a guarantee (*y*), and post-office orders (*z*), but not letters of ordination (*a*).
Of wills (*b*).
Of bills of exchange and promissory notes (*c*).

(*c*) 24 & 25 Vict. c. 96, ss. 12, 13.
(*d*) 29 & 30 Vict. c. 109.
(*e*) 44 & 45 Vict. c. 58.
(*f*) R. v. Cumming, 19 Q. B. D. 13; 57 L. T. 477; 56 L. J. Q. B. 287; In re Hearson, 7 T. L. R. 307; 64 L. T. 535.
(*g*) 24 & 25 Vict. c. 96, ss. 68 and 70.
(*h*) See post, p. 87.
(*i*) 4 Black. 130; 1 Hale, 23.
(*j*) 24 & 25 Vict. c. 97, ss. 9, 10.
(*k*) 46 Vict. c. 3, ss. 2-5.
(*l*) R. v. Weil, 9 Q. B. D. 701.
(*m*) 24 & 25 Vict. c. 99, ss. 18, 19, 21.
(*n*) 24 & 25 Vict. c. 98.
(*o*) 4 Black. 247.
(*p*) 1 Hawk. c. 70, s. 2.
(*q*) R. v. Lewis, Fost. 116; R. v. Bolland, 3 E. P. C. 958.
(*r*) R. v. Bontien, R. & R. 260.
(*s*) R. v. Closs, D. & B. 460; 27 L. J. M. C. 54.
(*t*) R. v. Palmer, 1 N. R. 96; R. & R. 72; R. v. Giles, 1 Moo. C. C. 166.
(*u*) 24 & 25 Vict. c. 98, ss. 1-8.
(*v*) Sect. 12.
(*w*) Sect. 20.
(*x*) R. v. Ritson, 1 C. C. R. 200; 30 L. J. M. C. 10.
(*y*) R. v. Coelho, 9 Cox, C. C. 8.
(*z*) R. v. Vanderstein, 10 ib. 177.
(*a*) R. v. Morton, 42 L. J. M. C. 58; L. R. 2 C. C. 22; 28 L. T. 452; 21 W. R. 629.
(*b*) Sect. 21.
(*c*) Sect. 22.

This does not extend to forging an acceptance where the bill had not been signed by the drawer *(d)*.

Of orders and receipts for money *(e)*.

It is sufficient if the party to whom it is addressed has been in the habit of treating similar documents as orders *(f)*. A guarantee *(g)*, a dividend warrant *(h)*, and a pawnbroker's duplicate *(i)*, are within the section. But not a request to pay money *(j)*, nor a certificate that a person is gaining his livelihood by certain means *(k)*. It must be made by a person who might command the payment to a person who was compellable to obey it *(l)*, and it must purport to be directed to the person having possession of the money *(m)*.

Of marriage licence *(n)*.

It matters not that the marriage is void *(o)*.

Of registers *(p)*.

Gold coin impairing, colouring to represent, counterfeiting or dealing in, having three or more pieces after previous conviction *(q)*. Gold coin.

Goods in manufacture, malicious injury to *(r)*. Goods.

Grievous bodily harm, with intent to maim, resist apprehension, or by explosion *(s)*. Grievous harm.

This applies to firing recklessly at a group *(t)*; but not to a man who has communicated a venereal disease to his wife *(u)*.

Hopbinds destroying *(v)*. Hopbinds.

Housebreaking or attempt *(w)*. Housebreaking.

Larceny *(x)*. Larceny.

At common law this is the wrongful or fraudulent taking or carrying away the personal goods of another from any place with a felonious intent to convert them to the taker's own use, and make them permanently his own property without the consent of the owner *(y)*. Wherever there is a *bonâ fide* claim of right, however groundless, it is no felony *(z)*, and the

---

(d) R. v. *Mopsey*, 11 Cox, C. C. 143.
(e) Sect. 23.
(f) R. v. *Kay*, L. R. 1 C. C. 257; 39 L. J. M. C. 118.
(g) R. v. *Joyce*, 1 L. & C. C. C. 576; 34 L. J. M. C. 168; 13 W. R. 662; 11 Jur. N. S. 472; 12 L. T. 351; 10 Cox, C. C. 100.
(h) R. v. *Autey*, 1 D. & B. C. C. 294; 26 L. J. M. C. 190; 7 Cox, C. C. 329; 3 Jur. N. S. 697.
(i) R. v. *Fitchie*, 7 Cox, C. C. 257; 29 L. T. 99; 1 D. & B. C. C. 175; 3 Jur. N. S. 419; 26 L. J. M. C. 90.
(j) R. v. *Thorn*, 2 Moo. C. C. 210; C. & M. 206.
(k) R. v. *Mitchell*, 2 F. & F. 44.
(l) R. v. *Clinch*, 2 E. P. C. 938.
(m) Ibid.
(n) Sect. 35.
(o) R. v. *Asplin*, 12 Cox, C. C. 391.
(p) Sect. 36.
(q) 24 & 25 Vict. c. 99, ss. 2, 3, 4, 11.
(r) 24 & 25 Vict. c. 97, s. 14.
(s) 24 & 25 Vict. c. 100, ss. 18, 28–30.
(t) R. v. *Fretwell*, 33 L. J. M. C. 128; 9 Cox, C. C. 471; 10 Jur. N. S. 595; 12 W. R. 751; 28 J. P. 344; 10 L. T. 428.
(u) R. v. *Clarence*, 22 Q. B. D. 23; 58 L. J. M. C. 10; 59 L. T. 780; 37 W. R. 166; 53 J. P. 149; 16 Cox, C. C. 511; 5 Ti. Rep. 61.
(v) 24 & 25 Vict. c. 97, s. 19.
(w) 24 & 25 Vict. c. 96, ss. 56, 57.
(x) 24 & 25 Vict. c. 96.
(y) 2 East, P. C. c. 16, s. 2.
(z) 1 Hale, 509.

88   EXECUTIVE OFFICERS.

intention to steal is of the essence of the act (*a*). There must be a taking either actual or constructive (*b*). As to goods lost, if the finder appropriate them believing that the owner can be found, it is larceny (*c*); but not on a subsequent appropriation with such knowledge (*d*). Where the owner of his own free will parts with the *property* there is no larceny, however fraudulent were the means employed (*e*); but this does not apply to a trick or artifice (*f*). There must be a carrying away; but a bare removal is sufficient (*g*).

Of horses, cows, sheep, &c. (*h*).
Of oysters in fishery (*i*).
Of bonds, bills, notes, &c. (*j*).
Of wills and codicils (*k*).
Of records or other legal documents (*l*).

This extends to the case of depriving an officer of the law of his warrant (*m*).

Of metal, glass, &c., fixed to house or land (*n*).
Of trees in pleasure-ground to the value of £1, or elsewhere £5 (*o*).
Of ore, metal, coal, &c. (*p*).
Of goods in dwelling-house to the value of £5 (*q*), or with menaces (*r*).
Of goods in process of manufacture (*s*), from ships, docks, or wharfs (*t*), or wreck (*u*).
By clerks and servants (*v*).

This constitutes embezzlement (*w*).

It applies to a female servant (*x*), and an apprentice though under age (*y*), and a son acting as clerk (*z*), and is not confined to servants of persons in trade (*a*). The mode by which the defendant is remunerated is immaterial (*b*). A commercial

(*a*) *R.* v. *Crump*, 1 C. & P. 658.
(*b*) 1 Hale, 514.
(*c*) *R.* v. *Thurborn*, 1 Den. 388; 2 C. & K. 831.
(*d*) *R.* v. *Pearson*, 2 Den. 353; 21 L. J. M. C. 41; *R.* v. *Mathews*, 12 Cox, 489.
(*e*) *R.* v. *Macgrath*, L. R. 1 C. C. 205; 39 L. J. M. C. 7; 2 E. P. C. 668; *R.* v. *Lovell*, 8 Q. B. D. 185; *R.* v. *Adams*, R. & R. 225.
(*f*) *R.* v. *Middleton*, L. R. 2 C. C. 38; 42 L. J. M. C. 73; *R.* v. *Hollis*, 12 Q. B. D. 25.
(*g*) 4 Bl. 231.
(*h*) 24 & 25 Vict. c. 96, ss. 10-13.
(*i*) Sect. 26.
(*j*) Sects. 27, 28.
(*k*) Sect. 29.
(*l*) Sect. 30.
(*m*) *R.* v. *Bailey*, L. R. 1 C. C. 347; 41 L. J. M. C. 61; 12 Cox, C. C. 129; 25 L. T. 882; 20 W. R. 301; 36 J. P. 324.
(*n*) Sect. 31.
(*o*) Sect. 32.
(*p*) Sect. 38.
(*q*) Sect. 60.
(*r*) Sect. 61.
(*s*) Sect. 62.
(*t*) Sect. 63.
(*u*) Sect. 64.
(*v*) Sect. 67.
(*w*) *R.* v. *Gibbs*, D. C. C. 415; 24 L. J. M. C. 62; 6 Cox, C. C. 455; 1 Jur. N. S. 118.
(*x*) *R.* v. *Smith*, R. & R. 267.
(*y*) *R.* v. *Mellish*, *ib.* 80.
(*z*) *R.* v. *Foulkes*, L. R. 2 C. C. 150; 44 L. J. M. C. 65.
(*a*) *R.* v. *Squire*, R. & R. 349; *R.* v. *Townsend*, 1 Den. 167; 2 C. & K. 168; *R.* v. *Adey*, 1 Den. 578; 19 L. J. M. C. 149.
(*b*) *R.* v. *Carr*, R. & R. 198; *R.* v. *Higgins*, *ib.* 145.

traveller is within the section (*c*); but not a commission agent (*d*). The employment need not be permanent (*e*); but for a single purpose is not sufficient (*f*).

By public officers (*g*).

Of fixtures by tenants (*h*).

Machines, malicious injury to (*i*).   *Machines.*

The destruction of any part whether it works or not (*j*), is within the section (*k*); but if a part be destroyed through fear the remaining parts are not so (*l*). It extends to ploughs and water-wheels (*m*), and the damage need not be permanent (*n*).

Manslaughter (*o*).   *Manslaughter.*

This is (1) involuntary—where a man doing an unlawful act not amounting to felony by accident kills another, or where by culpable neglect of duty he is the cause of the death of another, or, (2) voluntary—where in a sudden quarrel two persons fight, and one of them kills the other, or where a man greatly provokes another by some personal violence and the other immediately kills him (*p*).

Mines, malicious injury (*q*).   *Mines.*

If a workman stop up an airway by order of the master it is no felony unless they knew the act to be malicious (*r*). If the act be done under a *bonâ fide* claim of right it is not within the section (*s*).

Murder or attempts (*t*).   *Murder.*

This is where a person of sound memory and discretion unlawfully killeth any reasonable being, and under the king's peace with malice aforethought, express or implied (*u*).

Mutiny (*v*).   *Mutiny.*

Oaths unlawful (*w*).   *Oaths.*

This extends to oaths of secret societies (*x*), and to unlawful combinations (*y*).

Penal servitude, at large during (*z*).   *Penal servitude.*

(*c*) *R.* v. *Bailey*, 12 Cox, 56; *R.* v. *Tite*, L. & C. 29; 30 L. J. M. C. 142.
(*d*) *R.* v. *Bowers*, L. R. 1 C. C. 41; 35 L. J. M. C. 266.
(*e*) *R.* v. *Spencer*, R. & R. 299; *R.* v. *Smith, ib.* 516.
(*f*) *R.* v. *Nettleton*, 1 Moo. C. C. 259.
(*g*) Sects. 69–73. Not applicable to county court bailiff: *R.* v. *Parsons*, 16 Cox, C. C. 498.
(*h*) Sect. 74.
(*i*) *Ibid.* c. 97, s. 15.
(*j*) *R.* v. *Bartlett*, 2 Deac. C. L. 1517.
(*k*) *R.* v. *Mackerel*, 4 C. & P. 448.
(*l*) *R.* v. *West*, 2 D. C. L. 1518.
(*m*) *R.* v. *Gray*, L. & C. 365; 33 L. J. M. C. 78; 9 Cox, C. C. 417; 10 Jur. N. S. 160; 9 L. T. 733; 12 W. R. 350; *R.* v. *Fidler*, 4 C. & P. 449.
(*n*) *R.* v. *Fisher*, L. R. 1 C. C. 7; 35 L. J. M. C. 57.
(*o*) 4 Black. 193.
(*p*) Arch. C. C., 19th ed., p. 678.
(*q*) 24 & 25 Vict. c. 97, s. 28.
(*r*) *R.* v. *James*, 8 C. & P. 131.
(*s*) *R.* v. *Matthews*, 14 Cox, C. C. 5.
(*t*) 24 & 25 Vict. c. 100, ss. 11–15.
(*u*) 3 Inst. 47.
(*v*) 37 Geo. 3, c. 70, s. 1; 44 & 45 Vict. c. 58, s. 7.
(*w*) 37 Geo. 3, c. 123, s. 1; 52 Geo. 3, c. 104, s. 1.
(*x*) *R.* v. *Burgess*, L. & C. 258; 32 L. J. M. C. 55.
(*y*) *R.* v. *Marks*, 3 East, 157.
(*z*) 5 Geo, 4, c. 84, s. 22.

Personation.	Personation at elections, of bail, owners of stock, soldiers, sailors, &c., to obtain property (a).
Piracy.	Piracy (b).
Poison.	Poison, administering with intent or so as to endanger (c).
Prison breach.	Prison, breach of, or rescue, if for felony (d).
Prisoner of war.	Prisoner of war, aiding to escape (e).
Railway.	Railway, injuring with intent to obstruct, or endangering safety of passengers (f).
Rape.	Rape (g). This must take place by force, and without consent, and if the consent be through fear or duress it is void (h). So also is it probably if obtained by fraud (i). There must be penetration (j).
Rescue.	Rescue of a traitor or felon from custody (k), after conviction (l).
Riot.	Riot (m), or opposing making of proclamation. There must be some sort of resistance to lawful authority (n).
River-banks.	River- or sea-banks, interfering with, or opening sluices (o).
Robbery.	Robbery by person armed, or by two or more (p).
Sacrilege.	Sacrilege, or attempt (q). The vestry is part of the church for this purpose (r).
Signals.	Signals, altering (s).
Silver.	Silver coin, impairing, colouring to represent, counterfeiting, or dealing in counterfeit (t).
Slaves.	Slave trade offences (u).
Smuggling.	Smuggling, shooting at vessels of Her Majesty, six or more together, three or more armed and assembled, two or more armed or disguised, wounding officers (v). The shooting must be malicious. Firing on a pursuing revenue vessel sailing without proper ensign is not (w) within the section.
Stolen property.	Stolen property, receiving or taking reward to help to (x).

(a) 2 & 3 Will. 4, c. 53, s. 49; 24 & 25 Vict. c. 98, ss. 3, 34; 28 & 29 Vict. c. 124, s. 8; 30 & 31 Vict. c. 131, s. 35; 33 & 34 Vict. c. 58, s. 4; 37 & 38 Vict. c. 36, s. 1; 46 & 47 Vict. 51, s. 6.
(b) 7 Will. 4, and 1 Vict. c. 88.
(c) 24 & 25 Vict. c. 100, s. 11.
(d) 1 Hale, 612; 1 & 2 Geo. 4, c. 88, s. 1.
(e) 16 Geo. 2, c. 31.
(f) 24 & 25 Vict. c. 97, s. 35.
(g) 24 & 25 Vict. c. 100, s. 48.
(h) 1 Hawk. c. 41, s. 6.
(i) R. v. Barrow, 1 L. R. 1 C. C. 156; 38 L. J. M. C. 20; R. v. Flattery, 2 Q. B. D. 410; 46 L. J. M. C. 130.
(j) R. v. Hill, 1 East, P. C. 439.
(k) 1 Hale, 607; 1 Geo. 4, c. 88, s. 1.
(l) 2 Hawk. c. 21, s. 8.
(m) 1 Geo. 1, stat. 2, c. 5, prosecution must be within twelve months.
(n) R. v. Hunt, 1 Cox, C. C. 177; R. v. Atkinson, 11 ib. 330.
(o) 24 & 25 Vict. c. 97, s. 30.
(p) 24 & 25 Vict. c. 96, ss. 40-43.
(q) Sect. 50.
(r) R. v. Evans, C. & M. 298.
(s) 24 & 25 Vict. c. 97, s. 47.
(t) 24 & 25 Vict. c. 99, ss. 2-4.
(u) 5 Geo. 4, c. 113; 36 & 37 Vict. c. 88.
(v) 39 & 40 Vict. c. 36, s. 193.
(w) R. v. Reynolds, R. & R. 465.
(x) 24 & 25 Vict. c. 96, ss. 91, 100.

The principal offender need not have been indicted (*y*), and the receipt need not be direct from the thief (*z*).

Stores, public, obliterating marks (*a*). Stores.
Threatening letter, sending, or extorting by (*b*). Threatening letter.
Treason or treason-felony (*c*). Treason.
Trees, destroying (*d*). Trees.
Unnatural crime, or attempt (*e*). Unnatural crime.

The evidence is as in rape, but (1) it is not necessary to negative consent, and (2) both parties if patient do consent are equally guilty (*f*), except the patient, if a boy, be under fourteen, or if a girl, under twelve (*g*). It may be committed with animals, and this includes a domestic fowl (*h*).

Vessels, injuring by explosion or otherwise (*i*). Vessels.
Wreck, impeding escape from, or interfering with (*j*). Wreck.

There are a number of statutes which authorize constables to arrest offenders provided they are "found committing" any offence against those Acts by such constable. These, therefore, like felonies, form a class, which will be conveniently arranged in alphabetical order. Found, committing.

With regard to what is the meaning of this term, it appears that the words "found committing" must be construed strictly (*k*). An arrest cannot take place a little time afterwards (*l*), much less after an interval of two or three hours (*m*). But an offence may be being committed at a place other than that of its inception, as in the case of a thief still in possession of property recently stolen. In such case he is found committing (*n*).

Hawking cards without licence (*o*). Cards.
Counterfeiting foreign coin other than gold or silver (*p*). Coin.
Exporting counterfeit coin (*q*).
Possessing three or more pieces of counterfeit coin (*r*), or more than five pieces of foreign counterfeit with intent (*s*).
Uttering counterfeit gold or silver (*t*), or uttering, accompanied by possession of other counterfeit coin, or followed by a second

(*y*) R. v. *Jervis*, 9 C. & P. 156; R. v. *Pullam*, ib. 280.
(*z*) R. v. *Reardon*, L. R. 1 C. C. 31; 35 L. J. M. C. 171; 12 Jur. N. S. 476; 14 L. T. 449; 14 W. R. 663.
(*a*) 38 & 39 Vict. c. 25, s. 5.
(*b*) 24 & 25 Vict. c. 100, s. 16; 24 & 25 Vict. c. 96, ss. 47–50. See cases under "Crime," *supra*.
(*c*) 25 Edw. 3, stat. 5, c. 2; 11 & 12 Vict. c. 12, s. 3. Treason must be prosecuted within three years, unless against the person of the sovereign.
(*d*) 24 & 25 Vict. c. 96, ss. 32, 33.
(*e*) 24 & 25 Vict. c. 100, s. 61.
(*f*) R. v. *Wiseman*, Fort. 91.
(*g*) 1 Hale, 670; 3 Inst. 59.
(*h*) R. v. *Brown*, 24 Q. B. D. 357.
(*i*) 24 & 25 Vict. c. 97, ss. 45, 46.

(*j*) 24 & 25 Vict. c. 100, s. 17.
(*k*) R. v. *Phelps*, C. & M. 180; 1 Russ. Cr. 715.
(*l*) *Simmons* v. *Milligen*, 2 C. B. 524; 10 Jur. 224; 15 L. J. C. P. 102.
(*m*) *Downing* v. *Capel*, 36 L. J. M. C. 97; L. R. 2 C. P. 461; 16 L. T. 323; *Leete* v. *Hart*, 37 L. J. C. P. 157; L. R. 3 C. P. 322; 32 J. P. 407.
(*n*) *Griffiths* v. *Taylor*, L. R. 2 C. P. D. 194; 25 W. R. 196.
(*o*) 25 & 26 Vict. c. 22, s. 31.
(*p*) 24 & 25 Vict. c. 99, s. 22.
(*q*) Sect. 8.
(*r*) Sect. 11.
(*s*) Sect. 23, and see R. v. *Owen*, 53 J. P. 822.
(*t*) Sect. 9.

uttering (*u*), or uttering foreign medals, &c., with intent (*v*), or foreign counterfeit gold or silver (*w*) or base copper coin (*x*).

There need be no impression (*y*), and genuine money which has been filed is within the section (*z*). "Ringing the changes" is an uttering (*a*), but it is doubtful whether it is so in the case of money given in charity (*b*).

Defacing coin by stamping words thereon (*c*).

Tendering such defaced coin (*d*).

It need not be accepted to complete the offence (*e*).

Contagious diseases. Arrest under the Contagious Diseases Act extends also to the case of persons reasonably suspected (*f*) of being engaged in committing an offence, and is only to be exercised on the refusal of the party to give his name and address (*g*).

The offences are:—

Contravention of Act, Order of Council, or regulation of local authority.

Failing to keep diseased animal separate, or to give notice to the police (*h*).

The person must be aware of the fact that the animal is diseased (*i*).

Failing to give, produce, observe, or do any notice, licence, rule or thing required by the Act, or order or regulation, doing anything unlawful or omitting where omission is unlawful under the Act, refusing admission to officer when entitled to enter, or obstructing or impeding or throwing carcase of any diseased animal into river or sea within three miles of shore (*j*).

Using expired or blank licence or falsifying, fraudulently attempting to obtain compensation from Privy Council or local authority for slaughtered animal, or aiding or abetting, digging up carcase buried by order, or using prohibited vehicles (*k*).

Explosives. Power to arrest under the Explosives Act is also conferred on officers of the local authority (*l*). Constables may remove from licensed factories unauthorized persons (*m*).

The offences are:—

Manufacture at or keeping at unauthorized place (*n*).

Carrying on factory contrary to licence except using, in case

---

(*u*) Sect. 10.
(*v*) Sect. 13.
(*w*) Sect. 20.
(*x*) Sect. 15.
(*y*) *R.* v. *Welsh*, 1 East, P. C. 87, 164; 1 Leach, C. C. 364; *R.* v. *Wilson*. ib. 285.
(*z*) *R.* v. *Herrmann*, 4 Q. B. D. 284; 48 L. J. M. C. 106; 14 Cox, C. C. 279; 27 W. R. 475; 40 L. T. 263; 43 J. P. 398.
(*a*) *R.* v. *Franks*, 2 Leach, 736.
(*b*) *R.* v. *Page*, 8 C. & P. 122; *R.* v. ——, 1 Cox, 250, and see *R.* v. *Ion*,

2 Den. C. C. 484.
(*c*) 24 & 25 Vict. c. 99, s. 16.
(*d*) Sect. 17.
(*e*) *R.* v. *Radford*, 1 Den. 59; *R.* v. *John*, 2 ib. 495; 21 L. J. M. C. 166.
(*f*) See ante, p. 82.
(*g*) 41 & 42 Vict. c. 74, s. 50.
(*h*) Sect. 61.
(*i*) *Nicols* v. *Hall*, 8 C. P. 322.
(*j*) Sect. 50.
(*k*) Sect. 62.
(*l*) 38 & 39 Vict. c. 17, s. 78.
(*m*) Sect. 77.
(*n*) Sects. 4 and 5.

of emergency or temporarily, one part of a building for another process of manufacture (*o*).

Factory to be kept for that purpose only, fittings of danger buildings to be covered, lightning conductors provided unless considered unnecessary, taking articles liable to spontaneous ignition into danger, except for immediate use, repairs not to be done in danger building until room cleansed, notice outside danger building of quantity of ingredients allowed and copy of rules; tools to be wood or copper, and covered, suitable working clothes to be provided, no smoking, except in part allowed, vehicles for conveyance to have no exposed iron or steel, person under sixteen not to be employed except under supervision of adult, ingredients when process complete to be removed to magazine and to be sifted before use (*p*).

Stores.—Provisions of Order in Council to be observed, amount not to exceed that on licence, stores to be kept for that purpose only, fittings of danger buildings to be covered, lightning conductors except store less than 1000 lbs., repairs not to be done in danger building until room cleansed, tools to be wood or copper and covered, suitable working clothes to be provided, no smoking except in part allowed, person under sixteen not to be employed except under supervision of adult (*q*).

Retail.—To be in house or safe, latter to be safe distance from highway, amount, detached safe 200 lbs., in dwelling-house 50 lbs., in safe in dwelling-house 100 lbs., explosive articles not to be kept in or near safe, no exposed iron or steel in interior of receptacle, or more than one pound to be in case or bag (*r*).

All precautions to be taken to prevent fire or explosion and unauthorized persons having access (*rr*).

Hawking on highway (*s*).

Selling to children under thirteen (*t*).

Sale to be in closed packages, labelled (*u*).

Packing and Conveyance.—Not exceeding five pounds in case, over five pounds, if single, box to be approved, if double, inner to be a case approved, interior to be free from grit, not used for any other purpose, no iron or steel unless covered, not to exceed 100 lbs., to be branded (*v*).

Manufacturing prohibited articles (*w*).

Gunmakers.—In filling room not more than five pounds, except in safety cartridges, no other work to be carried on, no fire or artificial light unless protected, room to be detached from magazine, notice of intention to use as filling room (*x*).

Mines and Quarries.—Not more than prescribed amount, no

(*o*) Sect. 9.
(*p*) Sect. 10.
(*q*) Sect. 17.
(*r*) Sect. 22.
(*rr*) Sect. 23.
(*s*) Sect. 30.

(*t*) Sect. 31.
(*u*) Sect. 32.
(*v*) Sect. 33.
(*w*) Sect. 43.
(*x*) Sect. 46.

other work to be carried on, room to be detached from magazine, one kind not to be made into another nor resolved into its ingredients, notice of intention to use as filling room (*y*).

Failing to admit Government inspector (*z*), or to give notice of dangerous practices (*a*), or of accidents (*b*).

Reconstructing buildings destroyed by accident without consent of Secretary of State (*c*).

Obstructing officers of local authority (*d*).

Throwing fireworks in public thoroughfares (*e*).

Forging licences (*f*).

Defacing notices (*g*).

Gaming. Persons agreeing to pay money or deliver goods on the event of a game or lottery may be apprehended (*h*).

Hawkers. So also may hawkers without licence, or not producing licence (*i*).

A travelling auctioneer is within the Act (*j*).

Highways. As to highways, see *post* (*k*).

Indecent advertisements. As to indecent advertisements, the offences are:—

Affixing to or inscribing on any house, &c, or delivering or attempting to deliver, or exhibiting to any inhabitant any picture or printed or written matter of an indecent or obscene nature (*l*), or procuring others to do so (*m*).

Industrial schools. Under the Industrial Schools Act children apparently under fourteen may be arrested for begging, wandering, being destitute, or frequenting the company of reputed thieves (*n*). Also children escaping from such school (*o*).

Larceny. The Larceny Act (*p*) is extended to naval (*q*) and public stores (*r*). The offences are:—

Larceny after a previous conviction for felony (*s*), or indictable misdemeanour (*t*).

Inducing to execute a deed by fraud (*u*).

Dog-stealing (*v*), or possession of stolen dogs (*w*), or taking money to restore (*x*).

Embezzlement by agents (*y*), bankers, attorneys, &c. (*z*).

Trust money paid off from a mortgage, and in the hands of a

(*y*) Sect. 47.
(*z*) Sect. 55.
(*a*) Sect. 56.
(*b*) Sect. 63.
(*c*) Sect. 64.
(*d*) Sect. 69.
(*e*) Sect. 80.
(*f*) Sect. 81.
(*g*) Sect. 82.
(*h*) 42 Geo. 3, c. 119, s. 6.
(*i*) 51 & 52 Vict. c. 33, s. 6.
(*j*) *Hudson* v. *Shooter*, 55 J. P. 325.
(*k*) Page 134, and *Bach* v. *Holmes*, 57 L. J. M. C. 37; 16 Cox, C. C. 263; 56 L. T. 713; 51 J. P. 693.

(*l*) 52 & 53 Vict. c. 18, s. 3.
(*m*) Sect. 4.
(*n*) 29 & 30 Vict. c. 118, s. 14.
(*o*) Sect. 33.
(*p*) 24 & 25 Vict. c. 96.
(*q*) 32 & 33 Vict. c. 12, s. 10.
(*r*) 38 & 39 Vict. c. 25, s. 12.
(*s*) 24 & 25 Vict. c. 96, s. 7.
(*t*) Sect. 8.
(*u*) Sect. 90.
(*v*) Sect. 18.
(*w*) Sect. 19.
(*x*) Sect. 20.
(*y*) Sect. 75, see *R.* v. *Bowerman*, 39 W. R. 207; 55 J. P. 373.
(*z*) Sect. 76.

solicitor is within the section (*a*), but money simply lent for investment is not (*b*).

By factors (*c*), trustees (*d*), directors (*e*), directors keeping fraudulent accounts (*f*), destroying books (*g*), or publishing fraudulent statements (*h*).

Setting engines for deer (*i*).

Obtaining money, chattels, or security by false pretences (*j*).

This includes a trailway ticket (*k*), and an order on the treasurer of a burial society (*l*), but not a dog (*m*). The goods need not be in existence at the time if they are subsequently delivered (*n*).

Stealing fences (*o*).

Taking fish in land belonging to dwelling-house, other than angling in the daytime (*p*).

Stealing fruit (*q*).

Killing hares, &c., in warren (*r*).

Stealing oysters from beds (*s*).

Shipwrecked goods, in possession without satisfactory account (*t*)—offering for sale (*u*).

Simple larceny (*v*).

This includes "ringing the changes." (*w*).

Stealing domestic animals or birds (*x*), or found in possession without satisfactory account (*y*).

Tree stealing (*z*).

Stealing vegetables (*a*).

Found in possession of venison without giving satisfactory account (*b*).

Found in possession of wood similarly (*c*).

Receiving any of the above (*d*).

As to offences against the Malicious Injury to Property Act, the damage done must be more than nominal, and done with

Malicious injury to property.

(*a*) R. v. *Fullagar*, 14 Cox, C. C. 370; 41 L. T. 448; 44 J. P. 57.
(*b*) R. v. *Newman*, 8 Q. B. D. 706; 51 L. J. M. C. 87; 46 L. T. 394; 20 W. R. 550; 46 J. P. 612. *Cf.* R. v. *Christian*, L. R. 2 C. C. 94; 43 L. J. M. C. 1; 24 L. T. 654; 22 W. R. 132; 12 Cox, 502.
(*c*) Sect. 78.
(*d*) Sect. 80.
(*e*) Sect. 81.
(*f*) Sect. 82.
(*g*) Sect. 83.
(*h*) Sect. 84.
(*i*) Sect. 15.
(*j*) Sect. 88.
(*k*) R. v. *Boulton*, 1 Den. C. C. 508; 19 L. J. M. C. 67; 3 Cox, C. C. 576; 13 Jur. 1034.
(*l*) R. v. *Greenhalgh*, 1 D. C. C. 267; 6 Cox, C. C. 257.

(*m*) R. v. *Robinson*, 28 L. J. M. C. 58.
(*n*) R. v. *Martin*, 1 C. C. R. 56; 36 L. J. M. C. 20; 10 Cox, C. C. 383; 15 W. R. 358; 15 L. T. 54.
(*o*) 24 & 25 Vict. c. 96, s. 34.
(*p*) Sect. 24.
(*q*) Sect. 36.
(*r*) Sect. 17.
(*s*) Sect. 26.
(*t*) Sect. 65.
(*u*) Sect. 66.
(*v*) Sect. 4.
(*w*) R. v. *Hollis*, 12 Q. B. D. 25.
(*x*) Sect. 21.
(*y*) Sect. 22.
(*z*) Sect. 33.
(*a*) Sect. 37.
(*b*) Sect. 14.
(*c*) Sect. 35.
(*d*) Sect. 95.

96   EXECUTIVE OFFICERS.

intent to damage (*e*). A trespass can only be wilful and malicious when it is committed by a person who knows he has no pretence of right to enter the land (*f*), and does not extend to playing bowls on the turf (*g*), nor placing poisoned flesh on inclosed land (*h*).

The offences are:—
Killing or maiming animals (*i*).
Rioters injuring buildings (*j*).
Destroying dams (*k*) or fences (*l*).
Poisoning fish (*m*).
Destroying fruit in gardens (*n*) or elsewhere (*o*).
Making gunpowder with intent (*p*).
Injuring telegraphs (*q*) or attempts (*r*).
Injury by tenants (*s*).
Obstructing trains (*t*).
Changing a signal (*u*) or stopping by holding up one's arms is within the section (*v*).
Damaging trees (*w*).
Destroying vegetables in gardens (*x*) or elsewhere (*y*).
Destroying works of art (*z*).
Any damage over £5 (*a*).
Aiding or abetting any of these (*b*).

Night offences. Anyone may apprehend persons found committing indictable offences (*c*) in the night time (*d*).

Vagrants. The offences under the Vagrant Act (*e*) are:—
Begging or causing children to do so (*f*).

The section does not apply to persons unless their habit and mode of life is to wander abroad and beg (*g*), nor to discharged

---

(*e*) *Eley* v. *Lythe*, 50 J. P. 308; *R.* v. *Pembliton*, L. R. 2 C. C. 119; 43 L. J. M. C. 912; see *R.* v. *Welch*, 1 Q. B. D. 23; 45 L. J. M. C. 17, and *Hall* v. *Richardson*, 54 J. P. 345; 6 T. L. R. 91.

(*f*) *Looker* v. *Halcomb*, 4 Bing. 183; 12 Moo. 416; *Usher* v. *Luxmore*, 62 L. T. 110; 38 W. R. 254; 54 J. P. 405.

(*g*) *Laws* v. *Eltringham*, 51 L. J. M. C. 13; 8 Q. B. D. 283; 46 L. T. 64.

(*h*) *Daniel* v. *James*, 2 C. P. D. 351.

(*i*) 24 & 25 Vict. c. 97, s. 41.
(*j*) Sect. 12.
(*k*) Sect. 32.
(*l*) Sect. 25.
(*m*) Sect. 32.
(*n*) Sect. 23.
(*o*) Sect. 24.
(*p*) Sect. 54.
(*q*) Sect. 37.
(*r*) Sect. 38.

(*s*) Sect. 13.
(*t*) Sect. 36.
(*u*) *R.* v. *Hadfield*, 39 L. J. M. C. 131; L. R. 1 C. C. 253; 33 J. P. 548; 18 W. R. 955; 22 L. T. 664.
(*v*) *R.* v. *Hardy*, 40 L. J. M. C. 62; L. R. 1 C. C. 278; 11 Cox, C. C. 656; 19 W. R. 359; 35 J. P. 198; 23 L. T. 785.
(*w*) Sect. 22.
(*x*) Sect. 23.
(*y*) Sect. 24.
(*z*) Sect. 39.
(*a*) Sect. 51.
(*b*) Sect. 63.
(*c*) See *ante*, p. 48.
(*d*) 9 P.M. to 6 A.M.: 14 & 15 Vict. c. 19, s. 11.
(*e*) 5 Geo. 4, c. 83.
(*f*) Sect. 3.
(*g*) *Pointon* v. *Hill*, 12 Q. B. D. 306; 53 L. J. M. C. 62; 50 L. T. 268; 32 W. R. 478; 48 J. P. 341; 15 Cox, 461.

soldiers and sailors *en route* to their homes or their wives, provided with certificate of settlement (*h*).

Exposing person indecently—to insult female.

Exposing wounds for alms, or fraudulently collecting the same.

Fortune-telling or other deception (*i*).

This extends to "spirit-rapping" (*j*) and astrology (*k*).

Found on enclosed premises for unlawful purpose (*l*).

The purpose must be criminal, not merely immoral (*m*). It applies if the person is seen in the house but gets out and is taken on fresh pursuit, although he was not seen getting out of the house, but was found concealed on other premises near (*n*).

In possession of burglarious instruments or any weapon with intent (*o*).

Not maintaining family (*p*).

This does not apply in case of desertion by wife (*q*) or if there be an offer to support (*r*).

Obscene pictures, shewing in streets or shops.

Pedlars unlicensed.

Prostitutes misbehaving in streets, &c. (*s*).

Playing or betting in street or public place with tables, coins, cards, tokens, &c. (*t*).

Depositing money with a betting agent is not within the section (*u*).

A railway carriage is a public place (*v*), and so is a place to which the public have access, though not of right (*w*).

A *pari mutuel* is an instrument of gaming (*x*).

Returning to parish after removal by order of justices (*y*).

Suspected person or reputed thief frequenting wharves, highways, and places of public resort with intent (*z*).

(*h*) 43 Geo. 3, c. 61.
(*i*) 5 Geo. 4, c. 83, s. 4.
(*j*) *Monck* v. *Hilton*, L. R. 2 Ex. D. 268; 46 L. J. M. C. 163; 36 L. T. 66; 41 J. P. 214; 25 W. R. 373.
(*k*) *Penny* v. *Hanson*, 18 Q. B. D. 478; 56 L. J. M. C. 41; 16 Cox, C C. 173; 56 L. T. 235; 35 W. R. 379; 51 J. P. 167.
(*l*) Sect. 4.
(*m*) *Hayes* v. *Stevenson*, 9 W. R. 53; 3 L. T. 296; 24 J. P. 740.
(*n*) *R.* v. *Howarth*, 1 Moo. C. C. 207.
(*o*) Sect. 4.
(*p*) Sect. 3. 7 & 8 Vict. c. 100, s. 6, renders the mother liable in case of an illegitimate child. But arrest without warrant is not valid in either case: *Horley* v. *Rogers*, 6 Jur. N. S. 605.
(*q*) *R.* v. *Flinton*, 1 B. & A. 227.

(*r*) *Flannagan* v. *Bishopwearmouth*, 27 L. J. M. C. 46; 8 E. & B. 451; 3 Jur. N. S. 1103; 6 W. R. 38; 22 J. P. 464.
(*s*) Sect. 3.
(*t*) 36 & 37 Vict. c. 38.
(*u*) *Hirst* v. *Molesbury*, L. R. 6 Q. B. 130; 40 L. J. M. C. 76; 19 W. R. 246; 35 J. P. 229; 23 L. T. 555.
(*v*) *Langrish* v. *Archer*, 10 Q. B. D. 44; 52 L. J. M. C. 47; 15 Cox, 194; 47 L. T. 548; 31 W. R. 183; 47 J. P. 295.
(*w*) *Turnbull* v. *Appleton*, 45 J. P. 469.
(*x*) *Tollett* v. *Thomas*, L. R. 6 Q. B. 514; 40 L. J. M. C. 209; 19 W. R. 890; 35 J. P. 359; 24 L. T. 508.
(*y*) Sect. 3.
(*z*) Sect. 4.

The person must be seen more than once to be frequenting (*a*).

A private house during a sale is a place of public resort (*b*), and so is a railway platform (*c*), but a steamboat is not (*d*).

Wandering without visible means of subsistence and not giving a good account of oneself (*e*).

Game.

Three persons or more, any of such persons being armed, entering land for the purpose of taking game or rabbits at night may be arrested (*f*).

All the persons need not have entered the land (*g*).

Gardens in towns.

Persons throwing any rubbish into any public garden, or trespassing, or climbing the fences, or stealing or damaging the flowers and plants, or committing any nuisance there, are liable to arrest (*h*)

Gun.

So are persons carrying a gun, refusing to give name and address when required (*i*).

Hue and cry.

A constable concurring in pursuit or hue and cry after an alleged felon is justified in arresting whether the party be innocent or a felony be committed or not (*j*).

Indecent exposure.

Indecent exposure in a public place (*k*). It is not necessary that the place be open to the public (*l*), and they may even be trespassers (*m*). But it must take place in the presence of more than one person (*n*). An omnibus is a place (*o*), and so is a urinal (*p*), and a booth at races (*q*), and bathing without covering is an offence (*r*).

Licensing.

Persons on licensed premises during closing hours refusing to give correct name and address may be arrested (*s*).

(*a*) *Re Cross*, 26 L. J. M. C. 28; 1 H. & N. 651; *R.* v. *Clark*, 14 Q. B. D. 92; 54 L. J. M. C. 66; 52 L. T. 136; 33 W. R. 226; 49 J. P. 246.
(*b*) *Sewell* v. *Taylor*, 29 L. J. M. C. 50; 6 Jur. N. S. 502; 6 C. B. N. S. 160; 8 W. R. 26; 23 J. P. 792; 1 L. T. 37.
(*c*) *Ex parte Davis*, 26 L. J. M. C. 178; 21 J. P. 280; 5 W. R. 522.
(*d*) *R.* v. *Taylor*, 21 J. P. 488.
(*e*) Sect. 4.
(*f*) 9 Geo. 4, c. 69, s. 9.
(*g*) *R.* v. *Whittaker*, 17 L. J. M. C. 127; 11 L. T. 310; *R.* v. *Vezzell*, 20 L. J. M. C. 192; *R.* v. *Wood*, 25 ib. 96; 1 D. & B. C. C. 1.
(*h*) 26 Vict. c. 13, s. 5. This Act only applies where land is irrevocably set apart for public use; *Tulk* v. *Metropolitan Board of Works*, 8 B. & S. 813; L. R. 3 Q. B. 682; 37 L. J. Q. B. 272; 32 J. P. 548; 16 W. R. 985.
(*i*) 33 & 34 Vict. c. 57, s. 9.
(*j*) Hawk. P. C. 62, c. 12, s. 16;

and see 50 & 51 Vict. c. 55, s. 8.
(*k*) See 14 & 15 Vict. c. 100, s. 29.
(*l*) *R.* v. *Thallman*, L. & C. 326; 33 L. J. M. C. 58; 9 Cox, C. C. 388; 9 L. T. 425; 12 W. R. 88.
(*m*) *R.* v. *Wellard*, 14 Q. B. D. 63; 54 L. J. M. C. 11; 51 L. T. 604; 33 W. R. 156; 49 J. P. 296; 15 Cox, C. C. 559.
(*n*) *R.* v. *Webb*, 1 Den. 338; 18 L. J. M. C. 39; 2 C. & K. 993; *R.* v. *Watson*, 2 Cox, C. C. 376. But see *R.* v. *Elliott*, L. & C. 103. As to baths, see 41 & 42 Vict. c. 14, s. 11.
(*o*) *R.* v. *Holmes*, D. C. C. 207; 3 C. & R. 360; 6 Cox, C. C. 216; 22 L. J. M. C. 122; 17 Jur. 562.
(*p*) *R.* v. *Harris*, L. R. 1 C. C. 282; 40 L. J. M. C. 67; 11 Cox, C. C. 659; 24 L. T. 74; 19 W. R. 360.
(*q*) *R.* v. *Saunders*, 1 Q. B. D. 1; 45 L. J. M. C. 11; 13 Cox. C. C. 116; 33 L. T. 677; 24 W. R. 348.
(*r*) *R.* v *Reed*, 11 Cox, C. C. 689; *R.* v. *Crunden*, 2 Camp. 89.
(*s*) 35 & 36 Vict. c. 94, s. 25.

Premises other than those under exceptional licences, if situate in the metropolitan district (*i.e.* in the city or within four miles of Charing Cross), must be closed on week days (other than Saturdays) from 12.30 to 5.30 A.M. If beyond that area, but in the metropolitan police district, or in a town or place with a population of not less than 1000, determined to be a populous place by the licensing committee, from 11 P.M. to 6 A.M. Elsewhere from 10 P.M. to 6 A.M.

On Saturday and Sunday—

In the met. dist. from	12 Sat. night	to	1 P.M. Sun.
„ „	11 Sun.	„	5 A.M. Mon.
In met. pol. dist. or populous place	„ 11 Sat.	„	12.30 P.M. Sun.
	„ 10 Sun.	„	6 A.M. Mon.
Elsewhere .	„ 10 Sat.	„	12.30 P.M. Sun.
„ .	„ 10 Sun.	„	6 A.M. Mon.

Sunday met. dist. 3.0, elsewhere 2.30 to 6 P.M.

There may be a sale to persons lodging in the house or in case of railway-stations to persons arriving or departing by train, and to *bonâ fide* travellers (*t*).

Persons misconducting themselves in public-houses may also be arrested (*u*).

Persons damaging or extinguishing street lamps are also liable (*v*). Lighting.

Lunatics wandering may be apprehended (*w*) and taken to the workhouse (*x*). Lunatics.

Merchant seamen deserting are liable to arrest (*y*). Merchant seamen.

So also are pedlars refusing to produce certificate, or to permit inspection of pack (*z*). Pedlar.

Commercial travellers, vendors of books authorized by publishers, sellers of articles of food and for charitable purposes are not within the Act (*a*).

Casual paupers may be removed from the ward to the workhouse (*b*). Poor.

Persons leaving without authority or escaping from ships liable to quarantine may be arrested (*bb*). Quarantine.

Where a constable arrests a person on a reasonable charge preferred by another person he is under no liability for so doing if he act purely ministerially. The liability (if any) rests with the party so giving in charge (*c*). Reasonable charge.

(*t*) 37 & 38 Vict. c. 49, ss. 3, 10.
(*u*) 35 & 36 Vict. c. 94, s. 18; *Howell* v. *Jackson*, 6 C. & P. 723; and see 37 & 38 Vict. c. 49, s. 17.
(*v*) 3 & 4 Will. 4, c. 90, s. 55.
(*w*) 53 & 54 Vict. c. 5, ss. 15, 20.
(*x*) 48 & 49 Vict. c. 52, s. 2.
(*y*) 17 & 18 Vict. c. 104, s. 246.
(*z*) 34 & 35 Vict. c. 96, s. 18.
(*a*) *R.* v. *Hodgkinson*, 10 B. & C. 74; 5 M. & R. 162; *Gregg* v. *Smith*, 42 L. J. M. C. 121; L. R. 8 Q. B. 302; 21 W. R. 737; 37 J. P. 679; 28 L. T. 555.
(*b*) See *post*, p. 133.
(*bb*) 6 Geo. 4, c. 78, s. 19.
(*c*) *Flewster* v. *Royle*, 1 Camp. 188; *Glynn* v. *Houston*, 2 M. & G. 337; 2 Sc. N. R. 554; 2 Jur. 125; and see *Creagh* v. *Gamble*, 24 L. R. Ir. 458; *Hogg* v. *Ward*, 3 H. & N. 417; and *cf.* *Grinham* v. *Willey*, 28 L. J. Ex. 242; 4 H. & N. 496; 5 Jur. 441.

Reformatory school. Offenders escaping from a reformatory school are liable to arrest (d).

Rescue. And so are persons who rescue or attempt to rescue persons from custody or who obstruct officers (e).

Rout. A rout is a breach of the peace. It is a meeting of persons, three or more, upon a purpose which if executed would make them rioters, and which they actually make a motion to execute (f).

Swearing. Constables may arrest any unknown person taking a profane oath in their hearing (g).

Canals and Rivers.

Canals and rivers. These officers may arrest disorderly persons, night loiterers, and persons suspected of having committed or being about to commit offences against the Act (h).

Persons found committing (i) offences may be arrested by any constable (j).

The offences are:—
Assaulting constables on duty (k).
Injuring contents of packages (l).
Possessing instruments, &c., for carrying away liquor, &c. (m).
Stolen property—offering in pawn (n).

Metropolitan.

Metropolitan. The following persons may be arrested in the Metropolitan Police District.

Animals shewn, fed, shod, or exercised in street. Every person who shall, to the annoyance of the inhabitants or passengers, expose for show or sale (except in market), or feed animals, or shew any caravan containing animal, or public entertainment, or shoe, &c., any animal (except in case of accident), or clean, &c., or break or exercise any animal (o).

This does not apply to cattle turned out under the supervision of a boy (p).

On footway. Or lead or ride any animal, or drive any carriage, &c., or fasten horse, &c., on footway.

Assembly unlawful. Persons taking part in open-air meetings (except for the election of members) within a mile of Westminster Hall during the sittings of, and with a view to intimidate Parliament or the

(d) 29 & 30 Vict. c. 117, s. 21.
(e) 48 & 49 Vict. c. 75, s. 2.
(f) 4 Black. 146. See unlawful assembly, *ante*, p. 79.
(g) 19 Geo. 2, c. 21, s. 3.
(h) 3 & 4 Vict. c. 50, s. 10.
(i) *Ante*, p. 91.
(j) Sect. 11.
(k) Sect. 6.
(l) Sect. 8.

(m) Sect. 7.
(n) Sect. 12.
(o) 2 & 3 Vict. c. 47, s. 54. The offences under this section must be committed within view of the constable in a thoroughfare or public place.
(p) See *Sherborn* v. *Wells*, 32 L. J. M. C. 179; 3 B. & S. 784; 11 W. R. 594; 27 J. P. 566; 8 L. T. 274.

INHERENT POWERS. 101

Courts of Law (*q*), or more than ten persons repairing to the Queen or Parliament to present a petition or address (*r*).

The public have no right to occupy Trafalgar Square for meetings if prohibited by the Commissioners of Works (*s*).

Three or more persons betting (*t*). — Betting.

In some cases arrest may take place for breach of bye-laws (*u*). — Bye-laws.

Causing carriages to stand longer than necessary or thereby causing obstructions (*v*), or cleaning or repairing (except in case of accident). — Carriages standing, repairing.

Persons misbehaving in the driving of cattle or unlawfully pelting or hunting them (*w*). — Cattle, negligent driving.

Or damaging person or property and refusing to make amends (*x*), or property of the local authority (*y*). — Damage to person or property.

Persons idle and disorderly (*z*). — Disorderly persons.

These words must be construed strictly (*a*).

Suffering ferocious dogs to be at large, or causing them to worry persons or animals (*b*). — Ferocious dog.

Booths open in fairs between 11 P.M. and 6 A.M., the owners or managers thereof (*c*), or when such fair has been declared illegal. — Fairs.

Persons furiously riding or driving (*d*). — Furious driving.

Persons damaging fences, or affixing placards thereto without consent of owner, or damaging trees, shrubs, or seats (*e*). — Fences, damaging.

Persons interfering with the operations of the fire brigade may be removed (*f*). — Fires.

Persons wantonly discharging fire-arms or throwing missiles or making bonfires, or throwing fireworks, may be arrested (*g*). — Fire arms, missiles, &c.

So also may persons selling, distributing or exhibiting indecent prints, songs or exhibitions. — Indecent prints, songs, or exhibitions.

And those, except guards of the Post Office, blowing or using any noisy instrument to announce a show, or to hawk or sell articles or obtain alms. — Noisy instruments.

And persons unlawfully knocking at doors, ringing bells, or extinguishing lamps. — Knocking at doors, &c.

Or rolling casks, &c., or carrying planks or ladders, &c., on any footway. — Ladders, &c., on footway.

Or using threatening or abusive or insulting words or behaviour (*h*). — Abusive language.

Or unknown persons acting in parks in contravention of the rules thereof. — Parks.

(*q*) 57 Geo. 3, c. 19, s. 23; and see 28 & 29 Vict. c. 48, s. 18.
(*r*) 13 Car. 2, c. 5.
(*s*) *Ex parte Lewis*, 21 Q. B. D. 191; 57 L. J. M. C. 108; 59 L. T. 338; 37 W. R. 13; 52 J. P. 773; *R.* v. *Graham*, 16 Cox, C. C. 420.
(*t*) 30 & 31 Vict. c. 134, s. 23; see 48 & 49 Vict. c. 18.
(*u*) 54 & 55 Vict. c. 76, s. 16.
(*v*) 2 & 3 Vict. c. 47, s. 54.
(*w*) Ibid.
(*x*) 2 & 3 Vict. c. 47, s. 62.
(*y*) 18 & 19 Vict. c. 120, s. 216.
(*z*) 2 & 3 Vict. c. 47, s. 58.
(*a*) *Stocken* v. *Carter*, 4 C. P. 477. And see 10 Geo. 4, c. 44, s. 7.
(*b*) 2 & 3 Vict. c. 47, s. 54.
(*c*) Sect. 38.
(*d*) Ibid.
(*e*) Ibid.
(*f*) 28 & 29 Vict. c. 90, s. 12.
(*g*) 2 & 3 Vict. c. 47, s. 54.
(*h*) Ibid.

These rules are:—

1. Driving vehicles not admitted, or when admitted otherwise than according to rule.
2. Riding contrary to rule, or exercising or training or riding or driving furiously, or on road closed by notice in writing.
3. Drilling, playing games, practising gymnastics, or selling or letting commodities other than according to rule.
4. Delivering addresses contrary to rule.
5. Intoxicated person.
6. Walking on beds or enclosed grounds.
7. Fishing, bathing or skating not according to rule.
8. Dogs at large other than according to rule.
9. Destroying trees, seats, railings, or exhibiting advertisements.
10. Indecency or profane language.
11. Discharging fire-arms, throwing missiles, or making bonfires or letting off fireworks.
12. Wilful interference with or annoyance of any other person.
13. Worrying animals grazing or birds in water.
14. Entering and remaining between sunset and sunrise except to pass along way kept open.

This Act applies to Hyde, St. James' and the Green Parks, Kensington Gardens, Parliament Square Garden, Regent and Kennington Parks, Primrose Hill, Battersea and Greenwich Parks, Kew Gardens Pleasure Grounds and Green, Hampton Court Park, Gardens and Green; Richmond Park and Green, and Bushey Park (*i*).

Playing games. Poor.
Persons playing games or making slides (*j*).
Destitute persons may be conducted to places of reception for paupers (*k*).

Prostitute.
Prostitutes soliciting may be apprehended (*l*).

Public stores.
Persons reasonably suspected of conveying stores stolen from Her Majesty may be stopped, searched, and detained (*m*).

Regulations, disobedience to.
Persons refusing to conform to regulations for traffic (*n*), or when specially approved by the Secretary of State, shall refuse to regard the same, and to give name and address (*o*), are liable to arrest.

Riding on shafts, &c.
So are persons riding on shafts, or not having proper control of horses or other animals drawing (*p*).

River, ships, on, &c.
Persons suspected of felony may be arrested on board ship by a superintendent, inspector, or serjeant (*q*); and any constable may arrest any one unloading or throwing into the Thames any rubbish or refuse, or on the shore thereof, or into the streams

(*i*) 35 & 36 Vict. c. 15, ss. 5, 7, 10. Park-keepers have the same powers as constables. Commons are managed under local Acts. See *ante*, p. 62.
(*j*) 2 & 3 Vict. c. 47, s. 54.
(*k*) 28 & 29 Vict. c. 34, s. 7.

(*l*) 2 & 3 Vict. c. 47, s. 54.
(*m*) 38 & 39 Vict. c. 25, s. 6.
(*n*) 2 & 3 Vict. c. 47, s. 54.
(*o*) 30 & 31 Vict. c. 134, s. 12.
(*p*) 2 & 3 Vict. c. 47, s. 54.
(*q*) Sect. 34.

communicating therewith, or suffering offensive matter to flow into the said river (*r*).

Unknown persons sweeping dirt into sewers (*s*), or interrupting workmen of the local authority (*t*), may be arrested. *Sewers, &c.*

So also may persons reasonably suspected of having or conveying things stolen (*u*). *Stolen goods.*

This applies only to possession in the streets (*v*); but the offender may be arrested subsequently on immediate pursuit not in a street (*w*).

And unknown offenders against this Act (*x*), or persons found committing any such offences (*y*). *Unknown persons and those found committing.*

The misdemeanours in this Act are—
Breaking packages in order to spill contents (on river) (*z*).
Cutting ropes, cables, &c. (*a*).
Being drunk and disorderly (*b*).
Framing false bills of parcels (*c*).
Letting articles fall into river with intent (*d*).
Piercing casks, opening packages (river) (*e*).
Possessing instruments for unlawfully carrying away wine, &c. (*f*).
Receiving ships' stores from seamen (*g*).

Persons arrested must be forthwith delivered into the custody of the constable in charge of the nearest station (*h*). *Delivery at station.*

Forthwith means with reasonable promptness (*i*).

County and Municipal.

The special powers of these officers are confined to the arrest of idle and disorderly persons, disturbers of the public *County and municipal.*

(*r*) 27 & 28 Vict. c. 113, s. 74.
(*s*) 18 & 19 Vict. c. 120, ss. 205, 229.
(*t*) Sect. 218.
(*u*) 2 & 3 Vict. c. 47, s. 66.
(*v*) *Hadley* v. *Perks*, L. R. 1 Q. B. 444; 12 Jur. N. S. 662; 35 L. J. M. C. 177; 14 W. R. 730; 14 L. T. 325; 6 B. & S. 375.
(*w*) *R.* v. *Fisher*, 32 L. T. 22.
(*x*) Sect. 63, and see the offences mentioned in s. 60, which consist of shortly, cleansing articles, &c., in street, throwing rubbish, beating mats (except door-mats before 8 A.M.), throwing litter, &c., except sand in frost or matter to prevent noise in sickness, emptying soil, &c., between 6 A.M. and 8 P.M., keeping pig-styes to the front of a street, occupiers not cleansing footways, selling articles in parks, &c., except by consent of authority, hanging goods over ways,
or setting up poles or awnings so as to obstruct, leaving open vaults or cellars dangerously or insufficiently fenced.
(*y*) Sect. 66.
(*z*) Sect. 32.
(*a*) Sect. 27.
(*b*) Sect. 58.
(*c*) Sect. 29.
(*d*) Sect. 28.
(*e*) Sect. 31.
(*f*) Sect. 30.
(*g*) Sect. 26.
(*h*) Sect. 69.
(*i*) *R.* v. *Ashton*, 1 L. M. & P. 491; 19 L. J. M. C. 236; 14 Jur. 1045; 15 L. T. 259; 15 J. P. 9; *Hancock* v. *Somes*, El. & El. 795; 28 L. J. M. C. 196; 8 Cox, C. C. 172; 7 W. R. 422; 23 J. P. 662; *Costar* v *Hetherington*, El. & El. 802; 28 L. J. M. C. 198; 8 Cox, C. C. 175; 7 W. R. 413; 23 J. P. 663.

peace, and persons reasonably suspected of intention to commit felony (*j*).

Towns.

The Towns Police Clauses Act applies to all urban authorities under the Public Health Act (*k*).

The powers of arrest here are—

Animals, &c., shewn, fed, in street. Persons shewing or selling (except in a market or fair) any animal, or shoeing, farrying, cleaning, exercising, or turning them loose, or shewing any public entertainment (*l*).

An auction caravan, for which the owner paid toll, is not within the section (*m*).

Awning. Or placing any awning over a footway less than eight feet from the ground.

Carriages, &c., standing. Or allowing carriages, barrows, &c., to stand longer than necessary, or thereby interrupting a crossing or footpath; or repairing carriages (except in case of accident) (*n*).

This has been held only to apply to carriages, &c., and not to persons (*o*).

Cattle slaughtering. Dogs. Persons slaughtering cattle, except when over-driven, and killing on the spot necessary (*p*).

Or allowing any unmuzzled ferocious dog to be at large, or sets on any dog to worry any person or animal, or suffers it to be at large believing it to be in a rabid state, or after a public notice to confine dogs has been issued by a justice.

Driving. Or driving two or more carts, not fastened together at a less distance than four feet between, or driving or riding furiously.

Fire-arms. Or wantonly discharging fire-arms or fireworks, throwing stones, or making bonfires.

Games. Or flying kites or making slides.

Goods projecting on footway. Or allowing goods to project on footway so as to incommode the passage thereof, or rolling any cask, &c., or carries any ladder or timber on any footway except crossing the same, or loading and unloading any carriage, or leaving any furniture, &c., or stool, bench, or stall on any footway.

Indecent exposure Or wilfully exposing the person (*q*).

This must take place in the presence of more than one person (*r*).

or publication. Or offering for sale or distribution or exhibiting any obscene books, prints, &c., or using any profane or obscene language (*s*).

(*j*) 45 & 46 Vict. c. 50, s. 193. See 19 & 20 Vict. c. 69, ss. 6, 31. And as to parish constables, see 3 & 4 Will. 4, c. 90, s. 41.
(*k*) 38 & 39 Vict. c. 55, s. 171.
(*l*) 10 & 11 Vict. c. 89, s. 28. The offences under this section must be committed in a street, to the obstruction, annoyance, or danger of the residents or passengers, and within view of the constable; and see *Sher-born* v. *Wells, ante,* p. 100.
(*m*) *Ball* v. *Ward,* 33 L. T. 170; 40 J. P. 213.
(*n*) 10 & 11 Vict. c. 89, s. 28.
(*o*) *R.* v. *Long,* 59 L. T. 33; 52 J. P. 308; 4 Ti. Rep. 584; *R.* v. *Williams,* 55 J. P. 406.
(*p*) 10 & 11 Vict. c. 89, s. 28.
(*q*) *Ibid.*
(*r*) *R.* v. *Webb,* 18 L. J. M. C. 39.
(*s*) 10 & 11 Vict. c. 89, s. 28.

Or wilfully disturbing any inhabitant by ringing bells, knocking at doors, or unlawfully extinguishing the light of any lamp. *Knocking at doors, &c.*

Being instructed to deliver papers is no sufficient answer to a disturbance by ringing bells (*t*).

Or placing any line across a street, or hanging clothes thereon. *Lines.*

Or beating carpets or mats (except door-mats before 8 A.M.). *Mats.*

Or throwing or allowing to run into any street any offensive matter, except the laying of sand in frost or litter in sickness, if removed when the occasion ceases (*u*). *Offensive matter.*

Or keeping pigstye open to any street, &c., so as to be a nuisance. *Pigs.*

Or leaving any pit, cellar, or vault unfenced (*v*). *Pits.*

In Birmingham, Bristol, Leeds, Liverpool, and Manchester, constables may conduct destitute persons to asylums for relief (*w*). *Poor.*

Prostitutes soliciting are liable to arrest (*x*). *Prostitute.*

So also are persons having charge of carriages riding on shafts, or not having proper control, or not keeping near side, or passing on off-side, or not allowing free passage, or riding or driving on any footway, or fastening animals across the same. *Riding on shafts, &c., on footway.*

Or throwing rubbish from roof, except snow thrown so as not to fall on persons. *Rubbish.*

Or working any timber, stones, lime, &c., or drawing any timber or iron without sufficient means for guiding the same. *Timber, &c.*

Or placing heavy articles in upper windows not sufficiently guarded. *Window boxes.*

Or allowing servant to stand on sill of window for cleaning same, unless in basement story. *Window sill.*

And persons found committing (*y*) offences punishable on indictment, or as a misdemeanour against this or the special (*z*) Act. *Found committing.*

Persons are to be taken before a justice as soon as convenient, and not detained without the order of a justice more than forty-eight hours (*a*).

The misdemeanours are—

Cab-drivers misbehaving (*b*).

Drunk and disorderly (*c*).

Persons allowing chimneys to take fire (*d*).

Victuallers harbouring constables on duty (*e*).

Coffee-shop keepers harbouring disorderly persons (*f*).

(*t*) *Clarke* v. *Higgins*, 11 C. B. N. S. 545.
(*u*) Refuse may be placed on curb before 8 A.M. in box in London in streets named by the Commissioners of Sewers: 30 & 31 Vict. c. 134, s. 25.
(*v*) 10 & 11 Vict. c. 89, s. 28.
(*w*) 7 & 8 Vict. c. 101, s. 53.
(*x*) 10 & 11 Vict. c. 89, s. 28.
(*y*) See *ante*, p. 91.
(*z*) I.e. any Act passed for the regulation of towns.
(*a*) Sect. 15.
(*b*) Sect. 61.
(*c*) Sect. 29.
(*d*) Sects. 30, 31.
(*e*) Sect. 34.
(*f*) Sect. 35. An ale-house is within this section: *Cole* v. *Coulton*, 29 L. J. M. C. 125; 6 Jur. N. S. 698; 8 W. R. 412; 36 L. T. 216.

Keeping places for bear-baiting (*g*).
Pound breach (*h*).

Entry.

Entry.
Lands.
Constables are authorized to enter on lands (other than a dwelling-house or the curtilage thereof) if about to demand the production of a licence from a person carrying a gun (*i*).

Licensing.
They may also enter any house, room, or place where any public table or board is kept for playing at billiards, bagatelle, or any game of the like kind, whenever they think proper (*j*). And to detect the violation of the provisions of the Licensing Acts, which it is their duty to enforce, enter any licensed premises or any premises in respect of which an occasional licence is in force (*k*).

This section applies only to places licensed by justices (*l*), but the constable may enter, although no one is inside, nor has he reason to think there is (*m*).

Slaughterhouses.
As to slaughter-houses, they may, either alone or accompanied by any inspector appointed under 26 Geo. 3, c. 71, at all reasonable times in the day-time, enter and view the same, and take an account of all horses or cattle found thereon (*n*).

Smuggling.
They may enter on lands to prevent any signal being made to smugglers (*o*).

Threshing-machines.
And on premises where they have reason to believe a threshing-machine is worked contrary to the Act (*p*).

Trespassers.
They may not of their own motion turn trespassers off land (*q*).

Canal and River.

Canal and river.
The power of these officers to enter vessels is limited to where they have just cause to believe that an offence against the Act has been or is about to be committed thereon (*r*).

Metropolitan.

Metropolitan.
Dockyards.
These constables, employed under the Dockyard Acts (*s*), have no right to demand entrance to a licensed house to search for absentees from the Navy (*t*).

Vessels.
A superintendent or inspector may at all times, with such constables as he shall think necessary, by night or day, enter any ship, boat, &c., in the Thames, or the creeks or docks, to

---

(*g*) Sect. 36.
(*h*) Sect. 26.
(*i*) 33 & 34 Vict. c. 57, s. 10.
(*j*) 8 & 9 Vict. c. 109, s. 14.
(*k*) 37 & 38 Vict. c. 49, s. 16.
(*l*) *Harrison* v. *McL'Meel*, 48 J. P. 469; 50 L. T. 210.
(*m*) *R.* v. *Dobbins*, 48 J. P. 182; and see *Caswell* v. *Hundred House, JJ.*, 54 J. P. 87.

(*n*) 7 & 8 Vict. c. 87, s. 4, repealed as to London; 54 & 55 Vict. c. 76, s. 142.
(*o*) 39 & 40 Vict. c. 36, s. 192.
(*p*) 41 & 42 Vict. c. 12, s. 4.
(*q*) *R.* v. *Cox*, 1 F. & F. 664.
(*r*) 3 & 4 Vict. c. 50, s. 9; see *ante*, p. 82.
(*s*) 23 & 24 Vict. c. 135.
(*t*) *Turner* v. *Ford*, 37 L. T. 352.

inspect the conduct of any constable there stationed, or of the persons employed to load or unload, and to take such measures as may be necessary to prevent fire or accident and preserve the peace, and effectually prevent or detect all felonies and misdemeanours (*u*).

Search.

There is no statutory power to search a person on his arrest, and it is not certain that there is any such power at common law. In practice, however, a person apprehended for felony is searched, as well as the room or lodgings where he is taken, or happens to be living (*v*). The presumption is that in this latter case a warrant is necessary. *Search.*

Any constable may in any highway, street, or public place search any person whom he may have good cause to suspect of coming from any land where he shall have been unlawfully in search or pursuit of game (*vv*), or any person aiding or abetting such person, and having in his possession any game unlawfully obtained, or any gun, part of a gun, or nets or engines used for the killing or taking game (*w*). *Game.*

It is not necessary that any game should be found in the nets (*x*), but it should be seized on the highway (*y*) and found on the defendant's person (*z*), though this is not absolutely necessary (*a*).

Seizure and Detention.

Where a person is arrested for committing a felony or misdemeanour, any property in his possession believed to have been used by him for the purpose of committing the offence may be seized and detained as evidence in support of the charge; and, if necessary, such property may be taken from him by force, provided no unnecessary violence is used (*b*). *Seizure and detention.*

But if the seizure extend to property to which the power does not apply, it is no defence to say that in the judgment of the officer such power did apply (*c*).

Counterfeit coin and coining tools are seizable (*d*). *Coin.*

Under the Contagious Diseases Act the constable may stop, detain, and examine any animal, vehicle, boat, or thing to which an offence, or suspected offence relates, and require the same to *Contagious diseases.*

(*u*) 2 & 3 Vict. c. 47. ss. 33, 34.
(*v*) See *Dillon* v. *O'Brien, infra.*
(*vv*) Includes persons seen poaching: *Hall* v. *Robinson*, 53 J. P. 310.
(*w*) 25 & 26 Vict. c. 114, s. 2. Game = pheasants, partridges, grouse, black-game and their eggs, hares, woodcocks, snipe, and rabbits.
(*x*) *Jenkins* v. *King*, L. R. 7 Q. B. 480.
(*y*) *Clarke* v. *Crowder*, L. R. 4 C. P. 638.

(*z*) *Turner* v. *Morgan*, L. R. 10 C. P. 587.
(*a*) *Lloyd* v. *Lloyd*, 14 Q. B. D. 725; 53 L. T. 536; 49 J. P. 630; 33 W. R. 457; 15 Cox, C. C. 767.
(*b*) *Dillon* v. *O'Brien*, 16 Cox, C. C. 245.
(*c*) *Warne* v. *Varley*, 6 T. R. 443. See *Grindley* v. *Baker*, 1 B. & P. 229.
(*d*) 24 & 25 Vict. c. 99, s. 27.

be forthwith taken back to any place wherefrom it was unlawfully removed and execute that requisition (*e*).

Cruelty to animals. Where any person having charge of any vehicle or animal is arrested for an offence against the Cruelty to Animals Act, the constable may take carge of such vehicle or animal and deposit the same in some place of safe custody (*f*).

Customs. If any goods liable to duties of Customs, or prohibited to be imported or restricted, are stopped on suspicion of felony, they may be taken to the same station as the offender (*g*).

Dogs. Dogs reasonably supposed to be savage straying may be detained until expenses paid (*h*).

Excise. A similar power to that above stated under Customs is extended to goods seized under the Excise laws (*i*), but forfeited goods are to be taken to the Excise Office.

Explosives. Any Government inspector, constable, or officer of the local authority having reasonable cause to believe that any explosive, or ingredient of an explosive, or substance found by him is liable to be forfeited, may seize and detain the same until a Court of summary jurisdiction has determined the question of forfeiture. In such case the officer seizing may either require the occupier of the place in which it was seized (whether a building or not, or a carriage, boat, or ship) to detain the same in such place, or in any place under the control of such occupier, or may remove it in such manner and to such place as will, in his opinion, least endanger the public safety, and there detain it.

The receptacles containing the same may be seized, and detained, and removed in like manner as the contents thereof.

The officers seizing the same may use for the purposes of the removal and detention thereof any ship, boat, or carriage in which the same was seized, and any tug, tender, engine, tackle, beasts, and accoutrements belonging to or drawing, or provided for drawing, such ship, boat, or carriage, and shall pay to the owner a reasonable compensation for such use, to be determined, in case of dispute, by a Court of summary jurisdiction, and to be recovered in like manner as penalties under the Act.

The same shall, so far as practicable, be kept and conveyed in accordance with the Act and with all due precaution to prevent accidents (*j*).

Game. Carts, &c., in or on which there shall be reason to suspect that game unlawfully obtained, or articles or things used for the purpose of taking the same are carried, may be stopped and searched, and if found therein, may be seized and detained (*k*).

If the game, gun, &c., is visible, a search of the person is not necessary to give jurisdiction to seize (*l*).

(*e*) 41 & 42 Vict. c. 74, s. 50.
(*f*) 12 & 13 Vict. c. 92, s. 19.
(*g*) 39 & 40 Vict. c. 36, s. 206.
(*h*) 34 & 35 Vict. c. 56, s. 1.
(*i*) 7 & 8 Geo. 4, c. 53, s. 108.
(*j*) 38 & 39 Vict. c. 17, s. 74.
(*k*) 25 & 26 Vict. c. 114, s. 2.
(*l*) *Hall* v. *Knox*, 32 L. J. M. C. 1.

Money which has nothing to do with the charge cannot be taken (*m*). *Money.*

Animals, carts, or goods in the possession of persons arrested under the Vagrant Act may be seized and detained (*n*). *Vagrants.*

Canal and River.

These officers may stop, search, and detain boats or carriages on which there is reason to suspect anything stolen (*o*), and such property may be taken charge of (*p*). *Canal and river.*

Metropolitan.

When persons in charge of animals or carriages are taken in custody under the Metropolitan Police Act, such animals or carriages may be deposited in some place of safe custody (*q*). *Metropolitan.*

Carts, &c., within five miles of the Post Office not having owner's name thereon may be seized (*r*). *Carts, &c.*

This does not apply to carriages liable to excise duty (*s*).

Dogs not under control may be detained until payment of expenses (*t*). *Dogs.*

Carts and carriages removing furniture between 8 P.M. and 6 A.M., or at any time to evade the payment of rent, may be stopped (*u*). *Furniture.*

And so also may boats, carts, or carriages, in or upon which there is reason to believe anything stolen or unlawfully obtained may be found (*v*). *Stolen goods.*

Swine found straying in a street or public place may be seized and removed (*w*). *Swine.*

Towns.

The police under the Towns Police Clauses Act may impound cattle found straying within the limits of the special Act (*x*). *Towns. Impounding cattle.*

Bail.

Where persons are brought to the station charged with offences punishable by summary jurisdiction, if it be not practicable to bring them before the justice within twenty-four hours, the superintendent or inspector must inquire into the *Bail.*

(*m*) *R.* v. *O'Donnel*, 7 C. & P. 138; *R.* v. *D'Eyncourt*, 21 Q. B. D. 109; 4 Ti. Rep. 455.
(*n*) 5 Geo. 4, c. 83, s. 8.
(*o*) 3 & 4 Vict. c. 50, s. 11.
(*p*) Sect. 9.
(*q*) 2 & 3 Vict. c. 47, s. 68.
(*r*) 1 & 2 Will. 4, c. 22, s. 60.
(*s*) *Danby* v. *Hunter*, 5 Q. B. D. 20; 49 L. J. M. C. 15; 41 L. T. 622; 28 W. R. 223; 44 J. P. 809.
(*t*) 30 & 31 Vict. c. 134, s. 18. See *Wren* v. *Pocock*, 34 L. T. 697; 40 J. P. 646.
(*u*) 2 & 3 Vict. c. 47, s. 67.
(*v*) *Ibid.* ss. 34, 66.
(*w*) 54 & 55 Vict. c. 76, s. 17.
(*x*) 10 & 11 Vict. c. 89, s. 24.

case, and, except where the offence appears to him to be serious, shall discharge the prisoner upon his entering into recognizance (*y*), with or without sureties, for a reasonable amount to appear before the Court (*z*).

Subject to this enactment, there is, generally speaking, no obligation to give bail on arrest. It is a matter which usually falls within the discretion of the officer in charge of the station (*a*).

Chimney-sweepers and Pedlars.

Chimney sweepers and pedlars.

Chimney-sweepers may be required to give their name and address, and to produce their certificate (*b*).

Pedlars may be required to produce their certificate and to permit their pack to be inspected (*c*).

Dogs.
Metropolitan.

Dogs. Metropolitan.

Constables may destroy dogs suspected to be rabid, or when detained for contravention of muzzling order, after three days (*d*).

Fairs.
Metropolitan.

Fairs. Metropolitan.

Booths, &c., may be removed from ground when a fair has been declared unlawful (*e*).

Gun.

Gun.

Persons not in Her Majesty's service carrying gun may be requested to produce licence, and on refusal or neglect to do so, to state his name and address (*f*).

Traffic.
Metropolis.

Traffic. Metropolis. Fires.

All constables are authorized to aid the Fire Brigade in the execution of their duties. They may close any street in or near which a fire is burning (*g*).

(*y*) Recoverable summarily as a fine: 42 & 43 Vict. c. 42, s. 9.
(*z*) Sect. 38; and see 52 & 53 Vict. c. 44, s. 4.
(*a*) As to Metropolis, 10 Geo. 4, c. 44, s. 9; 2 & 3 Vict. c. 47, ss. 70, 72. As to county and municipal, 19 & 20 Vict. c. 69, s. 6; 45 & 46 Vict. c. 50, s. 227.

(*b*) 38 & 39 Vict. c. 70, s. 16.
(*c*) Sect. 17.
(*d*) 2 & 3 Vict. c. 47, s. 61; 30 & 31 Vict. c. 134, s. 18.
(*e*) 2 & 3 Vict. c. 47, s. 39; 31 & 32 Vict. c. 106, s. 2.
(*f*) 33 & 34 Vict. c. 57, s. 9.
(*g*) 28 & 29 Vict. c. 90, s. 12.

GAOLERS.

These officers have while acting the same powers, authorities, protection, and privileges as constables (*h*). *Gaolers.*

In prisons where debtors are confined, they are to be separated altogether from criminal prisoners (*i*). *Debtors.*

A debtor may maintain himself, provided he do not sell to other prisoners; and, if not maintained at the expense of the prison, is to receive the whole of his earnings. If furnished with implements, or so maintained, a deduction is to be made, to be determined by a justice (*j*).

Prisoners ordered by a judge to be treated as first-class misdemeanants are not criminal prisoners (*k*). *First class misdemeanants.*

As to criminal prisoners, no cell is to be used for the separate confinement of a prisoner unless certified to be fit by the inspector, and furnished with the means of enabling the prisoner to communicate at any time with an officer (*l*). *Criminal prisoners.*

The gaoler can only order confinement in a punishment-cell for twenty-four hours (*m*) and it is the same with irons and other mechanical restraints in cases of urgent necessity (*n*). Punishments can only be awarded by the gaoler or a justice (*o*).

Prisoners may be brought up for trial or removed (*p*), provided surgeon do not certify unfitness (*q*). *Removal.*

On admission they are to be searched, and all dangerous weapons, articles calculated to facilitate escape, and prohibited articles, to be taken from them (*r*); but no prisoner is to be searched in the presence of any other prisoner (*s*). *Search.*

Money and other effects brought into the prison by him, or sent for his use, which he is not allowed to retain, to be placed in custody of gaoler, who is to keep an inventory thereof (*t*). It appears to be recoverable at expiration of sentence (*u*). *Money.*

Prisoners may before trial maintain themselves, provided they do not sell to others (*v*). *Maintenance.*

A convicted criminal prisoner shall be provided with a complete prison dress, and shall be required to wear it (*w*). Sufficient bed-clothes to be provided, but convicted prisoners may be required to sleep on a plank bed during time determined by rules (*x*). *Clothes. Beds.*

Prisoners required to keep clean and decent (*y*). *Cleanliness.*

Hair of female not to be cut without her consent, except on

(*h*) 28 & 29 Vict. c. 126, Sched. I. r. 6.
(*i*) Sect. 17.
(*j*) Sched. I. r. 16. These rules are as if embodied in the Act.
(*k*) Sect. 67.
(*l*) Sect. 18.
(*m*) Sect. 43.
(*n*) Sched. I. r. 59.
(*o*) Sect. 43.
(*p*) Sect. 63.
(*q*) Sched. I. r. 10.
(*r*) Rule 6.
(*s*) Rule 7.
(*t*) Rule 8.
(*u*) See 33 & 34 Vict. c. 23, ss. 9, 18.
(*v*) Sched. I. r. 19.
(*w*) Rule 23.
(*x*) Rule 26.
(*y*) Rule 28.

account of vermin or dirt, or when surgeon deems necessary for health. That of males not to be cut closer than necessary for health (*z*).

Hard labour.
Hard labour not to be imposed before trial (*a*), nor more than ten hours a day (exclusive of meals), nor if surgeon certify unfitness, nor on Sundays, Good Fridays, or public fasts and thanksgivings (*b*). No prisoner not sentenced to hard labour to be punished for neglect of work, except by alteration in scale of diet (*c*).

Exercise.
Exercise in open air to be permitted daily. If employed in cell, to take such exercise as surgeon deems necessary (*d*).

Illness.
Prisoners desiring to see surgeon, or appearing out of health, to be referred by officer to gaoler, and by him without delay to surgeon (*e*).

Religion.
No prisoner to be compelled to attend any service of a persuasion to which he does not belong (*f*). Minister of same persuasion not to be introduced if prisoner object (*g*).

Education.
Prisoners to be instructed in reading, writing, and arithmetic during hours prescribed (*h*).

Visitors.
Provision to be made for admission of persons with whom prisoner before trial may desire to communicate. So far as consistent with the interests of justice, legal adviser to be seen alone (*i*).

Gaoler may demand name and address of any visitor, and when he has any ground for suspicion, may search, or cause to be searched, male visitors; and direct the matron, or some other female officer to search female visitors, such search not to be in the presence of any prisoner or of another visitor; and in case of any visitor refusing to be searched, may deny admission (*j*).

Females.
Females to be attended by female officers (*k*).

Articles carried in or out.
The gate porter may examine all articles carried in or out, and may stop any person suspected of bringing in spirits or other prohibited articles, or of carrying out any property belonging to the prison (*l*).

(*z*) Rule 29.
(*a*) Rule 32.
(*b*) Rule 34.
(*c*) Rule 38.
(*d*) Rule 39.
(*e*) Rule 41.
(*f*) Rule 46.

(*g*) Rule 47.
(*h*) Rule 53.
(*i*) Rule 54. See *R.* v. *Simmonds,* 7 C. & P. 176.
(*j*) Rule 55.
(*k*) Rule 67.
(*l*) Rule 97.

Customs.

The inherent powers of customs officers are the following:— *Customs.*

Officers employed to prevent smuggling (*a*) may haul their vessels on the shore (not being a garden or pleasure-ground, or place ordinarily used for any bathing-machine (*b*)), or may patrol the coasts (not being a garden or pleasure ground) (*c*). *Entry on lands.*

Customs officers may board any ship arriving in port, and stay on board until all the goods laden therein are delivered therefrom, or until her departure, and shall have free access to every part thereof (*d*). So also may they, after clearance outwards, within the limits of the port, or within one league of the coast (*e*); and any ship carrying false colours in order to remove them (*f*). *Boarding ships.*

They may after boarding demand all documents which ought to be on board, and require them to be brought for inspection (*g*), and where the ship has cleared, the clearance (*h*). *Demand documents.*

The officers may search ships. or rummage all parts thereof, for uncustomed or prohibited goods (*i*); and those employed to prevent smuggling may search persons on board any ship or boat in port, or who shall have landed therefrom, if they have reason to suppose they are carrying uncustomed or prohibited goods (*j*). Such a person may require first to be taken before a justice or collector, or other superior customs officer, who may either discharge him or direct the search. And a female is to be searched only by a female (*k*). *Search.*

If the keys be withheld, the examining or superior officer may open any place, box, or chest (*l*). The officers may break packages for exportation, the contents of which are unknown (*m*), and examine all goods shipped or brought for shipment (*n*). *Breaking packages and places.*

They may also fasten down hatchways (*o*). *Fasten hatchway.*

All goods on board, and all goods lading or unlading, may be examined (*p*). And officers employed to prevent smuggling (*q*) *Examination.*

(*a*) These words include coast-guard.
(*b*) 39 & 40 Vict. c. 36, s. 194.
(*c*) Sect. 196.
(*d*) Sects. 47, 147, 182. As to commissioned ships, see s. 52.
(*e*) Sect. 134.
(*f*) 17 & 18 Vict. c. 104, s. 105.
(*g*) Sect. 147. And see 44 & 45 Vict. c. 12, s. 11; and 47 & 48 Vict. c. 62, s 3.
(*h*) 39 & 40 Vict. c. 36, s. 134.
(*i*) Sects. 147, 182. As to commissioned ships, see s. 52.

(*j*) 44 & 45 Vict. c. 12, s. 12.
(*k*) 39 & 40 Vict. c. 36, s. 185. If the officer shall without reasonable ground cause any person to be searched, he shall forfeit £10.
(*l*) Sect. 47.
(*m*) Sect. 54.
(*n*) Sect. 102. As to salmon parcels, see 28 & 29 Vict. c. 121, s. 65.
(*o*) Sect. 47.
(*p*) Sect. 147.
(*q*) Including excise, coast-guard, and constabulary.

Samples. may on reasonable suspicion or probable cause stop and examine any cart or other conveyance to ascertain whether any smuggled goods are contained therein (*r*).

They may take samples of margarine imported into or manufactured in the kingdom, if they have reason to believe that the provisions of the Act are infringed by conveyance under another title (*s*).

And also of tea imported; and if they find it mixed with other substances, or exhausted tea, shall not deliver it unless with the sanction of the Commissioners, and if it be unfit for food, it may be destroyed (*t*).

Seizure. Where a power to seize is conferred by statute, it must be exercised strictly; and if the seizure extend to property to which the power does not apply, although in the judgment of the officer it did apply, it is no justification (*u*).

All officers employed in the prevention of smuggling may seize all ships, boats, goods, carriages, or other conveyances, and horses, animals, and things liable to forfeiture, and all persons liable to be detained, in any place on land or water (*v*). And for this purpose they may apparently go outside the usual limits of their jurisdiction (*w*). There can be no alienation so as to avoid forfeiture (*x*).

But no ship is to be liable to forfeiture unless under 250 tons (*y*). In such cases the Commissioners may fine, and require a sum not exceeding £500 to be deposited with the Collector. In default, the ship may be detained (*z*). The goods in such ship are still liable to forfeiture (*a*).

Ships unduly assuming British character, or concealing British or assuming foreign character, or owner acquiring ownership if unqualified, or making false declaration of ownership, are liable to seizure (*b*). And iron steamships not built according to rules may be detained (*c*).

If a foreign ship having had goods on board liable to seizure has unshipped at more than one league from the coast, she is liable to forfeiture, but only by coming within the distance during the same voyage (*d*).

Goods, &c., prohibited or restricted are:—

Arms, &c., proclaimed (*e*); beer (*f*); books, copyright, cards; cattle or hides proclaimed (*g*); chicory; chloral hydrate

(*r*) Sect. 203.
(*s*) 50 & 51 Vict. c. 29, s. 8.
(*t*) 38 & 39 Vict. c. 63, s. 30.
(*u*) *Warne* v. *Varley*, 6 T. R. 443; *Grindley* v. *Baker*, 1 B. & P. 229.
(*v*) 39 & 40 Vict. c. 36, s. 202. See *Lord Advocate* v. *Crookshanks*, 15 Court of Sess. Cas. 995.
(*w*) *R.* v. *Barfoot*, 13 East, 506.
(*x*) *Lockyer* v. *Offlen*, 1 T. R. 252.
(*y*) 53 & 54 Vict. c. 56, s. 1.
(*z*) Sect. 2.

(*a*) Sect. 4.
(*b*) 17 & 18 Vict. c. 104, s. 103.
(*c*) Sect. 300.
(*d*) *Att.-Gen.* v. *Schiers*, 2 C. M. & R. 286; 1 Gale, 223; 5 Tyr. 1024. As to quarantine, see 6 Geo. 4, c. 78, ss. 14, 15.
(*e*) 39 & 40 Vict. c. 36, s. 138; 42 & 43 Vict. c. 21, s. 8.
(*f*) 44 & 45 Vict. c. 12, s. 5.
(*g*) See 40 & 41 Vict. c. 68, s. 1, as to destructive insects.

chloroform, chocolate, clocks, cocoa, coffee; coin, false or foreign proclaimed (*h*); collodion; ether; ethyl, iodide of; explosives (*i*); Foreign Enlistment Act, ships liable under (*j*); foreign manufactured articles, &c.; postal packages (*k*); fruit; malt extract; Merchandize Marks Act, goods liable under (*l*); rum; naphtha; prints, indecent; salmon (*m*); soap containing spirit; snuff; spirits; spruce; tea; tobacco; varnish; watches, British manufacture; wine (*n*).

The offences consist of—

Failing to export, import, or enter goods properly (*o*), or to report cargo (*p*), and smuggling (*q*).

The unshipping of goods, though in some cases not unlawful, may become so by reason of any subsequent fraud; but there must be a fraudulent removal to render the unshipment illegal (*r*).

Contraband goods may be seized in a river before they are landed or offered for sale (*s*).

Where masters refuse or neglect to give to officers declarations concerning aliens (other than seamen employed), and refuse to pay the penalty imposed, the ship may be detained (*t*). Aliens.

Proceedings for the recovery of penalties or for condemnation must be commenced within three years after the commission of the offence or seizure of the articles (*u*); but this does not apparently apply to indictments (*v*). Limitation.

A charge of 5*s*. a day may be made, and for removal of goods where that takes place, where a ship or goods importing remain more than fourteen days after arrival; and the like charge may be made on ships brought in under legal process or by stress of weather, or for safety or derelict, when actually guarded (*w*). Charges.

As to dues, none is to be charged in respect of deficiency in goods, unless there is reason to suppose they have been abstracted (*x*). Dues.

(*h*) 49 & 50 Vict c. 41, s. 2; and 52 & 53 Vict. c. 42, s. 2.
(*i*) 46 & 47 Vict. c. 10, s. 3.
(*j*) 33 & 34 Vict. c. 90, s. 21.
(*k*) 45 & 46 Vict. c. 74, s. 14.
(*l*) 50 & 51 Vict. c. 28, s. 16; and see *Stacey* v. *Chilworth Co.*, 24 Q. B. D. 90; 59 L. J. M. C. 13; 62 L. T. 73; 38 W. R. 204; 54 J. P. 436; 6 T. L. R. 95; and *Wood* v. *Burgess*, 24 Q. B. D. 162; 59 L. J. M. C. 11; 61 L. T. 583; 38 W. R. 331; 54 J. P. 325; 16 Cox, 729; and see 54 Vict. c. 15.
(*m*) 26 & 27 Vict. c. 10, s. 3; and 28 & 29 Vict. c. 121, s. 65.
(*n*) 51 & 52 Vict. c. 14, s. 6. The amount of duty payable varies.
(*o*) 39 & 40 Vict. c. 36.
(*p*) *Ibid.*
(*q*) *Ibid.*
(*r*) *R.* v. *Candy*, Ex. 15, 5, 1843,

M. S. Rep. See *Att.-Gen.* v. *Hurel*, 11 M. & W. 589.
(*s*) *Smith* v. *Reynolds*, 2 Wils. 257; *Johnson* v. *Saunders*, 1 B. & P. 267; *Att.-Gen.* v. *Delous*, 6 Price, 283.
(*t*) 6 & 7 Will. 4, c. 11, s. 2. No action will lie at the suit of an alien for being refused admission to the country: *Musgrove* v. *Toy*, [1891] A. C. 272.
(*u*) 39 & 40 Vict. c. 36 s. 257.
(*v*) *R.* v. *Thompson*, 16 Q. B. 832; 15 Jur. 654; 20 L. J. M. C. 183; and see *Att.-Gen.* v. *Radloff*, 10 Ex. 84; 18 Jur. 555; 23 L. J. Ex. 240; *R.* v. *Akers*, 6 Esp. 125, n.; *Att.-Gen.* v. *Briant*, 15 M. & W. 169; 15 L. J. Ex. 265; and *Van Boven*, 9 Q. B. 669.
(*w*) 39 & 40 Vict. c. 36, s. 75.
(*x*) Sect. 99.

I 2

The duties become a debt to the Crown immediately on the importation (*y*).

In case of dispute as to dues, the amount demanded must be paid, and an action commenced against the Collector within three months to ascertain what amount is payable (*z*).

Clearance. Where harbour dues remain unpaid, a clearance to the vessel may be withheld until security be given for their payment (*a*), and in any case if the master refuse to state her nationality (*b*).

Sale. Goods, in default of perfect entry, may be sold within one month after landing (*c*). If not entered within 14 days, they may be sold within three months (*d*); and those in warehouses, not cleared after five years, after one month's notice to the warehouse-keeper. Overplus, after payment of duties, to go to owner if known. If goods not worth the duty, they may be destroyed. In that case the duty is to be paid by the proprietor of the warehouse (*e*).

Arrest. As has been above stated, persons generally may be arrested for offences against the Customs Acts. So also may persons making signals to smugglers (*f*), and those found or discovered to have been on board vessels with contraband goods within three miles of the coast (except in the service of a foreign State) (*g*), and persons receiving forfeited goods or offenders, or assaulting or obstructing officers, or attempting to do so (*h*). The arrest may be effected at any place within three years of the commission of the offence (*i*).

Persons on board infected ships may be detained pending examination of the state of health of persons so on board (*j*).

Securing goods. Officers may secure goods before landing, and, if necessary, they may be placed in the Queen's warehouse (*k*).

Firing on ships. They may in pursuit of a ship or boat liable to seizure or examination (after signal) fire into her if she do not bring to (*l*).

Excise powers. Customs officers may exercise Excise powers when necessary (*m*).

Sea fisheries. Certain of these officers are employed to put into force the Convention to Regulate the Fisheries in the North Sea (*n*).

(*y*) *Leaper* v. *Smith*, Bun. 79; *Anon.* Lam. 15; *Salter* v. *Magapert*, 1 Roll. R. 380; *Att.-Gen.* v. *Weeks*, Bun. 223. See *Att.-Gen.* v. *Ansted*, 12 M. & W. 520.
(*z*) Sect. 30.
(*a*) 10 Vict. c. 27, s. 48.
(*b*) 17 & 18 Vict. c. 104, ss. 102, 103; and as to steamships not properly fitted, see s. 300.
(*c*) 39 & 40 Vict. c. 36, s. 61.
(*d*) Sect. 73.
(*e*) Sects. 93, 94.
(*f*) Sect. 190.
(*g*) Sect. 179.
(*h*) 44 & 45 Vict. c. 12, s. 12.
(*i*) 39 & 40 Vict. c. 36, s. 199.

(*j*) Sect. 234.
(*k*) Sects. 47, 51, 61, 73, and 74. See *Att.-Gen.* v. *Voudière*, 1 C. M. & R. 571; 5 Tyr. 211; *Love* v. *Att.-Gen.* 2 C. M. & R. 544; 5 Tyr. 133; 1 Gale, 249.
(*l*) Sect. 181.
(*m*) 7 & 8 Geo. 4, c. 53, s. 38.
(*n*) As to local sea-fishery officers, see 51 & 52 Vict. c. 59, s. 6; and *R.* v. *Cubitt*, 22 Q. B. D. 622; 58 L. J. M. C. 133; 60 L. T. 638; 37 W. R. 892; 53 J. P. 470; 16 Cox, C. C. 618. Close time for bream is March to June; sea trout, September to January; oysters, May to July; and lamprey, March inclusive.

INHERENT POWERS. 117

In such case, in exercise of their powers, they may, with respect to any sea-fishing boat within the exclusive limits of the British Isles, and with respect to any British sea-fishing boat outside those limits—(1) board the boat; (2) require the owner, &c., to produce certificates; (3) number the crew; (4) require explanations as to certificates from master; (5) examine sails, lights, small boats, anchors, grapnels, and fishing implements; (6) seize any instrument serving only or intended to damage or destroy fishing implements by cutting or otherwise found on board or in possession of any person belonging to her; (7) hold an examination; (8) and in case of any contravention, take the offender and the boat and the crew to the nearest or most convenient port, and there detain them until adjudication (*o*).

Where seal-fishing in Behring's Sea has been prohibited by Order in Council, any full-pay naval officer may stop and examine any British ship in such sea and detain her, or any portion of her equipment, or any of her crew, if, in his judgment, the ship is being or is preparing to be used contrary to the Act (*p*). Seals.

EXCISE.

The powers of excise officers are as follows:— Excise.

They may demand the production of a gun licence from any person using or carrying a gun (other than those in the service of Her Majesty), and if such licence is not produced they may demand a person's name and address (*q*). Gun licence.

They and their assistants may at any time by night or day (but if between 11 P.M. and 5 A.M. in the presence of a constable) enter into and remain so long as they think fit, for the purpose of ascertaining, where any offence has been committed, in any building or place belonging to or used by persons to carry on a trade subject to the excise laws, or by persons required by the same laws to make entry of such building (*r*). They may enter at any time of the day or night the entered premises of a brewer for sale (*s*), and if they find any concealed pipe may enter any adjoining house into which such pipe leads (*t*). They may also enter at any time the premises of a distiller or rectifier (*u*), and at all reasonable times the premises of a brewer other than a brewer for sale (*v*). Entry.
Brewer for sale.
Distiller.
Brewer other than for sale.

Where they see a person using or carrying a gun, they may enter and remain as long as necessary on any lands or premises Lands.

(*o*) 16 & 17 Vict. c. 22, s. 12. The convention forms the 1st schedule to the Act.

(*p*) 54 Vict. c. 19. As to the suppression of the Slave Trade, see 5 Geo. 4, c. 113; 36 & 37 Vict. c. 88; *R.* v. *Zulueta*, 1 C. & K. 215; *Buron* v. *Denman*, 2 Ex. 167; *Madrazo* v. *Willes*, 3 B. & Ald. 353; and *Tobin* v. *The Queen*, 16 C. B. 310.

(*q*) 33 & 34 Vict. c. 57, s. 9; and see *post*, p. 119.

(*r*) 7 & 8 Geo. 4, c. 53, s. 22. See *Hill* v. *Barnes*, 2 W. Bla. 1135.

(*s*) 43 & 44 Vict. c. 20, s. 29. Beer includes cider and perry.

(*t*) Sect. 30.

(*u*) 43 & 44 Vict. c. 21, s. 137.

(*v*) 43 & 44 Vict. c. 20, s. 35.

118   *EXECUTIVE OFFICERS.*

(other than a dwelling-house or the curtilage thereof) for the purpose of making the demand specified above (*w*).

Methylator.
Retail spirit.
They may in the daytime enter and inspect the premises of methylators, or retailers of methylated spirits, or of persons authorized to receive such spirits (*x*), and they may at any time enter the premises of a spirit dealer or retailer (*y*).

Tobacco.
They may also at any time (but between 10 P.M. and 6 A.M. with the assistance of a constable) enter any workhouse or shop of a manufacturer, dealer, or retailer of tobacco or snuff and inspect and examine all tobacco and snuff therein (*z*).

Wine retailer.
And during the hours in which any house licensed for the retail of wine to be consumed on the premises is kept open, may enter every house, cellar, room, or place entered for storing, keeping, or retailing wine (*a*).

Examination general.
As regards places subject to the laws of excise they may inspect the same and take account of all matters, things, works, vessels, utensils, goods, and materials appertaining to such trade (*b*); and also of the brewing materials, vessels, and utensils used by brewers (*c*).

Brewery.

Distillery.
In a distillery, they may test the quantity of spirits at proof in any wash by distillation, and require any charger or receiver to be emptied and cleansed and any quantity of the wash to be distilled, and the produce to be conveyed into the charger or receiver. The distiller must provide assistance and fuel (*d*); and the officer may examine, gauge, and take account of any still or other vessel or utensil, and the spirits or materials for their manufacture (*e*), and where a concealed pipe is discovered, examine whether it conveys liquor so as to prevent a true account being taken (*f*).

Methylator.
Spirit retailer.
Tobacco.
Wine.
A methylator's stock can only be examined in the daytime (*g*), but that of a spirit retailer at any time (*h*), or of a tobacco manufacturer, dealer, or retailer (*i*), but that of a wine retailer can only be examined while the house is open for the sale of liquor (*j*).

Spirits in transit.
Spirits in transit may be examined (*k*).

Samples.
Brewer.
As to samples, the officer may take such as he deems necessary of any worts, or beer, or materials for brewing, in possession of a brewer for sale, who may first stir up and mix together such worts, beer, or materials (*l*).

Margarine.
In the case of margarine in transit, he may take samples to

(*w*) 33 & 34 Vict. c. 57, s. 10.
(*x*) 43 & 44 Vict. c. 24, s. 127. By 53 & 54 Vict. c. 8, s. 31, the duty on methylated spirits is abolished, but the manufacture is still subject to the Excise laws.
(*y*) Sect. 141.
(*z*) 3 & 4 Vict. c. 18, s. 3; and see 30 & 31 Vict. c. 90, s. 10.
(*a*) 23 & 24 Vict. c. 27, s. 24.
(*b*) 7 & 8 Geo. 4, c. 53, s. 22.

(*c*) 43 & 44 Vict. c. 20, ss. 29, 35.
(*d*) 43 & 44 Vict. c. 24, s. 40.
(*e*) Sect. 137.
(*f*) Sect. 139.
(*g*) Sect. 127.
(*h*) Sect. 141.
(*i*) 3 & 4 Vict. c. 18, s. 3.
(*j*) 23 & 24 Vict. c. 27, s. 24.
(*k*) 43 & 44 Vict. c. 24, s. 145.
(*l*) Cap. 20, s. 26.

ascertain whether the provisions of the Act have been complied with (*m*).

And also of any wort, wash, low wines, feints, or spirits from any vessel or utensil in a distillery (*n*), or of any methylated spirits (*o*). *Spirits.*

And generally he may take any samples if he pay for them at the current price (*p*). *Generally.*

If there is reason to suspect the existence of concealed pipes, a brewer's premises may be searched (*q*). And so may a distiller's (*r*) or a wine retailer's (*s*). *Search. Brewery. Distiller. Wine retailer.*

In the case of either a brewer or distiller if they are refused admittance they may (but at night only in the presence of a peace officer) break in (*t*); and if there be reason to suspect concealed pipes, may break up the ground of that or adjoining premises. In the case of a distillery, if the search be unsuccessful the damage is to be made good (*u*). *Breaking. Damage when made good.*

Where a power to seize is conferred by statute it must be exercised strictly, and if the seizure extend to goods to which the power does not apply, although in the judgment of the officer it did apply, it is no justification (*v*). *Seizure.*

These officers, or any person acting in their aid, may seize any goods, commodities, and chattels, and any carts, horses, carriages, or other conveyances for carrying the same, forfeited by any act relating to excise (*w*). And mere possession seems sufficient without the intention to employ them illegally (*x*).

And stills, vessels, utensils, spirits, or materials for their manufacture, liable to forfeiture, may be seized (*y*), or spirits found on premises of a wine retailer (*z*). *Spirits*

Goods liable to duty are: Beer, cards, chicory, cider, coffee, patent medicines, perry, snuff, spirits, sweets, tobacco, and wine (*a*).

Persons discovered in unentered excise factories may be arrested and detained (*b*); and the officers here may do all that is necessary for the purpose of having the matter adjudicated on (*c*). *Arrest. Unentered factories.*

So also persons hawking cards may be apprehended (*d*), and persons carrying a gun who shall refuse their name and address (*e*). *Cards. Gun.*

(*m*) 50 & 51 Vict. c. 29, s. 8.
(*n*) 43 & 44 Vict. c. 24, s. 42.
(*o*) Scets. 127, 141.
(*p*) 51 Vict. c. 8, s. 6.
(*q*) 43 & 44 Vict. c. 20, s. 30.
(*r*) Cap. 24, s. 137.
(*s*) 23 & 24 Vict. c. 27, s. 24.
(*t*) 43 & 44 Vict. c. 20, ss. 29, 30; c. 24, ss. 137, 139.
(*u*) *Ibid.* s. 139.
(*v*) *Warne* v. *Varley*, 6 T. R. 443; *Grindley* v. *Baker*, 1 B. & P. 229.

(*w*) 53 & 54 Vict. c. 21, ss. 30, 31.
(*x*) *Att.-Gen.* v. *Lockwood*, 9 M & W. 378.
(*y*) 43 & 44 Vict. c. 24, s. 140.
(*z*) 23 & 24 Vict. c. 27, s. 24.
(*a*) The amount of duty varies.
(*b*) 7 & 8 Geo. 4, c. 53, s. 33.
(*c*) *Evans* v. *M'Cloughlan*, 4 Macq. H. L. C. 89; 7 Jur. N. S. 1253.
(*d*) 25 & 26 Vict. c. 22, s. 31.
(*e*) 33 & 34 Vict. c. 57, s. 9.

120 EXECUTIVE OFFICERS.

Unlawful removal.
Hawking.

Persons may also be arrested for:—
The unlawful removal of malt, wort, or wash (*f*), or spirits (*g*).
Hawking and sale of spirits (*h*), or generally without licence(*i*), or of tobacco (*j*).
And persons liable to arrest may be arrested subsequently after escape at any time (*k*).
The offences not previously mentioned are:—
Fraudulently removing goods liable to duty (*l*).
Making out false accounts and obstructing officers (*m*).

Limitation.

Proceedings for the recovery of penalties must be commenced within three years (*n*). But this does not apparently apply to indictments (*o*).

Ladders and lights.
Worm-tub.

Brewers and distillers must supply officers with ladders and lights to enable them to make their examination (*p*), and distillers may be required to draw off worm-tub (*q*).

Permits.

Manufacturers of tobacco must shew permits when demanded (*r*); and so must persons removing spirits in quantities of more than one gallon (*s*).

Customs. Powers.

Excise officers are authorized to use all the powers of customs officers when necessary (*t*).

Officers may oppose force by force.

If persons armed with offensive weapons resist officers, they may be opposed by force (*u*).
A hatchet caught up accidentally (*v*), or a horsewhip, or a stick (*w*), or a smuggler's pole (*x*) is not an offensive weapon within this section; but anything not in common use for any other purpose than a weapon is (*y*).

TAXES.

Taxes.
Distraint.

The power of a collector of taxes in case of non-payment is to distrain upon the messuages, lands, tenements, and premises charged with such sum of money, or the person so charged by his goods and chattels, and all such other goods and chattels as the collector is thereby authorized to distrain, without any further authority than the warrant delivered on his appointment (*z*).

Warrant.

Charges.

As to the amount that may be charged for such distress where

(*f*) 43 & 44 Vict. c. 24, s. 144.
(*g*) Sect. 145.
(*h*) Sect. 146.
(*i*) 51 & 52 Vict. c. 33, s. 6.
(*j*) 5 & 6 Vict. c. 93, s. 13. Not to extend to dealers.
(*k*) 4 & 5 Will. 4, c. 51, s. 25.
(*l*) 7 & 8 Geo. 4, c. 53, s. 32.
(*m*) 53 & 54 Vict. c. 21, s. 30.
(*n*) Sect. 31.
(*o*) R. v. Thompson, ante, p. 115.
(*p*) 43 & 44 Vict. c. 20, s. 28; c. 24, s. 138.

(*q*) Sect. 143.
(*r*) 3 & 4 Vict. c. 18, s. 5.
(*s*) 43 & 44 Vict. c. 24, s. 145.
(*t*) 7 & 8 Geo. 4, c. 53, s. 38.
(*u*) Sect. 40.
(*v*) R. v. Rose, 1 Leach, C. C. 342.
(*w*) R. v. Fletcher, ib. 23.
(*x*) R. v. Noakes, 5 C. & P. 326.
(*y*) R. v. Cosans, 1 Leach, C. C. 342.
(*z*) 43 & 44 Vict. c. 19, s. 86; and see R. v. Ford, 4 N. & M. 451; 2 A. & E. 588; 1 H. & W. 46.

the tax is under £20, see 57 Geo. 3, c. 93, s. 1, and 7 & 8 Geo. 4, c. 17 (a).

The collector has priority over ordinary judgment debtors, and over the landlord for rent due (b). Where bankruptcy or liquidation supervene, however, the power of distraint vanishes (c). The collector's claim must here be proved in the ordinary way, but is entitled to preferential payment (d). Priority.

To authorize a levy a demand of the specific sum must have been made and payment refused (e). Demand.

Constables cannot be introduced unless there be reasonable ground to suppose that an assault will be committed or resistance to the distress made (f). Introduction of constables.

Goods of a third person found on the premises are apparently seizable (g). Goods of third person.

A reasonable time must elapse between the demand and distraint in order to permit of complying with such demand or the distraint will be unlawful (h). Reasonable time to elapse.

So also will it be if it is made for a sum which is not actually due (i). Must be for sum actually due.

The duties of the collector on seizure will be found stated ante (j).

These officers collect income and land tax and house duty.

Post Officers.

The power of these officers is principally as to detention and opening of letters. Post officers.

This may be done in the case of a letter returned for want of true direction, or if the person to whom it is directed be dead, or cannot be found, or shall have refused the same (k), or if it be suspected to contain contraband goods (l), or is sent contrary to regulations (m). Detention and opening of letters.

A post-master is unable to charge for delivery of letters, any more than the established rates (n).

Officers may, after request and refusal to leave, remove persons wilfully obstructing business in a post office (o). Obstructing business.

(a) Post, p. 180.
(b) 43 & 44 Vict. c. 19, s. 88.
(c) The Regent Stores, 38 L. T. 130; 42 J. P. 279.
(d) Bankruptcy Act, 1883, s. 40.; Re Henley Co., 48 L. J. Ch. 147; 39 L. T. 53; 26 W. R. 885.
(e) R. v. Ford, 4 N. & M. 451; 2 A. & E. 588; 1 H. & W. 46; 42 & 43 Vict. c. 21, s. 25.
(f) R. v. Clarke, 4 N. & M. 671; 3 A. & E. 287; 1 H. & W. 252.
(g) Jason v. Dixon, 1 M. & G. 601.
(h) Gibbs v. Stead, 8 B. & C. 528.

(i) Charleton v. Alway, 11 A. & E. 993.
(j) Page 39.
(k) 7 Will. 4, c. 36, s. 25.
(l) 3 & 4 Vict. c. 96, s. 65.
(m) 10 & 11 Vict. c. 85, s. 10. These regulations are bye-laws; see ante, p. 62. As to the interception of letters, see R. v. James, 24 Q. B. D. 439; 17 Cox, 24.
(n) Smith v. Powditch, Cowp. 182. These rates are fixed by Treasury warrant, 38 & 39 Vict. c. 22, s. 1.
(o) 47 & 48 Vict. c. 76, s. 9.

Contagious Diseases Inspectors.

Contagious diseases inspectors. These officers, who are under the orders of the Board of Agriculture, have the same powers as inspectors have under the Act (*p*).

They may, on the representation of a local inspector that the Act or an order or local regulation has not been complied with, detain a vessel, a copy of the representation being delivered to the master (*q*).

Burial-Grounds Inspector.

Burial-grounds inspector. The duty of this officer is to inspect burial-grounds in order to ascertain whether the regulations (if any) made by the Secretary of State in respect thereto, have been complied with (*r*).

Inebriates. This officer also inspects retreats for inebriates for the same purpose (*s*). In this case non-compliance with the regulations constitutes an offence against the Act (*t*).

Cruelty to Animals Inspectors.

Cruelty to animals inspectors. These officers visit registered places to secure compliance with the provisions of the Vivisection Act (*u*).

Except under special certificate, experiments must be performed with a view to the advancement by new discovery of physiological knowledge by a person holding a licence, but not as an illustration of lectures, nor for the purpose of attaining manual skill. The animal must be under the influence of a sufficiently powerful anæsthethic (which does not include *urari* or *curare* (*v*)), and if it be seriously injured, be killed before it recovers from the influence thereof.

Explosives Inspectors.

Explosives inspectors. Entry. These officers may for the purpose of making necessary examination and inquiry, enter, inspect, and examine any factory, magazine, or store of any explosive, and every part thereof, at all times by day and night, but so as not to unnecessarily impede or obstruct the work therein, and make inquiries as to the observance of the Act, and all measures and things relating to the safety of the public or of the persons employed therein.

And they may enter, inspect, and examine any premises registered under the Act, and every part thereof in which any

---

(*p*) See *ante*, p. 66.
(*q*) 41 & 42 Vict. c. 74, s. 52, and see 53 & 54 Vict. c. 14, s. 4.
(*r*) 18 & 19 Vict. c. 128, s. 8. See bye-laws, *ante*, p. 62.
(*s*) 42 & 43 Vict. c. 19, s. 15;

51 & 52 Vict. c. 19.
(*t*) 42 & 43 Vict. c. 19, s. 17.
(*u*) 39 & 40 Vict. c. 77, s. 10.
(*v*) Sect. 4. As to Inspectors of Anatomy, see 2 & 3 Will. 4, c. 75, ss. 6, 17.

explosive is kept or is reasonably supposed by them to be kept at all reasonable times by day.

They may require the occupier of any such factory, magazine, store, or premises, or any person employed therein to give them samples of any explosive or ingredient or substance (*w*), paying therefor the market value thereof (*x*). *Samples.*

FACTORY INSPECTORS.

This officer may, on producing, if required, the certificate of his appointment, (1) enter, inspect, and examine at all reasonable times, by day and night, a factory and workshop, and every part thereof, when he has reasonable cause to believe that any person is employed therein, and by day any place which he has reasonable cause to believe is a factory or workshop; (2) take with him in either case a constable, if he has reasonable cause to apprehend serious obstruction; (3) require the production of documents kept in pursuance of the Act, and inspect, examine, and copy the same; (4) make necessary examination and inquiry as to whether this and the Public Health Acts, have been complied with; (5) enter any school in which he has reasonable cause to believe that children employed in a factory or workshop are educated; (6) examine any person in such factory, &c., or school as to matters under the Act, and require them to sign a declaration of the truth of their statements; (7) exercise other necessary powers (*y*). *Factory inspectors. Entry.*

This power may be exercised whether or not the factory or workshop is used as a dwelling (*z*).

The powers are not to be exercised as to retail bakehouses unless there is reasonable cause to believe that a child, young person, or woman is employed therein (*a*). *Bakehouses.*

But they may be extended (by direction of the Secretary of State) to any place of public entertainment at which the employment of a child is for the time being licensed (*b*). *Cruelty to children.*

MINES INSPECTORS.

This officer may (1) make such examination and inquiry as is necessary to ascertain whether the provisions of this Act are complied with; (2) enter, inspect, and examine any mine and *Mines inspectors.*

(*w*) 38 & 39 Vict. c. 17, s. 55; 46 & 47 Vict. c. 3, s. 8, and see *ante*, p. 92.
(*x*) 38 & 39 Vict. c. 17, s. 76.
(*y*) 41 & 42 Vict. c. 16, ss. 68, 70. This Act does not apply to workshops where no child, young person, or woman is employed, s. 93 (except under sanitary provisions, which extend also to laundries—54 & 55 Vict. c. 75, ss. 1, 2), nor to private house or room where straw-plaiting, pillow-lace, or glove-making is carried on— s. 97; or any trade where the labour is exercised at irregular intervals, and does not furnish the whole or principal means of living—s. 98.
(*z*) 54 & 55 Vict. c. 75, s. 25.
(*a*) 46 & 47 Vict. c. 53, s. 17; and see 54 & 55 Vict. c. 75, s. 37.
(*b*) 52 & 53 Vict. c. 44, s. 3.

any part thereof at all reasonable times by day and night, but so as not to impede or obstruct the working of the mine; (3) examine and make inquiry respecting the state and condition of any mine or part thereof, ventilation, sufficiency of special rules and all measures and things connected with the safety of persons employed in or contiguous thereto, or the care and treatment of the horses and other animals used therein; (4) exercise all other necessary powers (c).

MERCHANT SHIPPING INSPECTORS.

Merchant shipping inspectors. Every officer of the Board of Trade, commanding officer of any commissioned ship on full pay, consular officer, registrar general of seamen, chief officer of customs, and shipping master may, where he has reason to suspect that the provisions of the Merchant Shipping Act, or the laws relating to merchant seamen and navigation are not complied with, (1) require the owner, master, or any of the crew of a British ship to produce any official log-books or documents, or a list of persons on board; (2) muster the crew; or (3) require the master to answer questions concerning the ship, crew or documents (d).

Board of Trade inspectors. Inspectors of the Board of Trade appointed to report (a.) as to accidents to vessels; (b.) whether the Act is complied with; (c.) whether the hull or machinery of steamships are in good condition, may (1) go on board any ship and inspect the same or any of the machinery, boats, equipments, or articles on board thereof, not unnecessarily detaining her; (2) enter and inspect any premises necessary for the purpose of making his report; (3) and require the production of all books, papers, &c. (e).

Surveyors. The surveyors may board any passenger steamship at all reasonable times and inspect the same and all machinery, &c., certificates, thereof, not unnecessarily detaining her, and, if necessary, require the ship to be taken into dock for examination (f).

Receivers. On a ship being stranded or in distress the receiver may take command of all persons present and issue directions for the preservation of the ship, persons on board, and cargo (g). For these purposes he may summon assistance, require the master of a ship near to lend aid and demand the use of any wagon, cart, or horses near (h).

(c) 50 & 51 Vict. c. 58, s. 41. 35 & 36 Vict. c. 77, s. 17, is to the like effect, which Act refers to metalliferous mines. An inspector under this latter Act may exercise the powers under the former Act if directed to do so by the Secretary of State—50 & 51 Vict. c. 58, s. 39. The decision of the Secretary of State that either of these Acts applies to any particular mine is final—s. 71.
(d) 17 & 18 Vict. c. 104, s. 13.

(e) Sect. 15. As to explosives, see 38 & 39 Vict. c. 17, s. 58.
(f) 17 & 18 Vict. c. 104, s. 306. As to life-saving apparatus, see 51 & 52 Vict. c. 24, s. 5; and as to lights and signals, 25 & 26 Vict. c. 63, s. 30.
(g) 17 & 18 Vict. c. 104, s. 441. He cannot interfere between master and crew unless requested by master to do so.
(h) Sect. 442.

He may cause persons plundering, creating obstruction or disorder to be apprehended, and force to be used for the suppression of such plundering, disorder or obstruction (*i*). *Arrest.*

In such cases the receiver and his assistants may, unless there is a public road equally convenient, enter and pass over adjoining lands and deposit cargo, &c., thereon. Any damage is recoverable as salvage (*j*). And in the absence of the receiver, or principal officer of customs or coastguard, officers of inland revenue, sheriff, justice, or commissioned officers, may act in that capacity (*k*). *Entry.*

Whenever any salvage is due under this Act the receiver shall, if due for services rendered to save ship, persons or cargo, detain the ship and cargo until payment or process of detention issues from competent Court; if due for saving of wreck, detain wreck in like manner. But on security being given he may release the same (*l*). *Detention.*

In such cases of detention, if parties liable to pay are aware of it, he may, if amount not disputed and payment not made in twenty days after becoming due, sell the same or a sufficient part thereof, and out of the proceeds pay the expenses and salvage and the surplus, if any, to the owners. In other cases there must be a judgment of a competent tribunal before sale (*m*). *Sale.*

A detaining officer is to have the same powers as an inspector of the Board of Trade (*n*). *Detaining officer.*

For the purposes of survey, he may go on board the ship and inspect the same, and every part thereof, and the machinery, equipments, and cargo, and may require the unloading or removal of any cargo, ballast, and tackle (*o*).

And any officer of the Board may seize and detain any ship liable to detention under the Foreign Enlistment Act (*p*).

Harbours, Docks, and Piers.

With regard to harbours, docks, and piers, the collector of rates may either alone or with any other persons enter any vessel within the limits of the harbour, &c., to ascertain the rates payable in respect of such vessel or the goods therein (*q*). *Harbours, &c. Rate collector. Entry.*

The master of every registered vessel must on demand produce the certificate of the registry to the collector (*r*). Where goods are to be unshipped, the master must in case of the whole cargo furnish the collector with a copy of the bill of lading, and in case of part of the cargo, with the best account in his power of the goods to be unshipped, and give twelve hours' notice of the time of unshipment (*s*); and before shipment an account *Certificate. Unshipment. Shipment.*

(*i*) Sect. 444.
(*j*) Sect. 446.
(*k*) Sect. 445.
(*l*) Sect. 468.
(*m*) Sect. 469.
(*n*) 39 & 40 Vict. c. 80, s. 12.
(*o*) As to foreign ships overloading, see s. 13.
(*p*) 33 & 34 Vict. c. 90, s. 21.
(*q*) 10 Vict. c. 27, s. 31.
(*r*) Sect. 36.
(*s*) Sect. 37.

126 EXECUTIVE OFFICERS.

Dispute. must be delivered to the collector (*t*). In case of dispute between the master and collector, the goods are to be weighed or measured, the expense thereof if the weight, &c., be greater than that stated, to fall on the master (*u*).

Non-payment of rate for vessel.
Distraint.
Appraisement.
Sale.
If rate not paid the collector may with such assistance as he may deem necessary go on board and demand payment, and on non-payment distrain or arrest of his own authority such vessel, and the tackle, apparel, and furniture belonging thereto, and detain the same until payment. If not paid within seven days he may cause the same to be appraised by two sworn appraisers and afterwards sold, and with the proceeds satisfy the rates and expenses of taking, keeping, selling, and appraising, and render the overplus to the owner on demand (*v*).

Rate for goods. A similar power is conferred in case of non-payment of rate for goods, and if they have been removed, he may distrain any other goods within the harbour, dock, or pier belonging to the person liable to pay (*w*).

Duties. In either case dues to Her Majesty must be first deducted out of the proceeds of sale (*x*).

Dispute. If any dispute arise as to the rate or charges for distraint, the collector may detain the goods until the proper amount be ascertained by a justice (*y*).

Harbour master.
Entry of vessel and position.
The harbour, dock, or pier-master may give directions for regulating the time at which and the manner in which any vessel shall enter into, go out of, or lie in or at the harbour, &c., and its position, mooring, or unmooring, placing, and removing whilst therein.

As to indicating a spot at which the vessel might take the ground, he must apparently use due care to select a spot at which she might do so with safety (*z*).

For discharge or loading.
Dismantling.
Remove unserviceable vessels.
Ballast.
Removal by master.
The position for taking in or discharging cargo, passengers, or ballast.

The manner of dismantling.

For removing unserviceable vessels and other obstructions, and for regulating the quantity of ballast for a vessel during delivery or after discharge of cargo (*a*).

This officer may himself cause vessels to be removed if he put a sufficient number of persons on board for protection, and there be no person in charge to attend to his directions (*b*); or after three days' written notice to the master for the purpose of repairing the harbour (*c*).

Entry to search for lights. He may enter any vessel in the harbour, or dock, or near the

---

(*t*) Sect. 39.
(*u*) Sects. 40, 41.
(*v*) Sect. 44.
(*w*) Sect. 45.
(*x*) Ibid.
(*y*) Sect. 46.
(*z*) See *Little* v. *Port Talbot Co.*, 7 T. L. R. 699.

(*a*) Sect. 52. Nothing done must be repugnant to the Customs' laws or regulations. An unreasonable exercise of power is subject to a penalty not exceeding £5—s. 53.
(*b*) Sect. 55.
(*c*) Sect. 65.

pier, to search for fire or light, contrary to the provisions of this or the special (*d*) Act or any bye-law, and extinguish the same (*e*).

Harbour constables have the same powers, protection, and privilege as constables (*f*). Harbour constables.

Piers, &c., under provisional orders are subject to the Merchant Shipping Act (*g*), and any general Act passed relating to harbours and dues (*h*). Piers under provisional orders.

RAILWAY INSPECTORS.

These officers may enter and inspect any railway, and all the stations, works, buildings, offices, stock, plant, and machinery belonging thereto (*i*). Railway inspectors.

WATER BAILIFFS.

Any water bailiff may, acting within the limits of his district, on production of the instrument of his appointment (*j*), examine any weir, dam, fishing-weir, fishing-mill, fixed engine or obstruction on any artificial water-course connected with any salmon river; stop and search on any salmon river any boat, &c., used in fishing on which there is reason to suspect (*k*) contains salmon, and seize any fish, instruments of fishing, or other articles forfeited in pursuance of the Acts; and search and examine all nets, &c., and other instruments used in fishing or carrying fish by persons reasonably suspected of having fish illegally caught, and seize all fish and other articles forfeited (*l*). Water bailiffs. Examine weirs, &c. Search boats. Seize forfeited articles. Search persons.

Lights, spears, &c., are forfeited (*m*) and roe as bait (*n*), nets of improper mesh (*o*), fixed engines in tidal waters (*p*), or not removed within thirty-six hours after commencement of close season (*q*), and nets used at the tail-race of a mill, or below a dam where no fish pass (*r*), or during close time (*s*), and fish caught by such means, and unseasonable fish (*t*).

(*d*) This includes piers, &c., constructed under provisional orders.
(*e*) Sect. 72.
(*f*) Sect. 79, and see *ante*, p. 76, et seq.
(*g*) 17 & 18 Vict. c. 104.
(*h*) 25 & 26 Vict. c. 19, s. 21.
(*i*) 34 & 35 Vict. c. 78, s. 4.
(*j*) This is a condition precedent to the exercise of the power: *Barnacott* v. *Passmore*, 19 Q. B. D. 75; 56 L. J. M. C. 99; 35 W. R. 812; and see *Cowler* v. *Jones*, 54 J. P. 660.
(*k*) As to what is reasonable suspicion, see *ante*, p. 82.
(*l*) 36 & 37 Vict. c. 71, s. 36, extended to any fresh-water fish by 47 & 48 Vict. c. 11, s. 3, which applies these provisions to all waters frequented by such fish.
(*m*) 24 & 25 Vict. c. 109, s. 11.
(*n*) Sect. 9.
(*o*) Sect. 10.
(*p*) Sect. 11.
(*q*) 24 & 25 Vict. c. 109, s. 20. The close time for bream, grayling, gudgeon, perch, pike, and tench, is March to June; for salmon and trout, September to January inclusive.
(*r*) Sect. 12, and 36 & 37 Vict. c. 71, s. 17.
(*s*) 28 & 29 Vict. c. 121, s. 58.
(*t*) 24 & 25 Vict. c. 109, ss. 14-21: 28 & 29 Vict. c. 21, s. 64; and 36 & 37 Vict. c. 71, ss. 19, 20.

Nets, stationary by mechanical contrivance, are fixed engines (*u*), but not if merely stretched across river by corks (*v*).

Any one may destroy an illegal fixed engine (*w*), and in such case the person so destroying the engines is not liable to be proceeded against for damages (*x*).

As to unseasonable fish, it is necessary to secure a conviction that the taker should know them to be such (*y*). But to take fish unlawfully they must be alive (*z*).

Privileges as constables. While acting within their authority they are to have the same powers, privileges, and protection as constables (*a*).

Arrest of offenders. This officer and his assistants may arrest persons between the expiration of the first hour after sunset and the last hour before sunrise illegally taking or killing salmon, or found in or near a salmon river with intent (*b*), or persons putting noxious material into a river with intent to destroy fish (*c*).

Production of licence. They may require any person found fishing for salmon to produce his licence (*d*).

A licence is required where a man uses any device by which salmon may be caught, and not only a device for the purpose of catching salmon (*e*).

Thames.

Thames. On the river Thames any water bailiff may enter into any fishing-boat or other vessel employed, or about to be employed, in fishing, and therein search for fish unlawfully taken, and any unlawful or prohibited net or apparatus for taking or destroying fish, and may seize any such fish, apparatus, &c. (*f*).

The conservators are authorized to make bye-laws for the protection of fish (*g*).

ALKALI WORKS INSPECTORS.

Alkali works inspectors. These officers may at all reasonable times by day and night, without notice, but so as not to interrupt the manufacture, enter and inspect any work to which the Act applies, and examine any process for the evolution, or condensation, or rendering harmless of noxious gas, and any place where alkaline waste is treated,

---

(*u*) Gore v. The Special Commissioners, L. R. 6 Q. B. 561; 40 L. J. Q. B. 252; Olding v. Wild, 14 L. T. 402.

(*v*) Watts v. Lucas, 40 L. J. M. C. 73; L. R. 6 Q. B. 226; 24 L. T. 128; 19 W. R. 470; Thomas v. Jones, 34 L. J. M. C. 45; 13 W. R. 154; 11 L. T. 450: but see Rawstone v. Backhouse. 37 L. J. C. P. 26; L. R. 3 C. P. 67; 17 L. T. 441; 16 W. R. 249.

(*w*) 24 & 25 Vict. c. 109, s. 11.

(*x*) Williams v. Blackwall, 8 L. T. N. S. 252; 32 L. J. Ex. 174; 11 W. R. 621; 9 Jur. 579.

(*y*) Hopton v. Thirlwall, 9 L. T. 327; 3 N. R. 70; 12 W. R. 72.

(*z*) Gazard v. Cooke, 55 J. P. 102.

(*a*) 36 & 37 Vict. c. 71, s. 36.

(*b*) 36 & 37 Vict. c. 71, s. 38; and see 47 & 48 Vict. c. 11, s. 3, *supra*.

(*c*) 24 & 25 Vict. c. 97, s. 61.

(*d*) 28 & 29 Vict. c. 121, s. 37. This power is also vested in conservators.

(*e*) Lyne v. Leonard, L. R. 3 Q. B. 156; Watts v. Lucas, 6 *ib.* 226.

(*f*) 27 & 28 Vict. c. 113, s. 66.

(*g*) Sect. 65, and see *ante*, p. 62.

or any liquid containing acid is likely to come in contact with alkaline waste, and generally to ascertain whether the provisions of the Act are complied with (*h*). They may apply tests and make experiments. And the owner must render assistance, and furnish on demand plans of any process (*i*).

(*h*) 44 & 45 Vict. c. 37, s. 16.
(*i*) Sect. 17. These works are required to be registered by s. 11.

MINISTER.

Minister. With regard to the office of minister, it should be premised that the freehold of churches and churchyards is in the rector or vicar (*a*), and in consequence he is entitled to the possession of **Keys.** the keys, and a duplicate obtained by a churchwarden has been ordered to be given up (*b*). "The minister has, in the first instance, the right to the possession of the key, and the churchwardens have only the custody of the church under him. If the minister refuses access to the church on fitting occasions, he will be set right on application and complaint to higher authorities" (*c*).

The possession of the church is in the minister and churchwardens, and no person has a right to enter it when it is not open for divine service except with their permission and under their authority (*d*).

Bells. Subsidiary to this right is that of ringing the bells and play-
Organ. ing the organ at, or before, or after divine service or otherwise. The consent of the incumbent is necessary in both cases (*e*).

Burial. Every person is by the common law entitled to burial in the churchyard of the parish in which he died (*f*) without any fee, unless there be a custom to pay such fee (*g*). But where a district which has a burial-ground becomes a separate and distinct parish, there is no right of burial in the old parish (*h*).

The intervention of the High Court is confined to the enforcement of the common law right (*i*), and does not extend to the mode of burial (*j*) nor the spot at which it takes place (*k*).

Connected with this subject is that of monuments and inscriptions.

Monu- In the case of monuments, whether they are affixed to the
ments. wall or merely placed there as coats of arms are, the consent of the vicar or rector is necessary (*l*). But if he remove them after being properly erected, "he is subject to an action to the heir and his heirs in the honour and memory of whose ancestor

(*a*) Phil. Ec. Law, 1756.
(*b*) Dewdney v. Good, 7 Jur. N. S. 763; Ritchings v. Cordingley, L. R. 3 Ad. & Ec. 113.
(*c*) Per Sir J. Nicholl: Lee v. Matthews, 3 Cons. 173.
(*d*) Per Sir J. Nicholl: Jarratt v. Steele, 3 Phil. 167; and see Griffin v. Deighton, 5 B. & S. 93; 33 L. J. Q. B. 29, 181; 5 B. & S. 93.
(*e*) Phil. 1756, 1757. See Wyndham v. Cole, 1 P. D. 130.

(*f*) R. v. Taylor, 7 Davy, 278.MS.; R. v. Coleridge, 2 B. & A. 806.
(*g*) Andrews v. Cawthorne, Willes, 536.
(*h*) Hughes v. Lloyd, 22 Q. B. D. 157; 5 Ti. R. 145; 37 W. R. 380.
(*i*) R. v. Coleridge, ubi sup.
(*j*) R. v. Taylor, ubi sup.
(*k*) Prideaux, 15th ed., 452.
(*l*) Maidman v. Malpas, 1 Hagg. Cons. 208; 2 Str. 1080.

INHERENT POWERS. 131

they were set up" (m). As to gravestones, no consent appears to be necessary for their erection (n).

With reference to inscriptions, " no person has a right to inscribe on a tombstone what his fancy may suggest, e.g. if such inscription should impugn the doctrine or discipline of the Church of England . . . the inscription would be struck out " (o). But the words " The Rev." before H. K., Wesleyan Minister, in an inscription, otherwise unobjectionable, was held not a sufficient justification for the incumbent refusing to allow the tombstone to be erected (p). Inscriptions.

It seems doubtful whether there is any obligation on the minister to perform the ceremony of marriage (q). Marriage.

CHURCHWARDENS.

It is the duty of churchwardens to enforce proper and orderly behaviour during divine service (r), and for this purpose they may direct in what particular seats, whether free or otherwise, persons shall sit (s). There is apparently no such duty when no service is being held (ss). Churchwardens. Seats.

Pews belong to the parish for the use of the inhabitants, and cannot be sold or let but by special Act of Parliament. The churchwardens must exercise a just discretion in the allotment of pews (t). A pew can only be appropriated to a house by faculty or prescription. If allotted to an inhabitant who ceases to be such, he cannot let it with and thus annex it to his house (u).

No power but the Legislature can deprive the inhabitants of a parish of their general right to be seated in the church (v); and an action for damages will lie against these officers who refuse admission to a parishioner (w). Neither can they dispossess any one of a sitting which he has enjoyed for a time, without giving notice of their intention and offering an opportunity for objection and explanation (x).

These officers may apprehend any person guilty of riotous, violent, or indecent behaviour in any church, chapel or churchyard during divine service or otherwise (y). Brawling.

(m) Inst. 18 b.
(n) Brice, Pub. Wor. p. 229.
(o) Breeks v. Wolfrey, 1 Curt. 887.
(p) Keet v. Smith, 4 A. & E. 398; 1 P. D. 73.
(q) Davis v. Black, 1 Q. B. 900; R. v. Moorhouse James, 2 Dea. C. C. 1.
(r) Burder v. Selmes, 1 Ec. & Ad. 114; Burton v. Henson, 10 M. & W. 105; Hutchins v. Denziloe, 1 Hagg. Cons. 170.
(s) Asher v. Calcraft, 18 Q. B. D. 607; 56 L. J. M. C. 57; 56 L. T. 490; 35 W. R. 651; 51 J. P. 598; Fuller v. Lane, 2 Add. 425.

(ss) Worth v. Torrington, 13 M. & W. 781.
(t) Wyllie v. Mott, 1 Hagg. Ec. 28.
(u) Ibid. 39, 34; Halliday v. Phillips, 23 Q. B. D. 48; 4 Ti. R. 640; 1891, A. C. 228; 64 L. T. 745.
(v) Astley v. Biddle, 1 Hagg. Cons. 318, n.
(w) Taylor v. Timson, 20 Q. B. D. 671; 57 L. J. Q. B. 286; 52 J. P. 135.
(x) Horsfall v. Holland, 6 Jur. N.S. 278.
(y) 23 & 24 Vict. c. 32, ss. 2, 3.

K 2

The disturbance must be wilful and intentional (z), but includes the case of a person persisting in going to one part of the church when directed to sit in another (a).

They may also arrest persons molesting any clergyman ministering or celebrating any sacrament or other divine rite or service (b).

This does not apply to the case of a clergyman collecting alms after the service is over (c).

They may pull off a man's hat irreverently worn (d). But before a person is assaulted he should be requested to retire (e).

OVERSEERS.

Overseers. Arrest of lunatic. Every overseer or relieving officer having knowledge that any person wandering at large within the parish is deemed to be a lunatic may apprehend such person and take him before a justice (f) or remove him to the workhouse (g).

If the circumstances are such as to justify their interference, and an action for false imprisonment be successfully brought against them they are not necessarily liable to pay the damages and costs awarded personally (h).

Paupers. These officers may search paupers on admission to the workhouse, and deliver any money found upon them to the guardians (i).

Workhouse Officers.

Workhouse officers. This power of search is extended to workhouse officers (j).

Lunatics. Alleged lunatics brought to the workhouse may be detained for three days (k), or on a proper certificate for fourteen days (l) or more (m).

They may receive chronic lunatics (n), and within fourteen days of an escape they, or asylum officers, may retake an escaped lunatic (o).

Paupers. Paupers offending against the poor laws are deemed idle and disorderly under the Vagrant Act (p). These officers may take such offenders before justices without warrant, and, if required to do so, from thence to gaol, and while so acting, are to have all the powers and privileges of constables (q).

(z) *Williams* v. *Glenister*, 2 B. & C. 699.
(a) *Asher* v. *Calcraft, ubi sup.*
(b) 23 & 24 Vict. c. 32, s. 2.
(c) *Cope* v. *Barber*, L. R. 7 C. P. 393; 41 L. J. M. C. 137; 26 L. T. 891; 36 J. P. 439.
(d) 1 Hawk. P. C. c 63, s. 29; and see *Reynolds* v. *Monkton*, 2 M. & R. 384.
(e) *Ballard* v. *Bond*, 1 Jur. 7.
(f) 53 & 54 Vict. c. 5, ss. 15, 20.
(g) 48 & 49 Vict. c. 52, s. 2.
(h) *Att.-Gen.* v. *Pearson*, 10 Jur. 651.
(i) 10 & 11 Vict. c. 110, s. 10.
(j) *Ibid.*
(k) 53 & 54 Vict. c. 5, s. 20.
(l) Sect. 24.
(m) Sect. 25, 26.
(n) Sect. 26.
(o) Sect. 85.
(p) 34 & 35 Vict. c. 108, s. 7; and see *ante*, p. 96.
(q) *Ibid.* s. 8.

Casuals cannot discharge themselves before 9 A.M. the second morning after admission, nor where admitted more than once in a month before the fourth morning, and during the interval they may be removed by these officers or a constable to the workhouse from the casual ward (*r*).

Casuals.

HIGHWAY SURVEYORS.

A highway is any road dedicated expressly or impliedly to the public, and used, whether or not the necessary steps have been taken under the Highways Act of 1835, to make it repairable by the parish (*s*). But a mere occupation road is not a highway, although they may co-exist (*t*).

Highway surveyors.

Justices may unite parishes into districts and appoint district surveyors, who are to have the same powers as highway surveyors (*u*), and the powers as to getting materials and preventing nuisances are extended to surveyors of county bridges and roads at the end thereof (*v*).

Surveyors of districts and county bridges.

Highway surveyors and surveyors of county bridges are not responsible in damages to travellers who have sustained injury from the highway or bridge being out of repair (*w*).

Liability for non-repair.

The surveyor may make a road through the grounds adjoining any ruinous or narrow part of the highway (not being the site or ground whereon any house stands, nor being a garden, lawn, yard, court, park, paddock, plantation, planted walk or avenue to any house or inclosed ground set apart for building ground, or as a nursery for trees) to be used as a highway while the old road is repairing or widening (*x*).

Road through adjoining grounds.

Obstructions from snow or the falling of banks are to be removed by the surveyor within twenty-four hours after notice from a justice (*y*).

Obstructions.

Where the ratepayers convey the material to repair it is to be at such times and places as the surveyor may direct (spring, seed-time and harvest excepted) (*z*).

Ratepayers conveying material.

If the surveyor shall make pits for getting materials he shall forthwith cause the same to be sufficiently fenced off while the pit continues open, and within three days after opening where no materials found cause the same to be filled up and covered with the turf taken out of the same, and where materials are found, within fourteen days after sufficient materials are obtained, cause the same to be filled up, if so required by the

Fencing holes.

Filling up.

(*r*) 45 & 46 Vict. c. 36, s. 4.
(*s*) *Roberts* v. *Hunt*, 15 Q. B. 17; *Fawcett* v. *York Railway*, 16 *ib.* 641, n.
(*t*) *Brownlow* v. *Tomlinson*, 1 M. & G. 484.
(*u*) 5 & 6 Will. 4, c. 50, ss. 14, 16. This Act does not apply to the Metropolis.
(*v*) Sect. 22.
(*w*) *Young* v. *Davis*, 2 H. & C. 197; 7 H. & N. 760; 31 L. J. Ex.

254; *M'Kinnon* v. *Penson*, 9 Ex. 609.
(*x*) Sect. 25.
(*y*) Sect. 26, and as to nuisances, see s. 73, and *Mill* v. *Hawker*, L. R. 10 Ex. 62; 44 L. J. Ex. 49; 33 L. T. 177; 39 J. P. 195; 33 W. R. 346. There is no obligation to remove them: *Morgan* v. *Leech*, 10 M. & W. 558; 12 L. J. M. C. 4; 6 J. P. 818.
(*z*) Sect. 35.

owner, within twenty-one days after appointment. Pits not likely to be useful to be filled up, and those likely to be useful to be sufficiently fenced (*a*).

<small>Materials in heaps.</small>
He must not allow materials in heaps to remain at night to the danger of passengers (*b*). But he is apparently not liable under this section, nor at common law if a road under repair be left without fence or light (*c*).

<small>Damage to bridges, &c.</small>
He cannot dig for materials whereby any bridge, well, building, dam, highway, occupation road, ford, mines, tin works, or other works may be damaged (*d*).

<small>Cleanse watercourse.</small>
He may make, scour, cleanse and keep open all ditches, gutters, drains, or watercourses, and also make and lay such tracks, tunnels, plats or bridges as he shall deem necessary in and through any lands or grounds adjoining. The damage in such case payable to the owner to be settled by a justice (*e*).

Tender of satisfaction for damage done is not a condition precedent to entry (*f*).

<small>Encroachments.</small>
He may take away and remove any encroachment (*g*).

But the defendant must first be summoned (*h*).

This does not apply to buildings not actually on the highway (*i*), but it does apply to any erection which makes the highway less commodious (*j*).

<small>Arrest of unknown offenders.</small>
Any person witnessing the commission of an offence may seize and detain the offender if unknown (*k*).

The offences are:—

Carrying away materials belonging to surveyor (*l*).

Riding on footpaths by the side of roads (*m*), or leading animals, carriages, &c., upon them, or tethering animals thereon.

Obstructing footways.

This does not extend to a right to plough up (*n*), nor to a perambulator (*o*), but there can be no right to erect stalls for refreshments (*p*).

(*a*) Sect. 55—Penalty for default not to exceed £10.
(*b*) Sect. 56, a penalty not exceeding £5.
(*c*) *Taylor* v. *Greenhalgh*, L. R. 9 Q. B. 487. See *Pendlebury* v. *Greenhalgh*, 1 Q. B. D. 36; 45 L. J. Q. B. 3; but see *Fearnley* v. *Ormsby*, L. R. 4 C. P. D. 136; 43 J. P. 384.
(*d*) Sect. 57. Penalty £5, and civil liability to remain. See *Peters* v. *Clarson*, 13 L. J. M. C. 153; 7 M. & G. 548; 8 Jur. 648; 8 Sc. N. R. 384.
(*e*) Sect. 67.
(*f*) *Peters* v. *Clarson*, *ubi sup.*
(*g*) Sect. 69.
(*h*) *Cooper* v. *Wandsworth Board*, *ante*, p. 34.
(*i*) *Chapman* v. *Robinson*, 1 E. & E. 25; 28 L. J. M. C. 30; 22 J. P. 735; 7 W. R. 12; 5 Jur. 434.
(*j*) *Denny* v. *Thwaites*, L. R. 2 Ex. D. 21; 46 L. J. M. C. 141; 35 L. T. 628; 41 J. P. 164; *Evans* v. *Oakley*, 1 C. & K. 125; 7 J. P. 660; *Chapman* v. *Robinson*, 28 L. J. M. C. 30.
(*k*) Sect. 79.
(*l*) Sect. 47.
(*m*) Sect. 72.
(*n*) *Mercer* v. *Woodgate*, 39 L. J. M. C. 21; 10 B. & S. 833; L. R. 5 Q. B. 26; 21 L. T. 458; 23 J. P. 759; 18 W. R. 116; *Woolley* v. *Corbishley*, 24 J. P. 773.
(*o*) *R.* v. *Matthias*, 1 F. & F. 570.
(*p*) *Simpson* v. *Wells*, L. R. 7 Q. B. 214; 41 L. J. M. C. 105; 26 L. T. 163; 36 J. P. 774.

Destroying the surface.
This includes a footway over a field (*q*).
Damaging banks, causeways, direction posts, or milestones.
Playing games to annoyance of passengers (*r*).
Hawkers, or gypsies, pitching tents, or encamping. Making fires, or firing guns or fireworks within fifty feet of the centre of the road.
There must be here injury, interruption or damage to the passengers (*s*). A burning tar-barrel on Guy Fawkes' Day is not within the section (*t*).
Baiting bulls, laying timber, running filth, wilful obstructions.
Suffering underwood to grow (*u*), or rain-water to drop from the eaves (*v*) is not within the section, but no continuance will make an obstruction lawful (*w*). A roller is an obstruction (*x*), and so are small ditches (*y*), and a person collecting a crowd by addressing them (*z*).
Persons guilty of pound-breach (*a*).
Drivers causing damage to others, or quitting road, or driving carriage without owner's name, or not keeping left side, or interrupting free passage, or not having proper control, or driving furiously (*b*).
Where a carriage is liable to excise duty, the name is not necessary (*c*). A bicycle is a carriage (*d*), and furious driving is now punishable under the section (*e*).

District Surveyor (Metropolis).

Every building (other than public buildings), and every work done thereon is subject to the supervision of this officer (*f*). He may at all reasonable times during the progress of the building or work enter and inspect the same (*g*), or enter to see whether such building, &c., is exempt from the operation of the

District surveyor. Metropolis. Buildings.

(*q*) *Brackenbury* v. *Thorsby,* 19 L. T. 692.
(*r*) See *Pappin* v. *Maynard,* 9 L. T. 327; 27 J. P. 745.
(*s*) *Stinson* v. *Browning,* L. R. 1 C. P. 321; 35 L. J. M. C. 152; 12 Jur. N. S. 262; H. & R. 263; 13 L. T. 799; 14 W. R. 395.
(*t*) *Hill* v. *Somerset,* 51 J. P. 742.
(*u*) *Walker* v. *Homer,* 45 L. J. M. C. 34.
(*v*) *Croasdill* v. *Ratcliffe,* 5 L. T. 834.
(*w*) *Gerring* v. *Basfield,* 16 C. B. N. S. 597; 28 J. P. 615; 11 L. T. 270; *Gully* v. *Smith,* 12 Q. B. D. 121; 53 L. J. M. C. 35; *Simpson* v. *Wells,* L. R. 7 Q. B. 214; 41 L. J. M. C. 105.

(*x*) *Wilkins* v. *Day,* 12 Q. B. D. 110; 49 L. T. 399; 32 W. R. 123; 48 J. P. 6.
(*y*) *Nicol* v. *Beaumont,* 53 L. J. Ch. 853: 50 L. T. 112.
(*z*) *Homer* v. *Cadman,* 55 L. J. M. C. 110; 16 Cox, C. C. 51; 54 L. T. 421; 34 W. R. 413; 50 J. P. 454.
(*a*) Sect. 75.
(*b*) Sect. 78.
(*c*) *Danby* v. *Hunter,* 5 Q. B. D. 20; 49 L. J. M. C. 15; 44 J. P. 283; 41 L. T. 622; 28 W. R. 223.
(*d*) 51 & 52 Vict. c. 41, s. 85.
(*e*) *Williams* v. *Evans,* L. R. 1 Ex. 277; 35 L. T. 864; 41 J. P. 151.
(*f*) 18 & 19 Vict. c. 122, s. 31.
(*g*) Sect. 42.

Act (*h*). Where the building has been erected without notice to him, he may enter and inspect within a month after discovery of the erection (*i*).

Theatres, &c. Similar powers are conferred in the case of theatres, music-halls, &c. (*j*).

Fees. The following fees are payable:—

For New Buildings.

	s.	d.
Not exceeding 400 sq. ft. in area (including any attached building), nor more than two stories high	30	0
For every additional story	5	0
„ „ „ 100 ft. sq. or part thereof	2	6
No fee to exceed £10.		
Not exceeding 400 sq. ft. and 1 story high	15	0

For Additions or Alterations.

Made after roof covered in—half the fee charged in case of new building.

	s.	d.
Inspecting arches or stone floors over or under public ways	10	0
„ openings in party walls	10	0
„ dangerous structures	20	0 (*k*)

And special services may be charged for (*l*).

INSPECTOR OF WEIGHTS AND MEASURES.

Inspector of weights and measures. This officer may at all reasonable times enter any building or other place in which coal is sold or kept or exposed for sale and stop any vehicle carrying coal for sale or delivery, and may test any weights and weighing instruments found therein, and *Weighing coal.* weigh any load, sack, or other less quantity in any such place or vehicle which is in course of delivery to the purchaser (*m*).

The master is not liable for the representation of his servant (*n*).

Where constables act in this capacity they are not in the execution of their duties (*o*).

(*h*) Sect. 43.
(*i*) Sect. 105.
(*j*) 41 & 42 Vict. c. 32, s. 21.
(*k*) 18 & 19 Vict. c. 122, Sched. II.
(*l*) Sect. 50.
(*m*) 52 & 53 Vict. c. 21, s. 29.

(*n*) *Roberts* v. *Woodward*, 25 Q. B. D. 412; 59 L. J. M. C. 129; 63 L. T. 200; 38 W. R. 770.
(*o*) *R.* v. *Kesteven JJ.*, 58 L. J. M. C. 157; 61 L. T. 51; 37 W. R. 670; 53 J. P. 661.

PART III.

LIABILITIES.

Under Warrants and Orders of Superior Courts at Common Law.

The first point to consider in reference to the liability of officers when acting under warrants and orders of any kind which issue in a due and regular manner is this, that obviously the exercise of the power conferred may be either (1) accurate, or (2) inaccurate. Inaccuracy of performance again divides itself into two kinds, namely, that which occurs where the power has been exceeded, and that where the duty to be performed has to some extent at least been neglected. It is only in the case of accurate performance that protection is afforded to the officer by virtue of the warrant (*a*). As regards inaccuracy, where the power has been exceeded, it would expose the officer to proceedings either civil or criminal on account of the excess, and where there has been neglect of duty to the detriment of the public, an attachment, information, or action would be held to lie. But where there has been mere excess of authority by officers acting under warrant, the doctrine of trespass *ab initio* does not apply as in the case of an overcharge in the nature of extortion (*b*), nor does it in any event in the case of nonfeasance (*c*). On the other hand, where there is any grossness or culpability in the excess such doctrine is applicable. Where for instance a sheriff merely continued in possession longer than the time allowed by law, he was held a simple trespasser (*d*). But where he so continued after the return day of the writ, such excess was held to constitute him a trespasser *ab initio* (*e*). And the same was decided where under a writ of *ca. sa.* he had broken an outer door (*f*). And in this last-mentioned case Lord Abinger said: "Where a party by reason of any irregularity becomes a trespasser *ab initio*, he cannot justify at all."

Liabilities.
Under warrants and orders of Superior Courts at common law.
Performance may be (1) accurate or (2) inaccurate, which latter consists of either (a.) excess or (b.) neglect.
Trespass ab initio not applicable in cases of (1) mere excess or (2) nonfeasance, but is applicable where excess is grave. No justification here.

(*a*) *Money* v. *Leach,* 19 St. Tr. 1001; and *cf. Crozier* v. *Cundy,* 9 D. & R. 224; 6 B. & C. 232; and *Bell* v. *Oakley,* 2 M. & S. 259.
(*b*) *Lloyd* v. *Davies,* 2 Ex. 103. See this doctrine stated, *post,* p. 152.
(*c*) *Six Carpenters' Case,* 8 Coke, 146 a.
(*d*) *Ash* v. *Dawnay,* 8 Ex. 237.
(*e*) *Aitkenhead* v. *Blades,* 5 Taunt. 198.
(*f*) *Kerby* v. *Denbey,* 1 M. & W. 336.

Warrant or order must issue (1) within jurisdiction; (2) apparently so: or (3) without jurisdiction.	It has been already stated that the officer can claim the protection of the warrant only in those cases where there has been accurate performance. This proposition needs a further limitation. The execution of a warrant or order of a superior Court at common law must take place under one of three conditions. Either the warrant or order must be (1) within the jurisdiction of the Court which issues it, or (2) apparently so, or (3) clearly outside such jurisdiction. The rule of law is that where an officer is acting under a warrant issued subject to
Officers protected in either of the first two cases.	either the first or second conditions, he is under no liability whatever on account of the execution, provided with no unnecessary force or violence he does simply what he was directed to do (*g*).
Except those of the House of Commons.	But in the case of warrants and orders of the House of Commons the protection is confined to the first case only, namely, where such House had jurisdiction to issue the warrant or order.
Stockdale v. *Hansard*.	In *Stockdale* v. *Hansard* (*h*) it was held no defence to an action for publishing a libel that the defamatory matter was part of a document which was by order of the House of Commons laid before the House, and thereupon became part of the proceedings of the House, and which was afterwards by order of the House printed and published by the defendants, on the ground that the existence of such privilege as would support the plea was
Bradlaugh v. *Erskine*.	negatived. On the other hand, in *Bradlaugh* v. *Erskine* (*i*), to a claim for damages for an assault committed on the plaintiff, a member of parliament, while attempting to enter the House for the purpose of taking his seat, defendant pleaded in justification thereof that the House had previously resolved and ordered that the defendant should " remove plaintiff from the House until he should engage no further to disturb the proceedings of the House," and that acting in pursuance of such order, defendant insisted and removed plaintiff. It was held on demurrer that the plea was good on the ground that the right of the Houses to impose discipline within their walls was absolute and exclusive (*j*).
Rule in *Turner* v. *Felgate* and *Cotes* v. *Michill*.	" Writs issued by a superior Court not appearing to be out of the scope of their jurisdiction are valid and of themselves without any further allegation, a protection to all officers and others in their aid acting under them; and that although they be on the face of them irregular as a *capias* against a peeress (*jj*) or void in form as a *capias ad respondendum* not returnable the next term (*k*) for the officers ought not to examine the judicial

(*g*) *Howard* v. *Gossett*, 10 Q. B. 359; *cf. Andrews* v. *Morris*, 1 *ib.* 17; and see *Brown* v. *Watson*, 23 L. T. 745; *Tarlton* v. *Fisher*, Doug. 671.
(*h*) 9 Ad. & E. 1.
(*i*) 47 L. T. 618.
(*j*) See *Bradlaugh* v. *Gossett*, 12

Q. B. D. 271, and the remarks of Alderson, B., and Tindal, C.J., in *Gossett* v. *Howard*, 10 Q. B. 412, n.
(*jj*) *Countess of Rutland*, 6 Rep. 54 a.
(*k*) *Parsons* v. *Lloyd*, 3 Wils. 341.

act of the Court whose servants they are, nor exercise their judgment touching the validity of the process in point of law, but are bound to execute it, and are therefore protected by it" (*l*).

If the process issue from a Court or person having competent jurisdiction, it will confer an authority even though there be error or irregularity in the previous proceedings (*m*) or the charge contained in it be utterly unfounded (*n*). But if it be defective on the face of it, as if there be a mistake in the name of the party to be arrested, or if the name of the officer or party to be arrested be inserted without authority and after the issue of the process, the apprehension may be resisted and the killing of the officer will be manslaughter only (*o*). *Erroneous process.*

Defective process.

The phrase above quoted "for the officers ought not to examine the judicial act of the Court whose servants they are, nor exercise their judgment touching the validity of the process in point of law," is one which requires interpretation. It may be thus stated. Being satisfied that the act of which the process issuing in a due and regular manner is the consequence, is the judicial act of the Court whose servants they are, they are not to inquire further, but are bound to execute it. But it is quite clear that they are bound to inquire so far as to satisfy themselves that it is the judicial act of such Court. And it is obvious that it may prove *not* to be so in two modes—first, that the process is feigned, forged, or simulated, and is not the process or order of the Court (*p*), or second (which is the third condition under which such warrants and orders may issue) that the Court has in the specific instance manifestly exceeded its jurisdiction (*q*), inasmuch as it was unable to take cognizance of the cause or matter in which the process issued (*r*). *"The officers ought not to examine the judicial act of the Court."*

What is the judicial act.

Here it is no defence to the officer if he execute it, and he can derive no protection from it. *Where jurisdiction exceeded no protection.*

With regard to justification, it has been held that a man acting under legal authority is not confined to the authority under which he has professed to act at the time when he acted, but he may resort to any other authority which justified his proceeding (*s*). Again, where the judgment is subsequently reversed as being wrong in point of law, all irregular process under it before the appeal is heard is good, and affords a justification to all parties acting under it (*t*). *Justification, what.*

(*l*) *Turner* v. *Fellgate*, 1 Lev. 95; *Cotes* v. *Michill*, 3 *ib*. 20. See the judgment of Parke, B., in *Gossett* v. *Howard*, 10 Q. B. 453.
(*m*) 1 Hale P. C. 457.
(*n*) 1 East, P. C. 310; *Green* v. *Elgie*, 5 Q. B. 99; *Ex parte Fernandez*, 10 C. B. N. S. 3.
(*o*) *Ibid*.
(*p*) *Hooper* v. *Lane*, 6 H. L. C. 443; 3 Jur. N. S. 1026; 27 L. J. Q. B. 75.

(*q*) *Stockdale* v. *Hansard*, 9 Ad. & E. 1.
(*r*) *Rutland, ubi supra*; *Parsons* v. *Lloyd, ubi supra*; *Smith* v. *Bourchier*, 2 Stra. 994; *Perkins* v. *Proctor*, 2 Wils. 385; and see *R.* v. *Danser*, 6 T. R. 245.
(*s*) Per Williams, J., *Hooper* v. *Lane, ubi supra*.
(*t*) *Weiss* v. *Smith*, 14 C. B. N. S. 596; *Smith* v. *Sydney*, L. R. 5 Q. B. 203; 39 L. J. Q. B. 144.

EXECUTIVE OFFICERS.

Pleading. In pleading, the defendant is bound to set forth the warrant, and rest his justification upon it (*u*), but he need state nothing in the defence but the issue thereof (*v*).

The greater part of the cases which occur in which officers of the superior Courts are concerned are those in which the defendant is—

THE SHERIFF,

Sheriff. Employs agent. whose position in point of law is peculiar. Although he is the officer entrusted with the execution of the Queen's writs (*w*), practically he never executes in person, but employs under-sheriffs, bound bailiffs, and others, for that purpose. The writ which goes to the sheriff has upon its face an injunction to **Warrant to bailiff.** make out his warrant to his bailiff to levy the execution in question. The justification of the sheriff is the writ, of the bailiff the warrant (*x*).

Form thereof immaterial so far as liability of sheriff concerned. From this principle it follows that so far as the liability of the sheriff is concerned, it matters not what is the form of the warrant which he issues to the bailiff. He is not only liable for the acts of the bailiff done under the warrant (*y*), but also for any mistake or misconduct committed in the course of the execution (*z*). It is no defence for the sheriff to say that his orders were not attended to. He still remains liable, provided the act complained of be one which the officer was bound to do while acting in execution of the sheriff's orders (*a*), and an actual recognition by the sheriff of such acts is not necessary (*b*).

"There is no doubt that the sheriff is liable for all acts done and neglects of duty by the bailiff in the execution of a writ, on the ground that if the sheriff thinks fit to commit the execution of a writ, which he is bound to execute, to another, he is responsible if that person does not execute it properly, and is in the same condition as if he had executed it himself (*c*), the case of a sheriff differing in this respect from the liability of an ordinary principal, for the acts of an agent who does not pursue the authority committed to him" (*d*). And this is so "for the sake of securing a responsible recourse for indemnity in case of any wrong done in the execution of process" (*e*).

Evidence to connect the Sheriff.

Evidence to connect the sheriff. In order to render the sheriff liable for the act of his officer, it

(*u*) *Greene* v. *Jones*, 1 Wms. Saund. 298, n. 1.
(*v*) Lev. p. 191 a.; Com. Dig. Pl. 3 M. 24; *Britton* v. *Cole*, 1 Salk. 408.
(*w*) 50 & 51 Vict. c. 55, s. 8.
(*x*) *Hooper* v. *Lane*, *ubi supra*.
(*y*) *Crowder* v. *Long*, 8 B. & C. 605; 3 M. & R. 17.
(*z*) *Smart* v. *Hutton*, 8 A. & E. 568; 2 N. & M. 426.

(*a*) *Smith* v. *Pritchard*, 8 C. B. 588.
(*b*) *Sanderson* v. *Baker*, 3 Wils. 309; 2 W. Bl. 832.
(*c*) *Parrott* v. *Mumford*, 2 Esp. 585.
(*d*) Per Parke, B., *Woods* v. *Finnis*, 7 Ex. 371.
(*e*) Per Erle, J., *Hooper* v. *Lane*, *ubi supra*.

is sufficient to produce the warrant, without the writ, and it lies upon the sheriff to prove that no such writ issued (*f*), but the mere proof that the officer is the bailiff of the sheriff, without producing the warrant is not sufficient (*g*) unless there be recognition by the sheriff that the officer acted under his authority, which will dispense with the necessity of producing the warrant (*h*). If the officer swear that the warrant existed, though it be lost, it is sufficient (*i*), and in such cases secondary evidence is admissible (*j*). *Proof of warrant.*

Where the warrant recites the writ, evidence of the judgment is not necessary (*k*). And it has been held that the sheriff need not prove the writ where the plaintiff claims by virtue of an assignment which is void as against creditors (*l*). *Of writ.*

Where the sheriff is sued for removing goods without paying a year's rent in arrear, the plea of "not guilty" admits the seizure by the sheriff, and the production of the warrant is unnecessary (*m*).

Proof of the indorsement of the officer's name on the writ by a clerk in the under-sheriff's office is *prima facie* evidence to connect the sheriff (*n*). *Of Indorsement.*

Where the execution took place at the time of year when the sheriffs were changed, and a witness after the case was set down for trial saw a form of return signed by the defendant, as sheriff, indorsed on the writ, which had never been returned, it was held sufficient to show that he was the sheriff who executed the writ. The writ, when produced, having the name of the sheriff erased, it was held for the jury to say whether the erasure was made to correct a mistake, or to defeat the plaintiff (*o*). *After expiration of office.*

In an action against a surviving sheriff of London, a return to a writ directed to both sheriffs, purporting to be that of both is conclusive to show that the return was authorised by the survivor (*p*). *Return of survivor.*

Admissions made by an officer while in possession under a writ are evidence against the sheriff (*q*), and if the officer be guilty of excess, even though it be contrary to the orders of the under-sheriff, the sheriff will not be allowed to bring evidence which would tend to disclaim his responsibility (*r*). *Admissions. Disclaimer.*

(*f*) *Gibbins* v. *Phillips*, 2 M. & R. 238; 7 B. & C. 535; *Grey* v. *Smith*, 1 Camp. 387.
(*g*) *Drake* v. *Sykes*, 7 D. & E. 113.
(*h*) *Jones* v. *Wood*, 3 Camp. 228; *Shepherd* v. *Wheble*, 8 C. & P. 534; *Martin* v. *Bell*, 1 Stark. 413.
(*i*) *Moon* v. *Raphael*, 2 Scott, 489; 2 Bing. N. C. 310.
(*j*) *Minshall* v. *Lloyd*, 2 M. & W. 450; *Taplin* v. *Atty*, 3 Bing. 164.
(*k*) *Bessey* v. *Windham*, 6 Q. B. 166; 8 Jur. 124; 14 L. J. Q. B. 7; *White* v. *Morris*, 11 C. B. 1015; 21 L. J. C. P. 185.
(*l*) *Ogden* v. *Hesketh*, 2 C. & K. 772.
(*m*) *Reid* v. *Poyntz*, 8 Dowl. 410; 6 M. & W. 412; 9 C. & P. 515.
(*n*) *Scott* v. *Marshall*, 2 C. & J. 238; 2 Tyr. 257; *Fermor* v. *Phillips*, 5 Moo. 184; 3 B. & B. 27; Holt, 537.
(*o*) *Whitehouse* v. *Atkinson*, 3 C. & P. 344.
(*p*) *Carlile* v. *Parkins*, 3 Stark. 163.
(*q*) *Jacobs* v. *Humphrey*, 2 Cr. & M. 413.
(*r*) *Scarfe* v. *Halifax*, 7 M. & W 288.

142 EXECUTIVE OFFICERS.

Swearing officer. A sheriff's officer who is subpœnaed to produce his warrant, need not be sworn (s).

The Under-Sheriff.

Under-sheriff.
No liability.
Other than criminal.
With regard to the under-sheriff, it appears that he is, while acting in that capacity, not liable for any neglect of duty, nor will an action lie against him for any default in him. For all such neglect or default, the sheriff is alone responsible (t). But this rule does not extend to cases of extortion on the part of this officer when proceeded against criminally, nor to any other liability criminally for unauthorised acts (u).

Or where sheriff dies. Where the sheriff dies, the under-sheriff must, until a successor be appointed, execute the office of sheriff, and while so doing he is liable in all respects as the sheriff, and may appoint a deputy (v).

Proof of authority. Where an assignment of a lease by deed taken in execution was made in the name and under the seal of office of the sheriff, by A. B., acting as under sheriff, it was held that such assignment was sufficiently proved without further proving the appointment of A. B., as under-sheriff (w).

The Bailiff.

Bailiff.
Three kinds.
Bailiffs are of three kinds, namely, special bailiffs, bound bailiffs, and bailiffs of liberties.

Special. A special bailiff is one appointed by the sheriff for the execution of a particular writ at the instance of the execution-creditor, or some other person similarly interested or his agent (x).

Effect of appointment of. The effect of the selection of such a bailiff is to relieve the sheriff from responsibility to the party at whose instance he was appointed (y), but to all other persons he is liable in the usual manner (z).

How constituted. What constitutes a special bailiff is matter of evidence in each case (a). A mere request that a particular officer may be employed is not sufficient (b), nor is mere interference with the officer on the part of the debtor (c).

Bound bailiff. A bound bailiff is the one usually employed by the sheriff. It is no part of the duty of this officer to receive writs of execution from the parties (d).

(s) R. v. Menlis, M. & M. 515; Summers v. Moseley, 4 Tyr. 158; 2 C. & M. 477.
(t) Cameron v. Reynolds, Cowp. 406.
(u) Hescott, 1 Salk. 330; Laicock, Lat. 187.
(v) 50 & 51 Vict. c. 55, s. 25.
(w) James v. Brown, 5 B. & Ald. 243.
(x) Pallister v. Pallister, 1 Chit. 614.

(y) Pallister v. Pallister, 1 Chit. 614.
(z) Wat. 2nd ed. p. 41.
(a) Ford v. Leche, 6 A. & E. 699; 1 N. & P. 737; and see Wright v. Child, L. R. 1 Ex. 358.
(b) Triminger v. Keene, W. N. (1882) p. 106.
(c) Corbet v. Brown, 6 D. P. C. 794.
(d) Wright v. Child, L. R. 1 Ex. 358; 35 L. J. Ex. 209; 15 L. T. 141; 4 H. & C. 529.

LIABILITIES. 143

If the warrant be addressed to him alone, and not to him and his assistants, he must himself execute it (*e*), or, at any rate, be near at the time of execution (*f*). *Execution by.*

The receipt of money by the bailiff in satisfaction of a judgment-debt is receipt by the sheriff, and the sheriff is liable therefor, although there is no evidence of the money coming to his hands (*g*). *Receipt of money by.*

The bailiff would appear to be personally liable for a false return (*h*). *False return.*

There is no liability criminally on the part of the sheriff for the acts of the bailiff (*i*), and this includes proceedings for penalties for extortion against the officer (*j*). In such case the sheriff is irresponsible (*k*). *Criminal liability.*

A liberty is a district in regard to which grants have been anciently made by the Crown to individuals conferring on them or their bailiffs the exclusive privilege of executing legal process therein (*l*). Westminster and Pontefract are instances of such liberties. *Bailiffs of liberties.*

The powers, duties, and liabilities of a bailiff of a liberty are similar to those of a bound bailiff (*m*).

When the king is a party, or the writ contains a *non omittas* clause, the sheriff or his officer must enter the franchise and execute the writ. And in any other case he may enter, and the execution is not on that account irregular; but the lord may recover compensation from the sheriff, for an infringement of his right; though the party against whom the writ was issued has no remedy (*n*). *When sheriff to enter liberty.*

When the sheriff has made out his mandate to the bailiff of a liberty, the bailiff and not the sheriff is responsible (*o*). *Liability of bailiff.*

Process directed in the first instance to the bailiff of a franchise is void (*p*), and the bailiff executing it is guilty of a trespass against the party whose goods are taken in execution, for he is not the recognised officer of the Court, but the sheriff (*q*).

The sheriff's mandate requires the bailiffs of the liberty to make their return to the sheriff; but, in practice, such return is made direct to the Court (*r*). *Return of bailiff.*

(*e*) *R.* v. *Noonan*, 10 Ir. C. L. R. 505.
(*f*) Wat. p. 70.
(*g*) *Woodman* v. *Gist*, 8 C. & P. 213; *Jones* v. *Perchard*, 2 Esp. 507; *Gregory* v. *Cotterell*, 5 El. & Bl. 571; 2 Jur. N. S. 16; 25 L. J. Q. B. 33.
(*h*) *Jackson* v. *Hill*, 10 Ad. & E. 477; 2 P. & D. 455.
(*i*) *Sanderson* v. *Baker*, 3 Wils. 309; 2 W. Bl. 832; *Woodgate* v. *Knatchbull*, 2 D. & East, 154.

(*j*) 50 & 51 Vict. c. 55, s. 29.
(*k*) *Woodgate* v. *Knatchbull, ubi supra.*
(*l*) Steph. Comm. 8th ed. p. 632.
(*m*) 50 & 51 Vict. c. 55, s. 34.
(*n*) *Carrett* v. *Smallpage*, 9 East, 330.
(*o*) *Boothman* v. *Earl Surrey*, 2 D. & E. 4; see 27 Hen. 8, c. 24, s. 8.
(*p*) Except in Westminster.
(*q*) *Grant* v. *Bagge*, 3 East, 128.
(*r*) Wat. p. 61.

UNDER WARRANTS AND ORDERS OF SUPERIOR COURTS NOT AT
COMMON LAW, OF INFERIOR COURTS, AND OFFICERS GENERALLY.

A.—AFTER ADJUDICATION.

Under warrants and orders of superior Courts not at common law, of inferior Courts, and officers generally.
A. After adjudication.
Liability.

The liability of an officer when acting under a warrant or order of this class where there has been an adjudication is practically identical with that of an officer acting under warrant or order of a superior Court at common law, the main distinction being that which was pointed out at the commencement of the work, namely, that whereas the presumption in favour of jurisdiction is general in the case of warrants and orders of the kind last mentioned, it extends only to what appears on the face of the particular instrument in the case of these warrants and orders.

Putting aside this distinction, the rule as to liability is the same, namely, that where an officer acts under a warrant or order of the class we are now considering, which shews on its face to have been made (1) within the jurisdiction of the Court or person issuing it, or (2) apparently so, it is a complete justification to the officer (*a*). On the other hand, where it clearly appears to have been made without such jurisdiction, being beyond the scope of the powers delegated to the Court or officer issuing it, it is no protection to the officer, and he can derive no shelter from what is practically a piece of waste paper (*b*).

When made without jurisdiction.

Onus of proof as to jurisdiction on defendant.

It is necessary for a party who relies upon the decision of an inferior tribunal to shew that the proceedings were within the jurisdiction of the Court (*c*). An officer of an inferior Court may justify acting under process which is only voidable, but not under void process (*d*). But in an action by A. against B. for false imprisonment, B. cannot defend himself under a justice's warrant against C., although A. was charged for felony before the magistrate, and was the person against whom the warrant was intended to issue (*e*). "It would be dangerous if a person whose office is purely ministerial, were allowed to sit in judgment and say who is the unnamed person intended by the warrant which he is required to execute" (*f*).

No trespass for error in form.

Trespass is only maintainable where the process is an absolute

(*a*) *Andrews* v. *Morris*, 1 Q. B. 17; *Patchett* v. *Bancroft*, 1 East. 563, n.; *Goodwin* v. *Gibbons*, 4 Burr. 2108; *Olliet* v. *Bessey*, T. Jon. 214.
(*b*) *Carratt* v. *Morley*, 1 Q. B. 28; and see *R.* v. *Danser*, 6 T. R. 245.

(*c*) Per Alderson, B., *Stanton* v. *Styles*, 5 Ex. 583.
(*d*) *Morse* v. *James*, Will. 122; see *Ex parte Besset*, 6 Q. B. 481.
(*e*) *Hoye* v. *Bush*, 1 M. & G. 775.
(*f*) Per Tindal, C.J., S. C.

nullity, not where it is merely erroneous in form (*g*). Where there is no jurisdiction as above stated, the whole proceeding being *coram non judice*, process is no protection against such an action (*h*).

The doctrine of trespass *ab initio* is as applicable to cases arising under these warrants and orders as to those of superior Courts at common law (*i*); but since the greater part of these warrants are issued either by County Courts or by justices to both classes of which a special form of protection is afforded, the point becomes of little practical value. Moreover, under certain statutes, it is expressly laid down that officers acting under warrants issued thereunder shall not be liable as such trespassers (*j*). *Trespass ab initio.*

Special protection in some cases.

As to warrants of the County Court it is laid down that the high bailiff is by himself or by the bailiffs appointed to assist him to execute them, and he is to be responsible for the acts and defaults of himself and such bailiffs as the sheriff is for himself and his officers (*k*). *High bailiff. Liability.*

The high bailiff however of the Court out of which a warrant originally issues is not responsible for any irregularities in its execution by the bailiff of another Court, even though his own bailiff assisted therein (*l*).

And for the protection of this officer it is provided that no action shall be commenced against any bailiff or against any person acting by the order or in aid of any bailiff for anything done in obedience to any warrant under the hand of the registrar and the seal of the Court until demand has been made or left at the office of such bailiff by the party intending to bring such action or by his solicitor or agent in writing, signed by the party demanding the same, of the perusal and copy of such warrant and the same has been refused or neglected for the space of six days after such demand, and in case after such demand and compliance therewith by shewing the said warrant to and permitting a copy to be taken thereof by the party demanding the same any action shall be brought against such bailiff or other person acting in his aid for any such cause as aforesaid without making the registrar who signed or sealed the *Protection.*

(*g*) *Riddell* v. *Pakeman*, 5 Tyr. 721; 2 Cro. M. & R. 30; and see *R.* v. *Binney*, 1 El. & B. 810; 22 L. J. M. C. 110; 17 Jur. 854; 17 J. P. 440; *R.* v. *Ely JJ.*, E. & B. 489; 55 L. J. M. C. 1; 1 Jur. 1017; *Guy* v. *Matthews*, 4 B. & S. 440; 33 L. J. M. C. 14; 11 W. R. 922; 8 L. T. 674; *Keane* v. *Reynolds*, 2 El. & B. 748; 18 Jur. 242.

(*h*) *Marshalsea*, 10 Rep. 68 b, 76 a; *Perkin* v. *Proctor*, 2 Wils. 382; *Miller* v. *Seare*, 2 W. Bl. 1141; *Smith* v. *Bourchier*, 2 Str. 993; *Higginson* v. *Martin*, 2 Mod. 195. And see *Doswell* v. *Impey*, 1 B. & C. 163.

(*i*) See the cases cited, *ante*, p. 137.

(*j*) See *e.g.* 2 & 3 Vict. c. 71, s. 51; 8 & 9 Vict. c. 109, s. 21; 17 Geo. 2, c. 38, s. 8; and see also *Goodwin* v. *Gibbons*, 4 Burr. 2108; and *Olliet* v. *Bessey*, T. Jon. 214.

(*k*) 51 & 52 Vict. c. 43. s. 35, and see *ante*, p. 140; and *Burton* v. *Le Gros*, 34 L. J. Q. B. 91.

(*l*) *Smith* v. *Pritchard*, 8 C. B. 565. A registrar who performs the duties of high bailiff is under the same liability.

said warrant, defendant on producing or proving such warrant at the trial of such action, a verdict shall be given for the defendant notwithstanding any defect of jurisdiction or other irregularity in the said warrant, and if such action be brought jointly against such registrar and also against such bailiff or person acting in his aid as aforesaid, then on proof of such warrant the finding shall be for such bailiff and for such person so acting as aforesaid notwithstanding such defect or irregularity as aforesaid (*m*).

This section and section 53 (*n*) cover cases where the warrant has been made without jurisdiction (*o*).

Constables, &c. A similar enactment, substituting the words "constable or other officer" for "bailiff" and "justice" for "registrar" is in force for the protection of officers acting under warrants of justices (*p*).

With reference to this latter enactment, it has been held that it does not apply to warrants of the Queen's Bench (*q*) nor of the Secretary of State (*r*), nor of commissioners of taxes (*s*), and that it extends only to actions of tort (*t*).

It seems however to refer to all officers generally (*u*), although not in an action of *replevin* (*v*).

Where the statute applies. In order to obtain the benefit of the statute the officer must shew that he acted in obedience to the warrant, and did not exceed his authority (*w*), and that he has complied with the terms of the section (*x*); but if he has exceeded his duty, but such excess was committed in the *bonâ fide* belief that he was acting in execution thereof, he is equally entitled to the protection (*y*). And it applies though the warrant be granted without jurisdiction (*z*), or the magistrates without authority order the suspension of the execution (*a*).

If, however, the officer loses the protection of the statute, he must justify under the warrant (*b*).

Where statute does not apply. The statute does not apply unless there be a remedy over (supposing the warrant illegal) against the magistrate who issues it (*c*).

Nor does it where a wrong person is arrested or a person under a wrong name (*d*), or a door be broken in execution of

(*m*) 51 & 52 Vict. c. 43, s. 54.
(*n*) *Post,* p. 157.
(*o*) *Aspey* v. *Jones,* 54 L. J. Q. B. 98.
(*p*) 24 Geo. 2, c. 44, s. 6.
(*q*) *Gladwell* v. *Blake,* 1 C. M. & R. 636; 1 Tyr. 186.
(*r*) *Entick* v. *Carrington,* 19 St. Tr. 1030; 2 Wils. 275.
(*s*) *Charleton* v. *Alway,* 11 A. & E. 993.
(*t*) *Green* v. *Rowan,* 7 C. & P. 48 n.
(*u*) Per Kenyon, C.J., *Harper* v. *Carr,* 7 T. R. 274.
(*v*) See *post,* p. 194, note (*t*).
(*w*) *Bell* v. *Oakley,* 2 M. & S. 259.
(*x*) *Clark* v. *Woods,* 17 L. J. M. C. 189.
(*y*) *Parton* v. *Williams,* 3 B. & A. 330; *Gosden* v. *Elphick,* 4 Ex. 445; 7 D. & L. 194; 13 Jur. 989; 19 L. J. Ex. 9.
(*z*) *Atkins* v. *Kilby,* 11 Ad. & E. 784; 4 P. & D. 145; *Price* v. *Messenger,* 2 B & P. 158; 3 Esp. 96.
(*a*) *Barrons* v. *Luscombe,* 5 N. & M. 330; 3 A. & E. 589; 1 H. & W. 457.
(*b*) *Read* v. *Coker,* 13 C. B. 859; 22 L. J. C. P. 205.
(*c*) *Sly* v. *Stevenson,* 2 C. & P. 464; *Cotton* v. *Radwell,* 2 N. & M. 399.
(*d*) *Haye* v. *Bush,* 2 Sc. N. R. 86; 1 M. & S. 775; 1 Dru. 15.

civil process (*e*), or where goods are seized not mentioned in the warrant, and not likely to be of use as evidence (*f*), or where the officer has executed it outside his jurisdiction (*g*).

The demand is good if signed by the plaintiff, his attorney or agent, and served or left by any other person (*h*), and though it require the perusal and copy to be given within three days (*i*). *What a good demand.*

As regards the County Court it is enacted that no officer shall be deemed a trespasser by reason of any irregularity or informality in any proceeding on the validity of which such warrant depends, or in the form of such warrant, or in the mode of executing it (*j*). And the same rule applies to officers acting under warrants of justices (*k*). *Irregularity in proceedings, County Court. Officers acting under warrants of justices.*

And where constables execute warrants for the recovery of tenements, they are under no liability on account of the person on whose application the warrant is granted having no lawful right to the possession of the premises (*l*). *Recovery of tenements.*

B.—WHERE NO ADJUDICATION.

It has been already pointed out that in the case of warrants and orders other than those of superior Courts at common law, the officer is under no liability for executing them where it appears on the face of the instrument either (1) that the Court or person issuing them had, or (2) apparently had jurisdiction to do so. But this is confined to cases where there has been an adjudication. *B. Where no adjudication.*

Where, however, there has been no adjudication, the rule as to liability is a different one. Acting under such warrants and orders the officer is protected only where the person or body issuing them had jurisdiction to do so, *and* the execution thereof is strictly carried out. If there was apparently jurisdiction when none in fact or clearly none at all, the warrant or order is equally valueless (*m*). *Liability. Where (1) apparently jurisdiction when none, or (2) none at all.*

But with this rule must be coupled the statute passed for the protection of officers acting under warrants of justices, and which we have discussed above (*n*), the greater number of warrants of this class being issued by those judicial officers. *Special protection*

Where an act can be done in a legal manner, the person giving the direction is not responsible for the act done if it be carried out in an illegal manner unless the relation of master and servant (*o*) exists between the person giving the direction and the person executing it (*p*). *Distinction between these orders and those of principal and agent.*

(*e*) *Bell* v. *Oakley*, 2 M. & S. 259.
(*f*) *Crozier* v. *Cundy*, 9 D. & R. 224; 6 B. & C. 232.
(*g*) *Milton* v. *Green*, 5 East, 238.
(*h*) *Clark* v. *Woods*, 3 New Sess. Cas. 213.
(*i*) *Collins* v. *Rose*, 5 M. & W. 194; 7 D. P. C. 796.
(*j*) 51 & 52 Vict. c. 43, s. 52.
(*k*) See 11 & 12 Vict. c. 43, s. 3;
2 & 3 Vict. c. 71, s. 51.
(*l*) 1 & 2 Vict. c. 74, s. 5.
(*m*) *Foster* v. *Dodd*, L. R. 3 Q. B. 76; *Wilkins* v. *Hemsworth*, 7 A. & E. 807.
(*n*) *Ante*, p. 146.
(*o*) See pp. 62, 148.
(*p*) *Creagh* v. *Gamble*, 24 L. R. Ir. 458.

C.—OTHER ORDERS.

C. Under other orders.

In regard to the other orders which have been enumerated above (*a*), it is obvious that they divide themselves into two classes, namely, general and specific. In both of these the law of principal and agent strictly applies.

Liability of principal and agent.

Where an officer is appointed by some person or body to do a class of acts, he becomes by virtue of his appointment the general agent of such person or body while acting in the performance of his duty. The liability in such cases of the principal has been thus stated:—A person [or body] who puts another in his place to do a class of acts in his absence is answerable for the wrong of the person so entrusted, either in the manner of doing such an act or in doing such an act under circumstances in which it ought not to have been done; provided that what is done is not done from any caprice of the servant, but in the course of the employment (*b*).

General agent.

A local authority in their public capacity are liable for any negligence of their servants (*c*).

Particular agent.

Where, however, the officer is appointed or directed to do some particular thing and that only, the liability of the person or body so appointing or directing him is more limited. In such cases the agent only binds the principal when acting in strict accordance with his instructions (*d*).

Ratification, effect of.

Moreover, the principal is in any case liable if the act complained of be one which was done for his benefit, whether or not there was any precedent authority, if the principal subsequently ratify the act (*e*).

Where there is a violation of a right to property or to personal security, he who procures the wrong to be done is a joint wrongdoer, and may be sued either alone or jointly with the agent for the wrong done (*f*). If an assault or imprisonment of the plaintiff be the necessary or probable consequence of orders given by the defendant, he will be responsible, although he did not directly order it or contemplate the possibility of its occurrence (*g*).

Evidence as to limits of authority.

What is within or without the scope of the authority is matter of evidence. Where a servant wantonly and not in

(*a*) *Ante*, p. 62.
(*b*) Underhill, Torts. 3rd ed. p. 41. See *Bayley* v. *Manchester Railway Co.*, L. R. 7 C. P. 415; 42 L. J. C. P. 78; and *Laugher* v. *Pointer*, 5 B. & C. 547; 8 D. & R. 556; *Joyce* v. *Metropolitan Board of Works*, 44 L. T. 811; and *cf. Abrahams* v. *Deakin*, 39 W. R. 145; 63 L. T. 690.
(*c*) *Hall* v. *Batley*, 47 L. J. Q. B. 148; 37 L. T. 710; 42 J. P. 151.

(*d*) *Brady* v. *Todd*, 9 C. B. N. S. 592.
(*e*) *Wilson* v. *Tunman*, 6 M. & Gr. 242; 6 Sc. N. R. 894; 1 D. & L. 513; 12 L. J. C. P. 307; and see *Wilson* v. *Barker*, 4 B. & Ad. 617; 1 N. & M. 409.
(*f*) Per Erle, J., *Lumley* v. *Gye*, 2 El. & Bl. 216; 22 L. J. Q. B. 463; *Barker* v. *Braham*, 2 W. Bl. 868.
(*g*) *Glynn* v. *Houston*, 2 M. & G. 337; 2 Sc. N. R. 548; 5 Jur. 125.

order to execute the master's orders, struck the plaintiff's horses and thereby produced an accident, the master was held not liable; but if in the course of the employment he so struck, although injudiciously, it would have been otherwise (*h*). Again, where a servant wholly exceeded his authority in arresting a person and did an act which was illegal, not in the mode of doing it, but in the doing it at all, the principal was held irresponsible (*i*). But where the act was one which the agent must be assumed to have authority to do, if there was a mistake in the performance of it, such mistake was held within the scope of the authority (*j*).

The fact, however, of the principal becoming liable does not exonerate the agent from his liability for tortious acts done by him. He may therefore be sued either separately or jointly with his principal (*k*). *Liability of agent.*

The relationship of principal and agent is unknown to the criminal law. If the principal direct the agent to do a criminal act, they are both liable as principals (*l*). On the other hand, if the agent do a criminal act unknown to the principal but purporting to act by his authority, the principal is irresponsible (*m*). *Criminal liability.*

With regard to the principals which are referred to in this class, the general rule as to their liability inasmuch as the powers which they exercise are conferred upon them by law, is that they are liable for any damage which has resulted from the doing of the act as individuals are (*n*); but as the powers which are exercised are almost wholly derived from statute, due regard to the wording of the Act in question must be had in order to ascertain what liability exists in any particular case. And in such circumstances the general rule appears to be the following, namely, that where the duty imposed is discretionary, or at any rate not absolute, the ordinary law as to liability for damage occasioned obtains (*o*). On the other hand, where the duty to be performed is of an absolute character, such liability is under the special circumstances negatived (*p*). *Liability of principal.*

(*h*) *Croft* v. *Allison*, 4 B. & A. 590.
(*i*) *Poulton* v. *London and South Western Railway Co.*, L. R. 2 Q. B. 534; 36 L. J. Q. B. 294.
(*j*) *Goff* v. *Great Northern Railway Co.*, 3 E. & E. 672; 30 L. J. Q. B. 148; 7 Jur. N. S. 286; 3 L. T. 850.
(*k*) *Lumley* v. *Gye, ubi sup.*; and see *Snowden* v. *Davis*, 1 Taunt. 359.
(*l*) 24 & 25 Vict. c. 100, s. 67.
(*m*) *Chisholm* v. *Doulton*, 58 L. J. M. C. 133. In statute law this liability frequently depends on the wording of the particular Act. And see *Wilson* v. *Stewart*, 32 L. J. M. C. 198; 3 B. & S. 913; 8 L. T. 277; 11 W. R.

640; 27 J. P. 661; *Bosley* v. *Davies*, 45 L. J. M. C. 27; 1 Q. B. D. 84; 33 L. T. 528; 40 J. P. 550; 24 W. R. 140.
(*n*) *Vaughan* v. *Taff Vale Railway Co.*, 5 H. & N. 679. See *R.* v. *Essex*, 14 Q. B. D. 753.
(*o*) *Dunn* v. *B'mham Canal Co.*, L. R. 7 Q. B. 244; 8 *ib.* 42; *Broughton* v. *Midland and Great Western Railway Co.*, 1 Ir. C. L. R. 169; *Metropolitan Asylum District* v. *Hill*, 6 App. Cas. 193.
(*p*) *Brand* v. *Hammersmith Railway*, L. R. 1 Q. B. 130; 2 *ib.* 223; 4 H. L. 171; *Dixon* v. *Metropolitan Board of Works*, 7 Q. B. D. 423; and see *Dixon* v. *Farrer*, 18 *ib.* 43.

UNDER INHERENT POWERS.

Under inherent powers.
Liability.

Where a public officer acts, or purports to act, by virtue of the powers which the law confers upon him, and while so acting is guilty of any illegality by way of commission or omission, he is personally responsible to the individual who has sustained damage thereby (a).

Every one who is appointed to discharge a public duty and receives a compensation, whether from the Crown or otherwise, is constituted a public officer (b).

The liability, however, of such officers is not confined to cases where there has been either excess of the authority conferred or breach of the duty imposed by law. It extends also to cases where the officer is strictly within the powers conferred on him, but guilty of harsh and oppressive conduct in their exercise. Where a Governor and Vice-Admiral of a Crown Colony suspended the judge of the Vice-Admiralty Court, but maliciously and without reasonable and probable cause, although he had legal authority to do so until the King's pleasure became known and the King subsequently confirmed the suspension, he was held notwithstanding liable in damages (c). The gist of the action was, admitting the legality of the suspension thus confirmed, but complaining of the defendant's exercise of his original authority, and his malicious and false representations by which the suspension had been confirmed (d).

Joint wrong-doers.

Whoever assists in the doing of an unlawful act becomes answerable for all the consequences of it, and when several persons have been jointly concerned in its commission they may generally all be charged jointly as principals, or the plaintiff may sue any of the parties upon whom individually a separate trespass attaches (e). If several are jointly bound to perform a duty, they are liable jointly and severally for the failure or refusal (f). And the same measure of liability attaches where several commit a trespass (g).

Judgment in an action against one of several joint trespassers is a bar to an action against the others for the same cause,

(a) *Lane* v. *Cotton*, 1 Ray. 646; 1 Salk. 17; *Tobin* v. *The Queen*, 16 C. B. 310; 10 Jur. 1029; *Rowning* v. *Goodchild*, 2 W. Bl. 906; *Barry* v. *Arnaud*, 10 A. & E. 646; 2 P. & D. 633.

(b) *Irwin* v. *Grey*, L. R. 1 C. P. 171; 2 H. L. 20; 35 L. J. C. P. 43; 36 *ib.* 148; and see *Terry* v. *Huntington*, Hard. 480, n.; *Whitfield* v. *Ld. Despencer*, Cowp. 754.

(c) *Sutherland* v. *Murray*, cited in *Sutton* v. *Johnstone*, 1 T. R. 493.

(d) Per Erskine arguendo, *Sutton* v. *Johnstone, ubi sup.*

(e) *Mitchell* v. *Tarbutt*, 5 T. R. 651.

(f) *Fergusson* v. *Kinnoull*, 9 Cl. & F. 289.

(g) *Hume* v. *Oldacre*, 1 Stark. 352.

although such judgment remains unsatisfied (*h*). But the cause of action must in both suits be identical (*i*).

Connected with the subject of liability is the principle which was illustrated in the case of *Armory* v. *Delamirie* (*j*), namely, that contained in the maxim—

"*Omnia præsumuntur contra spoliatorem.*"

Every presumption shall be made to the disadvantage of a wrongdoer. If an officer use the powers which he possesses against an individual on any other than public grounds, he becomes a wrongdoer, and this principle is applicable. Where a person who wrongfully converted property, refused to produce it, it was presumed as against him to be of the best description (*k*). Where a person claimed a debt from another, the proof of which was to be found in certain documents which were sealed up and in his keeping, and he broke the packet without authority to do so, the claim was disallowed (*l*); and where a necklace was missed and part of it traced to the defendant, who was unable satisfactorily to account for it, the whole necklace was presumed to have come to his hands (*m*).

Omnia præsumuntur contra spoliatorem.

EVIDENCE.

As to evidence, it is laid down that the fact that a person has acted in an official capacity is presumptive evidence of his appointment, and the formal appointment need not be proved (*n*); and this rule applies to both civil and criminal cases (*o*).

Evidence. Of officer acting sufficient, without proof of appointment.

DAMAGES.

In general the damages will depend on the extent of the trespass or breach of duty committed. But where there is any high-handedness on the part of the officer, or attempt to use his powers unfairly to the prejudice of any member of the public, exemplary or vindictive damages will be recoverable (*p*); and these must depend on the particular circumstances of the case (*q*). And in such cases the Court will not interfere with the discretion of the jury unless they are grossly excessive or clearly founded upon a mistaken or improper view of the matter (*r*).

Damages.

Vindictive damages.

(*h*) *Brinsmead* v. *Harrison*, L. R. 7 C. P. 547; 41 L. J. C. P. 19.
(*i*) *Slade*, 4 Co. 94 b; *Guest* v. *Warren*, 9 Ex. 379; 23 L. J. Ex. 121.
(*j*) 1 Str. 504.
(*k*) *Ibid.*
(*l*) *Crisp* v. *Anderson*, 1 Stark. 35.
(*m*) *Mortimer* v. *Cradock*, 12 L. J. C. P. 166, and see *Wardour* v. *Beresford*, 1 Vern. 452; *Sanson* v. *Ramsey*, 2 *ib.* 561; *Dalston* v. *Coatsworth*, 1 P. Wms. 731; *Gartside* v. *Ratcliffe*, 1 Ch. Cas. 292.

(*n*) *M'Gahey* v. *Alston*, 2 M. & W. 211; *Marshall* v. *Lamb*, 5 Q. B. 123; *Doe* v. *Young*, 8 *ib.* 63.
(*o*) *M'Gahey* v. *Alston*, *ubi sup.*; *R.* v. *Gordon*, 1 Leu. 515; *R.* v. *Barrett*, 6 C. & P. 124.
(*p*) *Merest* v. *Harvey*, 5 Taunt. 441.
(*q*) *Brunswick* v. *Sloman*, 8 C. B. 321; 18 L. J. C. P. 299; *Huckle* v. *Money*, 2 Wils. 205.
(*r*) *Edgell* v. *Francis*, 1 M. & G. 222; 1 Sc. N. R. 121; *Tullidge* v. *Wade*, 8 Wils. 18.

EXECUTIVE OFFICERS.

Not chargeable on public funds.
Same with penalties.
But superannuation is chargeable.

There is no power to charge the damages and costs recovered against an officer upon the public funds (*s*); and it is the same with penalties (*t*).

A sum due to an officer in respect of superannuation may, in the absence of direction by statute to the contrary, be attached in execution (*u*).

Connected with the subject of damages is the doctrine of

Trespass ab initio.

Trespass ab initio.

Where a power to enter upon lands or tenements is conferred by law on an individual, and when he has entered in pursuance thereof he commits a misfeasance (*i.e.* exceeds his authority), it shall be presumed that he entered with the intention of exceeding his authority, and that the trespass committed shall have relation back to the time of entering. In other words, whatever privilege he previously possessed is, by the excess, annulled (*v*).

(*s*) *Stops* v. *Northampton JJ.*, 4 T. Rep. 78. 53 L. J. Q. B. 24; 49 L. T. 471; 32 W. R. 122.
(*t*) *R.* v. *Wilts JJ.*, 8 D. P. C. 717.
(*u*) *Booth* v. *Trail*, 12 Q. B. D. 8;
(*v*) *Six Carpenters*, 8 Coke, 146.

REMEDIES.

PROTECTION.

1. *Prerogative.*

The Crown may, in the case of action arising against any of its officers, for anything done to which it is a party (*a*), demand a trial at bar, on the ground that it has an interest in the subject-matter of the suit (*b*). In that case it will be for " the plaintiff to shew the Court that it is misinformed " (*c*), and that the statement of the Attorney-General that the Crown is interested is groundless. If he fails to satisfy the Court as to this, the suit will become a Crown suit, and be regulated by the Crown Suits Act, 1865. The procedure in a Crown suit does not come within the scope of this work.

Remedies. Protection.
1. *Prerogative.*
When available.

It may, however, be here observed that by the Crown electing to come in and defend, it necessarily takes upon itself the responsibility for the act complained of, on the ground of the maxim, " *Omnis ratihabitio retrotrahitur et mandato priori æquiparatur* " (*d*).

Crown becomes responsible.

But no damages can be obtained against the Crown, for " the Crown can do no wrong " (*e*). In the event, therefore, of judgment being given for the plaintiff, " the redress, if any, must be by petition of right, which is now regulated by 23 & 24 Vict. c. 34. Under sect. 9 of that Act, he obtains a judgment that he is entitled to such relief as the Court shall think just " (*f*).

Damages in that case.

2. *Statutory Absolute.*

Customs and Excise officers, wreck receivers, and officers acting under the Explosives and Public Health Acts, are furnished with absolute statutory protection in a few cases.

2. *Statutory absolute.*

Customs and Excise officers are so protected for seizing goods as liable to forfeiture where there was probable cause for such seizure (*g*); in stopping carts and wagons to search for smuggled goods, though none be found (*h*); for firing into ships liable to

Customs and excise.

(*a*) See *ante*, p. 5.
(*b*) *Buron* v. *Denman*, 2 Ex. 167; *Dixon* v. *Farrar*, 18 Q. B. D. 43.
(*c*) Per Tindal, C.J.: *Paddock* v. *Forester*, 8 Dowl. 834; *Rowe* v. *Brenton*, 3 M. & R. 133.
(*d*) *Buron* v. *Denman*, *ubi sup.*
(*e*) 2 Rolle, Rep. 304.

(*f*) Per Blackburn, J.: *Thomas* v. *The Queen*, L. R. 10 Q. B. 33; *Irwin* v. *Gray*, 3 F. & F. 635. See Clode on Petition of Right.
(*g*) 53 & 54 Vict. c. 21, s. 29, and see c. 56, s. 2.
(*h*) 39 & 40 Vict. c. 36, s. 203.

seizure or examination (*i*); and for detaining ships under the Foreign Enlistment Act (*j*).

A judge's certificate that there was probable cause for the seizure, covers the seizure only, and does not extend to damages for deterioration of the goods seized while in the officers' possession (*k*).

Receiver. The wreck receiver is so protected in case of a wreck where any person is killed, maimed, or hurt by reason of his resisting the receiver in the execution of his duty (*l*).

Explosives. And officers acting under the Explosives Acts are similarly protected where on reasonable cause to believe that any explosive, or ingredient of an explosive or substance found by them, is liable to forfeiture, they seize and detain the same (*m*).

Public health. And so are officers generally acting under the Public Health Acts (*n*).

3. *Statutory Ordinary.*

3. *Statutory ordinary.* Nearly the whole of the officers enumerated in this work have in certain cases a special protection conferred on them when acting in pursuance of their powers, which may, in order to distinguish it from the other kinds of protection referred to above, be termed the ordinary statutory protection. Its leading characteristics are notice, limitation, local venue, tender of amends, payment into Court, and, in some cases, special verdicts.

These enactments refer in their entirety to actions of tort. In the case of prosecutions, the protection is limited to limitation and a local venue.

Where Acts conferring powers refer to a principal Act containing protection, that protection is available under the subordinate Acts.

When available. The protective clauses usually open with the words: "In case any action shall be brought against any officer for anything done in pursuance of this Act." These words have been held to include the omission to do as well as the commission of an act or acts (*o*).

They are "required for the purpose of protecting these officers in those cases where they intended to act within the strict line of their duty, but by mistake exceeded it" (*p*). Their object is "clearly to protect persons acting illegally, but in supposed pursuance and with a *bonâ fide* intention of discharging their duty" (*q*).

(*i*) Sect. 181.
(*j*) 33 & 34 Vict. c. 90, ss. 28, 29.
(*k*) *Laugher v. Breffit*, 5 B. & Ald. 762; D. & R. 417.
(*l*) 17 & 18 Vict. c. 104, s. 444, and see s. 104.
(*m*) 38 & 39 Vict. c. 17, s. 74.
(*n*) 38 & 39 Vict. c. 55, s. 265; 54 & 55 Vict. c. 76, s. 124.

(*o*) *Jowle v. Taylor*, 7 Ex. 58; *Davis v. Curling*, 6 Q. B. 286; *Midland Railway Co. v. Withington Local Board*, 11 Q. B. D. 788.
(*p*) Per Kenyon, C.J.: *Greenway v. Hurd*, 4 T. R. 555.
(*q*) Per Ellenborough, C.J.: *Theobald v. Crichmore*, 1 B. & A. 229.

The defendant is entitled to the protection if he honestly believes in the existence of a state of things which, if it had existed, would have justified his doing the acts complained of under the statute. Some facts must exist such as might give rise to an honest belief, but it is not necessary that the belief should be reasonable (*r*).

A County Court officer is protected while acting under warrant of the Court, although there was no jurisdiction to make the order on which the warrant was founded (*s*). And so is a tax-collector if he *bonâ fide* believe a sum demanded to be due (*t*). But not if there was no colour for the demand, or he makes an improper seizure, and takes a bribe to deliver up the goods (*u*), or is guilty of extortion under threat of legal proceedings or distress (*v*).

A sheriff sued for an excessive levy is not within the protection (*w*); nor is a surveyor if, in obeying the orders of the Highway Board, he does an unlawful act (*x*); but a local authority for anything done, or intended to be done, under their Act is so (*y*).

NOTICE.

The cases in which notice is necessary have been discussed above when we were considering when protection is available. It is necessary whenever the officer purports to act in pursuance of the statute (*z*).

It appears, however, to apply only to such acts as the officer might at the date of the statute conferring the right to notice have been called upon to perform (*a*). And the officer is not deprived of his right because he has received an indemnity against the consequences of his act by the party interested (*b*).

An officer who takes under a County Court warrant the goods of B. by mistake for those of A. is entitled to notice (*c*).

But where a constable is authorized to arrest a person found committing an offence, to entitle to notice it must be shown that at the time of the arrest he believed the offence to have been

Notice.

(*r*) *Chamberlain* v. *King*, L. R. 6 C. P. 474. See *Booth* v. *Clive*, 10 C. B. 827; 2 L. M. & P. 283; *Smith* v. *Hopper*, 9 Q. B. 1014; *Beechey* v. *Sides*, 9 B. & C. 806; *Cunn* v. *Clipperton*, 10 A. & E. 589; *Griffith* v. *Taylor*, 2 C. P. D. 194; 46 L. J. C. P 15; 36 L. T. 5; 25 W. R. 196.

(*s*) *Aspey* v. *Jones*, 54 L. J. Q. B. 98; 33 W. R. 217; 48 J. P. 613.

(*t*) *Waterhouse* v. *Keen*, 4 B. & C. 211; 6 D. & R. 257.

(*u*) *Irving* v. *Wilson*, 4 T. R. 486.

(*v*) *Umphelby* v. *McLean*, 1 B. & A. 42.

(*w*) *Copland* v. *Powell*, 1 Bing. 369.

But see *post*, p. 157.

(*x*) *Mill* v. *Hawker*, L. R. 10 Ex. 92; 44 L. J. Ex. 49, and *cf. Peters* v. *Clarson*, 7 M. & G. 548; 13 L. J. M. C. 153; 8 Sc. N. R. 384; 8 Jur. 648.

(*y*) *Edwards* v. *Islington*, 22 Q. B. D. 338.

(*z*) *Cook* v. *Leonard*, 6 B. & C. 351.

(*a*) *Bryson* v. *Russell*, 14 Q. B. D. 720; 51 L. T. 90; 33 W. R. 34; 48 J. P. 360.

(*b*) *White* v. *Morris*, 11 C. B. 1015; 21 L. J. C. P. 185; 16 Jur. 500.

(*c*) *Burling* v. *Harley*, 3 H. & N. 271; 27 L. J. M. C. 258; 4 Jur. 789.

committed, and that he had found the person arrested in the act of committing it (*d*); unless taken *in flagrante delicto*, it must be shewn that an offence had been committed, that the plaintiff was on the spot, that there was reasonable ground for believing that the mischief was still going on, and that the plaintiff was the author and instigator of it (*e*).

Officers sued to recover back money paid which had been by mistake illegally demanded, are entitled to notice (*f*), and so are surveyors acting *bonâ fide* in a public capacity (*g*), although under an appointment in fact informal and illegal (*h*).

Length of notice. By 5 & 6 Vict. c. 97, s. 4, in all cases where notice is necessary, one calendar month is to be sufficient. And there may be a whole month between the date of the doing of the act complained of and the date of the commencement of the action (*i*). But this Act does not apply to enactments passed subsequent thereto (*j*).

What it should contain. The notice should set forth the substantial ground of complaint, and specify the time and place of the commission of the act complained of (*k*). It should also state that an action will be brought (*l*). It is not necessary, however, to name all the persons meant to be made parties, nor to express whether it is intended to be brought aghinst several persons jointly or against one person only (*m*); and a reference to a wrong statute has been held immaterial (*n*), and so has an inaccuracy as to the date of arrest (*o*).

If it fails clearly and explicitly to point out the nature of the cause of action, it will be bad (*p*). But it ought not to be construed with great strictness, its object being merely to inform the defendant of the substantial ground of complaint, but not of the mode or manner in which the injury has been sustained (*q*). And it may be contained in a series of letters, as well as in a single document (*r*).

Care must be taken to address the notice to the right parties, and to serve it in the proper quarter (*s*).

An action may apparently be brought without notice, when

(*d*) *Roberts* v. *Orchard*, 2 H. & C. 769; 33 L. J. Ex. 65.
(*e*) *Cann* v. *Clipperton*, ubi sup. See *Danvers* v. *Morgan*, 1 Jur. Ex. 1051.
(*f*) *Greenway* v. *Hurd*, 4 T. R. 553; *Selmes* v. *Judge*, L. R. 6 Q. B. 724; 40 L. J. Q. B. 287; 24 L. T. 905; 19 W. R. 1110.
(*g*) *Hardwick* v. *Moss*, 7 H. & N. 136; 31 L. J. Ex. 207.
(*h*) *Hughes* v. *Buckland*, 15 M. & W. 355.
(*i*) *Young* v. *Higgon*, 6 ib. 54.
(*j*) *Boden* v. *Smith*, 18 L. J. C. P. 121.
(*k*) *Breese* v. *Jerdein*, 4 Q. B. 585;

Martin v. *Upcher*, 3 ib. 668.
(*l*) *Mason* v. *Birkenhead Commissioners*, 6 H. & N. 72; 29 L. J. Ex. 406.
(*m*) *Bax* v. *Jones*, 5 Pr. 168.
(*n*) *Macgregor* v. *Galsworthy*, 1 C. & K. 8.
(*o*) *Green* v. *Broad*, 51 L. J. Q. B. 640; 46 L. T. 888 : 46 J. P. 599.
(*p*) *Taylor* v. *Nesfield*, 3 El. & Bl. 724; 23 L. J. M. C. 169.
(*q*) *Prickett* v. *Gratrex*, 8 Q. B. 1020.
(*r*) *Lamley* v. *E. Retford*, 55 J. P. 133.
(*s*) *Hider* v. *Dorrell*, 1 Taunt. 384.

its principal object is to restrain an immediate injury, although damages are also claimed (*t*).

Where damages are to be ascertained by a justice notice does not create a limitation of time in which to apply to the justice (*u*).

Notice is required as regards:—

County Courts, by	51 & 52 Vict. c. 43, s. 53 (General).
Constables . .	10 Geo. 4 c. 44, s. 41 (Metropolitan).
	3 & 4 Vict. c. 50, s. 18 (Canals and Rivers).
	8 & 9 Vict. c. 109, s. 23 (Gaming).
	12 & 13 Vict. c. 92, s. 27 (Cruelty to Animals).
	16 & 17 Vict. c. 119, s. 17 (Betting).
	24 & 25 Vict. c. 96, s. 113 (Larceny).
	24 & 25 Vict. c. 97, s. 71 (Malicious Injury).
	24 & 25 Vict. c. 99, s. 33 (Coin).
Customs . .	39 & 40 Vict. c. 36, s. 268 (General).
Excise. . .	53 & 54 Vict. c. 21, s. 28 (General).
Tax . . .	43 & 44 Vict. c. 19. s. 20 (General).
Post . . .	7 Will. 4, & 1 Vict. c. 36, s. 46 (General).
Highway surveyors	5 Will. 4, c. 50, s. 109 (General).
District surveyors .	18 & 19 Vict. c. 122, s. 108 (General).
Public Health Act	38 & 39 Vict. c. 55, s. 264 (General).

And in the case of prosecutions as regards:—

County Courts, by	51 & 52 Vict. c. 43, s. 53 (General).
Constables . .	8 & 9 Vict. c. 109, s. 23 (Gaming).

LIMITATION.

Some of these Acts provide that no action shall be brought except within a given time. An action is deemed to be commenced from the issue of the writ (*v*). *Limitation.*

The continuance of the act complained of, such as that of raising a wall, is not a fresh fact so as to extend the period of limitation (*w*). But where the damage is continual it is otherwise (*x*).

Limitation is imposed as regards:—

The sheriff, by	50 & 51 Vict. c. 55, s. 29 (General).
County Courts	51 & 52 Vict. c. 43, s. 53 (General).
Constables . .	57 Geo. 3, c. 19, s. 32 (Meetings—Metropolis).
	60 Geo. 3, c. 1, s. 5 (Drilling).
	5 Geo. 4, c. 83, s. 19 (Vagrants).
	10 Geo. 4, c. 44, s. 41 (Metropolis).
	3 & 4 Vict. c. 50, s. 18 (Canals and Rivers).
	12 & 13 Vict. c. 92, s. 27 (Cruelty to Animals).
	24 & 25 Vict. c. 96, s. 113 (Larceny).

(*t*) *Flower* v. *Low Leyton,* 5 Ch. D. 347; 46 L. J. Ch. 621; and see *Woodard* v. *Billericay,* 11 C. D. 214; *Chapman* v. *Auckland,* 23 Q. B. D. 294; *Bateman* v. *Poplar,* 33 C. D. 360.

(*u*) *Peters* v. *Clarson,* 13 L. J. M. C. 153; 7 M. & G. 548; 8 Jur. 648; 8 Sc. N. R. 384.

(*v*) *Original Company* v. *Gibb,* 5 Ch. D. 719; 46 L. J. Ch. 311; Order v. r. 11.

(*w*) *Wordsworth* v. *Harley,* 1 B. & Ad. 391.

(*x*) *Crumbie* v. *Wallsend,* 7 Ti. L. R. 229; 55 J. P. 421.

Gaolers . . .	24 & 25 Vict. c. 97, s. 71 (Malicious Injury).
	24 & 25 Vict. c. 99, s. 33 (Coin).
	41 & 42 Vict. c. 74, s. 55 (Contagious Diseases)
	45 & 46 Vict. c. 50, s. 226 (Municipal).
	28 & 29 Vict. c. 126, s. 50 (General).
Customs . . .	6 Geo. 4, c. 78, s. 37 (General).
	39 & 40 Vict. c. 36, s. 272 (General).
	40 & 41 Vict. c. 13, s. 5 (General).
	48 & 49 Vict. c. 49, s. 6 (General).
Excise . . .	53 & 54 Vict. c. 21, s. 28 (General).
Tax . . .	43 & 44 Vict. c. 19, s. 20 (General).
Post . . .	7 Will. 4, & 1 Vict. c. 36, s. 46 (General).
Contagious diseases inspector . .	41 & 42 Vict. c. 74, s. 55 (General).
Highway surveyors	5 Will. 4, c. 50, s. 109 (General).
District surveyors .	18 & 19 Vict. c. 122, s. 108 (General).
Public Health Act	38 & 39 Vict. c. 55, s. 264 (General).
Local . . .	5 & 6 Vict. c. 97, s. 5 (General).

And in the case of prosecutions, as regards:—

County Courts, by	51 & 52 Vict. c. 43, s. 53 (General).
Constables . .	10 Geo. 4, c. 44, s. 41 (Metropolis).
	3 & 4 Vict. c. 50, s. 18 (Canals and Rivers).
	8 & 9 Vict. c. 109, s. 23 (Gaming).
	24 & 25 Vict. c. 96, s. 113 (Larceny).
	24 & 25 Vict. c. 97, s. 71 (Malicious Injury).
	24 & 25 Vict. c. 99, s. 33 (Coin).
	41 & 42 Vict. c. 74, s. 55 (Contagious Disease).
	45 & 46 Vict. c. 50, s. 226 (Municipal).
Post . . .	7 Will. 4, & 1 Vict. c. 36, s. 46 (General).
Contagious diseases inspector . .	41 & 42 Vict. c. 74, s. 55 (General).

Amends.

Amends.

Most of the Acts also provide that the defendant may at any time after action brought tender a sum of money by way of amends and that in case such sum be not accepted by the plaintiff in satisfaction of his claim, that the same may be paid into Court and in a few cases pleaded by the defendant in bar of such action. Such payment into Court is to have the same effect in law as in other actions where defendants are allowed to pay money into Court (y).

The payment of money into Court by way of amends does not necessarily conclude the plaintiff (z).

Tender of amends and payment into Court is permitted as regards:—

County Courts by .	51 & 52 Vict. c. 43, s. 53 (General).
Constables . .	10 Geo. 4, c. 44, s. 41 (Metropolis).
	3 & 4 Vict. c. 50, s. 18 (Canals and rivers).
	8 & 9 Vict. c. 109, s. 22 (Gaming).

(y) As to the rules concerning payment into Court, see Order xxii. and County Court Rules, 1889, Order ix.

(z) *Boyfield* v. *Porter*, 13 East, 200.

LIABILITIES.

	10 & 11 Vict. c. 89, s. 72 (Towns).
	12 & 13 Vict. c. 92, s. 27 (Cruelty to animals).
	16 & 17 Vict. c. 119, s. 16 (Betting).
	17 & 18 Vict. c. 38, s. 13 (Gaming).
	18 & 19 Vict. c. 120, s. 224 (Metropolitan Management).
	24 & 25 Vict. c. 96, s. 113 (Larceny).
	24 & 25 Vict. c. 97, s. 71 (Malicious injury).
	24 & 25 Vict. c. 99, s. 33 (Coin)..
	41 & 42 Vict. c. 74, s. 55 (Contagious diseases).
	45 & 46 Vict. c. 50, s. 226 (Municipal).
Customs	39 & 40 Vict. c. 36, s. 271 (General).
	48 & 49 Vict. c. 49, s. 6 (General).
Excise.	53 & 54 Vict. c. 21, s. 28 (General).
Tax	43 & 44 Vict. c. 19, s. 20 (General).
Contagious disease inspectors	41 & 42 Vict. c. 74, s. 55 (General).
Harbour officers	10 & 11 Vict. c. 27, s. 91 (General).
Overseers	17 Geo. 2, c. 38, s. 10 (a) (Poor-rate).
Highway surveyors	5 Will. 4, c. 50, s. 109 (General).
District surveyors	18 & 19 Vict. c. 120, s. 224 (General).
Markets and Fairs Act	10 & 11 Vict. c. 14, s. 51 (General).
Public Health Act	38 & 39 Vict. c. 55, s. 264 (General).
Towns Clauses Act	10 & 11 Vict. c. 34, s. 219 (General).

Tender of amends may be pleaded in bar as regards:—

Constables by	41 & 42 Vict. c. 74, s. 55 (Contagious diseases).
	45 & 46 Vict. c. 50, s. 226 (Municipal).
Customs	39 & 40 Vict. c. 36, s. 271 (General).
Excise.	53 & 54 Vict. c. 21, s. 28 (General).
Tax	43 & 44 Vict. c. 19, s. 20 (General).
Contagious disease inspectors	41 & 42 Vict. c. 74, s. 55 (General).
Harbour officers	10 & 11 Vict. c. 27, s. 91 (General).
Public Health officers	38 & 39 Vict. c. 55, s. 264 (General).

VENUE.

The majority of the statutes provide that the action shall be tried in the county in which the fact complained of was committed. This has not been interfered with by the Judicature Acts (b).

The rule appears to apply only to such acts as the officer might, at the date of the statute conferring the right to venue, have been called on to perform (c). And a constable who arrests on suspicion of felony without reasonable ground for such suspicion seems to be within the rule (d).

Local venue is imposed as regards:—

County Courts by	51 & 52 Vict. c. 43, s. 53 (General).
Constables	7 Jac. 1. c. 5 (General).
	57 Geo. 3, c. 19, s. 32 (Meetings—Metropolis).
	60 Geo. 3, c. 1, s. 5 (Drilling).

(a) And sec 43 Eliz. c. 2.
(b) See Order xxxvi, r 1.
(c) *Bryson* v. *Russell, ubi sup.*
(d) *Slaight* v. *Gee,* 2 Stark. 445.

EXECUTIVE OFFICERS.

	10 Geo. 4, c. 44, s. 41 (Metropolis).
	3 & 4 Vict. c. 50, s. 18 (Canals and rivers).
	8 & 9 Vict. c. 109, s. 23 (Gaming).
	12 & 13 Vict. c. 92, s. 27 (Cruelty to animals).
	24 & 25 Vict. c. 96, s. 113 (Larceny).
	24 & 25 Vict. c. 97, s. 71 (Malicious injury).
	24 & 25 Vict. c. 99, s. 33 (Coin).
Gaolers	28 & 29 Vict. c. 126, s. 50 (General).
Customs	39 & 40 Vict. c. 36, s. 272 (General).
Excise	53 & 54 Vict. c. 21, s. 28 (General).
Tax	43 & 44 Vict. c. 19, s. 20 (General).
Post	7 Will. 4, & 1 Vict. c. 36, s. 46 (General).
Churchwardens Overseers	} 21 Jac. 1, c. 12, s. 3 (General).
Asylum officers	53 & 54 Vict. c. 5, s. 331 (General).
Highway surveyors	5 Will. 4, c. 50, s. 109 (General).
District surveyors	18 & 19 Vict. c. 122, s. 108 (General).
Public Health Act	38 & 39 Vict. c. 55, s. 264 (General).

And in the case of prosecutions as regards :—

County Court	51 & 52 Vict. c. 43, s. 53 (General).
Constables	3 & 4 Vict. c. 50, s. 18 (Canals and Rivers).
	24 & 25 Vict. c. 96, s. 113 (Larceny).
	24 & 25 Vict. c. 97, s. 71 (Malicious Injury).
	24 & 25 Vict. c. 99, s. 33 (Coin).
Post	7 Will. 4, & 1 Vict. c. 36, s. 46) General).

PLEADING.

Pleading. The defendant is allowed in some instances to plead the general issue (*e*), and in a few cases any other plea by leave of the Court (*f*).

The plea is in the form " The defendant says he is not guilty," and this may be pleaded whenever he honestly believed in the existence of a state of things which if it had existed would have justified his doing the acts complained of under the statute (*g*). In the margin must be inserted the words " by statute," and the year of the reign, chapter, and section of the Act on which he relies (*h*), except where he relies on the whole Act or Acts, in which case the sections need not be specified (*i*).

This may be pleaded by a constable who is sued in trespass for false imprisonment (*j*). But if an officer join in pleading with another who cannot justify, he loses the benefit of the justification (*k*).

In actions under statute. In actions under statutes, it is not necessary to recite the statute in the claim; it is enough to state that the thing was done contrary to the statute in that case made and provided (*l*).

(*e*) This puts the whole matter in issue: Archbold, 19th ed., p. 149.
(*f*) Order xix., r. 12.
(*g*) *Chamberlain* v. *King, ubi sup.*
(*h*) Order xxi., r. 19; County Court Rules, 1889, Order x., r. 18.
(*i*) *Saunders* v. *Warren*, 4 Ti. Rep. 552; and see *Edwards* v. *Hodges*, 24 L. J. C. P. 121; *Burridge* v. *Nicho-*

letto, 6 H. & N. 383; 30 L. J. Ex. 145.
(*j*) *McCloughan* v. *Clayton*, Holt, N. P. C. 478.
(*k*) *Smith* v. *Bourchier*, 2 Str. 993. But see *Parkins* v. *Proctor*, 2 Wils. 385.
(*l*) *Holmes* v. *Sparkes*, 12 C. B. 251; 15 Jur. 975; 21 L. J. C. P. 194.

LIABILITIES. 161

The general issue may be pleaded as regards:—

Sheriff by	21 Jac. 1, c. 4, s. 4 (Penalty).
Constables	7 Jac. 1, c. 5 (General).
	19 Geo. 2, c. 21, s. 11 (Swearing).
	42 Geo. 3, c. 119, s. 8 (Gaming).
	57 Geo. 3, c. 19, s. 32 (Meetings—Metropolis).
	60 Geo. 3, c. 1, s. 5 (Drilling).
	5 Geo. 4, c. 83, s. 19 (Vagrants).
	10 Geo. 4, c. 44, s. 41 (Metropolis).
	3 & 4 Vict. c. 50, s. 18 (Canals and Rivers).
	12 & 13 Vict. c. 92, s. 27 (Cruelty to Animals).
	24 & 25 Vict. c. 96, s. 113 (Larceny).
	24 & 25 Vict. c. 97, s. 71 (Malicious Injury).
	24 & 25 Vict. c. 99, s. 33 (Coin).
Gaolers	28 & 29 Vict. c. 126, s. 49 (General).
Customs	39 & 40 Vict. c. 36, s. 272 (General).
	6 Geo. 4, c. 78, s. 37 (Quarantine).
Excise	53 & 54 Vict. c. 21, s. 28 (General).
Churchwardens }	21 Jac. 1, c. 12, s. 3 (General).
Overseers }	17 Geo. 2, c. 38, ss. 8-10 (General).
Highway surveyor	5 Will. 4, c. 50, s. 109 (General).
District surveyor	18 & 19 Vict. c. 122, s. 108 (General).
Local	See 5 & 6 Vict. c. 97, s. 3 (General).

This last does not apply to local Acts passed subsequent thereto (*ll*).

EVIDENCE.

The evidence for the plaintiff is in actions against revenue officers confined to the facts set forth and contained in the notice and service of such notice must be proved (*m*).

Evidence.
For plaintiff.

The defendant is permitted under the plea of the general issue to give the Act and the special matter in evidence under the statutes enumerated below.

For defendant.

Where officers exceed their jurisdiction they can apparently avail themselves of this protection only in mitigation of damages and not as a substantive defence to the action (*n*).

Sheriff by	21 Jac. 1, c. 4, s. 4 (Penalty).
Constables	7 Jac. 1, c. 5 (General).
	19 Geo. 2, c. 21, s. 11 (Swearing).
	42 Geo. 3, c. 119, s. 8 (Gaming).
	57 Geo. 3, c. 19, s. 32 (Meetings—Metropolis).
	60 Geo. 3, c. 1, s. 5 (Drilling).
	5 Geo. 4, c. 83, s. 19 (Vagrants).
	10 Geo. 4, c. 44, s. 41 (Metropolis).
	3 & 4 Vict. c. 50, s. 18 (Canals and Rivers).
	12 & 13 Vict. c. 92, ss. 27, 28 (Cruelty to Animals).
	24 & 25 Vict. c. 96, s. 113 (Larceny).
	24 & 25 Vict. c. 97, s. 71 (Malicious Injury).
	24 & 25 Vict. c. 99, s. 33 (Coin).

(*ll*) *Boden* v. *Smith*, 18 L. J. C. P. 120; and see *Cock* v. *Gent*, 12 M. & W. 234; *Richards* v. *Easts*, 15 *ib.* 244; *Moore* v. *Shepherd*, 10 Ex. 424; *Carr* v. *Royal Exchange Co.*, 21 L. J. Q. B. 93; 1 B. & S. 956.

(*m*) See 7 & 8 Geo. 4, c. 53, s. 118; 39 & 40 Vict. c. 36, ss. 268, 269; 43 & 44 Vict. c. 19, s. 20.

(*n*) *Rowcliffe* v. *Murray*, 1 Car. & M. 513; and see *Wood* v. *Chessal*, 2 W. Bl. 1254.

Gaolers	28 & 29 Vict. c. 126, s. 49 (General).
Customs	39 & 40 Vict. c. 36, s. 272 (General). 6 Geo. 4, c. 78, s. 37 (Quarantine).
Excise	53 & 54 Vict. c. 21, s. 28 (General).
Tax	43 & 44 Vict. c. 19, s. 20 (General).
Churchwardens Overseers	} 21 Jac. 1, c. 12, s. 3 (General).
Highway surveyors	5 Will. 4, c. 50, s. 109 (General).
District surveyors	18 & 19 Vict. c. 122, s. 108 (General).
Local	See 5 & 6 Vict. c. 97, s. 3 (General).

Verdict.

Verdict. In the following cases the verdict is directed:—

Constables by	7 Jac. 1, c. 5 (General). 24 Geo. 2, c. 44, s. 6 (Warrants). 57 Geo. 3, c. 19. s. 32 (Meetings—Metropolis). 60 Geo. 3, c. 1, s. 5 (Drilling). 12 & 13 Vict. c. 92, s. 27 (Cruelty to Animals).
Customs	39 & 40 Vict. c. 36, s. 270 (General).
Excise	53 & 54 Vict. c. 21, s. 28 (General).
Churchwardens Overseers	} 21 Jac. 1, c. 12, s. 3 (General).
Highway surveyors	5 Will. 4, c. 50, s. 109 (General).
Public Health	38 & 39 Vict. c. 55, s. 264 (General).

Where a constable was sued for executing the warrant of a justice it was held that he was entitled to a verdict, the justice not having been made a co-defendant as required by 24 Geo. 2, c. 44, s. 6, on proof of the warrant, although the terms of the statute had not been literally complied with (*o*).

Damages.

Damages. Damages are dealt with in the following cases:—

Customs by	39 & 40 Vict. c. 36, s. 270 (General).
Excise	53 & 54 Vict. c. 21, s. 28, 29 (General).
Merchant Shipping Act	17 & 18 Vict. c. 104, s. 104 (General).

A judge's certificate that there was probable cause for seizure covers the seizure only, and does not extend to damages for a deterioration of the goods seized while in the officer's possession (*p*).

Costs.

Costs. Costs are dealt with as regards:—

County Court by	51 & 52 Vict. c. 43, s. 55 (General)
Constables	19 Geo. 2, c. 21, s. 11 (Swearing). 42 Geo. 3, c. 119, s. 8 (Gaming). 57 Geo. 3, c. 19, s. 32 (Meetings—Metropolis). 60 Geo. 3, c. 1, s. 5 (Drilling).

(*o*) *Jones* v. *Vaughan*, 5 East, 445; 2 Sm. 5.

(*p*) *Laugher* v. *Brefit*, 5 B. & Ald. 762; D. & R. 417.

LIABILITIES. 163

	10 Geo. 4, c. 44, s. 41 (Metropolis).
	3 & 4 Vict. c. 50, s. 18 (Canals and rivers).
	12 & 13 Vict. c. 92, s. 27 (Cruelty to animals).
	24 & 25 Vict. c. 96, s. 113 (Larceny).
	24 & 25 Vict. c. 97, s. 71 (Malicious injury).
	24 & 25 Vict. c. 99, s. 33 (Coin).
	41 & 42 Vict. c. 74, s. 55 (Contagious diseases).
	45 & 46 Vict. c. 50, s. 226 (Municipal).
Gaolers	28 & 29 Vict. c. 126, s. 49 (General).
Customs	39 & 40 Vict. c. 36, s. 270, 272 (General).
Excise	53 & 54 Vict. c. 21, ss. 28, 29 (General).
Post	7 Will. 4, c. 36, s. 46 (General).
Contagious disease inspectors	41 & 42 Vict. c. 74, s. 55 (General).
Merchant Shipping Act	17 & 18 Vict. c. 104, s. 104 (General).
Highway surveyors	5 Will. 4, c. 50, s. 109 (General).
Public Health Act	38 & 39 Vict. c. 55, s. 264 (General).

Where an action was for an injunction, it was held that costs as between solicitor and client could not be given to a successful defendant (*q*).

Treble costs were abolished (*r*) by statute, but the Act does not apply to enactments passed subsequently thereto (*s*).

Where the defendant makes an affidavit that the plaintiff if unsuccessful will be unable to pay costs, and the plaintiff fails thereupon to give security for such costs, the action may be remitted to the County Court (*t*).

(*q*) *Pullin* v. *Deffel*, 64 L. T. 134.
(*r*) 5 & 6 Vict. c. 97, s. 2. See *Butterton* v. *Furber*, 1 B. & B. 517.
(*s*) See *Hasker* v. *Wood*, 54 L. J. Q. B. 419.
(*t*) 51 & 52 Vict. c. 43, s. 66.

BREACH OF DUTY.

Civil Proceedings.

Action for Damages.

Breach of Duty. Civil proceedings. Action for damages.
Where a person undertakes a public office, he is bound to perform the duties of the office, and if he neglects or refuses so to do, and an individual in consequence sustains injury therefrom, that lays the foundation for an action for damages to recover compensation for the injury so sustained (a).

Duty at common law.
When a duty or obligation exists at common law independently of a statute, a new remedy given by a statute is simply cumulative, and does not preclude the ordinary common law remedy by way of action, unless there are express words to that effect (b).

Statutory duty.
When a statute creates a right or duty, then although it has not in express terms given a remedy, the remedy which by law is properly applicable follows as an incident (c). But if the right or duty is entirely the creature of the statute, and a specific remedy is provided by the statute for its enforcement, that remedy and that only must be pursued (d), unless the remedy does not cover the entire right (e).

Duty must be absolute.
These principles apply apparently only when the duty to be performed is an absolute one, and not within the discretion of the officer.

The rule as to liability may therefore be thus stated. Wherever the law confers upon an officer a power to do a certain act by an obligatory (f) as distinguished from an enabling (g) enactment, there is then a corresponding duty in the officer to perform the act required in which if he fail, he will be liable to an action at the suit of the person who has sustained damage by reason of his default. On the other hand if the duty is optional or discretionary, no such liability (in the absence of malice)

(a) *Sutton* v. *Johnstone*, 1 T. R. 493; *Fergusson* v. *Kinnoull*, 9 Cl. & F. 279.

(b) *Chapman* v. *Pickersgill*, 2 Wils. 145.

(c) Per Maule, B., *Braithwaite* v. *Skinner*, 5 M. & W. 327.

(d) *Stevens* v. *Jeacocke*, 11 Q. B. 741; 17 L. J. Q. B. 163; *St. Pancras Vestry* v. *Batterbury*, 2 C. B. N. S. 477; 26 L. J. C. P. 243.

(e) *Shepherd* v. *Hills*, 11 Ex. 67.

As to pleading in actions under statute, see *Holmes* v. *Sparkes, ante,* p. 160.

(f) *E.g.,* "is hereby required."

(g) *E.g.,* "may" or "it shall be lawful." See *Julius* v. *Oxford (Bishop of)*, 5 App. Cas. 214; *McDougall* v. *Paterson*, 11 C. B. 755; 21 L. J. C. P. 27; *Crake* v. *Powell*, 2 E. & B. 210; 21 L. J. Q. B. 183; *Bell* v. *Crane*, L. R. 8 Q. B. 481; 42 L. J. M. C. 122; *Re Newport Bridge*, 29 ib. 52.

exists (*h*). But to this there is an important qualification. "It has been so often decided as to have become an axiom, that in public statutes words only directory, permissory, or enabling, may have a compulsory force where the thing to be done is for the public benefit or in advancement of public justice" (*i*), and this has been held to mean that where a power is deposited with a public officer for the purpose of being used for the benefit of persons who are specifically pointed out, and with regard to whom a definition is supplied by the legislature of the conditions upon which they are entitled to call for its exercise that power ought to be exercised, and the Court will require its exercise (*j*).

In practice, however, where a duty is conferred, although it is possible, yet it is not very probable that action would arise owing to the fact that the plaintiff had sustained damage by reason of the officer's neglect.

But there is a notable exception in the case of civil execution. There a person is entitled to put an officer in motion to do a certain act or acts, and if he fails to perform the duty so required of him, it gives rise to this action. *Practically confined to civil execution.*

The officers concerned in civil execution are the sheriff, the Admiralty marshal, and the high bailiff, who so far as liability is in question may be considered one (*k*), and constables.

As regards the sheriff, it has been laid down that if he neglect or refuse to execute any writ when he has the opportunity and is required to do so, he is liable (*l*), but that he is not liable for not using extraordinary exertion or providing against an unexpected or unforeseen contingency (*m*). Accordingly, if he neglects to execute within a reasonable time (*n*), or to seize (*o*), or to sell or sells for less money than he ought to have obtained (*p*), or sells the goods of a third person (*q*), or relinquishes or abandons possession (*r*), although mere temporary absence (*s*), or withdrawing under a proper order is not sufficient (*t*), he is liable. So also is he if he negligently conduct a sale whereby the position of the execution creditor is prejudiced (*u*), or sells *Sheriff. Limit of liability. Neglect of duty. Seizure. Sale.*

(*h*) See *Partridge* v. *Council of Medical Education*, 25 Q. B. D. 90; 6 Ti. Rep. 313.
(*i*) Per Coleridge, J., *R.* v. *Tithe Commissioners*, 14 Q. B. 474.
(*j*) Per Cairns, C., *Julius* v. *Oxford (Bishop of)*, ubi sup.
(*k*) Judicature Act, 1873, s. 84; and see Wms. & B. Ad. Prac., 2nd ed. p. 249; 51 & 52 Vict. c. 43, s. 35.
(*l*) *Brown* v. *Jarvis*, 1 M. & W. 704; *Mason* v. *Paynter*, 1 Q. B. 974.
(*m*) *Hodgson* v. *Lynch*, 5 Ir. C. P. R. 353.
(*n*) *Clifton* v. *Hooper*, 6 Q. B. 468; 8 Jur. 958; 14 L. J. Q. B. 1; *Mason* v. *Paynter*, 1 Q. B. 974; 1 G. & D. 381; 6 Jur. 214.
(*o*) *Pitcher* v. *King*, 5 Q. B. 766;

D. & M. 584; 8 Jur. 401; 13 L. J. Q. B. 162. He must have notice that the goods are in his bailiwick; *Yourrell* v. *Proby*, 2 Ir. C. L. 460.
(*p*) *Jacobs* v. *Humphrey*, 2 C. & M. 413; 4 Tyr. 272; *Carlile* v. *Parkins*, 3 Stark. 163; *Gawler* v. *Chaplin*, 2 Ex. 506; 18 L. J. Ex. 42.
(*q*) *Oughton* v. *Seppings*, 1 B. & Ad. 241.
(*r*) *Blades* v. *Armidale*, 1 M. & S. 711.
(*s*) *Ackland* v. *Paynter*, 8 Price, 99.
(*t*) *Darby* v. *Waterlow*, L. R. 3 C. P. 453; 37 L. J. C. P. 203; 16 W. R. 864; 18 L. T. 523.
(*u*) *Mullett* v. *Challis*, 16 Q. B. 239; 15 Jur. 243; 20 L. J. Q. B. 161.

by private contract, when entitled to do so, before actual seizure (*v*), or retains the goods and pays the plaintiff (*w*), or delivers the goods to the plaintiff in satisfaction of the debt (*x*), or executes the writ and retains in his hands the proceeds (*y*). But the execution creditor cannot sue the sheriff before the issue of the *venditioni exponas* (*z*), nor is he liable if he sell under a *venditioni exponas* (*a*), under an extent which is in from the Crown at the same time (*b*).

An application for an order against a sheriff to pay money levied under an execution must be made by motion after notice (*c*).

False return.

He is also liable if he make a false return—that is a return to the writ which does not describe accurately the position of affairs (*d*). But if the sheriff merely return the answer of the bailiff which proves to be false, he is not, it appears, responsible (*e*). A writ is not now returned to by order, but a notice to return from the person issuing the writ or his solicitor issues (*f*). The return must answer the whole mandate of the writ. He may return *nulla bona* where the debtor has an equitable interest only (*g*), and also where the proceeds are exhausted in payment of prior rent and charges (*h*); but not where there are goods in his hands unsold (*i*), nor where he ought to have levied and neglected to do so (*j*). If he returns that he has seized certain goods, he ought to specify their value (*k*); but he cannot return that a house is barricaded and he cannot enter to see what goods are there (*l*).

Interpleader.

In order to claim the benefit of the Interpleader Act he must be in possession of the goods (*m*) as a whole (*n*), unless the property would be injured by seizure (*o*). He must not be an interested party (*p*), nor have been indemnified (*q*), but he need not wait for an action to be brought (*r*). Where he has exer-

(*v*) *Ex parte Hall*, 14 Ch. D. 132; *Ex parte Villars*, 9 Ch. Ap. 432.
(*w*) *Waller* v. *Weedale*, Noy. 107.
(*x*) *Thompson* v. *Clerk*, Cro. Eliz. 514.
(*y*) *Perkinson* v. *Gilford*, Cro. Car. 539; W. Jon. 430.
(*z*) *Clutterbuck* v. *Jones*, 15 East, 78; *Ruston* v. *Hatfield*, 2 B. & A. 204.
(*a*) *Swain* v. *Morland*, 1 B. & B. 370; Gow. 39; Moo. 740.
(*b*) *Thurston* v. *Mills*, 16 East, 254.
(*c*) Order lii., rr. 2, 3; and see *Delmar* v. *Freemantle*, 3 Ex. D. 237.
(*d*) *Wylie* v. *Birch*, 4 Q. B. 566.
(*e*) *Jackson* v. *Hill*, 10 Ad. & E. 477; 2 P. & D. 455; and see *ante*, p. 143.
(*f*) Order lii., r. 11.
(*g*) *Scarlett* v. *Hanson*, 12 Q. B. D. 213; 53 L. J. Q. B. 62; 32 W. R. 310; 1 C. & E. 53.

(*h*) *Wintle* v. *Freeman*, 11 A. & E. 539; *Shattock* v. *Carden*, 6 Ex. 725.
(*i*) *Slade* v. *Hawley*, 13 M. & W. 757.
(*j*) *Dennis* v. *Whetham*, L. R. 9 Q. B. 345; 43 L. J. Q. B. 129; 30 L. T. 514; 22 W. R. 571.
(*k*) *Barton* v. *Gill*, 12 M. & W. 315.
(*l*) *Monk* v. *Cass*, 9 Dowl. 332.
(*m*) *Inland* v. *Bushell*, 5 Dowl. 147; 2 H. & W. 118; *Scott* v. *Lewis*, 4 Dowl. 259; 2 C. M. & R. 289; 1 Gale. 204; 5 Tyr. 1083.
(*n*) *Braine* v. *Hunt*, 2 Dowl. 391; 2 C. & M. 418.
(*o*) *Lea* v. *Rossi*, 11 Ex. 13; 1 Jur. N. S. 384; 24 L. J. Ex. 280.
(*p*) *Braddick* v. *Smith*, 9 Bing. 84; *Ostler* v. *Bower*, 4 Dowl. 605; 1 H. & W. 653.
(*q*) *Ibid*.
(*r*) *Green* v. *Brown*, 3 Dowl. 337.

LIABILITIES.

cised his discretion he is not entitled to relief (*s*), nor where he is guilty of neglect (*t*) or laches (*u*), except under special circumstances (*v*). He must inquire into the *bona fides* of the claims before applying for relief (*w*).

For neglect of duty the representatives of a deceased sheriff are also liable (*x*). Representatives of sheriff.

An action against the sheriff in these cases cannot be maintained without shewing actual pecuniary damage (*y*), but where damages are alleged and proved, they are recoverable without proof of malice or want of probable cause (*z*). Pleading to shew damage when.

In an action for a false return, the sheriff may shew the facts in support of his defence (*a*), but he cannot go into circumstantial evidence to impeach the judgment on the ground of collateral fraud (*b*). False return.

Admissions of the bailiff in these cases are evidence against the sheriff (*c*), but not those of the under-sheriff, unless they accompany some official act or tend to charge himself (*d*). Admissions.

The measure of damages in cases of neglect of duty by the sheriff is usually the value of the goods (*e*). Measure of damages.

By 56 Geo. 3, c. 50, s. 9, the sheriff is not liable for damages for anything done under that Act (*f*) unless there be wilful omission on his part.

By 50 & 51 Vict. c. 55, s. 29 the sheriff or his officer for any breach of the provisions of the Act or neglect or default in the execution of his office is liable to forfeit £200 and to pay all damages suffered by any person aggrieved (*g*). Statutory liability.

This applies apparently only to personal misconduct or neglect on the part of the officer actually guilty thereof, and in such case the sheriff, therefore is not responsible for the act of his officer (*h*).

But if he make out a warrant prior to the receipt of the writ this action will lie against him (*i*), and so also will it if he omit to appoint a deputy (*j*).

As has been above stated, the liability of the Admiralty Marshal is identical with that of the sheriff. Admiralty marshal.

(*s*) *Crump* v. *Day*, 4 C. B. 760.
(*t*) *Brackenbury* v. *Laurie*, 3 Dowl. 180.
(*u*) *Crump* v. *Day*, ubi supra.
(*v*) *Dixon* v. *Ensell*, 2 Dowl. 621.
(*w*) *Bishop* v. *Hinzman*, 2 ib. 106.
(*x*) *Packington* v. *Culliford*, 1 Roll. 921; Ex. pl. H. 2; *Adair* v. *Shaw*, 1 Sch. & Lef. 265.
(*y*) *Hobson* v. *Thellusson*, L. R. 2 Q. B. 642; 8 B. & S. 476; 36 L. J. Q. B. 302; 15 W. R. 1037; 16 L. T. N. S. 837; *Stinson* v. *Farnham*, L. R. 7 Q. B. 175; 41 L. J. Q. B. 52; 25 L. T. N. S. 747; 20 W. R. 183; *Moon* v. *Raphael*, 2 Sc. 489; 2 Bing. N. C. 310; 1 Hod. 289; 7 C. & P. 115.
(*z*) *Brasyer* v. *Maclean*, L. R. 6 P. C. 398; 33 L. T. 1.
(*a*) *Wintle* v. *Freeman*, ubi supra.
(*b*) *Tyler* v. *Duke of Leeds*, 2 Stark. 222.
(*c*) *North* v. *Sheriff of Middlesex*, 1 Camp. 389.
(*d*) *Snowball* v. *Goodericke*, 4 B. & Ad. 541.
(*e*) *Tyler* v. *Leeds*, ubi supra.
(*f*) Ante, p. 23.
(*g*) See 21 Jac. 1, c. 4, s. 4; and *Spencer*, 3 M. & W. 154; *Jones* v. *Williams*, 4 ib. 375.
(*h*) *Bagge* v. *Whitehead*, 7 T. L. R. 698.
(*i*) *Hall* v. *Roche*, 8 D. & E. 187.
(*j*) *Brackenbury* v. *Laurie*, 3 Dowl. 180.

High bailiff.

As regards the high bailiff, besides the ordinary liability which is the same as that of the sheriff it is enacted that:—

In case any bailiff who shall be employed to levy any execution against goods and chattels shall by neglect or connivance or omission lose the opportunity of levying any such execution, then, upon complaint of the party aggrieved by reason of such neglect, connivance or omission (and the fact alleged being proved to the satisfaction of the Court on the oath of any credible witness), the judge shall order such bailiff to pay such damages as it shall appear that the plaintiff has sustained thereby (k).

This power of the judge does not extend over the high bailiff of a foreign Court (l).

Constables.

The only case in which constables are employed in civil execution at the suit of an individual is that for the recovery of tenements.

Other officers.

And, as regards other officers, it has been held that an action lies against a postmaster for non-delivery of letters (m), and a collector of customs for refusing to sign a bill of entry without payment of an excessive duty (n), and a highway surveyor for leaving large stones on a road under repair so placed as to cause an obstruction (o). But he is not bound to remove nuisances (p), nor liable for mere non-repair (q).

It lies also against a minister for refusing admission to the church on proper occasions (r), or for removing without authority a monument appended to the wall of the church (s), and against churchwardens for refusing admission to the church at service time of a parishioner (t).

Withholding evidence. Omnia præsumuntur contra spoliatorem.

As to evidence, if it is withheld it renders the maxim *Omnia præsumuntur contra spoliatorem* applicable (u). Where a party has the means in his power of rebutting and explaining the evidence against him, if it does not tend to the truth, the omission to do so furnishes a strong inference against him (v). Where a public officer produces an instrument the execution of which he was bound to procure, as against him it is presumed to have been duly executed (w). And if it be defaced or destroyed slight evidence of the contents will usually be sufficient (x). The general rule in these cases is that the law excludes such evidence as from the nature of the thing, supposes still better evidence in the party's possession or power (y).

(k) 51 & 52 Vict. c. 43, s. 49.
(l) R. v. *Shropshire County Court*, 20 Q. B. D. 242; 58 L. T. 86.
(m) *Rowning* v. *Goodchild*, 2 W. Bl. 906; *Scott* v. *Shearman*, ib. 977. But see *Hordern* v. *Dalton*, 1 C. & P. 181.
(n) *Barry* v. *Arnand*, 10 A. & E. 646; 2 P. & D. 633.
(o) *Fearnley* v. *Ormsby*, L. R. 4 C. P. D. 136; 43 J. P. 384.
(p) *Morgan* v. *Leach*, 10 M. & W. 558; 12 L. J. M. C. 4; 6 J. P. 818.
(q) *Young* v. *Davis*, 2 H. & C. 197; 9 L. T. 145; 10 Jur. 79.

(r) *Lee* v. *Matthews*, 3 Cons. 173.
(s) 1 Inst. 18 b.
(t) *Taylor* v. *Timson*, 20 Q. B. D. 671; 57 L. J. Q. B. 266; 52 J. P. 135.
(u) See ante, p. 151.
(v) 3 Stark. Evidence, 3rd ed. p. 937.
(w) *Scott* v. *Waithman*, 3 Stark. N. P. C. 168; *Plumer* v. *Brisco*, 11 Q. B. 52.
(x) 1 Phil. Evidence, 10th ed. pp. 477, 478.
(y) *Twyman* v. *Knowles*, 13 C. B. 222; *Lumley* v. *Wagner*, 1 De G. M. & G. 604, 633.

Criminal Proceedings.

Attachment.

In the case of the sheriff, Admiralty marshal, and high bailiff, all of whom are officers of the Court, this remedy is open to any person aggrieved by the neglect to perform the duty required of them (*a*). *Attachment.*

By 50 & 51 Vict. c. 55, s. 29, if any sheriff, under-sheriff, bailiff, or officer of a sheriff is guilty of any breach of the provisions of the Act, or of any neglect or default in the execution of his office, he may be punished by the Court as for a contempt (*b*). *Sheriff.*

In regard to the Admiralty marshal, as he is now an officer of the High Court, his liability is identical with that of the sheriff (*c*). *Admiralty marshal.*

As to the high bailiff, it is laid down by 51 & 52 Vict. c. 43, s. 131, that in case of refusal to act, any party requesting the act to be done may apply to the High Court for an order calling on the officer to shew why it should not be done, and that upon the officer's then making default, attachment may issue. *High bailiff.*

The incidents of attachment will be found stated below in the next chapter (*d*).

Information.

In the case of all officers other than those mentioned under the head of *attachment*, the remedy under the criminal law for breach of duty is by information at the suit of the party grieved. *Information. To what officers applicable.*

The majority of statutes which confer powers include penalties for breaches of public duty by the officers on whom the powers are conferred.

Every public officer commits a misdemeanour who wilfully neglects to perform any duty which he is bound either by common law or by statute to perform, provided that the discharge of such duty is not attended with greater danger than a man of ordinary firmness and activity may be expected to encounter (*e*).

(*a*) See *Brainard* v. *Connecticut Railway, infra.* Of course all officers who refuse to obey the mandates of the Courts are like other persons liable to attachment or committal. See *R.* v. *Winton,* 5 T. R. 89. An order for attachment or committal must be applied for on notice, Order xliv., r. 2: *Jupp* v. *Cooper,* 5 C. P. D. 26; *Fynde* v. *Gould,* 9 Q. B. D. 335.
(*b*) See Hawk. P. C. II. c. 22, ss. 2, 3, 4.
(*c*) Judicature Act, 1873, s. 84.
(*d*) *Post,* p. 201.
(*e*) Steph. Dig. Crim. Law, Art. 122; *R.* v. *Pinney,* 5 C. & P. 254; 3 B. & Ad. 946.

When open to individual.
Breaches of public duty are not, however, remediable at the suit of a private individual, unless he is able to prove that he has sustained actual damage by reason thereof (*f*).

Withholding evidence.
An instance of breach of public duty is the withholding of material evidence. This is presumably perjury (*g*).

Where information is obtained from a constable he is bound to state in cross-examination if required by the judge or presiding magistrate to do so, the circumstances under which he had seen the facts to which he testified (*h*).

Refusing admission to prisoner.
Another instance is where an officer refuses admission to a lock-up or place of detention, of a counsel or solicitor for a prisoner awaiting trial who is retained for his defence, or other person properly claiming to be admitted (*i*), or refuses to give bail when required by law to do so (*j*).

Bail.

Non-repair of highway, &c.
It has been held, however, that an indictment does not lie against a highway-surveyor for non-repair of the highway (*k*), but he may be summoned for this (*kk*) or for allowing heaps to remain on the highway at night to the danger of passengers (*l*), or for damaging mills, &c. (*m*) or reglect to fill up pits (*n*).

Mandamus.

Mandamus.
A word should be here inserted on *mandamus*. It is a prerogative writ issuing in the Queen's name and directed to a public officer requiring him to do a particular thing appertaining to his office and duty (*o*).

In its application it is confined to cases where no effectual relief can be obtained in the ordinary course of an action (*p*). And inasmuch as the cases in which damages could occur on account of breach of duty which are not obtainable by action are very rare; it is a remedy which for practical purposes need not be further discussed (*q*).

(*f*) Brainard v. Connecticut Railway, 7 Cush. U.S. 510.
(*g*) See Steph. Comm. 8th ed. p. 278, and *post*, p. 208.
(*h*) R. v. Richardson, 3 F. & F. 693; Webb v. Catchlove, 82 L. T. (N.) 103. See Marks v. Beyfus, 25 Q. B. D. 494; 63 L. T. 733; 6 Ti. Rep. 350.
(*i*) See 28 & 29 Vict. c. 126, Sch. I. r. 54; and 40 & 41 Vict. c. 21, r. 56.
(*j*) See *ante*, p. 109.
(*k*) R. v. Dixon, 12 Mod. 198.
(*kk*) 5 & 6 Will. 4, c. 50, s. 94.

(*l*) Fearnley v. Ormsby, L. R. 4 C. P. D. 136.
(*m*) 5 & 6 Will. 4, c. 50, ss. 56, 57, 72.
(*n*) Sect. 55.
(*o*) Steph. Comm. 8th ed. III. 615; R. v. Bank of England, 2 B. & Ald. 622.
(*p*) R. v. Chester, 1 T. R. 396; Ex parte Robins, 1 W. W. & H. 578.
(*q*) See R. v. Fox, 2 Q. B. 246; R. v. Scott, *ib.*, 248, n.; and R. v. Wilts JJ., 8 Dowl. P. C. 717.

EXCESS OF POWER.

Self-Defence.

The first remedy which the law permits a man, against whom an excess of legal authority is being committed, to resort to, is that which can be applied on the spur of the moment—namely, self-defence. The law in reference thereto is as follows: It sanctions the defence of a man's person, liberty, and property against illegal violence, and permits the use of force to prevent crimes... yet all this is subject to the restriction that the force used is necessary, that is, that the mischief sought to be prevented could not be prevented by less violent means, and that the mischief done by, or which might reasonably be anticipated from the force used is not disproportioned to the injury or mischief which it is intended to prevent (a). *[Excess of power. Self defence.]*

The rule that a man shall retreat from an assailant before he uses force applies only to the use of such force as may inflict grievous bodily harm or death (b). If an officer be killed while exceeding his authority it is manslaughter only (c).

Fabrication of Evidence.

It will be convenient to insert here a few words on this head. *[Fabrication of evidence.]*

The fabrication of evidence, from a civil point of view, renders the maxim *Omnia præsumuntur contra spoliatorem* applicable to the case (d). From a criminal point of view, if it consists in procuring false witnesses, it is subornation of perjury, and if the party tampered with does not actually take an oath, the person inciting him so to do, though not guilty of subornation, is still liable to punishment (e). In cases other than witnesses it is a misdemeanour at common law (f). *[Civil consequences. Criminal consequences.]*

Of fabrication, the following are examples: Placing a pistol-ball in a tree in order to shew that a pistol, when discharged, was loaded with ball; soiling clothes to give the appearance of a struggle; fitting shoes to marks in earth or snow to connect the owner of the shoes with the offence; putting a portion of a

---

(a) Crim. Code Rept. p. 11. See *Beatty v. Gillbanks, ante,* p. 80; *M'Clenaghan v. Waters, Times,* 18th July, 1882.
(b) Steph. Comm. 8th ed. IV. 53.
(c) *Dixon,* 1 E. P. C. 313; *Tooley,* 2 Ray. 1296.
(d) See *ante,* p. 157, and Broom

Leg. Max. 5th ed. 939, 942; and per Mountenay, B., 17 How. St. Tr. 1430; *Norden's Case,* Fost. Cr. Law, 129.
(e) 1 Hawk. P. C. c. 69, s. 2.
(f) Rept. Crim. Code Commission, p. 21; *R. v. Vreones,* [1891] 1 Q. B. 360; 39 W. R. 304; 60 L. J. 62.

newspaper into the pocket of a prisoner, his clothes being detained at a police-station, the corresponding portion being found at the scene of the crime; tampering with witnesses, including that of inducing another officer to swear falsely as to a fact.

Civil Proceedings.

Torts which are also crimes.

Where an excess of power has a twofold aspect—namely, tortious and criminal—it is remediable either by action or prosecution. The old rule that where a tort amounted to a felony no action could be maintained previous to prosecution is abrogated, and can no longer be set up as a defence to civil proceedings (*g*).

Assault and Battery.

Civil proceedings. Assault and battery.

An assault is an attempt or offer to beat another without touching him, as if one lifts up a cane or his fist in a threatening manner at another or strikes at but misses him (*h*). A battery (which includes an assault) is the unlawful beating of another—the least touching of another's person wilfully or in anger (*i*), and this whether with the person or with any missile or weapon (*j*).

The fact of an assault being unintentional does not make it less an assault (*k*); but it may be urged in mitigation of damages (*l*); but if the act be neither wilful nor negligent no action will lie (*m*).

In the following cases it was held that an assault had been committed:—

Assault.

Where A. was advancing in a threatening attitude with an intention to strike B. so that his blow would have almost immediately reached B. if he had not been stopped, though at the particular moment when A. was stopped he was not near enough for his blow to take effect (*n*).

An examination by medical men in pursuance of an order of a magistrate of the person of a female in custody upon the charge of concealing the birth of her illegitimate child (*o*).

Riding after a person and obliging him to run away into a garden to avoid being beaten (*p*). Striking a man in a crowd for refusing to stand back, which he was unable to do for the

---

(*g*) *Midland Insurance Company* v. *Smith*, 6 Q. B. D. 561; *Roope* v. *D'Avigdor*, 10 *ib.* 412; *Appleby* v. *Franklin*, 17 *ib* 93. As to pleading in actions under statute, see *Holmes* v. *Sparkes*, *ante*, p. 160.
(*h*) 3 Black. 120.
(*i*) *Ibid.*
(*j*) *Russell* v. *Horne*, 8 A. & E. 602.
(*k*) *Corell* v. *Laming*, 1 Camp. 477.
(*l*) *James* v. *Campbell*, 5 C. & P. 373.
(*m*) *Stanley* v. *Powell*, 7 T. L. R. 25.
(*n*) *Stephens* v. *Myers*, 4 C. & P. 349.
(*o*) *Agnew* v. *Johson*, 14 C. C. C. 625; 47 L. J. M. C. 67.
(*p*) *Martin* v. *Shoppee*, 3 C. & P. 373.

crowd behind him (*q*), or for interfering with an officer engaged in preventing a breach of the peace (*r*).

Where plaintiff being in defendant's workshop and refusing to quit when desired, the defendant and his servants surrounded him and threatened to break his neck if he did not go out, whereupon the plaintiff, apprehensive of violence, departed (*s*).

A threat to shoot a person, coupled with the act of presenting a loaded fire-arm at him, although it is half-cocked (*t*).

In the following cases, no assault was held to have been committed :—

Where A. comes up to attack B., and B. puts himself into a fighting attitude to defend himself (*u*). *No assault.*

Presenting a loaded pistol, coupled with words shewing no intention to shoot the plaintiff (*v*).

Where A. seized the bridle of the horse on which B. was riding, and B., after a request to desist, struck A. with his riding-whip, using no more force than was necessary to obtain his release (*w*).

Where a constable was wholly passive and merely obstructed the entrance of a person into a room as any inanimate object would (*x*).

As regards threatening gestures, if the parties at the time the gestures are used are so far distant from each other that immediate contact is impossible, there is no assault (*y*).

With reference to procedure it is laid down that where the assault has been heard and determined by justices, a certificate by such justices of conviction or acquittal is a bar to all further proceedings (*z*). *Procedure. Certificate of justices.*

Such a certificate cannot be granted on an *ex parte* statement (*a*), but to be valid it need not be granted at the time the summons is heard (*b*).

In a civil action, that the defendant consented to the assault is a good defence (*c*), and therefore the defence of leave and licence amounts to not guilty (*d*). *Pleading.*

The defence to complete justification must answer severally the assaults specified in the claim (*e*).

(*q*) *Imason* v. *Cope*, 5 *ib.* 193.
(*r*) *Levy* v. *Edwards*, 1 C. & P. 40.
(*s*) *Read* v. *Coker*, 13 C. B. 859; 22 L. J. C. P. 205; 17 Jur. 990.
(*t*) *Osborne* v. *Veitch*, 1 F. & F. 317.
(*u*) *Moriarty* v. *Brooks*, 6 C. & P. 684.
(*v*) *Blake* v. *Barnard*, 9 C. & P. 626.
(*w*) *Rowe* v. *Hawkins*, 1 F. & F. 91.
(*x*) *Jones* v. *Wylie*, 1 C. & K. 257.
(*y*) *Cobbett* v. *Grey*, 4 Ex. 744; 19 L. J. Ex. 137.
(*z*) 24 & 25 Vict. c. 100, ss. 44, 45. See *Holden* v. *King*, 46 L. J. Ex. 75; 35 L. T. 479; 25 W. R. 72; and *Masper* v. *Brown*, 1 C. P. D. 97; 45 L. J. C. P. 203; 34 L. T. 254; 24 W. R. 369.
(*a*) *Reed* v. *Nutt*, 24 Q. B. D. 669; 59 L. J. Q. B. 311; 62 L. T. 635; 38 W. R. 621; 54 J. P. 559; 6 L. T. R. 266.
(*b*) *Hancock* v. *Somes*, 28 L. J. M. C. 196; *Costar* v. *Hetherington*, *ib.* 198.
(*c*) *R.* v. *Coney*, 8 Q. B. D. 534; 51 L. J. M. C. 66; 15 Cox, C. C. 46; 46 L. T. 307; 30 W. R. 678; 46 J. P. 404.
(*d*) *Christopherson* v. *Barr*, 11 Q. B. 473; 17 L. J. Q. B. 109; 12 Jur. 374.
(*e*) *Bush* v. *Barker*, 4 M. & Sc. 588.

That of *molliter manus imposuit* is a good defence to a battery (*f*). But if there be violence it is negatived (*g*).

As to the defence of *son assault demesne*, this admits the assault (*h*). But it is a good defence provided there be no excess (*i*).

Where A. and B. are joint defendants, that does not prevent A. pleading a justification to another and separate assault (*j*).

Evidence. To justify a battery the defendant must shew that there was an unlawful resistance on the part of the plaintiff to the lawful acts of the defendant (*k*). A sheriff's officer, it has been held, can only justify laying his hand upon a man in order to arrest him on a writ of process (*l*), or in case of resistance or an attempt to rescue him (*m*).

A plea justifying an assault on the ground that it was committed in dispersing a meeting, must either allege as a fact that the meeting was unlawful, or state facts from which its unlawfulness can be inferred (*n*).

Where plaintiff sued defendant for assault in taking him under a *habeas corpus*, after he had requested him not to do so, the writ having issued at the instance of the plaintiff, there being no sufficient evidence that the defendant knew at whose instance the writ issued, the assault was held justifiable (*o*).

Upon issue taken on a plea of *son assault demesne* it is necessary to prove an assault commensurate with the trespass sought to be justified (*p*). But the defendant may give evidence of an assault by the plaintiff without this plea (*q*).

And in any action of assault, though he has not pleaded justification, he may in cross-examination extract evidence in mitigation of damages (*r*).

Damages. As to damages, the Court will seldom interfere with the discretion of the jury, and the jury may take into consideration circumstances which go to aggravate or mitigate the injury sustained (*s*).

Where the assault has been carried to the extent of *mayhem* or wounding, heavy damages will be recoverable unless it be excused or justified (*t*).

(*f*) Titley v. Foxall, 2 Ld. Ken. 308.
(*g*) Oakes v. Wood, 2 M. & W. 791; M. & H. 237; Gregory v. Hill, 8 T. R. 299; Johnson v. Northwood, 1 Moo. 420; 7 Taunt. 689.
(*h*) Hay v. Kitchen, 1 Wils. 171.
(*i*) Blunt v. Beaumont, 2 C. M. & R. 412; 4 D. P. C. 219; Dean v. Taylor, 11 Ex. 68. See Rimmer v. Rimmer, 16 L. T. 238.
(*j*) Kearney v. Tottenham, 15 W. R. 1020.
(*k*) Gregory v. Hill, ubi sup.
(*l*) Harrison v. Hodgson, 10 B. & C. 445.
(*m*) 1 Ray, 222; 2 Str. 1049.

(*n*) O'Kelly v. Harvey, 10 Ir. L. R. 285.
(*o*) Hemming v. Hudson, 3 Ex. 107.
(*p*) Reece v. Taylor, 4 N. & M. 470; 1 H. & W. 15.
(*q*) Syers v. Chapman, 2 C. B. N. S. 438.
(*r*) Moore v. Adam, 2 Chit. 198; Linford v. Lake, 3 H. & N. 276; 27 L. J. Ex. 334; De Gondouin v. Lewis, 10 A. & E. 120.
(*s*) Tullidge v. Wade, 8 Wils. 18; Perkins v. Vaughan, 4 M. & G. 989; 7 Sc. N. R. 886; Speck v. Phillips, 5 M. & W. 281; 7 Dowl. 470.
(*t*) Bac. Ab. Maihem.

Wherever the wrong is of a grievous nature, done with a high hand, or is accompanied with a deliberate intention to injure, or with words of contumely and abuse, the jury are authorized in giving vindictive damages (*u*).

This action must be commenced within four years next after the cause of such action, and not after (*v*). *Limitation.*

Extortion.

The cases which arise under this head are, as in the case of action for damages (*w*), mainly those concerned with civil execution. It will be advisable, therefore, to set out here the fees and charges which are payable to officers concerned in this process. *Extortion. Chiefly relates to civil execution.*

Those of other officers where there are any, will be found stated with the powers enumerated in former parts of the work.

As regards the sheriff, he is entitled to charge the fees and poundage which were charged, prior to the Sheriffs' Act, 1887, until altered in pursuance of this Act (*x*). *Sheriff.*

The poundage allowed is for the first £100, 5 per cent., and afterwards 2½ per cent. (*y*). *Poundage.*

The fees are as follows (*z*) :— *Fees.*

For every warrant which shall be granted by the sheriff to his officer upon any writ or process :—

	£	s.	d.
In London or Middlesex	0	2	6
And on outlawry process, an additional	0	2	6
In other counties, where the most distant part of the county shall not exceed 100 miles from London	0	5	0
Not exceeding 200 miles	0	6	0
Exceeding 200 miles	0	7	0
Where there are several defendants in a writ of *capias*, and warrants are issued thereon by the under-sheriff against more than one defendant, no more shall be charged in any case for each warrant, after the first, than	0	2	6
For an arrest in London	0	10	6
In Middlesex, not exceeding 1 mile from the G. P. O.	0	10	6
Not exceeding 7 miles from the same place	1	1	0
In other counties, not exceeding a mile from the officer's residence	0	10	6
Not exceeding seven miles	1	1	0
Exceeding seven miles	1	11	6
For conveying the defendant to gaol from the place of arrest (*a*), per mile	0	1	0
For an undertaking to give a bail bond	0	10	6

For a Bail Bond.

If the debt do not exceed £50	0	10	6
„ „ „ 100	1	1	0
„ „ „ 150	1	11	6

(*u*) *Thomas* v. *Harris*, 27 L. J. Ex. 353.
(*v*) 21 Jac. 1, c. 16, s. 3.
(*w*) *Ante*, p. 165.
(*x*) 50 & 51 Vict. c. 55, ss. 20, 30.
(*y*) 29 Eliz. c. 4.
(*z*) 7 Will. 4 & 1 Vict. c. 55, s. 3.
(*a*) See *Cooper* v. *Hill*, 6 C. B. N. S. 703; 28 L. J. C. P. 311; 6 Jur. N. S. 99.

		£	s.	d.
If the debt do not exceed £300		2	2	0
„ „ 400		3	3	0
„ „ 500		4	4	0
If it shall exceed 500		5	5	0
For receiving money under the statute upon deposit for arrest, and paying the same into Court, if in London or Middlesex		0	6	8
If in any other county		0	10	0

For Filing the Bail Bond.

	£	s.	d.
If the arrest be made in London or Middlesex	0	2	0
If in any other county	0	4	0

Assignment of Bail or other Bond.

	£	s.	d.
If in London or Middlesex	0	5	0
If in any other county, including postage	0	7	6
For the return to any writ of *habeas corpus*, if one action	0	12	0
For each action after the first	0	2	6
For the bailiff to conduct prisoner to gaol, per diem	0	10	6
And travelling expenses per mile	0	1	0
To the bailiffs for executing warrants on extent, *capias ultogatum*, *ne exeat*, attachment, elegit, possession, forfeited recognizance, and other like matters, for each, if the distance from the sheriff's office or the bailiff's residence do not exceed five miles	1	1	0
If beyond that distance, per mile	0	0	6
Bond of indemnity besides stamps	1	10	0
Certificate of execution having issued for record	0	5	0

Under *fieri facias*.   The following fees may now be charged for execution of writs of *fi. fa.*, under order of 31st of August, 1888:—

1. For expenses incurred by the sheriff's officer in making inquiries as to the goods of an execution debtor, and as to claims for rent and other claims on the goods, the actual expenses not exceeding under any circumstances £1 1s.
2. For seizure by the sheriff's officer. For each building or place separately rated at which a seizure is made, £1 1s.
3. For mileage, to include the mileage of the bailiff or the man in possession, per mile from the sheriff's officer's residence, 1s.
The foregoing shall be paid by the execution creditor, and shall not be recoverable by him, although the execution proves abortive.
4. For man in possession, per day, 5s.
To provide his own board in every case.
5. For removal of goods or animals to a place of safe keeping, when necessary, the actual cost.
6. When goods or animals are removed, for warehousing and taking charge of the same (including feeding of animals), 2½ per cent. on the value of the goods or animals removed, or the sum endorsed on the writ of execution, whichever is the less. No fees for keeping possession of the goods or animals to be charged after the goods or animals have been removed.
7. For the inventory and valuation, cataloguing, lotting and preparing for sale, when no sale takes place by reason of the execution being withdrawn, satisfied, or stopped, 2¼ per cent. on the value of the goods (*b*).
8. For advertising and giving publicity to the sale by auction, the sum actually and necessarily paid.
9. For commission to the auctioneer on a sale by auction, 7½ per cent. on the sum realized, not exceeding £100; £5 per cent. on the next £100, £4 per

---

(*b*) This does not apply to seizure of a ship: *Cohen* v. *De las Rivas*, 39 W. R. 539; 64 L. T. 661.

LIABILITIES. 177

cent. on the next £200, and on any sum exceeding in all £500, £3 per cent. up to £1000, and £2½ per cent. on any sum exceeding £1000.

10. For any sale by private contract, half the percentage allowed on a sale by auction.

11. Poundage and fee for delivery of writ as before.

The foregoing fees 2, 3, 4, 5, 6, 8, 9, 10, and 11, shall be levied in every case in which an execution is completed by sale, as fees payable to sheriffs were levied before the making of this order. In every case where an execution is withdrawn, satisfied, or stopped, the fees under this order shall be paid by the person issuing the execution, or the person at whose instance the sale is stopped, as the case may be; and the amount of any costs and charges payable under this scale shall be taxed by a Master of the Supreme Court or District Registrar of the High Court (as the case may be), in case the sheriff and the party liable to pay such costs and charges differ as to the amount thereof (c).

Proceeding against the sheriff for contempt does not preclude the plaintiff from bringing his action (*d*). — *Process of contempt does not preclude action.*

Fees are payable by the creditor (*e*), and whether the process be regular or irregular does not matter (*f*). — *Fees payable by creditor.*

As to levy for fees and poundage it is doubtful whether this extends to *elegit* (*g*). It is probably confined to the charges (*h*). — *Levy for fees.*

Where the sheriff claims more than he is entitled to, it is not necessarily extortion (*i*).

The sheriff is entitled to deduct poundage though the parties compromise before he sells (*j*), and when the execution has been set aside for irregularity after the levy and payment over of the proceeds have been made (*k*). But where he leaves goods taken in execution with a person who parts with the possession of them, he may not retake them merely to secure his own poundage where the execution was fraudulent (*l*). — *Excessive claim not always extortion. Poundage on compromise. Execution set aside.*

When he has seized and is in possession of the goods or lands, he is entitled to poundage (*m*). But the seizure must be actual and according to the writ (*n*). It is not necessary that he should proceed to a sale (*o*). — *Due on seizure.*

But a tender before seizure is equivalent to payment, and no poundage is payable in such cases (*p*), nor where after seizure and before sale the writ is set aside (*q*).

When bankruptcy supervenes after seizure and before sale, — *Bankruptcy*

(*c*) There is no appeal from this taxation: *Townend* v. *Sheriff of Yorkshire*, 24 Q. B. D. 621; 59 L. J. Q. B. 156; 62 L. T. 402; 38 W. R. 381; 54 J. P. 598.

(*d*) *Pilkington* v. *Cooke*, 16 M. & W. 615.

(*e*) Wat. p. 112.

(*f*) *Bullen* v *Ansley*, 6 Esp. 111.

(*g*) *Mahon* v. *Miles*, 30 W. R. 123.

(*h*) *Porter* v. *Wootton*, 28 Sol. J. 548.

(*i*) *Long* v. *Bray*, 10 W. R. 841. See *Stephens* v. *Rothwell*, 6 Moo 338.

(*j*) *Alchin* v. *Wells*, 5 D. & E. 470.

(*k*) *Rawstone* v. *Wilkinson*, 4 M. & S. 256.

(*l*) *Goode* v. *Langley*, 7 B. & C. 26.

(*m*) *Mortimore* v. *Cragg*, 3 C. P. D. 216; 47 L. J. C. P. 348; 38 L. T. 116; 26 W. R. 363.

(*n*) *Bissicks* v. *Bath Colliery Company*, 3 Ex. D. 174; 47 L. J. Ex. 408; 38 L. T. 163; 26 W. R. 215.

(*o*) *Re Sheriff of Surrey*, 38 L. T. 116.

(*p*) *Colls* v. *Coates*, 11 A. & E. 826; 3 P. & D. 511.

(*q*) *Miles* v. *Harris*, 12 C. B. N. S. 550; 31 L. J. C. P. 361.

no poundage is due as costs of the execution (r), nor are such costs expenses incurred while in possession for cutting, carrying, threshing, and dressing corn (s).

The sheriff is not entitled to the costs of preparing a sale which has been stayed by notice of a prior act of bankruptcy (t). But otherwise he is so entitled (u); and in determining the amount for which execution is levied possession-money may be taken into account even after an injunction has been granted restraining the sheriff from sale (v).

Winding-up.
Where, by reason of a winding-up order, the sheriff was ordered to deliver up money and goods seized by him, the liquidator was directed to pay the amounts due to the sheriff for levy and charges on the writs and the costs of his application for such an order (w).

Keeping possession.
He will be allowed his costs of keeping possession after applying to the Court, where it is for the benefit of the parties, though it be not in furtherance of his duty (x). But where he retained out of the proceeds of a sale, which were not sufficient to satisfy the plaintiff's claim, the expenses occasioned by keeping possession under an injunction, this was disallowed (y). If he levies and remains in possession of goods, other than those of the execution debtor without any special order from the execution creditor, he cannot recover such possession-money (z).

But if, after taking possession of the goods of a company which afterwards goes into liquidation, he is restrained from selling, he is entitled to his poundage and costs (a). And all incidental expenses may be charged where the sale takes place by order of the Court, even though it subsequently appear that the seizure was wrongful (b).

Where after seizure and before sale the execution creditor becomes disentitled to recover the debt, the sheriff cannot sell any portion of the goods in order to realize the amount of his possession-money, fees, and expenses (c).

Payment into exchequer.
Where a bailiff illegally compelled the plaintiff under a threat of distraining his goods to pay him a sum of money, it was held that the fact of the bailiff's having before the commencement of the action paid over the entire sum to the sheriff, who had paid it into the Exchequer, was no defence (d).

(r) 46 & 47 Vict. c. 52, s. 46. *In re Ludmore*, 13 Q. B. D. 415; and see *In re Levy*, 63 L. T. 291; 38 W. R. 784.
(s) *Ex parte Conder*, 20 Q. B. D. 40; 36 W. R. 526.
(t) *Searle* v. *Blaise*, 14 C. B. N. S. 856.
(u) *In re Craycraft*, 8 C. D. 596.
(v) *Ex parte Lithgow*, 10 ib. 169.
(w) *In re Opera, Limited*, 1891, 2 Ch. 154; but see 7 T. L. R. 655.
(x) *Underden* v. *Burgess*, 4 Dowl. 104.
(y) *Buckle* v. *Bewes*, 5 D. & R. 495; 4 B. & C. 154.
(z) *Newman* v. *Merriman*, 26 L. T. 397; *Royle* v. *Busby*, 6 Q. B. D. 171.
(a) *In re Perkins Beach Lead Mine*, W. N. 1877, 261.
(b) *Bland* v. *Delano*, 6 Dowl. 293; 1 W. W. & H. 75.
(c) *Sneary* v. *Abdy*, 1 Ex. D. 299.
(d) *Snowden* v. *Davis*, 1 Taunt. 359.

LIABILITIES. 179

The remedy by action in consequence of the smallness of the sums in dispute is not often resorted to (*e*). **Remedy not often resorted to.**

With regard to the Admiralty Marshal, the fees payable are:
On an arrest: 5*s.* a day, and if the officers be required to go a greater distance than five miles, reasonable expenses for travelling, board, and maintenance. **Admiralty marshal. Fees.**

On a sale: 40*s.* a day, and 10*s.* poundage for every £50 sold, and part thereof, together with necessary expenses (*f*).

As to the high bailiff, it is laid down that if any bailiff or officer of the Court acting under colour or pretence of the process of the said Court, shall be charged with extortion or misconduct, or with not duly paying or accounting for any money levied by him, the judge may inquire summarily and make such order as he thinks just (*g*). **High bailiff.**

The poundage is 6*d.* in the pound for appraisement, and 1*s.* in the pound on the proceeds of the sale (*h*). **Poundage.**

The following are the fees allowed (*i*): **Fees.**

s. d.

For keeping possession of goods till sale on any premises, per day (including expenses of removal, storage of goods, and all other expenses), not exceeding five days, 6*d.* in the pound on the value of the goods seized, to be fixed by appraisement, in case of dispute (*j*).

For every default summons where not served by a solicitor . . 1 0
For service of every judgment summons issued upon a judgment of a Court other than a County Court 5 0
For executing every warrant, order of commitment, precept, or writ issued, from or on a judgment of a Court, other than a County Court, 1*s.* in the pound on the amount for which it issues, so that the total fee does not exceed 20*s.*; and for keeping possession, appraisement and sale, the same allowances as under a warrant of execution by a County Court.

	Where subject-matter of the suit	
	does not exceed £100.	does exceed £100.
	s. d.	*s. d.*
For service within home district of every summons, petition, notice or order:—		
If within two miles of court-house . . .	4 6	6 6
If beyond, for every additional mile or part .	0 6	0 6
For service in a foreign district—each defendant	6 0	8 0
Where service ordered to be personal—additional	4 0	5 0
For execution of each warrant in home district .	7 6	10 0
Mileage double that on summons, *supra*.		

(*e*) *Longdill* v. *Jones; Pilkington* v. *Cooke, ubi sup.*; and see *ante,* p. 167; and *post,* p. 201.
(*f*) Supreme Court Funds, 1884, r. 100.
(*g*) 51 & 52 Vict. c. 43, s. 50.
(*h*) Sect. 154.
(*i*) Treasury Order, Dec. 86.
(*j*) The judge may allow this where the execution is non-effective, by reason of not being upon goods of the execution debtor: *Thomas* v. *Peek,* 20 Q. B. D. 727.

	Where subject-matter of the suit	
	does not exceed £100.	does exceed £100.
	s. d.	s. d.
For execution of each warrant in foreign district	10 0	15 0
Keeping possession for each day the man is actually in possession	6 0	7 6
Superintending sale, either by auction or private contract, making out account and paying money into Court, £2 per cent. on first £50 so paid, and £1 per cent. on all afterwards.		
In Admiralty Matters.		
For service of summons or subpœna, if served within three miles of registrar's office	5 0	5 0
Beyond that distance, whether for service or execution, all reasonable expenses.		
In execution of a warrant of arrest of a vessel or property	15 0	20 0
In keeping possession of a vessel or property, to include the cost of a vessel-keeper if required, per day	5 0	5 0
In sale of vessel or property including inventory, for every £50 or fraction thereof	10 0	10 0
For service of summons of commitment	4 0	8 0
Execution of warrant against body or goods	20 0	30 0
Conveyance to gaol, per mile	1 0	1 0
In all cases where the amount is not disclosed, it shall be taken not to exceed £100.		

Actions may be transferred. Actions by or against officers may at the request of the party other than the officer be transferred to an adjoining Court for trial (*k*).

Overseers. As to overseers, it is enacted that distresses for small rents (*l*) under £20 are not to be charged for otherwise than as follows:

                                                     s. d.
Levying distresses 3 0
Man in possession, per day 2 6
Appraisement, whether by one broker or more, 6*d*. in the pound on value of goods; stamp, the lawful amount thereof, all expenses of advertisements (if any) . . 10 0
Catalogues, sale and commission, and delivery of goods, 1*s*. in the pound on the net produce of the sale.

Aggrieved parties may apply to a justice, who may adjudge treble the amount unlawfully taken, and costs.

Action to recover moneys improperly paid. But, besides these special proceedings, an action lies generally against officers to recover moneys improperly paid to them.

(*k*) 51 & 52 Vict. c. 43, ss. 42, 43. See *Partridge* v. *Elkington*, L. R. 6 Q. B. 82; 10 L. J. Q. B. 49; 19 W. R. 385.

(*l*) 57 Geo. 3, c. 93, s. 1. Extended to rates and taxes by 7 & 8 Geo. 4, c. 17.

Where an officer obtains money from a person by means of oppression, imposition, or deceit, an action will lie for its recovery (*m*); as, for instance, where a sheriff obtains money under the pressure of an illegal arrest (*n*); or under a threat to sell goods under a *fi. fa.* which he has no right to sell (*o*); or receives money in excess of that due (*p*); or where a toll-collector exacts an illegal or unauthorized toll (*q*); or where an officer levies money by seizing and selling goods upon a magistrate's conviction, which is afterwards quashed (*r*); or a revenue officer unlawfully seizes goods as forfeited and unlawfully detains them, and takes money which he has no right to take as the condition of their release (*s*).

But an action does not apparently lie against a revenue officer to recover an overpayment (*t*), nor to recover duties received by him after the Act which imposed them is repealed, if he has paid them over to his superior (*u*). Nor does it lie against a highway surveyor for failing to restore an overplus of distress to the owner, if such restoration be not properly demanded (*v*). *When it does not lie.*

If assets in the hands of an officer have been increased by an honest mistake of law, the Court will compel him to recognize the rules of honesty, and to act accordingly (*w*). *General rule where money come to officer's hands.*

Under certain statutes an action lies for a penalty for taking money under colour of office (*x*).

Where a sheriff's officer was sued for a penalty for extortion (*y*) which was not proved, but the claim was held outrageous, the action against the officer was dismissed, but without costs (*z*). *Action for penalty.*

False Imprisonment (*a*).

Every confinement of the person is an imprisonment, whether it be in a common prison or in a private house, or even by forcibly detaining one in the public streets. Unlawful or false imprisonment consists in such confinement or detention without sufficient authority (*b*). *False imprisonment.*

False imprisonment commences from the time of arrest, and

(*m*) *Neate* v. *Hardinge*, 6 Ex. 349; 20 L. J. Ex. 250.
(*n*) *Payne* v. *Chapman*, 4 Ad. & E. 364; *Mesnil* v. *Dakin*, L. R. 3 Q. B. 18; 37 L. J. Q. B. 42.
(*o*) *Valpy* v. *Manley*, 1 C. B. 602.
(*p*) *Dew* v. *Parsons*, 2 B. & A. 562; 1 Chit. 295.
(*q*) *Lewis* v. *Hammond*, 2 B. & A. 206.
(*r*) *Feltham* v. *Terry*, Bull, N. P. 131 n.
(*s*) *Allen* v. *Backhouse*, 3 M. & W. 645; *Irving* v. *Wilson*, 4 T. R. 485.
(*t*) *Whitbread* v. *Brooksbank*, Cowp. 89; Lofft. 529. But see *Geraldes* v. *Donison*, Holt, 346.

(*u*) *Greenway* v. *Hurd*, 4 T. R. 553.
(*v*) *Charinton* v. *Johnson*, 14 L. J. Ex. 299.
(*w*) *In re Opera, Limited*, [1891] 2 Ch. 154, but see 7 T. L. R. 655.
(*x*) As to this, see *Edwards* v. *Salmon*, 23 Q. B. D. 531; 58 L. J. Q. B. 571; 38 W. R. 166.
(*y*) 50 & 51 Vict. c. 55, s. 29.
(*z*) *Woolford's Trustee* v. *Levy*, 7 T. L. R. 598.
(*a*) The remedy of a person falsely imprisoned is in the first instance, *i.e.* while under arrest to obtain a writ of *habeas corpus*.
(*b*) 3 Black. 127.

lasts until the plaintiff is before the magistrates. After that it becomes malicious prosecution (c).

Actual contact is not necessary to constitute an imprisonment. Any restraint put upon the freedom of another by shew of authority or force, is sufficient to constitute an imprisonment (d), so that if a person is restrained from leaving a room or going out of a house without the presence of a constable, this infringement of his personal liberty will constitute an imprisonment (e). If you put your hand on a man, or tell him he must go with you, and he goes, supposing you have the right and the power to compel him, that is an arrest (f).

By sheriff.
A person unlawfully imprisoned by a sheriff or any of his officers shall have an action against such sheriff in like manner as against any other person that should imprison him without warrant (g).

Where the bailiff having a writ of fi. fa. in his hands arrested the defendant, instead of levying on his goods, the sheriff was held liable (h). So also was he where he arrested a person who represented himself to be the person named in the writ, for detaining him after he had notice that he was not the real party (i). And he is also liable where he arrests after the return-day of the writ (j).

By constable.
If a bailiff who has a process against any one says to him, "You are my prisoner; I have a writ against you"; on which the person addressed submits, turns back, or goes with him, though the bailiff never touched him (k); or if a constable command a person to go with him, and the order is obeyed, and they walk together in the direction pointed out by the constable, in each case there is a constructive imprisonment (l). And in an action against a constable by A., he cannot defend himself under a magistrate's warrant against B., although A. was charged with felony before the magistrate, and was the person against whom the warrant was intended to issue (m); nor if

---

(c) *Austin* v. *Dowling*, 5 L. R. C. P. 534; 39 L. J. C. P. 260; 22 L. T. 721; 18 W. R. 1003.

(d) The practice of "shadowing" by the police, which has been the subject of debate on several occasions of late in Parliament, would appear to fall within these words. And even if the party be suspected of felony about to be committed on which arrest might take place, it seems doubtful whether this practice could be justified. Cases have occurred in which false charges have been made as a cover for this process.

(e) *Warner* v. *Riddiford*, 4 C. B. N. S. 206. The practice of watching premises would appear to come within these words.

(f) Per Tindal, C.J., *Wood* v. *Lane*, 6 C. & P. 774.

(g) 50 & 51 Vict. c. 55, s. 15.

(h) *Smart* v. *Hutton*, 8 A. & E. 568; 2 N. & M. 426.

(i) *Dunston* v. *Paterson*, 2 C. B. N. S. 495; 3 Jur. 982; 26 L. J. C. P. 267.

(j) *Parrott* v. *Mumford*, 2 Esp. 585.

(k) *Grainger* v. *Hill*, 4 Bing. N. C. 212; 5 Sc. 580.

(l) *Bird* v. *Jones*, 7 Q. B. 742; 15 L. J. Q. B. 82; 9 Jur. 870.

(m) *Haye* v. *Bush*, 2 Sc. N. R. 86; 1 M. & G. 775; 1 Drink. 15; and see *Creagh* v. *Gamble*, 24 L. R. Ir. 458.

he arrest a person on a charge from another person which is unreasonable (n).

But the forcibly preventing a party from proceeding in a particular direction, *e.g.* along a public footway, is not an imprisonment (o). And a constable on duty at a police station is justified in detaining a person brought there in charge and delivered to him by a constable, although he may have been illegally arrested (p).

The keeper of a prison who receives and detains one appre- By gaoler. hended and charged in custody under a warrant runs the risk of the warrant having been executed against the proper person, and if by mistake it be executed against authority, he is liable (q). So also is he if where a duty to discharge is cast upon him, he detain a person longer (r).

But where the cause does not appear on the face of the warrant or order and he complies with its terms, he is not liable (s).

Every unlawful detainer of a prisoner after he has gained a Generally. right to be discharged is a fresh imprisonment (t).

All persons aiding and assisting in the unlawful confinement of another are responsible in damages for the trespass, although they had nothing to do with the original arrest, and had no knowledge that the arrest and imprisonment were unlawful at the time they had a hand in it (u). But this does not apply to a constable arresting on a hue and cry (v), or on a reasonable charge made by another person (w). If a wrong person be arrested by mistake, all persons causing the arrest are liable for the injury, unless the party complaining has brought the injury on himself by his own misstatements and misrepresentations (x).

A justification of an imprisonment on the ground that the Procedure. Pleading. plaintiff had committed felony, and an abandonment of the plea at the trial, or a failure to prove it, are evidence of malice, and a great aggravation of the original wrong; but a justification on the ground that a felony had been committed, and that the defendant had reasonable and probable cause to suspect the plaintiff guilty of it is rather in the nature of an apology for the defendant's conduct (y). The onus of justification is on the defendant, and therefore in trespass for arrest on a warrant the plaintiff need not produce the warrant (z). It lies on the defendant to plead and prove affirmatively the existence of reasonable

---

(n) *Hogg* v. *Ward*, 3 H. & N. 417.
(o) *Bird* v. *Jones, ubi supra.*
(p) *Bowditch* v. *Fossbury*, 19 L. J. Ex. 339.
(q) *Aaron* v. *Alexander*, 3 Camp. 34.
(r) *Moone* v. *Rose*, L. R. 4 Q. B. 486; 38 L. J. Q. B. 236.
(s) *Greares* v. *Keene*, 4 Ex. D. 73.
(t) *Withers* v. *Healey*, Cro. Jac. 379; 2 Inst. 52.

(u) *Griffin* v. *Coleman*, 4 H. & N. 265; 28 L. J. Ex. 137.
(v) *Ante*, p. 98.
(w) *Ante*, p. 99.
(x) *Davies* v. *Jenkins*, 11 M. & W. 754.
(y) *Warwick* v. *Foulkes*, 12 M. & W. 509; 1 D. & R. 638; 13 L. J. Ex. 109; 8 Jur. 85.
(z) *Holroyd* v. *Doncaster*, 11 Moo. 441.

cause as his justification (*a*). A plea which professes to justify several assaults and false imprisonments laid in separate counts, must shew distinct occasions upon which the defendant was justified in committing each particular trespass (*b*).

The question of reasonable and probable cause is for the judge (*c*).

Where, under statutes, constables are authorized to arrest offenders in their view or found committing offences, a plea justifying an arrest must allege that the offence was committed within view of the constable, or the offender was found committing such offence, as the case may be (*d*). And where a statute authorized a constable to remove an offender, a plea stating that he was so removed and detained in custody, was held no justification, such detention having been unlawful (*e*).

Evidence. Proof must be given of circumstances from which the judge and jury may decide whether there was or was not a restraint or a detention of the person, and it is not enough for witnesses to swear that they considered the plaintiff was in custody, nor to shew that the defendant at a police office stood before the plaintiff and said, "You cannot go away till the magistrate comes," if it appears that he relinquished that attitude, and went to another part of the office before the plaintiff had made any attempt to depart (*f*).

If A. imprisons B., and in continuance of the imprisonment delivers him into the charge of C., who keeps him in custody, the acts and declarations of C. are evidence against A. (*g*). If a witness who admits that he stole similar property at the same time is called to sustain the defence, his testimony ought to receive some confirmation (*h*). The defendant cannot cross-examine as to the bad character of the plaintiff, nor as to previous charges against him (*i*).

A conviction of a third party for the same offence as that for which plaintiff was arrested cannot be put in, unless the defendant knew of it at the time of the arrest (*j*). And a conviction which when put in proves to be informal, has no weight (*k*).

Reasonable and probable cause of suspicion is good evidence in mitigation of damages under not guilty (*l*).

(*a*) *Hicks* v. *Faulkner*, 46 L. T. 127; 8 Q. B. D. 167; 51 L. J. Q. B. 268; 30 W. R. 545; 46 J. P. 420; *Mure* v. *Kaye*, 4 Taunt. 34; and see *M'Cloughan* v. *Clayton*, Holt, N. P. C. 478.
(*b*) *M'Curday* v. *Driscoll*, 1 C. & M. 618; 3 Tyr. 571; *Dawson* v. *Clark*, 1 Bin. 563.
(*c*) *Howard* v. *Clarke*, 20 Q. B. D. 558.
(*d*) *Simmons* v. *Milligen*, 2 C. B. 524; 10 Jur. 224; 15 L. J. C. P. 102.
(*e*) *Williams* v. *Glenister*, 4 D. & R. 217; 2 B. & C. 699.

(*f*) *Cant* v. *Parsons*, 6 C. & P. 504.
(*g*) *Powell* v. *Hodgetts*, 2 *ib.* 432.
(*h*) *Richards* v. *Turner*, Car. & M. 414.
(*i*) *Downing* v. *Butcher*, 2 M. & Rob. 374.
(*j*) *Thomas* v. *Russell*, 9 Ex. 764; 2 C. L. R. 542; 23 L. J. Ex. 233.
(*k*) *Justice* v. *Gosling*, 12 C. B. 39; 16 Jur. 429; 21 L. J. C. P. 94.
(*l*) *Perkins* v. *Vaughan*, 4 M. & G. 989; 5 Sc. M. R. 881; 12 L. J. C. P. 38; 6 Jur. 1114; *Chinn* v. *Morris*, 2 C. & P. 361.

LIABILITIES. 185

Every expense that the plaintiff necessarily incurs in order to Damages.
restore himself to a complete state of freedom is recoverable as
damages (*m*). But he cannot recover in respect of having been
detained whereby he missed an opportunity of being taken into
employment (*n*); nor for illness caused by refusal of defendant
to send for medical assistance, unless the jury find that the detention was unreasonable (*o*). The Court never interferes with
the discretion of the jury, unless the damages are grossly excessive or founded on a mistaken or improper view (*p*). Where
some working men were unlawfully imprisoned for six hours,
being in the meantime well fed and cared for, and the jury
awarded £300 to each, the Court refused to set aside the verdict (*q*). And where a person was arrested on a bad warrant
for arrears of poor-rate, the damages were held to be the amount
he had paid under protest on arrest (*r*).

The plaintiff may in his notice of trial, and the defendant may Jury.
within four days afterwards, or such extended time as may be
allowed, claim to have the action tried by a jury (*s*).

The action must be commenced within four years next after Limitation.
the cause thereof (*t*).

Malicious Prosecution.

A malicious prosecution is a prosecution instituted by one Malicious
person against another without reasonable and probable cause, prosecu-
and which has failed. It commences at the time the plaintiff tion.
is before the magistrates. Prior to this, it is false imprisonment (*u*).

Prosecuting a person with any other motive than bringing a
guilty party to justice is a malicious prosecution, as where it
is instituted with the view of terrifying parties from the
commission of some prevalent offence (*v*).

If there be no reasonable or probable cause for a charge, the
action lies (*w*), and so also does it for maliciously obtaining or
executing a warrant (*x*).

(*m*) *Foxall* v. *Barnett*, 2 El. & Bl. 298; 23 L. J. Q. B. 7.
(*n*) *Hoey* v. *Felton*, 11 C. B. N. S. 142; 31 L. J. C. P. 105; 9 Jur. 764; 5 L. T. 354; 10 W. R. 78.
(*o*) *O'Brien* v. *Brabner*, 49 J. P. 227; 78 L. T. (N.) 409.
(*p*) Per Tindal, C.J.; *Edgell* v. *Francis*, 1 M. & G. 222; 1 Sc. N. R. 121.
(*q*) *Huckle* v. *Money*, 2 Wils. 205.
(*r*) *Clark* v. *Woods*, 17 L. J. M. C. 189.
(*s*) Order xxxvi., r. 2.
(*t*) 21 Jac. 1, c. 16, s. 3.
(*u*) *Austin* v. *Dowling*, 5 L. R. C. P. 234; 39 L. J. C. P. 260; 22 L. T. 721; 18 W. R. 1003.

(*v*) *Stevens* v. *Midland Counties Railway*, 10 Ex. 352; 2 C. L. R. 130; 23 L. J. Ex. 328; 18 Jur. 932. Cases are not unknown of prosecution instituted by an officer in order to divert suspicion from himself.
(*w*) *Clark* v. *Postan*, 6 C. & P. 423; *Fitzjohn* v. *Mackinder*, 9 C. B. N. S. 505; 30 L. J. C. P. 257; 7 Jur. N. S. 1283; 4 L. T. 149; 9 W. R. 477.
(*x*) *Booth* v. *Cooper*, 1 T. R. 535; 3 Esp. 135; 4 Doug. 339; *Elsie* v. *Smith*, 1 D. & R. 97; 2 Chit. 304; and see *Hope* v. *Evered*, 17 Q. B. D. 338; 55 L. J. M. C. 146, 55 L. T. 320; 34 W. R. 742; *Utting* v. *Burney*, 5 Ti. Rep. 39; and *Creagh* v. *Gamble*, 24 L. R. Ir. 458.

Counsel's opinion is of no avail to a man who has instituted such a prosecution (*y*).

On the principle that *nemo bis vexari debet pro eadem causa* it has been held that there can be no appeal from an acquittal (*z*). Any such proceedings, therefore, would appear to be in the nature of a malicious prosecution.

The necessary ingredients in this action are:—

1. Malice.

1. Malice, which may be either express or implied.

To sustain the averment of malice the charge must be wilfully false (*a*). But if in the opinion of the judge there was no reasonable or probable cause, the jury may from that fact alone infer malice (*b*).

Scandalous charges and accusations made by the defendant against the plaintiff in connection with the prosecution are evidence of malice. And so are any statements or declarations made by the defendant tending to shew that he was actuated by spite and ill-will in instituting the prosecution (*c*).

It is no answer to shew that the charge preferred against the plaintiff was not sustainable in point of law (*d*).

The question of malice is never in terms left to the jury (*e*).

2. Want of reasonable and probable cause.

2. Want of reasonable and probable cause.

Reasonable and probable cause has been defined by a learned judge as an honest belief in the guilt of the accused based upon a full conviction founded upon reasonable grounds of the existence of a state of circumstances, which, assuming them to be true, would reasonably lead any ordinarily prudent and cautious man, placed in the position of the accuser, to the conclusion that the prisoner charged was probably guilty of the crime imputed (*f*).

Information received from persons apparently respectable and believed to be credible is sufficient (*g*). The disbelief of the party making the charge is some want of probable cause, notwithstanding other evidence may have shewn that there was *primâ facie* probable cause (*h*). The evidence need not be sufficient to convict, nor need it be confirmed at the time of the plaintiff's arrest (*i*).

Similarity of handwriting has been held not *per se* reasonable and probable cause for preferring a charge (*j*).

(*y*) *Hewlett* v. *Crutchley*, 5 Taunt. 283.
(*z*) See *The Queen* v. *Lowdon*, JJ., 6 Ti. Rep. 389; *Cox* v. *Hakes*, *ib.* 465; 39 W. R. 145.
(*a*) *Cohen* v. *Morgan*, 6 D. & R. 8.
(*b*) *Busst* v. *Gibbons*, 30 L. J. Ex. 75.
(*c*) *Mitchell* v. *Williams*, 11 M. & W. 217; 12 L. J. Ex. 193.
(*d*) *Wicks* v. *Fentham*, 4 T. R. 248.
(*e*) *Payne* v. *Revans*, 9 W. R. 693.
(*f*) *Hicks* v. *Faulkner*, 8 Q. B. D. 167; 51 L. J. Q. B. 268; 30 W. R. 545; 46 L T. 127; 46 J. P. 420.
(*g*) *Chatfield* v. *Comeford*, 4 F. & F. 1008.
(*h*) *Broad* v. *Ham*, 5 Bing. N. C. 722; 8 Sc. 40.
(*i*) *Dawson* v. *Vansandau*, 11 W. R. 516.
(*j*) *Clements* v. *Ohrly*, 2 C. & K. 686.

The question of reasonable and probable cause is for the judge (*k*).

3. *Prosecution determined in plaintiff's favour.* — The plaintiff, to recover in this action must have had judgment in his favour in the prosecution (*l*). An acquittal through defect in the indictment is sufficient (*m*), but if it be the result of deliberation, and the evidence be such as to cause the jury to pause, it is doubtful whether it is so (*n*). The prosecution being non-proved is not of itself evidence of malice (*o*).

3. Prosecution determined in plaintiff's favour.

4. Allegation and proof of damage having been sustained by the plaintiff is essential (*p*).

4. Damage.

The plaintiff must in this action allege and prove affirmatively the non-existence of reasonable and probable cause (*q*). Every allegation proper to support the action, namely, that the defendant falsely, maliciously, and without any reasonable or probable cause, caused the plaintiff to be indicted, and the trial and acquittal must be pleaded (*r*).

Procedure.

It is not necessary to state that there was an information, if the defendants procured a warrant to issue; but if the claim state that the defendant made information on oath, on which the magistrate granted the warrant, the information must be proved and a recital of it in the warrant is not sufficient (*s*). But the claim is sustained, although it appear that the defendant preferred the indictment unwillingly and solely because he was bound over to do so, if it appear that he was himself the cause of his being bound over by originally making a malicious charge (*t*).

Where the bill has not been found, an action cannot be supported without evidence of express malice as well as the want of probable cause (*u*).

The defendant cannot plead probable cause with not guilty, as the two pleas are incompatible (*v*).

The plaintiff must give evidence of malice express or implied. It cannot be implied from mere proof of the prosecutor not appearing when called (*w*).

Evidence.

In an action for maliciously procuring plaintiff to be arrested on a charge of larceny, defendant cannot give evidence to show

---

(*k*) *Howard* v. *Clarke*, 20 Q. B. D. 558.

(*l*) *Taylor* v. *Ford*, 29 L. T. 392; 22 W. R. 47. See *Castrique* v. *Behrens*, 3 El. & El. 709; 30 L. J. Q. B. 163; and *Barber* v. *Lewis*, 7 C. B. N. S. 183; 29 L. J. C. P. 161.

(*m*) *Wicks* v. *Fentham*, 4 T. R. 247.

(*n*) *Smith* v. *Macdonald*, 3 Esp. 7. But see *Willans* v. *Taylor*, 3 Moo. & P. 350.

(*o*) *Sinclair* v. *Eldred*, 4 Taunt. 7.

(*p*) *Freeman* v. *Arkell*, 3 D. & R. 669; 1 C. & P. 137.

(*q*) *Hicks* v. *Faulkner*, *ubi sup.*

(*r*) *Carman* v. *Truman*, 1 Bro. P. C. 101; *De Medina* v. *Grove*, 10 Q. B. 152.

(*s*) *Gregory* v. *Derby*, 8 C. & P. 749.

(*t*) *Dubois* v. *Keates*, 3 P. & D. 367; 11 A. & E. 329; 4 Jur. 148.

(*u*) *Byne* v. *Moon*, 1 Marsh. 12.

(*v*) *Cotton* v. *Brown*, 4 N. & M. 831; 3 A. & E. 312.

(*w*) *Purcell* v. *Macnamara*, 9 East, 361; 1 Camp. 199; *Abrath* v. *North Eastern Railway Company*, 11 Q. B. D. 440.

that the plaintiff's character was suspicious, and that his house had been searched on former occasions (*x*). If the defendant gives evidence of probable cause, a witness may, however, be asked whether the plaintiff was not a man of notoriously bad character (*y*). But where the plaintiff does not expressly claim damages in respect of injury to reputation, general evidence as to his character is inadmissible (*z*).

Damages. There are three sorts of damages in these cases, either of which is sufficient to sustain an action, namely, damage to a man's reputation, person or property (*a*). And every expense which the plaintiff has necessarily incurred in order to defend himself from the false and malicious charge is recoverable (*b*).

Jury. The right to trial by jury is the same as that in actions for false imprisonment (*c*).

Limitation. The action must be commenced within four years after the cause of such action and not after (*d*).

Public Nuisance.

Public nuisance. Every injury to public rights which affects all persons alike, such as an obstruction in a public thoroughfare merely impeding the right of passage and rendering the way less convenient, is remediable only by indictment (*e*). But for any special injury which affects an individual beyond his fellows, such as being delayed in making a journey and compelled to take a circuitous route (*f*), or driving against the obstruction during a dark night, compensation in damages may be obtained (*g*).

Special damage.

The prevention of customers from going to a colliery by obstructing the highway *per quod*, the benefit of the colliery was lost, and the coals dug up depreciated in value, is such a special and particular damage as to enable the owner of the colliery to maintain an action for the private injury resulting from the nuisance (*h*).

Limitation. The limitation for actions of the first kind is four, and for those of the second kind six years (*i*).

Slander.

Slander. Slander is a false and malicious defamation of character (*j*),

(*x*) *Newsam* v. *Carr*, 2 Stark. 69.
(*y*) *Rodriguez* v. *Tadmire*, 2 Esp. 721.
(*z*) *Downing* v. *Butcher*, 2 M. & Rob. 374.
(*a*) *Per* Holt, C.J., *Sairle* v. *Roberts*, 1 Ld. Ray. 378.
(*b*) *Foxall* v. *Barnett*, 2 El. & Bl. 298; 23 L. J. Q. B. 7.
(*c*) See *ante*, p. 185.
(*d*) 21 Jac. 1, c. 16, s. 3.
(*e*) *Hart* v. *Bassett*, T. Jon. 156.
(*f*) *Wickes* v. *Hungerford Market Company*, 2 Bing. N. C. 281; 2 Sc. 462. But see *Ricket* v. *Metropolitan Railway*, 2 H. L. 175.
(*g*) *Iveson* v. *Moore*, 1 Ld. Ray. 486; 1 Salk. 15. See *Harris* v. *Mobbs*, 2 Ex. D. 268; *Wilkins* v. *Day*, 12 Q. B. D. 110; 49 L. T. 399.
(*h*) *Iveson* v. *Moore*, *ubi sup.*
(*i*) 21 Jac. 1, c. 16, s. 3.
(*j*) By s. 56 of the County Courts Act, this action does not lie in that Court. But by s. 64 it may be there taken by agreement.

LIABILITIES.

expressed verbally, tending to injure the reputation of another and expose him to public ridicule, hatred, or contempt (*k*).

The action is not maintainable without proof of actual damage caused to the plaintiff, *except* where the words impute the commission of a crime, unfitness for society, or misconduct in business (*l*).

And to call a man a felon after he has been convicted but received a pardon or undergone his sentence is actionable (*m*), without proof of such damage.

Words merely conveying suspicion will not sustain the action (*n*), but it is otherwise if they impute a crime, though it is described in vulgar language and not in technical terms (*o*), and the offence imputed need not be an indictable offence (*p*).

However honestly the party who publishes a libel believes it to be true, if it is untrue in fact, the law implies malice, unless the occasion justifies the act, and this is a question of law (*q*). A publication may be a libel on a private person which would not be so on a person in a public capacity, but any imputation of unjust or corrupt motives is equally libellous in either case (*r*).

Allegorical terms of a defamatory character or of evil import, such as imputing to a person the qualities of a "frozen snake" in the fable, are libellous *per se* without innuendoes to explain their meaning (*s*).

Repetition of injurious rumour is actionable unless the occasion be privileged, and it is no justification that the rumour existed (*t*). Where slanderous words are not actionable *per se*, no action will lie against the original utterer for damages resulting from a repetition unauthorized by him (*u*), nor where the special damage was due not to the slander as uttered by the defendant, but to its repetition (*v*). It is no answer to shew that the slander was heard from another, naming the person and the time without shewing that the defendant believed it to be true, and spoke the words on a justifiable occasion (*w*). If the defendant at the time of speaking the words give the name of the person from whom he heard it, this is no justification; but if he did this, and at the trial proves this fact, it will go in mitigation of damages (*x*).

(*k*) Broom, Com. Law, 9th ed. 731.
(*l*) Rowcliffe v. Edmunds, 7 M. & W. 12; Foulger v. Newcomb, L. R. 2 Ex. 327.
(*m*) Leyman v. Latimer, L. R. 3 Ex. D. 352; 47 L. J. Ex. 470.
(*n*) Simmons v. Mitchell, 6 App. Cas. 156.
(*o*) Colman v. Goodwin, 3 Doug. 90.
(*p*) Webb v. Beavan, 1 Q. B. D. 609; 52 L. J. Q. B. 544; 49 L. T. 201; 47 J. P. 488.
(*q*) Darby v. Ouseley, 1 H. & N. 1.

(*r*) Parmiter v. Coupland, 6 M. & W. 105.
(*s*) Hoare v. Silverlocke, 12 Q. B. 625; and see Jacobs v. Schmaltz, 62 L. T. 121; 6 T. L. R. 155.
(*t*) Watkin v. Hall, L. R. 2 Q. B. 396.
(*u*) Parkins v. Scott, 1 H. & C. 153; 31 L. J. Ex. 331.
(*v*) Speight v. Gosnay, 55 J. P. 501.
(*w*) M'Pherson v. Daniel, 10 B. & C. 263; Ecklin v. Little, 6 Ti. Rep. 366.
(*x*) Bennett v. Bennett, 6 C. & P. 586.

Privileged Communications.

Privileged communications.
Privileged communications comprehend all statements made *bonâ fide* in the performance of a duty, or with a fair and reasonable purpose of protecting the interests of the person making them. In such cases the onus of proving malice lies on the plaintiff (*y*).

Charges and communications which would otherwise be slanderous are protected if made *bonâ fide* in the prosecution of an inquiry into a suspected crime. It is for the jury to say whether the circumstances warranted the charge made by the defendant, whether it was made *bonâ fide* or before more persons than was necessary, or in language stronger than the occasion justified (*z*). A criminatory communication made by a public officer is privileged if it is confined to a statement of facts which it is his duty to investigate, and contains nothing but what he believes to be true. But if he imputes improper motives to others, and accuses them of attempts to extort money by misrepresentation, if irrelevant calumny is introduced, or if it contains strictures upon the motives and conduct of others which the facts stated do not warrant, he will exceed his privilege, and subject himself to an action for damages (*a*).

Words spoken by a medical officer to the steward of a public school to the effect that the plaintiff, a butcher, who supplied meat to the school, sold bad meat, were held privileged in the absence of malice (*b*).

A witness in a court of justice is absolutely privileged as to anything he may say as a witness, having reference to the inquiry on which he is called, and a statement as to another matter made to justify him in consequence of a question going to his credit is within the rule (*c*).

Injunction.
The Court has jurisdiction to restrain a person making slanderous statements, but such jurisdiction will be exercised with great care (*d*).

Procedure.
Where a plea of justification contains several charges, and the prosecutor replies generally denying the whole, the prosecutor is entitled to a verdict, unless the defendant proves to the satisfaction of the jury the truth of all the material allegations; and if the defendant fails to do this, it is no ground for a new trial that with respect to some of the charges on which the jury gave a verdict against the defendant, the finding was against the weight of evidence (*e*). A defence stating the matter com-

---

(*y*) *Somerville* v. *Hawkins*, 10 C. B. 583; *Harrison* v. *Bush*, 5 El. & Bl. 344; 25 L. J. Q. B. 25; and see *Stuart* v. *Bell*, 7 T.L. Rep. 502; 64 L. T. 633; 39 W. R. 613; [1891] 2 Q. B. 341.

(*z*) *Primrose* v. *Lawrence*, 11 Ad. & E. 282.

(*a*) *Cooke* v. *Wildes*, 5 El. & Bl. 340; 24 L. J. Q. B. 367; *Popham* v. *Pickburn*, 7 H. & N. 891; 31 L. J. Ex. 133.

(*b*) *Humphreys* v. *Stillwell*, 2 F. & F. 590.

(*c*) *Seaman* v. *Netherclift*, 2 C. P. D. 53; 46 L. J. C. P. 128.

(*d*) *Loog* v. *Bean*, 26 C. D. 306.

(*e*) *Reg.* v. *Newman*, Dears. C. C. 85.

plained of "is true in substance and effect" means true in every particular, and if the defendant does not prove such statement to be true, the defence is not proved, although he proves facts of the same description (*f*). Where the claim alleged that one, at the request and by the direction of the defendant, uttered the slander, the plaintiff was ordered to give particulars of the names of the persons to whom, and of the place at which such slander was uttered (*g*).

But where a slander imputing a specific charge is justified in the defence, particulars of such plea are unnecessary, and will not be ordered (*h*).

Evidence will be rejected where the particular facts and circumstances sought to be proved are not stated or referred to in the defence (*i*). A communication being shewn to be privileged, it lies on the plaintiff to prove malice in fact; in order, however, to entitle him to have the question of malice left to the jury, he need not shew circumstances necessarily leading to the conclusion that malice existed, or such as are inconsistent with its non-existence, but they must be such as raise a probability of malice, and be more consistent with its existence than with its non-existence (*j*). *Evidence.*

The defendant may (after notice to the plaintiff delivered with his defence) give in evidence in mitigation of damages, that he made or offered an apology before the commencement of the action, or as soon thereafter as he had opportunity to do so (*k*). Where the defendant does not by his defence assert the truth of the statement complained of, he cannot give evidence in chief to mitigate damages as to the circumstances of publication or the character of the plaintiff unless by leave of the judge or seven days before trial he furnish particulars to the plaintiff of the matters as to which he intends to give evidence (*l*).

Whenever injury has been done to the fair fame, reputation, or character of the plaintiff, the jury is justified in giving such a sum by way of damages as marks their sense of the maliciousness or recklessness of the wrongdoer in offering the insult and injury, their belief in the groundlessness of the charge and their desire to vindicate the character of the plaintiff (*m*), and the Court will never interfere unless the damages are manifestly outrageous and extravagant (*n*). *Damages.*

Where the plaintiff obtained a verdict with nominal damages, he was held entitled to his full costs (*o*). *Costs.*

(*f*) *Weaver* v. *Lloyd,* 4 D. & R. 230.
(*g*) *Bradbury* v. *Cooper,* 12 Q. B. D. 94; 32 W. R. 92.
(*h*) *Cumming* v. *Green,* 7 T. L. R. 408.
(*i*) *Scott* v. *Sampson,* 8 Q. B. D. 491; *Wood* v. *Durham,* 59 L. T. 142.
(*j*) *Somerville* v. *Hawkins, ubi supra*; *Jenoure* v. *Delmege,* 63 L. T. 814; [1891] A. C. 73; 39 W. R. 388; 55 J. P. 500.
(*k*) 6 & 7 Vict. c. 96, s. 1.
(*l*) Order xxxvi., r. 37; County Court Rules, Order x., rr. 16, 17.
(*m*) *Doe* v. *Filliter,* 13 M. & W. 51.
(*n*) *Gilbert* v. *Burtenshaw,* Cowp. 230; Lofft. 771.
(*o*) *Garnett* v. *Bradley,* 48 L. J. Q. B. 186.

Trespass to Personalty.

Jury. The right to trial by jury is the same as in actions of false imprisonment (*p*).

Limitation. The action must be commenced within two years next after the words spoken, and not after (*q*).

Trespass to personalty. Every direct forcible injury or act disturbing the possession of goods without the owner's consent is a trespass; and if it amount to a deprivation of possession to such an extent as to be inconsistent with the rights of the owner, it then becomes a wrongful conversion (*r*). A person who has moved the goods of another without a lawful right to do so, even to put them out of the way, is liable for the natural consequences of the removal (*s*).

Every interference with a man's lawful business or occupation without lawful excuse is actionable, such as driving the plaintiff's tenants from their holdings by menaces (*t*), or preventing people by the use of threats and intimidation from trading with the plaintiff's vessel in a foreign port (*u*), or from dealing at the plaintiff's shop, or from sending their children to the plaintiff's school, or placing obstructions and impediments in the way of the exercise of the right of free access to a man's place of business (*v*).

Sheriff. Execution against wrong person. With regard to the sheriff, it is laid down that if he seize goods after a tender of the debt and costs, he is liable (*w*), but not if he take goods on an execution which is afterwards set aside for irregularity (*x*), or if he merely seize goods which are privileged from seizure (*y*).

Trespass *vi et armis* lies against a sheriff for taking the goods of A. instead of B. by his bailiff upon a *fi. fa.* (*z*). And if there are two persons of the same name and address, and a writ issues against one of them, and the sheriff through inadvertence or mistake executes the writ against the wrong person, he is liable (*a*).

Where under a *fi. fa.* against A. the furniture in his house was seized and sold, where he lived with a woman with whom

(*p*) See *ante*, p. 185. As to withdrawing the case from the jury, see *O'Brien* v. *Salisbury*, 54 J. P. 215; 6 T. L. R. 133.
(*q*) 21 Jac. 1, c. 16, s. 3.
(*r*) Underhill, Torts, 5th ed. 265. Possession is sufficient title to maintain the action: *Smith* v. *Miller*, 1 T. R. 480.
(*s*) *Walker* v. *Sharman*, 3 F. & F. 259.
(*t*) 1 Roll. Abr. 108, pl. 21.
(*u*) *Tarleton* v. *M'Gawley*, Peake, 270.
(*v*) *Bell* v. *Midland Railway Co.*,

10 C. B. N. S. 307; 30 L. J. C. P. 273.
(*w*) *Lefans* v. *Moregreen*, 1 Keb. 655; *Barker* v. *St. Quintin*, 12 M. & W. 441; 1 D. & L. 542; 13 L. J. Ex. 144.
(*x*) *Doe* v. *Thorn*, 1 M. & S. 425.
(*y*) *Rideal* v. *Fort*, 11 Ex. 847.
(*z*) *Sanderson* v. *Baker*, 3 Wils. 309; 2 W. Bl. 842; *Ackworth* v. *Kempe*, 1 Doug. 40.
(*a*) *Jarmain* v. *Hooper*, 1 D. & L. 769; 7 S. N. R. 663; 6 M. & G. 827; 8 Jur. 127; 13 L. J. C. P. 63.

he had gone through the ceremony of marriage, and to whom the goods belonged before marriage, it was held that the woman having afterwards discovered that the marriage was void, might maintain an action against the sheriff, and recover the value of the goods, although it exceeded the price for which they were sold (*b*).

But where the property belonged to a woman who cohabited with the debtor, assumed his name, and represented herself as his wife, the action was not maintainable (*c*).

The sheriff is liable to an action by the owner of goods lent on hire if having seized them under an execution against the hirer, he sells the entire property in them; but the hirer must have given notice to the sheriff on the seizure (*d*), and for the mere seizure without sale he is not liable (*e*).

As to interpleader proceedings, see *ante* (*f*). Where neither the premises nor the goods belong to the debtor, the sheriff may on such proceedings be protected against an action for trespass, or for wrongful seizure if no substantial grievance has been done (*g*).

And where the sheriff is directed to levy on the goods of a wrong person, he is under no liability for so doing (*h*).

An action lies at the suit of an administrator for taking away the goods of an intestate (*i*). But where an executrix used the goods of her testator as her own, and afterwards married, and then treated them as the goods of the husband, it was held that the action was not maintainable (*j*).

A landlord may maintain an action against him for removing goods before the rent has been satisfied (*k*). Where the bailiff in possession of goods under a landlord's distress received a *fi. fa.* from a sheriff and sold the goods under it, the sheriff was held liable to action at the suit of the landlord (*l*). Landlord.

Where the sheriff sells more than sufficient to satisfy the debt and costs he is liable for the excess (*m*). And he is also liable, if he sell for less money than ought to have been obtained (*n*). But if a judgment debtor have a qualified interest only as a bailee in goods seized, and the sheriff, having no notice thereof, sells them absolutely, he is not guilty of a conversion by the Seizure.

(*b*) *Glasspoole* v. *Young*, 9 B. & C. 696.

(*c*) *Edwards* v. *Farebrother*, 2 M. & P. 293.

(*d*) *Dean* v. *Whitaker*, 1 C. & P. 347.

(*e*) *Duffil* v. *Spottiswoode*, 3 *ib.* 435.

(*f*) Page 166.

(*g*) *Smith* v. *Critchfield*, 14 Q. B. D. 873.

(*h*) *Morris* v. *Salberg*, 22 Q. B. D. 615; 58 L. J. Q. B. 275; 61 L T. 283; 37 W. R. 460; 53 J. P. 772; 5 Ti. Rep. 376.

(*i*) *Thorpe* v. *Stallwood*, 1 D. P. C. 24.

(*j*) *Quick* v. *Staines*, 1 B. & P. 293.

(*k*) *Calvert* v. *Joliffe*, 2 B. & Ad. 418; *Haythorn* v. *Bush*, 2 Dowl. 641; 2 C. & M. 689; *Cocker* v. *Musgrove*, 15 L. J. Q. B. 365.

(*l*) *Reddell* v. *Stowey*, 2 M. & Rob. 358.

(*m*) *Batchelor* v. *Vyse*, 4 M. & Sc. 552; *Aldred* v. *Constable*, 8 Jur. 956; 6 Q. B. 370.

(*n*) *Gawler* v. *Chaplin*, 2 Ex. 506; 18 L. J. Ex. 42.

194   EXECUTIVE OFFICERS.

mere act of selling. It must be shewn that he parted with the possession of the goods and caused them to be used by the purchaser (*o*). And if he sell goods under a *fi. fa.*, and afterwards the judgment is reversed, the defendant cannot have restitution, but the value for which they were sold (*p*).

County Court.
In the County Court, where the judge had adjudicated in favour of a claimant whose house had been broken and entered and his goods seized and taken away as the goods of an execution debtor, it was held that the claimant could not afterwards proceed in an action of trespass for taking away the goods (*q*).

Water bailiff.
And where a water-bailiff removed what proved to be an illegal fixed engine from a salmon-river, it was held that an action against him for such removal was not sustainable (*r*).

Surveyor.
Nor does an action lie against a surveyor for removing a bar to a public way (*s*).

Distress (*t*).
With regard to wrongful distress, it has been held that the jurisdiction of the High Court is not ousted by the Taxes Act (*u*). And where the plaintiff who was the owner and occupier of the vicarial tithes and occupier of the rectorial tithes on which the land-tax had been redeemed, was assessed to land-tax for a gross sum for both, which, on demand, he refused to pay, whereupon the collector distrained, it was held that trespass lay for the distress, and that the plaintiff was not bound to appeal (*v*). A conviction on a statute on the face of it, not pursuing the previous statute, nor shewing that any offence had been committed, is bad, and although it has not been quashed, its invalidity may be taken advantage of on the trial of an action of trespass for a distress taken under a warrant grounded upon it (*w*). But a party making a wrongful distress for two causes as to one of which he is entitled to notice of action, is liable in trespass as to the other (*x*). And parties executing distress for poor-rate are liable if they commit any excess not excused by law (*y*). And so is a highway surveyor if he execute a warrant for highway-rate against a person not chargeable (*z*).

Detention.
Where a revenue officer unlawfully seizes goods as forfeited, and unlawfully detains them, and takes money which he has no

(*o*) *Lancashire Co.* v. *Fitzhugh*, 6 H. & N. 502; 30 L. J. Ex. 231.
(*p*) *Hoe.* 5 Co. 90 b.
(*q*) *Chater* v. *Chigwell*, 14 Jur. 697; 19 L. J. Q. B. 520; 15 Q. B. 217.
(*r*) *Williams* v. *Blackwall*, 8 L. T. 252; 9 Jur. 579; 32 L. J. Ex. 174; 11 W. R. 621.
(*s*) *Pullin* v. *Deffel*, 64 L. T. 134.
(*t*) The ancient remedy for wrongful distress was *replevin*, which is now practically obsolete except as regards the County Court: Gilbert on Repl. p. 138; County Court Rules, 1889, Order xxxiv.; Pollock, Torts, 2nd ed.

299. In such an action 24 Geo. 2, c. 44, s. 6, is inapplicable: *Milward* v. *Caffin*, 2 Bl. 1331; and see *ante*, p. 146.
(*u*) *Shaftesbury* v. *Russell*, 1 B. & C. 666.
(*v*) *Charleton* v. *Alway*, 11 A. & E. 993.
(*w*) *Gimbert* v. *Coyney*, M'Lel. & Y. 46.
(*x*) *Lamont* v. *Southall*, 7 D. P. C. 569.
(*y*) *Bell* v. *Oakley*, 2 M. & S. 259.
(*z*) *Freeman* v. *Read*, 32 L. J. M. C. 226; 10 Jur. 149.

right to take as the condition of their release, he is liable to action (*a*). But where goods liable to duty have been landed and warehoused and examined by officers in the regular execution of their duty, no action can be maintained against such officers for the detention of goods under a belief that they are liable to forfeiture, though it ultimately appears that they were not so liable (*b*). And condemnation in the Exchequer is conclusive against any such action being maintainable (*c*).

And where a police officer came into possession of a ring which the plaintiff was supposed to have stolen, but was acquitted on the hearing of the charge, and no order having been made by the magistrate with regard to it, refused to give it up, it was held that the officer was not liable to action at the suit of the plaintiff for the detention (*d*).

Where a postmaster delivered up letters of a bankrupt to a trustee believing *bonâ fide* that he was entitled to them, it was held he was not liable under 9 Anne c. 10, s. 40, for wittingly, willingly, and knowingly detaining letters and causing them to be detained and opened (*e*).

The Court will not, in the absence of a trust, restrain the sheriff from selling the goods of a stranger found upon the land of a person against whom execution had issued (*f*). But if goods have been wrongfully seized by him it is otherwise, and he may be restrained from selling or remaining in possession, but the execution creditor should either be made a party to the action or notice should be served on him before the injunction is granted. The plaintiff will not get his costs of such an action prematurely brought (*g*). Injunction.

In an action against the sheriff the claim after reciting that two writs of *fi. fa.* had been delivered to him to be executed stated that defendant as such sheriff, under colour of the writs, wrongfully seized the goods of the plaintiff to a much greater value than necessary to satisfy, and sold the same. This was held sufficient (*h*). Procedure.

In actions for removing goods seized without paying the rent after notice of its being due, no averment of notice to the execution-creditor is necessary (*i*). But if the action is founded on the statute, notice to the sheriff is always alleged and should not be omitted (*j*). The defence of "not guilty" admits the seizure by the sheriff, and it is not necessary to

(*a*) *Irving* v. *Wilson*, 4 T. R. 485.
(*b*) *Jacobson* v. *Blake*, 7 Sc. N. R. 772; 6 M. & G. 919; 13 L. J. C. P. 89; 8 Jur. 272; *De Gondonin* v. *Lewis*. 2 P. & D. 283.
(*c*) *Scott* v. *Shearman*, 2 W. Bl. 977.
(*d*) *Bullock* v. *Dunlop*, 2 Ex. D. 43; 46 L. J. Ex. 156; 36 L. T. 191; 25 W. R. 293.
(*e*) *Meirelles* v. *Banning*, 2 B. & Ad. 909.

(*f*) *Garstin* v. *Asplin*, 1 Madd. 151; *Jackson* v. *Stanhope*, 15 L. J. Ch. 466.
(*g*) *Hilliard* v. *Hanson*, 21 Ch. D. 69; *Aylwin* v. *Evans*, 47 L. T. 568.
(*h*) *Gawler* v. *Chaplin, ubi. sup.*
(*i*) *Risely* v. *Ryle*, 11 M. & W. 16; 12 L. J. Ex. 322.
(*j*) *Thurgood* v. *Richards*, 7 Bing. 428; 4 C. & P. 481.

produce the warrant to connect him with the officer (*k*). And where in such an action the defence was that the sheriff seized goods which were alleged to belong to S., but which did not, in fact, belong to him, the plaintiff was nevertheless held entitled to a verdict (*l*). It is not sufficient for the defendant to shew in mitigation of damages that the goods realized less than the amount of the rent, but he must prove that their actual value to the landlord at the time of removal was less (*m*).

Where a sheriff's officer, having a *fi. fa.* against A. called at his house when he was from home waited till he returned, and then informed him of his business, this was held sufficient to warrant the jury in finding that the writ was executed at the time of the officer's entry (*n*).

A sheriff justifying in trespass under a writ of *fi. fa.* need not shew his authority (*o*).

Evidence.

In an action for abusing the process of the Court in order illegally to compel a party to give up his goods, it is not necessary to prove that the action under which the process was improperly employed has determined, nor to aver that the process was sued out without reasonable and probable cause (*p*).

An affidavit made by a sheriff's officer under the Interpleader Act respecting the goods is admissible to prove the officer to be the servant of the sheriff (*q*).

And where plaintiff, being owner and occupier of the vicarial tithes and occupier of the rectorial tithes, on which latter tithe the land-tax had been redeemed, was assessed to land-tax on a gross sum for which on refusal, the collector distrained, it was held that the demand having been made for a sum alleged to be due for a quarter then expired, defendant could not justify the distress by shewing that a sum was due at the expiration of the current quarter for vicarial tithes which would cover the sum distrained for (*r*).

In an action for excessive distress it is not necessary to prove express malice (*s*).

Damages.

Damages must be both alleged and proved in action against the sheriff for wrongful seizure (*t*), and any special damage that has been sustained is recoverable (*u*).

Where the defendants had become trespassers *ab initio* by breaking the door, the jury were rightly directed that they

(*k*) *Reid* v. *Poyntz*, 6 M. & W. 210; 8 Dowl. 410.
(*l*) *Fowler* v. *Cookson*, 1 Q. B. 419.
(*m*) *Thomas* v. *Mirehouse*, 19 Q. B. D. 563; 36 W. R. 104.
(*n*) *Bird* v. *Bass*, 6 M. & G. 143; 6 Sc. N. R. 928.
(*o*) *Cheasley* v. *Barnes*, 10 East, 73; *Ogden* v. *Hesketh*, 2 C. & K. 772.
(*p*) *Grainger* v. *Hill*, 4 Bing. N. C.
212; 5 Sc. 261.
(*q*) *Brickill* v. *Hulse*, 2 N. & P. 426.
(*r*) *Charleton* v. *Alway*, 11 A. & E. 993.
(*s*) *Field* v. *Mitchell*, 6 Esp. 71.
(*t*) *Tancred* v. *Allgood*, 4 H. & N. 444; 28 L. J. Ex. 362.
(*u*) *Keene* v. *Dilke*, 4 Ex. 388; 18 L. J. Ex. 440.

might, even on the defence of not guilty, give damages in respect of all the injuries complained of (v).

In an action for removing goods without paying the rent due the measure of damages is *primâ facie* the amount of rent, but the sheriff may prove that the value of the goods removed was less than that amount (w). The price of the goods sold is not necessarily, but is usually, the measure of damages if the sale be wrongful (x).

In an action for taking goods under irregular process, where special damage is alleged and claimed but not proved, the plaintiff is entitled to nominal, or such substantial damages as the jury thinks fit (y).

Whenever a public officer has wrongfully seized and detained goods from the owner, the latter is entitled to recover the loss resulting from the wrongful act, so that if the property detained has fallen in value in the market, the plaintiff is entitled to add the amount of that to the damage he has sustained (z).

The action must be commenced within four years after the cause thereof, and not after (a). Limitation.

Trespass to Realty.

Every unauthorized entry upon or direct interference with another's land is a trespass for which an action lies without proof of actual damage (b). And if a man abuse an authority given him by the law as distinguished from that of the party, as in leave and licence, he becomes a trespasser *ab initio* (c). But mere non-feasance does not constitute him such a trespasser (d). Trespass to realty.

If there is an abuse of authority by which the party becomes a trespasser *ab initio* the plaintiff is entitled to recover damages as well for the part or injury which would have been justified if there had been no abuse as for the part which is directly caused by the abuse (e). And the rule that a party cannot be made a trespasser by relation is only applicable where the act complained of was lawful at the time (f).

This action will lie for continuing on the premises and disturbing the plaintiff's possession after the time allowed by law (g), or after distress made (h).

If a sheriff remain on premises for the purpose of putting the Sheriff.

(v) *Kerbey* v. *Denby*, 1 M. & W. 336; 2 Gale, 31.
(w) *Thomas* v. *Mirehouse, ubi sup.*
(x) *Whitehouse* v. *Atkinson*, 3 C. & P. 244.
(y) *Doss* v. *Doss*, 14 L. T. 646.
(z) *Barry* v. *Arnand*, 8 Q. B. 609.
(a) 21 Jac. 1, c. 16, s. 3.
(b) Underhill, p. 253. Possession is a sufficient title to maintain the action: *Jones* v. *Chapman*, 2 Ex. 821.

(c) As to this doctrine, see *ante*, pp. 137, 152.
(d) *Six Carpenters' Case*, 8 Co. 146 a.
(e) *Kerbey* v. *Denby*, 1 M. & W. 341; 2 Gale, 31.
(f) *Thorpe* v. *Stallwood*, 5 M. & G. 760.
(g) *Winterbourne* v. *Morgan*, 2 Camp. 117.
(h) *Ladd* v. *Thomas*, 4 P. & D. 9.

purchaser of a lease in possession he would be liable to this action at the suit of the debtor if in possession, although the premises had been sold and transferred (*i*).

County Court.
Where a judge of the County Court adjudicated in favour of a claimant whose house had been broken and entered and his goods seized and taken away as those of the execution debtor, it was held that the claimant was afterwards entitled to proceed for the special damage occasioned by the wrongful breaking and entry (*j*).

Constables.
Where a search warrant was executed by a constable to whom it was not addressed, this was held the proper form of action (*k*). But where a constable on hearing a noise in a public house at one o'clock in the night, entered the house, the door being open, the action was held not to lie (*l*).

Overseers.
Overseers executing a distress for poor-rate are liable if they commit any excess not excused by law (*m*).

Highway surveyor.
A surveyor who had removed by order of the highway board the locks from a gate placed across a footpath by the occupier of the land through which it ran, was held liable to this action notwithstanding the order of the board (*n*), and so also was he where he dug away the plaintiff's bank without authority, although evidence was given that the property was thereby improved (*o*), and where on an order to lop trees he topped them (*p*).

Forcible entry.
An attempt to eject by force a person having a legal title to land brings the person who makes it within the statute against forcible entry (*q*), and damages cannot be recovered in such case (*r*), except for independent wrong committed in the course of such entry (*s*). But an allegation *vi et armis* in an action for breaking and entering does not imply a forcible entry (*t*).

Injunction.
The Court will not, it appears, grant an injunction in respect of an interference with a church way at the suit of a parishioner, the ecclesiastical courts having jurisdiction in such cases (*u*). But a local authority interfering with property in an unauthorized manner, as, *e.g.* when not authorized under the Public Health Act, will be restrained, and the plaintiff will not be left to his remedy under the compensation clauses (*v*). An

(*i*) *Playfair* v. *Musgrove*, 14 M. & W. 239; 15 L. J. Ex. 26; 3 D. & L. 72; 9 Jur. 783.
(*j*) *Chater* v. *Chigwell*, 14 Jur. 697; 19 L. J. Q. B. 520; 51 Q. B. 217.
(*k*) *Freegard* v. *Barnes*, 7 Ex. 827; 21 L. J. Ex. 320.
(*l*) *R.* v. *Smith*, 6 C. & P. 136.
(*m*) *Bell* v. *Oakley*, 2 M. & S. 259.
(*n*) *Mill* v. *Hawker*, L. R. 10 Ex. 62; 44 L. J. Ex. 49; 33 L. T. 177; 39 J. P. 195; 38 W. R. 346.
(*o*) *Alston* v. *Scales*, 9 Bing. 3.
(*p*) *Unwin* v. *Hanson*, [1891] 2 Q. B. 115; 7 T. L. R. 488.
(*q*) *Laws* v. *Telford*, 13 C. C. C. 226; 1 App. Cas. 414; 45 L. J. Ex. 613; 35 L. T. 69; and see *infra*, p. 209.
(*r*) *Newton* v. *Harland*, 1 M. & G. 244.
(*s*) *Beddall* v. *Maitland*, 17 Ch. D. 174.
(*t*) *Harvey* v. *Bridges*, 3 D. & L. 55; 14 M. & W. 442; 1 Ex. 261.
(*u*) *Batten* v. *Gedge*, 41 C. D 507.
(*v*) *Grand Junction Canal* v. *Shugar*, 6 Ch. App. 483.

appeal to a superior board does not oust the jurisdiction of the Court (w).

If a public board exceed the due limits of their authority, and commit acts of nuisance, whether of a public or private (x) nature, the Court may restrain by injunction (y), unless the jurisdiction is expressly negatived (z).

As regards apprehended injury, the Court will not usually interfere unless the damage will be irreparable (a).

If the defendant relies upon the defence of leave and licence, he must prove either an express permission from the plaintiff (b), or circumstances from which such permission may fairly be implied (c). Procedure.

The defendant may justify under a sufficient legal process, if he had it in fact at the time, although he declared then that he entered for another cause (d).

To render a defendant liable as a trespasser *ab initio*, facts sufficient to support this must be stated in the claim (e).

The action may be well laid to have been done under a false charge and assertion, for that is laid only as a matter of aggravation, and the jury may give damages for the trespass, as it is aggravated by such false charge (f). In an action for breaking and entering plaintiff's house and expelling him therefrom, the breaking and entering are the gist of the action, and the expulsion is merely aggravation; therefore a justification as to the breaking and entering will cover the whole claim (g).

The defendant may give in evidence under not guilty that he entered by virtue of a warrant, and was turned out, whereupon he committed the trespasses complained of (h). But a party who insists on remaining on the land of another against his will, and therefore *primâ facie* against right, ought to shew all the circumstances which make such possession lawful and abridge the just rights of property (i). Evidence.

Where the defendant put in an informal affidavit to the effect that he had entered under a warrant to search for dutiable goods, it was held no defence (j). And where a local authority

(w) *Tinkler* v. *Wandsworth*, 2 D. & J. 261.
(x) *Box* v. *Allen*, 1 Dick. 49.
(y) *Att.-Gen.* v. *Forbes*, 2 M. & C. 133.
(z) *Birley* v. *Chorlton*, 3 Beav. 499.
(a) *Palmer* v. *Paul*, 2 L. J. Ch. 154; *Fletcher* v. *Bealey*, 28 Ch. D. 688. See also as to injunctions, *Att.-Gen.* v. *Metropolitan Board of Works*, 1 H. & M. 320; *Macey* v. *ib.*, 33 L. J. Ch. 377; *Bateman* v. *Poplar*, 37 Ch. D. 272; *Att.-Gen.* v. *Richmond*, 2 Eq. 306; *Ellis* v. *Bridgworth*, 2 J. & H. 67.
(b) *Kavanagh* v. *Gudge*, 7 M. & G. 316.
(c) *Ditcham* v. *Bond*, 3 Camp. 524.
(d) *Crowther* v. *Ramsbottom*, 7 T. R. 654; and *cf. Playfair* v. *Musgrove*, 14 M. & W. 239; 3 D. & L. 72; 9 Jur. 783; 15 L. J. Ex. 26.
(e) *Shoreland* v. *Govett*, 8 D. & R. 257; 5 B. & C. 485; and see *Morrish* v *Murray*, 2 D. & L. 199; 13 M. & W. 52; 13 L. J. Ex. 261; and *Johnson* v. *Leigh*, 1 Marsh. 565; 6 Taunt. 246.
(f) *Bracegirdle* v. *Orford*, 2 M. & S. 77.
(g) *Taylor* v. *Cole*, 3 T. R. 292.
(h) *Eagleton* v. *Gutteridge*, 11 M. & W. 465.
(i) *Hayling* v. *Okey*, 8 Ex. 531.
(j) *R.* v. *Moseley*, 1 C. & K. 718.

is sued for a trespass, it is incumbent on them to prove affirmatively from the statute the existence of the power which they claim to exercise (*k*).

Damages. Where the defendants had become trespassers *ab initio* by breaking the door, the jury were rightly directed that they might, even on the defence of not guilty, give damages in respect of all the injuries complained of (*l*).

The true criterion of damages has been held to be the whole injury which the plaintiff has received (*m*). If the entry is made after notice or warning not to trespass or is a wilful or impertinent intrusion upon a man's domestic privacy, or an insulting invasion of his proprietary rights, a very serious cause of action will arise, and exemplary damages be recoverable (*n*).

But it has been held that a plaintiff is not entitled to recover as damages the costs of setting aside a warrant, and all subsequent proceedings under which the trespass was committed (*o*).

Limitation. The action must be commenced within six years next after the cause thereof, and not after (*p*).

(*k*) See *Sutton* v. *Norwich*, 27 L. J. Ch. 741; *Simpson* v. *Staffordshire Railway*, 34 ib. 387.
(*l*) *Kerby* v. *Denbey*, *ubi supra*.
(*m*) *Clark* v. *Newsam*, 1 Ex. 131; 16 L. J. Ex. 297.
(*n*) *Merest* v. *Harvey*, 5 Taunt. 443.
(*o*) *Holloway* v. *Turner*, 6 Q. B. 928.
(*p*) 21 Jac. 1, c. 16. s. 3.

CRIMINAL PROCEEDINGS.

Attachment.

Attachment is the punitive process to which the High Court resorts for excess of public duty on the part of its officers. As a remedy to an individual it is like all other public process only available where damage has been sustained through such excess of duty, by such individual (*a*).

Being confined to officers of the Court it is only available against the Sheriff, the Admiralty Marshal, the Tipstaff, and the High Bailiff (*b*).

As against the sheriff it has been laid down that attachment may be moved for in any of the following cases:—

Arrest without authority.
Breaking doors without excuse.
Corrupt practices.
Detaining person till he pays money for his release.
Extortion.
False return, where circumstances of hardship to plaintiff.
Force, using needless.
Illtreating persons arrested.
Neglecting to execute (*c*).

The process cannot be executed on Sunday (*d*). But it must be moved for within a reasonable time (*e*).

If the sheriff has executed the writ and has in his hands or possession, the proceeds of the execution, he is at once liable to this process (*f*). But the old rule as to attachment absolute in the first instance is abrogated (*g*).

The death of the defendant will not remove the sheriff's liability (*h*); but if any of the proceedings against the sheriff be irregular, the Court will set aside the attachment (*i*).

The service of the writ must be personal on the sheriff or his deputy (*j*).

An order for attachment or committal must be applied for on notice (*k*).

Criminal proceedings. Attachment.

(*a*) *Brainard* v. *Connecticut Railway Co.*, 7 Cush. (U.S.) R. 510.
(*b*) See *ante*, p. 165. As to officers other than the sheriff, the process is rarely or never resorted to.
(*c*) Hawk. P. C. Bk. II. c. 22, ss. 2, 3 and 4; and see 50 & 51 Vict. c. 55, s. 29.
(*d*) *R.* v. *Myers*, 1 T. R. 266.
(*e*) *R.* v. *Perring*, 3 B. & P. 151.
(*f*) *Phillips* v. *Canterbury*, 11 M. & W. 619; *Botten* v. *Tomlinson*, 16 L. J. C. P. 138.
(*g*) *Jupp* v. *Cooper*, 5 C. P. D. 26; *Eynde* v. *Gould*, 9 Q. B. D. 335.
(*h*) *R.* v. *Sheriff of Middlesex*, 3 T. R. 133.
(*i*) *R.* v. *Sheriff of Middlesex*, 2 M. & S. 562.
(*j*) *Woodland* v. *Fuller*, 11 A. & E. 859; 2 P. & D. 570.
(*k*) Tidd. 8th ed. 314; Chit. Arch. 7th ed. 556.

Information (m).

Information.

Every public officer commits a misdemeanour who in the exercise or under colour of exercising the duties of his office, does any illegal act, or abuses any discretionary power with which he is invested by law, from an improper motive, the existence of which motive may be inferred, either from the nature of the act or the circumstances of the case. But an illegal exercise of authority caused by a mistake as to the law, made *bonâ fide*, is not a misdemeanour (n).

An officer executing a warrant upon a person absolutely privileged would render himself liable to this process (o).

If police officials appear as advocates before justices in cases in which they are not properly prosecutors, they are guilty of misdemeanour by virtue of 6 & 7 Vict. c. 73, s. 2, and the proceedings being irregular, a conviction will be quashed (p).

Refusing admission to persons into a Court of petty sessions, when an open Court is another instance (q).

Where, some few years since, a murder had been committed, a police official held a sort of informal inquiry into the circumstances attending the murder. This was clearly an excess of authority, and rendered the officer liable to this process (r).

And the same would apply in the case of the illegal practice of interrogating persons under arrest (s). In the case of any persons whether under arrest or not, there is of course no obligation to answer. Such obligation is usually confined to witnesses in open Court.

An information lies also against officers employed by or under the post office if they suffer letters to be hindered, delayed, or opened (t), and also against persons not so employed (u).

It also lies against highway surveyors for not filling up and fencing holes within due time (v), for causing stones or other obstructions to remain at night on the highway to the danger of passengers (w), for digging for materials whereby any bridge,

The process is directed to the coroner when it issues against the sheriff, and to the present sheriff when it issues against his predecessor (l).

(l) Order xliv. r. 2: *Jupp* v. *Cooper*, ubi supra.
(m) In the case of offences not cognisable by a Court of Summary Jurisdiction, the remedy is of course by indictment.
(n) Steph. Dig. Crim. Law, Art. 121; 1 Salk. 380; Cro. Eliz. 654.
(o) See ante, p. 7.
(p) *Nicholson* v. *Naylor*, 57 L. J. M. C. 43; 58 L. T. 157; 52 J. P. 162; 16 Cox, C. C. 373; and see *Kyle* v. *Barber*, 58 L. T. 229; 52 J. P. 541, 725; 16 Cox, C. C. 378; and *R.* v. *Bushell*, 52 J. P. 136; 16 Cox, 367. In the case of revenue officers they are entitled to conduct cases before justices. See 53 & 54 Vict. c. 21, s. 27, and 39 & 40 Vict. c. 36, s. 273.
(q) 11 & 12 Vict. c. 42, ss. 17, 19.
(r) See Amos on the Constitution, 3rd ed. pp. 131, 134.
(s) Taylor, Evidence, 6th ed. 779.
(t) 9 Anne, c. 10, s. 40; 7 Will. 4, c. 36, s. 25.
(u) 54 & 55 Vict. c. 46, s. 10.
(v) 5 & 6 Will. 4, c. 50, s. 55.
(w) Sect. 56.

building, &c., is damaged (*x*), and in these cases the civil liability remains.

Tax collectors and overseers are also liable to this process for taking more than the fees allowed on a distress (*y*). And so are workhouse and asylum officers for unlawful detention of a lunatic (*z*), or for illtreatment (*a*), or abuse of a female lunatic (*b*). But the mode of procedure in these cases is limited to that of prior consent of the Crown law officers, except where commenced by superior officers (*c*).

As has been above stated, inasmuch as the sheriff, Admiralty Marshal, Tipstaff, and High Bailiff are liable to attachment, this remedy is not open against them (*d*).

Assault and Battery.

An assault is an attempt to offer with force and violence to do a corporal hurt to another as by striking at him with or without a weapon, or presenting a gun at him at such a distance to which the gun will carry, or pointing a pitchfork at him standing within reach of it, or by holding up one's fist to him, or by any such like act done in an angry, threatening manner (*e*). *Assault and battery.*

Any injury whatsoever, be it ever so small, being actually done to the person of a man, in an angry, revengeful, rude, or insolent manner, as by spitting in his face, or anyway touching him in anger, or violently jostling him out of the way, are batteries (*f*).

A magistrate has no right to order the examination of the person of a prisoner. Any officer making examination in pursuance of such order is therefore guilty of assault (*g*), and so are officers who cut unnecessarily the hair of a pauper in the poorhouse (*h*).

But it is doubtful whether the mere presentation of a pistol, which is in fact not loaded, at another is an assault (*i*), and it is no battery to lay one's hand gently on another whom an officer has a warrant to arrest (*j*). But if more force than necessary be used it is otherwise (*k*).

A person charged with assault and battery may be found guilty of either offence (*l*).

(*z*) Sect. 57.
(*y*) 57 Geo. 3, c. 93, s. 6.
(*z*) 53 & 54 Vict. c. 5, s. 315.
(*a*) Sect. 322.
(*b*) Sect. 324.
(*c*) Sect. 325. Cases may possibly arise where officers with a view to gain, may cause to be published false news as to sedition. This is a misdemeanour: Steph. Dig. C. L. Art. 95.
(*d*) See *ante*, pp. 169, 201.
(*e*) Hawk. P. C. c. xv. s. 1; *R.* v.

St. *George,* 9 C. & P. 483; *R.* v. *Baker,* 1 C. & K. 254.
(*f*) Hawk. P. C. c. xv. s. 2.
(*g*) *Agnew* v. *Jobson,* 13 Cox, C. C. 625.
(*h*) *Forde* v. *Skinner,* 4 C. & P. 239.
(*i*) *R.* v. *Brown,* 10 Q. B. D. 381.
(*j*) Hawk. P. C. c. xv. s. 2.
(*k*) *R.* v. *Mabel,* 9 C. & P. 474; *Levy* v. *Edwards,* 1 C. & P. 40.
(*l*) Hawk. P. C. c. xv., s. 1.

A battery cannot be justified by an officer unless there was resistance in the party (*m*), and though one cannot justify by pleading *son assault demesne* in the indictment, this may be given in evidence upon not guilty (*n*).

It is a good defence to prove that the battery occurred by misadventure (*o*), or that it occurred in arrest on legal process (*p*), provided no greater force than necessary was used (*q*).

It is also a good defence to shew that the complaint has been heard and determined by two justices (*r*).

Common Nuisance.

Common nuisance.

A common nuisance is indictable at common law.

Every injury to public rights which affects all parties alike, such as an obstruction in a public thoroughfare merely impeding the right of passage and rendering the way less convenient, is only remediable by indictment (*s*). And all injuries to a highway such as digging a ditch or making a hedge across it, laying timber upon it, or doing any act whereby it is rendered less commodious to the public, are nuisances at common law (*t*).

Although an Act of Parliament authorizes alterations or blocking up of a highway, yet if these are not carried out with reasonable care and cause unnecessary danger to persons using the highway, the person carrying out such alterations, &c., may be indicted for obstruction (*u*).

Eavesdropping.

Another instance of common nuisance is eavesdropping, which consists in loitering under walls or eaves of a house, to hearken after discourse and thereupon to frame slanderous and mischievous tales. Offenders are apparently indictable at the sessions, and liable to be fined and bound over to good behaviour (*v*).

Conspiracy.

Conspiracy.

By the common law, liberty of a man's mind and will, how he should bestow himself and his means, his talents and his industry, is as much the subject of the law's protection as is that of his body. Therefore, if two or more persons agreed to

---

(*m*) *Williams* v. *Jones*, Ca. temp. Hard. 301.
(*n*) Per Holt, C.J., *R.* v. *Cotesworth*, 6 Mod. 172.
(*o*) *Gibbons* v. *Pepper*, 2 Salk. 637; and see *Coward* v. *Baddeley*, 4 H. & N. 478; 5 Jur. N. S. 414; 28 L. J. Ex. 260.
(*p*) 2 Roll. Abr. 547a.
(*q*) 1 Ld. Ray. 222; 2 Str. 1049; 1 C. & P. 40.

(*r*) 24 & 25 Vict. c. 100, ss. 44, 45. See *ante*, p. 173.
(*s*) *Hart* v. *Basset*, T. Jon. 156; *R.* v. *Cross*, 3 Camp. 224; *R.* v. *Russell*, 6 East, 427.
(*t*) 1 Hawk. P. C. C. 76, s. 48.
(*u*) *R.* v. *Burt*, 11 Cox, 399; and see *Lewis* v. *Vaughan*, 4 Ti. Rep. 649.
(*v*) 4 Bl. Com. 168.

co-operate against that liberty of thought and freedom of will, they would be guilty of a conspiracy (*w*).

A conspiracy is an agreement between two or more persons:—

1. Falsely to charge another with a crime either from a malicious or vindictive motive or feeling towards the party, or for the purpose of extorting money from him.

This does not extend to the case where persons consult and agree to prosecute a person who is guilty, or against whom there are reasonable grounds of suspicion (*x*).

2. Wrongfully to injure or prejudice a third person or any body of men in any other manner.

Such as that to injure a man in his trade or profession (*y*), or to charge a man as the reputed father of a bastard (*z*); but not to commit a mere civil trespass (*a*).

3. To commit any offence (*b*).

This would apply to the case of officers conspiring with others (not officers) (*c*) to do that which would be illegal in themselves such as "shadowing" and watching premises (*d*); and also to perpetrate outrages—as appears to have been done in Ireland, and perhaps in this country also. This latter would constitute in the officer concerned misprision of felony (*e*), which consists in knowledge that a felony has been committed and concealment of the fact.

4. To do any act with intent to pervert the course of justice.

Such as that of justices to certify that a highway was in repair when they knew it was otherwise (*f*), and that of procuring persons to commit offences, or to spread rumours that offences are about to be committed, with a view to create general alarm, and in order to obtain rewards for the discovery of offenders or supposed offenders (*g*).

5. To effect a legal purpose with a corrupt intent or by improper means (*h*).

Nothing need be done in pursuance of the conspiracy (*i*), and the indictment need not state the overt acts used to effect the intended mischief (*j*). The word "falsely" need not be used

(*w*) Per Bramwell, B., *R.* v. *Druitt*, 10 C. C. C. 592.
(*x*) *R.* v. *Best*, 1 Salk. 177; 2 Ld. Ray. 1167. See *Ex parte Wolf*, 28 J. P. 23; and also the cases cited, *ante*, p. 82.
(*y*) *R.* v. *Eccles*, 1 Leach, 274.
(*z*) 1 Hawk. c. 72, s. 2.
(*a*) *R.* v. *Turner*, 13 East, 228. But see *R.* v. *Kerrick*, 5 Q. B. 49; Dav. & M. 208; 12 L. J. M. C. 135.
(*b*) See *Lewis* v. *Vaughan*, 4 Ti. Rep. 649; and *R.* v. *Pollman*, 2 Camp. 229 n.
(*c*) These other persons are usually "common informers." History from

28 Ed. I. downwards shows us that this phrase is frequently not easily distinguishable from "false witness."
(*d*) And see *cf.* 38 & 39 Vict. c. 86, s. 7.
(*e*) 3 Ed. I. c. 9.
(*f*) *R.* v. *Mawbey*, 6 T. R. 619.
(*g*) *R.* v. *Macdaniel*, 1 Leach, 45; Fost. 130; *R.* v. *Jolliffe*, 4 T. R. 265; *R.* v. *Thompson*, 16 Q. B. 832; 20 L. J. M. C. 183; and see *R.* v. *Taylor*, 15 Cox, C. C. 265.
(*h*) See *R.* v. *Parnell*, 14 Cox, 508.
(*i*) *R.* v. *Best*, *ubi sup.*
(*j*) *R.* v. *Eccles*, *ubi sup.*; *R.* v. *Kimmersley*, Stra. 193.

in the indictment, nor the particular charge be specified, nor need it be laid that the party charged was acquitted (*k*).

A defence attempting to justify one of the overt acts is bad (*l*).

It is not necessary to prove any direct or immediate injury, or even to shew any specific overt act (*m*). The fact of conspiring need not be proved, but may be collected from other circumstances (*n*).

Individuals doing individual acts, but with a combined end previously determined on, is evidence of a conspiracy (*o*).

Extortion.

Extortion. This offence, which is punishable by fine and imprisonment, consists in the taking of money by any officer by colour of his office, either where none is due at all, or not so much as is due, or where it is not yet due (*p*).

A threat to accuse a man of a crime with intent to extort money is a felony (*q*). The threat may be made personally or to a third person with intent that it should be communicated (*r*). It must be a threat to accuse or an accusation. If A. be in custody for an offence, and the defendant threaten to procure witnesses to prove the charge, it is not sufficient (*s*), but it need not be a threat to accuse before a judicial tribunal (*t*). And it is immaterial whether the prosecutor be innocent or guilty of the offence imputed (*u*), if the object be to extort money by means of the accusation (*v*).

With regard to the sheriff, he is not liable for the act of his officer in this case (*w*). The under-sheriff is, however, personally liable to this process if he refuse to execute until he has received his fees (*x*).

It is extortion to arrest a man in order to obtain a release for him (*y*), or to obtain money from a prisoner by any colourable means (*z*); and so also was it held to be where a collector of duty obtained a sum of money from a person on the allegation, contrary to the fact, that it was due. And in the same case it was held that the mere fact of the officer having paid the money over to his principal made it none the less extortion (*a*).

Where an officer of the local authority under the Public

(*k*) R. v. *Spragg*, 2 Burr. 993.
(*l*) *Gregory* v. *Brunswick*, 6 M. & G. 205.
(*m*) R. v. *Robinson*, 1 Leach, 37.
(*n*) R. v. *Parsons*, Black. 392.
(*o*) R. v. *Cope*, Strn. 144. The employment by the police of decoys, or of marked money, where the cause of suspicion is not reasonable, would amount to a conspiracy.
(*p*) 1 Hawk. P. C. 418, s. 1.
(*q*) 24 & 25 Vict. c. 96, s. 1.

(*r*) R. v. *Peddle*, R. & R. 484.
(*s*) R. v. *Gill*, 1 Arch. P. A. 302.
(*t*) R. v. *Robinson*, 2 M. & Rob. 14.
(*u*) R. v. *Gardner*, 1 C. & P. 479.
(*v*) R. v. *Richards*, 11 Cox, 43.
(*w*) Per Ashurst, J.: *Woodgate* v. *Knatchbull*, 2 D. & East, 154; and see *Bagge* v. *Whitehead*, ante, p. 167.
(*x*) *Hescott*, 1 Salk. 330.
(*y*) *Williams* v. *Lyons*, 8 Mod. 189.
(*z*) R. v. *Colvin*, ib. 226.
(*a*) R. v. *Higgins*, 4 C. & P. 247.

Health Act was paid extra for work not included in his original agreement, it was held he was not liable for penalties as for extortion (*b*). But the remedy is available as against tax collectors and overseers (*c*).

On an indictment it is not necessary to prove that the defendant took the exact sum laid. It is for the jury to say whether the excesses were really taken as a fair charge or not (*d*).

There can be no accessories in this offence (*e*).

False Imprisonment.

False imprisonment is a misdemeanour at common law.

Every restraint of the liberty of a free man is an imprisonment (*f*), though it be in the high street or elsewhere, and he be not put into any prison or house (*g*); but merely preventing a man from proceeding along a particular way is not (*h*), nor if the person escape before actual arrest (*i*).

The officer need not to complete the arrest actually touch the person. If he lock the door of the room in which he is, it is sufficient (*j*).

Where a warrant has been shewn to a party who goes at the desire of the officer without compulsion, it is an imprisonment (*k*).

Where a prisoner in custody for a civil offence escapes, if the escape be negligent, the officer may retake him at any time without warrant (*l*); if voluntary, or the offender be a criminal prisoner, he cannot afterwards be retaken without a new warrant, unless the offence be one for which he might have been arrested originally without warrant (*m*), or it be on fresh pursuit (*n*).

If a prosecutor fail in proving an imprisonment, he may still prove an assault and battery (*o*).

Inciting to Commit an Offence.

This is indictable at common law.

The offence of soliciting and inciting a man to commit a felony, is, where no such felony is actually committed, a misdemeanour only. Where the felony is committed, it is a felony (*p*).

(*b*) *Edwards* v. *Salmon*, 23 Q. B. D. 531; 58 L. J. Q. B. 571; 38 W. R. 166.
(*c*) See *ante*, pp. 121, 180.
(*d*) *R.* v. *Gilham*, 6 T. R. 265.
(*e*) *R.* v. *Loggen*, 1 Str. 73.
(*f*) 2 Inst. 482.
(*g*) Fitz. Bar. 501. As to the practices of "shadowing" and watching premises, see *ante*, p. 182, n.n.
(*h*) *Bird* v. *Jones*, 7 Q. B. 742.
(*i*) *Russen* v. *Lucas*, Ry. & M. 26; 1 C. & P. 153.

(*j*) *Williams* v. *Jones*, Ca. temp. Hard. 301.
(*k*) *Chinn* v. *Morris*, 2 C. & P. 361; *Pocock* v. *Moore*, Ry. & M. 321.
(*l*) Dalt. 169.
(*m*) 2 Hawk. c. 14, s. 9.
(*n*) 10 St. Tr. 462.
(*o*) See *ante*, p. 203.
(*p*) *R.* v. *Gregory*, L. R. 1 C. C. R. 77; 36 L. J. M. C. 60; 16 L. T. 388; 10 Cox, C. C. 459; 24 & 25 Vict. c. 94, s. 2.

To solicit a servant to steal his master's goods is a misdemeanour, though it be not charged in the indictment that the servant stole the goods, nor that any other act was done than the soliciting and inciting. Such offence is indictable at the sessions, having a tendency to a breach of the peace (*q*); and it is no defence that the servant purposely submitted himself to the incitement with intent to betray the inciter (*r*).

An attempt to suborn a man to commit perjury is a misdemeanour (*s*), and so is the mere attempt to solicit a person to attempt to commit an offence (*t*), or to pervert the course of justice by withholding evidence.

Where a defendant is indicted for a misdemeanour committed by the soliciting another to do an act which if done would amount to a felony and render the defendant also guilty of felony, it is unnecessary to negative the doing of the act, for it cannot be intended that a felony has been committed where none is charged (*u*).

Where a person uses words or behaviour of or in the presence of another which are calculated to provoke a breach of the peace, he may be summoned before a justice and bound over to keep the peace for a certain time (*v*).

But this has been held not to apply to the case of a man going about using insulting words to another (*w*). There must apparently be fear of corporal injury (*x*).

Where officers incite persons to commit crimes it is of course a conspiracy (*y*). The incitement which is here chiefly alluded to is that which exists in some other countries of provoking persons to offend against the law that the powers of the law may with some colour be employed against them.

The attempt to force a government reporter into a public meeting would appear to savour of this offence.

Perjury.

Perjury.

Perjury consists in the wilful taking a false oath before a Court or person having competent jurisdiction to administer it

---

(*q*) *R.* v. *Higgins*, 2 East, 5. The practice of "shadowing" must have a similar tendency, and would therefore appear to fall into this category; as also would that of employing powers not *bonâ fide* but simply *in terrorem*, on account of some motive other than the extortion of money.

(*r*) *R.* v. *Quail*, 4 F. & F. 1076.

(*s*) Referred to in *R.* v. *Scofield*, Cald. 397.

(*t*) *R.* v. *Ransford*, 13 C. C. C. 9.

(*u*) 1 Stark. Cr. Pl. 148.

(*v*) Steph. Comm., 8th ed. 288,
vol. iv.

(*w*) *Phillips* v. *JJ. of Gateshead*, L. T. (N.) 19, 7, 79. In the Met. Pol. Dist. such conduct is subject to a fine, and in default imprisonment: 2 & 3 Vict. c. 47, s. 54.

(*x*) 1 Hawk. c. 60, ss. 6, 7; Dalt. c. 116.

(*y*) See *ante*, p. 205. Disturbances and even riots have, it is said, been at times fomented by the police. This would constitute misdemeanour or felony on the part of the officers, as the case might be.

in reference to a matter then pending in a judicial proceeding, and on a point material to the issue (z).

This and the taking a false oath in a matter not of a judicial nature or where not material are both common law misdemeanours (a).

A false affirmation is punishable in like manner (b).

The necessary points to establish are:—
1. The false oath must be taken deliberately and intentionally (c).
2. It must be either false in fact, or if true the defendant must have known it to be so (d), or if false and he swears that he *believes* it to be true (e).
3. The oath must have been taken before a Court or officer having competent jurisdiction to administer it (f).
4. It must be made in reference to a material part of the matter then under consideration (g).

Two or more cannot be jointly indicted for this offence (h).

Some one or more of the assignments must be proved by two witnesses, or by one witness, corroborated by proof of other material and relevant facts (i).

Fabrication of evidence when it consists of the procurement of false witnesses is subornation of perjury, and if the party tampered with does not actually take an oath, the person inciting him to do so is still liable to punishment (j). Fabrication in cases other than witnesses is a misdemeanour at common law (k). Swearing up to a point (which does not exist) in a charge, essential to its establishment, would appear to savour both of fabrication and perjury.

Subornation of perjury is punishable as perjury (l).

Trespass to Realty.

Trespass to realty is an offence under the criminal law only in the case of forcible entry.

There is no doubt an indictment will lie at common law for a forcible entry, although it is generally brought on the Act of Parliament (m). In this case there must be proof of such a force as constitutes a public breach of the peace (n).

An entry by breaking the doors or windows whether any

(z) See 2 Geo. 2, c. 25, s. 2.
(a) R. v. *Chapman*, 1 Den. 432; 2 C. & K. 846.
(b) 3 & 4 Will. 4, cc. 49, 82.
(c) 1 Hawk. c. 69, s. 2.
(d) Ibid. s. 6.
(e) R. v. *Pedley*, 1 Leach, 327.
(f) 3 Inst. 166; 1 Hawk. c. 69, ss. 3, 4; and see R. v. *Aylett*, 1 T. R. 69, and R. v. *Hughes*, 4 Q. B. D. 614.
(g) R. v. *Griepe*, 1 Ld. Ray. 256; R. v. *Nichol*, 1 B. & Ald. 21.
(h) R. v. *Phillips*, 2 Str. 921.

(i) R. v. *Boulter*, 2 Den. 396; 21 L. J. M. C. 57; 3 C. & K. 236; R. v. *Shaw*, L. & C. 579; 34 L. J. M. C. 169.
(j) Hawk. P. C. I. c. 69, s. 2.
(k) R. v. *Vreones*, 1891, 1 Q. B. 360; 39 W. R. 364; 60 L. J. 62. See Crim. Code Com. Report, p. 21.
(l) Arch., 19th ed., p. 857.
(m) Per Wilmot, J.: R. v. *Bake*, 3 Burr. 1731; 5 Ric. 2, c. 8.
(n) R. v. *Wilson*, 8 T. R. 357.

person be in the house or not, especially if it be a dwelling-house, or where personal violence is done to the prosecutor or any of his family or servants or caretakers, or when it is accompanied with such threats of personal violence that it is calculated to prevent the prosecutor from defending his possession, has been held within the statute (o).

A mere trespass is not sufficient. There must be some shew of force calculated to prevent resistance (p).

Where the party has no right of entry, all persons in his company, as well those who do not use violence as those who do are equally guilty; but if he have a right of entry, then only those who use or threaten violence or actually abet those who do, are guilty (q). And where the defendants broke and entered the plaintiff's house to prevent him from murdering his wife, they were held justified (r).

(o) 1 Hawk. c. 64, ss. 20, 21, 26, 27.
(p) R. v. *Smyth*, 5 C. & P. 201.
(q) 3 Bac. Abr. Forc. Ent. (B).
(r) *Handcock* v. *Baker*, 2 B. & P. 260.

APPENDIX.

I.—WARRANTS AND ORDERS OF SUPERIOR COURTS AT COMMON LAW.

No. 1.

"Ordered by the Lords spiritual and temporal in Parliament assembled that the Sergeant-at-Arms attending this House shall forthwith attach the person of   and bring him in safe custody to the Bar of this House [to-morrow at 10 of the clock in the forenoon] and this shall be a sufficient Warrant on that behalf."

HENRY GRAHAM,
Cler. Parl.

To the Sergeant-at-Arms attending this House, his Deputy and Deputies, and to all Mayors, Justices and other Her Majesty's Officers, to be aiding and assisting in the execution thereof.

No. 1A.

Whereas by the judgment [or order] dated, &c., it was ordered [recite direction required to be performed]. Now upon motion, &c., by counsel, &c. who alleged that [   ] and upon reading the said judgment [or, order] &c. This Court doth order that the Sergeant-at-Arms attending this Court do [insert order]; [and thereupon such further order shall be made as shall be just].

No 2.

Whereas the House of Commons have this day resolved that   having been guilty of a contempt and breach of privilege of this House be committed to the custody of the Sergeant-at-Arms attending this House; these are, therefore, to require you to take into your custody the body of the said   and him safely to keep during the pleasure of the House; for which this shall be your sufficient warrant.

Signed
SPEAKER.

To the Sergeant-at-Arms attending this House and his Assistants and to all Mayors, Sheriffs, Bailiffs, Justices and other Her Majesty's officers.

No. 3.
ASSISTANCE.

Victoria, &c.

Whereas according to the tenour and true meaning of an order made in a certain action depending in our High Court of Justice between   and   the said C. D., was ordered and enjoined   yet, nevertheless, he the said C. D. and other ill-disposed persons his accomplices have refused to pay obedience thereto and detain and keep the possession of the said   in manifest contempt of us and our said Court, and whereas by an order made in the said action bearing date   , it was ordered that a writ of assistance should issue directed to the Sheriff of the County of   to put the said A. B. into possession of the premises in question pursuant to the said hereinbefore recited order and : Know ye, therefore, that we being willing and desirous that justice should be done to the said A. B. in this behalf, do give unto you full power and authority to place and put the said A. B. or his assigns without delay into the full, peaceable and quiet possession of all and singular the said   according to the intent and true meaning of the said orders of our said Court, and, therefore, we do hereby command and enjoin you that immediately after your receipt of this writ you do go and repair to   and take possession of the said   and that you do place and put the said A. B. and his assigns into the full, peaceable and quiet possession thereof according to the true intent and meaning of the said orders, and herein you are not in any wise to fail.

Witness, &c.

No. 4.
ATTACHMENT.

Victoria, &c., to the Sheriff of   greeting.

We command you to attach A. B. so as to have him before us in the   Division of our High Court of Justice, wheresoever the said Court shall then be, there to answer to us, as well touching a contempt which he it is alleged hath committed against us, as also such other matters as shall be then and there laid to his charge, and further to perform and abide such order as our said Court shall make in this behalf, and hereof fail not and bring this writ with you.

Witness, &c.

No. 5.
BENCH WARRANT.

England, to wit:

Whereas it is certified to me by the Clerk of the Peace for the County of   that at the general sessions of the Peace of our lady the Queen holden in and for the County of   on the   , 189 , J. B. late of   , was and now stands indicted for making an assault upon W. T., gent, and unlawfully violently and injuriously seizing and taking from the said W. T. against his consent, a receipt bearing date the   last purporting to be the receipt of one E. W., &c., to which indictment the said J. B. hath not as yet appeared or pleaded, these are therefore to will, require and in Her Majesty's name, strictly to charge and command you and every of you upon sight hereof to apprehend and take the body of the said J. B. and bring him before me or one of the other judges of Her Majesty's High Court of Justice being taken in or near the cities of London or Westminster, if elsewhere before some Justice of the Peace near to the place where he shall be found to the end that the said J. B., may become bound with sufficient sureties for his personal appearance at the next general quarter sessions of the Peace of our lady the Queen to be

holden in and for the County of   to answer the said indictment and be
further dealt with according to law.   Hereof fail not at your peril.
                                        Given under my hand and seal,
To
Sheriff of
and to all Chief and Petty Constables,
    headboroughs and all others whom
    it may concern.

No. 6.

CONTUMACE CAPIENDO.

Victoria, &c.   greeting.
Whereas A. B. has signified to us, &c., that C. D. of   in your County of
        is manifestly contumacious and contemns the jurisdiction and authority
of the law and jurisdiction ecclesiastical of   nor will C. D. submit to the
ecclesiastical jurisdiction, but forasmuch as the royal power ought not to be
wanting to enforce such jurisdiction. We command you that you attach the
said C. D. by his body until he shall have made satisfaction for the said
contempt, and how you shall execute this our precept, notify unto us on the
        at our Royal Courts of Justice in London, and in no wise omit this and
have you then there this writ.
                                        Witness, &c.

Indorsement.

This writ is allowed and delivered of record before our lady the Queen in
the Queen's Bench Division of the High Courts of Justice at the Royal Courts
of Justice, London, the   day of   according to the form of the
statute in such case made and provided.

No. 7.

EXTENT.

Victoria, &c.
Whereas, A. B. and C. D. of   , by their writing obligatory sealed with
their seals bearing date   became bound jointly and severally to us in
the sum of £   of good and lawful money of Great Britain, payable at a
day now past, which said sum of money they have not, nor have either of
them yet paid or caused to be paid to us, as we are informed, and we being
willing to be satisfied, the same with all the speed we can, as is just, do
command you that you omit not by reason of any liberty in your bailiwick,
but enter the same and take the said A. B. and C. D. by their bodies wherever
they shall be found in your bailiwick, and keep them safely and securely in
prison till we shall be fully satisfied the said debt, and that as well by the
oaths and testimony of any other good and lawful men by whom the truth
may be better known, as by all other lawful means you diligently inquire
what lands and tenements, and of what yearly values the said A. B. and C. D.,
or either of them, had in your bailiwick on the said   , on which day
they first became our debtors as aforesaid, or, at any time since, and what
goods and chattels, and of what sorts and prices, and what debts, credits,
specialties, and sums of money the said A. B. and C. D., or, either of them,
or what pers n or persons to their or either of their use, or in trust for them
or either of them now hath or have in your bailiwick, and that all and singular
such goods and chattels, lands and tenements, debts, credits, specialties, and
sums of money in whose hands soever the same now are, you diligently
appraise and extend on the oaths of the said good and lawful men, and do
take and seize the same into your hands there to remain until we shall be
fully satisfied the said debt according to the form of the statute made for

such recovery of such our debts; and lest this, our command, should not be fully executed, we further command and empower you by these presents to summon before you such persons as you shall think proper, and carefully examine them in the premises, and that you distinctly and openly make appear to the justices of the   Division of our High Court of Justice, on the   day of   , in what manner you shall have executed this our command, and that you then have there this writ provided, that what goods and chattels you shall seize into your hands by virtue hereof, you do not sell or cause to be sold until we shall otherwise command you.

Witness, &c.

No. 8.

NE EXEAT REGNO.

Victoria, &c.

Whereas, it is represented to us in our High Court of Justice on the part of A. B. plaintiff, against C. D. defendant, amongst other things, that the said defendant is   and designs quickly to go into parts beyond the seas, as by oath made in that behalf appears which tends to the great prejudice and damage of the said plaintiff; therefore, in order to prevent this injustice, we do hereby command you that you do without delay cause the said C. D. personally to come before you, and give sufficient bail or security in the sum of £   , that he the said C. D. will not go or attempt to go into parts beyond the seas, without leave of our said Court; and, in case the said C. D. shall refuse to give such bail or security, then you are to commit him the said C. D. to our next prison, there to be kept in safe custody until he shall do it of his own accord, and when you shall have taken such security, you are forthwith to make and return a certificate thereof to our said Court, distinctly and plainly under your seal, together with this writ.

Witness, &c.

No. 9.

NOCUMENTO AMOVENDO.

Victoria, &c.

Whereas, on the   day of   , at   , which said indictment we afterwards for certain reasons caused to be brought before us in the Queen's Bench Division of our High Court of Justice to be determined according to the law and custom of England, and whereas, thereupon at the Assizes holden at, and in and for the County of   , on the   day of   , before Justices   , upon the trial of an issue joined between us and the said   , he, the said   was in due manner convicted of the   contained in the said indictment, in manner and form as in and by the said indictment was alleged against him, as in the said Queen's Bench Division before us more fully appears upon record; whereupon, on the   day of   , it was adjudged and ordered by our said Court before us that the said   for the nuisances aforesaid charged upon him by the said indictment, whereof, he was so convicted as aforesaid, should pay a fine of £   , and that such nuisances should be abated as in our said Court before us also appears upon record; we therefore command you that the said   so erected and built upon the said highway at the parish of   , in the County of   , and so as aforesaid continued as in the said indictment mentioned, you do without delay remove or cause to be removed, and how you shall execute this, our writ, make known to us in our said Court immediately after the execution thereof, and have then there this writ.

Witness, &c.

No. 10.
Warrant of Committal.

Victoria, &c.
Whereas, by an order bearing date   and made   in a certain action, wherein A. is plaintiff, and B. defendant, it was ordered that   these are therefore in pursuance of the said order to will and require you forthwith upon receipt thereof, to make diligent search and inquiry after the body of the said   , and wheresoever you shall find him to arrest and apprehend him, and bring him to the bar in this Court to answer his contempt in the said order mentioned, willing, and requiring all and singular mayors, sheriffs, justices, bailiffs, constables, gaolers, headboroughs, and all other Her Majesty's officers and loving subjects to be aiding in the execution of the premises as they tender Her Majesty's service, and will answer to the contrary at their peril, and this shall be your warrant.
To
         Tipstaff,
of this Court.
The order absolute for committal is, after reciting the circumstances that this Court doth order that   do stand committed to   prison for his said contempt.

No. 11.
Order of Lords to Gaoler.

"Ordered by the Lords spiritual and temporal in Parliament assembled, that the Constable of Her Majesty's Tower of London, his deputy, or deputies, shall receive the body of   [member of this House], and keep him in safe custody within the said Tower during the pleasure of this House for his contempt committed against this House; and this shall be a sufficient warrant on that behalf."

         H. Graham,
           Cler., Parl.

To the Constable, &c.

No. 12.
Warrant of Speaker to Gaoler.

Whereas, the House of Commons have this day resolved that   having been guilty of a contempt and breach of privilege of this House, be committed to the custody of the Sergeant-at-Arms attending this House. These are therefore to require you to receive into custody the body of the said   and him safely to keep during the pleasure of this House.
To the Constable, &c.,
         Speaker.

No. 12A.

The defendant   being this day, brought to the bar of this Court, by the Sergeant-at-Arms attending this Court, to answer his contempt in not [stating default], and still persisting in his said contempt. It is upon motion, &c., ordered, that the said   be turned over to   prison, and do remain there until he shall [state what required] clear his contempt, and this Court make other order to the contrary.

No. 13.
PARDON.

Victoria, &c.
Whereas, A. B. was at the Sessions of the Peace [or Assizes] holden at   , in and for the County of   , on the   day of   , convicted of   , and was sentenced to be imprisoned and kept to hard labour for the period of   [or, convicted of murder and sentenced to death].

We, in consideration of some circumstances, humbly represented unto Us, are Graciously pleased to extend Our Grace and Mercy unto him, and to Grant unto him Our [Free] Pardon for the crime of which he so stands convicted [or, on condition that he be kept in penal servitude for the remainder of his natural life]. Our Will and Pleasure, therefore is, that you cause the said A. B. to be forthwith discharged out of custody [or give the necessary directions accordingly]. And, for so doing, this shall be your Warrant. Given at Our Court, at St. James, the   day of   , 189 , in the   year of Our Reign.

To Our Trusty and Well beloved Our Justices of the Peace, acting in and for the County of   , The Governor of our Prison at   , and all others whom it may concern. } By Her Majesty's Command.

Secretary of State.

NOTE.—Where the original sentence is of penal servitude, &c., the same form is used with the necessary alterations and with various conditions.

No. 14.
REMISSION.

Victoria, &c.
Whereas, A. B. was at the Sessions of the Peace holden at   , in and for the County of   , on the   day of   , convicted of   , and was sentenced to be imprisoned and kept to hard labour for the period of   .

We, in consideration of some circumstances, humbly represented unto Us, are Graciously pleased to extend Our Grace and Mercy unto the said A. B., and to Remit unto him such part of his [or, *e.g.*, one month of his aforesaid sentence], said sentence as remains yet to be undergone and performed.

Our Will and Pleasure therefore is, that you cause the said A. B.   to be forthwith discharged out of Custody [or, that you do take due notice hereof]. And for so doing, this shall be your Warrant. Given at Our Court at St. James's, the   day of   , 189 , in the   year of Our Reign.

To Our Trusty and Well-beloved The Governor of our Prison of   , and all others whom it may concern. } By Her Majesty's Command.

Secretary of State.

No. 15.
HABEAS CORPUS AD SUBJICIENDUM.

Victoria, etc., to the Keeper, &c.
We command you that you have the body of C. D. detained in our prison under your custody as it is said under safe and secure conduct together with the date and cause of his being taken and detained by whatsoever name he may be called before (Lord Chief Justice) at his Chambers in   immediately after the receipt of this writ to do and receive all and singular those things which our said (Chief Justice) shall then and there consider of him in this behalf and have you then there this writ.

Witness, &c.

No. 16.
Writ of Delivery.

Victoria, &c., to the Sheriff of   greeting.
We command you that without delay you cause the following chattels, that is to say [here enumerate the chattels recovered by the judgment or order for the return of which execution has been ordered to issue] to be returned to A. B., which the said A. B. lately in our High Court of Justice recovered against C. D. [or, C. D. was ordered to deliver to the said A. B.] in an action in the   division of our said Court.* And we further command you that if the said chattels cannot be found in your bailiwick, you distrain the said C. D. by all his lands and chattels in your bailiwick, so that neither the said C. D. nor any one for him do lay hands on the same until the said C. D. render to the said A. B. the said chattels. And in what manner, &c. And have you there then this writ.

Witness, &c.

The like, but instead of a distress until the chattel is returned, commanding the sheriff to levy on defendant's goods the assessed value of it.
[Proceed as in the preceding form until the * and then thus:—]
And we further command you, that if the said chattels cannot be found in your bailiwick, of the goods and chattels of the said C. D. in your bailiwick you cause to be made £   [the assessed value of the chattels] † And in what manner, etc. And have you there then this writ.

Witness, &c.

[If on either of the preceding forms it is wished to include damages, costs, and interest, proceed to the † and continue thus:—]
And we further command you that of the goods and chattels of the said C. D. in your bailiwick, you cause to be made the sum of £   (damages), and also interest thereon at the rate of £4 per centum per annum, from the   day of   which said sum of money and interest were in the said action by the judgment therein [or, by order] dated the   day of   adjudged (or, ordered) to be paid by the said C. D. to A. B. together with certain costs in the said judgment (or, order) mentioned, and which costs have been taxed and allowed by one of the taxing officers of our said Court at the sum of £   as appears by the certificate of the said taxing officer, dated the   day of   , and that of the goods and chattels of the said C. D. in your bailiwick you further cause to be made the said sum of £   (costs), together with interest thereon at the rate of £4 per centum per annum from the   day of   , and that you have that money and interest before us in our said Court immediately after the execution hereof to be paid to the said A. B. in pursuance of the said judgment (or order). And in what manner, &c. And have you there this writ.

Witness, &c.

No. 17.
Elegit.

Victoria, &c., to the Sheriff of   greeting.
Whereas lately in our High Court of Justice in a certain action (or, certain actions as the case may be) there depending, wherein A. B. is plaintiff and C. D. defendant (or, in a certain matter there depending, intituled "In the matter of E. F.", as the case may be) by a judgment [or, order as the case may be] of our said Court made in the said action [or, matter as the case may be] and bearing date the   day of   it was adjudged [or, ordered, as the case may be] that C. D. should pay unto A. B. the sum of £   together with interest thereon after the rate of £   per centum per annum from the   day of   , together also with certain costs as in the said

judgment [or, order, as the case may be] mentioned, and which costs have been taxed and allowed by   one of the taxing officers of our said Court, at the sum of £   as appears by the certificate of the said taxing officer, dated the   day of   . And afterwards the said A. B. came unto our said Court, and according to the statute in such case made and provided, chose to be delivered to him all such lands, tenements, rectories, tithes, rents, and hereditaments, including lands and hereditaments of copyhold or customary tenure, in your bailiwick as the said C. D. or any one in trust for him, was seised or possessed of on the   day of   in the year of our Lord   * or at any time afterwards, or over which the said C. D. on the said   day of   or at any time afterwards, held any disposing power which he might without the assent of any other person exercise for his own benefit, to hold to him the said goods and chattels as his properties, goods, and chattels, and to hold the said lands, tenements, rectories, tithes, rents, and hereditaments respectively, according to the nature and tenure thereof, to him and to his assigns until the said two several sums of £   and £   together with interest upon the said sum of £   , at the rate of £   per centum per annum from the said   day of   and on the said sum of £   (costs) at the rate of £4 per centum per annum from the   day of   shall have been levied. Therefore we command you that without delay you cause to be delivered to the said A. B. all such lands and tenements, rectories, tithes, rents, and hereditaments, including lands and hereditaments of copyhold or customary tenure in your bailiwick as the said C. D or any person or persons in trust for him was or were seised or possessed of on the said   day of   † or at any time afterwards, or over which the said C. D. on the said   day of   † or at any time afterwards, had any disposing power which he might without the assent of any other person exercise for his own benefit to hold the said lands, tenements, rectories, tithes, rents, and hereditaments respectively, according to the nature and tenure thereof, to him and to his assigns until the said two several sums of £   and £   together with interest as aforesaid, shall have been levied. And in what manner you shall have exercised this our writ make appear to us in our Court aforesaid, immediately after the execution thereof, under your seals, and the seals of those by whose oath you shall make the said extent and appraisement. And have there then this writ.

Witnesses, &c.

* The day on which the judgment or order was made.
† The date of the certificate of taxation. The writ must be so moulded as to follow the substance of the judgment or order.

No. 18.

FIERI FACIAS.

Victoria, &c., to the Sheriff of   greeting.

We command you that of the goods and chattels of C. D. in your bailiwick you cause to be made the sum of £   and also interest thereon at the rate of £   per centum per annum from the   day of   *, which said sum of money and interest were lately before us in our High Court of Justice in a certain action [or, certain actions as the case may be] wherein A. B. is plaintiff and C. D. defendant [or, in a certain matter there depending, intituled "In the matter of E. F." as the case may be] by a judgment [or order as the case may be] of our said Court bearing date the   day of   adjudged [or, ordered as the case may be] to be paid by the said C. D. to A. B. together with certain costs in the said judgment [or, order as the case may be] mentioned, and which costs have been taxed and allowed by one of the taxing officers of our said Court at the sum of £   as appears by the certificate of the said taxing officer, dated the   day of   , and that of the goods and chattels of the said C. D. in your bailiwick you further cause to be made the said sum of £   (costs), together with interest

APPENDIX. 219

thereon at the rate of £4 per centum per annum from the   day of   *
and that you have that money and interest before us in our said Court
immediately after the execution hereof to be paid to the said A. B. in
pursuance of the said judgment [or, order as the case may be]. And in what
manner you shall have executed this our writ make appear to us in our said
Court immediately after the execution thereof. And have there then this
writ.

Witness, &c.

* Day of the Judgment or order, or day on which money directed to be paid, or day from which interest is directed by the order to run, as the case may be.

No. 19.
VENDITIONI EXPONAS.

Victoria, &c., to the Sheriff of   greeting.
Whereas by our writ we lately commanded you that of the goods and
chattels of C. D. [here recite the *fieri facias* to the end], and on the
day of   you returned to us in the   division of our High Court of
Justice aforesaid, that by virtue of the said writ to you directed you had
taken goods and chattels of the said C. D. to the value of the money and
interest aforesaid, which said goods and chattels remained in your hands
unsold for want of buyers. Therefore we, being desirous that the said A. B.
should be satisfied his money and interest aforesaid, command you that you
expose to sale and sell, or cause to be sold, the goods and chattels of the said
C. D. by you in form aforesaid taken, and every part thereof, for the best
price that can be gotten for the same, and have the money arising from such
sale before us in our said Court of justice immediately after the execution
hereof to be paid to the said A. B. And have then there this writ.

Witnesses, &c.

No. 20.
DISTRINGAS AGAINST AN EX-SHERIFF.

Victoria, &c., to the Sheriff of   greeting.
We command you that you distrain   , late sheriff of your county
aforesaid by all his land and chattels in your bailiwick, so that neither he
nor any one by him do lay hands on the same until you shall have another
command from us in that behalf, and that you answer to us for the issues of
the same, so that the said   expose for sale and sell or cause to be sold
for the best price that can be gotten for the same, those goods and chattels
which were of   in your bailiwick to the value of £   * the sum of
£   which lately before us in our High Court of Justice in a certain
action wherein   plaintiff and   defendant   by a †   of our
said court bearing date the   day of   was ‡   to be paid by the
said   to the said   and of the sum of £   the amount at which
the costs in the said †   mentioned have been taxed and allowed, and of
interest on the said sum of £   at the rate of £4 per centum per annum
from the   day of   and on the said sum of £   at the same rate
from the   day of   which goods and chattels he lately took by virtue
of our writ, and which remain in his hands for want of buyers, as the said
late sheriff hath lately returned to us in our said Court, and have the money
arising from such sale before us in our said Court immediately after the
execution hereof, to be paid to the said   . And have there then this
writ.

Witnesses, &c.

This writ was issued by, &c.
The defendant is a   and resides at   in your bailiwick.

* "The amount of" or "part of."
† "Judgment" or "order."
‡ "Adjudged" or "ordered."

No. 21.
POSSESSION.

Victoria, &c.

Whereas lately in our High Court of Justice, by a judgment of the Division of the same Court, A. B. recovered [or, E. F. was ordered to deliver to A. B.] possession of all that   with the appurtenances in your bailiwick. Therefore we command you that you do not by reason of any liberty of your County but that you enter the same, and without delay you cause the said A. B. to have possession of the said land and premises with the appurtenances. And in what manner, &c. And have you then there this writ.

Witness, &c.

No. 22.
SUPERSEDEAS.

Victoria, &c.

Whereas A. B. has [appeared in the Queen's Bench Division of our High Court of Justice to an indictment against him for certain misdemeanours]. We therefore command you that you wholly supersede the distraining or otherwise molesting any longer the said A. B. on account of the premises aforesaid, and if you have distrained the said A. B. that then you do without delay deliver or cause to be delivered to him that which you have so distrained, if he be thereby distrained for the reasons aforesaid and no other, and this you are not to omit.

Witness, &c.

No. 23.
ARREST—ADMIRALTY.

Victoria, &c.

To the Marshal, &c. [or to the Collector of Customs at the port of   ]. We hereby command you to arrest the ship or vessel   of the port of   (and the cargo and freight as the case may be) and to keep the same under safe arrest until you shall receive further orders from us.

Witness, &c.

No. 24.
RELEASE—ADMIRALTY.

Victoria, &c.

To the Marshal, &c., and to all and singular his substitutes, greeting. Whereas in an action of possession commenced in our said High Court on behalf of   against the   or vessel called the   , her tackle, apparel, and furniture [and against   intervening], the Judge has ordered possession of the said   or vessel to be delivered up to the said   or to his lawful attorney for his use. We therefore hereby command you to release the said vessel, her tackle, apparel, and furniture, from the arrest made by virtue of our warrant in that behalf, and to deliver possession thereof to the said   or to his lawful attorney for his use.

Witness, &c.   Seal.

Writ of possession
    Taken out by

No. 25.

COMMISSION OF APPRAISEMENT AND SALE.

Victoria, &c.

To the Marshal of the Probate, Divorce, and Admiralty Division of our said High Court, and to all and singular his substitutes, greeting : Whereas in an action of   commenced in our said high Court on behalf of against   [and against   intervening], the Judge has ordered the said   to be appraised and sold. We therefore hereby authorize and command you to reduce into writing an inventory of the said   , and having chosen one or more experienced person or persons, to swear him or them to appraise the same according to the true value thereof, and upon a certificate of such value having been reduced into writing to cause the said   to be sold by public auction for the highest price, not under the appraised value thereof, that can be obtained for the same. And we further command you, immediately upon the sale being completed, to pay the proceeds arising therefrom into the Registry of the said Division, and to file the certificate of appraisement signed by you and the appraiser or appraisers, and an account of the sale signed by you, together with this commission.

Witness, &c.

Commission of Appraisement and Sale.
Taken out by   .

Seal.

II.—WARRANTS AND ORDERS OF SUPERIOR COURTS NOT AT COMMON LAW: OF INFERIOR COURTS AND OFFICERS GENERALLY.

A. AFTER ADJUDICATION.

No. 1.
Writ to levy Fine.

Victoria, &c.
To the Sheriff, &c.
You are hereby required and commanded as you regard yourself and all yours, that you omit not by reason of any liberty in your County, but that you enter the same, and of all the goods and chattels, of all and singular the persons in the roll to this writ annexed, you cause to be levied all and singular the debts and sums of money upon them in the same roll severally charged, so that the money may be ready for payment at (time of return to writ) to be paid over in such manner as the Commissioners of Her Majesty's Treasury may direct; and if any of the several debts cannot be levied by reason of no goods or chattels being to be found belonging to the parties, then in all cases that you take the bodies of the parties refusing to pay the aforesaid debts and lodge them in the gaol of   , there to remain until they pay the same, or be discharged by the authority of the said Commissioners or otherwise in due course of law.
Dated.

Clerk of { Assize
Crown.

No. 2.
Bankruptcy—Warrant to Search.

Whereas by evidence duly taken upon oath it hath been made to appear to the Court that there is reason to suspect and believe that the property of the said debtor is concealed in the house   of one X. M. of   such house, &c.   not belonging to the said debtor.

These are therefore to require you to enter in the daytime into the house of the said X. M., situate as aforesaid, and there diligently to search for the said property, and if any property of the said debtor shall be there found by you on such search that you seize the same to be disposed of and dealt with according to the provisions of the Bankruptcy Act, 1883.
Dated.

Registrar.
To X. Y., Officer of this Court, and his Assistants [or, H. Bailiff, and others the bailiffs of this Court].

No. 3.

WARRANT TO SEIZE.

Whereas on the   a receiving order was made against the said debtor, these are therefore to require you forthwith to enter into and upon the house and houses and other the premises of the said debtor, and also on all other place or places belonging to the said debtor, wherein all his goods and money are or are reputed to be, and there to seize all the ready money, jewels, plate, household effects, goods, merchandize, books of accounts, and all other things whatsoever belonging to the said debtor, except his necessary wearing apparel, bedding, and tools, as excepted by the Bankruptcy Act, 1883. And that which you shall so seize you shall safely detain and keep in your possession until you shall receive other orders in writing for the disposal thereof from the trustee (or official receiver), and in case of resistance, or of not having the key or keys of any door or lock of any premises belonging to the said debtor wherein all his goods are or are supposed to be, you shall break open or cause the same to be broken open for the better execution of this warrant.

Dated, &c.

No. 4.

WARRANT AGAINST DEBTOR ABOUT TO QUIT ENGLAND.

To (the above officer), and to the Governor or Keeper of   prison.

Whereas by evidence taken on oath it hath been made to appear to the satisfaction of the Court that there is probable reason to suspect and believe that the said A. B. of   is about to go abroad (or quit his place of residence) with the view of avoiding service of a Bankruptcy petition (or appearing thereto, &c.).

These are therefore to require you, the said   and others, to take the said A. B., and to deliver him to the Governor or Keeper of the above-mentioned prison, and you the said Governor or Keeper to receive the said A. B. and him safely to keep in the said prison until such time as this Court may order.

Dated, &c.

No. 5.

WARRANT TO APPREHEND PERSON NOT APPEARING.

Whereas by summons or subpœna dated   and directed to the said A. B., of   he was required personally to be and appear on the at this Court to be examined, and such said summons or subpœna was afterwards on the   as hath been proved by oath duly served upon the said   and a reasonable sum was tendered to him for his expenses, and whereas the said   having no lawful impediment made known to or allowed by this Court, hath not appeared before me, as by the said summons or subpœna he was required, but therein has wholly made default, these are therefore to will and require, and authorise you, and either of you, to whom this warrant is directed, immediately upon receipt hereof, to take the said   and bring him before this Court on the   in order to his being examined as aforesaid, and for your so doing this shall be your sufficient warrant.

Dated, &c.

No. 6.

ORDER OF COMMITMENT.

The Debtors Act, 1869.

In the [title of Court ordering committal]
   Between A. B. Plaintiff, and
             C. D. Defendant.

To X. Y. The Officer of this Court and his Assistants (or, to the High Bailiff and others the Bailiffs of the said Court, and all Peace Officers within the jurisdiction of the said Court, to the Governor of the [prison used by the Court].

Whereas the plaintiff obtained a judgment (or order) against the defendant in the High Court of Justice [or, as the case may be] on the   day of   , for the sum of £   , and there is now due and payable upon the said judgment the sum of   , and whereas a summons was, at the instance of the plaintiff, duly issued out of this Court, by which the defendant was required to appear personally at this Court on the   day of   189 , to be examined on oath, touching the means he had then or had had since the date of the judgment (or order) to pay the said sum, which summons was proved to this Court to have been personally and duly served on the defendant.

And whereas, at the hearing of the said summons, it has now been proved to the satisfaction of the Court that the defendant now has [or, has had] since the date of the judgment (or order) the means to pay the sum in respect of which he made default as aforesaid, or an instalment or instalments thereof as ordered by the said judgment, and has refused (or neglected) (or then refused or neglected) to pay the same.

Now, therefore, it is ordered that the defendant shall be committed to prison for   days, unless he shall sooner pay the sums, in payment of which he has so made default, together with the prescribed costs hereinafter mentioned, or shall file such affidavit as is mentioned in Order xxv., Rule 30 of the County Court Rules, 1889.

These are, therefore, to require you the said High Bailiff, Bailiffs and others to take the defendant and to deliver him to the governor or keeper of the [prison used by the Court] and you the said governor or keeper to receive the defendant, and him safely keep in the said prison for   days from the arrest under this order, or until he shall be sooner discharged by due course of law.

Given under the seal of ·   this [insert date of order] day of   189.
   E. F.
           Registrar of the Court.

	£	s.	d.
Amount of payment or order remaining due . . .			
Costs of judgment, summons and poundage on this order.			
Amount upon the payment given, the prisoner is to be discharged			

This order remains in force one year from the date hereof, unless such time is altered under Order xxv., Rule 33.—Add when so ordered.—The time during which this order is to remain in force was on the   day of   extended by order of the Judge for   months.

           Registrar.

No. 7.

ORDER OF COMMITTAL FOR NEGLECT TO OBEY ORDER.

Whereas by an order of this Court, dated the   day of   , 189 , (here recite the order). Now upon the application of the plaintiff, and upon hearing the defendant [or, if the defendant does not appear, reading the affidavit of X. Y., or where service has been by bailiff, the indorsement of L. M., a bailiff of this Court, or the County Court of   holden at shewing, or being satisfied on oath, that a copy of the said order, and notice of this application have been severally served upon the defendant C. D.] and upon reading the affidavit of, &c. [enter evidence], the Court being of opinion, upon consideration of the facts disclosed by the said affidavit [or affidavits] that the defendant C. D. has been guilty of a contempt of this Court by neglecting to obey the said order, doth order that the said defendant C. D. do stand committed to [here insert prison used by the Court] for his said contempt.

It is further ordered that any application for his release from custody shall be made to the Judge.

No. 8.

WARRANT OF ATTACHMENT.

To the High Bailiff and others, the Bailiffs of the said Court and all Peace Officers within the jurisdiction of the said Court, and to the Governor of the [here insert prison used by the Court].

Whereas by an order bearing date the   day of   , it was ordered that the defendant C. D. should stand committed to prison for contempt of this Court.

These are, therefore, to require you forthwith to arrest and apprehend the defendant C. D., and him safely convey and deliver to the Governor of the [prison used by this Court], and you, the said Governor, to receive the defendant C. D. until the further order of this Court.

Dated this   day of   189 .

E. F.
Registrar of the Court.

No. 9.

WARRANT OF ATTACHMENT FOR INSULT OR MISBEHAVIOUR.

To the High Bailiff and others, the Bailiffs of the said Court, and all Peace Officers within the jurisdiction of the said Court, and to the Governor of the [prison used by the Court].

Whereas at a Court holden on this day, A. B. wilfully insulted His Honor, the Judge, during his sitting in Court [or, C. D., the Registrar, High Bailiff, Bailiffs, or Officer] (as the case may be) of the said Court during his attendance in Court, or wilfully interrupted the proceedings of the said Court, or wilfully misbehaved in the said Court.

These are, therefore, to require you, the said High Bailiff, Bailiff and others to take the said A. B., and to deliver him to the Governor of the above-named prison, and you the said Governor, to receive the said A. B., and him safely to keep in the said prison for   days from the arrest under this warrant, or until he shall be sooner discharged by due course of law.

Given under the seal of the Court this   day of   , 189 .

Judge of the Court.

No. 9A.

ORDER OF DISCHARGE FROM CUSTODY.

Upon application made this   day of   by   for the defendant who was committed to prison for contempt, by order of this Court dated the   day of   , 189 , and upon reading the affidavit of the defendant, filed the   day of   , 189 , shewing that he is desirous of clearing his contempt, and upon hearing   the plaintiff [or, if no one appears for

Q

plaintiff, then upon being satisfied that notice of this application has been duly served upon the plaintiff], it is ordered that the said defendant be discharged out of the custody of the Governor of [here insert name of prison] as to the said contempt, but not as to the costs of the said contempt.
    Dated this   day of   , 189 .

                                       E. F.
                                    Registrar of the Court.

No. 10.
CORONER.—WARRANT OF ARREST.

To all Constables, &c.
To Wit :
    Whereas by an inquisition taken before me, &c.   on view of the body of R. F. then and there lying dead one   late of the parish of, &c., stands charged with the wilful murder of the said R. F., these are, therefore, by virtue of my office in Her Majesty's name to charge and command you and every of you, that you or some or one of you, without delay, do apprehend and bring before me, or one of Her Majesty's Justices of the Peace, for said County, the body of the said   of whom you shall have notice that he may be dealt with according to law, and for your so doing this is your warrant.

                                      Given, etc.
                                          Coroner.

No. 11.
COMMITMENT.

To all Constables, &c., and to the Keeper, &c.
    [As last, to "every of you"] forthwith safely to convey the body of the said   to Her Majesty's gaol of   and safely to deliver the same to the keeper of the said gaol, and these are likewise by virtue of my said office in Her Majesty's name to will and require you the said keeper to receive the body of the said   into your custody, and him safely to keep in the said gaol until he shall be thence discharged by due course of law, and for your so doing this shall be your warrant.

                                       Given, &c.

No. 12.
AGAINST WITNESS IN CONTEMPT OF SUMMONS.

To all Constables, &c.
    Whereas I have received credible information that A. B., of the parish of   can give evidence on behalf of our Sovereign lady the Queen, touching the death of R. F., now lying dead in the said parish of   , and whereas the said A. B. (having been duly summoned to appear, and give evidence before me and my inquest, touching the premises, at the time and place in the said summons specified, of which oath hath been duly made before me) hath refused and neglected so to do, to the great hindrance and delay of Justice, these are, therefore, by virtue of my office in Her Majesty's name to charge and command you, or one of you, without delay, to apprehend and bring before me, &c.   now sitting at the parish aforesaid, by virtue of my said office, the body of the said A. B., that he may be dealt with according to law, and for your so doing this is your warrant.

                                       Given, &c.

No. 13.

COMMITMENT OF WITNESS FOR REFUSING TO GIVE EVIDENCE.

[That for refusing to sign information or enter into recognizances the same *mutatis mutandis*.]

Whereas, I heretofore issued my summons under my hand directed to A. B. requiring his personal appearance before me, &c., at the time and place therein mentioned, to give evidence and be examined on Her Majesty's behalf, touching the death of R. F., then and there lying dead, of the personal service of which summons, oath hath been duly made before me, and whereas the said A. B, having neglected and refused to appear pursuant to the contents of the said summons, I therefore afterwards issued my warrant under my hand and seal, in order that the said A. B. by virtue thereof, might be apprehended and brought before me, to answer the premises, and whereas the said A. B. in pursuance thereof, hath been apprehended and brought before me now duly sitting by virtue of my office, and hath been duly required to give evidence and be examined before me and my inquest on Her Majesty's behalf, touching the death of the said R. F.; yet the said A. B. notwithstanding, hath wilfully and absolutely refused, and still doth wilfully and absolutely refuse to give evidence and be examined, touching the premises, or to give sufficient reason for his refusal, in wilful and open violence and delay of justice, these are therefore, &c., the said constables, &c., forthwith to convey the body of the said A. B. to the gaol of   and safely to deliver the same to the keeper of the said prison there, and these are likewise, &c., to request you the said keeper to receive the body of the said A. B. into your custody, and him safely to keep in the prison, until he shall consent to give his evidence and be examined before me and my inquest on Her Majesty's behalf, touching the death of the said R. F., or until he shall be discharged from thence by due course of law, and for so doing this is your warrant.

Given, &c.

No. 14.

JUSTICES—ARREST FOR NOT APPEARING.

To the Constable of, &c.

Whereas, on the   last past, A. B. of   was charged before the undersigned, &c.   (and, whereas, I then issued my summons to the said A. B., commanding him, &c., to be and appear before me on, &c.,   or before such other Justice of the Peace for the same County as might then be there, to answer the said charge, and be further dealt with, according to law), and whereas the said A. B. hath neglected to be, or appear at the time and place appointed, in and by the said summons, although it hath now been proved to me upon oath that the said summons was duly served upon the said A. B., these are therefore, &c.; forthwith to apprehend the said A. B., and to bring him before me or some other Justice of the Peace, &c., to answer the said charge, and be further dealt with according to law.

Given, &c.

No. 15.

COMMITMENT.

To the Constable of, &c., and to the Keeper, &c.

Whereas, A. B. was this day charged before me, &c., on the oath of C. D. of   , and others, for that [offence]. These are therefore to command you, the said Constable of   , to take the said A. B. and him safely to convey to the   gaol at   aforesaid, and there to deliver him to the keeper thereof, together with this precept, and I do hereby command you the said keeper of the said   to receive the said A. B. into your custody in the said   , and there safely to keep him until he shall be thence delivered by due course of law.

Given, &c.

No. 16.
DISTRESS.

To the Constable, &c.

Whereas, A. B., late of   , was on this day duly convicted before the undersigned, &c.,   and it was thereby adjudged that the said A. B. should for such offence forfeit and pay   , and should also pay to the sa'd C D. the sum of   , for his costs in that behalf, and it was thereby ordered that, if the said several sums should not be paid (forthwith), the same should be levied by distress and sale of the goods and chattels of the said A. B., and it was thereby also adjudged that in default of sufficient distress, the said A. B. should be imprisoned in the   at   (and there kept to hard labour) for the space of   , unless the said several sums and all costs and charges of the said distress, and of the commitment and conveying of the said A. B. to the said   should be sooner paid   . And whereas the said A. B., being so convicted, as aforesaid, and being now required to pay the said sums of   , hath not paid the same, or any part thereof, but therein hath made default; these are therefore, &c., forthwith to make distress of the goods and chattels of the said A. B., and, if within the space of   days next after the making of such distress, the said sums, together with the reasonable charges of taking and keeping the distress shall not be paid, that then you do sell the said goods and chattels so by you distrained, and do pay the money arising by such sale into   clerk of the Justices, &c.,   , that he may pay and apply the same as by law is directed, and may render the overplus, if any, on demand to the said A. B.; and if no such distress can be found, then that you certify the same unto me to the end, that such further proceedings may be had thereon, as to the law doth appertain.

Given, &c.

No. 17.
TAXES. WARRANT TO BREAK OPEN.

To   , and   , Collectors of the duties hereinafter mentioned   , for the   of   in the district of   .

Whereas, in and by the   Assessments of the duties of Income Tax, and the duties on inhabited houses for the aforesaid   for the year ending   , of   , hath been duly charged to the said duties in the sum of   . And whereas it appears by the oath of   , Collector of the said duties taken before us, whose hands and seals are hereunto subscribed, and the said   , being two Collectors of the Income Tax and Inhabited House Duties acting, &c.   , that the said sum of   hath been duly demanded of the said   , and that he hath refused or neglected to pay the same, and that the same now remains due and unpaid. And whereas, it further appears by the oath aforesaid, that divers goods and chattels, liable by law to be distrained for the said duties, are lying, and being in a certain house situate   in the district   , now in the possession of   .

These are therefore to authorize and require you, the above-named collectors, and either of you, calling to your assistance a constable, or other peace officer within the   and for the   of the foresaid, and in the presence of the said constable, or other peace officer, to demand entrance into the said house of   , and, in case of resistance, or neglect, or refusal, to open the same, to break open in the daytime the said house, and enter the same, and to distrain therein the said goods and chattels, and the distress there found to keep by the space of five days at the costs and charges of

the said   , and if the whole of the said sum of   , together with the said costs and charges be not paid within the said five days, then the said distress having been first duly valued and appraised by two inhabitants of the said   , or other sufficient persons, be sold by you, and the overplus [if any] moneys arising by such sale after paying and deducting the said sum of   , and the costs and charges of taking, keeping, and selling the said distress be restored to the owner thereof.
Given, &c.
Commissioners for the said Duties.

No. 18.

TAXES. COMMITMENT.

To (as last)   and to the Keeper, &c.
[As last to   " unpaid "] and that no sufficient distress can or may be found, whereby the same may be levied, now therefore we, the said Commissioners, &c., hereby command you, the above-mentioned collectors of the said duties, or either of you, to apprehend the said   , and to take him to Her Majesty's prison at   and to deliver him to the keeper thereof, together with this warrant. And we do hereby command you, the said keeper, to receive him, the said   into your custody in the said prison, there to be kept without bail until payment shall be made, or security to our satisfaction be given for the payment of the said sum of   remaining due and unpaid as aforesaid, and also of the further sum of   which we, the said Commissioners do adjudge to be reasonable for the costs and expenses of apprehending the said   , and conveying him to prison.
Given, &c.
Commissioners of the said Duties.

No. 19.

WARRANT TO BRING UP PRISONER.

To [officer in whose custody the prisoner is]
Whereas, the plaintiff [or defendant] hath made application to me, by affidavit, for a warrant to bring up before this Court E. F., who, it is said, is detained as a prisoner in your custody, in order that the said E. F. may be examined as a witness on behalf of the said plaintiff (or defendant) in a certain action depending in this Court between the said A. B. plaintiff, and C. D. defendant: You are therefore hereby required to bring the said E. F. before this Court at (Court-house) on the   day of   , 189 , at o'clock in the   noon, then and there to be examined as a witness on behalf of the said plaintiff (or defendant); and, immediately after the said E. F. shall have given his testimony before this Court, that you safely conduct him the said E. F. to the prison from which he shall have been brought under this warrant.

No. 19A.

SECRETARY OF STATE—WARRANT TO BRING UP PRISONER TO GIVE EVIDENCE.

The Right Honourable   One of Her Majesty's Most Honourable Privy Council, and Principal Secretary of State, &c., &c., &c.
Whereas, by an Act passed in the sixteenth year of Her Majesty's reign, intituled "An Act for the better prevention and punishment of Aggravated Assaults upon Women and Children, and for preventing delay and expense in the Administration of certain parts of the Criminal Law." It is amongst other things enacted that "It shall be lawful for one of Her Majesty's Principal Secretaries of State, or any Judge of the Court of Queen's Bench,

or Common Pleas, or any Baron of Exchequer, in any case where he may see fit to do so, upon application by affidavit, to issue a warrant or order under his hand for bringing up any prisoner or person confined in any gaol, prison, or place, under any sentence, or under commitment for trial, or otherwise (except under process in any civil action, suit, or proceeding), before any court, judge, justice, or other judicature, to be examined as a witness in any cause or matter, civil or criminal, depending, or to be enquired of, or determined in or before such Court, judge, justice, or other judicature, and the person required by any such warrant or order to be so brought before such Court, judge, justice, or other judicature, shall be so brought under the same care and custody, and be dealt with in like manner in all respects as a prisoner required by any writ of *habeas corpus* awarded by any of Her Majesty's Superior Courts of Law at Westminster, to be brought before such Court to be examined as a witness in any cause or matter depending before such Court, is now by law required to be dealt with."

And whereas application has been made to me by affidavit for bringing up A. B. who was convicted at the   on the   day of   , of   and sentenced to   imprisonment   before the Court of Quarter Sessions to be holden at   , in and for the County of   , at the hour of   o'clock in the forenoon, on the   day of   , and on such subsequent days as the said Court may direct to be examined as a witness in a criminal matter then and there to be enquired into. I do hereby in pursuance of the power vested in me by the before-mentioned Act, authorize and require you to cause the said A. B. to be brought before the said Court at the place and time, and for the purposes aforesaid. And for so doing this shall be your warrant.

Given at Whitehall, the   day of   , 189 , in the year of H.M. Reign.

To the Governor of Her Majesty's Prison at   , and all others whom it may concern.

No. 20.

WARRANT TO REMOVE TO ASYLUM—CRIMINAL LUNATICS ACT, 1884.

47 & 48 Vict. c. 64, s. 2.

(*a*.) Registered No. of Prisoner _____
(*b*.) Name _____
(*c*.) Offence of which convicted _____
(*d*.) Date of conviction _____
(*e*.) Court _____
(*f*.) Sentence _____
(*g*.) Date when certified to be insane _____
(*h*) Prison in which confined at date of this warrant _____

WARRANT OF REMOVAL FROM PRISON TO ASYLUM.

Whereas, the prisoner above described, now in the above-named prison, has been duly certified to be insane; this warrant is to authorize and require you, the Governor of the said prison, to cause the said prisoner to be removed from the said Prison to   Lunatic Asylum; and you the Superintendent of the said Lunatic Asylum, to receive and there to detain the said prisoner as a criminal lunatic until further order, or, until the expiration of the sentence of penal servitude or imprisonment.

To the Governor of Her Majesty's Prison at   and
      To the Superintendent of
          Lunatic Asylum.

Under Secretary of State, Whitehall,
          day of   189 .

No. 20A.

CRIMINAL LUNATIC ASYLUMS ACT, 1860.

23 & 24 Vict. c. 75, s. 2.

WARRANT OF REMOVAL OF A CRIMINAL LUNATIC ORDERED TO BE DETAINED DURING HER MAJESTY'S PLEASURE, FROM PRISON TO BROADMOOR.

I hereby authorize and require you, the Governor of the above-named prison, to cause the criminal lunatic above described to be removed from the said prison to Broadmoor Lunatic Asylum, and to transmit with the same a certificate in the form annexed, duly filled up and authenticated; and you, the Superintendent of Broadmoor Lunatic Asylum, to receive and there to detain the said criminal lunatic until further order.

To the Governor of Her Majesty's Prison at
and
To the Superintendent of Broadmoor Lunatic
    Asylum.

                                  One of Her Majesty's Principal
                                  Secretaries of State, Whitehall,
                                      day of   189 .

20B.

39 & 40 Geo. iii. c. 94; 46 & 47 Vict. c. 38.

[Description as above.]

WARRANT OF REMOVAL OF A CRIMINAL LUNATIC ORDERED TO BE DETAINED DURING HER MAJESTY'S PLEASURE FROM PRISON TO ASYLUM.

Her Majesty having been pleased to direct the removal of the criminal lunatic above described from the above-named prison to   Lunatic Asylum, I hereby authorize and require you the Governor of the said prison, to cause the said criminal lunatic to be removed from the said prison to the said lunatic asylum, and to transmit with the same a certificate in the form annexed, filled up and authenticated: and you, the Superintendent of the said lunatic asylum, to receive and there to detain the said criminal lunatic until further order.

To the Governor of Her Majesty's Prison at
and
    To the Superintendent of
        Lunatic Asylum.

                                  One of Her Majesty's Principal
                                Secretaries of State, Whitehall.
                                    day of   189 .

No. 21.

JUSTICES. WARRANT TO REMOVE TO REFORMATORY SCHOOL.

[Usual form for detention.] And we further command you the said Keeper to send the said A. B. at the expiration of his term of imprisonment aforesaid, as, and in the manner directed by the Reformatory Schools Act, 1866, to the   Reformatory School at   , and, for so doing, this shall be your sufficient warrant.

                                       Given, &c.

No. 22.

COUNTY COURT. WARRANT OF ARREST AND DETENTION.

Admiralty Jurisdiction.

In the County Court of   , holden at   .

(Seal)

[Title of Action.]

Whereas, an action has been instituted in this Court on behalf of A. B., of   , against [state description and name of vessel or property] in the sum of [state sum in letters] pounds. These are therefore to require and order you to arrest the said   , and to keep the same under safe arrest until you shall receive further orders from this Court.

Given under the seal of the Court this   day of   , 189 .

To the High Bailiff of the said Court,
and others the Bailiffs thereof.

Registrar.

No. 22A.

ORDER OF RELEASE.

Admiralty Jurisdiction.

In the County Court of   , holden at   .

(Seal)

[Title of Action.]

You are hereby authorized and directed to release the   now under arrest of this Court by virtue of its warrant, upon the payment of all costs, charges, and expenses, attending the custody thereof.

Given under the seal of the Court, this   day of   . 189 .

By the Court,

Registrar.

To the High Bailiff of the said Court,
and others the Bailiffs thereof.

No. 23.

WARRANT OF DELIVERY.

Whereas, at a Court holden at   , on the   day of   , 189 , the plaintiff obtained a judgment against the defendant for the recovery of   , [here enumerate the goods and chattels which the Court has ordered to be recovered of the defendant], and thereupon it was ordered by the Court, that the defendant should return the said goods and chattels to the plaintiff on the said   day of   , 189 , and that in default a warrant of delivery should issue. And whereas the defendant did not on the said   day of   189 , return the said goods and chattels to the plaintiff. These are therefore to require and order you forthwith to seize the said goods and chattels so not returned as aforesaid, wheresoever they may be found within the district of this Court, and to deliver the same to the plaintiff. And if the same cannot be found by you within such district, you are required and ordered to distrain all the lands and chattels of the defendant, wheresoever they may be found within the district of this Court, and them hold until the defendant shall deliver the said goods to you, and to make return of what you have done under this warrant immediately upon the execution thereof.

Application was made to the Registrar for this warrant at   minutes past the hour of   , on the   noon of the   day of   189 .

No. 24.

WARRANT OF EXECUTION AGAINST THE GOODS OF DEFENDANT.

Whereas on the   day of   189 , the plaintiff obtained a judgment in this Court against the defendant for the sum of £   for debt (or damages) and costs; and it was thereupon ordered by the Court that the defendant should pay the same to the registrar on the   day of   (or by instalments of   for every   days). And whereas default has been made on payment according to the said order: These are therefore to require and order you forthwith to make and levy by distress and sale of the goods and chattels of the defendant, wheresoever they may be found, within the district of the Court (except the wearing apparel and bedding of him or his family, and the tools and implements of his trade, if any, to the value of five pounds), the sum stated at the foot of this warrant, being the amount due to the plaintiff under the said order, including the costs of this execution, and also to seize and take any money or bank notes (whether of the Bank of England or of any other bank), and any cheques, bills of exchange, promissory notes, bonds, specialties, or securities for money of the defendant which may there be found, or such part or so much thereof as may be sufficient to satisfy this execution, and the costs of making and executing the same, and to pay what you shall have so levied to the registrar of this Court, and make return of what you have done under this warrant immediately upon the execution thereof.

Given under the seal of the Court this   day of   189 .
By the Court.

Registrar.

To the High Bailiff of the said Court,
and others the Bailiffs thereof.

	£	s.	d.
Amount for which judgment was obtained			
Paid into Court.			
Remaining due			
Poundage for issuing this warrant			
Total amount to be levied			

NOTICE.—The goods and chattels are not to be sold until after the end of five days next following the day on which they were seized, unless they be of a perishable nature, or at the request of the said defendant.

Application was made to the Registrar for the warrant at   minutes past the hour of   in the   noon of the   day of   189 .

No. 24A.

WARRANT OF EXECUTION AGAINST THE VESSEL OR PROPERTY OF DEFENDANT.

Admiralty Jurisdiction.

In the County Court of   holden at   ,

(Seal)

[Title of Action.]

Whereas on the   day of   189 , the plaintiff obtained a judgment in this Court against the defendant for the sum of £   for   and costs; and it was thereupon ordered by the Court that the defendant should pay the same to the plaintiff on the   day of   .
And whereas default has been made in payment according to the said order. These are therefore to require and order you forthwith to make and levy by distress and sale of the goods and chattels, including the [state description and name of vessel] of the defendant, wheresoever they may be

found within the district of this Court (except the wearing apparel and bedding of him or his family, and the tools and implements of his trade, if any, to the value of five pounds) the sum stated at the foot of this warrant, being the amount due to the plaintiff under the said order, including the costs of this execution; and also to seize and take any money or bank notes (whether of the Bank of England or of any other bank), and any cheques, bills of exchange, promissory notes, bonds, specialties, or securities for money of the defendant which may there be found, or such part or so much thereof as may be sufficient to satisfy this execution, and the costs of making and executing the same, and to pay what you shall have so levied to the Registrar of this Court, and make return of what you have done under this warrant immediately upon the execution thereof.

Given under the seal of the Court this   day of   189 .
By the Court.
Registrar.

To the High Bailiff of the said Court,
and others the Bailiffs thereof.

	£	s.	d.
Amount for which judgment was obtained			
Costs			
Poundage for issuing this warrant			
Total amount to be levied			

No. 25.
WARRANT OF POSSESSION.

Whereas according to the tenor and true meaning of an order, bearing date the   day of   189 , made in this action, the said defendant C. D. was ordered to deliver up possession to A. B. in the said order named of all that, &c. [as in order]. And whereas a copy of such order was duly served upon the said C. D., yet nevertheless he the said C. D., and other ill disposed persons, his accomplices, have refused to pay obedience thereto, and detain and keep the possession of the said house [or tenement and premises]. These are, therefore, to authorize and require you to forthwith enter into and upon the said messuage [or tenement and premises], and that you do remove, eject, and expel the said C. D., his tenants, servants, and accomplices, each and every of them, out of and from the said messuage [or tenement and premises], and every part and parcel thereof, and that you do place and put the said A. B. and his assigns into the full, peaceable, and quiet possession thereof, and defend and keep him and his said assigns in such peaceable and quiet possession when and as often as any interruption may or shall from time to time be given or offered to them or any of them, according to the true intent and meaning of the said order; and herein you are not in any wise to fail.

Given under the seal of the Court this   day of   189 .
By the Court.
Registrar.

To the High Bailiff of the said Court,
and others the Bailiffs thereof.

[NOTE.—The above form is given as an example of a warrant of possession issued pursuant to an order in an action other than an action of ejectment.]

No. 25A.
WARRANT OF POSSESSION IN EJECTMENT FOR POSSESSION AND COSTS.

Whereas at a Court holden at   on the   day of   189 , it was adjudged that the plaintiffs were on the   day of   189 , and still are entitled to the possession of the property mentioned in the statement annexed to the summons in this action; that is to say [describe the property as set out in the statement]; and it was ordered that the defendants should give the plaintiffs possession of the said above-mentioned property forthwith [or, on the   day of   ], and it was adjudged that the plaintiffs should recover against the defendants the sum of £   for costs; and it was ordered that the defendants should pay the said sum to the Registrar of this Court forthwith [or, on the   day of   ].

And whereas the defendants have not obeyed the said order: These are, therefore, to authorize and require you to forthwith give possession of the said hereinbefore mentioned property to the plaintiff. And these are, therefore, further to require and order you forthwith to make and levy by distress and sale of the goods and chattels of the defendant, wheresoever they may be found within the district of this Court (excepting the wearing apparel and bedding of the defendant or his family, and the tools and implements of his trade, if any, to the value of five pounds), the said sum and the costs of this warrant and execution; and also to seize and take any money or bank notes (whether of the Bank of England or any other bank), and any cheques, bills of exchange, promissory notes, bonds, specialties, or securities for money, of the defendant, which may be there found, or such part or so much thereof as may be sufficient to satisfy this execution and the costs of making and executing the same, and to pay the amount so levied to the Registrar of this Court, and make return of what you have done under this warrant immediately upon the execution thereof.

To the High Bailiff of
   the said Court.

No. 26.

COMMITMENT—POOR RATES.

To the Overseers of the Poor of the Parish of   in the County of   and to the Constable of   , and to all other peace officers in the said County   , and to the Keeper of the House of Correction at   in the said County   to wit:

Whereas, on the   day of   last past, a complaint was made before   one of Her Majesty's Justices of Peace in and for the said County of   , by the churchwardens and overseers of the poor of the parish   of   , in the said County,   that   being a person duly rated to the relief of the poor of the said parish   in and by [or several] Rate   made on the   day of   , in the year of Our Lord, 189 , and on the   day of   , in the year, &c., 189   , and on the day of   , in the year, &c., 189   , in the   sum of [or, several sums of   and of   and of]   , hath not paid the same or any part thereof, but hath refused so to do; and afterwards, on the   day of   , in the year, &c., 189 , at   in the said County,   the parties aforesaid appeared before   and   two of Her Majesty's justices of the peace, in and for the said County [the said churchwardens and overseers by   one of the said overseers   appeared before   and   Two of Her Majesty's Justices of Peace in and for the said County; but the said   although duly called, did not appear by himself, his counsel, or attorney, and it was then satisfactorily proved to the said justices that the said   had been duly served with the summons in that behalf which required him to be and appear there at that day before such two or more justices of the peace as should then be there to answer the said complaint, and to be further dealt with according to law], and then having heard the matter of the said complaint, and it being then duly proved to the said justices upon oath (in the presence and hearing of the said   ), that an assessment for the relief of the poor of the said parish   of   dated the   day of   , in the year, &c., 189 , was duly made, allowed, and published, and that the said   was therein and thereby assessed at the sum of   aforesaid, and that a certain other assessment for the relief of the poor of the said parish   of   dated the   day of   in the year, &c., 189   , was duly made, allowed, and published, and that the said   was therein and thereby assessed at the sum of   aforesaid, and that a certain other assessment for the relief of the poor of the said parish of   , dated the   day of   in the year, &c., 189   , was duly made, allowed, and published, and that the said   was therein and thereby assessed at the sum of   aforesaid, and that the said   sums had been duly demanded of the said   , but that he had not paid and had refused and still refused to pay the same, and the said   then not shewing to the said   and   any sufficient cause for not paying the same, the said justices thereupon then issued a warrant to   commanding them to levy the said   sums of   and the sum of   for the costs incurred in obtaining that warrant, by distress and sale of the goods and chattels of the said   . And whereas it now appears to the undersigned   of Her Majesty's Justices of the Peace, in and for the said County   as well by the return of the said   to the said warrant of distress as otherwise, that the said   hath made diligent search for the goods and chattels of the said   , but that no sufficient distress whereon to levy the said sums above-mentioned could be found. These are therefore to command you, the said churchwardens and overseers and constables, peace officers, or some or one of you, to take the said   and him safely to convey to the House of Correction   at   in the County   aforesaid, and there deliver him to the said keeper, together with this precept.

And,   do hereby command you, the said Keeper of the said House of Correction   to receive the said   into your custody in the said House of Correction   there to imprison him for the space of   unless the said   sums of   , and   together with the sum of   for the costs attending the said distress, and the further sum of   , being the costs and charges of this commitment, and of taking and conveying the said   to prison, making on the whole the sum of   , shall be sooner paid unto you the said keeper; and for your so doing, this shall be your sufficient warrant.

Given, &c.

No. 27.

Justices—Warrant for Recovery of Tenements.

Whereas (set forth complaint) we two of Her Majesty's justices, &c. in petty sessions assembled, acting for   do authorize and command you on any day within   days from the date hereof (except on Sunday, Christmas Day, and Good Friday) between the hours of nine in the forenoon and four in the afternoon to enter (by force if needful), and with or without the aid of   owner (or agent), or any other person or persons, whom you may think requisite to call to your assistance, into and upon the said tenement, and to eject thereout any person, and of the said tenement full and peaceable possession to deliver to the said   (owner or agent).

Given, &c.

No 28.

Settlement—Order.

To the Churchwardens and Overseers of   and to the Churchwardens and Overseers of   .

Whereas complaint hath been made unto us whose names are hereunto and seals affixed, &c.,   by the churchwardens and overseers, &c.

We, the said justices, on due proof thereof   do adjudge the same to be true, and that the place of the last local settlement of the said pauper is in the said parish of   .

These are therefore to command you, the churchwardens and overseers of   , or some one of you, at such time and in such manner as by law is provided and directed in that behalf, to remove and convey the said paupers from and out of your parish of, &c.   and them deliver, together with this your order, or a duplicate or true copy thereof, unto the overseers of the poor there, or at the workhouse of the said last-mentioned union at   , and the guardians of the said last-mentioned union are hereby required to receive and provide for them according to law.

Given, &c.

No. 29.

JUSTICES—CERTIFICATE FOR STOPPING OR DIVERTING HIGHWAY.

Whereas [recite meetings of inhabitants, resolution to stop up or divert, chairman directed surveyor to apply to justices to view, view thereon adjudged unnecessary, notices of proceedings duly published, said highway measured by metes and bounds].

Now we, whose names are hereunto set, so being such justices as aforesaid, in pursuance of the aforesaid statute, do hereby certify that on the   we together and in the presence of each other at the same time viewed the said highway, &c.,   and that upon such view we found that the said highway is unnecessary, and we the said justices further certify that the reasons why the said public highway is unnecessary are as follows, that is to say   .

Given, &c.

No. 30.

LICENCE TO GET STONES, &C.

To the Surveyor, &c.

Whereas by an Act passed, &c.   and whereas it appears to us, &c. that he hath applied to A. B. for his consent to take stones and carry away materials from the land called or known, &c.   within the said parish for the purposes aforesaid, and that the said materials are necessary for the repair of highways, and that the said A. B. hath refused to permit the same to be dug, got, taken, and carried away, and the said A. B. having been duly summoned to appear before us to shew cause why such permission should not be granted, and having appeared before us accordingly, we have heard what has been alleged, &c., and are of opinion that the said materials are necessary and ought to be dug, got, taken, and carried away for the purposes aforesaid, therefore we do hereby give our licence to the said surveyor to dig, get, take, and carry away the same accordingly, the said surveyor making satisfaction for the same and also for the damage done to such land in manner directed by the said Act, &c.

Given, &c.

No. 30A.

ORDER TO PRUNE HEDGES, &C.

To the Surveyor, &c.

Whereas (summons to owner to appear, &c.) and the said offence having been fully proved before us upon the oath of   &c., now we, upon duly considering the circumstances of the case, do hereby order and direct that such hedges be cut, plashed, and pruned, so as not to exceed the height of   from the surface of the land on which the same are situate, and that all such trees as grow in and near such hedges in the lands of the said   adjoining the said carriageway or cartway (not being trees planted for ornament or for shelter to any hop-ground, house, building, or courtyard of the said   ) be pruned or lopped so that the said carriageway or cartway shall not be prejudiced by the shade thereof, and so that the sun and wind may not be excluded from such carriageway or cartway to the damage thereof: And we do further order that in case the said   shall not comply with this order within ten days after a copy thereof shall have been left at the usual place of abode of the said   or of his steward or agent, that then the said   the surveyor aforesaid do cut, prune, or plash such hedges, and prune or lop such trees in manner directed by this order.

Given, &c.

B. WHERE NO ADJUDICATION.

No. 31.
SECRETARY OF STATE—TREASON.

I, &c.,   one of the Lords of Her Majesty's most honourable Privy Council, and principal Secretary of State, &c.,   These are in Her Majesty's name to authorize and require you, taking a constable to your assistance, to make strict and diligent search for (defendant, and state cause of committal), and, him having found, you are to seize and apprehend, and to bring in safe custody before me to be examined, concerning the premises, and further dealt with according to law, in the due execution whereof all mayors, sheriffs, justices of the peace, constables, and others, Her Majesty's officers, civil, and military, and loving subjects whom it may concern, are to be aiding and assisting to you, as there shall be occasion, and for so doing this shall be your warrant.

Given at St. James, &c.

To   and   ,
    [two] of Her Majesty's Messengers in ordinary.

No. 32.
CORONER—EXHUMATION.

To wit:
Whereas complaint hath been made unto me, one of Her Majesty's Coroners for   that on the   day of this instant the body of one R. F. was privately and secretly buried in your parish in the said county, and that the said R. F. died not of a natural but a violent death, and whereas no notice of the violence of the death of the said R. F. hath been given to either of Her Majesty's coroners for the said county, whereby on Her Majesty's behalf an inquisition might have been taken, on view of the body of the said R. F. before his interment, as by law is required; these are therefore by virtue of my office in Her Majesty's name, to charge and command you, that you forthwith cause the body of the said R. F. to be taken up, and safely conveyed to   in the said parish, that I, with my inquest may have a view thereof, and proceed therein according to law. Hereof fail not as you will answer the contrary at your peril.
    To the Minister, Churchwardens,
        and Overseers.

No. 33.
SECRETARY OF STATE.—ORDER TO REMOVE BODY.

Application having been made to me, the   , one of Her Majesty's Principal Secretaries of State, for permission to remove the remains of   , I do hereby, in virtue of the power vested in me by the 25th section of the Act 20 & 21 Vict. c. 81, grant licence for the removal of the remains of   from   on condition (1) that the removal be effected with due care and attention to decency, early in the morning, that McDougall's Disinfecting

Powder or chloride of lime be freely sprinkled over the coffin, the soil, or any matter that may be offensive, and (2) that .

This licence simply exempts from the penalties which would be incurred if the removal took place without a licence; it does not in any way alter civil rights. It does not, therefore, confer the right to bury the remains in any place where such right does not already exist.

This licence shall, if any of the conditions on which it is granted be not complied with, be deemed to have been void from the beginning, and, if not acted upon within twelve months from this date, shall become void.

Given under my hand at Whitehall, this .

No. 34.

SECRETARY OF STATE.—EXTRADITION WARRANT.

To the keeper of , and to L. M., constable of .
Whereas, A. B., late of , accused (or convicted) of the commission of the crime of , within the jurisdiction of , was delivered into the custody of you, C. D., keeper of , by warrant dated , pursuant to the Extradition Acts, now I do hereby, in pursuance of the said Acts, order you the said keeper to deliver the body of the said A. B. into the custody of the said L. M., and I command you, the said L. M., to receive the said A. B. into your custody, and to convey him within the jurisdiction of the said , and there place him in the custody of any person or persons appointed by the said to receive him, for which this shall be your warrant.

Given, &c.,

Secretary of State.

No. 35.

SECRETARY OF STATE.—FUGITIVE OFFENDERS.

To the Keeper of .
Whereas on the , a warrant was issued by , being a person having lawful authority to issue the same within that part of Her Majesty's dominions for the apprehension of A. B., charged with , and whereas, it having been proved to me by affidavit that the signature to the said warrant is the signature of the said , I did on the indorse the said warrant in the manner prescribed by the statute, &c., and whereas, under and by virtue of the said warrant, the said A. B. was apprehended and conveyed before , who upon such evidence of criminality as would have justified the committal of the said A. B. if the offence had been committed in England, did commit him to your custody in the said prison at aforesaid, and immediately gave information thereof in writing under his hand accompanied by a copy of the aforesaid warrant to me, &c., . Now I do hereby by this warrant under my hand and seal order that the said A. B. shall be delivered into the custody of L. M., a constable of the police force, for the purpose of his being conveyed to , and delivered into the custody of the proper authorities, there to be dealt with in due course of law, and you are hereby ordered and required to deliver him accordingly to the said L. M.

Secretary of State.

No. 36.

JUSTICES.—ARREST.

Whereas A. B. of , hath this day been charged upon oath before the undersigned, one, &c., , for that he ; these are, therefore, to command you in Her Majesty's name forthwith to apprehend the said A. B., and

APPENDIX.

to bring him before me or some other of Her Majesty's justices, in and for the said county, to answer unto the charge, and to be further dealt with according to law.

Given, &c.

No. 37.
SEARCH.

Whereas it appears to me, &c., by the information on oath of A. B. of   , that the house known as   , is kept and used as a   , this is therefore to require you in Her Majesty's name, with such assistance as you may find necessary, to enter into the said house and premises (and if necessary to use force for making such entry, whether by breaking open doors or otherwise), and there diligently to search for   who may be therein, and for so doing this shall be your warrant.

Given, &c.

No. 38.
REMAND.

To the Constable of   , and to the Keeper of   .
Whereas A. B. was this day charged before me   , for that   , and it appears to me to be necessary to remand the said A. B., these are therefore to command you, the said constable, in Her Majesty's name forthwith to convey the said A. B. to the   at   , in the said county, and there to deliver him to the keeper thereof, together with this precept, and I hereby command you, the said keeper, to receive the said A. B. into your custody in the said   , and there safely to keep him, until   day of   instant, when I hereby command you to have him at   , at   o'clock   , before me or before such other justice, &c., as may then be there, to answer further to the said charge, and be further dealt with according to law, unless you shall be otherwise ordered in the meantime.

Given, &c.

No. 39.
BETTING OR GAMING HOUSE.—ENTRY.

Whereas it appears to me on the report in writing of   , a superintendent in the Metropolitan Police Force, that there are good grounds for believing, and that he does believe, that the house, room, or place known as   , is kept and used as a   , within the meaning of an Act passed, &c.   ; this is, therefore, in the name of Our Lady the Queen to require you with such assistants as you may find necessary, to enter into the said house, room, or place, and, if necessary, to use force for making such entry, whether by breaking open doors or otherwise, and there diligently to search for all instruments of unlawful (betting or gaming) which may be therein, and to arrest, search, and bring before some one of the magistrates sitting at   , as well the keepers of the same, as also the persons their haunting, resorting, and playing, to be dealt with according to law, and for so doing this shall be your warrant.

Commissioner,
Metropolitan Police.

No. 40.
ASSISTANCE.—CUSTOMS.

Victoria, &c.
To all and singular our officers and ministers who now have or hereafter shall have any office, power, or authority derived from or under the Commis-

sioners of our Admiralty or our High Admiral of our United Kingdom for the time being; as also all and every our Vice-Admiral, Justices of the Peace, Mayors, Sheriffs, Constables, Bailiffs, and all other our officers and subjects whomsoever within every city, borough, town, and county of England and Wales and the Islands, and territories thereto belonging, and to every of you; greeting.

[Recite letters patent appointing Commissioners and authorizing them to appoint subordinate officers to collect Customs.]

We therefore strictly enjoin and command you and every one of you that all excuses apart, you and every one of you permit and suffer the [said commissioners] and the deputies, ministers, servants, and other officers of them the said commissioners or of their successors in office, as aforesaid, from time to time as they shall think proper as well by night as by day to enter and go on board any ship, boat, or other vessel riding, lying, or being within and coming into any port, creek, or harbour of England and Wales or of the islands and territories thereunto belonging, and such ship, boat, or vessel then and there found to search and survey and the persons therein being strictly to examine touching and concerning the premises aforesaid according to the laws and statutes in that behalf made and provided; and in the daytime to enter and go into the houses, shops, cellars, warehouses, rooms, and other places where any goods, wares, or merchandises lie concealed or are suspected to be concealed, which are prohibited, or for which the duties of customs and other rates and sums of money aforesaid are not or shall not be duly paid, and duly satisfied, answered and paid unto our collectors or deputy collectors or other person or persons duly appointed for that purpose or otherwise agreed for according to the true intent of the laws in force or hereafter to be made; and such houses, shops, cellars, warehouses, rooms, and other places to search and survey for the said goods, wares, and merchandises, and further to do and execute all things which of right and according to the laws and statutes in force in this behalf shall be to be done.

[Injunction to aid and assist the commissioners and their successors.]

In witness, &c.

No. 41.

ORDER—TO DETAIN SHIP.

To   [Officer of Customs or Board of Trade], &c.

I, an officer having the authority of the Board of Trade to order the provisional detention of unsafe ships have reason to believe that the ship named below is unsafe, and *I hereby order* that such ship be provisionally detained for the purpose of being surveyed.

I have, therefore, to request that you will take the necessary steps for detaining her forthwith, taking care that the accompanying notification (Surveys 85a) embodying a written statement of the grounds of the ship's detention is served at once.

Given, &c.

Officer having special authority to order the detention of unsafe ships.

(A.) SHIP.

Name and Port of Registry.	Official No.	Where lying.
.		

No. 42

Excise.—Warrant of Distraint.

Collection. } To   Officers of Inland Revenue, or, either of them.

Whereas, the sum of   has been charged in respect of Duties of Excise upon, and is payable by   for beer, by   , brewed at   , in the   of   , and within the collection called   collection, and the said sum remains unpaid.

Now, I,   the   Collector of Inland Revenue, for the said Collection, by virtue of the power and authority to me given by the statute in that behalf, Do, by this warrant, signed by me, empower you the above-named officer of Inland Revenue, or, either of you, to distrain upon all the beer, malt, and other materials for brewing, and vessels and utensils belonging to the said   , or in any premises in the use or possession of the said   , or, of any person on   behalf, or in trust for   , and to levy the said sum of   so charged upon the said   , and remaining unpaid as aforesaid, together with all the costs and expenses attending the distress. And, I do hereby empower you, or either of you, to sell by public auction the said beer, malt, materials, vessels, and utensils, or so much thereof, as will be sufficient to levy the said sum of   , with all the costs and expenses attending the distress, and to apply the proceeds of the sale in and towards payment of the costs and expenses of the distress and sale, and in and towards payment of the said sum of   , so due from the said   , and to return the surplus, if any, to the said   .

Given under my hand at   in the   of   , this   day of   , in the year of Our Lord One Thousand Eight Hundred and Ninety   .

[Note.—The sale must not take place without six days' previous notice.]

No. 43.

Justices—Removal of Infected Persons.

To the Inspector of Nuisances for, &c.,   and to all other persons whom it may concern.

Whereas information on oath has been made before me, the undersigned, &c.,   that   residing at   in the said City, is suffering from a dangerous, infectious disorder, and is without proper lodging and accommodation there (or, is lodged in a room in the house aforesaid occupied by more than one family).

And whereas the certificate of   a legally qualified medical practitioner is now produced and shewn to me, dated this day, certifying to the above facts   . Now, therefore, I, the said Justice, do hereby in pursuance of the Public Health Act, 1875, s. 124, order and direct you to forthwith remove the said   from the said house to the Sanatorium of and belonging to the Sanitary Authority of the said City at   wherein he is to be received and detained by the Superintendent thereof.

Dated this,

J. P.

No. 44.

Justices—Removal of Body.

To the Inspector of Nuisances, &c.,   and to all whom it may concern.

Whereas it has been made to appear to me on oath that the dead body of   now lying in the dwelling-house, No   , in the parish of   in the said City, is in such a state from decomposition as to endanger the health of the inmates of the said house.

And whereas a certificate is now produced and shewn to me signed by _____ , a legally qualified medical practitioner, dated this day, confirming the facts alleged on oath as above.

Now, therefore, in pursuance of the statute 36 & 37 Vict. c. 55, s. 142, I do order that the aforesaid dead body be forthwith removed to the public mortuary for the said parish, and the same be buried within the period of twenty-four hours from the making of this order.

Dated, &c.

J. P.

No. 45.

ORDER TO EXAMINE PREMISES.

Whereas (local authority) have by their officer (name) made appear to me, &c., and the said officer has made oath to me that demand has been made pursuant to the provisions of the Public Health Act, 1875, for admission to _____ for the purpose of _____ and that such demand has been refused. Now, therefore, I, the said A. B. do hereby require you _____ (having the custody of the premises) to admit the said (authority) (or officers) to the said premises for the purpose aforesaid.

J. P.

No. 46.

DEALERS IN OLD METALS.

We the undersigned, &c. _____ do by this order in writing made pursuant to [Act] authorise you as such Inspector of Police to visit at any time the several places of business, and inspect the goods and chattels of all dealers in old metals, who are for the time being subject to the regulations of the said Act, and who carry on business as such dealers within your district, you recording in the book, required to be kept by such dealers, the day and hour of your visiting, and placing, opposite the entry of every article examined by you, your initials or name in attestation of the same.

Given, &c.

No. 47.

JUSTICES—ORDER TO APPREHEND LUNATIC.

To E. F., one of the Overseers (or Relieving Officer).

Whereas, I, the undersigned, one of Her Majesty's Justices, &c., have received notice from you that A. B., a person wandering at large within your parish, is deemed to be a lunatic: These, are therefore to order and require you to apprehend the said person so wandering, if he be found within your said parish, and to bring him before me on the _____ , or, before such other justice of the peace as may then be there to be dealt with according to law.

Given, &c.

No. 48.

ORDER TO DETAIN LUNATIC IN WORKHOUSE.

I, &c., being satisfied that A. B. a pauper in the _____ workhouse of _____ , is a lunatic (or idiot), and a proper person to be taken charge of under care and treatment in the workhouse, and being satisfied that the accommodation in the workhouse is sufficient for his proper care and treatment, separate from the inmates of the workhouse, not lunatics (or, that his condition is such that it is not necessary for the convenience of the lunatic, or, of the other inmates, that he should be kept separate), hereby authorize you to take charge of, and if the workhouse medical officer shall certify it to be necessary to detain the said A. B. as a patient in your workhouse.

Subjoined is a statement of particulars respecting the said A. B.

Given, &c.

To
    Master of the Workhouse at

No. 49.

PAUPER—REMOVAL TO ASYLUM.

To the Overseers, &c.
  and to the Superintendent of the
    Lunatic Asylum at

Whereas, one C. D., a pauper lunatic chargeable upon the common fund of the   Union, in the County of   , is now confined as a lunatic in the   , and it is desirable that he should be removed from thence to the County Lunatic Asylum aforesaid, at

We, therefore, the undersigned, being two visitors of the said Asylum at   , or   , and being also two of Her Majesty's Justices of the Peace in and for the said County, do hereby order you the said proprietor of (the house in which confined) to deliver the said C. D. to the said overseers of the parish of   aforesaid, or, one of them upon this order being presented to you by them, or any one of them, and We hereby order that you the said overseers, do forthwith thereupon remove the said C. D. to the said lunatic asylum at   , and, We further order you the said Superintendent, &c., do receive the said C. D. as a patient into the said last-mentioned asylum.

Given, &c.

[Similar forms are employed for conveyance from one asylum to another, or, in case of discharge.]

No. 50.

ORDER TO REMOVE FROM DANGEROUS STRUCTURES [METROPOLIS].

[After Certificate of Danger.]

To
    One of the Constables of the Metropolitan Police Force.

Upon the foregoing application of the London County Council, duly made on their behalf unto me, the undersigned, one of the Magistrates of the Police Courts of the Metropolis, sitting at the   Police Court in the City of London, and within the Metropolitan Police District, I, being satisfied of the correctness of the certificate of the said surveyor, hereby direct that the inmates of the structure named in such certificate, be forthwith removed therefrom by you the said constable; and, if they have no other abode, I do hereby require that they be received into the workhouse established for the reception of the poor of the parish of   , the said County and district in which the said structure is situate.

Given, &c.

No. 51.

JUSTICES—WEIGHTS.

Whereas you, the said A. B., have been duly appointed and now are Inspector of Weights and Measures for the District of   now I, the undersigned,   in pursuance of the statute in such case made and provided, do hereby authorize you, the said A. B., as such inspector as aforesaid, at all reasonable times to enter any shop, store, warehouse, stall, yard, or place, whatsoever within your district and jurisdiction, wherein goods shall be exposed or kept for sale, or shall be weighed for conveyance or carriage, and there to examine all weights, measures, steelyards, or weighing machines, and to compare and try the same with the Government Imperial Standard of weights and measures, required and authorized to be provided under the statute in such case made and provided, and for your so doing this shall be your sufficient warrant and authority.

Given, &c.

No. 52.

JUSTICES—ORDERS TO WATER BAILIFFS.

Whereas it has been made appear on oath before me, of   , a Water Bailiff, duly appointed for by the Fishery District of   , that he has good reason to suspect, and does suspect, that acts in contravention of the Fishery Acts, 1861 and 1865, are being done (or, are likely to be done) on certain land in the occupation of   situate at the parish of   in the said County, being on and near a salmon river, to wit, the   river.

Now, therefore, I, the said justice, do hereby, in pursuance of the Salmon Fishery Act, 1865, authorize the said bailiff for a period not exceeding twenty-four hours to enter upon, and remain on the aforesaid land during any hour of the day or night for the purpose of detecting the persons, who may be then and there committing any offence as aforesaid.

Given, &c.
J. P.

No. 53.

JUSTICES—WARRANT TO ENTER PREMISES UNDER PUBLIC HEALTH ACT, LONDON.

Whereas, A. B., being a person authorized under the Public Health Act [London], 1891, to enter certain premises [   ] has made application to me, &c., having jurisdiction in and for [   ] to authorize the said A. B. to enter the said premises; and, whereas, I, C. D., am satisfied by information on oath that there is reasonable ground for such entry, and that there has been a refusal or failure to admit to such premises, and either that reasonable notice of the intention to apply to a justice for a warrant has been given, or, that the giving of notice of such intention would defeat the object of the entry [or, that there is on the said premises a contravention of the said Act, or, of a bye-law made thereunder, and that an application for admission, or notice of an application for a warrant, would defeat the object of the entry].

Now, therefore, I the said C. D., do hereby authorize the said A. B. to enter the said premises, and if need be by force, with such assistants as he may require, and therein execute his duties under the said Act.

Given, &c.

INDEX.

ABDUCTION, 48

ABETTORS IN MISDEMEANOUR, 48

ABORTION, 48

ABSOLUTE DUTIES, 5

ABUSIVE LANGUAGE: See CONSTABLE—ARREST—METROPOLIS.

ACCUSING OF CRIME WITH INTENT: See EXTORTION.

ACTION AGAINST OFFICER: See LIABILITIES.
    limitation of time, 157
    notice of, 155
    tender of amends, 158

ADJUDICATION DEFINED, 34
    to what applicable, 34

ADMINISTERING CHLOROFORM with intent, 48, 85

ADMIRALTY, uttering false certificates, 48
    personating person entitled, 48

ADMIRALTY MARSHAL,
    appraisement, 31
    arrest, effect of, 30
        after departure, 30
    cargo, arrest of, 30
        when included in that of ship, 30
            not, 30
    attachment liable to for breach of duty, 169
    caveat, effect of, 30
    commission of appraisement, 31
            removal, 31
            unlivery, 31
    duty of, 31
    fees, 31
    jurisdiction, 30
    priority, 30
    release, 30
    safe custody, 30
    sale, 31
        must be by auction, 31
    service, how effected and when, 30
    warrant of arrest, 29
    notice of issue, 29

ADULTERATION, 65
    division of article, 65
    drugs, 65
    food, 65
    margarine, 65

ADULTERATION—*continued*.
 milk, 66
 notification, 65, 66
 samples, 65
 what constitutes an offence under Act, 65

ADVERTISEMENTS, INDECENT: *See* CONSTABLES—ARREST.

AFFRAY, officer may arrest without warrant: *See* CONSTABLES—ARREST.
 Affrayers running away and dispersing cannot be pursued: *See* CONSTABLES—ARREST.

ALIEN, false declaration, 48: *See* CUSTOMS—SEIZURE.

ALKALI INSPECTORS,
 Powers, 128

AMBASSADOR, privilege from arrest of, 7, 16
 Servant of, 7, 16

AMENDS, TENDER OF: *See* ACTION.

ANALYST, PUBLIC, 65

ANATOMY, INSPECTORS OF, 122

ANGLING IN DAYTIME, 95

ANIMALS, CRUELTY TO: *See* CRUELTY TO ANIMALS INSPECTOR.
 diseased: *See* CONTAGIOUS DISEASE—ANIMALS.
 impounding, 109
 killing or maiming, 48
 obstructing thoroughfare, 134
 shewn in street—Metropolis: *See* CONSTABLE—ARREST.
  Towns: *See* CONSTABLE—ARREST.
 tethering on highway: *See* SURVEYOR OF HIGHWAYS.

APPEAL AGAINST RATE,
 sum assessed may, notwithstanding be levied, 44

APPRAISEMENT: *See* HIGH BAILIFF—ORDER OF RELEASE—SHIP.
  See ADMIRALTY—MARSHAL.

APPRAISER appointed by high bailiff,
 bailiff may act as, 42
 remuneration, 179

AQUEDUCTS, INJURING, 48

ARMS, TRAINING TO USE, 48

ARREARS OF DUTIES OR LAND TAX,
 goods not liable to be taken on other process while claim outstanding, 25
 of rent while claim outstanding, 25

ARREST: *See* ADMIRALTY—MARSHAL.
  See CONSTABLES.
  See HIGH BAILIFF.
  See OVERSEERS.
  See REVENUE—CUSTOMS.
  See REVENUE—EXCISE.
  See SHERIFF.
  See SURVEYOR—HIGHWAYS.
  See WATER BAILIFFS.
  WRECK RECEIVER.
 privilege from, 7, 16

ARSON, 48

ASSAULT, actual violence not necessary, 172
   aggravated: *See* CONSTABLE—ARREST—METROPOLITAN.
   common, 172
   on county constable, 48
   on female, 48
   on officer in execution of his duty: *See* CONSTABLE—ARREST.
   on parish officer, 48
   on person arresting, 48
   power of bailiff to arrest for, 40
   promoting another to, 48
   with intent to rob, 84
   person armed, 90

ASSAULT AND BATTERY: *See* LIABILITIES—CIVIL PROCEEDINGS—CRIMINAL PROCEEDINGS.

ASSEMBLY, UNLAWFUL, DEFINED: *See* CONSTABLE—ARREST.
   verbal order of justice, 48, 59

ASSISTANCE, WRIT OF; *See* SHERIFF—WRITS.

ASSIZE PRISONERS, COPY OF CALENDAR,
   signed by judge, takes place of warrant to gaoler, 13

ASYLUM, REMOVAL OF INSANE, 40, 59, 61
   discharge, 61

ASYLUM OFFICERS: *See* GAOLER.
                 See OVERSEERS.

ATTACHMENT, WRIT OF: *See* SHERIFF—WRITS.
   of officers, 169

ATTEMPT TO COMMIT FELONY, 48

AUCTIONEER, commission of sale under writ, 176

AUDI ALTERAM PARTEM,
   maxim where applicable, 34

BAIL, ORDER TO: *See* GAOLER.
   admission to: *See* CONSTABLES.

BAILIFF: *See* HIGH BAILIFF.
        See SHERIFF.

BAKEHOUSE, INSPECTION OF: *See* PUBLIC HEALTH.
                               See FACTORY INSPECTORS.

BANK NOTES, MAKING, 48

BANKRUPT ABSCONDING, 48
   fraudulent, 48

BANKRUPTCY offences, for which judge has power to commit, 35, 36
   collector of taxes and rates entitled to preferential payment, 44, 121
   warrants in County Court, 36

BATHS AND WASH-HOUSES: *See* PUBLIC HEALTH.

BATTERY, DEFINITION OF, 70

BELLS, RINGING: *See* CONSTABLE—ARREST.
                 See MINISTER.

BENCH WARRANT: *See* SHERIFF—WRITS.

250　　　　　　　　　　　INDEX.

BETTING, ARREST FOR: *See* CONSTABLE—ARREST.
　　　　　　　　　　See CONSTABLE—ARREST—METROPOLITAN.
　　documents, seizure of, 54
　　house believed by superintendent of police to be used for, 54

BIGAMY, 48

BILL OF SALE,
　　Admiralty Marshal and High Bailiff shall (if required) execute to purchaser of ship, 31
　　of goods made by officer of sheriff, presumption as to property which has passed under, exempt from seizure, 23
　　registration of, 23

BILLETING SOLDIERS, 48

BISHOP, POWERS, &c., OF, 19

BLACK ROD: *See* SERGEANT-AT-ARMS (LORDS).

BLASPHEMOUS LIBEL, 48

BOARD OF AGRICULTURE: *See* CONTAGIOUS DISEASES INSPECTORS.

BOARD OF TRADE,
　　power of officer under Merchant Shipping Act, 124

BOARDING SHIPS, 113

BODY, EXHUMATION OF: *See* MINISTER—CHURCHWARDEN—OVERSEERS.

BOOK DEBTS,
　　not saleable by sheriff under writ of *fi. fa.*, 20

BOOKS, commitment for not delivering up, 43
　　obscene, 52

BRAWLING: *See* CONSTABLE—ARREST.

BREAKING DOORS,
　　after escape, 6
　　breaking out, 7, 16
　　breaking window, 16
　　brewers' premises: *See* REVENUE—EXCISE.
　　distillery: *See* REVENUE—EXCISE.
　　during what hours, 7, 16
　　entering aperture, 16
　　felony or breach of peace: *See* CONSTABLE—ARREST.
　　inner doors, 6, 15
　　trunks, cupboards, &c., 15
　　outhouses, 6, 15
　　party's own house, definition of, 16
　　power as to, 6, 15
　　previous request and denial, 6, 15
　　remaining on premises, 7, 16
　　third party's house, 6, 15
　　what constitutes, 15

BREAKING PACKAGES, 113

BREWER,
　　breaking premises: *See* REVENUE, EXCISE.
　　distraint on: *See* REVENUE, EXCISE.
　　entry on premises of: *See* REVENUE, EXCISE.
　　examination of stock,
　　　　materials: *See* REVENUE, EXCISE.
　　officer may take samples of beer: *See* REVENUE, EXCISE.
　　other than for sale, entry on premises of: *See* REVENUE, EXCISE.
　　search of premises: *See* REVENUE—EXCISE.

BRIBERY AT ELECTIONS, 48
BRIDGE,
    damage to: *See* SURVEYOR, HIGHWAYS.
    repair of: *See* SURVEYOR, HIGHWAYS.
    malicious injury to, 48
BRITISH CONSULAR OFFICER,
    power under Merchant Shipping Act, 124
BROKER,
    appointed by high bailiff,
    bailiff may act as, 42
    remuneration, 179
BUILDINGS,
    dangerous, 61
BULLION,
    conveying out of mint, 85
BUOYS,
    interfering with, 48
BURGLARY, 48
BURIAL,
    minister refusing to allow, 130
    right of, where district becomes a separate parish, 130
BURIAL-GROUNDS INSPECTORS,
    powers, 122
BYE-LAWS,
    confirmation, 65
    definition, 63
    dispensing power, 64
    good or bad in part, 64
    necessary ingredients, 63
        consistent, 63
        certain, 63
        general, 63
        reasonable, 63
        not *ultrà vires*, 64
    power to mitigate penalty, 63
        make, 62
    what, 64
        burial-grounds, 62
        gaols, 62
        local, 62
        post office, 62
        revenue, 62
        traffic, 62

CANAL BOATS,
    inspection under order, 66
    master to render assistance, 66
CANALS: *See* CONSTABLE, ARREST.
    list of misdemeanours for which arrest without warrant, 100
CAPIAS UTLAGATUM: *See* SHERIFF (WRITS).
CARDS,
    hawking: *See* CONSTABLE, ARREST.
        See REVENUE, EXCISE.

CARGO,
  may be arrested as security for freight due, 30
  seizure of, under warrant, 30
  service, how effected, 30
  where landed and warehoused or transhipped, 30

CARNAL KNOWLEDGE,
  attempt, 48

CARNALLY ABUSING,
  child under thirteen, 48

CARRIAGES,
  driving on footway : *See* CONSTABLE, ARREST.
  repairing or cleaning in street : *See* CONSTABLE, ARREST.
  standing in street : *See* CONSTABLE, ARREST.

CATTLE,
  diseased, 69
  maiming or killing : *See* CONSTABLE, ARREST.
  negligent driving of : *See* CONSTABLE, ARREST.
  slaughtering in street : *See* CONSTABLE, ARREST.
  turning loose : *See* CONSTABLE, ARREST.
  impounding, 109

CAUSEWAYS,
  damaging : *See* SURVEYOR, HIGHWAYS : ARREST.

CAVEAT,
  entered against release of property—duty of Admiralty Marshal, 30

CELL,
  for separate confinement : *See* GAOLER.
  punishment : *See* GAOLER.

CELLARS,
  inspection of : *See* DISTRICT SURVEYOR.

CHAIN CABLES, &c.,
  injuring, 48

CHALLENGE TO FIGHT, 48

CHATTELS NOT CAPABLE OF ACTUAL DELIVERY,
  sold under writ of *fi. fa.*, 21, 27

CHEATING,
  by false weights, 48

CHILD,
  exposure : *See* CONSTABLE, ARREST.
  ill-treatment of : *See* CONSTABLE, ARREST.
  stealing, 48
  under thirteen—carnally abusing, 48

HIMNEY-SWEEPER, 110

CHLOROFORM,
  administering with intent, 48

CHOKE,
  attempt to, with intent, 48

CHURCH OR MEETING-HOUSE,
  disturbing, 48

CHURCHWARDENS,
    brawling, 131
    duti· s, 131
    protection, 160
    seats, 131
  warrants and orders, 46
    coroner, 46
    privy council, 46
    dangerous vaults or burying-places, 46
    Secretary of State, 47

CLERGYMAN,
  privilege from arrest, 7

CLOTHES OF PRISONERS, 111
  prisoners entitled to their clothes upon discharge, 14
    proper clothing where clothes destroyed, 14

CLUB,
  gaming in, 55
  the Park Club case, 55

COCK-FIGHTING,
  power of local authority as to: *See* CONSTABLE, ARREST.

COIN,
  offences, 49: *See* CONSTABLE, ARREST.
  possessing clippings or tools for making, 85

COLLECTORS OF LIGHTING AND WATCHING RATE: *See* OVER-
SEERS.

COLLECTORS OF TAXES,
  execute distress warrants for non-payment of taxes, 39

COMBINATIONS,
  unlawful, 49

COMMISSION: *See* ADMIRALTY MARSHAL.
  of appraisement, 31
    removal, 31
    unlivery, 31

COMMISSIONERS OF TAXES,
  may commit defaulter to prison, 40

COMMITTAL: *See* ATTACHMENT.

COMPANY,
  being wound-up, not liable to attachment, sequestration, or distress, 25
  offences, 57
  (railway) liability of rolling stock to execution, 25
  (cost book mining) a partnership merely, 25

COMPOUNDING,
  felony, 49
  informations, 49
  misdemeanour, 49

CONSERVATORS, BOARD OF,
  order,
    how long in force, 61
  powers (Thames), 128

CONSPIRACY, 49

254 INDEX.

CONSTABLES,
  Inherent powers,
    duty, 76
    force, use of, 76
    aiding other officers, 76
    infants, &c., 76
  Arrest, 76
    abduction, 82
    abortion, 83
    affray, 78
    aqueducts, 83
    arson, 83
    assault and battery, 78, 84
    assembly, unlawful, 79
    bank-notes, making, 84
    bankrupt, 84
    bigamy, 84
    brawling, 80
    breach of the peace, 80
    breaking doors, 77
    buoys, 84
    burglary, 84
    cards, hawking, 91
    cattle, 85
    child abuse, 85
        exposure, 80
    chloroform 85
    choking, 85
    coin offences, 85, 91
    contagious diseases, 92
    convicted persons, 81
    copper offences, 85
    crime, accusing of, 85
    cruelty to animals, 81
            children, 82
    deer, 86
    desertion, 86
    dice, false, 82
    drunkenness, 82
    embezzlement, 86
    escape, 82, 86
    explosives, 82, 86, 92
    extradition, 86
    felonies, list of, for which arrest without warrant, 82
    foreign gold, 86
    forgery, 86
    found committing, 91
    list of offences for which arrest without warrant, 78
    game, 98
    gaming, 94
    gardens in towns, 98
    general powers, 76
    gold coin, 87
    goods, injury to, 87
    grievous harm, 87
    gun, 98
    handcuffs, 77
    hawkers, 94
    highways, 94
    hop-binds, 87
    housebreaking, 87
    hue and cry, 98

CONSTABLES—*continued.*
  Arrest—*continued.*
    illegal drilling, 79
    indecency, 98
    indecent advertisements, 94
        exposure, 98
    industrial schools, 94
    jurisdiction, 77
    larceny, 87, 94
    licensed premises, hours of closing in default of name and address, 98
    lighting, 99
    limitation, laying information, 77
    lunatics, 99
    machines, injury to, 89
    malicious injury to property, 95
    manslaughter, 89
    merchant seamen, 99
    mines, 89
    murder, 89
    mutiny, 89
    night offenders, 96
    oaths, 89
    pedlars, 99
    penal servitude, 89
    personation, 90
    piracy, 90
    poison, 90
    poor, 99
    prison breach, 90
    prisoner of war, 90
    quarantine, 99
    railway, 90
    rape, 90
    reasonable charge, 99
        suspicion, 82
    reformatory schools, 100
    rescue, 90, 100
    ringing bells, 80, 101
    riot, 90
    river-banks, damage, 90
    robbery, 90
    rout, 100
    sacrilege, 90
    signals, 90
    silver, 90
    slaves, 90
    smuggling, 90
    stating cause, 77
    stolen property, 90
    stores, 91
    Sunday, 76
    swearing, 100
    threatening letters, 91
    time, 76
    treason, 91
    trees, damage to, 91
    unnatural crime, 91
    vagrants,
        Act, list of offences under, 96
    vessels, 91
    wreck, 91

CONSTABLES—*continued.*
 canals and rivers :—
  disorderly persons, 100
  offenders, 100
 metropolitan :—
  abusive language, 101
  animals shewn in street, 100
   on footway, 100
  assembly unlawful, 100
  betting, 101
  bye-laws, 101
  carriages on footway, 101
   repairing, 101
   standing, 101
  cattle, negligent driving, 101
   turning loose, 101
  damage to person, 101
  cellars left open, 103
  cleaning articles, 103
   property, 101
  delivery at station, 103
  disorderly persons, 101
  fairs, 101
  fences, damaging, 101
  ferocious dogs, 101
  found committing, 103
  furious driving, 101
  fire-arms in street, 101
  fires, 101
  fireworks in street, 101
  indecent prints, 101
  instruments, noisy, 101
  knocking at doors, 101
  ladders on footway, 101
  licensed premises,
   hours of closing, 98
  litter throwing, 103
  mats, beating, 103
  obstructions, 103
  parks, regulations, 101, 103
  pig-styes, 103
  playing games in street, 102
  poor, 102
  prostitute soliciting, 102
  public entertainment—street, 100
  public stores, 102
  regulations of traffic, non-observance, 102
  riding on shafts, 102
  river, throwing refuse, 102
  rubbish throwing, 103
  sewers, 103
  soil emptying, 103
  stolen goods, 103
  suspected offences (river), 102
  unknown offenders, 103
County, 103
Municipal:—
 disorderly persons, 103
Towns :—
 animals shewn in street, 104
 awnings, 104

CONSTABLES—*continued.*
   Towns—*continued.*
      carriages standing, 104
      cattle-slaughtering—street, 104
      dogs, ferocious, 104
      driving more than two carts, 104
      fire-arms, discharging, 104
      furious driving or riding, 104
      found committing, 105
      games, street, 104
      goods projecting,
          on footway, 104
      indecent exposure, 104
          publication, 104
      knocking at doors, 105
      lines across street, 105
      mats, shaking, 105
      matter, offensive, 105
      pigs, 105
      pits unfenced, 105
      poor, 105
      prostitute importuning, 105
      riding on footway, 105
         shafts, 105
      rubbish thrown from roof, 105
      timber, stones, lime, &c., 105
      window boxes, 105
      window-sill, standing on, 105
  bail, 109
  chimney sweeps and pedlars, 110
  dogs, sale and destruction of,
             (metropolitan), 110
  duties generally, 76
  entry
      lands, 106
      licensed premises, generally, 106
             occasional, 106
      slaughter-houses, 106
      smuggling, 106
      threshing-machines, 106
      trespassers, 106
    canals and rivers :—
      vessels, 106
    Metropolitan :—
      licensing (dockyards), 106
      vessels, 106
  fairs (metropolitan), 110
  gun, 110
  powers generally, 76
  search, 107
      game, 107
  seizure and detention, 107
      coining tools, 107
      contagious diseases, 107
      cruelty to animals, 108
      customs, 108
      dogs, stray, 108
      excise, 108
      explosives, 108
      game, 108
      money, 109
      property on person arrested, 108

CONSTABLES—*continued.*
  seizure and detention—*continued.*
    vagrants, 109
    Canals and rivers :—
      boats and carriages, 109
    Metropolitan :—
      carts, 109
      dogs, 109
      furniture removing, 109
      generally, 109
      stolen goods, 109
      swine, 109
    Towns :—
      cattle, 109
  Traffic (metropolitan) :—
    Fires, 110
  Liabilities :—
    action against—notice, 155
    when necessary, 155
    appearing as advocate before justices where not prosecutors, 202
    interrogating persons arrested, 202
    refusing admission to defendants to open Court, 202
    assuming judicial functions, 202
    protection, 154
      canals and rivers, 157
      county, 158
      customs and excise, 157
      metropolitan, 157
      municipal, 158
      towns, 159
      pleading, 160
  Under warrant
    of Justice,
      officer must act within
        limits of particular county, 50, 146
    of Queen's Bench, 146
    cases under statute, 146
      not under statute, 146
    demand of copy of warrant, 146
    recovery of tenements, 147 : *See also* LIABILITIES.
Warrants and orders,
  Arrest, 50
    addressed to particular officer, he must have warrant in his possession, 52
    backing, 50
    explosives, 53
    jurisdiction, 50
    resistance, lawful when, 52
    Metropolitan,
      betting, 54
      cock-fighting, 60
      dramatic entertainments, 60
      gaming houses, persons in, 54
    Towns :—
      cock-fighting, 60
  Entry :—
    Public Health Act, 58
      London, 61
    stolen goods, 53
    recovery of tenements, 43

CONSTABLES—*continued.*
  Warrants and orders—*continued.*
    Entry—*continued.*
      recovery of tenements—*continued.*
        Sundays, 43
        during what hours, 43
     Metropolitan,
      betting houses, 54
        what is house for this purpose, 54
      cock-fighting, 60
      dealers in old metals, 59
      dramatic entertainment, 60
      gaming house, 54
      nuisance, 43
     Towns,
      cock-fighting, 60
    Search, 52
     explosives, 53
       entry, case of emergency,
         wharves and ships, 53
     petroleum,
      seizure and detention, 53
     premises occupied by convicted persons, 53
     seizure must be limited to property named, 52
     stolen property, 53
  Remand,
    duty under, 54
  Of coroner, 37
    commitment by quarter sessions, 36
    distress, 37
      how executed, 37
      sale by auction, 37
        within what time, 37
        extent of, 37
      goods not to be removed, 38
        but impounded, 38
      costs, 38
      overplus, 38
      superseded, 38
      what not to be taken, 38
      priority, 38
      in civil cases, 43
      copy if demanded must be given,
        where not necessary to demand, 146
    in indictable offences, 37, 48
    in civil cases, 43
      non-payment of rates, 43
    inferior Courts, 37
    police magistrate (in extradition), 51
    Secretary of State (in extradition), 47
      criminal lunatics, 47
      fugitive offenders, 47
    quarter sessions (bench warrant), 48
      calendar, 37
  Orders :—
    commissioner (metrop.),
      betting house, 54
      gaming house, 54
      cock-fighting, 60
      dramatic entertainment, 60
    chief officer of police,

CONSTABLES—*continued.*
　Warrants and orders—*continued.*
　　Orders—*continued.*
　　　chief officers of police—*continued.*
　　　　to examine premises, 53
　　　　　　old metals, 59
　　　　industrial school as to, 59
　　　　lunatics, 59
　　　　local authority,
　　　　　cock-fighting, 60
　　　　secretary of state, 47, 59
　　　　justices, 58
　　　　　(Metrop.) dangerous structures, 60
　　　　to remove children to workhouse, 59
　　　　lunatics, 59
　　　verbal,
　　　　disturbing petty sessions, 59
　　　　　　revising barristers' court, 59
　　　　coroner, 59
　　　　justice, 59
　　　　justice not sitting, 59
　　　　returning officer, 59
　　　　rout, 59
　　　　local authorities, 59
　　　　witnesses, 59
　　　　unlawful assembly, 59

CONSTABLE,
　refusing to assist when required, 49

CONTAGIOUS DISEASES INSPECTORS,
　powers, 122
　protection, 158
　orders of privy council issued by board of agriculture, 122

CONTAGIOUS DISEASES ACT: See CONSTABLE, ARREST.
　entry, 66
　seizure and detention, 92, 107
　offences under, 92
　powers of inspectors, 66

CONTEMPT,
　jurisdiction of inferior Courts to punish for, 37
　　　　superior Courts to punish for, 12
　warrant of committal for, 12, 36

CONTRACT OF SERVICE, breaking, 49

CONTUMACE CAPIENDO: See SHERIFF WRITS.

CONVICTED PERSONS,
　arrest of: See CONSTABLE, ARREST.
　premises occupied by, may be searched, 53

COPPER, counterfeiting, 85

COPYRIGHT, false registration, 49

CORONER,
　warrant of,
　　exhumation of body, 46
　　offences for which he may issue, 37
　may order forcible exclusion of party from Court, 59
　officer of, 37

COSTS: See LIABILITIES, PROTECTION.

INDEX.

COUNCILS OF CONCILIATION, 58

COUNTERFEIT COIN,
    exporting, 91 : *See* CONSTABLE, ARREST.
    foreign coins other than gold or silver, 91
    possessing three or four pieces with intent, 91

COUNTY COURT,
    statutory protection to officers, notice of action required, 155
    warrants of, in equity and admiralty, 36

COURT,
    wilful interruption of proceedings, 12, 36
    order to produce: *See* GAOLER.

COURTS,
    officers attending,
    power, 75

CRIME,
    extortion by accusing of, 49
    tort which is also a, 172
    unnatural, 91

CRIMINAL LUNATICS,
    prisoner: *See* GAOLER.
    warrant of Secretary of State : *See* CONSTABLE, WARRANTS.

CRUELTY TO ANIMALS: *See* CONSTABLE, ARREST.

CRUELTY TO CHILDREN : *See* CONSTABLE, ARREST.

CRUELTY TO THOSE UNDER ONE'S CONTROL, 49

CRUELTY TO ANIMALS INSPECTORS,
    powers, 122
    vivisection, 122

CUSTOMS : *See* REVENUE.
    offences, 49

DAIRIES, 70

DAMAGES: *See* LIABILITIES.

DANGEROUS STRUCTURES,
    order for removal from: *See* DISTRICT SURVEYOR.
    vaults or burying places: *See* MINISTER ; CHURCHWARDEN.

DEAD BODY, disinterring, 49

DEALERS IN OLD METALS,
    powers to visit places of business registered, 59

DEALERS IN SPIRITS,
    power to visit premises, 118

DEALERS IN TOBACCO,
    power to visit premises, 118

DEBT,
    imprisonment for, 17
        debts at suit of Crown, 10
    payment of, and costs to sheriff, 20
        will supersede distress warrant, 20

DEBTORS, 111

DEBTORS ACT, orders under, 35, 36

DEBTS, BOOK-,
    may be taken under writ of extent, 10
    not saleable by sheriff under *fi. fa.*, 20

DECLARATION, making false, 49

DEER TAKING, 49

DELIVERY, writ of: *See* SHERIFF (WRITS); HIGH BAILIFF (WRITS).

DEPARTMENTAL REGULATIONS: *See* BYE-LAWS.

DESERTION FROM ARMY, 49
    navy, 49

DESTITUTE PERSON,
    constable may conduct to ward or other such place: *See* CONSTABLE—ARREST—METROPOLIS.

DICE, FALSE: *See* CONSTABLE—ARREST—METROPOLIS.

DIRECTION POSTS, DAMAGING: *See* SURVEYOR—HIGHWAYS—ARREST.

DISEASED CATTLE: *See* CONTAGIOUS DISEASES.
    orders issued by board of agriculture, 122

DISOBEDIENCE OF ORDER OF JUSTICE, 49
    direction under statute, 49
    where no penalty, 49

DISORDERLY PERSONS: *See* CONSTABLE—ARREST—METROPOLIS.
                     See CONSTABLE—MUNICIPAL.
    house keeping, 49

DISTILLER,
    breaking premises of: *See* REVENUE—EXCISE.
    entry on premises, 117
    examination of material, 118
    must supply officer with ladders and lights, 120
    search of premises, 119

DISTRESS, WARRANT OF,
    against estate of company in liquidation, void, 25
    brewer for unpaid duty, 56
    distiller for unpaid duty, 57
    costs and charges, 38
    for rates under £20—charges, 180
    for taxes in arrear where refusal to pay, 39
        goods of third person, 121
        previous demand necessary, 121
        sum must be actually due, 121
    for tolls, 71
    goods to be impounded, 38
    goods not to be removed till sale, 38
    how executed, 37
    payment or tender of debt and costs will supersede, 38
    penalty for exaction in effecting sale, 38
        for excessive charges, 38
    priority, 38
    sale within what time, 38
    ship, 126
    what may not be taken, 38

DISTRINGAS, WRIT OF: *See* SHERIFF—WRITS.

DISTURBING A COURT,
    election court, 59

DISTURBING A COURT—*continued.*
   meeting of justices, 59
   revising barristers' court, 59
   petty sessions, 59

DOCUMENTS, DEMAND OF, 66, 113, 124

DOG, FEROCIOUS: *See* CONSTABLE—ARREST.
   rabid or otherwise, 108, 109
   constable may destroy, when, 110

DOORS, BREAKING: *See* BREAKING DOORS.
   knocking at: *See* CONSTABLE—ARREST.

DRAINS: *See* PUBLIC HEALTH—LOCAL AUTHORITY.

DRAMATIC ENTERTAINMENT,
   order of commissioner of police as to, 60

DRIVING: *See* CONSTABLE—ARREST.
   carriage on footway, 100
   cattle negligently, 101
   causing damage, 101
   more than two carts or wagons, 104
   without owner's name, 135

DRUGS, ADULTERATION OF, 65

DRUNKENNESS: *See* CONSTABLE—ARREST.

DUES: *See* REVENUE—CUSTOMS.

DUTIES: *See* REVENUE—CUSTOMS.
       See REVENUE—EXCISE.
   in arrear, 25
      goods and chattels not liable to other process, 25
      absolute, 5
      relative, 5

DWELLINGS UNDERGROUND, INSPECTION: *See* DISTRICT SURVEYOR.

EAVES-DROPPING, 204

ELECTION OFFENCES, 49
   municipal, 49

ELEGIT, WRIT OF: *See* SHERIFF—WRITS.

EMBEZZLEMENT, 49

ENTERTAINMENT, DRAMATIC, 60
   public in street, 100, 104

ENTRY, FORCIBLE, 49

EPIDEMIC: *See* PUBLIC HEALTH.

EQUITABLE INTEREST IN TERM OF YEARS,
   liability to seizure of, 18

EQUITY OF REDEMPTION,
   may be taken under writ extent, 10
   may not be taken under writ elegit, 18

ESCAPE: *See* CONSTABLE—ARREST.
   aiding in, 49
   of felon, 49
   rescue in felony, 49
      misdemeanour, 49

ESTATE HELD FROM CROWN,
    in execution under writ elegit, 18

EVIDENCE,
    Act and special matters may be given, when: *See* LIABILITIES—PROTECTION.
    of officer acting sufficient, 151
    fabrication of, 171, 209
    withholding of, 168, 170

EXACTION,
    in effecting sale under distress: *See* DISTRESS WARRANT.
    penalty for: *See* DISTRESS WARRANT.

EXAMINATION OF GOODS, 113, 118

EXCESSIVE CHARGES,
    in effecting sale under distress
    warrant, penalty for, 38

EXCISE: *See* REVENUE.
    offences, 49

EXECUTION,
    against goods valid, although sheriff liable to action for breaking civil, 16
    property remains in defendant until, 17
    Sunday, 7, 16

EXHUMATION OF BODY,
    warrant of coroner, 46
    order of Secretary of State, 47

EXIGENT, WRIT OF: *See* SHERIFF—WRITS.

EXPLOSION WITH INTENT OR ATTEMPT, 49

EXPLOSIVES INSPECTORS,
    entry, 122
        factory magazine or store, 122
        registered premises, 122
        wharves and ships, 122
    powers general, 122
    samples may take, 123
        payment for, 123
        expenses of testing, 123
    seizure, 108
    under warrants and orders, 57, 67
    entry in case of emergency, 57
    seizure, 57
    local authority, 67
    arrest, 67
    petroleum, 67
    samples, 67

EXPOSURE OF CHILD, 80
    indecent, 98

EXTENT, WRIT OF: *See* SHERIFF—WRITS.

EXTORTION,
    action against sheriff: *See* SHERIFF.
    by accusing of crime, 49
    by colour of office, 49

EXTRADITION, 49
    warrant of Secretary of State: *See* CONSTABLE—WARRANTS.
    warrant of police magistrate: *See* CONSTABLE—WARRANTS.

FABRICATION OF EVIDENCE: *See* LIABILITIES.

FACTORY INSPECTORS,
    entry, 123
    bakehouses, 123
    certificate to be produced to occupier, 123
    cruelty to children, 123
    powers, 123
    may take constable, when, 123
    school, 123
    examination, 123
    production of certificates, registers, &c., 123

FAIRS WHERE DECLARED ILLEGAL: *See* CONSTABLE—ARREST—METROPOLITAN.
    booth open in such fair, 110

FALSE IMPRISONMENT, 49

FALSE NEWS, 203

FALSE PRETENCES, 49

FALSIFICATION OF ACCOUNTS, 49

FARM STUFFS,
    duty of sheriff as to, 23

FELONY,
    misprision of, 49
    tort, which is also a, 172

FELONIES,
    list of, for which arrest without warrant, 82

FENCES,
    damaging: *See* CONSTABLE, ARREST.

FI. FA.,
    writ of: *See* SHERIFF, WRITS.

FILTH,
    removal of: *See* PUBLIC HEALTH.

FINES,
    recovery of, 35

FIRES: *See* PUBLIC HEALTH (METROPOLIS).

FIRE-ARMS: *See* CONSTABLE, ARREST (METROPOLIS).
    discharge of, in street: *See* CONSTABLE, ARREST (METROPOLIS).

FIRE BRIGADE,
    powers, 74

FIREWORKS,
    in street, 101
    nuisance by, 49

FIRST-CLASS MISDEMEANANT, 13, 111

FISH,
    stealing, 49

FISHING,
    illegal: *See* WATER BAILIFFS.
    person to produce licence, 128

FIXTURES,
  agricultural, 23
    (landlords), list of, 23
    (tenants), list of, 21
  mortgaged by tenant, 24
  no power to remove after determination of tenancy, 24
  tenant may remove—liable to be taken in execution against tenant, 24

FOOD,
  inspection of, 70, 74
  adulteration of, 65

FOOTWAY,
  awning or projection over, 104
  driving cart or carriage on, 100, 104
  goods projecting over, 104
  ladders, casks, &c., on, 101, 104
  riding on, 100, 105

FORCE,
  Lord Ellenborough on: *See* BREAKING DOORS.
  employment of, 5
  officers may use . . . to recover possession of warrant, 7
  officers may use, in what cases, 76, 120

FORCIBLE ENTRY, 209

FOREIGN ENLISTMENT ACT,
  aiding equipment, 49
  shipbuilding, 49
  warrant of Secretary of State, 56

FOREIGN GOLD AND SILVER COUNTERFEITING, 87, 90, 91

FORGERY, 49

FOUND COMMITTING
  list of offences under, 91
  notice of action against officer, 155

FREIGHT,
  Warrant, Admiralty,
    cargo may be arrested for freight due, 30
    freight not to be arrested, note to be appended to præcipe, 30
    service, how effected, 30
    where cargo has been landed and warehoused, or transhipped, 30

FRIENDLY SOCIETIES,
  circulation of false copies of rules, 49

FUGITIVE OFFENDERS, 49: *See* CONSTABLE, WARRANTS.
  warrant of Secretary of State, 47

FURIOUS DRIVING, 101, 104

FURNITURE,
  removing, 109

GAME, 50: *See* CONSTABLE, ARREST AND DETENTION. *See* SEIZURE AND DETENTION.

GAMES,
  playing in street: *See* CONSTABLE, ARREST.
    on highway: *See* SURVEYOR, HIGHWAYS.
  unlawful, 55

INDEX.   267

GAMING,
    arrest for, 94, 97, 101
    cheating at play, 50
    club, 55
    house, keeping, 50
    house, believed by superintendent of police to be used for, 54
    seizure of tables, instruments, &c., 54

GAOLERS,
    articles carried in or out of prison, 112
    duties, 111
    liability, 150
    pleading, 160
    privileges, 111
    protection, 153
    prisoners, 111
        admission of visitors, 112
        assize prisoners, practice as to, 13
        cleanliness, 111
        clothes, 111
        debtors, 43, 111
        discharge of prisoner, 13, 40
        education, 112
        exercise, 112
        females, 112
        first-class misdemeanant, 13, 40, 111
        hair cutting, 111
        hard labour, 112
        illness, 112
        maintenance, 111
        mechanical restraints, 111
        money, 111
        punishment, 111
        religion, 112
        removal of prisoner, 111
        search, 111
        separate confinement, cell for, 111
        sleeping, 111
    warrants and orders,
        of Lords, 12
        of Speaker, 13
        of High Court, 13
            (warrant to sheriff contains order to gaoler),
        of Secretary of State,
            to bring up prisoner to give evidence,
                for trial, 40
            to remove to asylum, 40
        of County Court, 40
        of justices, 40
        reformatory schools, 40
        bail, to admit to, 13
        commitment in civil cases, 43
            in default of sureties, 40
                penalty under Customs Acts, 40
            copy to be delivered, 14
        habeas corpus, 14
        pardon, 13
        release, 13
        to produce in Court, 40
        when term of imprisonment should be specified, 13
        wrong person executed against, 183

268   INDEX.

GAS-PIPES,
   removal, 68

GENERAL ISSUE, 160

GIPSIES ENCAMPING : See SURVEYOR, HIGHWAYS.

GOLD COIN,
   colouring to represent, 87
   impairing, 87

GOODS,
   deposited with another as security, not seizable, 24
   distraint of, by collector, for non-payment of rates—ship : See MERCHANT SHIP INSPECTOR.
   forfeiture of : See REVENUE, CUSTOMS.
   in custody of law, not seizable, 24
   in hands of executor, liability to seizure of, 25
   in manufacture, malicious injury to, 87
   impounded under distress warrant, 38
   lent on hire, liability to seizure of, 24
   list of, importation of which prohibited or restricted : See REVENUE CUSTOMS.
   list of, liable to duty, 114, 119
   may be detained, even though seizure illegal, 16
   not actually defendants, not seizable under writ *fi. fa*, 23
   not leviable under writ of extent, 10
   not sold, return of sheriff, 27
   previously assigned, sheriff not bound to interplead, 23
   sold, 23
      under distress warrant, 37
   subject to lien, seizure of, 24
   taken in execution, if claimed, duty of bailiff as to, 41
   securing : See REVENUE, CUSTOMS.

GOOD-WILL,
   not saleable by sheriff under *fi. fa.*, 20

GRIEVOUS BODILY HARM,
   with intent, 87

GUN,
   carrying : See CONSTABLE, ARREST.
   licence : See REVENUE, EXCISE.
      entry on land to demand, 117

GUNPOWDER : See CONSTABLE, SEIZURE AND DETENTION.

HABEAS CORPUS AD SUBJICIENDUM, writ of, 181 : See GAOLER.

HACKNEY CARRIAGE,
   standing : See CONSTABLE, ARREST (METROPOLIS).

HARBOUR MASTERS : See MERCHANT SHIP, INSPECTION.

HATCHWAY,
   fastening, 113

HAWKERS WITHOUT LICENCE : See CONSTABLE, ARREST.

HAWKING CARDS : See CONSTABLE, ARREST.

HAWKING PETROLEUM : See PETROLEUM.

HEDGES,
   pruning : See SURVEYOR, HIGHWAYS.

HIGH BAILIFF,
    duties,
        sometimes performed by registrar, 36
    liabilities,
        action in another Court, 180
    default,
        remedy for, 169
    extortion, 179
    fees allowed, 179
    position of compared with sheriff, 145
    protection, 145, 153
    warrants and orders,
        Admiralty, 41
        arrest, 41
            appraisement when necessary, 41
            execution on Sunday, 41
            release, 41
            service, 41
    committal,
        Admiralty and Equity, 36
        bankruptcy, 36
        contempt, 36
        Debtors Act, 36
        verbal, 36
    delivery, 41
    execution on goods, 41
        bailiffs may act as brokers, 42
        custody of goods, 41
        goods claimed, 41
        landlord, 42
        partners, 20
        sale, 42
        securities to hold, 41
        ship,
            sale, 42
                appraisement, 42
                duty on completion, 42
                inventory, 42
        superseded by payment or tender, 41
        tithe rent charge, 41
        what may be taken, 41
    possession, 42
        continuance of warrant, 42
        entry, 42
            during what hours, 42
        fees, 42
    bailiff,
        arrest, 40
            assault in execution of duty, 40
            liability of high bailiff, 40
            rescue of goods, 40
        broker acting as, 42

HIGHWAY, SURVEYOR OF: *See* SURVEYOR.
    tethering animals on, 134

HIGHWAYS, 67
    entry, 67
    inspection, 67

HOP-BINDS,
    destroying, 50
    falsely marked bags, 50

HORSE FLESH: *See* PUBLIC HEALTH.

HOUSE,
    believed by superintendent of police to be used for betting, power to enter, 54
    believed by superintendent of police to be used as common gaming, power to enter, 54
    betting, 54
    breaking, 50
        after escape, 6
        party's own house, 6, 15
        third party's, officer breaks in at peril, 6, 15
    common lodging, 74
    demolishing, 96
    entering at night with intent, 84
    gaming, 54
    malicious injury to, 96
    purification of, 68, 73
    sanctity of a man's, 15

HUSBAND,
    liability of for wife's debts, 25

ILL-TREATMENT OF CHILD: *See* CONSTABLE, ARREST, CRUELTY.

IMPOUNDING ANIMALS,
    food and water to be provided, 81

IMPOUNDING OF GOODS: *See* DISTRESS WARRANT.

IMPRISONMENT FOR DEBT: *See* DEBT.

INCITING TO COMMIT OFFENCE, 207

INDECENT ADVERTISEMENTS: *See* CONSTABLE, ARREST.

INDECENT EXPOSURE, 50: *See* CONSTABLE, ARREST.

INDECENT PRINTS, SONGS, &c., 50: *See* CONSTABLE, ARREST (METROPOLIS).

INDEMNITY,
    usually given by lessor of plaintiff to sheriff for executing writ of possession, 29

INDICTABLE OFFENCES, 48

INDUSTRIAL SCHOOLS, 50: *See* CONSTABLE, ARREST.

INEBRIATES ACTS,
    duty of inspector, 122
    powers, 122

INFECTED PERSONS,
    removal of: *See* PUBLIC HEALTH.
    ships: *See* REVENUE, CUSTOMS.

INFORMATION,
    remedy for breach of duty under criminal law, 169
    for excess of power, 202

INHERENT POWERS,
    to be pursued strictly, 75

INJUNCTION,
    when available, 195, 198

INJURY, MALICIOUS, TO PROPERTY: *See* CONSTABLE, ARREST.

INQUISITION,
    to ascertain lands, 18

INSANE PERSONS,
    removal to asylum of, 40, 59, 61

INSCRIPTIONS ON TOMBSTONES,
    rights of individuals, 131

INSTRUMENT, NOISY, IN STREET: *See* CONSTABLE, ARREST.

INSULT, WILFUL, TO JUDGE, &c.,
    warrant of committal for, 12, 36

INTEREST,
    recoverable on a judgment, 20

INTERPLEADER: *See* SHERIFF, LIABILITIES.

INTERRUPTION, WILFUL, OF PROCEEDINGS OF COURT,
    warrant of committal for, 36

INVENTORY: *See* SHIP.

JESUITS, 50

JUDGE,
    wilful insult to, 12, 36

JUDGMENT,
    against partners, 20

JUROR,
    wilful insult to, 36

JURY,
    directed for whom to find verdict, in what cases: *See* LIABILITIES, PROTECTION.

JUSTICE OF THE PEACE,
    warrant of, 48
    may order forcible exclusion of party from Court in preliminary enquiry, 59

KIDNAPPING, 50

KILLING CATTLE, 85

KILLING CONSTABLE,
    when manslaughter, 52
    when murder, 52

LADDERS, CASKS, &c.,
    on footway: *See* CONSTABLE, ARREST (METROPOLIS).
    duty to supply: *See* REVENUE, EXCISE.

LAND TAX IN ARREAR,
    goods and chattels not liable to other process, 25

LANDS,
    elegit, seizable under, 18
        copyhold, 18

LANDS—*continued.*
    freehold estates held from Crown, 18
        mansion, excepted from leasing power of tenant for life, 18
        public, 18
        subject to appointment, 18
        trust (simple), 18
        wife's lands,
            not seizable, 18
        ecclesiastical, 19
        equity of redemption, 19
        mortgage, 18
        remainder, 19
        reversion, 19
        sold, 18
        trust, long term (rent-charge), 18
    extent, seizable under, 10
        equity of redemption, 10
        freehold, 10
        leasehold (may be extended as lands), 11
        trust,
            not seizable, 10
        copyhold, 11
        judgment obtained against, 11
        mortgaged, 11
        sold, 11
    entry on: *See* CONSTABLES.
        See REVENUE.

LANDLORD,
    claim over goods taken in execution, duty of sheriff, 25
                                          high bailiff, 42
    consenting to a sale by sheriff, 26
    fixtures, 23, 26
    priority over collector of taxes, 121
    recovery of tenements, 43
    tenancy, yearly, 25
        other terms, 26
    tenement let by week, 26

LARCENY,
    found committing, 94
    list of misdemeanours under Act for which arrest without warrant, 94
    list of felonies under Act for which arrest without warrant, 87

LEASE,
    taken under writ of extent, 10
                fi. fa., 21

LETTERS,
    Non-delivery of, action for opening, detaining or delaying, 195
    misdemeanour, 202
        express warrant necessary for every separate case, 46
    postmaster's duty as to delivery, 121
    sending threatening, 91

LEVARI FACIAS, WRIT OF: *See* SHERIFF, WRITS.

LEVY WARRANT: *See* REVENUE, EXCISE.

LIABILITIES
    under warrants and orders of Superior Courts
        at common law, 137
        jurisdiction exceeded, 137
        justification, 137, 139
            pleading, 140
        "officer ought not to examine judicial act of Court," 139

LIABILITIES—*continued.*
    under warrants and orders of Superior Courts—*continued.*
        performance accurate, 137
            inaccurate, 137
        process defective, 139
            erroneous, 139
        trespass *ab initio*, 137
        warrant within jurisdiction, 138
            within apparently, 138
            without jurisdiction, 139
    Sheriff:—
        acts of bailiff liable for, 140
        evidence to connect, 140
            admissions, 141
            after expiration of office, 141
            disclaimer, 141
            handwriting, 141
            indorsement on writ, 141
            plea of "not guilty," 141
            privity, 141
            production of copy precept, 141
                warrant, 141
            proof of authority, 141
                warrant, 141
            return of two sheriffs, 141
            secondary evidence, 141
            subsequent recognition by sheriff's officer of illegal execution, 141
            swearing sheriff's officer, 142
        evidence against officer, 142, 143
    under-sheriff—
        no liability except,
            criminal, 142
            extortion, 142
            where sheriff dies, 142
    Bailiff—
        assistant, 143
        bound, 142
            criminal liability, 143
            false return, 143
            receipt of money, 143
        special, 142
            effect of appointment, 142
            how constituted, 142
        of liberty, 143
            bailiff of franchise liable, 143
                return of, 143
            Crown or party, 143
            process directed to bailiff generally void, 143
                high bailiff, Westminster, 143
            when sheriff to send to lord, 143
                bailiff, 143
                    enters without a *non-omittas* clause, 143
            writs for execution within franchise, 143
        liability of, 143
        no criminal liability of sheriff, 143
    under warrants and orders of superior Courts not at common law, of inferior Courts and officers generally, 144
    after adjudication, 144
        jurisdiction, 144
            onus of proof as to, 144
            presumption as to, 144

T

LIABILITIES—*continued.*
 after adjudication—*continued.*
  liability,
   general rule as to, 144
  special protection, 145, 146
   constables, &c., under warrant, justice, 146
   extends only to actions of tort, 146
   good demand, what, 147
   justice sued jointly with constable, 146
   Queen's Bench warrants, 146
   statute held to apply, 146
    not to apply, 146
  trespass,
   ab initio, 145
   process must be absolute nullity, 144
 high bailiff, 145
  duties, 145
  liabilities, 145
 constable,
  Recovery of tenements, 146
 officer proceeding under warrant, 145, 146, 147
 where no adjudication, 147
 Distinction between these orders and those enumerated as "other orders" as to liability, 147
  jurisdiction apparent, when none in fact, 147
 special protection, 147
 under other orders,
  principal and agent, 148
   general agent, 148
   particular, 148
    effect of ratification, 148
    evidence as to limit of authority, 148
    liability of agent, 149
     principal, 149
     criminal liability, 149
 under inherent powers,
  personal liability, 150
  joint wrong-doers, 150
  omnia præsumuntur contra spoliatorem, 151
  evidence, 151
  damages, 151
   not chargeable on public funds, 152
   trespass, *ab initio,* 152
   penalties, 152
   superannuation, 152
Breach of duty, 164
 evidence, withholding, 168
Civil proceedings, 164
 civil execution, 165
 action for damages, 164
 duty,
  absolute, 164
  common law, 164
  public officer, 164
  statutory, 164
 admiralty marshal, 167
 churchwardens, 168
 constables, 168
 customs, 168
 High Bailiff, 168
  summary remedy against defaulting, 168
  highway surveyor, 168, 170

LIABILITIES—*continued.*
  Civil proceedings—*continued.*
    High Bailiff—*continued.*
      minister, 168
    Sheriff, 165
      application to Court to be by motion, when, 195
      action for false return, 166, 167
      admissions, 167
      after bankruptcy, 177
      delaying sale, 165
        execution, 165
        statutory liability, 167
      goods of third person, 192
      improperly conducting sale, 165
      interpleader, 166
      liability of representative, 167
      limit of liability, 165
      neglect of duty, 165, 167
      pleading must shew damage, 167
      withdrawing from possession, 165
      Return "*nulla bona*," 166
    postmaster, 168
      non-delivery letters, 168
  Criminal Proceedings :—
    attachment, 169
      against admiralty marshal, 169
        high bailiff, 169
        sheriff, 169
    information, 169
      against all other officers, 169
      withholding evidence, 170
      refusing admission of visitors to prisoner, 170
        bail, 170
    mandamus, 170
  Excess of Power :—
    self-defence, 171
    fabrication of evidence, 171
  Civil Proceedings :—
    torts which are also crimes, 172
    action to recover moneys improperly paid, 180
      when it does not lie, 181
      when money comes to officer's hands—rule, 181
    assault and battery, 172
      mayhem, 174
      when none, 173
      procedure, 173
      plea,
        certificate of justices, 173
        committed in dispersing meeting, 174
        moll. manus imposuit, 174
        son assault demesne, 174
      limitation, 175
      damages, 174
    extortion, 175, 179
      sheriff, 175
        abusing process of Court, 178
        bankruptcy, 177
        compromise, 177
        creditor becoming disentitled, 177
        due on seizure, 177
        excess, 177
        execution set aside, 177

LIABILITIES—*continued.*
    extortion—*continued.*
        sheriff—*continued.*
            keeping possession, 178
            motion to refund and for attachment, 201
            incidental costs, 178
            fees, 175
            under *fi. fa.*, 176
            poundage, 175
            payment into exchequer, 178
            Proceedings for contempt do not preclude action, 177
            restrained from selling, 178
            winding-up, 178
        Under Sheriff:—
            fees, 175
        admiralty marshal, 179
            fees, 179
        officers' fees,
        high bailiff, 179
            fees, 179
            action may be transferred, 180
            poundage, 179
        overseers, 180
            fees, 180
        penalty,
            action for, 181
    false imprisonment, 181
        arrest, 182
            after return-day of writ, 182
            wrong person, 182
            by constable, 182
                gaoler, 183
                sheriff, 182
            generally, 183
        procedure, 183
            pleadings, 183
            evidence, 184
            damages, 185
            jury, 185
            limitation, 185
        remedy by *habeas corpus*, 181
        shadowing, 182
        watching premises, 182
    malicious prosecution, 185
        distinguished from false imprisonment, 185
        necessary ingredients, 186
            malice, 186
            probable cause, 186
            prosecution determined in plaintiff's favour, 187
            damage, 187
        prosecution improperly instituted, 185
        procedure, 187
            pleading, 187
            bad indictment, no answer, 181
            damages, 188
            evidence as to plaintiff's character, 187
            jury, 188
            limitation, 188
    Public Nuisance, 188
        damages, 188
        limitation, 188
        replevin, 194

LIABILITIES—*continued*.
- Slander, 188
    - privileged communications, 190
        - criminating communication by public officer, 190
        - apology offered,
        - injunction, 190
    - procedure, 190
        - jury, 192
        - evidence, 191
        - Damages, 191
        - Costs, 191
        - limitation, 192
        - plea of justification, 190
    - repetition of, 189
- Trespass to Personalty, 192
    - sheriff, 192
        - action maintainable by representative, 193
        - excessive seizure, 193
        - execution afterwards set aside against wrong person, 192, 193
        - goods, detention of, 194
            - forfeited, 194
            - privileged, 194
            - sale of, 194
        - landlord, 193
        - seizure after tender of debt, 192
        - sheriff selling goods lent on hire, 192
    - County Court, 194
    - water bailiff, 194
    - Surveyor of highways, 194
        - distress, 194
        - detention, 194
        - injunction, 195
    - Procedure, 195
        - damages, 196
        - evidence, 196
        - justification, 196
        - landlord, 196
        - limitation, 197
        - measure of damages, 197
        - removing goods before paying rent, 195
        - trespass *ab initio*, 196
        - wrongful seizure, 195
- Trespass to Realty, 197
    - breaking and entering, 197
    - forcible entry not included, 198
    - injunction, 198
    - limitation, 200
    - trespass, *ab initio*, 197
    - County Court, 198
    - constables, 198
    - overseers, 198
    - highway surveyors, 198
    - Procedure, 199
        - damages, 200
        - evidence, 199
        - pleading, 199
        - sheriff remaining on premises to put purchaser of lease in possession, 197
- Criminal Proceedings, 201
    - Attachment, 201
        - after expiration of office, 202
        - death of defendant, 201

278   INDEX.

LIABILITIES—*continued.*
   Criminal proceedings—*continued.*
      Attachment—*continued.*
         service, 201
         Sunday execution, 201
         when available, 201
         within reasonable time, 201
         writ of predecessor, 202
      Information, 202
         misdemeanour, 202
         advocate where not properly prosecutor, 202
         refusing admission to open Court, 202
         holding enquiry, 202
         interrogation, 202
         post office, 202
         highway surveyors, 202
         tax officer, 203
         overseers, 203
         workhouse officers, 203
         asylum officers, 203
      Assault and battery, 203
      Common nuisance, 204
         eaves-dropping, 204
      Conspiracy, 204
         what, 204
         decoys of police, 206
      extortion, 206
      fabricating evidence, 171
      false imprisonment, 207
      inciting to commit offence, 207
         power used not *bonâ fide*, 208
         shadowing, 208
      perjury, 208
         fabrication, 209
      trespass to realty, 209
         forcible entry, 209
   Damages generally, 151
      limited to actual damage, 151
      exemplary, 151
   Local authority, 148
      officers acting under, 149
   Nemo bis vexari debet, 186
   Omnia præsumuntur contra spoliatorem, 151
   personal, 150
   principal and agent, 148
      general agent, 148
      particular agent, 148
   protection, 153
   prerogative, 153
      Crown responsible, 153
      damages, 153
      when available, 153
   statutory absolute, 153
      Revenue officer, 153
         where probable cause for seizure, 153
         foreign enlistment, 154
         ships liable to seizure, 154
         stop carts and wagons, 153
      explosives, 154
      officer under Public Health, 154
      wreck receiver, 154
   statutory, ordinary, 154

LIABILITIES—*continued.*
   statutory, ordinary—*continued.*
      available, when, 154
      costs, 162
      damages, 162
      evidence, 161
         act and special matter may be given, 161
      leading characteristics, 154
      limitation, 157
      notice, 155
         length of, 156
         necessary when, 156
         unnecessary when, 156
         what it should contain, 156
      pleading, 160
         statute not necessary to recite, 160
      tender of amends, 158
         payment into Court, 158
      venue, 159
      verdict, 162

LIBEL
   against Queen, 50
   against administration of justice, 50
   publishing, against person, 50

LICENCE,
   gun, demand of : *See* REVENUE—EXCISE.
   officer may enter on lands or premises to demand, 106, 117

LICENSED PREMISES,
   persons found during close hours on : *See* CONSTABLE—ARREST.
      „   „   *See* CONSTABLE—METROPOLIS.

LIEN
   of Crown under Excise laws, 11
   seizure of goods subject to, 24

LIMITATION,
   penalties can be recovered, 115, 120
   period within which action against officer may be brought : *See* LIABI-
      LITIES.

LIQUIDATION,
   company in, not liable to attachment, sequestration, &c., 25

LOCAL ACTS,
   liability under, 148
   limitation, 158
   power to seize wares, 62

LOCAL AUTHORITIES,
   orders of : *See* BYE-LAWS.

LOCAL OFFICERS,
   agents of local authority, 62
   orders of justices to, 61
      infectious disease, 61
      detention in hospital, 61
   metropolis :—
      infectious disease, 73
      detention in hospital, 73
      underground dwellings, 73

LODGER,
   false declaration, 50

LODGING-HOUSE, COMMON,
    inspection of, 74

LOTTERIES, 50

LUNATIC,
    apprehension of: *See* OVERSEERS; CONSTABLE—ARREST; CONSTABLE—WARRANT.
    criminal, 50
    offences against, 50

MACHINES,
    malicious injury to, 89

MAGISTRATE,
    military under direction of, 6

MAIMING CATTLE, 85

MAINTENANCE, 50

MALICIOUS INJURY TO PROPERTY: *See* CONSTABLE—ARREST.
    list of misdemanours for which arrest without warrant, 96
    of felonies for which arrest without warrant, 83

MANDAMUS, 170

MANSLAUGHTER, 50

MARGARINE: *See* ADULTERATION; REVENUE—EXCISE.
    samples for analyses, 66, 114

MARKETS AND FAIRS, 71

MARRIAGE,
    minister refusing to perform, 131

MARRIED WOMAN,
    no power to commit, for receiving separate estate, 35

MASTERS AND WORKMEN: *See* COUNCILS OF CONCILIATION.

MATS,
    shaking or beating, 105

MAYHEM: *See* LIABILITIES, ASSAULT, &c.

MEDICAL PRACTITIONER,
    false registration, 53

MERCHANDISE MARKS, 50: *See* REVENUE—CUSTOMS—SEIZURE.

MERCHANT SHIPPING ACTS: *See* REVENUE—CUSTOMS.
    offences, 50

MERCHANT SHIPPING INSPECTORS,
    Board ship. 124
    enter premises, 124
    false colours, 114
    foreign enlistment, 125
    inspection of life-saving apparatus, 124
        of lights, 124
        of explosives, 124
    master to answer questions, 124
    muster crew, 124
    national character, 114
    passenger ships, 114

MERCHANT SHIPPING INSPECTORS—*continued.*
    require attendance, 124
        production of books, 124
           of log-books, 124
        list of persons on board, 124
    ship subject to forfeiture, power to detain, 114
    steamships, 114
    survey, extent of, 124
constables, 127
detaining officer,
    ship unsafe, survey of, 125
harbour masters,
    directions as to ballast, 126
        cargo, 126
        dismantling, 126
        entry and position, 126
        unserviceable vessel, 126
    entry and search for lights, 126
    Merchant Shipping Act, when incorporated, 127
    penalty for excess, 126
    removal of vessels, 126
protection, 159
rate collectors,
    account of shipment, 125
    bill of lading, 125
    certificate of registry, 125
    dispute with master, 126
    entry, 125
    non-payment of rates, 126
        appraisement, 126
        demand, 126
        distraint of goods, 126
           other goods, 126
           vessel, 126
    dues to Her Majesty, 126
    entry, 126
    overplus, 126
    sale, 126
receiver,
    absence of,
        what officers may exercise his powers, 125
    arrest plunderers, 125
    demand vehicles, 124
    detain ship or wreck, 125
    entry on land, 125
    require master of ship near to aid, 124
    sale, 41, 125
    salvage, 125
    summon assistance, 124
    warrant of justice, 58
surveyor,
    board and inspect, 124

METHYLATED SPIRITS,
    entry on premises of methylator: *See* REVENUE, EXCISE.
    examination of stock only in daytime, 118

MILESTONES DAMAGING: *See* SURVEYOR—HIGHWAYS—ARREST.

MILITARY, EMPLOYMENT OF, 6, 80

MILK, ADULTERATION OF, 66

MINES INSPECTORS,
    powers, 123

MINISTER,
    bells, 130
    burial duty as to, 130
        refusing right of, where district becomes a separate parish, 130
    dangerous vaults or burying-places, 46
    keys, 130
    inscriptions on tombstones, 131
    marriage, no duty as to, 131
    monuments, 130
    organ, 130
    warrant of coroner, 46
    Order of Privy Council, 46
        Secretary of State, 47

MINT, conveying bullion or tools out of, 50

MISDEMEANANT, FIRST-CLASS, 13, 111
    person acting as solicitor, though not duly qualified, not entitled to be treated as, 13

MISDEMEANOURS,
    list of, for which arrest without warrant, 76

MONUMENTS,
    consent of incumbent or rector in churches necessary to their erection, 130

MUNICIPAL CORPORATION,
    appropriating money of, 50

MURDER OR ATTEMPT, 50

MUSEUMS AND GYMNASIUMS, 71

MUSIC AND DANCING, 50

MUTINY, 50

NE EXEAT REGNO, writ of: See SHERIFF (WRITS).

NEGOTIABLE INSTRUMENTS,
    not arrived at maturity not leviable under writ extent, 11

NOCUMENTO AMOVENDO: See SHERIFF (WRITS).
    writ of, 12

NEMO BIS VEXARI DEBET, 186

NON EST INVENTUS,
    return of, 8

NOTICE,
    necessary to defeat title of *bonâ fide* purchaser, 24
    of action against officer: See LIABILITIES.
        where necessary, 155
        where unnecessary, 155
    of writ of execution or attachment, 20, 165, 169

NUISANCE,
    abatement of, 69
    alleged. Order to examine premises, 58
    on highway, 50

NUISANCE INSPECTOR,
    Order of justice, 58

OATHS,
    taking unlawful, 50

OBSCENE BOOKS, 52

OBSTRUCTING THOROUGHFARE—ANIMALS, 134

OFFENCES, INDICTABLE, 48
    inciting to commit, 207
    not yet committed: See WARRANTS AND ORDERS.

OFFICE, buying or selling, 50

OFFICERS ATTENDING COURTS,
    to preserve decorum, 75
        cases of indecency, 75

OLD METALS, DEALERS IN,
    power to visit places of business, 59

OMNIA PRÆSUMUNTUR,
    contra spoliatorem, 151, 168
    ritè esse acta, 32

OMNIS RATIHABITIO RETROTRAHITUR, 153

OPEN AIR MEETING,
    within mile of Westminster Hall: See CONST. ARREST.

ORDERS OF DEPARTMENTS: See BYE-LAWS.

ORGAN,
    playing, 130

OVERSEERS,
    arrest of lunatic, 132
    paupers, 132
        removal, 44
        search of, 132
    warrants and orders, 43
    distress,
        bankruptcy, 44
        bill of sale—effect of, 44
        company in liquidation, 44
        cost of levy, 44
        excessive charges, 44
        levy, 44
            in another county, 44
            notice of appeal does not prevent, 44
            previous demand, 44
    local collectors, 43
    paid assistant, 43
    poor-rate,
        appeal against, 44
    protection, 159
    warrant of coroner, 46
    Order of Privy Council, 46
            Secretary of State, 47
            justices—lunatics, 61

284 INDEX.

PARDON : *See* GAOLER.

PARK-KEEPER (METROP.),
    powers, 102

PARKS REGULATIONS (METROP.), 101

PARLIAMENT,
    prisoner under Speaker's warrant entitled to discharge on prorogation of, 13

PARTNERS,
    judgment against, 20

PAWNBROKERS' PLEDGES,
    may be taken under writ of *fi. fa.*, 21

PEACE,
    breach of—Justices not sitting may verbally commit, 59
        arrest without warrant, 80
    commitment in default of finding sureties for, 40
    disturbing justices, 75

PEDLAR, 97
    refusing to produce certificate : *See* CONSTABLE—ARREST.

PENAL SERVITUDE,
    at large during term of, 50

PENALTY,
    action for, 181
    for excessive charges or exaction in effecting sale under distress warrant, 38, 180

PERJURY, 50, 208

PERMIT,
    manufacturer of tobacco must shew : *See* REVENUE—EXCISE.
    persons removing spirits to produce   „   „   „

PERSON UNKNOWN: *See* WARRANTS & ORDERS.
            CONSTABLES—ARREST.
            HIGHWAY SURVEYORS.

PERSONATION, 50

PETITION OF RIGHT, 153

PETROLEUM,
    hawking, 93
    officer may take samples for testing, 67
    regulations as to conveying, 93

PETTY SESSIONS,
    disturbing, 75

PHARMACY,
    false registration, 50

PIGS,
    near any street so as to be nuisance, 70

PILES, CUTTING, 51

PIRACY, 51

PITS,
    not sufficiently fenced, 133

PLEADING: *See* LIABILITIES; PROTECTION.
    benefit of writ or warrant in justification may be foregone where officer pleads jointly with another, 160
    general issue, 160
    in actions under statute, 160

POLICE: *See* CONSTABLES.

POLICY OF ASSURANCE,
    may be taken under writ $fi. fa.$, 21

POOR,
    false evidence to Assessment Committee, 50
    injuring rate-book, 50
    officer promoting marriage of mother of bastard, 50

POSSE COMITATUS,
    who may raise, 6, 17

POSSESSION, WRIT OF: *See* SHERIFF—WRITS.

POST OFFICE, 51. *See* REVENUE.

POUND BREACH, 51

PREMISES,
    entry, 117
        brewing, 117
            other than for sale, 117
        distiller, 117
        licensing, 106
        methylator's, 118
        old metals, dealer in, 59
        spirit dealer, 118
        slaughter houses, 106
        threshing machines, 106
        tobacco, 118
        wine retailer, 118
    noxious trade—power to enter, 69, 72
    occupied by convicted persons may be searched, 53
    order to examine case of alleged nuisance, 59

PREROGATIVE: *See* LIABILITIES—PROTECTION.

PRISON,
    breach of, 90
    rescue, 51

PRISONERS,
    assize, 13
    insane, 40
    of war, aiding to escape, 90
    removal to another prison, 111
        to another part of prison, 62, 64
    rules as to: *See* GAOLER.

PRIVILEGE,
    from arrest, 7, 16
        ambassador, 7, 16
        clergyman, 7, 16

PRIZE-FIGHTS, 51, 78

PRODUCE IN COURT, ORDER TO: *See* GAOLER.

PROHIBITION,
    of landing diseased cattle, 69

286   INDEX.

PROSECUTION,
    limitation, 77, 91, 115, 120

PROSTITUTE SOLICITING : See CONSTABLE, ARREST.

PROTECTION : See LIABILITIES—PROTECTION.

PRUNING HEDGES : See SURVEYOR, HIGHWAYS.

PUBLIC ENTERTAINMENT : See CONSTABLE, ARREST.
    in street, 100, 104

PUBLIC HEALTH,
    bakehouses, 71
    baths and wash-houses, 71
    dairies, 70
    food, inspection of, 70
        horse-flesh, 71
        seizure of unwholesome, 70, 74
    lodging-houses, 74
    markets and fairs, 71
    museums and gymnasiums, 71
    nuisances, 69
    parks, 71
    prevention of disease epidemic, 69, 70
    Public Health Amendment, 70
    removal of infected persons, 68, 73
    slaughter-houses, 71
    tents and vans, 71
    tolls, distress for, 71
    weighing goods, 71
    working classes, 70
    workshops, 72
  Liability of officer, 148
    protection, 153
  Orders of local authority, 69
    compensation to owner, 69
    dangerous buildings, 69
    diseased cattle, 69
    drains, 68
    factories, 69
    filth, 68
    gas and water, 68
    houses, 68, 69
    infection, 68
    meat, unsound, 69
    nuisances, 69
    streets, 68
    water-mains, 68
    wells, 69
  METROPOLIS :—
    Powers of vestry, 74
    common lodging-houses, 74
    fires, 74
    infectious disease, 73
    epidemics, 73
    tents and vans, 74
    underground rooms, 74
    inspection of premises, 72
    drains, 74
    entry, 72
    manure, 72
    nuisance, 72
    opening of ground, 73, 74

PUBLIC HEALTH—*continued.*
  METROPOLIS—*continued.*
    order of justice, 73
    orders of local authority, 72
    ditches, 73
    food, 74

PURCHASER,
  bonâ fide without notice, 23, 24
  writ of execution or attachment does not prejudice, 23
  plaintiff in sale under vendee by sheriff may be . . . ., 27
  title to goods of, 24

QUARTER SESSIONS,
  calendar, 37
  power to commit by, 36
  warrant—bench, 48

QUEEN'S MESSENGERS,
  warrant of Secretary of State, 46

QUEEN, FIRING AT, 51

RAILWAY,
  insuring, with intent to obstruct, 90
  offences, 51

RAILWAY COMPANY,
  rolling-stock not liable to execution, 25

RAILWAY INSPECTORS,
  powers, 127

RAPE, 51

RATES,
  appeal against, sum assessed may notwithstanding be levied, 44
  commitment for non-payment of, 43

REAL ESTATE,
  false statement as to title, 51

REASONABLE SUSPICION,
  what, 82

RECEIVING ORDER,
  duty of sheriff before sale of goods, having notice of, 26

RECEIVING STOLEN PROPERTY, 51

RECOGNIZANCES,
  not entering into, 37
  recovery of, 35, 110

RECOVERY OF TENEMENTS, 43

REFORMATORY SCHOOL, 51: *See* CONSTABLE; ARREST.
  removal of prisoners to, 40

REFUSE THROWING: *See* CONSTABLE; ARREST (METROP.).
  into Thames, 102

REGISTRAR,
  wilful insult to, 36: *See also* HIGH BAILIFF.

REGISTRAR-GENERAL OF SEAMEN,
    power under Merchant Shipping Act, 124

REGISTRATION OF MARRIAGE,
    false declaration, 51

REGULATIONS OF DEPARTMENTS: *See* BYE-LAWS.

REGULATIONS AS TO TRAFFIC: *See* CONSTABLE—ARREST (METROP.).

RELATIVE DUTIES, 5

RELEASE, ORDER OF: *See* GAOLERS.

RELIEVING OFFICER: *See* OVERSEERS.
    powers, 132

RELIGIOUS HOUSES, 46

REMAINDER,
    not seizable under writ of elegit, 19

REMAND WARRANT: *See* CONSTABLE'S WARRANTS.

REMEDIES, 153

RENT,
    in arrear,
        yearly tenancy,
            goods and chattels not liable to other process till one year paid, 25
        weekly tenancy,
            goods and chattels not liable to other process till four weeks paid, 25
        term any other less than a year,
            goods and chattels not liable to other process till two terms paid, 25

RESCUE, 57
    felony, 90
    misdemeanour, 100

RESCUE OF GOODS,
    powers of bailiff to arrest for, 40

RESISTANCE,
    to officer attempting to force his way in house in execution of writ, 15
    process, 6
    generally, 76, 120, 171

REVENUE OFFICERS,
    Customs,—
        inherent powers,
            arrest, 46
                assaulting officers, 116
                found with contraband goods, 116
                infected ships, 116
                receiving forfeited goods or offenders, 116
                signal to smugglers, 116
                subsequent, 116
            board ship, 113
            break open, 113
                packages or boxes, 113
                contents unknown, 113
                goods for shipment, 113
                      salmon parcels, 113
            charges, 115
            clearance withheld, 116

REVENUE OFFICERS—*continued.*
  Customs—*continued.*
    inherent powers—*continued.*
      demand documents, 113
      detention of goods, 114
      disputed rates, 116
      dues, 115
      duties, list of goods liable to, 114
      entry, 113
        lands, 113
      expenses watching, &c., ship, 115
        after fourteen days, 115
      examination, 113
        carts, &c., 114
      excise powers, 116
      fasten down hatchway, 113
      fire on ship, 116
      goods, conveyances, &c., forfeited, 115
        importation prohibited or restricted, 114
        sold, 116
      limitation, 115
      merchant shipping powers, 124
      offences, 115
      sale, 116
      Sea Fisheries Act, 116
        arrest offender, 117
        board, 117
        demand documents, 117
        examine tackle, 117
        lights, 117
        make inquiry, 117
        muster crew, 117
        seize destructive instruments, 117
      seals, 117
      search, 113
        commissioned ships, 113
        persons, 113
      securing goods, 116
        Queen's warehouse, 116
      seizure, 114
        aliens, 115
        for harbour dues, 116
        merchandize marks, 114
        power must be exercised strictly, 114
      take samples, 114
        margarine, 114
        tea, 114
    warrants and orders,
      arrest, 55
      detention of ship, 56
      entry, 55
        lands, 55
        premises, 55
      Sea Fisheries Act, 56
      search, 55
        foreign enlistment, 56
        houses, 56
        writ of assistance, 55
  Excise—
    Inherent powers,
      arrest, 119
        cards, hawking, 119

U

REVENUE OFFICERS—*continued.*
  Excise—*continued.*
    Inherent powers—*continued.*
      arrest—*continued.*
        gun, carrying, 119
        making out false accounts, 120
        obstructing officers, 120
        persons on unlicensed premises, 119
        removing fraudulently goods,
          liable to duty, 120
          malt, 120
          spirits, 120
        selling spirits, 120
          tobacco, 120
        subsequent, 120
      breaking, 119
        brewer's premises, 119
          adjoining premises, 119
        distillery, 119
      customs, powers, 120
      demand gun licence, 117
      distiller to draw off warm tub, 120
        supply ladders, &c., 120
      entry, 117
        brewery, 117
          adjoining premises, 117
        brewing premises other than for sale, 117
        distillery, 117
        lands, 117
        methylator's premises, 118
        spirit-dealer, 118
        tobacco, 118
        wine retailer, 118
      examination, 118
        brewing, 118
        distillery, 118
        methylator, 118
        spirit retailer, 118
        spirits in transit, 118
        tobacco, 118
        wine retailer, 118
    force to force, 120
    gun-licence—demand, 117
    goods—list of, liable to duty, 119
    ladders, &c., 120
    limitations, 120
    offences, list of, 120
    production of permit, 120
      spirits, 120
      tobacco, 120
    samples, 118
      beer, 118
      margarine, 118
      payment for, 119
      spirits, 119
    search, 119
      brewery, 119
      distillery, 119
      wine retailer, 119
    seizure, 119
      deposit of goods, 119
      spirits, 119

REVENUE OFFICERS—*continued.*
  Excise—*continued.*
    seizure—*continued.*
      unlawful—of goods as forfeited, 119
    worm-tub, 120
  Warrants and Orders,
    Levy, 38
      How executed, 38
      sale, 38
        within what time, 38
        overplus to owner, 38
        warrant to be shewn, 38
        demand a condition precedent to action for illegal detention, 39
    commitment, 39
    arrest, 56
    search, 56
    distraint, 56
Post Office,
  detention and opening letters, 121
  duty of postmaster, 121
  non-delivery of letters, 121
  obstructing business, 121
  offences, 51
  removal of offenders, 121
Warrants and Orders,
  detention and opening letters, 46
    separate warrant for every case, 46
liability, 150
  notice of action, 157
  protection, 157
Taxes.
  bankruptcy collector entitled to preferential payment, 121
  constable—introduction of, 121
  distraint, 120
    charges, 120
    demand, 121
    goods of third person, 121
    priority, 121
    reasonable time to elapse, 121
    sum must be actually due, 121
Warrants and Orders,
  warrant of commissioners, 40
  —of committal of defaulter, 40
  —of distress, 39
    appeal, neglect to, 39
    appraisement, 39
    bill of sale—effect of, 39
    breaking doors, 39
    charges, 39
    for several distresses—one warrant, 39
    how executed, 39
      in foreign jurisdiction, 39
    no seizure but by landlord valid against collector, 39
    overplus, 39
    sale, 39
    to be kept five days, 39
Liability, 150
  protection, 157
    damages, 151
    evidence, 151
    personal, 150
    protection, 153

REVENUE OFFICERS—*continued.*
   Liability—*continued*
      protection—*continued.*
         absolute, 153
         limitation, 157
         notice, 155

REVERSION,
   not seizable under writ of elegit, 19

RIDING, FURIOUS: *See* CONST. ARREST.
   on shafts: *See* CONST. ARREST.
   on footway: *See* CONST. ARREST.

RINGING BELLS: *See* CONST. ARREST.

RIOT, 51: *See* MINISTER.
   verbal orders of justice in, 48

RIVER OR SEA BANKS,
   interfering with, 90

ROBBERY, 51
   by person armed, 90
   by two or more, 90

ROUT: *See* CONST. ARREST.

RUBBISH THROWN FROM ROOF, 105

SACRILEGE, 51

SALE,
   by receiver of ship or wreck: *See* MERCHANT SHIP INSP.
   custody of goods until, 27, 30, 38, 39, 42, 116
   duty of sheriff having notice of receiving order prior to, 26
   Payment to sheriff before—a bar to further execution, 28
   period to elapse after seizure, 27, 37, 38, 39, 42
   To defeat expected execution not necessarily fraudulent, 23
   under distress warrant excessive charges, 38
   under execution exceeding £20 must be by public auction, 28
   under levy warrant, 38
   by Customs officer, 116

SALMON,
   illegally taken—warrant to seize: *See* WATER BAILIFFS.

SALVAGE,
   appraisement to be made before release of cargo by high bailiff, 41
   personal luggage of passengers and clothes of seamen exempt, from arrest, 30
   when due—duty of receiver: *See* MERCHANT SHIP INSPEC.

SAMPLES,
   Adulteration Act, 65
      division of article, 65
      food or drugs for analysis, 65
      margarine, 65, 114
      milk, 66
      notification, 65, 66
      where to be procured, 65
   beer or worts, 118
   explosives, 53
   spirits, 119
   payment for—as to, 119

SAVINGS BANKS, 51

SEA BANKS,
    interfering with, 51

SEA FISHERIES ACT,
    power of Customs officers : *See* CUSTOMS.
    seal fishing : *See* CUSTOMS.

SEAMEN,
    preventing loading of ship, 51 : *See* CONSTABLE.

SEARCH : *See* REVENUE.

SEARCH WARRANT : *See* CONSTABLES ; WARRANTS.

SEIZURE : *See* CONSTABLES ; REVENUE.

SERGEANT-AT-ARMS—LORDS,
    black rod, order where to, 7
    fees appear to have been abolished, 8
    powers under order of the House, 7
        warrant of the Chancellor, 8
    verbal orders, 8
    ward of Court, order for, 8

SERGEANT-AT-ARMS—COMMONS,
    fees, 8
    House of Commons not strictly a superior Court, 8
    powers under warrant of the Speaker, 8
        Inherent, 75
    verbal orders, 8

SEPARATE ESTATE,
    anticipation of which married woman restrained from power to commit for receiving, 35

SHERIFF,
    writs,
        assistance, 8
            duty of sheriff, 8
            fees, 9
            form of, 8
            when issued, 8
        attachment, 9
            breaking doors, 9
            endorsement necessary, 9
            duty of sheriff, 9
            fees, 9
            no poundage, 9
            when issued, 9
        bench warrant, 9
            when issued, 9
        capias ad resp., 9
            when issued, 9
        capias utlagatum, 9
            when issued, 9
        contumace capiendo, 10
            form of, 10
            to be produced in Court, 10
            when issued, 10
        delivery, 17
            effect of judgment, 17
            fees, 17
            when issued, 17

SHERIFF—*continued.*
  writs—*continued.*
    distringas, 28
      when issued, 28
    elegit, 18
      execution invalid, 18
      fees, 175
      inquisition to be held, 18
      no sale, 19
      poundage, 19
      return to writ, 19
      what may be taken, 18
        lands, 18
          estates held from Crown, 18
          generally, 18
          in trust, 18
          mansion, 18
          public, 18
          subject to appointment, 18
          wife's, 18
        no interest for subsequent writ, 18
      what may not be taken, 18
        lands, 18
          ecclesiastical, 19
          equity of redemption, 18
      what may not be taken, 18
        lands, 18
          mortgaged, 18
          remainder, 19
          rent, 19
          reversion, 19
          sold, 18
          trust, 19
      when issued, 18
    exigent, 10
      when issued, 10
    extent, 10
      appraisement, 11
      execution valid, 10
        invalid, 10
      fees, 175
      imprisonment for debt, 10
      no poundage, 11
      priority, 11
      what may be taken, 10
        debts, 10
        goods and chattels, 10
          of partners, 11
            conveyed away fraudulently, 10
        term of years as goods or as lands, 10
        lands, 10
          equity of redemption, 10
          equitable mortgage by deposit, 10
          freehold, 10
          trust, 10
      what may not be taken, 10
        goods, 11
          assigned to creditors, 11
          pawned or pledged, 11
          subject to lien, 11
          vested in trustee for bankrupt, 11
          negotiable instrument not at maturity, 11

SHERIFF—*continued.*
  writs—*continued.*
    extent—*continued.*
      what may not be taken—*continued.*
        lands, 11
          copyhold, 11
          judgment obtained against, 11
          mortgaged, 11
          sold, 11
      when issued, 19
  fieri facias, 10
    death of debtor, 20
      creditor, 20
    duty of sheriff, 20
      enquire in *bond fides* of claim for rent, 26
      execution against partners, 20
        can sell only debtor's right, 20
        cannot sell book debts or goodwill, 20
        further levy, 21
      payment of debt or tender, effect of, 20
      seizure,
        man to be in possession till sale, 20
        of part, 20
        of third person's goods, 23
    ecclesiastical, 19
    partners, 20
    priority, where several writs, 19
    property in defendant until execution, 20
    what may be taken, 21
      goods and chattels, 21
        corn, &c., which yield annual profit, 21
        fixtures, 21
          removable by tenant during term, what, 21
        lease, 21
        money, 21
        not capable of delivery, 21
        saleable, 21
        ship, 21
          seizure before sale apparently not necessary, 21
        term of years, 21
    what may not be taken, 23
      crops produced without labour, 23
      effects of company in liquidation, 25
      farm stuffs, 23
      fixtures, 23
        landlord's, what, 23
        tenant's, renounced, &c., 24
          mortgaged, 24
          removable under Agricultural Holdings Act, 23, 26
      goods,
        ambassador's, 7
        assigned previously,
          sheriff may withdraw, 23
        deposited as security, 24
        ecclesiastical, 19
        in custody of law, 24
        in hands of executors, 25
          trustee or agent (money), 24
          sheriff (money), 24

SHERIFF—*continued.*
   writs—*continued.*
      fieri facias—*continued.*
         what may not be taken—*continued.*
           goods—*continued.*
              lent, 24
              necessaries, 23
              not defendants, 23
              of wife, 25
              sold, 24
              subject to lien, 24
                  bill of sale, 23
                      to be registered, 23
              rent in arrear, 25
                  term of rental, 26
                      return of sheriff, 26
                      sheriff must withdraw, 26
                      sale consented to by landlord, 26
                taxes in arrear, 25
              rolling stock of railway company, 25
              tools, bedding, &c., to £5, 23
        when issued, 19
        writ to agree with judgment, 20
      levari facias, 11
        when issued, 11
      ne exeat regno, 12
        fees, 12
        when issued, 12
      nocumento amovendo, 12
        when issued, 12
      possession, 28
        breaking doors, 28
        duty of sheriff, 29
        fees, 29
        indemnity usually given by lessor of plaintiff, 29
        part-delivery of, 29
        persons to be removed, 29
          left on premises must attorn to plaintiff, 29
        plaintiff recovering only undivided portion, 29
          must point out precise lands, 29
        poundage, 29
        when employed, 28
      recovery of fines, escheats, &c., 35
        when issued, 35
          offender out of jurisdiction, 35
      supersedeas, 29
        when issued, 29
      venditioni exponas, 26
        assignment of term, 28
        bankruptcy supervening, 26
        before return of *ven. ex.*, 26
        farm stuffs, 28
        fees and poundage, 28
        lease and fixtures, 27
        must be sold, when, 27
        must hold proceeds for 14 days, 27
        must not sell for much below real value, 27
        payment before sale, 28
        plaintiff may be purchaser, 27
        public auction, 28
        receiving order within 14 days—only writs for less than £20
          entitled to be paid, 27

SHERIFF—*continued.*
  writ—*continued.*
    venditioni exponas—continued.
      return of sheriff, 27
      safe custody, 27
      sale by sheriff indefeasible, 27
        must be for ready money, 27
        stopped when enough realized, 27
        within reasonable time, 27
    liabilities,
      under warrants and orders of superior Courts at Common Law,
        justification, 139
        liability for bailiff,
          form of warrant immaterial, 140
        position,
          employs agent, 140
      evidence to connect sheriff, 140
        after expiration of office, 141
        disclaimer, 141
        evidence against officer, 143
        handwriting, 141
        indorsement on writ, 141
        plea of "Not guilty," 141
        privity must be established, 141
        production of copy-precept, 141
            warrant, 141
            writ, 141
        proof of warrant, 141
        recognition subsequent by officer, 141
        return of two sheriffs, 141
        secondary evidence,
          recital of writ on warrant, 141
        swearing sheriffs' officer, 142
    Breach of duty,
      civil proceedings, 164
        action for false return, 166
        admissions, 167
        delaying execution, 165
        duties, statutory, 167
        limit of liability, 143
        interpleader, 166
        measure of damages, 167
        neglect of duty, 165
          to seize, 165
        pleading must shew damage, 167
        return of *nulla bona*, 166
        sale, 165
          after bankruptcy, 165
          delaying, 165
          goods of third person, 165
          improperly conducting, 165
        withdrawing from possession, 165
      criminal proceedings, 169
        attachment, 169
    Excess of Power,
      civil proceedings, 172
        extortion, 175
          arrangement between parties, 177
          excessive payment, 177
          execution set aside, 177
          fees allowed, 175
            by whom payable, 177

SHERIFF—*continued.*
   writ—*continued.*
      Excess of Power—*continued.*
         civil proceedings—*continued.*
           extortion—*continued.*
              incidental costs, 178
              keeping possession, 178
              motion to refund, and for attachment, 166
              poundage, when due, 177
              proceedings for contempt, 177
              restrained from selling, 177
              tender before seizure, 177
              where bankruptcy supervenes, 177
                  winding-up supervenes, 178
              where creditor disentitled, 178
           abusing process of Court, 178
           false imprisonment, 182
              arrest after return day of writ, 182
                  of wrong person, 182
           trespass to personalty, 192
              action maintainable by representative, 167
              excessive seizure, 193
                  sale, 193
              execution against wrong person, 192
                  goods lent on hire, 192
              execution set aside, 192
              procedure, 195
                  evidence, 196
                  landlord, 193
                  limitation, 157
                  measure of damages, 196
                  removing goods before paying rent, 193
                  special damage, 196
                  wrongful seizure, 193
              seizure after tender of debt, 192
           trespass to realty, 197
              breaking and entering, 197
              limitation, 157
              measure of damages, 200
              remaining on premises to put purchaser of lease in
                  possession, 197
              trespass *ab initio*, 200
        criminal proceedings, 201
           attachment, 201
              available, when, 201
              after expiration of office, 202
              death of defendant, 201
              reasonable time, motion for within, 201
              service, 201
              set aside, 201
              Sunday execution, 201
              writ of predecessor, 202
           extortion, 206
           false imprisonment, 182, 207
   powers and duties,
      duty of incoming, 17
         outgoing, 17
      entering liberty, 17
      posse comitatus may raise, 6, 17
      receipt for writ, 17

SHERIFF—*continued.*
  powers and duties—*continued.*
    return to writ, 17
      limit as to, 17
      not within given time, 17
      notice as to, 17
    juries, 76
  bailiff,
    bound, 142
      assistant, 143
        liability for, 143
      evidence against, 143
        of warrant, 143
      fees, 175
      liable for extortion, 143
        false return, 143
      process directed to, 142
      receipt of money by, 143
    of liberty, 143
      mandate made out—sheriff not liable, 143
      process must in first instance be directed to sheriff, 143
        exception to this, 143
    special, 142
      effect of appointment, 142
      how constituted, 142
  Under-sheriff:—
    death of sheriff, 142
    duties, 142
    fees, 175
    liabilities, 142
    may raise *posse comitatus*, 6

SHIP,
  Customs officer boarding, 113
  damage to : *See* REVENUE—MERCHANT SHIP.
  distraint of for non-payment rates, 126
  directions of harbour-master, 126
  false colours, 114
  firing on, 116
  high bailiff if required to execute bill of sale to purchaser of, 42
  inspection of lights, 124
        signals, 124
  inventory before sale, 42
  infected, 114
  loss of, 125
  master to deliver name of consignee or copy of bill of lading to collector,
    125
      give notice of unshipment to collector, 125
      produce certificate of registry to collector, 125
      declare to customs officers nation to which ship belongs, 114
  passenger ship, rules as to, 114
  power to board and inspect : *See* MERCHANT SHIP INSPECTOR.
      seize and detain : *See* MERCHANT SHIP INSPECTOR.
  Queen's, not liable to arrest, 30
  receiver, duty of,
    when stranded within limits of United Kingdom, 124
    when salvage due, 125
    sale by, 125
  skipper to give statement of accounts to collector, 125
  steamship, rules as to, 114
  under writ of *fi. fa.*, sale of, 21
  under warrant, Admiralty Marshal,

SHIP—*continued.*
  under warrant, Admiralty Marshal—*continued.*
    service how effected, 30
  unsafe, detention of, 56
  what warrant of arrest extends to, 30

SIGNALLING TO SMUGGLERS, 116

SIGNALS, ALTERING, 51

SILVER COIN,
  impairing, 90
  colouring to represent, 90

SLAVE TRADE OFFENCES, 51, 117

SLAUGHTER
  of cattle in street: *See* CONSTABLE, ARREST.
  of diseased cattle: *See* CONTAGIOUS DISEASE INSPECTOR.

SLAUGHTERHOUSE,
  entry of constable: *See* CONSTABLE, ENTRY.
  inspection: *See* PUBLIC HEALTH.

SLUICES, OPENING, 81

SMOKE,
  power to enter building or steam vessel for purposes of inspection, 70

SMUGGLING, 51

SOLDIERS,
  employment of, 6, 80
  billeting, 48

SOLICITING COMMISSION OF OFFENCE, 51

SPIRIT RETAILER,
  entry on premises, 118
  examination of stock, 118

SPIRITS,
  removal of, production of permit: *See* REVENUE, EXCISE.
  seizure: *See* REVENUE, EXCISE.

STILL VESSEL,
  seizure of: *See* REVENUE, EXCISE.

STOLEN PROPERTY,
  receiving, 90

STORES, PUBLIC,
  obliterating marks, 91

STREET,
  animals, shown in, 100, 104
  carriages standing, being cleaned or repaired in, 101, 104
  discharge of fire-arms in, 101, 104
    fireworks in, 101, 104
  lines placed across, 105
  maiming or killing cattle in, 101, 104
  noisy instrument in, 101
  offensive matter thrown upon, 105
  pigs kept near to, 105
  playing games in, 102
  public entertainment in, 100, 104
  slaughtering cattle in, 101, 104
  turning cattle loose in, 101, 104

STRUCTURES,
    dangerous, 60, 61

SUICIDE,
    attempt at, 51

SUMMONS, 62

SUNDAY,
    arrest on, 77
    execution of warrant on, 7, 16

SUPERSEDEAS,
    writ of: *See* SHERIFF, WRITS.

SURETIES FOR THE PEACE,
    commitment in default of, 40

SURVEYOR OF HIGHWAYS,
    arrest of unknown offender, 134
    certificate to divert or stop up, 45
    cleanse watercourses, 134
    county bridges, 134
    damage to bridges, 134
    districts, 133
    entry platforms, 67
    housing working classes, 67
    fencing holes, 133
    filling holes, 133
    injury through bridge or highway out of repair, 133
    make road in adjoining ground, 133
    liability, 150
        notice of action, 157
        protection, 153
    licence to get stones, 45
    obstructions at night, 133, 134
    pruning hedges, order for, 45
    rate levy, 45
    ratepayers convey material, 133
    remove encroachments, 134
        remove banks, 134
        snow, 134
    warrant of distress, 45
  District surveyor,
    dangerous structures, 61
    fees, 136
    inspect buildings, 135
        theatres, 136
    liability, 150
        notice of action, 157
        protection, 153

SUSPICION REASONABLE,
    what, 82

SWEARING,
    arrest for: *See* CONSTABLE, ARREST.

TAMPERING WITH WITNESS, 51

TAXES: *See* REVENUE.

TENANTS' FIXTURES: *See* FIXTURES.

TENDER,
    of amends, 158

TENT,
    inspection of: *See* PUBLIC HEALTH.
    pitching on highway, 135

THEATRES,
    inspection of: *See* DISTRICT SURVEYORS.

THOROUGHFARE,
    animals obstructing, 100, 104, 134

THREATENING LETTER,
    sending, 91

THRESHING-MACHINE,
    entry on premises: *See* CONSTABLE, ENTRY.

TIPSTAFF,
    duties, 12
    fees, 12
    warrant of committal, 12
        in bankruptcy, 35
    order under Debtors Act, 35
        how long in force, 35
        evidence of means to pay, 35
        extends to what, 35

TITHE,
    recovery where premises occupied by owner, 41

TITLE DEEDS,
    may not be taken under writ of *fi. fa.*, 21

TOBACCO DEALER,
    entry on premises: *See* REVENUE, EXCISE.
    examination of stock: *See* REVENUE, EXCISE.
    manufacturer to show, permit: *See* REVENUE, EXCISE.

TOLL COLLECTOR,
    exacting illegal toll, 181

TOLLS,
    distress for, 71

TORTS,
    amounting to crimes, 172

TRADES UNION OFFENCES, 51

TRADE OFFENCES, 51

TRAFALGAR SQUARE,
    holding public meetings in, 79, 101

TRAFFIC, 110

TREASON, 51
    arrest without warrant: *See* CONSTABLE, ARREST.
    warrant of Secretary of State: *See* QUEEN'S MESSENGER.

TREASON-FELONY, 57

TREASURE-TROVE,
    selling, 51

TREES,
    destroying, 91, 96

TRESPASS,
    to personalty, 192
    to realty, 197, 209
    ab initio, 152
        liability of officer acting inaccurately under warrant, 137

TRESPASSERS : *See* CONSTABLE, ENTRY.

TRUSTEES,
    estate vested in—sheriff may seize under writ, 10, 18

UNDER SHERIFF : *See* SHERIFF.

UNNATURAL CRIME, 51

UNWHOLESOME MEAT,
    offering for sale, 51

VACCINATION,
    false certificate, 51

VAGRANTS : *See* CONSTABLE, ARREST.
              See CONSTABLE, SEIZURE AND DETENTION.

VANS, INSPECTION OF : *See* PUBLIC HEALTH.

VENDITIONI EXPONAS: *See* SHERIFF (WRITS).
    writ of, 26

VENDORS SELLING DEEDS, 51

VENUE : *See* LIABILITIES—PROTECTION.

VERDICT,
    jury directed : *See* LIABILITIES—PROTECTION.

VESSELS,
    detention of, 56, 114, 125, 126
    entry on, 106, 113, 124, 125
    injury by explosion, 91
    malicious injury to, 51

VESTRY,
    powers as to inspection of drains, &c.: *See* PUBLIC HEALTH (METROPOLITAN).

VIADUCTS,
    malicious injury to, 51

VIVISECTION : *See* CRUELTY TO ANIMALS INSPECTORS.

WAR-STORE OFFENCES, 51

WARD OF COURT, ORDER FOR, 8

WARRANTS AND ORDERS,
    cause of issue must appear when, 3
    definition of warrant, 3
    jurisdiction to issue, 3, 7
    offence not yet committed relating to, 3 *n.*
    period of detention specified, when, 3
    presumption as to jurisdiction to issue, 3
    production of—not condition-precedent to execution, 7
    sealed—when, 3 *n.*

WARRANTS AND ORDERS—*continued*.
   search warrants—peculiarities, 3 *n*.
   unknown persons, 3 *n*.
   void when, 3 *n*.
  Orders,
    authority co-extensive with validity, 4
    constituting relationship of principal and agent, 4
    definition of, 4
    jurisdiction to make, must appear when, 4
    of Courts of Record, 4
    resemble warrants when, 4
    validity of proceedings on essential, 4
    verbal presumed written, when, 4
    Of Superior Courts at Common Law :—
      1. The King a Party,
        this phrase explained, 5
        force—what amount may be employed, 5
        breaking doors, power as to, 6
          after escape, 6
          breaking out, 7
          during what hours, 7
          inner doors, 6
          party's own house, 6
          previous request and denial, 6
          third party's house, 6
          remaining on premises, 7
        Lord Ellenborough on, use of force, 5
        evidence to prove necessity for using admissible, 6
        military if employed to be under magistrate, 6
        necessity of resorting to must be shown, 5
        officer may recover possession of warrant, 7
        posse comitatus—who may raise, 6
        privilege from arrest, 7
        Sunday execution, 7
        gaoler ⎫
        sergeant-at-arms, Lords ⎬ As to powers, see under head
        sergeant-at-arms, Commons ⎬ of each officer.
        sheriff ⎬
        tipstaff ⎭
      2. The King not a Party,
        breaking doors, 15
        does not affect validity of execution, 16
          liability of officer for, 16
          out, 16
          window, 16
          cupboards, trunks, &c., 15
          entering aperture, 16
          entry obtained by fraud, 16
          inner doors, 15
          ordinary entry not a breaking, 16
          outhouses, 6
          previous request and denial, third party's house, 15
          what constitutes, 15
        continuance in possession, 16
        privilege from arrest, 16
        Sunday execution, 16
        whether now arrest for debt, 17
        Admiralty marshal ⎫ As to powers, see under these officers
        sheriff   ⎭ respectively.
    Of Superior Courts not at Common Law: Of Inferior Courts and Officers
      generally,
        distinction between, and those of Superior Courts at Common Law, 32

WARRANTS AND ORDERS—*continued.*
  Of Superior Courts not at Common Law—*continued.*
    apt conclusion, 32
    certain date, 32
    cause of issue to appear, 32
    erroneous process, effect of, 33
    jurisdiction to make, to appear, 32
    killing of officer when not murder, 52
    must be executed by person to whom addressed, 33
    no distinction between warrants and orders as to jurisdiction, but between those made after adjudication and without adjudication, 33
    liability of officers under these, 34
    omnia præsumuntur ritè esse acta, not applicable, 32
    period of detention to appear, 32
  proceedings regular when a presumption as to, 33
  resistance to bad warrant lawful, 52
  to arrest to become bound next sessions, 33
  A.—After adjudication :—
    1.—The King a Party :—
       sheriff ⎫
       tipstaff ⎪
       high bailiff ⎪
       constables ⎬ As to powers, see under these officers
       excise ⎪ respectively.
       taxes ⎪
       gaoler ⎭
    2.—The King not a Party :—
       high bailiff ⎫
       constables ⎪
       gaolers ⎬ As to powers, see under these officers
       overseers ⎪ respectively.
       highway surveyors ⎭
  B.—Where no adjudication :—
    1.—The King a Party :—
       Queen's messenger ⎫
       post officers ⎪
       minister, churchwarden, and overseers ⎪
       constables ⎪
       customs ⎬ As to powers, see
       excise ⎪ under these officers
       explosives inspectors ⎪ respectively.
       wreck receiver ⎪
       nuisance inspector ⎭
    2.—The King not a Party :—
       constables ⎫
       weights inspectors ⎪
       water bailiffs ⎬ As to powers, see under
       overseers and workhouse officers ⎪ these officers respec-
       district surveyors ⎪ tively.
       local officers ⎭
  C.—Other orders :—
    constitute relation of principal and agent, 62
       local acts ⎫
       bye-laws ⎪
       adulteration ⎪
       canal-boats ⎪
       contagious disease ⎬ See under these heads respectively.
       explosives ⎪
       highways ⎪
       public health ⎪
       weights and measures ⎭

x

306 INDEX.

WATER BAILIFFS,
    arrest offenders, 128
    examine weirs and dams, 127
    privileges as constables, 128
    production of licence, 128
    putting noxious material into river, 128
    search nets, 127
    stop and search boats, 127
            persons, 127
    seize fish forfeited, 127
        unlawful engines, 127
        salmon illegally taken or killed, 127
    warrant of justices, 60
    order of justices, 60
        of conservators, 61
    Thames :—
        powers, 128

WATERCOURSES, CLEANSING : *See* SURVEYOR, HIGHWAYS.

WATERMAINS : *See* PUBLIC HEALTH.

WEIGHTS, INSPECTORS,
    powers, 136
    warrant of justice, 60

WEIGHTS AND MEASURES,
    power of officers to weigh coal, 74

WIFE,
    exposing for sale, 51
    liability of husband for debts of, 25

WINDOW BOXES,
    not sufficiently guarded, 105
    sill,
        standing on, 105

WINE RETAILER,
    entry on premises : *See* REVENUE—EXCISE.
    search of premises : *See* REVENUE—EXCISE.
    spirits on premises may be seized : *See* REVENUE—EXCISE.
    stock, examined only during hours of sale : *See* REVENUE—EXCISE.

WITCHCRAFT, PRETENDING, 37

WITNESS,
    contempt of summons, 37
    refusing to enter into recognizances, 37
        give evidence, 37
        sign information, 37
    required to leave Court, 59
    wilful insult to, 36
    tampering with, 172, 209

WORKSHOP REGULATION,
    offences against, 51

WORKHOUSE OFFICERS : *See* OVERSEERS.
    lunatics, 132
    offenders, 132
    paupers, 132

WORKHOUSE OFFICERS—*continued.*
    search, 132
    order of justices, 61
    right of guardians to sit with closed doors, 61

WRECK,
    impeding escape from, 51
    interfering with, 51
    sale, by receiver, 41, 125
    within limits of United Kingdom,
        duty of receiver, 124

WRECK RECEIVERS: *See* MERCHANT SHIP INSPECTORS.

www.ingramcontent.com/pod-product-compliance
Lightning Source LLC
Chambersburg PA
CBHW030000240426
43672CB00007B/772